THE FILM ANTHOLOGIES INDEX

by
STEPHEN E. BOWLES

The Scarecrow Press, Inc.
Metuchen, N.J., & London
1994

British Library Cataloguing-in-Publication Data available

Library of Congress Cataloging-in-Publication Data

Bowles, Stephen E., 1943-
    The film anthologies index / by Stephen E. Bowles
      p. cm.
    Includes bibliographical references.
    ISBN 0-8108-2896-0 (alk. paper)
    1. Motion pictures--Bibliography. 2. Anthologies--Indexes.
  I. Title.
  Z5784.M9B637 1994 <PN1994>
  086.79143 '75--dc20   94-13541

For

Janis Lippincott Guyon

and

Naomi Lippincott Bowles

without whom the titles and filmmakers in

The Film Anthologies Index

would have no personal meaning

TABLE OF CONTENTS

THE FILM ANTHOLOGIES INDEX

INTRODUCTION

WHY *THE FILM ANTHOLOGIES* INDEX IS NEEDED

The present volume, like most reference works, was born more out of frustration than love.

For those, like me, who began their film studies in the 1960s, the respectable literature of film scholarship consumed, maybe, one shelf worth of books while the periodicals remained a buried treasure. By the mid-1970s, however, the literature on film had multiplied to the point where systematic and exhaustive bibliographical references were essential. Bibliographies of books, bibliographies of articles, bibliographies of reviews and even bibliographies of bibliographies appeared by the late-1970s to fill this need.

As the literature of film studies probed continually deeper into the medium, so have the various anthologies designed to (1) snare shorter pieces scattered throughout the scores of periodicals, (2) provide excerpts from longer—often book length—works, and (3) include essays specifically written for the anthologies. The missing bibliographical link was to index the contents of these anthologies, making their contents conveniently accessible.

That was the impetus behind *The Film Anthologies Index*.

THE ORGANIZING PRINCIPLE

Above all other considerations, the purpose of *The Film Anthologies Index* is usefulness to the potential researcher in locating particular pieces within these available anthologies. *The Film Anthologies Index* does this in two fundamental ways:

- First, when the author's name is known, the AUTHOR ENTRIES section is designed so that a user looking for a particular piece can easily find the appropriate author entry, locate the particular title and then have a listing of all the anthologized sources where that piece can be found.

- Second, if the author is not known, the FILMS, NAMES AND KEY WORDS section is a means to locate the films (by title), names (of persons), and key words and phrases cited within the individual titles collected for the AUTHOR ENTRIES section.

There are a few other parameters that need to be mentioned.

- As with most reference books, this one is *non-interpretative*.

  That is, *The Film Anthologies Index* goes by the title of the piece (rather than its contents). If the title is cryptic or nonspecific, then it has either been left that way in the entry or, where appropriate, a [RE: ...] is appended to clarify the contents.

- It is also *non-judgmental*.

  No subjective criteria have been imposed on the quality of any entry. All sources that fall within the definition of "anthology" have been included, from gossipy recollections by now-forgotten individuals to the well-researched scholarly investigations.

- Every effort has been made to be *comprehensive*.

  Ideally, one might argue, to avoid the subjective question of quality (which is always suspect), everything should be included. The counter to this argument is that to include everything would make the volume unwieldy and immense. Those volumes that have been excluded are explained later.

The purpose of *The Film Anthologies Index* is NOT to provide an annotated or classified reference to the *contents* of each entry. Rather, *The Film Anthologies Index* works exclusively from the title of an essay or excerpt (over 15,000 listed under 6,563 entries). This provides a convenient source for the user to find any piece published in one of the included anthologies.

SECTION I
BOOKS INCLUDED

DEFINING AN ANTHOLOGY

When I began this project, it seemed that defining an anthology would be the easiest part of the project. After all, the conventions of an anthology have long been associated with publishing.

- On the simplest level, an anthology is a collection of writings that have a shared orientation, usually written by various authors. The essays can be either original to the volume or reprinted (and sometimes edited or altered) from a previous publication. Most typically these pieces are complete and self-contained.

- By a short extension, the definition was expanded to include books composed of complete and self-contained essays by a single author (for example, Dudley Andrew's *Film in the Aura of Art* or Stuart Kaminsky's *American Film Genres*) and books composed of excerpts that may or may not be complete or self-contained (for example, selections from books on film theory that are often anthologized).

- And, then, what about those anthologies that cover more than just film topics? There are dozens of anthologies on the competitive market whose boundaries touch such wider topics as mass media, popular culture and communications research, or those anthologies centered around individuals whose contributions extend beyond film. Should those be absorbed into the definition?

The short definition quickly proved either inadequate or confining, certainly less than useful to provide anything like a comprehensive approach. Therefore, I freely extended the definition.

WHAT'S INCLUDED AND EXCLUDED

There are 716 books included in *The Film Anthologies Index*. Of those, 649 have their complete contents included and 67 have selected items included.

I have included:

- All relevant volumes published through 1991 (with about a dozen entries drawn from 1992). These works have been collected from library holdings, used bookstores, private collections ... wherever I could locate the books.

- Anthologies that comprise a broader sweep than just film—that is, readers in mass entertainment, communication studies, media analysis—have been included on a *selective* basis. Generally, if there is a section devoted to film, I have included the essays.

- Books that are devoted to filmmakers in which the chapters are self-contained and written by various authors; for example, the *Focus On* ... series.

Within those books that have been included:

- I have generally omitted such items as introductions, conclusions, afterwords, bibliographies, filmographies and glossaries.

- I have also omitted, on several occasions, certain chapters which are simply not germane to the boundaries of this book. An example is a book like *Re-Interpreting Brecht*, which has several chapters related to film and others devoted to non-film topics (theater, literature).

    In those instances where selected chapters have been included, I have attached an explanatory NOTE to the bibliographical entry.

I have generally excluded:

- Volumes of film reviews. The exceptions are those books with a defined theme (for example: feminism or Marxism) so that they can double as—in the widest sense—a doctrine or thesis.

- Volumes whose contents are limited to capsule summaries of films or filmmakers.

- Single-author books on specific filmmakers.

- Books written in languages other than English (unless, of course, they have been translated into English).

An unexpected problem arose when a book's title had changed. On rare occasions, this can happen when a book goes into its original printing to a reprinted edition or from hardcover to paperback or from a foreign to American release. For example, Jay Leyda's volume *Voices of Film Experience* was originally published in 1977 in hardback but was subsequently reissued in 1984 in paperback under the title *Film Makers Speak* "supplemented with corrections and additions by Doug Tomlinson." (Curiously, however, the copyright date did not change.)

SECTION II
AUTHOR ENTRIES

ORGANIZATION

The organizing principle of the AUTHOR ENTRIES is to identify and collect all anthologized sources of a single piece under the author's name. The process was to extract the contents of each anthology and order the individual pieces by author, arranged alphabetically by name. (Occasionally, where there was no "author," I used an editor or respondent.)

- First priority: Under the author's name, entries are grouped by the title of the particular piece.

  For example, Robert Warshow's essay on "The Westerner" appears in nine different anthologies. The piece is listed as an individual entry under Warshow's name (# 6167) with all the anthologized sources in which this essay can be found.

- Second priority: If other essays in, say, Warshow's own anthology of essays, *The Immediate Experience*, do not appear in multiple sources, they are grouped together (# 6165), excluding the previously identified essay on "The Westerner."

There are a few identifiable problems in this manner of organization. For example:

- The same article may have different titles in different sources. For example, William Rothman's analysis of the Hemingway novel/Hawks film *To Have and Have Not* is titled "To Have and Have Not Adapted a Film from a Novel" in his own collected writings *The "I" of the Camera* (# 5087); it is titled "To Have and Have Not Adapted a Novel" in the anthology *The Modern American Novel and the Movies* (# 5088).

  Because it is the same essay in concept but revised in wording, it is listed separately (with an explanatory [NOTE: ...] attached).

- Even under the same author and title, the entries may not be the same—one may be an excerpt or edited version of the complete piece. For example, Sergei Eisenstein's essay on "Dickens, Griffith, and the Film Today" is printed in its entirety in *Film Form* and several other volumes (# 1762) but is abridged and somewhat altered when published in *Film Theory and Criticism: Introductory Readings* (# 1763).

  Similar in reasoning to the former item, these have been treated as separate entries.

- A non-English-language article from an original source may have different translators/translations. For example, Jean Douchet's piece on Alfred Hitchcock from *Cahiers du Cinéma* is translated by David Wilson as "Hitch and his Audience" and the same source piece translated by Verena Conley as "Hitch and His Public."

  For convenience, these translations have been grouped together under Douchet's entry (# 1625), with an explanatory NOTE.

- Then there is the case in which the same piece has completely different titles in separate reprints. For example, Irving Pichel's essay on camera movement is entitled "Change of Camera Viewpoint" in *The Movies as Medium* and appears as "Seeing with the Camera" in both *A Casebook on Film* and *Hollywood Directors*.

  Elusive as this practice can be, I have tried to catch these and bundle them together with an explanatory [NOTE: ...] in the entry.

APPARENT INCONSISTENCIES

I have attempted, as much as reasonably possible, to preserve entries exactly as they are presented in the anthologized source. (For example, I have not altered any of the wording in any title.) Because I have <u>not</u> taken the liberty to conform entries into a single (arbitrary) standard, this can sometimes lead to *apparent* inconsistencies in:

- Variant spellings of certain established words (for example: filmmaker, film maker and film-maker).

- Different British and American spellings (for example: "colour" and "color").

- Different stylistic conventions and idiosyncrasies (for example: 1930s and 1930's).

- Whether the proper diacritical marks are used or omitted (for example: Luis Bunuel and Luis Buñuel).

- Even film titles and author names can have different appearances (for example: *Blowup, Blow-up, Blow-Up* and *Blow Up* / I.C. Jarvie, Ian C. Jarvie and Ian Jarvie).

Despite apparent differences in the AUTHOR ENTRIES section, in the FILMS, NAMES AND KEY WORDS section, all variant spellings have been integrated to a single standard spelling.

There are, however, some liberties I have taken for the sake of continuity in the AUTHOR ENTRIES section.

- In *The Film Anthologies Index*, I have attempted to place all film/book titles in italics. In the various anthologies, film/book titles can be designated by single quotation marks, double quotation marks, bold print, all capitalization, or sometimes without any special type style.

- Because the titles of all individual pieces appearing in *The Film Anthologies Index* are placed within double quotation marks, there are occasional discrepancies in the use of single/double quotation marks from their source anthology.

- Finally, I have occasionally had to include a date or reference in brackets after the title, name or entry to avoid potential confusion.

ABBREVIATIONS

/rev ed = revised edition
/1 ed = first edition (/2 ed, ...)
[*sic*] = as it appears in the original. This can indicate either an error or a deliberate usage.

SECTION III
FILMS, NAMES AND KEY WORDS

This section does NOT attempt to create general categories into which large clusters of entries are categorically or thematically grouped together. Rather, this is an index to films, names and key words *as they appear* in the titles of the individual entries.

In this section, I have not included references to filmmakers where s/he is identified as the maker of a specific film. For example, the AUTHOR ENTRY for "Fassbinder's *Ali: Fear Eats the Soul*," is about the film rather than Fassbinder. It is, therefore, referenced under the film title only.

Finally, I have not included author names. Therefore, to find all the available anthologized material by or about, say, Alfred Hitchcock, the user will need to check the AUTHOR ENTRIES section under "Hitchcock, Alfred" to find pieces that Hitchcock has written or where he has been interviewed <u>and</u> in the FILMS, NAMES AND KEY WORDS section under "Hitchcock, Alfred" to find those citations that contain a reference to his name.

ACKNOWLEDGMENTS

Although this has been almost entirely a one-person production, there are several people who need to be thanked for their contributions.

Omar Melo, a computer genius and *Star Trek* fanatic, provided invaluable assistance in working with the complicated page layout programs needed to finalize *The Film Anthologies Index*.

Sharon Schwartz assisted in compiling the entry numbers for the third section. Her meticulous energy took up the slack when mine wavered.

Finally, thanks to Cheryl Anker and Noelle Bowles for their proofreading efforts and helpful suggestions.

Academy All the Way.
Lewis, Grover.
San Francisco, CA: Straight Arrow, 1974.
[NOTE: Selected entries from this book.]

Acting in the Cinema.
Naremore, James.
Berkeley, CA: University of California, 1988.
[NOTE: Selected entries from this book.]

Africa on Film: Myth and Reality.
Maynard, Richard A. (editor).
Rochelle Park, NJ: Hayden Book Company, 1974.

Against Interpretation (and Other Essays).
Sontag, Susan.
New York: Farrar, Straus & Giroux, 1966.
[NOTE: Selected entries from this book.]

The Age of the Dream Palace: Cinema and Society in Britain, 1930-1939.
Richards, Jeffrey.
New York: Routledge and Kegan Paul, 1984.
[NOTE: Selected entries from this book.]

Alfred Hitchcock's High Vernacular: Theory and Practice.
Sharff, Stefan.
New York: Columbia University, 1991.
[NOTE: Selected entries from this book.]

Algerian Cinema.
Salmane, Hala, Simon Hartog and David Wilson (editors).
London: British Film Institute, 1976.

Alice Doesn't: Feminism, Semiotics, Cinema.
de Lauretis, Teresa.
Bloomington, IN: Indiana University, 1984.

Alien Zone: Cultural Theory and Contemporary Science Fiction Cinema.
Kuhn, Annette (editor).
New York: Verso, 1990.

All Our Yesterdays: 90 Years of British Cinema.
Barr, Charles (editor).
London: British Film Institute, 1986.

The Ambiguous Image: Narrative Style in Modern European Cinema.
Armes, Roy.
Bloomington, IN: Indiana University, 1976.

The American Animated Cartoon: A Critical Anthology.
Peary, Danny and Gerald Peary (editors).
New York: E.P. Dutton, 1980.

American Directors (Volume One).
Coursodon, Jean-Pierre with Pierre Sauvage (editors).
New York: McGraw-Hill Book Co., 1983.

American Directors (Volume Two).
Coursodon, Jean-Pierre with Pierre Sauvage (editors).
New York: McGraw-Hill Book Co., 1983.

American Film Directors: The World As They See It.
Lloyd, Ronald.
New York: New Viewpoints, 1976.

American Film Genres: Approaches to a Critical Theory of Popular Film (first edition).
Kaminsky, Stuart M.
Dayton, OH: Pflaum Publishing, 1974.

American Film Genres (second edition).
Kaminsky, Stuart M.
Chicago, IL: Nelson-Hall, 1985.

The American Film Heritage: Impressions from The American Film Institute Archives.
American Film Institute (editor).
Washington, DC: American Film Institute/Acropolis Books, 1972.

The American Film Industry (first edition).
Balio, Tino (editor).
Madison, WI: University of Wisconsin, 1976.

The American Film Industry (revised edition).
Balio, Tino (editor).
Madison, WI: University of Wisconsin, 1985.

American Film Makers Today.
Smith, Dian G.
New York: Julian Messer, 1983.

American Film Melodrama: Griffith, Vidor, Minnelli.
Lang, Robert.
Princeton, NJ: Princeton University, 1989.

American History/American Film: Interpreting the Hollywood Image.
O'Connor, John E. and Martin A. Jackson (editors).
New York: Continuum/Frederick Ungar, 1988.

American Horrors: Essays on the Modern American Horror Film.
Waller, Gregory A. (editor).
Urbana, IL: University of Illinois, 1987.

American Media: The Wilson Quarterly Reader.
Cook, Philip S., Douglas Gomery and Lawrence W. Lichty (editors).
Washington, DC: The Wilson Center Press, n.d.
[NOTE: Selected entries from this book.]

The American Movie Industry: The Business of Motion Pictures.
Kindem, Gorham (editor).
Carbondale, IL: Southern Illinois University, 1982.

American Nightmare: Essays on the Horror Film.
Britton, Andrew, Richard Lippe, Tony Williams and Robin Wood.
Toronto (Canada): Festival of Festivals, 1979.

Before the Wall Came Down: Soviet and East European Filmmakers Working in the West.
Petrie, Graham and Ruth Dwyer (editors).
Lanham, MD: University Press of America, 1990.

Behind the Screen: How Films Are Made.
Watts, Stephen (editor).
London: Arthur Barker Ltd, 1938.

Bertolt Brecht, *Cahiers du Cinéma* and Contemporary Film Theory.
Lellis, George.
Ann Arbor, MI: UMI Research Press, 1976, 1982.

Bertolucci's Dream Loom: A Psychoanalytic Study of Cinema.
Kline, T. Jefferson.
Amherst, MA: University of Massachusetts, 1987.

The Best of *Rob Wagner's Script*.
Slide, Anthony (editor).
Metuchen, NJ: Scarecrow Press, 1985.

Between Action and Cut: Five American Directors.
Thompson, Frank (editor).
Metuchen, NJ: Scarecrow Press, 1985.

Beyond Formula: American Film Genres.
Solomon, Stanley J.
New York: Harcourt Brace Jovanovich, 1976.

Black Film as Genre.
Cripps, Thomas.
Bloomington, IN: Indiana University, 1978.

The Black Man on Film: Racial Stereotyping.
Maynard, Richard A. (editor).
Rochelle Park, NY: Hayden Book Company, 1974.

Blue Skies and Silver Linings: Aspects of the Hollywood Musical.
Babington, Bruce and Peter William Evans.
Manchester (England): Manchester University, 1985.

Blueprint on Babylon.
Marshall, J.D. (editor).
Tempe, AZ: Phoenix House, 1978.

Borges in/and/on Film.
Borges, Jorge Luis (Edgardo Cozarinsky, notes and editor; Gloria Waldman and Ronald Christ, translators).
New York: Lumen Books, 1988.

Brazilian Cinema.
Johnson, Randal and Robert Stam (editors).
East Brunswick, NJ: Associated University Presses, 1982.

Breaking the Glass Armor: Neoformalist Film Analysis.
Thompson, Kristin.
Bloomington, IN: Indiana University, 1988.

Breaking the Frame: Film: Film Language and the Experience of Limits.
Hedges, Inez.
Bloomington, IN: Indiana University, 1991.

The Brechtian Aspect of Radical Cinema.
Walsh, Martin (Keith M. Griffith, editor).
London: British Film Institute, 1981.

Britain and the Cinema in the Second World War.
Taylor, Philip M. (editor).
New York: St. Martin's Press, 1988.

Britain Can Take It: The British Cinema in the Second World War.
Aldgate, Anthony and Jeffrey Richards.
Oxford (England): Basil Blackwell, 1986.

British Cinema and Society 1930-1970.
Richards, Jeffrey and Anthony Aldgate.
Totowa, NJ: Barnes & Noble Books, 1983.

British Cinema History.
Curran, James and Vincent Porter (editors).
London: Weidenfeld & Nicolson, 1983.

British Cinema Now.
Auty, Martin and Nick Roddick (editors).
London: British Film Institute, 1985.

***Cahiers du Cinéma*, The 1950s: Neo-Realism, Hollywood, New Wave.**
Hillier, Jim (editor).
Cambridge, MA: Harvard University, 1985.

***Cahiers du Cinéma*, 1960-1968: New Wave, New Cinema, Reevaluating Hollywood.**
Hillier, Jim (editor).
Cambridge, MA: Harvard University, 1986.

***Cahiers du Cinéma*, 1969-1972: The Politics of Representation.**
Browne, Nick (editor).
London: Routledge, 1990.

Caligari's Children: The Film as Tale of Terror.
Prawer, S.S.
New York: Oxford University Press, 1980.
[NOTE: Selected entries from this book.]

Canned Goods as Caviar: American Film Comedies of the 1930s.
Weales, Gerald.
Chicago, IL: University of Chicago, 1985.

Capturing the Culture: Film, Art, and Politics.
Grenier, Richard.
Washington, DC: Ethics and Public Policy Center, 1991.
[NOTE: Selected entries from this book.]

A Casebook on Film.
Samuels, Charles Thomas.
New York: Van Nostrand Reinhold, 1970.

Celebrity Articles from "The Screen Guild Magazine".
Sterling, Anna Kate (editor).
Metuchen, NJ: Scarecrow Press, 1987.

Celebrity Circus.
Higham, Charles.
New York: Delacorte Press, 1979.

Celluloid and Symbol.
Cooper, John C. and Carl Skrade (editors).
Philadelphia, PA: Fortress Press, 1970.

The Celluloid Muse: Hollywood Directors Speak.
Higham, Charles and Joel Greenberg.
Chicago, IL: Henry Regnery, 1969.

The Censorship Papers: Movie Censorship Letters from the Hays Office, 1934 to 1968.
Gardner, Gerald (editor).
New York: Dodd, Mead, 1987.

Charlie Chaplin: His Reflection in Modern Times.
Nysenholc, Adolphe (editor).
New York and Berlin: Mouton de Gruyter, 1991.
[NOTE: Selected entries from this book (excludes entries in French).]

Chicano Cinema: Research, Reviews, and Resources.
Keller, Gary D. (editor).
Binghamton, NY: Bilingual Review/Press, 1985.

The Child Stars.
Zierold, Norman J.
New York: Coward-McCann, 1965.
[NOTE: Selected entries from this book.]

Children's Novels and the Movies.
Street, Douglas (editor).
New York: Frederick Ungar Publishing, 1983.

Chilean Cinema.
Chanan, Michael (editor).
London: British Film Institute, 1976.

Chinese Film: The State of the Art in the People's Republic.
Semsel, George Stephen (editor).
New York: Praeger, 1987.

Chinese Film Theory: A Guide to the New Era.
Semsel, George S., Xia Hong and Hou Jianping (editors).
New York: Praeger Publishers, 1990.

The Cineaste Interviews: On the Art and Politics of the Cinema.
Georgakas, Dan and Lenny Rubenstein (editors).
Chicago, IL: Lake View Press, 1983.

Cinema: A Critical Dictionary (2 volumes).
Roud, Richard (editor).
London: Secker & Warburg, 1980.

Cinema and Cultural Identity: Reflections on Films from Japan, India, and China.
Dissanayake, Wimal (editor).
Lanham, MD: University Press of America, 1988.

Cinema and History.
Ferro, Marc (Naomi Greene, translator).
Detroit, MI: Wayne State University, 1988 (English trans.).
[NOTE: Selected entries from this book.]

Cinema and Language.
Heath, Stephen and Patricia Mellencamp (editors).
Los Angeles: American Film Institute, 1983.

Cinema and Social Change in Latin America: Conversations with Filmmakers.
Burton, Julianne (editor).
Austin, TX: University of Texas, 1986.

The Cinema Book: A Complete Guide to Understanding the Movies.
Cook, Pam (editor with James Donald, Christine Gledhill, Sheila Johnston, Paul Kerr, Annette Kuhn, Andy Medhurst, Geoffrey Nowell-Smith, Jane Root and Terry Stapes).
London: British Film Institute, 1985.

Cinema Drama Schema: Eastern Metaphysics in Western Art.
Currie, Hector.
New York: Philosophical Library, 1985.
[NOTE: Selected entries from this book.]

Cinema East: A Critical Study of Major Japanese Films.
McDonald, Keiko I.
East Brunswick, NJ: Associated University Presses, 1983.

Cinema Examined: Selections from 'Cinema Journal'.
MacCann, Richard Dyer and Jack C. Ellis (editors).
New York: E.P. Dutton, 1982.

Cinema Eye, Cinema Ear: Some Key Film-Makers of the Sixties.
Taylor, John Russell.
New York: Hill and Wang, 1964.

Cinema Histories, Cinema Practices.
Mellencamp, Patricia and Philip Rosen (editors).
Frederick, MD: University Publications of America, 1984.

Cinema in Finland: An Introduction.
Hillier, Jim (editor).
London: British Film Institute Publishing, 1975.

Cinema in Revolution: The Heroic Era of the Soviet Film.
Schnitzer, Luda and Jean, and Marcel Martin (editors).
New York: Hill and Wang, 1973.

Cinema Novo x 5: Masters of Contemporary Brazilian Film.
Johnson, Randal.
Austin, TX: University of Texas, 1984.

The Cinema of Adventure, Romance & Terror (from the archives of *American Cinematographer*).
Turner, George E. (editor).
Hollywood, CA: The ASC Press, 1989.

The Cinema of Cruelty: From Bunuel to Hitchcock.
Bazin, Andre.
New York: Seaver Books, 1982.

A Cinema of Loneliness: Penn, Kubrick, Coppola, Scorsese, Altman.
Kolker, Robert Phillip.
New York: Oxford University Press, 1980.

Cinema, Politics and Society in America.
Davies, Philip and Brian Neve (editors).
New York: St. Martin's Press, 1981.

Cinema Stylists.
Belton, John.
Metuchen, NJ: Scarecrow Press, 1983.

Cinema Verite in America: Studies in Uncontrolled Documentary.
Mamber, Stephen.
Cambridge, MA: MIT Press, 1974.

The Cinematic Apparatus.
de Lauretis, Teresa and Stephen Heath (editors).
New York: St. Martin's Press, 1980, 1985.

The Cinematic Imagination: Writers and the Motion Pictures.
Murray, Edward.
New York: Frederick Ungar Publishing, 1972.

The Cinematic Muse: Critical Studies in the History of French Cinema.
Thiher, Allen.
Columbia, MO: University of Missouri, 1979.

The Cinematic Text: Methods and Approaches.
Palmer, R. Barton (editor).
New York: AMS Press, 1989.

The Cinematic Vision of F. Scott Fitzgerald.
Dixon, Wheeler Winston.
Ann Arbor, MI: UMI Research Press, 1986.

Circles of Confusion (Texts 1968-1980): Film, Photography, Video.
Frampton, Hollis.
Rochester, NY: Visual Studies Workshop, 1983.

The Citizen Kane Book.
No author/editor provided.
Boston, MA: Little, Brown, 1971.

The Civil War on the Screen and Other Essays.
Spears, Jack.
Cranbury, NJ: A.S. Barnes, 1977.

The Classic American Novel and the Movies.
Peary, Gerald and Roger Shatzkin.
New York: Frederick Ungar Publishing, 1977.

The Classic Cinema: Essays in Criticism.
Solomon, Stanley J. (editor).
New York: Harcourt Brace Jovanovich, 1973.

Classic Movie Monsters.
Glut, Donald F.
Metuchen, NJ: Scarecrow Press, 1978.

The Classical Hollywood Cinema: Film Style & Mode of Production to 1960.
Bordwell, David, Janet Staiger and Kristin Thompson.
New York: Columbia University, 1985.

Close Encounters: Film, Feminism, and Science Fiction.
Penley, Constance, Elisabeth Lyon, Lynn Spigel and Janet Bergstrom (editors).
Minneapolis, MN: University of Minnesota, 1991.

Close-Up: A Critical Perspective on Film.
Kinder, Marsha and Beverle Houston.
New York: Harcourt Brace Jovanovich, 1972.

Close-Up: The Contemporary Director.
Tuska, Jon (editor).
Metuchen, NJ: Scarecrow Press, 1981.

Close Up: The Contract Director.
Tuska, Jon (general editor).
Metuchen, NJ: Scarecrow Press, 1976.

Close-Up: The Hollywood Director.
Tuska, Jon (general editor).
Metuchen, NJ: Scarecrow Press, 1978.

Close Viewings: An Anthology of New Film Criticism.
Lehman, Peter (editor).
Gainesville, FL: University Presses of Florida, 1990.

Closely Watched Films: The Czechoslovak Experience.
Liehm, Antonín J.
White Plains, NY: International Arts and Sciences, 1974.

Columbia Pictures: Portrait of a Studio.
Dick, Bernard F. (editor).
Lexington, KY: The University Press of Kentucky, 1992.

Combat Films: American Realism, 1945-1970.
Rubin, Steven Jay.
Jefferson, NC: McFarland & Company, 1981.

Comedy/Cinema/Theory.
Horton, Andrew (editor).
Berkeley, CA: University of California, 1991.

A Comparative Study of Selected American Film Critics, 1958-1974.
Blades, Jr., Joseph Dalton.
New York: Arno Press, 1976.

The Compleat [*sic*] Guide to Film Study.
Poteet, G. Howard (editor).
Urbana, IL: National Council of Teachers of English, 1972.

The Composer in Hollywood.
Palmer, Christopher.
New York: Marion Boyars, 1990.

Concepts in Film Theory.
Andrew, Dudley.
New York: Oxford University Press, 1984.

Confessions of an Ex-Fan Magazine Writer.
Wilke, Jane.
Garden City, NY: Doubleday and Company, 1981.

Conflict and Control in the Cinema: A Reader in Film and Society.
Tulloch, John (editor).
Melbourne and Sydney (Australia): Macmillan Company of Australia, 1977.

Contemporary Literary Criticism (Volume 16).
Gunton, Sharon R. (compiler and editor).
Detroit, MI: Gale Research, 1981.

Contemporary Literary Criticism (Volume 20).
Gunton, Sharon R. (compiler and editor).
Detroit, MI: Gale Research, 1982.

Conversations in the Raw.
Reed, Rex.
New York: World Publishing, 1969.

Courtroom's Finest Hour in American Cinema.
Harris, Thomas J.
Metuchen, NJ: Scarecrow Press, 1987.

The Craft of the Screenwriter: Interviews with Six Celebrated Screenwriters.
Brady, John.
New York: Simon and Schuster (Touchstone), 1981.

Creative Differences: Profiles of Hollywood Dissidents.
Zheutlin, Barbara and David Talbot.
Boston, MA: South End Press, 1978.

A Critical Cinema: Interviews with Independent Filmmakers.
MacDonald, Scott.
Berkeley, CA: University of California, 1988.

A Critical Cinema 2: Interviews with Independent Filmmakers.
MacDonald, Scott.
Berkeley, CA: University of California, 1992.

Critical Perspectives on Black Independent Cinema.
Cham, Mbye B. and Claire Andrade-Watkins (editors).
Cambridge, MA: MIT Press, 1988.

A Critique of Film Theory.
Henderson, Brian.
New York: E.P. Dutton, 1980.

Crossroads to the Cinema.
Brode, Douglas (editor).
Boston, MA: Holbrook Press, 1975.

The Cubist Cinema.
Lawder, Standish D.
New York: New York University, 1975.

The Cult Film Experience: Beyond All Reason.
Telotte, J.P. (editor).
Austin, TX: University of Texas, 1991.

Current Research in Film: Audiences, Economics and Law, Volume One.
Austin, Bruce A. (editor).
Norwood, NJ: Ablex Publishing, 1985.

Current Research in Film: Audiences, Economics and Law, Volume Two.
Austin, Bruce A. (editor).
Norwood, NJ: Ablex Publishing, 1986.

Current Research in Film: Audiences, Economics and Law, Volume Three.
Austin, Bruce A. (editor).
Norwood, NJ: Ablex Publishing, 1987.

Current Research in Film: Audiences, Economics and Law, Volume Four.
Austin, Bruce A. (editor).
Norwood, NJ: Ablex Publishing, 1988.

Cut!: Horror Writers on Horror Film.
Golden, Christopher (editor).
New York: Berkley Books, 1992.

The Czechoslovak New Wave.
Hames, Peter.
Berkeley, CA: University of California, 1985.

Dada and Surrealist Film.
Kuenzli, Rudolf E. (editor).
New York: Willis Locker & Owens, 1987.

The Dame in the Kimono: Hollywood, Censorship, and The Production Code from the 1920s to the 1960s.
Leff, Leonard J. and Jerold L. Simmons.
New York: Grove Weidenfeld, 1990.

Dance in the Hollywood Musical.
Delamater, Jerome.
Ann Arbor, MI: UMI Research Press, 1978, 1981.
[NOTE: Selected entries from this book.]

Dark Romance: Sex and Death in the Horror Film.
Hogan, David J.
Jefferson, NC: McFarland & Company, 1986.
[NOTE: Selected entries from this book.]

Dark Visions: Conversations with the Masters of the Horror Film.
Wiater, Stanley.
New York: Avon Books, 1992.

The Dead That Walk: Dracula, Frankenstein, the Mummy, and Other Favorite Movie Monsters.
Halliwell, Leslie.
New York: Continuum, 1988.
[NOTE: Selected entries from this book.]

Debrett Goes to Hollywood.
Kidd, Charles.
New York: St. Martin's Press, 1986.

The Deep Red Horror Handbook.
Balun, Chas. [*sic*] (editor).
Albany, NY: Fantaco Books, 1989.

Dictionary of Literary Biography (Volume 26: American Screenwriters).
Morseberger, Robert E., Stephen O. Lesser and Randall Clark (editors).
Detroit, MI: Gale Research, 1984.

Dictionary of Literary Biography (Volume 44: American Screenwriters).
Clark, Randall (editor).
Detroit, MI: Gale Research, 1986.

Directing the Film: Film Directors on Their Art.
Sherman, Eric, compiler.
Boston, MA: Little, Brown, 1976.

Directors and Directions: Cinema for the Seventies.
Taylor, John Russell.
New York: Hill and Wang, 1975.

The Director's Event: Interviews with Five American Film-Makers.
Sherman, Eric and Martin Rubin.
New York: Atheneum, 1969.

Directors in Action.
Thomas, Bob (editor).
Indianapolis, IN: Bobbs Merrill, 1973.

Do You Sleep in the Nude?.
Reed, Rex.
New York: New American Library, 1968.

The Documentary Conscience: A Casebook in Film Making.
Rosenthal, Alan.
Berkeley, CA: University of California, 1980.

Documentary Explorations: 15 Interviews with Film-Makers.
Levin, G. Roy.
Garden City, NY: Doubleday and Company, 1971.

The Documentary Tradition (first edition).
Jacobs, Lewis (editor).
New York: Hopkinson and Blake, 1971.

The Documentary Tradition (second edition).
Jacobs, Lewis (editor).
New York: W.W. Norton & Company, 1979.

Don't Shoot the Best Boy! The Film Crew at Work.
Shand, John and Tony Wellington.
Sydney (Australia): Currency Press, 1988.

Dostoevsky and Soviet Film: Visions of Demonic Realism.
Lary, N. M..
Ithaca, NY: Cornell University, 1986.

Double Exposure: Fiction into Film.
Boyum, Joy Gould.
New York: New American Library, 1985.

Dreams and Dead Ends: The American Gangster/Crime Film.
Shadoian, Jack.
Cambridge, MA: MIT Press, 1977.

The Dreams and the Dreamers.
Alpert, Hollis.
New York: The Macmillan Company, 1962.

Early Cinema: Space, Frame, Narrative.
Elsaesser, Thomas with Adam Barker (editors).
London: British Film Institute, 1990.

Early Women Directors.
Slide, Anthony.
Cranbury, NJ: A.S. Barnes, 1977.

Easy Pieces.
Hartman, Geoffrey H.
New York: Columbia University, 1985.
[NOTE: Selected entries from this book.]

Echo and Narcissus: Women's Voices in Classical Hollywood Cinema.
Lawrence, Amy.
Berkeley, CA: University of California, 1991.

The Education of the Film-maker: An International View.
UNESCO/American Film Institute.
Paris (France): The UNESCO Press/Los Angeles: American Film Institute, 1975.

Eisenstein at Ninety.
Christie, Ian and David Elliott (editors).
London: Museum of Modern Art Oxford, 1988.

The Emergence of Film Art (first edition).
Jacobs, Lewis (editor).
New York: Hopkinson and Blake, 1969.

The Emergence of Film Art (second edition).
Jacobs, Lewis (editor).
New York: W.W. Norton & Company, 1979.

An Empire of Their Own: How the Jews Invented Hollywood.
Gabler, Neal.
New York: Crown Publishers, 1988.

Encountering Directors.
Samuels, Charles Thomas.
New York: Capricorn Books, 1972.

Encounters with Filmmakers: Eight Career Studies.
Tuska, Jon.
Westport, CT: Greenwood Press, 1991.

The English Novel and the Movies.
Klein, Michael and Gillian Parker (editors).
New York: Frederick Ungar Publishing, 1981.

Eros in the Mind's Eye: Sexuality and the Fantastic in Art and Film.
Palumbo, Donald (editor).
Westport, CT: Greenwood Press, 1986.
[NOTE: Selected entries from this book.]

Essays on Chaplin.
Bodon, Jean (editor).
New Haven, CT: University of New Haven Press, 1985.

The Essential Cinema: Essays on the Films in the Collection of Anthology Film Archives (Volume One).
Sitney, P. Adams (editor).
New York: Anthology Film Archives & New York University, 1975.

Ethnic Images in American Film and Television.
Miller, Randall M. (editor).
Philadelphia, PA: The Balch Institute, 1978.

Euripides in Cinema: The Heart Made Visible.
McDonald, Marianne.
Philadelphia, PA: Centrum Philadelphia, 1983.

Experiment in the Film.
Manvell, Roger (editor).
London: The Grey Walls Press, 1949.

Explorations in Film Theory: Selected Essays from *Ciné-Tracts*.
Burnett, Ron (editor).
Bloomington, IN: Indiana University, 1991.

Explorations in National Cinemas.
Lawton, Ben and Janet Staiger (editors).
Pleasantville, NY: Redgrave Publishing, 1977.

Fabrications: Costume and the Female Body.
Gaines, Janet and Charlotte Herzog (editors).
Los Angeles/New York: American Film Institute/Routledge, 1990.

Fair Use and Free Inquiry: Copyright Law and the New Media.
Lawrence, John Shelton and Bernard Timberg (editors).
Norwood, NJ: Ablex Publishing, 1980.

Fallen Angels: The Lives and Untimely Deaths of 14 Hollywood Beauties.
Crivello, Kirk.
Secaucus, NJ: Citadel, 1988.

Fantasy and the Cinema.
Donald, James (editor).
London: British Film Institute, 1989.

Fashion in Film.
Engelmeier, Regine and Peter W. (editors).
Munich (Germany): Prestel-Verlag, 1990.
[NOTE: Selected entries from this book.]

Fassbinder.
McCormick, Ruth, translator.
New York: Tanam Press, 1981.

Faulkner, Modernism, and Film: Faulkner and Yoknapatawpha, 1978.
Harrington, Evans and Ann J. Abadie (editors).
Jackson, MS: University Press of Mississippi, 1979.
[NOTE: Selected entries from this book.]

Feature Films as History.
Short, K.R.M. (editor).
Knoxville, TN: University of Tennessee, 1981.

Federico Fellini: Essays in Criticism.
Bondanella, Peter (editor).
New York: Oxford University Press, 1978.

The Female Gaze: Women as Viewers of Popular Culture.
Gamman, Lorraine and Margaret Marshment (editors).
Seattle, WA: The Real Comet Press, 1989.
[NOTE: Selected entries from this book.]

Female Spectators: Looking At Film and Television.
[NOTE: The title printed on the title-page on the paperback edition is erroneously spelled "Female Spectactors"].
Pribram, E. Deidre (editor).
New York: Verso, 1988.

Feminism and Film Theory.
Penley, Constance (editor).
New York: Routledge, Chapman and Hall, 1988.

Feminist in the Dark: Reviewing the Movies.
Maio, Kathi.
Freedom, CA: The Crossing Press, 1988.

Fiction, Film, and Faulkner: The Art of Adaptation.
Phillips, Gene D.
Knoxville, TN: University of Tennessee, 1988.

50 Major Film-Makers.
Cowie, Peter (editor).
New York: A.S. Barnes, 1975.

Figures of Desire: A Theory and Analysis of Surrealist Film.
Williams, Linda.
Urbana, IL: University of Illinois, 1981.

The Film.
Sarris, Andrew (editor).
Indianapolis, IN: The Bobbs-Merrill Company, 1968.

Film: A Montage of Theories.
MacCann, Richard Dyer (editor).
New York: E.P. Dutton, 1966.

Film: An Anthology.
Talbot, Daniel (editor).
New York: Simon and Schuster, 1959.

Film and Dream: An Approach to Bergman.
Petric, Vlada (editor).
Pleasantville, NY: Redgrave Publishing, 1981.

Film and Literature: A Comparative Approach to Adaptation.
Aycock, Wendell and Michael Schoenecke (editors).
Lubbock, TX: Texas Tech University, 1988.

Film and Literature: Contrasts in Media.
Marcus, Fred H. (editor).
Scranton, PA: Chandler Publishing Company, 1971.

Film and Politics in the Third World.
Downing, John D.H. (editor).
New York: Praeger, 1987.

Film and Politics in the Weimar Republic.
Plummer, Thomas G., Bruce A. Murray, Linda
    Schulte-Sasse, Anthony K. Munson and Laurie Loomis
    Perry (editors).
New York: Holmes & Meier, 1982.

Film and Propaganda in America: A Documentary History (Volume 1: World War I).
Wood, Richard (editor).
Westport, CT: Greenwood Press, 1990.

Film and Propaganda in America: A Documentary History (Volume 2: World War II--Part 1).
Culbert, David (editor).
Westport, CT: Greenwood Press, 1990.

Film and Propaganda in America: A Documentary History (Volume 3: World War II--Part 2).
Culbert, David (editor).
Westport, CT: Greenwood Press, 1990.

Film & Radio Propaganda in World War II.
Short, K.R.M. (editor).
Knoxville, TN: University of Tennessee, 1983.

Film and Revolution.
MacBean, James Roy.
Bloomington, IN: Indiana University, 1975.

Film and Society.
MacCann, Richard Dyer (editor).
New York: Charles Scribner's Sons, 1964.

Film and the Arts in Symbiosis: A Resource Guide.
Edgerton, Gary R. (editor).
Westport, CT: Greenwood Press, 1988.

Film and the Critical Eye.
DeNitto, Dennis and William Herman.
New York: Macmillan Publishing Company, 1975.
[NOTE: Selected entries from this book.]

Film and the Interpretive Process.
Boyd, David.
New York: Peter Lang Publishing, 1989.

Film and the Liberal Arts.
Ross, T.J. (editor).
New York: Holt, Rinehart and Winston, 1970.

Film And/As Literature.
Harrington, John (editor).
Englewood Cliffs, NJ: Prentice-Hall, 1977.

Film at Wit's End: Eight Avant-Garde Filmmakers.
Brakhage, Stan.
Kingston, NY: McPherson, 1989.

Film Before Griffith.
Fell, John L. (editor).
Berkeley, CA: University of California, 1983.

Film Biographies.
Brakhage, Stan.
Berkeley, CA: Turtle Island, 1977.

Film: Book 1 (The Audience and the Filmmaker).
Hughes, Robert (editor).
New York: Grove Press, 1959.

Film: Book 2 (Films of Peace and War).
Hughes, Robert (editor).
New York: Grove Press, 1962.

Film Criticism: A Counter Theory.
Cadbury, William and Leland Poague.
Ames, IA: Iowa State University, 1982.

Film, Culture, and the Black Filmmaker: A Study of Functional Relationships and Parallel Developments.
Diakité, Madubuko.
New York: Arno Press, 1980.

Film/Culture: Explorations of Cinema in Its Social Context.
Thomas, Sari (editor).
Metuchen, NJ: Scarecrow Press, 1982.

Film Culture Reader.
Sitney, P. Adams (editor).
New York: Praeger, 1970.

The Film Director as Superstar.
Gelmis, Joseph.
Garden City, NY: Doubleday and Company, 1970.

Film Directors on Directing.
Gallagher, John Andrew.
New York: Praeger, 1989.

Film Essays and a Lecture.
Eisenstein, Sergei (Jay Leyda, editor).
Princeton, NJ: Princeton University, 1968, 1982.

The Film Factory: Russian and Soviet Cinema in Documents.
Taylor, Richard (translator and editor) and Ian Christie (editor).
Cambridge, MA: Harvard University, 1988.

Film Feminists: Theory and Practice.
Gentile, Mary C.
Westport, CT: Greenwood Press, 1985.

Film Flam: Essays on Hollywood.
McMurtry, Larry.
New York: Simon and Schuster, 1987.

Film Form.
Eisenstein, Sergei M. (Jay Leyda, translator and editor).
New York: Harcourt, Brace, 1949.

Film Form: Thirty-Five Top Filmmakers Discuss Their Craft.
Oumano, Ellen.
New York: St. Martin's Press, 1985.

Film Genre Reader.
Grant, Barry Keith (editor).
Austin, TX: University of Texas, 1986.

Film Genre: Theory and Criticism.
Grant, Barry K..
Metuchen, NJ: Scarecrow Press, 1977.

The Film Greats.
Norman, Barry.
London: Hodder & Stoughton, 1985.

Film Hieroglyphs: Ruptures in Classical Cinema.
Conley, Tom.
Minneapolis, MN: University of Minnesota, 1991.

Film: Historical-Theoretical Speculations.
Lawton, Ben and Janet Staiger (editors).
Pleasantville, NY: Redgrave Publishing, 1977.

Film in Society.
Berger, Arthur Asa (editor).
London: Transaction Books, 1980.

Film in the Aura of Art.
Andrew, Dudley.
Princeton, NJ: Princeton University, 1984.

Film India: The New Generation 1960-1980.
Cunha, Uma da (editor).
New Delhi (India): Directorate of Film Festivals, 1981.
[NOTE: Selected entries from this book.]

Film Lighting: Talks with Hollywood's Cinematographers and Gaffers.
Malkiewicz, Kris.
Englewood Cliffs, NJ: Prentice-Hall, 1986.

Film Makers on Film Making: Statements on Their Art by Thirty Directors.
Geduld, Harry M. (editor).
Bloomington, IN: Indiana University, 1970.

Film Notes.
Hammen, Scott.
Louisville, KY: Hamilton Printing Co, 1979.

Film on the Left: American Documentary Film from 1931 to 1942.
Alexander, William.
Princeton, NJ: Princeton University, 1981.

Film Plots: Scene-By-Scene Narrative Outlines for Feature Film Study (Volume 1).
Leff, Leonard J.
Ann Arbor, MI: Pierian Press, 1983.

Film Plots: Scene-By-Scene Narrative Outlines for Feature Film Study (Volume 2).
Leff, Leonard J.
Ann Arbor, MI: Pierian Press, 1988.

Film Propaganda: Soviet Russia and Nazi Germany.
Taylor, Richard.
New York: Barnes & Noble, 1979.
[NOTE: Selected entries from this book.]

Film: Readings in the Mass Media.
Kirschner, Allen and Linda (editors).
New York: The Odyssey Press, 1971.

Film Score: The View from the Podium.
Thomas, Tony (editor).
South Brunswick, NJ: A.S. Barnes and Company, 1979.

The Film Sense.
Eisenstein, Sergei M. (Jay Leyda, translator and editor).
New York: Harcourt, Brace, 1942, 1947.

Film Sound: Theory and Practice.
Weis, Elisabeth and John Belton (editors).
New York: Columbia University, 1985.

Film Study in Higher Education.
Stewart, David C. (editor).
Washington, DC: American Council on Education, 1966.

Film Study in the Undergraduate Curriculum.
Grant, Barry Keith (editor).
New York: Modern Language Association, 1983.

Film Style and Technology: History and Analysis.
Salt, Barry.
London: Starword, 1983.

Film: The Front Line 1983.
Rosenbaum, Jonathan.
Denver, CO: Arden Press, 1983.

Film: The Front Line 1984.
Ehrenstein, David.
Denver, CO: Arden Press, 1984.

Film Theory and Criticism: Introductory Readings (first edition).
Mast, Gerald and Marshall Cohen (editors).
New York: Oxford University Press, 1974.

Film Theory and Criticism: Introductory Readings (second edition).
Mast, Gerald and Marshall Cohen (editors).
New York: Oxford University Press, 1979.

Film Theory and Criticism: Introductory Readings (third edition).
Mast, Gerald and Marshall Cohen (editors).
New York: Oxford University Press, 1985.

Film Theory and Criticism: Introductory Readings (fourth edition).
Mast, Gerald, Marshall Cohen and Leo Braudy (editors).
New York: Oxford University Press, 1992.

Filming Literature: The Art of Screen Adaptation.
Sinyard, Neil.
New York: St. Martin's Press, 1986.

The Filming of the West.
Tuska, Jon.
Garden City, NY: Doubleday and Company, 1976.

Filming Shakespeare's Plays: The Adaptations of Laurence Olivier, Orson Welles, Peter Brook and Akira Kurosawa.
Davies, Anthony.
New York: Cambridge University, 1988.

Filmmakers in Conversation.
Loeb, Anthony (editor).
Chicago, IL: Columbia College, 1982.

Filmmakers on Filmmaking (Volume 1).
McBride, Joseph (editor).
Los Angeles: J.P. Tarcher (for the American Film Institute), 1983.

Filmmakers on Filmmaking (Volume 2).
McBride, Joseph (editor).
Los Angeles: J.P. Tarcher (for the American Film Institute), 1983.

Films Deliver: Teaching Creatively with Film.
Schillaci, Anthony and John M. Culkin (editors).
New York: Citation Press, 1970.
[NOTE: Selected entries from this book.]

Films for Women.
Brunsdon, Charlotte (editor).
London: British Film Institute, 1986.

Films of Commitment: Socialist Cinema in Eastern Europe.
Nemes, Károly.
Budapest (Hungary): Corvina, 1985.
[NOTE: Selected entries from this book.]

The Films of G.W. Pabst: An Extraterritorial Cinema.
Rentschler, Eric (editor).
New Brunswick, NJ: Rutgers University, 1990.

The Films of the Seventies: A Social History.
Palmer, William J.
Metuchen, NJ: Scarecrow Press, 1987.
[NOTE: Selected entries from this book.]

The Films of Werner Herzog: Between Mirage and History.
Corrigan, Timothy (editor).
New York: Methuen, 1986.

The Films You Don't See on Television.
Schlossheimer, Michael.
New York: Vantage Press, 1979.

The First Film Makers.
MacCann, Richard Dyer (editor).
Metuchen, NJ: Scarecrow Press, 1989.

The First Tycoons.
MacCann, Richard Dyer (editor).
Metuchen, NJ: Scarecrow Press, 1987.

Five for Five: The Films of Spike Lee.
No author/editor provided.
New York: Stewart, Tabori & Chang, 1991.

Flights of Fancy: The Great Fantasy Films.
Von Gunden, Kenneth.
Jefferson, NC: McFarland & Company, 1989.

Focus on *Blow-Up*.
Huss, Roy (editor).
Englewood Cliffs, NJ: Prentice-Hall, 1971.

Focus on *Bonnie and Clyde*.
Cawelti, John G. (editor).
Englewood Cliffs, NJ: Prentice-Hall, 1973.

Focus on Chaplin.
McCaffrey, Donald W. (editor).
Englewood Cliffs, NJ: Prentice-Hall, 1971.

Focus on *Citizen Kane*.
Gottesman, Ronald (editor).
Englewood Cliffs, NJ: Prentice-Hall, 1971.

Focus on D.W. Griffith.
Geduld, Harry M. (editor).
Englewood Cliffs, NJ, 1971.

Focus on Film and Theatre.
Hurt, James (editor).
Englewood Cliffs, NJ: Prentice-Hall, 1974.

Focus on Godard.
Brown, Royal S. (editor).
Englewood Cliffs, NJ: Prentice-Hall, 1972.

Focus on Hitchcock.
LaValley, Albert J. (editor).
Englewood Cliffs, NJ: Prentice-Hall, 1972.

Focus on Howard Hawks.
McBride, Joseph (editor).
Englewood Cliffs, NJ: Prentice-Hall, 1972.

Focus on Orson Welles.
Gottesman, Ronald (editor).
Englewood Cliffs, NJ: Prentice-Hall, 1976.

Focus on *Rashomon*.
Richie, Donald (editor).
Englewood Cliffs, NJ: Prentice-Hall, 1972.

Focus on Shakespearean Films.
Eckert, Charles W. (editor).
Englewood Cliffs, NJ: Prentice-Hall, 1972.

Focus on *Shoot the Piano Player*.
Braudy, Leo (editor).
Englewood Cliffs, NJ: Prentice-Hall, 1972.

Focus on *The Birth of a Nation*.
Silva, Fred (editor).
Englewood Cliffs, NJ: Prentice-Hall, 1971.

Focus on The Horror Film.
Huss, Roy and T.J. Ross (editors).
Englewood Cliffs, NJ: Prentice-Hall, 1972.

Focus on The Science Fiction Film.
Johnson, William (editor).
Englewood Cliffs, NJ: Prentice-Hall, 1972.

Focus on *The Seventh Seal*.
Steene, Birgitta (editor).
Englewood Cliffs, NJ: Prentice-Hall, 1972.

Focus on The Western.
Nachbar, Jack (editor).
Englewood Cliffs, NJ: Prentice-Hall, 1974.

Footnotes to the Film.
Davy, Charles (editor).
London: Lowe & Brydone Ltd, 1938 (reprint New York: Arno Press, 1970).

Forbidden Films: The Filmmaker and Human Rights (In Aid of Amnesty International).
Glassman, Marc and W.W. Barker (editors).
Toronto (Ontario): Toronto Arts Group for Human Rights, 1984.
[NOTE: Selected entries from this book.]

Framing the Past: The Historiography of German Cinema and Television.
Murray, Bruce A. and Christopher J. Wickham (editors).
Carbondale, IL: Southern Illinois University Press, 1992.

French Cinema of the Occupation and Resistence: The Birth of a Critical Esthetic.
Bazin, André (Stanley Hochman, translator).
New York: Frederick Ungar Publishing, 1975.
[NOTE: Selected entries from this book.]

French Cinema Since 1946 (Volume 1: The Great Tradition).
Armes, Roy.
Cranbury, NJ: A.S. Barnes, 1966, rev. 1970.

French Cinema Since 1946 (Volume 2: The Personal Style).
Armes, Roy.
Cranbury, NJ: A.S. Barnes, 1966, rev. 1970.

French Film: Texts and Contexts.
Hayward, Susan and Ginette Vincendeau (editors).
New York: Routledge, 1990.

French Film Theory and Criticism: A History/Anthology (Volume 1: 1907-1929).
Abel, Richard (editor).
Princeton, NJ: Princeton University, 1988.

French Film Theory and Criticism: A History/Anthology (Volume 2: 1929-1939).
Abel, Richard (editor).
Princeton, NJ: Princeton University, 1988.

The French Literary Filmmakers.
Michalczyk, John J.
Philadelphia, PA: The Art Alliance Press, 1980.

Fritz Lang: Genre and Representation in His American Films.
Humphries, Reynold.
Baltimore, MD: Johns Hopkins University, 1982; trans. 1989.
[NOTE: Selected entries from this book.]

Fritz Lang: The Image and the Look.
Jenkins, Stephen (editor).
London: British Film Institute, 1981.

From Enchantment to Rage: The Story of Surrealist Cinema.
Kovács, Steven.
Cranbury, NJ: Associated University Presses, 1980.
[NOTE: Selected entries from this book.]

From Hanoi to Hollywood: The Vietnam War in Film.
Dittmar, Linda and Gene Michaud (editors).
New Brunswick, NJ: Rutgers University, 1990.

From Limelight to Satellite: A Scottish Film Book.
Dick, Eddie (editor).
Edinburgh (Scotland): Scottish Film Council and British Film Institute, 1990.

The Future of the Movies.
Ebert, Roger and Gene Siskel.
New York: Andrews & McMeel, 1991.

Games of Terror: *Halloween, Friday the 13th*, **and the Films of the Stalker Cycle.**
Dika, Vera.
Cranbury, NJ: Associated University Presses, 1990.

Garbo and the Night Watchmen.
Cooke, Alistair (editor).
New York: McGraw-Hill Book Co., 1971.

Gays and Film (first edition).
Dyer, Richard (editor).
London: British Film Institute Publication, 1977.

Gays and Film (revised edition).
Dyer, Richard (editor).
New York: New York Zoetrope, 1984.

Genre: The Musical/A Reader.
Altman, Rick (editor).
Boston, MA: Routledge & Kegan Paul, 1981.

German Film and Literature: Adaptations and Transformations.
Rentschler, Eric (editor).
New York: Methuen, 1986.

Ginger, Loretta and Irene Who?.
Eells, George.
New York: Putnam, 1976.

Godard and Others: Essays on Film Form.
Giannetti, Louis D.
Cranbury, NJ: Associated University Presses, 1975.

Godard on Godard.
Godard, Jean-Luc (Tom Milne, translator).
New York: The Viking Press, 1972.

The Gospel from Outer Space.
Short, Robert.
New York: Harper & Row, 1983.

Graham Greene: The Films of His Fiction.
Phillips, Gene D.
New York: Teachers College Press, 1974.

Great American Directors.
Smith, Dian G.
New York: Julian Messner, 1987.

The Great Cartoon Directors.
Lenburg, Jeff.
Jefferson, NC: McFarland & Company, 1983.

Great Film Directors: A Critical Anthology.
Braudy, Leo and Morris Dickstein (editors).
New York: Oxford University Press, 1978.

The Great Movie Comedians (from Charlie Chaplin to Woody Allen).
Maltin, Leonard.
New York: Crown Publishers, 1978.

The Great Movie Shorts.
Maltin, Leonard.
New York: Bonanza Books, 1972.
[NOTE: Selected entries from this book.]

Greenhorns: Foreign Filmmakers Interpret America.
Kagan, Norman.
Ann Arbor, MI: Pierian Press, 1982.

Grierson on Documentary.
Grierson, John (Forsyth Hardy, editor).
New York: Praeger, 1966.

Grierson on the Movies.
Grierson, John (Forsyth Hardy, editor).
London: Faber and Faber, 1981.

Guts & Glory: Great American War Movies.
Suid, Lawrence H.
Reading, MA: Addison-Wesley Publishing Co., 1978.

Halliwell's Hundred.
Halliwell, Leslie.
New York: Charles Scribner's Sons, 1982.

The Hand That Holds the Camera: Interviews with Women Film and Video Directors.
Miller, Lynn Fieldman.
New York: Garland Publishing, 1988.

Handbook of American Film Genres.
Gehring, Wes D. (editor).
Westport, CT: Greenwood Press, 1988.

Harlan Ellison's Watching.
Ellison, Harlan.
Los Angeles: Underwood-Miller, 1989.
[NOTE: Selected entries from this book.]

Hemingway and Film.
Phillips, Gene D.
New York: Frederick Ungar Publishing, 1980.

Hemingway and the Movies.
Laurence, Frank M.
Jackson, MS: University of Mississippi, 1981.
[NOTE: Selected entries from this book.]

The Historian and Film.
Smith, Paul (editor).
New York: Cambridge University, 1976.

A History of the American Avant-Garde Cinema.
No author/editor provided.
New York: The American Federation of Arts, 1976.

A Hitchcock Reader.
Deutelbaum, Marshall and Leland Poague (editors).
Ames, IA: Iowa State University, 1986.

The Hitchcock Romance: Love and Irony in Hitchcock's Films.
Brill, Lesley.
Princeton, NJ: Princeton University, 1988.

Hitchcock's Re-Released Films: From *Rope* to *Vertigo*.
Raubicheck, Walter and Walter Srebnick (editors).
Detroit, MI: Wayne State University, 1991.

Hollywood 1920-1970.
Cowie, Peter (editor).
London: Tantivy Press, 1977.

Hollywood as Historian: American Film in a Cultural Context.
Rollins, Peter C. (editor).
Lexington, KY: University Press of Kentucky, 1983.

Hollywood Cameramen: Sources of Light.
Higham, Charles.
Bloomington, IN: Indiana University, 1970.

Hollywood Destinies: European Directors in America, 1922-1931.
Petrie, Graham.
London: Routledge & Kegan Paul, 1985.

Hollywood Directors 1914-1940.
Koszarski, Richard (editor).
New York: Oxford University Press, 1976.

Hollywood Directors 1941-1976.
Koszarski, Richard (editor).
New York: Oxford University Press, 1977.

The Hollywood Film Industry.
Kerr, Paul (editor).
London: Routledge & Kegan Paul, 1986.

Hollywood Genres: Formulas, Filmmaking, and the Studio System.
Schatz, Thomas.
Philadelphia, PA: Temple University, 1981.

The Hollywood Greats.
Norman, Barry.
London: Hodder & Stoughton, 1979.

The Hollywood Hall of Shame: The Most Expensive Flops in Movie History.
Medved, Harry and Michael.
New York: Putman, 1984.

Hollywood in the Age of Television.
Balio, Tino (editor).
Cambridge, MA: Unwin Hyman, 1990.

Hollywood: Legend and Reality.
Webb, Michael (editor).
Boston, MA: New York Graphics Society, 1986.

The Hollywood Murder Casebook.
Munn, Michael.
London: Robson Books, 1987.

The Hollywood Professionals (Volume 1).
Canham, Kingsley.
London: Tantivy Press, 1973.

The Hollywood Professionals (Volume 2).
Denton, Clive, Kingsley Canham and Tony Thomas.
London: Tantivy Press, 1974.

The Hollywood Professionals (Volume 3).
Belton, John.
London: Tantivy Press, 1974.

The Hollywood Professionals (Volume 4).
Rosenthal, Stuart and Judith Kass.
London: Tantivy Press, 1975.

The Hollywood Professionals (Volume 5).
Denton, Clive and Kingsley Canham.
London: Tantivy Press, 1976.

The Hollywood Professionals (Volume 6).
Estrin, Allen.
London: Tantivy Press, 1980.

The Hollywood Professionals (Volume 7).
Poague, Leland.
London: Tantivy Press, 1980.

Hollywood Renaissance.
Jacobs, Diane.
New York: A.S. Barnes, 1977.

The Hollywood Screenwriters.
Corliss, Richard (editor).
New York: Avon Books, 1972.

Hollywood Speaks!: An Oral History.
Steen, Mike (editor).
New York: G.P. Putnam's Sons, 1974.

The Hollywood Studio System.
Gomery, Douglas.
New York: St. Martin's Press, 1986.

The Hollywood Studios: House Style in the Golden Age of the Movies.
Mordden, Ethan.
New York: Alfred A. Knopf, 1988.

Hollywood: The Golden Era.
Spears, Jack.
Cranbury, NJ: A.S. Barnes, 1971.

Hollywood: The Pioneers.
Brownlow, Kevin.
New York: Alfred A. Knopf, 1979.

Hollywood Tragedy.
Carr, William H.A..
New York: Fawcett Crest, 1962, 1976.

Hollywood Voices: Interviews with Film Directors.
Sarris, Andrew (editor).
Indianapolis, IN: Bobbs-Merrill, 1967, 1971.

Home Is Where the Heart Is: Studies in Melodrama and the Woman's Film.
Gledhill, Christine (editor).
London: British Film Institute, 1987.

Horizons West: Studies of Authorship within the Western.
Kitses, Jim.
Bloomington, IN: Indiana University, 1969.

The Horror People.
Brosnan, John.
New York: New American Library, 1976.

Hound & Horn: Essays on Cinema.
Amberg, George (editor).
New York: Arno Press & The New York Times, 1972 (reprint).

How Do I Look: Queer Film and Video.
Bad Object-Choices [*sic*].
Seattle, WA: Bay Press, 1991.

How Scripts Are Made.
Karetnikova, Inga.
Carbondale, IL: Southern Illinois University, 1990.

The "I" of the Camera: Essays in Film Criticism, History, and Aesthetics.
Rothman, William.
New York: Cambridge University, 1988.

Icons: Intimate Portraits.
Worrell, Denise.
New York: The Atlantic Monthly Press, 1989.

Ideas of Order in Literature & Film.
Ruppert, Peter (editor).
Tallahassee, FL: University Presses of Florida, 1980.

Ideas on Film: A Handbook for the 16mm Film User.
Starr, Cecile (editor).
New York: Funk & Wagnalls, 1951.

Ideology and the Image: Social Representation in the Cinema and Other Media.
Nichols, Bill.
Bloomington, IN: Indiana University, 1981.
[NOTE: Selected entries from this book.]

The Idols of Silence.
Slide, Anthony.
Cranbury, NJ: A.S. Barnes, 1976.

Illuminating Shadows: The Mythic Power of Film.
Hill, Geoffrey.
Boston, MA: Shambhala, 1992.

Image and Likeness: Religious Visions in American Film Classics.
May, John R. (editor).
Mahwah, NJ: Paulist Press, 1992.

Image as Artifact: The Historical Analysis of Film and Television.
O'Connor, John E. (editor).
Malabar, FL: Robert E. Krieger Publishing, 1990.

Image Ethics: The Moral Rights of Subjects in Photographs, Film, and Television.
Gross, Larry, John Stuart Katz, and Jay Ruby (editors).
New York: Oxford University Press, 1988.

The Image Maker.
Henderson, Ron (editor).
Richmond, VA: John Knox Press, 1971.

"Image" on the Art and Evolution of the Film: Photographs and Articles from the Magazine of the International Museum of Photography.
Deutelbaum, Marshall (editor).
New York: Dover Publications, 1979.

Image, Sound and Story: The Art of Telling in Film.
Potter, Cherry.
London: Secker & Warburg, 1990.
[NOTE: Selected entries from this book.]

Images in Our Souls: Cavell, Psychoanalysis, and Cinema.
Smith, Joseph H. and William Kerrigan (editors).
Baltimore, MD: Johns Hopkins University, 1987.

Images of Alcoholism.
Cook, Jim and Mike Lewington (editors).
London: British Film Institute, 1979.

Images of Madness: The Portrayal of Insanity in the Feature Film.
Fleming, Michael and Roger Manvell.
Cranbury, NJ: Associated University Presses, 1985.

Imitations of Life: A Reader on Film and Television.
Landy, Marcia (editor).
Detroit, MI: Wayne State University, 1991.

The Immediate Experience: Movies, Comics, Theatre and Other Aspects of Popular Culture.
Warshow, Robert.
New York: Atheneum, 1970.

Indelible Images: New Perspectives on Classic Films.
Cardullo, Bert.
Lanham, MD: University Press of America, 1987.

Indian Cinema Superbazaar.
Vasudev, Aruna and Philippe Lenglet (editors).
New Delhi (India): Vikas Publishing House Pvt Ltd, 1983.

Inner Views: Filmmakers in Conversation.
Breskin, David.
New York: Faber and Faber, 1992.

Inner Views: Ten Canadian Film-Makers.
Hofsess, John.
Canada: McGraw-Hill Ryerson Ltd., 1975.

Inside the Film Factory: New Approaches to Russian and Soviet Cinema.
Taylor, Richard and Ian Christie (editors).
New York: Routledge, 1991.

Interviews with B Science Fiction and Horror Movie Makers.
Weaver, Tom.
Jefferson, NC: McFarland & Company, 1988.

Interviews with Film Directors.
Sarris, Andrew.
Indianapolis, IN: Bobbs-Merrill, 1967.

Introduction to Film Criticism: Major Critical Approaches to Narrative Film.
Bywater, Tim and Thomas Sobchack.
New York: Longman, 1989.

Introduction to the Art of the Movies.
Jacobs, Lewis (editor).
New York: The Noonday Press, 1960.

Introduction to the Photoplay: Contemporary Account of the Transition to Sound in Film.
Tibbetts, John C. (editor).
Los Angeles: A National Film Society Publication, 1929.

Inventing Vietnam: The War in Film and Television.
Anderegg, Michael (editor).
Philadelphia, PA: Temple University, 1991.

The Israeli Film: Social and Cultural Influences 1912-1973.
Jacob-Arzooni, Gloria.
New York: Garland, 1983.
[NOTE: Selected entries from this book.]

Issues in Feminist Film Criticism.
Erens, Patricia (editor).
Bloomington, IN: Indiana University, 1990.

Italian and Irish Filmmakers in America: Ford, Capra, Coppola, and Scorsese.
Lourdeaux, Lee.
Philadelphia, PA: Temple University, 1990.

Italian Cinema: Literary and Socio-Political Trends.
Lawton, Benjamin Ray, Jr. (editor).
Los Angeles: Center for Italian Studies (Department of Italian, UCLA), 1973.

Italian Film in the Light of Neorealism.
Marcus, Millicent.
Princeton, NJ: Princeton University, 1986.

The Italian Political Filmmakers.
Michalczyk, John J.
Cranbury, NJ: Associated University Presses, 1986.

Japanese Film Directors.
Bock, Audie.
New York: Kodansha International, 1978.

Jean Renoir: Essays, Conversations, Reviews.
Gilliatt, Penelope.
New York: McGraw-Hill, 1975.

Journey To a Legend and Back: The British Realistic Film.
Orbanz, Eva (editor).
Berlin (Germany): Verlag Volker Spiess, 1977.

Jump Cut: Hollywood, Politics and Counter Cinema.
Steven, Peter (editor).
New York: Praeger, 1985.

The Kaleidoscopic Lens: How Hollywood Views Ethnic Groups.
Miller, Randall M. (editor).
Englewood, NJ: Jerome S. Ozer, 1980.

Kings of the Bs: Working within the Hollywood System.
McCarthy, Todd and Charles Flynn (editors).
New York: E.P. Dutton, 1975.

Kings of Tragedy.
Wayne, Jane Ellen.
New York: Manor Books, 1976.

Kino and the Woman Question: Feminism and Soviet Silent Film.
Mayne, Judith.
Columbus, OH: Ohio State University, 1989.

Kino-Eye: The Writings of Dziga Vertov.
Vertov, Dziga (Annette Michelson, editor).
Berkeley, CA: University of California, 1984.

A Kiss Is Still a Kiss.
Ebert, Roger.
New York: Andrews, McMeel & Parker, 1984.

Kuleshov on Film: Writings of Lev Kuleshov.
Kuleshov, Lev (Ronald Levaco, editor and translator).
Berkeley, CA: University of California, 1974.

Landmark Films: The Cinema of Our Century.
Wolf, William.
New York: Paddington Press, 1979.

Landscapes of Contemporary Cinema.
Lewis, Leon and William David Sherman.
Buffalo, NY: State University of New York, 1967.

The Last New Wave: The Australian Film Revival.
Stratton, David.
Sydney (Australia): Angus & Robertson, 1980.

The Latin Image in American Film.
Woll, Allen L.
Los Angeles: UCLA Latin American Center, 1977.
[NOTE: Selected entries from this book.]

Lessons with Eisenstein.
Nizhny, Vladimir (Ivor Montagu and Jay Leyda, translators and editors).
New York: Hill and Wang, 1962, 1969.

Light Moving in Time: Studies in the Visual Aesthetics of Avant-Garde Film.
Wees, William C..
Berkeley, CA: University of California Press, 1992.

The Living and the Undead: From Stoker's 'Dracula' to Romero's 'Dawn of the Dead'.
Waller, Gregory A.
Urbana, IL: University of Illinois, 1986.

The Logic of Images: Essays and Conversations.
Wenders, Wim.
London: Faber and Faber, 1991.

Made Into Movies: From Literature to Film.
McDougal, Stuart Y.
New York: Holt, Rinehart and Winston, 1985.

Magical Reels: A History of Cinema in Latin America.
King, John.
London and New York: Verso, 1990.
[NOTE: Selected entries from this book.]

Major Film Directors of the American and British Cinema.
Phillips, Gene D..
Cranbury, NJ: Lehigh University/Associated University Presses, 1990.

The Major Film Theories: An Introduction.
Andrew, J. Dudley.
New York: Oxford University Press, 1976.

Making a Monster: The Creation of Screen Characters by the Great Makeup Artists.
Taylor, Al and Sue Roy.
New York: Crown Publishers, 1980.

The Making of the Great Westerns.
Meyer, William R.
New Rochelle, NY: Arlington House, 1979.

Making Visible the Invisible: An Anthology of Original Essays on Film Acting.
Zucker, Carole (editor).
Metuchen, NJ: Scarecrow Press, 1990.

Man and the Movies.
Robinson, W.R. (editor).
Baton Rouge, LA: Louisiana State University, 1967.

Mastering the Film and Other Essays.
Samuels, Charles Thomas.
Knoxville, TN: University of Tennessee, 1977.

Masters of Light: Conversations with Contemporary Cinematographers.
Schaefer, Dennis and Larry Salvato.
Berkeley, CA: University of California, 1984.

Masters of the American Cinema.
Giannetti, Louis.
Englewood Cliffs, NJ: Prentice-Hall, 1981.

Masters of the Soviet Cinema: Crippled Creative Biographies.
Marshall, Herbert.
Boston, MA: Routledge & Kegan Paul, 1983.

The Melody Lingers On: The Great Songwriters and Their Movie Musicals.
Hemming, Roy.
New York: Newmarket Press, 1986.

The Men Who Made the Movies.
Schickel, Richard.
New York: Atheneum, 1975.

The Mexican Cinema: Interviews with Thirteen Directors.
Reyes Nevares, Beatrice.
Albuquerque, NM: University of New Mexico, 1976.

The Mindscapes of Art: Dimensions of the Psyche in Fiction, Drama, and Film.
Huss, Roy.
Cranbury, NJ: Associated University Presses, 1986.
[NOTE: Selected entries from this book.]

The Modern American Novel and the Movies.
Peary, Gerald and Roger Shatzkin (editors).
New York: Frederick Ungar Publishing, 1978.

Modern European Filmmakers and the Art of Adaptation.
Horton, Andrew S. and Joan Magretta, eds.
New York: Frederick Ungar Publishing, 1981.

Modernism in the Narrative Cinema: The Art Film as a Genre.
Siska, William C.
New York: Arno Press, 1980.
[NOTE: Selected entries from this book.]

Modernist Montage: The Obscurity of Vision in Cinema and Literature.
Sitney, P. Adams.
New York: Columbia University, 1990.

The Moguls.
Zierold, Norman.
New York: Coward-McCann, 1969.

More of Hollywood's Unsolved Mysteries.
Austin, John.
New York: Shapolsky Publishers, 1991.

The Movie Business Book.
Squire, Jason E. (editor).
Englewood Cliffs, NJ: Prentice-Hall, 1983.

Movie Comedy.
Byron, Stuart and Elisabeth Weis (editors).
New York: Grossman, 1977.

Movie Comedy Teams.
Maltin, Leonard.
New York: New American Library, 1970, 1974.

The Movie Greats.
Norman, Barry.
Kent (England): Hodder & Stoughton, 1985.

The Movie Makers: Artists in an Industry.
Phillips, Gene D.
Chicago, IL: Nelson-Hall Company, 1973.

Movie People: At Work in the Business of Film.
Baker, Fred and Ross Firestone (editors).
New York: Douglas Book Co., 1972.

Movie Reader.
Cameron, Ian (editor).
New York: Praeger, 1972.

Movie Star: A Look at the Women Who Made Hollywood.
Mordden, Ethan.
New York: St. Martin's Press, 1983.

The Movie Star: The National Society of Film Critics on 'The Movie Star'.
Weis, Elisabeth (editor).
New York: Penguin Books, 1981.

The Movie That Changed My Life.
Rosenberg, David (editor).
New York: Viking Press, 1991.

Moviemakers at Work: Interviews.
Chell, David.
Redmond, WA: Microsoft Press, 1987.

The Moviemakers.
Fleming, Alice.
New York: St. Martin's Press, 1973.

The Movies: An American Idiom (Readings in the Social History of the American Motion Picture).
McClure, Arthur F. (editor).
Cranbury, NJ: Associated University Presses, 1971.

Movies and Methods: An Anthology.
Nichols, Bill (editor).
Berkeley, CA: University of California, 1976.

Movies and Methods (Volume 2).
Nichols, Bill (editor).
Berkeley, CA: University of California, 1985.

Movies and Money: Financing the American Film Industry.
Wasko, Janet.
Norwood, NJ: Ablex Publishing, 1982.

Movies as Artifacts: Cultural Criticism of Popular Film.
Marsden, Michael T., John G. Nachbar and Sam L. Grogg, Jr., (editors).
Chicago, IL: Nelson-Hall, 1982.

The Movies as Medium.
Jacobs, Lewis (editor).
New York: Farrar, Straus & Giroux, 1970.

The Movies in Our Midst: Documents in the Cultural History of Film in America.
Mast, Gerald (editor).
Chicago, IL: University of Chicago, 1982.

Movies of the Silent Years.
Lloyd, Ann (editor).
London: Orbis, 1984.

The Movies on Your Mind: Film Classics on the Couch from Fellini to Frankenstein.
Greenberg, Harvey R.
New York: E.P. Dutton, 1975.

A Moving Picture Feast: The Filmgoer's Hemingway.
Oliver, Charles M. (editor).
New York: Praeger, 1989.

Narration in Light: Studies in Cinematic Point of View.
Wilson, George M.
Baltimore, MD: Johns Hopkins University, 1986.

Narrative, Apparatus, Ideology: A Film Theory Reader.
Rosen, Philip (editor).
New York: Columbia University, 1986.

Narrative Strategies: Original Essays in Film and Prose Fiction.
Conger, Syndy M. and Janice R. Welsch (editors).
Macomb, IL: Western Illinois University, 1980.

Native Informant: Essays on Film, Fiction, and Popular Culture.
Braudy, Leo.
New York: Oxford University Press, 1991.
[NOTE: Selected entries from this book.]

The New American Cinema: A Critical Anthology.
Battcock, Gregory (editor).
New York: E.P. Dutton, 1967.

The New Australian Cinema.
Murray, Scott (editor).
Australia: Thomas Nelson Australia Pty Ltd, 1980.

New Challenges for Documentary.
Rosenthal, Alan (editor).
Berkeley, CA: University of California, rev. 1988.

The New Documentary in Action: A Casebook in Film Making.
Rosenthal, Alan.
Berkeley, CA: University of California, 1971.

New German Cinema: From Oberhausen to Hamburg.
Franklin, James.
Boston, MA: Twayne Publishers, 1983.

The New German Cinema.
Sandford, John.
London: Oswald Wolff, 1980.
[NOTE: Selected entries from this book.]

New German Film: The Displaced Image.
Corrigan, Timothy.
Austin, TX: University of Texas, 1983.

New German Filmmakers: From Oberhausen Through the 1970s.
Phillips, Klaus (editor).
New York: Frederick Ungar Publishing, 1984.

The New Hollywood: What the Movies Did with the New Freedoms of the Seventies.
Bernardoni, James.
Jefferson, NC: McFarland & Company, 1991.

The New Italian Cinema: Studies in Dance and Despair.
Witcombe, R.T..
New York: Oxford University Press, 1982.

The New Poverty Row: Independent Filmmakers as Distributors.
Ray, Fred Olen (editor).
Jefferson, NC: McFarland & Company, 1991.

The New Screenwriter Looks at the New Screenwriter.
Froug, William.
Los Angeles: Silman-James Press, 1991.

New Vocabularies in Film Semiotics: Structuralism, Post-Structuralism and Beyond.
Stam, Robert, Robert Burgoyne and Sandy
   Flitterman-Lewis.
New York: Routledge, 1992.

The New Wave: Critical Landmarks.
Graham, Peter (editor).
Garden City, NY: Doubleday and Company, 1968.

The New Wave: Truffaut, Godard, Chabrol, Rohmer, Rivette.
Monaco, James.
New York: Oxford University Press, 1976.

Nonfiction Film: Theory and Criticism.
Barsam, Richard Meran (editor).
New York: E.P. Dutton, 1976.

Nonindifferent Nature.
Eisenstein, Sergei (Herbert Marshall, translator).
New York: Cambridge University, 1987.

Notes of a Film Director.
Eisenstein, Sergei.
New York: Dover Publications, 1970.

The Novel and the Cinema.
Wagner, Geoffrey.
Cranbury, NJ: Associated University Presses, 1975.
[NOTE: Selected entries from this book.]

Novels into Film.
Bluestone, George.
Berkeley, CA: University of California Press, 1961.

Nuclear War Films.
Shaheen, Jack G. (editor).
Carbondale, IL: Southern Illinois University, 1978.

Of Mice and Magic: A History of American Animated Cartoons.
Maltin, Leonard.
New York: New American Library, 1980, rev. 1986.

Off Hollywood: The Making and Marketing of Independent Films.
Rosen, David and Peter Hamilton.
New York: Grove Weidenfeld, 1987, 1990.

Off Screen: Women and Film in Italy.
Bruno, Giuliana and Maria Nadotti (editors).
New York: Routledge, 1988.

Omni's Screen Flights/Screen Fantasies: The Future According to Science Fiction Cinema.
Peary, Danny (editor).
Garden City, NY: Doubleday and Company, 1984.

On the Verge of Revolt: Women in American Films of the Fifties.
French, Brandon.
New York: Frederick Ungar Publishing, 1978.

The Once and Future Film: British Cinema in the Seventies and Eighties.
Walker, John.
London: Methuen, 1985.

Opera, Ideology and Film.
Tambling, Jeremy.
Manchester (England): Manchester University, 1987.

The Parade's Gone By.
Brownlow, Kevin.
New York: Alfred A. Knopf, 1968.

Passport to Hollywood: Film Immigrants Anthology.
Whittemore, Don and Philip Alan Ceccettini.
New York: McGraw-Hill Book Co., 1976.

People Are Crazy Here.
Reed, Rex.
New York: Delacorte Press, 1974.

People Will Talk.
Kobal, John.
New York: Alfred A. Knopf, 1986.

Personal Views: Explorations in Film.
Wood, Robin.
London: Gordon Fraser, 1976.

Perspectives on Chinese Cinema.
Berry, Chris (editor).
London: British Film Institute Publishing, 1991.

Perspectives on the Study of Film.
Katz, John Stuart (editor).
Boston, MA: Little, Brown, 1971.

Pieces of Time: Peter Bogdanovich on the Movies.
Bogdanovich, Peter.
New York: Arbor House/Esquire, 1973.

Planks of Reason: Essays on the Horror Film.
Grant, Barry Keith (editor).
Metuchen, NJ: Scarecrow Press, 1984.

The Poetics of Cinema (Volume 9: Russian Poetics in Translation).
Taylor, Richard (editor).
Oxford (England): RPT Publications (in association with the Department of Literature, University of Essex), 1982 (orig. 1927).

Points of Resistence: Women, Power & Politics in the New York Avant-Garde Cinema, 1943-71.
Rabinovitz, Lauren.
Urbana, IL: University of Illinois, 1991.

The Political Language of Film and the Avant-Garde.
Polan, Dana B.
Ann Arbor, MI: UMI Research Press, 1981, 1985.

Politics and Film.
Furhammar, Leif and Folke Isaksson (Kersti French, translator).
New York: Praeger, 1968, trans 1971.
[NOTE: Selected entries from this book.]

Politics, Art and Commitment in East European Cinema.
Paul, David W. (editor).
New York: St. Martin's Press, 1983.

Politics of the Self: Feminism and the Postmodern in West German Literature and Film.
McCormick, Richard W.
Princeton, NJ: Princeton University, 1991.
[NOTE: Selected entries from this book.]

Popcorn and Sexual Politics.
Maio, Kathi.
Freedom, CA: The Crossing Press, 1991.

Popular Television and Film.
Bennett, Tony, Susan Boyd-Bowman, Colin Mercer and Janet Woollacott (editors).
London: British Film Institute Publishing, 1981.
[NOTE: Selected entries from this book.]

Post New Wave Cinema in the Soviet Union and Eastern Europe.
Goulding, Daniel J. (editor).
Bloomington, IN: Indiana University, 1989.

Powell, Pressburger and Others.
Christie, Ian (editor).
London: British Film Institute Publication, 1978.

The Power of the Image: Essays on Representation and Sexuality.
Kuhn, Annette [with Frances Borzello, Jill Pack and Cassandra Wedd].
London: Routledge & Kegan Paul, 1985.

The Pretend Indians.
Bataille, Gretchen M. and Charles L.P. Silet (editors).
Ames, IA: Iowa State University, 1980.
[NOTE: Selected entries from this book.]

Produced and Abandoned: The Best Films You've Never Seen.
Sragow, Michael (editor).
San Francisco, CA: Mercury House, 1990.

Producers on Producing: The Making of Film and Television.
Broughton, Irv.
Jefferson, NC: McFarland & Company, 1986.

Profiles: Five Film-makers from India.
Banerjee, Shampa.
New Delhi (India): Directorate of Film Festivals, 1985.

Projections: A Forum for Film Makers (Issue No. 1).
Boorman, John and Walter Donohue, eds..
London: Faber and Faber, 1992.

Propaganda and the German Cinema, 1933-1945.
Welch, David.
New York: Oxford University Press, 1983.

Propaganda on Film: A Nation at War.
Maynard, Richard A. (editor).
Rochelle Park, NJ: Hayden Book Company, 1975.

Propaganda, Politics and Film, 1918-45.
Pronay, Nicholas and D.W. Spring (editors).
London: Macmillan Press, 1982.

Psychiatry and the Cinema.
Gabbard, Krin and Glen O. Gabbard.
Chicago, IL: University of Chicago, 1987.
[NOTE: Selected entries from this book.]

Psychoanalysis and Cinema.
Kaplan, E. Ann (editor).
New York: Routledge, 1990.

Pursuits of Happiness: The Hollywood Comedy of Remarriage.
Cavell, Stanley.
Cambridge, MA: Harvard University, 1981.

Questions of Third Cinema.
Pines, Jim and Paul Willemen (editors).
London: British Film Institute, 1989.

Radical Innocence: A Critical Study of the Hollywood Ten.
Dick, Bernard F.
Lexington, KY: University Press of Kentucky, 1989.

Raymond Chandler on Screen: His Novels Into Film.
Pendo, Stephen.
Metuchen, NJ: The Scarecrow Press, 1976.

Readings and Writings: Semiotic Counter-Strategies.
Wollen, Peter.
London: Verso, 1982.

Readings in Philippine Cinema.
Guerrero, Rafael Ma (editor).
Manila (Philippines): Experimental Cinema of the
    Philippines (Manila Film Center), 1983.

The Real Tinsel.
Rosenberg, Bernard and Harry Silverstein (editors).
New York: The Macmillan Company, 1970.

Rediscovering French Film.
Bandy, Mary Lea (editor).
New York: Museum of Modern Art, 1983.

**Reel Politics: American Political Movies from *Birth of a
Nation* to *Platoon*.**
Christensen, Terry.
New York: Basil Blackwell, 1987.

**Reel Power: The Struggle for Influence and Success in
the New Hollywood.**
Litwak, Mark.
New York: William Morrow, 1986.

**Re-interpreting Brecht: His Influence on Contemporary
Drama and Film.**
Kleber, Pia and Colin Visser (editors).
New York: Cambridge University, 1990.
[NOTE: Selected entries from this book.]

Religion in Film.
May, John R. and Michael Bird (editors).
Knoxville, TN: University of Tennessee, 1982.

Renaissance of the Film.
Bellone, Julius (editor).
New York: The Macmillan Company, 1970.

Renoir on Renoir: Interviews, Essays, and Remarks.
Renoir, Jean (Carol Volk, translator).
New York: Cambridge University, 1989.

Resisting Images: Essays on Cinema and History.
Sklar, Robert and Charles Musser (editors).
Philadelphia, PA: Temple University, 1990.

**Reviewing Histories: Selections from New Latin
American Cinema.**
Fusco, Coco (editor).
Buffalo, NY: Hallwalls, 1987.

Re-vision: Essays in Feminist Film Criticism.
Doane, Mary Ann, Patricia Mellencamp and Linda Williams
    (editors).
Frederick, MD/Los Angeles: University Publications of
    America/American Film Institute, 1984.

The Rhetoric of Filmic Narration.
Browne, Nick.
Ann Arbor, MI: UMI Research Press, 1976, 1982.

Ribbons in Time: Movies and Society since 1945.
Monaco, Paul.
Bloomington, IN: Indiana University, 1987.

The Rivals of D.W. Griffith: Alternate Auteurs 1913-1918.
Koszarski, Richard (editor).
Minneapolis, MN: Walker Art Center, 1976.

Rolling Breaks (and Other Movie Business).
Harmetz, Aljean.
New York: Alfred A. Knopf, 1983.

**Romantic Comedy: In Hollywood from Lubitsch to
Sturges.**
Harvey, James.
New York: Alfred A. Knopf, 1987.

**Rotha on the Film: A Selection of Writings about the
Cinema.**
Rotha, Paul.
Fair Lawn, NJ: Essential Books, 1958.

**The Runaway Bride: Hollywood Romantic Comedy of
the 1930s.**
Kendall, Elizabeth.
New York: Alfred A. Knopf, 1990.

Russian Formalist Film Theory.
Eagle, Herbert (editor).
Ann Arbor, MI: Michigan Slavic Materials (University of
    Michigan), 1981.

**S.M. Eisenstein: Selected Works (Volume 1: Writing,
1922-34).**
Eisenstein, Sergei (Richard Taylor, translator and editor).
London: British Film Institute, 1988.

Schickel on Film.
Schickel, Richard.
New York: William Morrow, 1989.

Scotch Reels: Scotland in Cinema and Television.
McArthur, Colin (editor).
London: British Film Institute, 1982.
[NOTE: Selected entries from this book.]

Screen Experience: An Approach to Film.
Feyen, Sharon (editor).
Dayton, OH: Pflaum Publishing, 1969.

Screen Reader 1: Cinema/Ideology/Politics.
No editor provided.
London: The Society for Education in Film and Television,
    1977.

Screening America: Reflections on Five Classic Films.
Blake, Richard A.
Mahwah, NJ: Paulist Press, 1991.

**Screening America: Using Hollywood Films to Teach
History.**
Rebhorn, Marlette.
New York: Peter Lang, 1988.

Screening Out the Past: The Birth of Mass Culture and the Motion Picture Industry.
May, Lary.
New York: Oxford University Press, 1980.

Screening the Novel: Rediscovered American Fiction in Film.
Miller, Gabriel.
New York: Frederick Ungar Publishing, 1980.

Screening the Novel: The Theory and Practice of Literary Dramatization.
Giddings, Robert, Keith Selby and Chris Wensley.
New York: St. Martin's Press, 1990.

The Screenwriter Looks at the Screenwriter.
Froug, William.
New York: Dell Publishing, 1972; reprint Los Angeles: Silman-James Press, 1991.

Screenwriter: Words Become Pictures (Interviews with Twelve Screenwriters from the Golden Age of American Movies).
Server, Lee.
Pittstown, NJ: The Main Street Press, 1987.

The Screenwriter's Handbook: What to Write, How to Write It, Where to Sell It.
Nash, Constance and Virginia Oakey.
New York: Barnes & Noble Books, 1978.
[NOTE: Selected entries from this book.]

Screwball Comedy: A Genre of Madcap Romance.
Gehring, Wes D..
Westport, CT: Greenwood Press, 1986.

Second Wave.
Cameron, Ian, et al.
New York: Praeger, 1970.

Seeing is Believing: How Hollywood Taught Us to Stop Worrying and Love the Fifties.
Biskind, Peter.
New York: Pantheon Books, 1983.

Seeing Through Movies.
Miller, Mark Crispin (editor).
New York: Pantheon Books, 1990.

Selected Takes: Film Editors on Editing.
LoBrutto, Vincent (editor).
New York: Praeger, 1991.

Self and Cinema: A Transformalist Perspective.
Houston, Beverle and Marsha Kinder.
Pleasantville, NY: Redgrave Publishing, 1980.

Selling a Screenplay: The Screenwriter's Guide to Hollywood.
Field, Syd.
New York: Dell Publishing, 1989.
[NOTE: Selected entries from this book.]

Sex Goddesses of the Silent Screen.
Zierold, Norman.
Chicago, IL: Henry Regnery, 1973.

Sexual Stratagems: The World of Women in Film.
Erens, Patricia (editor).
New York: Horizon Press, 1979.

Sexuality in the Movies.
Atkins, Thomas R. (editor).
Bloomington, IN: Indiana University, 1975.

The Shadow and Its Shadow: Surrealist Writing on Cinema.
Hammond, Paul (editor).
London: British Film Institute, 1978.

Shadows of the Magic Lamp: Fantasy and Science Fiction in Film.
Slusser, George and Eric S. Rabkin (editors).
Carbondale, IL: Southern Illinois University, 1985.

Shakespeare and the Film.
Manvell, Roger.
New York: Praeger, 1971.

Shakespeare on Film.
Jorgens, Jack J.
Bloomington, IN: Indiana University, 1977.

Shakespearean Films/Shakespearean Directors.
Donaldson, Peter S.
Boston, MA: Unwin Hyman, 1990.

Shooting Stars: Heroes and Heroines of Western Film.
McDonald, Archie P. (editor).
Bloomington, IN: Indiana University, 1987.

Shot/Countershot: Film Tradition and Women's Cinema.
Fischer, Lucy.
Princeton, NJ: Princeton University, 1989.

"Show Us Life": Toward a History and Aesthetic of the Committed Documentary.
Waugh, Thomas (editor).
Metuchen, NJ: Scarecrow Press, 1984.

Sight and Sound: A Fiftieth Anniversary Selection.
Wilson, David (editor).
London: Faber and Faber, 1982.

Sight, Sound, and Society: Motion Pictures and Television in America.
White, David Manning and Richard Averson (editors).
Boston, MA: Beacon Press, 1968.

Signatures of the Visible.
Jameson, Fredric.
London: Routledge, Chapman & Hall, 1990.

Signs and Meaning in the Cinema.
Wollen, Peter.
Bloomington, IN: Indiana University, 1969 (rev. 1972).

The Silent Voice: The Golden Age of the Cinema.
Lennig, Arthur.
Albany, NY: State University of New York, 1966.

The Silent Voice: A Sequel.
Lennig, Arthur.
Troy, NY: Walter Snyder, Printer, 1967.

Six European Directors: Essays on the Meaning of Film Style.
Harcourt, Peter.
London: Penguin, 1974.

The Social Documentary in Latin America.
Burton, Julianne (editor).
Pittsburgh, PA: University of Pittsburgh, 1990.

The Sociology of Film Art.
Huaco, George A.
New York: Basic Books, 1965.

Some Time in the Sun.
Dardis, Tom.
New York: Charles Scribner's Sons, 1976.

Sound and the Cinema: The Coming of Sound to American Film.
Cameron, Evan William (editor).
Pleasantville, NY: Redgrave Publishing, 1980.

The Sound Film: An Introduction.
Lennig, Arthur (editor).
Troy, NY: Walter Snyder (Printer), 1969.

The South and Film.
French, Warren (editor).
Jackson, MI: University Press of Mississippi, 1981.

Souvenir Programs (of Twelve Classic Movies 1927-1941).
Kreuger, Miles (editor).
New York: Dover Publications, 1977.

Spanish Film Directors (1950-1985).
Schwartz, Ronald.
Metuchen, NJ: Scarecrow Press, 1986.

Spanish Film Under Franco.
Higginbotham, Virginia.
Austin, TX: University of Texas, 1988.

Spellbound in Darkness: A History of the Silent Film.
Pratt, George C. (text and editor).
Greenwich, CT: New York Graphic Society, 1966, rev. 1973.

Springtime in Italy: A Reader on Neo-Realism.
Overbey, David (editor and translator).
Hamden, CT: Archon, 1978.

Stage to Screen: Theatrical Origins of Early Film, David Garrick to D.W. Griffith.
Vardac, A. Nicholas.
Cambridge, MA: Harvard University, 1949.
[NOTE: Selected entries from this book.]

Star Acting: Gish, Garbo, Davis.
Affron, Charles.
New York: E.P. Dutton, 1977.

Star Texts: Image and Performance in Film and Television.
Butler, Jeremy G. (editor).
Detroit, MI: Wayne State University, 1991.

Stardom: Industry of Desire.
Gledhill, Christine (editor).
New York: Routledge, 1991.

Stars of the Silents.
Wagenknecht, Edward.
Metuchen, NJ: Scarecrow Press, 1987.

Steinbeck and Film.
Millichap, Joseph R.
New York: Frederick Ungar Publishing, 1983.
[NOTE: Selected entries from this book.]

Stephen King's Danse Macabre.
King, Stephen.
New York: Berkley Books, 1981.
[NOTE: Selected entries from this book.]

Sternberg.
Baxter, Peter.
London: British Film Institute Publishing, 1980.

Still in Movement: Shakespeare on Screen.
Buchman, Lorne M.
New York: Oxford University Press, 1991.

The Story of the Films (as told by Leaders of the Industry).
Kennedy, Joseph P. (editor).
New York: A.W. Shaw Company, 1927 (reprinted Jerome S. Ozer, 1971).

The Story of the Lost Reflection: The Alienation of the Image in Western and Polish Cinema.
Coates, Paul.
London: Verso, 1985.
[NOTE: Selected entries from this book.]

Stranded Objects: Mourning, Memory, and Film in Postwar Germany.
Santner, Eric L.
Ithaca, NY: Cornell University, 1990.

Structural Film Anthology.
Gidal, Peter (editor).
London: British Film Institute, 1976.

Studies in Documentary.
Lovell, Alan and Jim Hillier.
New York: Viking Press, 1972.

Styles of Radical Will.
Sontag, Susan.
New York: Farrar, Straus and Giroux, 1969.
[NOTE: Selected entries from this book.]

Subversive Pleasures: Bakhtin, Cultural Criticism, and Film.
Stam, Robert.
Baltimore, MD: Johns Hopkins University, 1989.

Surrealism and American Feature Films.
Matthews, J.H.
Boston, MA: Twayne Publishers, 1979.

Surrealism and the Cinema: Open-Eyed Screening.
Gould, Michael.
London: A.S. Barnes, 1976.

Take 10: Contemporary British Film Directors.
Hacker, Jonathan and David Price.
London: Oxford University Press, 1991.

Take 22: Moviemakers on Moviemaking.
Crist, Judith.
New York: Viking Press, 1984 (expanded edition, New York: Continuum, 1991).

The Talking Clowns: From Laurel and Hardy To the Marx Brothers.
Manchel, Frank.
New York: Franklin Watts, 1976.

Talking Pictures.
Norman, Barry.
London: Hodder & Stoughton, 1987.

Talking Pictures: Screenwriters in the American Cinema 1927-1973.
Corliss, Richard.
Woodstock, NY: The Overlook Press, 1974.

The Taste for Beauty.
Rohmer, Eric (Carol Volk, translator).
New York: Cambridge University Press, 1989.

A Technological History of Motion Pictures and Television.
Fielding, Raymond (editor).
Berkeley, CA: University of California, 1967.

Technologies of Gender: Essays on Theory, Film, and Fiction.
de Lauretis, Teresa.
Bloomington, IN: Indiana University, 1987.

Ten Film Classics: A Re-Viewing.
Murray, Edward.
New York: Frederick Ungar Publishing, 1978.

Tennessee Williams and Film.
Yacowar, Maurice.
New York: Frederick Ungar Publishing, 1977.

That's Hollywood: A Behind-the-Scenes Look at 60 of the Greatest Films of All Time.
Gelder, Peter van.
New York: Harper Perennial, 1990.

Theatre and Film: A Comparative Study.
Manvell, Roger.
Cranbury, NJ: Associated University Presses, 1979.

Theories of Authorship: A Reader.
Caughie, John (editor).
London: Routledge & Kegan Paul, 1981.

Theories of Film.
Tudor, Andrew.
New York: Viking Press, 1973.
[NOTE: Selected entries from this book.]

Three European Directors.
Wall, James M. (editor).
Grand Rapids, MI: William B. Eerdman's Publishing, 1973.

Three-Quarter Face: Reports and Reflections.
Gilliatt, Penelope.
New York: Coward, McCann & Geoghegan, 1980.

Through a Freudian Lens Deeply: A Psychoanalysis of Cinema.
Dervin, Daniel.
Hillsdale, NJ: The Analytic Press, 1985.

To Desire Differently: Feminism and the French Cinema.
Flitterman-Lewis, Sandy.
Urbana, IL: University of Illinois, 1990.

Tower of Babel: Speculations on the Cinema.
Rhode, Eric.
Philadelphia, PA: Chilton Books, 1967.

The Tragic and Mysterious Deaths of Hollywood's Most Remarkable Legends.
Jacobson, Laurie.
New York: Simon and Schuster, 1984.

Transcendental Style in Film: Ozu, Bresson, Dreyer.
Schrader, Paul.
Berkeley, CA: University of California, 1972.

Travolta to Keaton.
Reed, Rex.
New York: William Morrow, 1979.

Twenty-five Black African Filmmakers.
Pfaff, Françoise.
Westport, CT: Greenwood Press, 1988.

Underworld U.S.A..
McArthur, Colin.
New York: Viking Press, 1972.

Unheard Melodies: Narrative Film Music.
Gorbman, Claudia.
London: British Film Institute, 1987.
[NOTE: Selected entries from this book.]

Unholy Fools (Wits, Comics, Disturbers of the Peace: Film and Theater).
Gilliatt, Penelope.
New York: The Viking Press, 1973.
[NOTE: Selected entries from this book.]

Unspeakable Images: Ethnicity and the American Cinema.
Friedman, Lester D. (editor).
Urbana, IL: University of Illinois, 1991.

Valentines and Vitriol.
Reed, Rex.
New York: Delacorte Press, 1977.

A Variable Harvest: Essays and Reviews of Film and Literature.
Tuska, Jon.
Jefferson, NC: McFarland & Company, 1990.
[NOTE: Selected entries from this book.]

A Viewer's Guide to Film Theory and Criticism.
Eberwein, Robert T.
Metuchen, NJ: Scarecrow Press, 1979.

Virgins, Vamps, and Flappers: The American Silent Movie Heroine.
Higashi, Sumiko.
St. Albans, VT: Eden Press Women's Publications, 1978.

Visual and Other Pleasures.
Mulvey, Laura.
Bloomington, IN: Indiana University, 1989.

Voices from the Japanese Cinema.
Mellen, Joan.
New York: Liveright, 1975.

The War, The West, and The Wilderness.
Brownlow, Kevin.
New York: Alfred A. Knopf, 1979.
[NOTE: Selected entries from this book.]

West German Filmmakers on Film: Visions and Voices.
Rentschler, Eric (editor).
New York: Holmes & Meier, 1988.

Western Films: A Brief History.
Etulain, Richard W. (editor).
Manhattan, KS: Sunflower University, 1983, 1988.

Western Movies.
Pilkington, William T. and Don Graham (editors).
Albuquerque, NM: University of New Mexico, 1979.

What Is Cinema? (Volume 1).
Bazin, André (Hugh Gray, translator and editor).
Berkeley, CA: University of California, 1967.

What Is Cinema? (Volume 2).
Bazin, André (Hugh Gray, translator and editor).
Berkeley, CA: University of California, 1971.

What Is Cinéma Vérité?.
Issari, M. Ali and Doris A. Paul.
Metuchen, NJ: Scarecrow Press, 1979.

Women and Film.
Todd, Janet (editor).
New York: Holmes & Meier Publishers, 1988.

Women and Film: Both Sides of the Camera.
Kaplan, E. Ann.
New York: Methuen, 1983.

Women and the Cinema: A Critical Anthology.
Kay, Karyn and Gerald Peary (editors).
New York: E.P. Dutton, 1977.

Women Directors: The Emergence of a New Cinema.
Quart, Barbara Koenig.
New York: Praeger, 1988.

Women Filmmakers: A Critical Reception.
Heck-Rabi, Louise.
Metuchen, NJ: Scarecrow Press, 1984.

Women in Film Noir.
Kaplan, E. Ann (editor).
London: British Film Institute, 1978.

Women on Film: The Critical Eye.
McCreadie, Marsha.
New York: Praeger, 1983.

The Women Who Knew Too Much: Hitchcock and Feminist Theory.
Modleski, Tania.
New York: Methuen, 1988.

Women's Film and Female Experience, 1940-1950.
Walsh, Andrea S..
New York: Praeger, 1984.

Wonderful Inventions: Motion Pictures, Broadcasting, and Recorded Sound at the Library of Congress.
Newsom, Iris (editor).
Washington, DC: Library of Congress, 1985.
[NOTE: Selected entries from this book.]

Words and Images: Australian Novels into Film.
McFarlane, Brian.
Melbourne (Australia): Heinemann Publishers Australia Pty Ltd, 1983.

Working Cinema: Learning from the Masters.
Madsen, Roy Paul.
Belmont, CA: Wadsworth Publishing, 1989.

Working in Hollywood: 64 Professionals Talk about Moviemaking.
Brouwer, Alexandra and Thomas Lee Wright (editors).
New York: Crown Publishers, 1990.

World Cinema Since 1945.
Luhr, William (editor).
New York: Frederick Ungar Publishing, 1987.

The World of Entertainment!: Hollywood's Greatest Musicals.
Fordin, Hugh.
Garden City, NY: Doubleday and Company, 1975.

The World of Luis Bunuel: Essays in Criticism.
Mellen, Joan (editor).
New York: Oxford University Press, 1978.

Writing in a Film Age: By Contemporary Novelists.
Cohen, Keith (editor).
Boulder, CO: University Press of Colorado, 1991.

Yesterday's Clowns: The Rise of Film Comedy.
Manchel, Frank.
New York: Franklin Watts, 1973.

Young British and Black: The Work of Sankofa and Black Audio Film Collective.
Fusco, Coco.
Buffalo, NY: Hallwalls, 1988.

Young Soviet Film Makers.
Vronskaya, Jeanne.
London: George Allen and Unwin, 1972.
[NOTE: Selected entries from this book.]

1   **anonymous.**
"'The True Story of Bonnie and Clyde'."
"Barrow and Woman Are Slain by Police in Louisiana Trap." [RE: Bonnie and Clyde.]
"Barrow's Killings Date from Parole." [RE: Clyde Barrow.]
"Changes and Revisions from Original Script to Film." [RE: *Bonnie and Clyde.*]
"Frank Hamer's Story."
IN: <u>Focus on Bonnie and Clyde</u>

2   **anonymous.**
"*Rashomon.*"
IN: <u>Focus on Rashomon</u>

3   **anonymous.**
"A Discussion with the Audience of the 1970 Chicago Film Festival." [RE: Howard Hawks.]
IN: <u>Focus on Howard Hawks</u>

4   **anonymous.**
"Capitalizing Race Hatred." [RE: *Birth of a Nation.*]
"Censorship: The Curse of a Nation." [RE: *Birth of a Nation.*]
"Fighting Race Calumny." [RE: *Birth of a Nation.*]
IN: <u>Focus on The Birth of a Nation</u>

5   **anonymous.**
"Communications Act of 1934."
IN: <u>Film and Society</u>

6   **anonymous.**
"Declaration of the Association of Revolutionary Cinematography."
"Film-Makers' Letter to Stalin."
"First Congress of Soviet Writers (extracts)."
"For a Great Cinema Art: Speeches to the All-Union Creative Conference of Workers in Soviet Cinema (extracts)."
"Party Cinema Conference Resolution: The Results of Cinema Construction in the USSR and the Tasks of Soviet Cinema."
"RAPP Resolution on Cinema." [RE: Russian Association of Proletarian Writers.]
"Reactions to Stakhanov's Article (extracts)." [SEE: Alexei Stakhanov, "My Suggestion to Soviet Cinema".]
"Resolution of Thirteenth Party Congress on Cinema."
"Russfilm Script Competition."
"To the Party Conference on Cinema From a Group of Film Directors."
IN: <u>The Film Factory</u>

7   **anonymous.**
"Fighting a Vicious Film: Protest Against The Birth of Nation."
IN: <u>Focus on D.W. Griffith</u>

8   **anonymous.**
"Film Notes: Middle Class Security vis-à-vis 'The Street' (*Dirnentragödie*; *Jenseits der Strasse*; *Der Blaue Engel*)."
"Film Notes: The Search for Harmony (*Metropolis*; *Niemandsland*; *M*)."
"Film Notes: The Plight of the Working Class (*Brüder*; *Mutter Krausens Fahrt ins Glück*; *So is das Leben* [and] *Kuhle Wampe, oder Wem gehört die Welt?*)."
IN: <u>Film and Politics in the Weimar Republic</u>

9   **anonymous.**
"Filmmakers and the Popular Government: A Political Manifesto." [RE: Chile.]
IN: <u>Reviewing Histories</u>

10   **anonymous.**
"From What Strange Source." [RE: farces.]
IN: <u>Image on the Art ...</u>

11   **anonymous.**
"In Memory of Harry Alan Potamkin, 1900-1933."
IN: <u>Hound & Horn</u>

12   **anonymous.**
"Interim Report of the Film Committee to the Australian Council for the Arts, 1969."
IN: <u>An Australian Film Reader</u>

13   **anonymous.**
"Letter of Clearance from the Production Code Office."
IN: <u>Focus on Citizen Kane</u>

14   **anonymous.**
"Loew's Inc."
"Color and Sound on Film."
"The Drama of the People."
"The Moving Picture and the National Character."
"The Nickelodeon."
"The Sins of Hollywood."
"Pictures That Talk."
"*The Birth of a Nation.*"
IN: <u>The Movies in Our Midst</u>

15   **anonymous.**
"Newsreel."
IN: <u>Perspectives on the Study of Film</u>

16   **anonymous.**
"RKO Cutting Continuity of the Orson Welles Production, *Citizen Kane.*"
IN: <u>The Citizen Kane Book</u>

17   **anonymous.**
"Schoedsack Tells of Making *Dr. Cyclops.*"
IN: <u>Focus on The Science Fiction Film</u>

18   **anonymous.**
"Stanley and Livingstone." [NOTE: Two articles with the same title.]
"Trader Horn." [NOTE: Two articles with the same title.]
IN: <u>Africa on Film</u>

19   **anonymous.**
"The 'Make-Believe' Indian."
IN: <u>The Pretend Indians</u>

20   **anonymous.**
"The Hamburg Declaration (1979)."
"The Manifesto of Women Film Workers (1979)."
"The Munich Declaration (1983)."
"The Oberhausen Manifesto (1962)."

IN: The Movies in Our Midst

47 **Adler, Mortimer J.**
"Art and Prudence."
IN: The Movies in Our Midst

48 **Adler, Mortimer.**
"[From:] Research: The Immature."
"[From:] The Problem in Practical Philosophy."
IN: Film and Society

49 **Adler, R.**
"Critic Keeps Her Cool on *Up Tight*."
IN: The Black Man on Film

50 **Adler, Renata.**
"On Reviewing, I: Turnstiles."
IN: Film: Readings in the Mass Media

51 **Adrian.**
"Clothes." [RE: costume.]
IN: Behind the Screen

52 **Affron, Charles.**
"The Actress as Metaphor: Gish in *Broken Blossoms*."
"The Actress as Auteur: Gish and Griffith." [RE: Lillian Gish.]
"Before Glamour at MGM: Gish, Vidor, and Seastrom."
"From Orchids to Roses: Garbo's Silent Films."
"A Career for *Camille*."
"A Star Is Made: Davis, Warners, and Wyler."
"'I detest cheap sentiment': Davis and the Tear Jerker."
IN: Star Acting

53 **Affron, Charles.**
"[From:] *Cinema and Sentiment*: Voice and Space."
IN: Film Theory and Criticism /4 ed

54 **Affron, Charles.**
"Generous Stars."
IN: Star Texts

55 **Affron, Charles.**
"Identifications."
IN: Imitations of Life

56 **Affron, Charles.**
"Order and the Space for Spectacle in Fellini's *8-1/2*."
IN: Close Viewings

57 **Agar, John.**
"John Agar." [An interview.]
IN: Interviews with B ...

58 **Agcaoili, T.D.**
"Lamberto V. Avellana: A National Artist and His Times."
IN: Readings in Philippine Cinema

59 **Agee, James.**
"Comedy's Greatest Era."
IN: Film Theory and Criticism /1 ed
Film Theory and Criticism /2 ed
Film Theory and Criticism /3 ed
Awake in the Dark
Film: An Anthology
Film: Readings in the Mass Media

60 **Agee, James.**
"*Notorious*."
IN: Focus on Hitchcock

61 **Agee, James.**
"*The Bride Comes to Yellow Sky*–the Shooting Script." [NOTE: Preceded by Stephen Crane's short story, "The Bride Comes to Yellow Sky."]
IN: Film and the Liberal Arts

62 **Agee, James.**
"David Wark Griffith."
IN: Great Film Directors
Awake in the Dark
Focus on The Birth of a Nation
The Black Man on Film

63 **Agee, James.**
"So Proudly We Fail."
IN: Propaganda on Film
The Movies in Our Midst

64 **Agee, James.**
"Three Short Reviews." [RE: *God Is My Co-Pilot*; *Till the Clouds Roll By*; *Carnegie Hall*.]
"Undirectable Director: John Huston."
IN: Awake in the Dark

65 **Agee, James.**
"*Farrebique*."
"*Monsieur Verdoux*."
IN: Renaissance of the Film

66 **Agee, James.**
"*Henry V*."
IN: Focus on Shakespearean Films
Film Theory and Criticism /1 ed

67 **Agee, James.**
"*Mission to Moscow*."
IN: Propaganda on Film

68 **Agee, James.**
"*Sunset Boulevard*."
IN: Sight and Sound

69 **Agee, James.**
"*Wilson*."
IN: Film and Society

70 **Agel, Geneviève.**
"*Il Bidone*."
IN: Federico Fellini

71 **Ager, Cecelia.**
"Cecelia Ager." [Collected film capsules.]
IN: Garbo and the Night Watchmen

72 **Agosta, Lucien L.**
"*Tom Brown's Schooldays* [novel by] Thomas Hughes. Pride and Pugilism: The Film Versions of *Tom Brown*."
IN: Children's Novels and the Movies

73 **Aguilar, Richard 'Aggie'.**
"Richard 'Aggie' Aguilar." [Interview by Kris Malkiewicz.]

"Van Dyke, Lorentz, Ivens, and Dick: Variations on the Sponsored Film and *Men and Dust*, 1938-1940."
IN: <u>Film on the Left</u>

99   **Alexandrov, Grigori Vassilievitch.**
"Working with Eisenstein."
IN: <u>Cinema in Revolution</u>

Alexandrov, Grigori. SEE: Eisenstein, Sergei.

100   **Alicata, Mario and Giuseppe De Santis.**
"Truth and Poetry: Verga and the Italian Cinema."
IN: <u>Springtime in Italy</u>

101   **Allan, Blaine.**
"The Only Voice in the World: Telling *The Saga of Anatahan*."
IN: <u>Sternberg</u>

102   **Allas, Denise Chou.**
"Dolphy: The Way of a Clown."
IN: <u>Readings in Philippine Cinema</u>

103   **Allen, Dede.**
"Dede Allen." [Interview by Vincent LoBrutto.]
IN: <u>Selected Takes</u>

104   **Allen, Douglas.**
"Workers' Films: Scotland's Hidden Film Culture."
IN: <u>Scotch Reels</u>

105   **Allen, Jay Presson.**
"Jay Presson Allen." [Interview by Judith Crist.]
IN: <u>Take 22</u>

106   **Allen, Jeanne Thomas.**
"Copyright and Early Theater, Vaudeville, and Film Competition."
IN: <u>Film Before Griffith</u>

107   **Allen, Jeanne Thomas.**
"Afterward." [RE: A reply to Ralph Cassady, Jr., "Monopoly in Motion Picture Production and Distribution..."]
IN: <u>The American Movie Industry</u>

108   **Allen, Jeanne Thomas.**
"The Decay of the Motion Pictures Patents Company."
IN: <u>The American Film Industry</u>

109   **Allen, Jeanne Thomas.**
"Fig Leaves in Hollywood: Female Representation and Consumer Culture."
IN: <u>Fabrications</u>

110   **Allen, Jeanne Thomas.**
"The Industrial Context of Film Technology: Standardisation and Patents." [SEE: Jean-Louis Comolli, "Discussion".]
IN: <u>The Cinematic Apparatus</u>

111   **Allen, Jeanne Thomas.**
"*The Turn of the Screw* [novel by] Henry James. *Turn of the Screw* and *The Innocents*: Two Types of Ambiguity."
IN: <u>The Classic American Novel ...</u>

112   **Allen, Jeanne.**
"Looking Through *Rear Window*: Hitchcock's Traps and Lures of Heterosexual Romance."
IN: <u>Female Spectators</u>

113   **Allen, Jeanne.**
"Self-Reflexivity in Documentary."
IN: <u>Explorations in Film Theory</u>

114   **Allen, Jim.**
"The Way Back from the Legend." [RE: British Free Cinema.]
IN: <u>Journey To a Legend and Back</u>

115   **Allen, Robert C.**
"Contra the Chaser Theory."
IN: <u>Film Before Griffith</u>

116   **Allen, Robert C.**
"A Reader-Oriented Poetics of the Soap Opera." [RE: television.]
IN: <u>Imitations of Life</u>

117   **Allen, Robert C.**
"Film History: The Narrow Discourse."
IN: <u>Film: Historical-Theoretical ...</u>

118   **Allen, Robert C.**
"Motion Picture Exhibition in Manhattan, 1906-1912: Beyond the Nickelodeon."
"Vitascope/Cinématographe: Initial Patterns of American Film Industrial Practice."
IN: <u>The American Movie Industry</u>
    <u>Film Before Griffith</u>

119   **Allen, Robert C.**
"The Movies in Vaudeville: Historical Context of the Movies as Popular Entertainment."
IN: <u>The American Film Industry /rev ed</u>

120   **Allen, Steve.**
"Steve Allen." [An interview.]
IN: <u>Producers on Producing</u>

121   **Allouache, Merzak.**
"The Necessity of a Cinema Which Interrogates Everyday Life." [RE: Algeria.]
IN: <u>Film and Politics in the Third World</u>

122   **Alloway, Lawrence.**
"Monster Films."
IN: <u>Focus on The Horror Film</u>

123   **Alloway, Lawrence.**
"The Iconography of the Movies."
IN: <u>Movie Reader</u>

124   **Almario, Virgilio S.**
"Cinderella Superstar: The Life and Legend of Nora Aunor."
IN: <u>Readings in Philippine Cinema</u>

125   **Almendros, Nestor.**
"[From:] *Man with a Camera*: Some Thoughts on My Profession."
IN: <u>Film Theory and Criticism /3 ed</u>

150   **Amis, Kingsley.**
      "A Decade of New Heartbreakers."
         IN: <u>Film and the Liberal Arts</u>

151   **Anderegg, Michael.**
      "Hollywood and Vietnam: John Wayne and Jane
         Fonda as Discourse."
         IN: <u>Inventing Vietnam</u>

152   **Anderson, Carolyn.**
      "The *Titicut Follies* Audience and the Double Bind of
         Court-Restricted Exhibition."
         IN: <u>Current Research in Film /v. 3</u>

153   **Anderson, Carolyn.**
      "Biographical Film."
         IN: <u>Handbook of American Film Genres</u>

154   **Anderson, Carolyn.**
      "Film and Literature."
         IN: <u>Film and the Arts in Symbiosis</u>

155   **Anderson, Carolyn and Thomas W. Benson.**
      "Direct Cinema and the Myth of Informed Consent:
         The Case of *Titicut Follies*."
         IN: <u>Image Ethics</u>

156   **Anderson, Howard A.**
      "Miniatures in Special Visual Effects."
         IN: <u>The ASC Treasury ...</u>

157   **Anderson, J.L.**
      "Japanese Swordfighters and American Gunfighters."
         IN: <u>Cinema Examined</u>

158   **Anderson, Joseph and Barbara.**
      "Motion Perception in Motion Pictures."
         IN: <u>The Cinematic Apparatus</u>

159   **Anderson, Lindsay.**
      "The Situation of the Serious Filmmaker."
         IN: <u>Film: Book 1</u>

160   **Anderson, Lindsay.**
      "Lindsay Anderson on Censorship: A Letter to Martin
         Heavisides."
         IN: <u>Forbidden Films</u>

161   **Anderson, Lindsay.**
      "Alfred Hitchcock."
         IN: <u>Great Film Directors</u>
             <u>Focus on Hitchcock</u>

162   **Anderson, Lindsay.**
      "Some Aspects of the Work of Humphrey Jennings."
         IN: <u>The Documentary Tradition /1 ed</u>
             <u>The Documentary Tradition /2 ed</u>

163   **Anderson, Lindsay.**
      "Lindsay Anderson." [Interview by Joseph Gelmis.]
         IN: <u>The Film Director as Superstar</u>

164   **Anderson, Lindsay.**
      "Interview [with] Lindsay Anderson." [Interview by Eva
         Orbanz, Gisela Tuchtenhagen and Klaus
         Wildenhahn.]
         IN: <u>Journey To a Legend and Back</u>

165   **Anderson, Lindsay.**
      "Free Cinema."
      "Only Connect: Some Aspects of the Work of
         Humphrey Jennings."
         IN: <u>Nonfiction Film Theory and Criticism</u>

166   **Anderson, Lindsay.**
      "*The Seventh Seal*."
         IN: <u>Focus on The Seventh Seal</u>

167   **Anderson, Lindsay.**
      "The Method of John Ford."
         IN: <u>The Emergence of Film Art /1 ed</u>
             <u>The Emergence of Film Art /2 ed</u>

168   **Anderson, Lindsay.**
      "Lindsay Anderson." [Interview by G. Roy Levin.]
         IN: <u>Documentary Explorations</u>

169   **Anderson, Lindsay.**
      "*The Searchers*."
         IN: <u>Theories of Authorship</u>

170   **Anderson, Lindsay, J.A. Bardem, Luis Buñuel,
      David Lean, Satyajit Ray, and Jean Renoir.**
      "The Film Maker and the Audience."
         IN: <u>Film Makers on Film Making</u>

171   **Anderson, Robert.**
      "*The Nun's Story*."
         IN: <u>Africa on Film</u>

172   **Anderson, Robert.**
      "The Motion Pictures Patents Company: A
         Reevaluation."
         IN: <u>The American Film Industry /rev ed</u>

      Anderson, Robert. SEE: Jacoby, Irving.

173   **Andreadis, A. Harriette.**
      "*Pippi Longstocking* [novel by] Astrid Lindgren. The
         Screening of Pippi Longstocking."
         IN: <u>Children's Novels and the Movies</u>

174   **Andrew, J. Dudley.**
      "Hugo Musterberg."
      "Rudolf Arnheim."
      "Sergei Eisenstein."
      "Béla Balázs and the Tradition of Formalism."
      "Siegfried Kracauer."
      "André Bazin."
      "Jean Mitry."
      "Christian Metz and the Semiology of the Cinema."
      "The Challenge of Phenomenology: Amédée Ayfre
         and Henri Agel."
         IN: <u>The Major Film Theories</u>

175   **Andrew, Dudley.**
      "The State of Film Theory."
      "Perception."
      "Representation."
      "Signification."
      "Narrative Structure."
      "Valuation (of Genres and Auteurs)."
      "Identification."
      "Figuration."

"Interpretation."
IN: <u>Concepts in Film Theory</u>

176   Andrew, Dudley.
"*Broken Blossoms*: The Vulnerable Text and the
Marketing of Masochism."
"The Turn and Return of *Sunrise*."
"The Fever of an Infectious Film: *L'Atalante* and the
Aesthetics of Spontaneity."
"Productive Discord in the System: Hollywood *Meets*
[sic, *Meet*] *John Doe*."
"*La Symphonie pastorale*, Performed by the French
Quality Orchestra."
"Private Scribblings: The Crux in the Margins around
Diary of a Country Priest."
"Realism, Rhetoric, and the Painting of History in
Henry V."
"Echoes of Art: The Distant Sounds of Orson Welles."
"The Passion of Identification in the Late Films of
Kenji Mizoguchi."
IN: <u>Film in the Aura of Art</u>

177   Andrew, Dudley.
"[From:] *Concepts in Film Theory*: Adaptation."
IN: <u>Film Theory and Criticism /4 ed</u>
<u>Concepts in Film Theory</u>

178   Andrew, Dudley.
"An Open Approach to Film Study and the Situation at
Iowa."
IN: <u>Film Study in the Undergraduate Curriculum</u>

179   Andrew, Dudley.
"Desperation and Meditation: Bresson's *Diary of a
Country Priest* from the Novel by Georges
Bernanos."
"Ice and Irony: Delannoy's *La Symphonie Pastorale*
from the Novel by André Gide."
IN: <u>Modern European Filmmakers ...</u>

180   Andrew, Dudley.
"France."
IN: <u>World Cinema Since 1945</u>

181   Andrew, Dudley.
"Hermeneutics and Cinema: The Issue of History."
IN: <u>The Cinematic Text</u>

182   Andrew, Dudley.
"Sound in France: The Origins of a Native School."
"Poetic Realism."
IN: <u>Rediscovering French Film</u>

183   Andrew, Dudley.
"The Primacy of Figure in Cinematic Signification."
IN: <u>Cinema and Language</u>

184   Andrew, Dudley.
"The Well-Worn Muse: Adaptation in Film History and
Theory."
IN: <u>Narrative Strategies</u>

185   Andrew, Dudley.
"The Neglected Tradition of Phenomenology in Film
Theory."
IN: <u>Movies and Methods /v. 2</u>

186   Andrew, Dudley.
"The Post-War Struggle for Colour."
IN: <u>The Cinematic Apparatus</u>

186a   Andrew, Dudley.
"*Casque d'or, casquettes*, a cask of aging wine:
Jacques Becker's *Casque d'or* (1952)."
IN: <u>French Film: Texts and Contexts</u>

187   Andrews, Julie.
"Julie Andrews." [Interview by Charles Higham.]
IN: <u>Celebrity Circus</u>

188   Andrews, Terry L.
"John Thomas Sayles."
IN: <u>Dictionary of Literary Biography /v. 44</u>

189   Andreyev, Leonid.
"First Letter on Theatre (extracts)."
"Second Letter on Theatre (extract)."
IN: <u>The Film Factory</u>

190   Ang, Ien.
"*Dallas* and the Melodramatic Imagination."
IN: <u>Imitations of Life</u>

191   Anger, Kenneth.
"Interview in 'Spider'."
IN: <u>Film Makers on Film Making</u>

192   Anhalt, Edward.
"'Gentlemen, This Is A Corpse.' There's Kind Of A
Silence--" [RE: an interview.]
IN: <u>Blueprint on Babylon</u>

193   Anhalt, Edward.
"Edward Anhalt." [Interview by William Froug.]
IN: <u>The Screenwriter Looks ...</u>

194   Anka, Paul.
"Paul Anka." [Interview by Charles Higham.]
IN: <u>Celebrity Circus</u>

195   Anoshchenko, Nikolai.
"Sound Cinema in the Service of the Cultural
Revolution."
IN: <u>The Film Factory</u>

196   Ansen, David.
"*Baby, It's You*."
"*Hearts of the West*."
"*Never Cry Wolf*."
"*September 30, 1955*."
"*Straight Time*."
IN: <u>Produced and Abandoned</u>

197   Ansen, David.
"Peter Sellers."
IN: <u>The Movie Star: The National ...</u>

198   Anstey, Edgar.
"Development of Film Technique in Britain."
IN: <u>Experiment in the Film</u>

199   Anstey, Edgar.
"Interview [with] Edgar Anstey." [Interview by Eva
Orbanz, Helmut Wietz and Klaus Wildenhahn.]

IN: <u>Journey To a Legend and Back</u>

200 **Antheil, George.**
"New Tendencies in Composing for Motion Pictures."
IN: <u>Film and the Liberal Arts</u>

201 **Anthony, Barry.**
"Music-Hall Mirth-Makers."
IN: <u>Movies of the Silent Years</u>

202 **Antin, David.**
"Video: The Distinctive Features of the Medium."
IN: <u>Film Theory and Criticism /3 ed</u>

203 **Antoine, André.**
"A Proposal on the Cinema."
IN: <u>French Film Theory and Criticism /v. 1</u>

204 **Antongini, Tom.**
"D'Annunzio and Film."
IN: <u>Authors on Film</u>

205 **Antonioni, Michelangelo.**
"Concerning a Film about the River Po."
IN: <u>Springtime in Italy</u>

206 **Antonioni, Michelangelo.**
"Two Statements."
IN: <u>Film Makers on Film Making</u>

207 **Antonioni, Michelangelo.**
"Reflections on the Film Actor."
IN: <u>Film: Readings in the Mass Media</u>

208 **Antonioni, Michelangelo.**
"Antonioni in the English Style: A Day on the Set."
IN: <u>Focus on Blow-Up</u>

209 **Antonioni, Michelangelo.**
"The Event and the Image."
IN: <u>The Emergence of Film Art /1 ed</u>
<u>The Emergence of Film Art /2 ed</u>

210 **Antonioni, Michelangelo.**
"Michelangelo Antonioni." [Interview by Andrew Sarris.]
IN: <u>Interviews with Film Directors</u>

211 **Antonioni, Michelangelo.**
"Michelangelo Antonioni." [Interview by Charles T. Samuels.]
IN: <u>Encountering Directors</u>

212 **Anwell, Maggie.**
"Lolita Meets the Werewolf: *The Company of Wolves*."
IN: <u>The Female Gaze</u>

212a **Apostolos-Cappadona, Diane.**
"The Art of 'Seeing': Classical Paintings and *Ben-Hur* [1959]."
IN: <u>Image and Likeness</u>

213 **Apseloff, Marilyn.**
"*Charlotte's Web* [novel by] E.B. White. *Charlotte's Web*: Flaws in the Weaving."
IN: <u>Children's Novels and the Movies</u>

214 **Aragon [Aragon, Louis].**
"What Is Art, Jean-Luc Godard?"

IN: <u>Authors on Film</u>
<u>Focus on Godard</u>

215 **Aragon, Louis.**
"On Décor."
IN: <u>The Shadow and Its Shadow</u>
<u>French Film Theory and Criticism /v. 1</u>

216 **Aranda, J. Francisco.**
"Out of Innocence."
IN: <u>The World of Luis Buñuel</u>

217 **Arbogast, Roy.**
"Roy Arbogast [on Special Effects: Mechanical Effects]." [Interview by David Chell.]
IN: <u>Moviemakers at Work</u>

218 **Arbuthnot, Lucie and Gail Seneca.**
"Pre-text and Text in *Gentlemen Prefer Blondes*."
IN: <u>Issues in Feminist Film Criticism</u>

219 **Archer, Eugene.**
"Director of Enigmas: Alain Resnais."
IN: <u>The Emergence of Film Art /1 ed</u>
<u>The Emergence of Film Art /2 ed</u>

220 **Archer, Eugene.**
"Elia Kazan--The Genesis of a Style."
IN: <u>The Film</u>

221 **Archer, Eugene.**
"Where Are the Stars of Yesteryear?"
IN: <u>The Movies: An American Idiom</u>

222 **Arié, Marie-Laure.**
"Author's Rights (Le Droit D'Auteur) and Contemporary Audiovisual Techniques in France."
IN: <u>Fair Use and Free Inquiry</u>

223 **Aristarco, Guido.**
"Guido Aristarco Answers Fellini." [RE: *La Strada*; neo-realism.]
"Italian Cinema." [RE: *La Strada*; neo-realism.]
IN: <u>Federico Fellini</u>

224 **Aristarco, Guido, Claude Autant-Lara, Robert Bresson, Noel Burch, André Cayatte, Samuel Fuller, Sergei Gerasimov, Jean-Luc Godard, Richard Griffith, Alexander Hammid, Kurt Hoffmann, Stanley Kauffmann, Stanley Kramer, Len Lye, Roger Manvell, Louis Marcorelles, Marshall McLuhan, Arthur Miller, Robert Osborn, Gian-Luigi Polidoro, Herbert Read, Jean Renoir, Tony Richardson, Paul Rotha, Dore Schary, George Stoney, François Truffaut, Archer Winsten, Robert Wise.**
"The Issue: Questions and Answers on Peace and War."
IN: <u>Film: Book 2</u>

225 **ARK (member).**
"ARRK Must Be Reorganized." [RE: Association of Workers of Revolutionary Cinematography.]
IN: <u>The Film Factory</u>

226 **Arkoff, Samuel Z.**
"Samuel Z. Arkoff." [An interview.]
IN: <u>Interviews with B ...</u>

227 **Arlen, Michael J.**
"The Prosecutor."
    IN: New Challenges for Documentary

228 **Arletty.**
"Arletty." [Interview by John Kobal.]
    IN: People Will Talk

229 **Arliss, George.**
"Stop Cruelty to Animals!"
    IN: Celebrity Articles ...

230 **Armat, Thomas.**
"My Part in the Development of the Motion Picture
    Projector."
    IN: A Technological History ...

231 **Armatage, Kay.**
"Interview with Joyce Wieland."
    IN: Women and the Cinema

232 **Armes, Roy.**
"René Clair."
"Jean Renoir."
"Marcel Carné."
"Max Ophuls."
"Jean Cocteau."
"Henri-Georges Clouzot."
"René Clément."
"Jacques Becker."
"Claude Autant-Lara."
"Jacques Tati."
"Jean Grémillon."
"Georges Rouquier."
"Roger Leenhardt."
    IN: French Cinema Since 1946 /v. 1

233 **Armes, Roy.**
"Georges Franju."
"Jean-Pierre Melville."
"Claude Chabrol."
"François Truffaut."
"Jean-Luc Godard."
"Jacques Rivette."
"Agnès Varda."
"Alain Resnais."
"Chris Marker."
"Alexandre Astruc."
"Roger Vadim."
"Louis Malle."
"Jean Rouch."
"Alain Robbe-Grillet."
"Jacques Demy."
"Pierre Etaix."
"Claude Lelouch."
    IN: French Cinema Since 1946 /v. 2

234 **Armes, Roy.**
"Luis Buñuel: Surrealism and Narrative."
"Jean-Pierre Melville: Appearance and Identity."
"Michelangelo Antonioni: Figures in a Mental
    Landscape."
"Jacques Tati: The Open Window of Comedy."

"Robert Bresson: An Anachronistic Universe."
"Ingmar Bergman: The Disintegrated Artist."
"Alain Resnais: The Simultaneous Experience."
"Alain Robbe-Grillet: The Reality of Imagination."
"Miklós Jancsó: Dialectic and Ritual."
"Pier Paolo Pasolini: Myth and Modernity."
"Walerian Borowczyk: Space, Style and Fable."
"Jean-Luc Godard: Identity and Communication."
"Dusan Makavejev: Collage and Compilation."
"Jean-Marie Straub: Strict Counterpoint."
"May 1968: Towards a Political Cinema."
    IN: The Ambiguous Image

235 **Armes, Roy.**
"François Truffaut and *Shoot the Piano Player*."
    IN: Focus on Shoot the Piano Player

236 **Armes, Roy.**
"Robert Bresson."
    IN: Great Film Directors
        French Cinema Since 1946 /v.1

237 **Armour, Robert A.**
"*A Portrait of the Artist as a Young Man* [novel by]
    James Joyce; *A Portrait of the Artist as a Young
    Man* [film by] Joseph Strick. The 'Whatness' of
    Joseph Strick's *Portrait*."
    IN: The English Novel and the Movies

238 **Armour, Robert A.**
"History Written in Jagged Lightning: Realistic South
    vs. Romantic South in *The Birth of a Nation*."
    IN: The South and Film

239 **Armstrong, Dan.**
"Wiseman's *Model* and the Documentary Project:
    Toward a Radical Film Practice."
    IN: New Challenges for Documentary

240 **Armstrong, F. Jeffrey.**
"Rod Serling."
    IN: Dictionary of Literary Biography /v. 26

241 **Arnaz, Desi.**
"The Birth of Little Ricky."
    IN: Bedside Hollywood

242 **Arnheim, Rudolf.**
"[From:] *Film as Art*: The Making of a Film."
    IN: Film Theory and Criticism /1 ed
        Film Theory and Criticism /2 ed
        Film Theory and Criticism /3 ed
        Film Theory and Criticism /4 ed

243 **Arnheim, Rudolf.**
"[From:] *Film as Art*: The Complete Film."
    IN: Film Theory and Criticism /1 ed
        Film Theory and Criticism /2 ed
        Film Theory and Criticism /3 ed
        Film Theory and Criticism /4 ed

244 **Arnheim, Rudolf.**
"[From:] *Film as Art*: Film and Reality."
    IN: Film Theory and Criticism /1 ed
        Film Theory and Criticism /2 ed
        Film Theory and Criticism /3 ed
        Film Theory and Criticism /4 ed

245   **Arnheim, Rudolf.**
       "Film and Reality."
          IN: <u>Film: Readings in the Mass Media</u>

246   **Arnheim, Rudolph [*sic*, Rudolf].**
       "Art Today and the Film."
          IN: <u>The New American Cinema</u>
             <u>Crossroads to the Cinema</u>
             <u>Film and the Liberal Arts</u>

247   **Arnheim, Rudolf.**
       "A New Laocoön: Artistic Composites and the Talking
          Film."
          IN: <u>Film Sound</u>

248   **Arnheim, Rudolf.**
       "Epic and Dramatic Film."
          IN: <u>Film: A Montage of Theories</u>
             <u>Film And/As Literature</u>

249   **Arnheim, Rudolf.**
       "Fiction and Fact."
          IN: <u>Sight and Sound</u>

250   **Arnheim, Rudolf.**
       "Josef von Sternberg."
          IN: <u>Sternberg</u>

251   **Arnheim, Rudolf.**
       "Portrait of an Artist."
       "To Maya Deren."
          IN: <u>Film Culture Reader</u>

252   **Arnheim, Rudolph [*sic*, Rudolf].**
       "Fifty Years of Film."
          IN: <u>Ideas on Film</u>

253   **Arnheim, Rudolph [*sic*, Rudolf].**
       "Film as Art."
          IN: <u>Film: An Anthology</u>

254   **Arnold, Edward.**
       "I Prefer the Screen to the Stage."
          IN: <u>Celebrity Articles ...</u>

255   **Arnold, Gary.**
       "*Blazing Saddles*."
       "*Sleeper*."
       "*The Miracle of Morgan's Creek*."
       "For Woody." [RE: Woody Allen.]
          IN: <u>Movie Comedy</u>

256   **Arnold, James W.**
       "Musical Fantasy: *The Little Prince*."
          IN: <u>Shadows of the Magic Lamp</u>

257   **Arnold, James W.**
       "The Western."
       "The Comedy."
          IN: <u>Screen Experience</u>

258   **Arnold, James.**
       "The Present State of the Documentary."
          IN: <u>The Documentary Tradition /1 ed</u>
             <u>The Documentary Tradition /2 ed</u>

259   **Aron, Robert.**
       "Films of Revolt."
          IN: <u>French Film Theory and Criticism /v. 1</u>

260   **Arrowsmith, William.**
       "Film as Educator."
          IN: <u>Perspectives on the Study of Film</u>

261   **Artaud, Antonin.**
       "Cinema and Reality."
          IN: <u>French Film Theory and Criticism /v. 1</u>

262   **Artaud, Antonin.**
       "Sorcery and the Cinema."
          IN: <u>The Avant-Garde Film</u>

263   **Artaud, Antonin.**
       "The Premature Old Age of the Cinema."
          IN: <u>French Film Theory and Criticism /v. 2</u>

264   **Artaud, Antonin.**
       "Witchcraft and the Cinema."
          IN: <u>The Shadow and Its Shadow</u>

265   **Artel, Linda and Susan Wengraf.**
       "Positive Images: Screening Women's Films."
          IN: <u>Issues in Feminist Film Criticism</u>
             <u>Jump Cut</u>

266   **Arthur, Paul S.**
       "1959-1963 (*Science Fiction, Prelude, Dog Star Man,
          Notebook, Little Stabs at Happiness, Mass for the
          Dakota Sioux*)."
       "1967-1970 (*T,O,U,C,H,I,N,G, Runaway, 69,
          Diploteratology or Bardo Folly, Our Lady of the
          Sphere, Bleu Shut*)."
          IN: <u>A History of the American Avant-Garde Cinema</u>

267   **Arvidson, Linda.**
       "Griffith Directs His First Movie."
       "How Griffith Came to Make *The Birth of a Nation*."
          IN: <u>Focus on D.W. Griffith</u>

268   **Asakura, Setsu.**
       "Setsu Asakura." [Interview by Joan Mellen.]
          IN: <u>Voices from the Japanese Cinema</u>

269   **Ashby, Hal.**
       "*The Landlord*."
          IN: <u>Directors in Action</u>

270   **Ashley, Elizabeth.**
       "A Bad Girl."
          IN: <u>Bedside Hollywood</u>

271   **Ashley, John.**
       "John Ashley." [An interview.]
          IN: <u>Interviews with B ...</u>

272   **Ashmore, Harry S.**
       "An Outside Conscience for Television."
          IN: <u>Sight, Sound, and Society</u>

273   **Asimov, Isaac.**
       "Movie Science."
          IN: <u>Omni's Screen Flights ...</u>

274   **Aspinall, Sue.**
       "Women, Realism and Reality in British Films,
          1943-53."
          IN: <u>British Cinema History</u>

"Elvis: The Mystery Lingers and Deepens." [RE: Elvis Presley.]

"Thomas Harper Ince—Death by Indigestion or a Bullet."

"The Strange and Unsolved Death of Thelma Todd."

"Carol Wayne: 'The Matinee Lady' and Her Mysterious Death."

"The Tragic Death of Carole Landis."

"Marilyn Monroe: The Mystery Which Won't Disappear."

"Jean Harlow's Infantile Husband."

"'The Mexican Spitfire' Laughed No More." [RE: Carmen Miranda.]

"The Lonely Death of 'Johnny Yuma': Nick Adams."

"And There Are Still More Unsolved Mysteries ... Coercion Is Also a Hollywood Way of Life."
IN: More of Hollywood's Unsolved Mysteries

306 **Austin, Wade.**
"The Real Beverly Hillbillies."
IN: The South and Film

307 **Autry, Gene.**
"Ten Commandments of the Cowboy."
IN: The American West on Film

308 **Autry, Gene.**
"The Most Famous Reindeer of All."
IN: Bedside Hollywood

309 **Auty, Martin [sic, Martyn].**
"*Sunrise.*"
"*The Great Train Robbery.*"
"*The Big Parade.*"
"*Un Chien Andalou.*"
"*Wings.*"
IN: Movies of the Silent Years

310 **Auty, Martyn.**
"But Is It Cinema?"
IN: British Cinema Now

311 **AuWerter, Russell.**
"John Frankenheimer."
"Robert Altman."
"John Cassavetes."
IN: Directors in Action

312 **Avakian, Aram.**
"The Editor."
IN: Movie People

313 **Aveline, Claude.**
"Apropos the Prix Louis Delluc."
"Films and Milieux."
"John Ford."
IN: French Film Theory and Criticism /v. 2

314 **Avellar, José Carlos.**
"Seeing, Hearing, Filming: Notes on the Brazilian Documentary."
IN: Brazilian Cinema

315 **Avildsen, John G.**
"John G. Avildsen." [Interview by John Andrew Gallagher.]
IN: Film Directors on Directing

316 **Axelrod, Jonathan.**
"Jonathan Axelrod." [Interview by William Froug.]
IN: The Screenwriter Looks ...

317 **Ayer, Douglas, Roy E. Bates, and Peter J. Herman.**
"Self-Censorship in the Movie Industry: A Historical Perspective on Law and Social Change."
IN: The American Movie Industry

318 **Ayfre, Amédée.**
"Neo-Realism and Phenomenology."
IN: Cahiers du Cinéma, The 1950s

319 **Ayfre, Amedée.**
"The Religious Scope of *The Seventh Seal.*"
IN: Focus on The Seventh Seal

320 **Azmi, Shabana.**
"Shabana Azmi." [Interview.]
IN: Indian Cinema Superbazaar

321 **B, Beth and Scott B.**
"Beth B and Scott B." [Interview by Scott MacDonald.]
IN: A Critical Cinema

322 **Babbitt, Art.**
"Character Analysis of the Goof--June 1934."
IN: The American Animated Cartoon

323 **Babington, Bruce and Peter William Evans.**
"Reading a Musical—*Easter Parade.*"
"*Gold Diggers of 1933* and the Busby Berkeley Backstage Musical."
"*The Merry Widow* and Operetta."
"*Swing Time* and the Astaire-Rogers Musical."
"*Jolson I* and *II* and the Musical Biopic."
"*Summer Holiday* and the Pastoral Musical."
"*It's Always Fair Weather* and the Gene Kelly Musical."
"*Carousel* and the Rodgers & Hammerstein Musical."
"*On A Clear Day You Can See Forever*--Minnelli and the Introspective Musical."
"*Hair* and the Contemporary Musical."
IN: Blue Skies and Silver Linings

324 **Babuscio, Jack.**
"Camp and the Gay Sensibility."
IN: Gays and Film
Gays and Film /rev. ed.

325 **Baby, Yvonne.**
"I Wanted to Treat *Shoot the Piano Player* Like a Tale by Perrault: An Interview with François Truffaut."
IN: Focus on Shoot the Piano Player

326 **Baby, Yvonne.**
"Shipwrecked People from the Modern World: Interview with Jean-Luc Godard on *Le Mepris.*"
IN: Focus on Godard

327 **Bacall, Lauren.**
"You Know How to Whistle ..."
IN: Bedside Hollywood

328 **Bachmann, Gideon.**
"Jancsó Plain."

IN: The Emergence of Film Art /2 ed

329 **Bachmann, Gideon, Robert Drew, Richard Leacock and D.A. Pennebaker.**
"The Frontiers of Realist Cinema."
IN: Film: A Montage of Theories

330 **Baclanova, Olga.**
"Olga Baclanova." [Interview by John Kobal.]
IN: People Will Talk

331 **Badger, Clarence C.**
"Reminiscences of the Early Days of Movie Comedies."
IN: Image on the Art ...

Badger, David P. SEE: Wyatt, Robert O.

332 **Badham, John.**
"*WarGames* and the Real World."
IN: Omni's Screen Flights ...

Badham, John. SEE: Dreyfuss, Richard.

333 **Bahadur, Satish.**
"Aesthetics: From Traditional Iconography to Contemporary Kitsch."
IN: Indian Cinema Superbazaar

334 **Bailey, John.**
"John Bailey." [Interview by Dennis Schaefer and Larry Salvato.]
IN: Masters of Light

334a **Baillie, Bruce.**
"Bruce Baillie." [Interview by Scott MacDonald.]
IN: A Critical Cinema 2

335 **Bakshi, Ralph.**
"Ralph Bakshi." [Interview by Charles Higham.]
IN: Celebrity Circus

336 **Bakshy, Alexander.**
"The Cinematograph as Art."
IN: Introduction to the Art of the Movies

337 **Bakshy, Alexander.**
"*The Circus*."
IN: Focus on Chaplin

338 **Bakshy, Alexander.**
"Dynamic Composition."
IN: The Movies as Medium

339 **Balázs, Béla.**
"The Future of Film."
IN: The Film Factory

340 **Balázs, Béla.**
"The Script."
IN: Film And/As Literature

341 **Balázs, Béla.**
"[From:] *Theory of the Film*: Art Form and Material."
IN: Film Theory and Criticism /1 ed
Film And/As Literature

342 **Balázs, Béla.**
"Theory of the Film."

IN: Film: An Anthology

343 **Balázs, Béla.**
"The Faces of Men."
IN: Film: A Montage of Theories

344 **Balázs, Béla.**
"[From:] *Theory of the Film*: The Face of Man."
IN: Film Theory and Criticism /1 ed
Film Theory and Criticism /2 ed
Film Theory and Criticism /3 ed
Film Theory and Criticism /4 ed

345 **Balázs, Béla.**
"[From:] *Theory of the Film*: The Close-Up."
IN: Film Theory and Criticism /1 ed
Film Theory and Criticism /2 ed
Film Theory and Criticism /3 ed
Film Theory and Criticism /4 ed

346 **Balazs, Bela.**
"[From:] *Theory of the Film*."
IN: Film and Literature: Contrasts ...

347 **Balazs, Bela.**
"Der Sichtbare Mensch."
"In Praise of Theory."
IN: Perspectives on the Study of Film

348 **Balazs, Bela.**
"Theory of the Film: Sound."
IN: Film Sound

349 **Belazs [*sic*, Balazs], Bela.**
"The Acoustic World."
IN: The Movies as Medium

350 **Baldwin, James.**
"Life Straight in de Eye."
IN: The Black Man on Film

351 **Baldwin, James.**
"Sidney Poitier."
IN: Authors on Film

352 **Balio, Tino.**
"New Producers for Old: United Artists and the Shift to Independent Production."
IN: Hollywood in the Age of Television

353 **Balio, Tino.**
"Stars in Business: The Founding of United Artists."
IN: The American Film Industry
The American Film Industry /rev ed

354 **Balio, Tino.**
"The Kinetoscope."
"United Artists Takes Shape."
IN: The First Tycoons

355 **Ball, J.A.**
"Scientific Foundations." [RE: the photoplay.]
IN: Introduction to the Photoplay

356 **Ball, Lucille.**
"Lucille Ball." [Interview by Rex Reed.]
IN: Travolta to Keaton

357 **Ball, Lucille.**
"Lucille Ball." [Interview by Charles Higham.]
IN: Celebrity Circus

358 **Ball, Lucille.**
"The Actress."
IN: Filmmakers on Filmmaking /v. 1

359 **Ball, Robert Hamilton.**
"Shakespeare by Vitagraph (1908-1911)."
IN: The First Film Makers

360 **Ball, Tevvy.**
"Evolution of Vision in the Films of Luchino Visconti."
IN: Italian Cinema

360a **Ballard, Lucien.**
"Interview with Lucien Ballard." [Interview by Leonard Maltin.]
IN: The Art of the Cinematographer

361 **Balshofer, Fred and Arthur Miller.**
"Going Into the Film Business."
IN: The First Film Makers

361a **Balun, Chas.**
"Inside the Head of Stuart Gordon."
"I Spit in Your Face: Films That Bite."
IN: The Deep Red Horror Handbook

362 **Bambara, Toni Cade.**
"Programming with *School Daze*."
IN: Five for Five

362a **Bamps, Yvan and Ralph Heyndels.**
"*Modern Times* in the Light of Adorno and Beckett."
IN: Charlie Chaplin

363 **Bandy, Philip.**
"'NET Journal': *Hiroshima-Nagasaki*."
IN: Nuclear War Films

364 **Banerjee, Shampa.**
"V. Shantaram."
"Raj Kapoor."
"Mrinal Sen."
"Guru Dutt."
"Ritwik Ghatak."
IN: Profiles: 5 Film-makers ...

365 **Bankhead, Tallulah.**
"Tallulah Bankhead." [Interview by John Kobal.]
IN: People Will Talk

366 **Banks, Russell.**
"*Bambi*."
IN: The Movie That Changed My Life

367 **Barabáš, Stanislav.**
"Stanislav Barabáš." [Interview by Antonín J. Liehm.]
IN: Closely Watched Films

368 **Barbarow, George.**
"*Rashomon* and the Fifth Witness."
IN: Focus on Rashomon

369 **Barbera, Jack.**
"Tomorrow and Tomorrow and *Tomorrow*."

IN: The South and Film

370 **Bardèche, Maurice and Robert Brasillach.**
"Méliès."
IN: Film: An Anthology

371 **Bardeche, Maurice and Robert Brasillach.**
"The Films of René Clair."
IN: The Emergence of Film Art /1 ed
The Emergence of Film Art /2 ed

372 **Bardem, J.A.**
"The Situation of the Serious Filmmaker."
IN: Film: Book 1

Bardem, J.A. SEE: Anderson, Lindsay.

Barka, Souhail Ben. SEE: Ben Barka, Souhail.

373 **Barker, Clive.**
"Clive Barker." [Interview by Stanley Wiater.]
IN: Dark Visions

374 **Barker, Clive and Peter Atkins.**
"Other Shelves, Other Shadows: A Conversation (An Interview with Clive Barker)."
IN: Cut!: Horror Writers ...

Barlow, John D. SEE: Wallis, Victor.

375 **Barnard, Tim.**
"Pasolini, Pier Paolo: Dossier on Censorship."
IN: Forbidden Films

376 **Barnard, Tim.**
"Popular Cinema and Popular Politics."
IN: Argentine Cinema

377 **Barnouw, Eric [*sic*, **Erik**].**
"*Hiroshima-Nagasaki*: The Case of the A-Bomb Footage."
IN: New Challenges for Documentary

378 **Barnouw, Erik.**
"Propaganda at Radio Luxembourg: 1944-1945."
IN: Film & Radio Propaganda ...

379 **Barnouw, Erik.**
"The Sintzenich Diaries." [RE: Arthur H.C. "Hal" Sintzenich.]
"Lives of a Bengal Filmmaker: Satyajit Ray of Calcutta."
IN: Wonderful Inventions

380 **Barr, Alfred H., Jr.**
"Nationalism in German Films."
IN: Hound & Horn

381 **Barr, Charles.**
"CinemaScope: Before and After." [NOTE: Also called "Cinemascope: Before and After."]
IN: Film Theory and Criticism /1 ed
Film Theory and Criticism /2 ed
Film Theory and Criticism /3 ed
Film: A Montage of Theories

382 **Barr, Charles.**
"*Hercules Conquers Atlantis*."
"*King & Country*."

IN: Movie Reader

383 **Barr, Charles.**
"Broadcasting and Cinema: 2: Screens within
   Screens."
"Introduction: Amnesia and Schizophrenia."
   IN: All Our Yesterdays

384 **Barri, Diana.**
"Diana Barri." [Interview by Scott MacDonald.]
   IN: A Critical Cinema

385 **Barrios, Gregg.**
"*Alambrista!*: A Modern Odyssey."
"*Zoot Suit*: The Man, the Myth, Still Lives (A
   Conversation with Luis Valdez)."
"A Cinema of Failure, a Cinema of Hunger: The Films
   of Efraín Gutiérrez."
   IN: Chicano Cinema

386 **Barron, Arthur.**
"*Sixteen in Webster Groves* and *The Berkeley
   Rebels*." [Interview by Alan Rosenthal.]
   IN: The New Documentary in Action

387 **Barron, Arthur.**
"Arthur Barron." [Interview by G. Roy Levin.]
   IN: Documentary Explorations

388 **Barron, Arthur.**
"Toward New Goals in Documentary."
   IN: The Documentary Tradition /1 ed
       The Documentary Tradition /2 ed

389 **Barry, Iris.**
"*A Diary for Timothy*."
   IN: The Documentary Tradition /1 ed
       The Documentary Tradition /2 ed

390 **Barry, Iris.**
"Georges Méliès, Magician and Film Pioneer."
   IN: Rediscovering French Film

391 **Barry, Iris and Eileen Bowser.**
"The Scope of *Intolerance*."
   IN: The Classic Cinema

392 **Barrymore, Lionel.**
"The Actor - II."
   IN: Behind the Screen

393 **Barsam, Richard Meran.**
"[From:] *Nonfiction Film: A Critical History*: Defining
   Nonfiction Film."
   IN: Film Theory and Criticism /1 ed

394 **Barsam, Richard Meran.**
"Nonfiction Film: The Realist Impulse."
   IN: Film Theory and Criticism /2 ed

395 **Barsam, Richard Meran.**
"This Is America: Documentaries for Theaters,
   1942-1951."
"Leni Riefenstahl: Artifice and Truth in a World Apart."
   IN: Nonfiction Film Theory and Criticism

396 **Barsam, Richard.**
"*Ulysses* [novel by] James Joyce; *Ulysses* [film by]
   Joseph Strick. When in Doubt Persecute Bloom."
   IN: The English Novel and the Movies

397 **Barshop, Mark.**
"An Introduction to Federico Fellini."
   IN: Italian Cinema

398 **Bartel, Paul.**
"*Death Race 2000*: New World's Violent Future."
   IN: Omni's Screen Flights ...

399 **Barthes, Roland.**
"Diderot, Brecht, Eisenstein."
   IN: Narrative, Apparatus, Ideology

400 **Barthes, Roland.**
"The Face of Garbo."
   IN: Film Theory and Criticism /1 ed
       Film Theory and Criticism /2 ed
       Film Theory and Criticism /3 ed
       Film Theory and Criticism /4 ed

401 **Barthes, Roland.**
"The Death of the Author."
   IN: Theories of Authorship

402 **Barthes, Roland.**
"Toward a Semiotics of Cinema [Barthes in interview
   with Michel Delahaye, Jacques Rivette]."
   IN: Cahiers du Cinéma, 1960-1968

403 **Barthes, Roland.**
"Upon Leaving the Movie Theatre."
   IN: Apparatus

404 **Basinger, Jeanine.**
"Ten That Got Away."
   IN: Women and the Cinema

404a **Basinger, Jeanine.**
"*Anatomy of a Murder*: Life and Art in the Courtroom."
   IN: Columbia Pictures

405 **Bass, Ronald.**
"Ronald Bass." [Interview by William Froug.]
   IN: The New Screenwriter Looks ...

406 **Bass, Warren.**
"Filmic Objectivity and Visual Style."
   IN: Film/Culture: Explorations ...

407 **Bataille, Gretchen and Charles L.P. Silet.**
"The Entertaining Anachronism: Indians in American
   Film."
   IN: The Kaleidoscopic Lens

408 **Batchan, Alexander.**
"The 'Alienation' of Slava Tsukerman."
   IN: Before the Wall Came Down

409 **Bates, Robin.**
"The Ideological Foundations of the Czech New
   Wave."
   IN: The Emergence of Film Art /2 ed

Bates, Roy E. SEE: Ayer, Douglas.

410   **Bathrick, David.**
"Melodrama, History, and Dickens: *The Love of Jeanne Ney*."
IN: <u>The Films of G.W. Pabst</u>

411   **Bathrick, Serafina K.**
"Starring Shirley MacLaine ... A Beauty and a Buddy."
IN: <u>Jump Cut</u>

412   **Bathrick, Serafina K.**
"The Female Colossus: The Body as Facade and Threshold."
IN: <u>Fabrications</u>

413   **Bathrick, Serafina Kent.**
"*In This Our Life* [novel by] Ellen Glasgow. Independent Woman, Doomed Sister."
IN: <u>The Modern American Novel ...</u>

414   **Battcock, Gregory.**
"Four Films by Andy Warhol."
IN: <u>The New American Cinema</u>

415   **Battestin, Martin C.**
"Osborne's *Tom Jones*: Adapting a Classic."
IN: <u>Man and the Movies</u>
<u>Film And/As Literature</u>
<u>Film and Literature</u>

416   **Baudry, Jean-Louis.**
"The Apparatus: Metapsychological Approaches to the Impression of Reality in Cinema."
IN: <u>Narrative, Apparatus, Ideology</u>
<u>Apparatus</u>
<u>Film Theory and Criticism /4 ed</u>

417   **Baudry, Jean-Louis.**
"Ideological Effects of the Basic Cinematographic Apparatus."
IN: <u>Apparatus</u>
<u>Movies and Methods /v. 2</u>
<u>Narrative, Apparatus, Ideology</u>
<u>Film Theory and Criticism /4 ed</u>

418   **Baudry, Jean-Louis.**
"Author and Analyzable Subject."
IN: <u>Apparatus</u>

419   **Baughman, James L.**
"The Weakest Chain and the Strongest Link: The American Broadcasting Company and the Motion Picture Industry, 1952-60."
IN: <u>Hollywood in the Age of Television</u>

420   **Baumbach, Jonathan.**
"*King Lear*." [RE: Jean-Luc Godard's version.]
IN: <u>Produced and Abandoned</u>

421   **Baumbach, Jonathan.**
"From A to Antonioni: Hallucinations of a Movie Addict."
IN: <u>Man and the Movies</u>
<u>Great Film Directors</u>

422   **Baumbach, Jonathan.**
"*Breathless* Revisited."
IN: <u>Great Film Directors</u>

422a **Baumbach, Jonathan.**
"Seeing Myself in Movies."
IN: <u>Writing in a Film Age</u>

423   **Bauso, Thomas M.**
"*Rope*: Hitchcock's Unkindest Cut."
IN: <u>Hitchcock's Re-Released Films</u>

424   **Baxandall, Lee.**
"Toward an East European Cinemarxism?"
IN: <u>Politics, Art and Commitment ...</u>

425   **Baxter, John.**
"Screen Sexuality: Flesh, Feathers, and Fantasies."
IN: <u>Sexuality in the Movies</u>

426   **Baxter, John.**
"The Gangster Film."
IN: <u>Crossroads to the Cinema</u>

427   **Baxter, John.**
"The Sternberg Style."
IN: <u>Great Film Directors</u>

428   **Baxter, John.**
"The Sixties."
"The Thirties."
IN: <u>Hollywood 1920-1970</u>

429   **Baxter, Peter.**
"On the Naked Thighs of Miss Dietrich."
IN: <u>Movies and Methods /v. 2</u>

430   **Bazelon, David T.**
"The Louder Reality: Behind the Busy Mirror."
IN: <u>Sight, Sound, and Society</u>

431   **Bazin, André.**
"The Virtues and Limitations of Montage."
"*Le Journal d'un curé de campagne* and the Stylistics of Robert Bresson."
"Charlie Chaplin."
"Cinema and Exploration."
"Painting and Cinema."
IN: <u>What Is Cinema? /v. 1</u>

432   **Bazin, André.**
"An Aesthetic of Reality: Cinematic Realism and the Italian School of the Liberation."
"*La Terra Trema*."
"*Bicycle Thief*."
"*Umberto D*: A Great Work."
"In Defense of Rossellini."
"The Myth of Monsieur Verdoux."
"*Limelight*, or the Death of Molière."
"The Grandeur of *Limelight*."
"The Western, or the American Film *par excellence*."
"Entomology of the Pin-Up Girl."
"*The Outlaw*."
"Marginal Notes on *Eroticism in the Cinema*."
IN: <u>What Is Cinema? /v. 2</u>

433   **Bazin, André.**
"Pierre Prévert's *Audieu Léonard*."
"For a Realistic Esthetic."
"Jean Delannoy's *L'Eternel Retour*."

"Marcel Carné's *Les Visiteurs du Soir* and Robert
    Bresson's *Les Anges du Péché*."
"Pierre Blanchar's *Un Seul Amour*."
"Toward a Cinematic Criticism."
"Jean Grémillon's *Le Ciel Est à Vous*."
"To Create a Public."
"On Realism."
"The Art of Not Seeing Films."
"Marcel L'Herbier's *La Nuit Fantastique*."
"The Cinema and Popular Art."
"Revival of Marcel Carné's *Quai des Brumes*."
"Marcel Carné's *Les Enfants du Paradis*."
"Jaubert and French Cinema."
"Julien Duvivier's *Untel Père et Fils*."
"Christian-Jaque's *Boule de Suif*."
"René Chanas' *Le Jugement Dernier*."
"René Clément's *La Bataille du Rail*."
"Henri Calef's *Jéricho*."
"Yves Allégret's *Les Démons de l'Aube*."
"Louis Daquin's *Patrie*."
"On *L'Espoir*, or Style in the Cinema."
    IN: <u>French Cinema of the Occupation ...</u>

434 Bazin, André.
"*A King in New York*."
"*Monsieur Verdoux* or Charlot Martyred."
"If Charlot Hadn't Died." [RE: *Limelight*.]
"Immortal Charlot!" [Re: Charles Chaplin.]
"Pastiche or Postiche, or Nothingness over a
    Mustache." [RE: *The Great Dictator*.]
"Time Validates *Modern Times*."
    IN: <u>Essays on Chaplin</u>

435 Bazin, André.
"Erich von Stroheim."
"Carl Theodor Dreyer."
"Preston Sturges."
"Luis Buñuel."
"Alfred Hitchcock."
"Akira Kurosawa."
    IN: <u>The Cinema of Cruelty</u>

436 Bazin, André.
"[From:] *What Is Cinema?*: The Myth of the Total
    Cinema."
    IN: <u>Film Theory and Criticism /1 ed</u>
        <u>Film Theory and Criticism /2 ed</u>
        <u>Film Theory and Criticism /3 ed</u>
        <u>Film Theory and Criticism /4 ed</u>
        <u>What Is Cinema? /v. 1</u>

437 Bazin, André.
"[From:] *What Is Cinema?*: The Evolution of the
    Language of Cinema." [NOTE: Also called "The
    Evolution of Film Language."]
    IN: <u>What Is Cinema? /v. 1</u>
        <u>Film Theory and Criticism /1 ed</u>
        <u>Film Theory and Criticism /2 ed</u>
        <u>Film Theory and Criticism /3 ed</u>
        <u>Film Theory and Criticism /4 ed</u>
        <u>The New Wave: Critical Landmarks</u>
        <u>Film and the Liberal Arts</u>

438 Bazin, André.
"[From:] *What Is Cinema?*: Theater and Cinema."
    IN: <u>Film Theory and Criticism /1 ed</u>
        <u>Film Theory and Criticism /2 ed</u>
        <u>Film Theory and Criticism /3 ed</u>
        <u>Film Theory and Criticism /4 ed</u>
        <u>Film And/As Literature</u>
        <u>What Is Cinema? /v. 1</u>

439 Bazin, André.
"*Cabiria*: The Voyage to the End of Neorealism." [RE:
    The Nights of Cabiria.]
    IN: <u>Federico Fellini</u>
        <u>What Is Cinema? /v. 2</u>

440 Bazin, André.
"*La Strada*."
    IN: <u>Federico Fellini</u>

441 Bazin, André.
"*Los Olvidados*."
    IN: <u>The World of Luis Buñuel</u>

442 Bazin, André.
"*Othello*." [RE: Orson Welles, 1951.]
    IN: <u>Film Theory and Criticism /1 ed</u>
        <u>Focus on Shakespearean Films</u>

443 Bazin, André.
"*Umberto D*."
"An Exemplary Western." [RE: *Seven Men from Now*.]
"The Death of Humphrey Bogart."
"Beauty of a Western." [RE: *The Man from Laramie*.]
    IN: <u>Cahiers du Cinéma, The 1950s</u>

444 Bazin, André.
"Hitchcock versus Hitchcock."
    IN: <u>Focus on Hitchcock</u>

445 Bazin, André.
"In Defense of Mixed Cinema."
    IN: <u>Film And/As Literature</u>
        <u>What Is Cinema? /v. 1</u>

446 Bazin, André.
"La Politique des Auteurs." [NOTE: Also called "On
    the *politique des auteurs*".]
    IN: <u>The New Wave: Critical Landmarks</u>
        <u>Cahiers du Cinéma, The 1950s</u>

447 Bazin, André.
"Neorealism and Pure Cinema: *The Bicycle Thief*."
    IN: <u>The Classic Cinema</u>

448 Bazin, André.
"The Originality of Welles as a Director."
    IN: <u>Focus on Citizen Kane</u>

449 Bazin, André.
"The Destiny of Jean Gabin."
    IN: <u>What Is Cinema? /v. 2</u>
        <u>Rediscovering French Cinema</u>

450 Bazin, André.
"The Stalin Myth in Soviet Cinema (with an
    Introduction by Dudley Andrew)."
    IN: <u>Movies and Methods /v. 2</u>

451　**Bazin, André.**
"The French Renoir."
IN: <u>Great Film Directors</u>

452　**Bazin, André.**
"The Evolution of the Western."
IN: <u>Movies and Methods: An Anthology</u>
<u>What Is Cinema? /v. 2</u>

453　**Bazin, André.**
"The Pagnol Case."
"The Destiny of Jean Gabin."
"The Disincarnation of Carné."
IN: <u>Rediscovering French Film</u>

454　**Bazin, André.**
"The Ontology of the Photographic Image."
IN: <u>Crossroads to the Cinema</u>
<u>What Is Cinema? /v. 1</u>

455　**Bazin, André.**
"De Sica: Metteur-en-scène."
IN: <u>What Is Cinema? /v. 2</u>
<u>Film Theory and Criticism /4 ed</u>

456　**Bazin, André, Jacques Doniol-Valcroze, Pierre Kast, Roger Leenhardt, Jacques Rivette, Eric Rohmer.**
"Six Characters in Search of *auteurs*: A Discussion about the French Cinema."
IN: <u>Cahiers du Cinéma, The 1950s</u>

　　　Bazin, André. SEE: Moullet, Luc.

457　**Beale, Alison.**
"*Song of the Shirt*: The Film and History Project."
IN: <u>Explorations in Film Theory</u>

458　**Beaton, James F.**
"*Deliverance* [novel by] James Dickey. Dickey Down the River."
IN: <u>The Modern American Novel ...</u>

459　**Beauchamp, Thomas and Stephen Klaidman.**
"A Study in Multiple Forms of Bias." [RE: *The Uncounted Enemy: A Vietnam Deception.*]
IN: <u>Image Ethics</u>

460　**Beaufort, John.**
"*Rashomon*."
IN: <u>Focus on Rashomon</u>

461　**Beaupré, Lee.**
"How to Distribute a Film."
IN: <u>The Hollywood Film Industry</u>

462　**Beauvoir, Simone de.**
"[From:] *Brigitte Bardot and the Lolita Syndrome*."
IN: <u>Women and the Cinema</u>

463　**Beaver, Frank E.**
"*Chulas fronteras*."
"*Del mero corzón*."
IN: <u>Chicano Cinema</u>

464　**Beck, Bernard.**
"The Overdeveloped Society: *THX 1138*."
IN: <u>Film in Society</u>

465　**Becker, Boris W., Barbara Brewer, Bodie Dickerson, and Rosemary Magee.**
"The Influence of Personal Values on Movie Preferences."
IN: <u>Current Research in Film /v. 1</u>

466　**Becker, Edith, Michelle Citron, Julia Lesage and B. Ruby Rich.**
"Lesbians and Film."
IN: <u>Jump Cut</u>

467　**Becker, Lawrence.**
"A Minor Masterpiece—Dušan Makavejev's *WR: Mysteries of the Organism*."
IN: <u>The Emergence of Film Art /2 ed</u>

468　**Becker, Lawrence.**
"Sex, Morality, and the Movies."
IN: <u>Sexuality in the Movies</u>

469　**Beckerman, Jim.**
"*The Man Who Would Be King* [novel by] Rudyard Kipling; *The Man Who Would Be King* [film by] John Huston. On Adapting 'The Most Audacious Thing in Fiction'."
IN: <u>The English Novel and the Movies</u>

470　**Beggs, Neil.**
"The Heart Seems to Have Gone ..."
IN: <u>An Australian Film Reader</u>

471　**Beh, Siew Hwa.**
"*The Woman's Film*."
"*Vivre Sa Vie*."
IN: <u>Movies and Methods: An Anthology</u>

472　**Behlmer, Rudy.**
"In His Own Image: *Frankenstein* (1931)."
"A Dream and a Vision: *Lost Horizon* (1937)."
"They Called It 'Disney's Folly': *Snow White and the Seven Dwarfs*."
"'Welcome to Sherwood!': *The Adventures of Robin Hood*."
"The Rover Boys in India: *Gunga Din*."
"Bret Harte in Monument Valley: *Stagecoach* (1939)."
"'We're the People': *The Grapes of Wrath*."
"'The Stuff That Dreams Are Made Of': *The Maltese Falcon* (1941)."
"George Raft in *Casablanca*?"
"The Face in the Misty Light: *Laura*."
"Waves of Love Over the Footlights: *All About Eve*."
"The Ravishment of the Tender: *A Streetcar Named Desire*."
"'Remember Eleanor Roosevelt's Serene Smile': *The African Queen*."
"All Talking! All Singing! All Dancing!: *Singin' in the Rain*."
"Do Not Forsake Me, Oh My Darlin': *High Noon*."
IN: <u>America's Favorite Movies</u>

473　**Behlmer, Rudy.**
"*Tarzan* at MGM." [RE: Tarzan series.]
IN: <u>The Cinema of Adventure, Romance & Terror</u>

IN: <u>Film and Politics in the Third World</u>

501 Benayoun, Robert.
"The King is Naked." [RE: Nouvelle Vague.]
IN: <u>The New Wave: Critical Landmarks</u>

502 Benchley, R.
"Hearts in Dixie."
IN: <u>The Black Man on Film</u>

503 Benchley, Robert.
"Confessions of a Writer-Actor."
IN: <u>Celebrity Articles ...</u>

504 Benedek, Laslo.
"Directing *Death of a Salesman* for the Screen."
IN: <u>Hollywood Directors 1941-1976</u>

505 Benegal, Shyam.
"Shyam Benegal." [Interview.]
IN: <u>Indian Cinema Superbazaar</u>

506 Benelli, Dana.
"The Cosmos and Its Discontents."
IN: <u>The Films of Werner Herzog</u>

507 Benjamin, Burton.
"The Documentary Heritage."
IN: <u>The Documentary Tradition /1 ed</u>
<u>The Documentary Tradition /2 ed</u>
<u>Nonfiction Film Theory and Criticism</u>

508 Benjamin, Walter.
"The Work of Art in the Age of Mechanical
Reproduction."
IN: <u>Film Theory and Criticism /1 ed</u>
<u>Film Theory and Criticism /2 ed</u>
<u>Film Theory and Criticism /3 ed</u>
<u>Film Theory and Criticism /4 ed</u>

509 Bennett, Charles.
"Charles Bennett: First-Class Constructionist."
[Interview by Pat McGilligan.]
IN: <u>Backstory</u>

510 Bennett, Charles.
"Charles Bennett." [Interview by Lee Server.]
IN: <u>Screenwriter: Words Become Picture</u>

511 Bennett, Charles.
"The Jules Verne Influence on *Voyage to the Bottom
of the Sea* and *Five Weeks in a Balloon*."
IN: <u>Omni's Screen Flights ...</u>

512 Bennett, Colin.
"Our Film-makers Reach Out."
IN: <u>An Australian Film Reader</u>

513 Bennett, Joseph.
"The Essences of Being." [RE: *L'Avventura*.]
IN: <u>Renaissance of the Film</u>

513a Benning, James.
"James Benning." [Interview by Scott MacDonald.]
IN: <u>A Critical Cinema 2</u>

514 Benoit-Levy, Jean.
"[From:] Universal Influences and Objectives of the
Motion Picture."

IN: <u>Film and Society</u>

515 Benson, Edward.
"Leisure and Monopoly Capital: Concentration and
Standardization in Franco-U.S. Trade in Film."
IN: <u>Current Research in Film /v. 3</u>

516 Benson, Harold.
"Movies Without a Camera." [RE: Norman McLaren.]
IN: <u>The Emergence of Film Art /1 ed</u>
<u>The Emergence of Film Art /2 ed</u>

517 Benson, Sheila.
"Choose Me."
"Mike's Murder."
"This Is Spinal Tap."
IN: <u>Produced and Abandoned</u>

Benson, Thomas W. SEE: Anderson, Carolyn.

518 Bentley, Eric.
"Realism and the Cinema."
IN: <u>Focus on Film and Theatre</u>

519 Bentley, Eric.
"The Political Theatre of John Wayne."
IN: <u>Conflict and Control in the Cinema</u>

520 Beranger, Clara.
"The Story."
IN: <u>Introduction to the Photoplay</u>

521 Béranger, Jean.
"Meeting with Ingmar Bergman: An Interview."
IN: <u>Focus on The Seventh Seal</u>

522 Berg, Angelika and Regine Engelmeier.
"Design or No Design: Costume Designers and
Couturiers in the Great Days of Hollywood."
"Major Costume Designers in Hollywood."
IN: <u>Fashion in Film</u>

523 Berg, Charles Ramírez.
"Zoot Suit."
IN: <u>Chicano Cinema</u>

524 Berg, Charles.
"Film and Photography."
IN: <u>Film and the Arts in Symbiosis</u>

525 Berg, Rick.
"Losing Vietnam: Covering the War in an Age of
Technology."
IN: <u>From Hanoi to Hollywood</u>

526 Bergen, Candice.
"Candice Bergen." [Interview by Rex Reed.]
IN: <u>Travolta to Keaton</u>

527 Berger, Arthur Asa.
"Introduction: *Society* on Film, Film in *Society*."
IN: <u>Film in Society</u>

528 Berger, John.
"The screenwriter as collaborator ..."
IN: <u>The Cineaste Interviews</u>

529 **Bergman, Andrew.**
"[From:] *We're in the Money*: Frank Capra and Screwball Comedy, 1931-1941."
IN: Film Theory and Criticism /2 ed

530 **Bergman, Ingmar.**
"A Program Note to *The Seventh Seal*."
IN: Focus on The Seventh Seal

531 **Bergman, Ingmar.**
"Bergman on Bergman."
"Ingmar Bergman." [Interviewed by John Reilly.]
IN: The Image Maker

532 **Bergman, Ingmar.**
"Bergman Discusses Film-Making."
IN: Film And/As Literature

533 **Bergman, Ingmar.**
"Film Has Nothing To Do With Literature."
IN: Film: A Montage of Theories

534 **Bergman, Ingmar.**
"Ingmar Bergman." [Interview by Andrew Sarris.]
IN: Interviews with Film Directors

535 **Bergman, Ingmar.**
"Ingmar Bergman." [Interview by Charles T. Samuels.]
IN: Encountering Directors

536 **Bergman, Ingmar.**
"On Dreams, the Subconscious, and Filmmaking."
IN: Film and Dream

537 **Bergman, Ingmar.**
"The Director."
IN: Filmmakers on Filmmaking /v. 1

538 **Bergman, Ingmar.**
"What Is 'Film Making'?"
IN: Film Makers on Film Making
Film: Readings in the Mass Media

539 **Bergman, Ingmar.**
"Why I Make Movies."
IN: The Emergence of Film Art /1 ed
The Emergence of Film Art /2 ed

540 **Bergman, Ingrid.**
"*Casablanca*'s Other Ending."
IN: Bedside Hollywood

541 **Bergman, Ingrid.**
"Ingrid Bergman." [Interview by John Kobal.]
IN: People Will Talk

542 **Bergman, Mark.**
"*The Phenix City Story*: 'This Will Happen to Your Kids, Too'."
IN: Kings of the Bs

543 **Bergstrom, Janet.**
"Androids and Androgyny."
IN: Close Encounters

544 **Bergstrom, Janet.**
"Enunciation and Sexual Difference."
"Rereading the Work of Claire Johnston."

"Alternation, Segmentation, Hypothesis: Interview with Raymond Bellour—An Excerpt."
IN: Feminism and Film Theory

545 **Bergstrom, Janet.**
"Psychological Explanation in the Films of Lang and Pabst."
IN: Psychoanalysis and Cinema
Bergstrom, Janet. SEE: Penley, Constance.

546 **Berkeley, Busby.**
"Director of Musical Numbers."
IN: Hollywood Speaks!

547 **Berman, Pandro S.**
"The Producer."
IN: Hollywood Speaks!

Berman, Rick. SEE: Hinds, Nanda.

548 **Berman, Russell A.**
"Hans-Jürgen Syberberg: Of Fantastic and Magical Worlds."
"Hellmuth Costard: The Undisturbed Course of Events."
IN: New German Filmmakers

549 **Berman, Russell A.**
"A Return to Arms: Käutner's *The Captain of Köpenick*."
IN: German Film and Literature

550 **Berman, Russell A.**
"A Solidarity of Repression: *Kameradschaft*."
IN: The Films of G.W. Pabst

551 **Bern, Paul.**
"Theory of the Silent Motion Picture."
IN: Introduction to the Photoplay

552 **Bernardet, Jean-Claude.**
"Trajectory of an Oscillation."
IN: Brazilian Cinema

553 **Bernardet, Jean-Claude.**
"The Sociological Model, or His Master's Voice: Ideological Form in *Viramundo*."
"The Voice of the Other: Brazilian Documentary in the 1970s."
IN: The Social Documentary ...

553a **Bernardoni, James**
"The Television Fallacy (*Bananas*; *American Graffiti*)."
"The Literary Fallacy (*All That Jazz*; *Apocalypse Now*)."
"The Hitchcockian Fallacy (*Carrie*; *Taxi Driver*)."
"The Hawksian Fallacy (*M*A*S*H*; *Jaws*; *Raiders of the Lost Ark*)."
"Redeemers of the Lost Art (*McCabe and Mrs. Miller*; *Annie Hall*; *Breaking Away*; *Escape from Alcatraz*)."
IN: The New Hollywood

554 **Bernds, Edward.**
"Edward Bernds." [An interview.]
IN: Interviews with B ...

555 **Bernhardt, Curtis.**
"Curtis Bernhardt."
IN: The Celluloid Muse

556 **Bernstein, Barbara.**
"That's Not Brave, That's Just Stupid."
IN: Women and the Cinema

557 **Bernstein, Elmer.**
"What Ever Happened to Great Movie Music?"
IN: Crossroads to the Cinema

558 **Bernstein, Matthew.**
"Hollywood Martyrdoms: *Joan of Arc* and Independent Production in the Late 1940s."
IN: Current Research in Film /v. 4

559 **Bernstein, Sidney L.**
"Walk Up! Walk Up! Please."
IN: Footnotes to the Film

560 **Berry, Chris.**
"Market Forces: China's 'Fifth Generation' Faces the Bottom Line."
"Sexual Difference and the Viewing Subject in *Li Shuangshuang* and *The In-Laws*."
IN: Perspectives on Chinese Cinema

561 **Bertino, Tom.**
"Hugh Harman and Rudolf Ising at Warner Brothers."
IN: The American Animated Cartoon

562 **Bertolucci, Bernardo.**
"Bernardo Bertolucci." [Interview by Joseph Gelmis.]
IN: The Film Director as Superstar

563 **Bertolucci, Bernardo.**
"The poetry of class struggle ..."
"I am not a moralist ..."
IN: The Cineaste Interviews

564 **Bessy, Maurice.**
"[From:] Méliès."
IN: Focus on The Science Fiction Film

565 **Betjeman, John.**
"Settings, Costumes, Backgrounds."
IN: Footnotes to the Film

566 **Beylie, Claude.**
"*Macbeth*, or the Magical Depths." [RE: *Macbeth*, 1948.]
IN: Focus on Shakespearean Films

567 **Bezanson, Mark.**
"*Little Big Man* [novel by] Thomas Berger. Berger and Penn's West: Visions and Revisions."
IN: The Modern American Novel ...

568 **Bezzerides, A.I.**
"A.I. Bezzerides." [Interview by Lee Server.]
IN: Screenwriter: Words Become Pictures

569 **Bhabba, Homi K.**
"The Commitment to Theory."
IN: Questions of Third Cinema

570 **Bharucha, Rustom.**
"The 'Boom' of David Lean's *A Passage to India*."
IN: Before His Eyes

571 **Bhattacharya, Basu.**
"Basu Bhattacharya." [Interview.]
IN: Indian Cinema Superbazaar

572 **Bia Jingsheng.**
"Throwing Away the Walking Stick of Drama."
IN: Chinese Film Theory

573 **Bierce, Ambrose.**
"*An Occurrence at Owl Creek Bridge*." [RE: the short story.]
IN: Film and Literature: Contrasts ...

Biette, Jean-Claude. SEE: Rohmer, Eric.

Biggers, Thompson. SEE: Shapiro, Mitchell E.

574 **Bill, Tony.**
"Tony Bill." [Interview by John Andrew Gallagher.]
IN: Film Directors on Directing

575 **Billard, Pierre.**
"*Chimes at Midnight*."
IN: Focus on Shakespearean Films

576 **Billman, Carol.**
"*The Wonderful Wizard of Oz* [novel by] L. Frank Baum. 'I've seen the movie': Oz Revisted."
IN: Children's Novels and the Movies

577 **Binford, Mira Reym.**
"The Two Cinemas of India."
IN: Film and Politics in the Third World

578 **Binford, Mira Reym.**
"Innovation and Imitation in the Indian Cinema."
IN: Cinema and Cultural Identity

579 **Bird, Michael.**
"Film as Hierophany."
"Ingmar Bergman."
IN: Religion in Film

580 **Birdsall, Eric R. and Fred H. Marcus.**
"Schlesinger's *Midnight Cowboy*: Creating a Classic."
IN: Film and Literature: Contrasts ...

581 **Biró, Yvette.**
"Pathos and Irony in East European Films."
IN: Politics, Art and Commitment ...

582 **Birri, Fernando.**
"For a Nationalist, Realist, Critical and Popular Cinema."
"For a Cosmic Cinema, Raving and Lumpen: The First Cosmunist (Cosmic Communist) Manifesto."
IN: Argentine Cinema

583 **Birri, Fernando.**
"The Roots of Documentary Realism." [RE: Argentina.]
IN: Cinema and Social Change ...
    Argentine Cinema

604 **Blair, Patricia.**
"Films in Public Libraries."
IN: Ideas on Film

605 **Blaise, Clark.**
"*The Thing* [1951]."
IN: The Movie That Changed My Life

606 **Blake, Richard A.**
"The Screwball Comedy: *It Happened One Night*."
"The Gangster Film: *Scarface*."
"The Western: *Stagecoach*."
"The Detective Story: *The Maltese Falcon*."
"The Horror Film: *Frankenstein*."
IN: Screening America: Reflections on ...

607 **Blake, Robert.**
"Robert Blake." [Interview by Charles Higham.]
IN: Celebrity Circus

608 **Blakeston, Oswell.**
"Two Vertov Films." [RE: *The Eleventh Year, Man with the Movie Camera*.]
IN: The Documentary Tradition /1 ed
The Documentary Tradition /2 ed

609 **Blanchard, Simon and Sylvia Harvey.**
"The Post-war Independent Cinema—Structure and Organisation."
IN: British Cinema History

610 **Blankfort, Michael.**
"The Film Writer and Freedom."
IN: Sight, Sound, and Society

611 **Blatty, William Peter.**
"William Peter Blatty." [Interview by Charles Higham.]
IN: Celebrity Circus

612 **Bletcher, Billy.**
"Billy Bletcher: The Voice Animator."
IN: The Real Tinsel

613 **Bliven, Bruce.**
"*The Covered Wagon*."
IN: The First Tycoons

614 **Bloch, Robert.**
"The Special Effectiveness of George Pal."
"The Master of *Metropolis*."
IN: Omni's Screen Flights ...

615 **Block, Ralph.**
"Not Theater, Not Literature, Not Painting."
IN: Introduction to the Art of the Movies
Film: A Montage of Theories

616 **Blondell, Joan.**
"Joan Blondell." [Interview by John Kobal.]
IN: People Will Talk

617 **Blondell, Joan.**
"Joan Blondell." [Interview by Charles Higham.]
IN: Celebrity Circus

618 **Bloom, Harold.**
"*The Fatal Glass of Beer*."
IN: The Movie That Changed My Life

619 **Bloom, Harry S.**
"The Copyright Position in Britain."
IN: Fair Use and Free Inquiry

620 **Blotner, Joseph.**
"Faulkner in Hollywood."
IN: Man and the Movies

621 **Blue, James.**
"One Man's Truth--An Interview With Richard Leacock."
IN: The Documentary Tradition /1 ed
The Documentary Tradition /2 ed

622 **Bluem, A. William.**
"The Documentary Idea: A Frame of Reference."
IN: Nonfiction Film Theory and Criticism

623 **Bluem, A. William.**
"Television and the Documentary."
IN: Film: A Montage of Theories

624 **Bluestone, George.**
"The Limits of the Novel and the Limits of the Film."
"*Wuthering Heights*."
"*Pride and Prejudice*."
"*The Ox-Bow Incident*."
"*Madame Bovary*."
IN: Novels into Film

625 **Bluestone, George.**
"[From:] *Novels into Film*: Limits of the Novel and the Film." [NOTE: This excerpt is different from the other excerpts of the same title.]
IN: Film Theory and Criticism /1 ed
Film Theory and Criticism /2 ed
Film Theory and Criticism /3 ed

626 **Bluestone, George.**
"The Limits of the Novel and the Limits of the Film." [NOTE: This excerpt is different from the other excerpts of the same title.]
IN: Film And/As Literature

627 **Bluestone, George.**
"Novels Into Film." [NOTE: This excerpt is different from the other excerpts of the same title.]
IN: Film: A Montage of Theories

628 **Bluestone, George.**
"The Limits of the Novel and the Limits of the Film." [NOTE: This excerpt is different from the other excerpts of the same title.]
IN: Film and the Liberal Arts

629 **Bluestone, George.**
"Editing."
IN: A Casebook on Film

630 **Bluestone, George.**
"Filming Novels: The Hemingway Case."
IN: A Moving Picture Feast

631 **Bluestone, George.**
"*The Informer*."

"A Few Favorites."
"B-Movies."
"The Best American Films of 1939."
"Sex and Violence."
"The Autumn of John Ford."
"Leo McCarey."
"Capra vs. Selznick."
"That's All, Folks." [RE: Chuck Jones.]
"Screenwriters and Preston Sturges."
"Ernst Lubitsch."
"To the Western White House."
"Q and A."
"On Location."
"Mr. Zukor's 100th Birthday Party."
  IN: Pieces of Time

658   Bogdanovich, Peter.
"Peter Bogdanovich." [Interview by Judith Crist.]
  IN: Take 22

659   Bogdanovich, Peter.
"Edgar G. Ulmer." [Interview].
  IN: Kings of the Bs

660   Bogdanovich, Peter.
"El Dorado."
  IN: Focus on Howard Hawks

661   Bogdanovich, Peter.
"The Kane Mutiny." [RE: Citizen Kane.]
  IN: Focus on Orson Welles

662   Bogdanovich, Peter.
"John Ford."
  IN: The American West on Film

663   Bogdanovich, Peter.
"Peter Bogdanovich." [Interview by Eric Sherman and Martin Rubin.]
  IN: The Director's Event

664   Bogdanovich, Peter.
"Fate, Murder, and Revenge." [RE: Fritz Lang.]
  IN: Great Film Directors

665   Bogdanovich, Peter.
"Interview with Alfred Hitchcock."
  IN: Focus on Hitchcock

666   Bogdanovich, Peter.
"The Hollywood B Movie."
  IN: Crossroads to the Cinema

667   Bohannan, Paul.
"The Myth and the Fact."
  IN: Africa on Film

668   Bohm, Hark.
"Taking Leave of the Security of Esoteric Aesthetics."
  IN: West German Filmmakers on Film

669   Bohn, Thomas.
"Nunnally Johnson."
  IN: Dictionary of Literary Biography /v. 26

670   Boland, Elena.
"Honesty or Hokum--Which Does the Public Want?"
[RE: Billy the Kid, 1930.]
  IN: The American West on Film

Bolton, H. Philip. SEE: Lellis, George.

671   Boltyansky, Grigori.
"Cinema and the Soviet Public."
  IN: The Film Factory

672   Bond, Kirk.
"Formal Cinema."
  IN: Introduction to the Art of the Movies

673   Bond, Kirk.
"Spoliation of 'Que Viva Mexico!'"
  IN: Hound & Horn

674   Bond, Ralph.
"Interview [with] Ralph Bond." [Interview by Eva Orbanz.]
  IN: Journey To a Legend and Back

675   Bondanella, Peter.
"Italy."
  IN: World Cinema Since 1945

676   Bondanella, Peter.
"Early Fellini: Variety Lights, The White Sheik, The Vitelloni."
  IN: Federico Fellini

677   Bonitzer, Pascal.
"Off-screen Space."
"'Reality' of Denotation."
  IN: Cahiers du Cinéma: 1969-1972

678   Bonitzer, Pascal.
"The Silences of the Voice."
  IN: Narrative, Apparatus, Ideology

679   Bonitzer, Pascal, Jean-Louis Comolli, Serge Daney, Jean Narboni and Jean-Pierre Oudart.
"La Vie est à nous: A Militant Film."
  IN: Cahiers du Cinéma: 1969-1972

Bonitzer, Pascal. SEE: Aumont, Jacques.

Bontemps, Jacques. SEE: Godard, Jean-Luc; SEE: Rohmer, Eric.

679a   Boorman, John.
"Bright Dreams, Hard Knocks: A Journal for 1991."
  IN: Projections: A Forum ...

680   Booth, Margaret.
"The Cutter." [RE: editor.]
  IN: Behind the Screen

681   Borde, Raymond.
"'The Golden Age': French Cinema of the '30s."
  IN: Rediscovering French Film

681a   Borden, Lizzie.
"Lizzie Borden." [Interview by Scott MacDonald.]
  IN: A Critical Cinema 2

706 Bourget, Jean-Loup.
"Faces of the American Melodrama: Joan Crawford."
IN: Imitations of Life

707 Bourget, Jean-Loup.
"Social Implications in the Hollywood Genres."
IN: Film Genre
Film Genre Reader
Film Theory and Criticism /4 ed

707a Bourget, Jean-Loup.
"Chaplin and the Resistance to 'Talkies'."
IN: Charlie Chaplin

708 Bowen, Elizabeth.
"Why I Go to the Cinema."
IN: Footnotes to the Film
Film: A Montage of Theories

709 Bowen, Elizabeth.
"*Things to Come*: A Critical Appreciation."
IN: Focus on The Science Fiction Film

710 Bowen, Harold G.
"Thomas Alva Edison's Early Motion-Picture
Experiments."
IN: A Technological History ...

711 Bowen, Kevin.
"'Strange Hells': Hollywood in Search of America's
Lost War."
IN: From Hanoi to Hollywood

712 Bowers, William.
"William Bowers." [Interview by William Froug.]
IN: The Screenwriter Looks ...

713 Bowser, Eileen.
"Toward Narrative, 1907: *The Mill Girl*."
"Griffith's Film Career Before *The Adventures of
Dollie*."
IN: Film Before Griffith

714 Bowser, Eileen.
"*Isn't Life Wonderful*."
IN: The First Film Makers

715 Bowser, Eileen.
"*Wild and Woolly*."
IN: The Rivals of D.W. Griffith

Bowser, Eileen. SEE: Barry, Iris.

716 Boyd, David.
"Images of Interpretation: *Blow-Up*."
"Positions and Perspectives: *Rashomon*."
"Identity and Textuality: *Citizen Kane*."
"Autobiography and Interpretation: *8-1/2*."
"Doubling and Deconstruction: *Vertigo*."
"Images Beyond Interpretation: *Persona*."
IN: Film and the Interpretive Process

717 Boyer, Jay.
"Daniel Taradash."
IN: Dictionary of Literary Biography /v. 44

718 Boyer, Jay.
"Delmer Daves."
"Sidney Buchman."
IN: Dictionary of Literary Biography /v. 26

719 Boyle, Barbara D.
"Independent Distribution: New World Pictures."
IN: The Movie Business Book

720 Boyum, Joy Gould.
"Biases and Preconceptions [of adaptation]."
"Film as Literature."
"The Viewer as Reader: Varieties of Interpretation."
"The Filmmaker as Reader: The Question of Fidelity."
"Point of View (*The Innocents*: Point of View as
Puzzle; *The Great Gatsby*: The Breakdown of
Distance; *The French Lieutenant's Woman*: Dual
Perspective; *Apocalypse Now*: Misguided Journey
to the Heart of Darkness)."
"Style and Tone (*Women in Love*: Style as Daring;
Ragtime: Missing the Beat; *Tess*: Romantic Strains
and Tragic Rhythms; *Daisy Miller*: The Loss of
Innocence)."
"Metaphor, Symbol, Allegory (*A Clockwork Orange*:
Viddying Metaphor; *Lord of the Flies*: Boys Will Be
Boys; *Wise Blood*: Wise Choice; *Death in Venice*:
The Seductiveness of the Sensual)."
"Interiors: Thought, Dream, Inner Action
(*Slaughterhouse-Five*: Pilgrim's Progress through
Time and Space; *Under the Volcano*: Looking
Outward; *The Day of the Locust*: Hollywood as a
State of Mind; *Swann in Love* and *The Proust
Screenplay*. Proust Outside and In)."
"Afterward—*The Magnificent Ambersons*: Reversing
the Bias."
IN: Double Exposure

721 Boyum, Joy Gould.
"*Blume in Love* and A Touch of Class."
"*Love and Death*."
"*The Phantom of Liberté*."
IN: Movie Comedy

722 Boyum, Joy Gould.
"*The White Dawn*."
"*The Conversation*."
IN: Produced and Abandoned

723 Boyum, Joy Gould.
"Dustin Hoffman."
IN: The Movie Star: The National ...

723a Boyum, Joy Gould.
"Columbia's Screwball Comedies: Wine, Women and
Wisecracks."
IN: Columbia Pictures

724 Brackett, Leigh.
"Leigh Brackett: Journeyman Plumber." [Interview by
Steve Swires.]
IN: Backstory 2

725 Brackett, Leigh.
"Working with Hawks."
IN: Women and the Cinema

748 Braudy, Leo.
"[From:] *The World in a Frame*: Acting: Stage vs. Screen."
IN: <u>Film Theory and Criticism /4 ed</u>

749 Braudy, Leo.
"[From:] *The World in a Frame*: Genre: The Conventions of Connection."
IN: <u>Film Theory and Criticism /2 ed</u>
<u>Film Theory and Criticism /3 ed</u>
<u>Film Theory and Criticism /4 ed</u>

750 Braudy, Leo.
"Genre and Resurrection of the Past."
IN: <u>Shadows of the Magic Lamp</u>
<u>Native Informant</u>

751 Braudy, Leo.
"Hitchcock, Truffaut, and the Irresponsible Audience."
IN: <u>Focus on Hitchcock</u>
<u>Native Informant</u>

752 Braudy, Leo.
"On Two Fronts." [RE: politics.]
IN: <u>Perspectives on the Study of Film</u>

753 Braudy, Leo.
"Renoir's Theater Films of the 1950s."
"Rossellini: From *Open City* to *General della Rovere*."
IN: <u>Great Film Directors</u>

754 Brauer, Ralph A.
"When the Lights Went Out—Hollywood, the Depression, and the Thirties."
IN: <u>Movies as Artifacts</u>

755 Brauer, Ralph.
"Who Are Those Guys? The Movie Western During the TV Era."
IN: <u>Focus on The Western</u>

Braun, B. Vivian. SEE: Wright, Basil.

756 Brautigam, Otto.
"Double Exposures in the Early Days."
IN: <u>The ASC Treasury ...</u>

757 Braverman, Richard.
"John Milius."
IN: <u>Dictionary of Literary Biography /v. 44</u>

758 Braver-mann, B.G.
"Josef von Sternberg."
IN: <u>Sternberg</u>

759 Brecher, Irving.
"Irving Brecher." [Interview by Lee Server.]
IN: <u>Screenwriter: Words Become Pictures</u>

760 Brecht, Bertolt.
"Concerning Music for the Film."
"Concerning the Film."
"On *The Gold Rush*: 'Less Security'."
IN: <u>Authors on Film</u>

761 Brecht, Bertolt.
"Short Description of a New Technique of Acting Which Produces an Alienation Effect."

IN: <u>Star Texts</u>

761a Breer, Robert.
"Robert Breer." [Interview by Scott MacDonald.]
IN: <u>A Critical Cinema 2</u>

762 Breese, Eleanor.
"The Story Editor."
IN: <u>The Movie Business Book</u>

Bremond, C. SEE: Morin, E.

763 Brennan, William J.
"The Irish in American Film and Television."
IN: <u>Ethnic Images ...</u>

764 Brenon, Herbert.
"Must They Have Temperament?"
IN: <u>Hollywood Directors 1914-1940</u>

765 Brent, Evelyn.
"Evelyn Brent." [Interview by John Kobal.]
IN: <u>People Will Talk</u>

766 Bresson, Robert.
"Notes on the Cinematographer."
IN: <u>Star Texts</u>

767 Bresson, Robert.
"Notes on Sound."
IN: <u>Film Sound</u>

768 Bresson, Robert.
"Rhythm Comes from Within."
IN: <u>Rediscovering French Film</u>

769 Bresson, Robert.
"Robert Bresson." [Interview by Andrew Sarris.]
IN: <u>Interviews with Film Directors</u>

770 Bresson, Robert.
"Robert Bresson." [Interview by Charles T. Samuels.]
IN: <u>Encountering Directors</u>

771 Bretherton, David.
"David Bretherton." [Interview by Vincent LoBrutto.]
IN: <u>Selected Takes</u>

772 Breton, André.
"As in a Wood." [RE: disorientation.]
IN: <u>The Shadow and Its Shadow</u>

Brewer, Barbara. SEE: Becker, Boris W.

773 Brewster, Ben (prepared).
"Documents from *Novy Lef*, with Biographical Notes, Etc."
"Notes on the Text 'John Ford's *Young Mr. Lincoln*' by the Editors of *Cahiers du Cinéma*."
IN: <u>Screen Reader 1</u>

774 Brewster, Ben.
"Deep Staging in French Films 1900-1914."
"A Scene at the 'Movies'."
IN: <u>Early Cinema ...</u>

775 Brewster, Ben.
"The Fundamental Reproach: Bertolt Brecht and the Cinema."

"Jack Arnold."
"Hammer."
"American International Productions and Roger Corman."
"William Castle."
"Vincent Price."
"Christopher Lee."
"Peter Cushing."
"Writing Horror: Richard Matheson and Robert Bloch."
"Directing Horror: Freddie Francis and Roy Baker."
"Producing Horror: Milton Subotsky and Kevin Francis."
"The Horror Fans."
IN: The Horror People

802 **Broughton, James.**
"Two Notes on *Mother's Day*."
IN: The Avant-Garde Film

803 **Broullon, R., G. Crowdus and A. Francovich.**
"'5 Frames are Frames, Not 6, But 5': An Interview with Santiago Alvarez."
IN: Conflict and Control in the Cinema

804 **Brouwer, Alexandra and Thomas Lee Wright (editors).**
"Head of Production (Michael Medavoy)."
"Producer (Kathleen Kennedy)."
"Screenwriter (Alvin Sargent)."
"Director (Taylor Hackford)."
"Agent (Jeremy Zimmer)."
"Business Affairs Executive (Wm. Christopher Gorog)."
"Entertainment Attorney (Tom Hansen)."
"Story Editor (Dan Bronson)."
"Titles Registrar (Dan Furie)."
"Script Supervisor (Meta Wilde)."
"Production Manager (C. O. 'Doc' Erickson)."
"Auditor (Sandra Rabins)."
"Casting Director (Janet Hirshenson and Jane Jenkins)."
"Dialect Coach (Robert Easton)."
"Stunt Coordinator (Kerry Rossall)."
"Choreographer (Jeffrey Hornaday)."
"Teacher (Adria Later)."
"Animal Trainer (Clint Rowe)."
"Production Designer (Polly Platt)."
"Set Designer (David Klassen)."
"Set Decorator (Marvin March)."
"Property Master (Emily Ferry)."
"Lead Man/Swing Gang (Paul Meyerberg)."
"Costume Designer (Rosanna Norton)."
"Key Costumer (Jim Tyson)."
"Makeup Artist (Ben Nye, Jr.)."
"Hair Stylist (Lynda Gurasich)."
"Production Illustrator (Ed Verreaux)."
"Matte Painter (Albert Whitlock)."
"Production Coordinator (Lisa Cook)."
"Construction Coordinator (George Stokes)."
"First Assistant Director (David Sosna)."
"Second Assistant Director (Victoria Rhodes)."
"Transportation Coordinator (Dan Marrow)."

"Location Manager (Ron Quigley)."
"Caterer (Steve Michaelson)."
"Wrangler (Rudy Ugland)."
"Key Grip (Tom Ramsey)."
"Gaffer (Steve Mathis)."
"Director of Photography (Laszlo Kovacs)."
"Camera Operator (Walt Lloyd)."
"Film Editor (Freeman and Carmel Davies)."
"Negative Cutter (Diane Jackson)."
"Color Timer (Aubrey Head)."
"Titles and Optical Effects Coordinator (Richard Gernand)."
"Studio Projectionist (Sal Olivas)."
"Visual Effects Producer (Richard Edlund)."
"Visual Effects Researcher (Jonathan Erland)."
"Special Makeup Designer (Chris Walas)."
"Model and Miniature Builder (Greg Jein)."
"Creature Design (Carlo Rambaldi)."
"Production Sound Mixer (Jim Webb)."
"Boom Operator (Forrest Williams)."
"Supervising Sound Editor (Cecelia Hall)."
"Rerecording Mixer (Robert 'Buzz' Knudson)."
"Composer (Bill Conti)."
"Music Editor (Richard Stone)."
"Scoring Mixer (Dan Wallin)."
"Unit Publicist (Stanley Brossette)."
"Still Photographer (Ralph Nelson)."
"Acquisitions Executive (Henry Seggerman)."
"Distribution Executive (Leo Greenfield)."
"Marketing Executive (Sidney Ganis)."
"Theater Owner (Henry Plitt)."
IN: Working in Hollywood

805 **Brown, Clarence.**
"The Producer Must Be Boss."
IN: Hollywood Directors 1941-1976

806 **Brown, Constance.**
"Olivier's *Richard III*: A Reconsideration."
IN: Focus on Shakespearean Films

Brown, David. SEE: Zanuck, Richard.

807 **Brown, Geoff.**
"Harry Langdon and Larry Semon--Two Silent Comics."
IN: Movies of the Silent Years

808 **Brown, Geoff.**
"Musicals."
IN: Anatomy of the Movies

809 **Brown, Geoff.**
"'Sister of the Stage': British Film and British Theatre."
IN: All Our Yesterdays

810 **Brown, Karl.**
"The Great D.W."
"The Proof of the Pudding." [RE: D.W. Griffith.]
IN: The First Film Makers

811 **Brown, Royal S.**
"Hermann [*sic*, Herrmann], Hitchcock, and the Music of the Irrational."

IN: <u>Film Theory and Criticism /3 ed</u>

812 Brown, Royal S.
"Introduction: One Plus One Equals."
"*La Chinoise*: Child's Play?"
"Jean-Luc Godard: Nihilism versus Aesthetic
   Distantiation."
   IN: <u>Focus on Godard</u>

813 Brown, Royal.
"Film and Classical Music."
   IN: <u>Film and the Arts in Symbiosis</u>

814 Brown, S.
"Imitation of Life: Once a Pancake."
   IN: <u>The Black Man on Film</u>

815 Browne, Nick.
"Representation and Story: Significance in *The 39
   Steps*."
"Narration as Interpretation: The Rhetoric of *Au
   Hasard, Balthazar*."
   IN: <u>The Rhetoric of Filmic Narration</u>

816 Browne, Nick.
"The Spectator-in-the-Text: The Rhetoric of
   Stagecoach."
   IN: <u>Narrative, Apparatus, Ideology</u>
      <u>Movies and Methods /v. 2</u>
      <u>The Rhetoric of Filmic Narration</u>
      <u>Film Theory and Criticism /4 ed</u>

817 Browne, Nick.
"The Rhetoric of the Specular Text with Reference to
   Stagecoach." [NOTE: A variation on the essay
   "The Spectator-in-the-Text: The Rhetoric of
   Stagecoach."]
   IN: <u>Theories of Authorship</u>

818 Browne, Nick.
"Griffith's Family Discourse: Griffith and Freud."
   IN: <u>Home Is Where the Heart Is</u>

819 Brownlow, Kevin.
"The Primitive Years."
"Early Days at Vitagraph."
"The Experimenters."
"Early Hollywood."
"From *Birth of a Nation* to *Intolerance*."
"Directors."
"D.W. Griffith."
"Allan Dwan."
"Henry King."
"Mary Pickford."
"Clarence Brown."
"The Lost Work of Edward Sloman."
"William Wellman."
"Cecil B. De Mille."
"Josef von Sternberg."
"The Cameraman."
"Charles Rosher."
"Art Direction."
"Douglas Fairbanks in *Robin Hood*."
"The Golden Path; or, The Curse of Melodrama."
"Scenario."

"Editing: The Hidden Power."
"Two Unique Processes: Tinting and Titling."
"Margaret Booth."
"William Hornbeck."
"Stunt Men of Silent Pictures."
"You Can't Make a Picture without 'em." [RE: grips;
   carpenters; property men; electricians; assistants.]
"It Was a Tough Life."
"The Silents Were Never Silent."
"Acting."
"The Stars."
"Geraldine Farrar."
"Gloria Swanson."
"Betty Blythe."
"The Heroic Fiasco: *Ben-Hur*."
"Producers."
"Louis B. Mayer and Irving Thalberg."
"David O. Selznick."
"We're Not Laughing Like We Used To." [RE: Harry
   Langdon; Raymond Griffith.]
"Reginald Denny."
"Harold Lloyd."
"Buster Keaton."
"Chaplin."
"The Silent Film in Europe."
"Abel Gance."
"The Talking Picture."
   IN: <u>The Parade's Gone By</u>

820 Brownlow, Kevin.
"Substance from Shadow: Pre-Cinema."
"Suspension of Disbelief: Edison and Invention."
"The Route to Respectability: Edwin Porter and the
   Theatrical Phase."
"Guiding Light: D.W. Griffith and Biograph."
"A New World for a Nickel: Nickelodeons."
"Lawful Larceny: The Patents War."
"The Mesmeriser: Griffith's Masterpieces."
"Expanding Empire: The Production of *Intolerance*."
"Intolerance Flourishes: World War One."
"Why Hollywood?: Sun, Space and Somnolence."
"'Our Night to Howl': Social Life in
   Hollywood--Scandal."
"The Cleavage Crisis: The March of Censorship."
"The Iodine Squad: Stunt Men and Women."
"Leave 'em Laughing: Comedy."
"Cult of the Personality: Stardom."
"Great Lover of the Silver Screen: Rudolph Valentino."
"The Rise and Fall of John Gilbert: Gilbert and Garbo."
"The Fellow Who Can't Do Anything Else: The
   Director."
"When Hollywood Ruled the World: On Location
   Abroad."
"Trick of the Light: Salute to the Cameraman."
"More than Meets the Eye: Salute to the Art Director."
"The Man You Will Love to Hate: Erich von Stroheim."
"Sunny Siberia: The European Community."
"Unaccustomed as We Are...: The Arrival of Talking
   Pictures."
   IN: <u>Hollywood: The Pioneers</u>

821 **Brownlow, Kevin.**
"*The Battle Cry of Peace*."
"The Chaplin Craze."
"*Britain Prepared*."
"The Creel Committee."
"*My Four Years in Germany*."
"Erich von Stroheim."
"Griffith."
"King Vidor and *The Big Parade*."
"*What Price Glory?*."
"*Wings*."
"*Barbed Wire*."
"*All Quiet*."
"Broncho Billy Anderson."
"Bison 101 and Thomas Ince."
"William S. Hart."
"Al Jennings."
"Emmett Dalton."
"Tom Mix."
"Will Rogers."
"The American Indian."
"Edward S. Curtis."
"*The Vanishing American*."
"*Redskin*."
"*The Devil Horse*."
"Yakima Canutt."
"*Sundown*."
"*The Wind*."
"*The Covered Wagon*."
"*North of 36*."
"*The Iron Horse*."
"*The Big Trail*."
"Burton Holmes."
"The Kolb Brothers."
"Herbert Ponting."
"Cherry Kearton."
"Lowell Thomas."
"Captain Noel."
"Mr. and Mrs. Martin Johnson."
"Robert Flaherty."
"*Frozen Justice*."
"*White Shadows in the South Seas*."
"*Stark Love*."
"*Stampede*."
"*Grass*."
"*Chang*."
"*The Viking*."
"*The Silent Enemy*."
"*Trader Horn*."
    IN: <u>The War, The West, and The Wilderness</u>

822 **Brownlow, Kevin.**
"*The Wishing Ring*."
    IN: <u>The Rivals of D.W. Griffith</u>

823 **Brownlow, Kevin.**
"Allan Dwan."
    IN: <u>The First Film Makers</u>

824 **Brownlow, Kevin.**
"Silent Films—What Was the Right Speed?"

    IN: <u>Early Cinema ...</u>

825 **Brownlow, Kevin.**
"William Beaudine."
"*Stark Love*."
"*The Wishing Ring*."
    IN: <u>The American Film Heritage</u>

826 **Broyles, Yolanda Julia.**
"Chicano Film Festivals: An Examination."
    IN: <u>Chicano Cinema</u>

827 **Bruce, David.**
"Hollywood Comes To the Highlands."
    IN: <u>From Limelight to Satellite</u>

828 **Bruce, Graham.**
"Alma Brasileira: Music in the Films of Glauber
    Rocha."
    IN: <u>Brazilian Cinema</u>

829 **Brückner, Jutta.**
"Women's Films Are Searches for Traces."
    IN: <u>West German Filmmakers on Film</u>

830 **Brunette, Peter.**
"The Three Stooges and the (Anti-)Narrative of
    Violence: De(con)structive Comedy."
    IN: <u>Comedy/Cinema/Theory</u>

831 **Brunette, Peter.**
"*Snow White and the Seven Dwarfs*."
    IN: <u>The American Animated Cartoon</u>

832 **Brunette, Peter.**
"*Native Son* [novel by] Richard Wright. Two Wrights,
    One Wrong."
    IN: <u>The Modern American Novel ...</u>

833 **Brunette, Peter.**
"Filming Words: Wenders's *The Goalie's Anxiety at
    the Penalty Kick* from the Novel by Peter Handke."
    IN: <u>Modern European Filmmakers ...</u>

834 **Brunette, Peter.**
"Toward a Deconstructive Theory of Film."
"Unity and Difference in *Paison*."
    IN: <u>The Cinematic Text</u>

835 **Brunette, Peter.**
"Visual Motifs in Rossellini's *Voyage to Italy*."
    IN: <u>Close Viewings</u>

836 **Brunette, Peter.**
"*The Prince and the Pauper* [novel by] Mark Twain.
    Faces in the Mirror: Twain's Pauper, Warner's
    Prince."
    IN: <u>The Classic American Novel ...</u>

837 **Brunius, Jacques.**
"Crossing the Bridge."
"The Lights Go Up."
"The Screen's Prestige."
    IN: <u>The Shadow and Its Shadow</u>

838 **Brunius, Jacques.**
"Every Year in Marienbad; or The Discipline of
    Uncertainty." [RE: *Last Year at Marienbad*.]

IN: <u>Renaissance of the Film</u>

839 Brunius, Jacques B.
"Experimental Film in France."
IN: <u>Experiment in the Film</u>

840 Bruno, Giuliana.
"Ramble City: Postmodernism and *Blade Runner*."
IN: <u>Alien Zone</u>

841 Bruno, Giuliana and Maria Nadotti.
"Off Screen: An Introduction."
"On the Margins of Feminist Discourse: The
Experience of the '150 Hours Courses'."
"Filmography: Women in Film in Italy."
IN: <u>Off Screen</u>

842 Brunsdon, Charlotte.
"*Crossroads*: Notes on Soap Opera." [RE: television.]
IN: <u>Imitations of Life</u>

843 Brustein, Robert.
"Out of This World." [RE: *Dr. Strangelove...*]
IN: <u>Renaissance of the Film</u>

844 Brustein, Robert.
"The New Hollywood: Myth and Anti-Myth."
IN: <u>A Casebook on Film</u>
    <u>The Movies in Our Midst</u>

845 Brustellin, Alf.
"The Other Tradition."
IN: <u>West German Filmmakers on Film</u>

**846 Brustellin, Alf, Rainer Werner Fassbinder,
Alexander Kluge, Volker Schlöndorff and
Bernhard Sinkel.**
"*Germany in Autumn*: What Is the Film's Bias?"
IN: <u>West German Filmmakers on Film</u>

847 Bryan, Bill.
"Bill Bryan." [Interview by William Froug.]
IN: <u>The New Screenwriter Looks ...</u>

848 Bryan, Julien.
"Face to Face."
IN: <u>Ideas on Film</u>

849 Bryan, Julien.
"War Is, Was, and Always Will Be, Hell."
IN: <u>The Documentary Tradition /1 ed</u>
    <u>The Documentary Tradition /2 ed</u>

850 Bryant, M. Darrol.
"Cinema, Religion, and Popular Culture."
IN: <u>Religion in Film</u>

851 Brynych, Zbynek.
"Zbynek Brynych." [Interview by Antonín J. Liehm.]
IN: <u>Closely Watched Films</u>

852 Buchman, Lorne M.
"Spatial Multiplicity: Patterns of Viewing in Cinematic
Space."
"Inside-Out: Dynamics of *Mise-en-scène*."
"Houseless Heads: The Storm of *King Lear* in the
Films of Peter Brook and Grigory Kozintsev."
"Expanding Secrets: The Space of the Close-up."

"Local Habitations: The Dialectics of Filmic and
Theatrical Space."
"Temporal Multiplicity: Patterns of Viewing in
Cinematic Time."
"Naming Time: Orson Welles's *Othello*."
IN: <u>Still in Movement</u>

853 Buchsbaum, Jonathan.
"Richard Brooks."
IN: <u>Dictionary of Literary Biography /v. 44</u>

854 Buchsbaum, Jonathan.
"Left Political Filmmaking in the West: The Interwar
Years."
IN: <u>Resisting Images</u>

855 Buck, Pearl S.
"Films for Neighbors."
IN: <u>Ideas on Film</u>

856 Budd, Mike.
"*The Cabinet of Dr. Caligari*: Production, Reception,
History."
IN: <u>Close Viewings</u>

857 Bukatman, Scott.
"Paralysis in Motion: Jerry Lewis's Life as a Man."
IN: <u>Comedy/Cinema/Theory</u>

858 Bukatman, Scott.
"Who Programs You? The Science Fiction of the
Spectacle."
IN: <u>Alien Zone</u>

859 Bunnell, Charlene.
"The Gothic: A Literary Genre's Transition to Film."
IN: <u>Planks of Reason</u>

860 Buñuel, Juan.
"A Letter on *The Exterminating Angel*."
IN: <u>The World of Luis Buñuel</u>

861 Buñuel, Luis.
"The Situation of the Serious Filmmaker."
IN: <u>Film: Book 1</u>

862 Buñuel, Luis.
"Luis Buñuel." [Interview by Beatrice Reyes Nevares.]
IN: <u>The Mexican Cinema</u>

863 Buñuel, Luis.
"A Statement."
IN: <u>Film and the Liberal Arts</u>
    <u>The Great Film Directors</u>

864 Buñuel, Luis.
"Buster Keaton's *College*."
IN: <u>The Shadow and Its Shadow</u>
    <u>The Great Film Directors</u>

865 Buñuel, Luis.
"Poetry and Cinema."
"On *Viridiana*."
IN: <u>The World of Luis Buñuel</u>

866 Buñuel, Luis.
"Cinema, Instrument of Poetry."
IN: <u>The Shadow and Its Shadow</u>

867 **Buñuel, Luis.**
"*Metropolis*."
"Carl Dreyer's *Jeanne d'Arc*."
IN: Great Film Directors

868 **Buñuel, Luis.**
"Luis Bunuel." [Interview by Andrew Sarris.]
IN: Interviews with Film Directors

869 **Bunuel, Luis.**
"Notes on the Making of *Un Chien Andalou*."
IN: Art in Cinema
The World of Luis Buñuel

Buñuel, Luis. SEE: Anderson, Lindsay.

870 **Burch, Glen.**
"Film Councils at Work."
IN: Ideas on Film

871 **Burch, Noel.**
"Four French Documentaries."
IN: The Documentary Tradition /1 ed
The Documentary Tradition /2 ed

872 **Burch, Noël.**
"A Primitive Mode of Representation?"
IN: Early Cinema

873 **Burch, Noël.**
"Akira Kurosawa."
"Carl Theodor Dreyer: The Major Phase."
"Fritz Lang: German Period."
"Léonce Perret."
"Marcel L'Herbier."
"Marcel Hanoun."
"Nagisa Oshima and Japanese Cinema in the 60s."
"Sergei M. Eisenstein."
IN: Cinema: A Critical Dictionary

874 **Burch, Noël.**
"On the Structural Use of Sound."
IN: Film Sound

875 **Burch, Noël.**
"Primitivism and the Avant-Gardes: A Dialectical Approach."
IN: Narrative, Apparatus, Ideology

876 **Burch, Noël.**
"Approaching Japanese Film."
IN: Cinema and Language

877 **Burch, Ruth.**
"Casting."
IN: Hollywood Speaks!

878 **Burchard, John E.**
"Doubts."
IN: Film Study in Higher Education

879 **Burdick, Dolores.**
"*Persona*: Facing the Mirror Together."
IN: Close Viewings

Burgoyne, Robert. SEE: Stam, Robert.

880 **Burgschmidt, Hans.**
"Open Letter from a Projectionist: An Open Letter to Rick Jackson of the Ontario Theatres Branch."
IN: Forbidden Films

881 **Burke, Frank.**
"The Three-Phase Process and the White Clown–Auguste Relationship in Fellini's *The Clowns*."
IN: Explorations in National Cinemas

882 **Burnett, Charles.**
"Inner City Blues."
IN: Questions of Third Cinema

883 **Burnett, Ron.**
"The Crisis of the Documentary Film in Quebec."
IN: Explorations in Film Theory

884 **Burnett, Ron.**
"The Practice of Film Teaching: Vanier College."
IN: Film Study in the Undergraduate Curriculum

885 **Burnett, W.R.**
"W.R. Burnett: The Outsider." [Interview by Ken Mate and Pat McGilligan.]
IN: Backstory

886 **Burnley, Fred.**
"*The Dream Divided*." [Interview by Alan Rosenthal.]
IN: The New Documentary in Action

887 **Burns, E. Jane.**
"Nostalgia Isn't What It Used To Be: The Middle Ages in Literature and Film."
IN: Shadows of the Magic Lamp

888 **Burns, Fred.**
"Achieving the Fantastic in the Animated Film."
IN: Shadows of the Magic Lamp

889 **Burns, Gary.**
"Film and Popular Music."
IN: Film and the Arts in Symbiosis

890 **Burroughs, Edgar Rice.**
"[From:] *Tarzan of the Apes* [the book]."
IN: Africa on Film

890a **Burroughs, William S.**
"Screenwriting and the Potentials of Cinema."
IN: Writing in a Film Age

891 **Burrows, Elaine.**
"Live Action: A Brief History of British Animation."
IN: All Our Yesterdays

892 **Burrud, Bill.**
"Bill Burrud." [An interview.]
IN: Producers on Producing

893 **Burstall, Tim.**
"Twelve Genres of Australian Film."
IN: An Australian Film Reader

894 **Burton, Julianne.**
"Bridging Past and Present: Legend and Politics in *The Promised Land*."

IN: Reviewing Histories

895   Burton, Julianne.
"Cultures of Silence, Cultures of Visibility."
IN: Forbidden Films

896   Burton, Julianne.
"Film and Revolution in Cuba: The First 25 Years."
IN: Jump Cut

897   Burton, Julianne.
"Latin America."
IN: World Cinema Since 1945

898   Burton, Julianne.
"Democratizing Documentary: Modes of Address in
the Latin American Cinema, 1958-72." [NOTE:
See the entry in *The Social Documentary ...*]
IN: Show Us Life

899   Burton, Julianne.
"Transitional States: Creative Complicities with the
Real in *Man Marked to Die: Twenty Years Later*
and *Patriamada*."
"Toward a History of Social Documentary in Latin
America."
"Democratizing Documentary: Modes of Address in
the New Latin American Cinema, 1958-1972."
[NOTE: An altered version of essay in the book
"Show Us Life".]
IN: The Social Documentary ...

**Burton, Julianne. SEE: Guzmán, Patricio; SEE:
Ranucci, Karen.**

900   Burton, Richard.
"Liz at First Sight."
IN: Bedside Hollywood

900a   Burton, Tim.
"Tim Burton." [Interview by David Breskin.]
IN: Inner Views

901   Busch, Niven.
"Niven Busch: A Doer of Things." [Interview by David
Thomson.]
IN: Backstory

902   Buschmann, Christel.
"Response to H.C. Blumenberg."
IN: West German Filmmakers on Film

903   Buscombe, Edward.
"A New Approach to Film History."
IN: Film: Historical-Theoretical ...

904   Buscombe, Edward.
"Bread and Circuses: Economics and the Cinema."
IN: Cinema Histories, Cinema Practices

905   Buscombe, Edward.
"Coca-Cola Satellites? Hollywood and the
Deregulation of European Television."
IN: Hollywood in the Age of Television

906   Buscombe, Edward.
"Ideas of Authorship."
IN: Theories of Authorship

907   Buscombe, Edward.
"Notes on Columbia Pictures Corporation 1926-41."
IN: The Hollywood Film Industry

908   Buscombe, Edward.
"Sound and Color."
IN: Movies and Methods /v. 2

909   Buscombe, Edward.
"The Idea of Genre in the American Cinema."
IN: Film Genre
Film Genre Reader

910   Buscombe, Edward.
"The Representation of Alcoholism on Television."
IN: Images of Alcoholism

911   Bush, W. Stephen.
"*The Birth of a Nation*."
IN: Focus on The Birth of a Nation

912   Bush, W. Stephen.
"Moving Picture Absurdities."
IN: The Pretend Indians

913   Butler, Bill.
"Bill Butler." [Interview by Dennis Schaefer and Larry
Salvato.]
IN: Masters of Light

913a   Butler, Bill.
"Bill Butler." [Interview by Anthony Loeb.]
IN: Filmmakers in Conversation

914   Byars, Jackie.
"Gazes/Voices/Power: Expanding Psychoanalysis for
Feminist Film and Television Theory."
IN: Female Spectators

915   Byers, Thomas B.
"Commodity Futures."
IN: Alien Zone

915a   Byg, Barton.
"Generational Conflict and Historical Continuity in
GDR Film."
IN: Framing the Past

916   Bygrave, Mike.
"The New Moguls."
IN: Anatomy of the Movies

917   Byrge, Duane.
"Donald Ogden Stewart."
IN: Dictionary of Literary Biography /v. 26

918   Byrne, Richard B.
"An Outline History of Film Styles."
IN: Screen Experience

919   Byrne, Richard B. and Sharon Feyen.
"Documentary: Film as Social Commentary."
IN: Screen Experience

920   Byron, Stuart.
"*The Discreet Charm of the Bourgeoisie*."
"Blake Edwards."
"Frank Tashlin."

"Jerry Lewis."
IN: Movie Comedy

921 Bywater, Tim and Thomas Sobchack.
"The Journalistic Approach: Film Reviews for the
Mass Audience."
"The Humanistic Approach: Traditional Aesthetic
Responses to the Movies."
"The Auteurist Approach: Analysis of Filmmakers and
Their Films."
"The Genre Approach: Analysis of Formula Films."
"The Social Science Approach: Films as Social
Artifacts."
"The Historical Approach: Viewing the Past."
"The Ideological/Theoretical Approach: Using Basic
Principles to Uncover Deeper Meanings."
IN: Introduction to Film Criticism

922 Cabarga, Leslie.
"Strike at the Fleischer Factory."
IN: The American Animated Cartoon

923 Cabot, Susan.
"Susan Cabot." [An interview.]
IN: Interviews with B ...

924 Cadbury, William.
"Story, Pleasure, and Meaning in *The Scarlet
Empress*."
IN: Narrative Strategies

925 Cadbury, William and Leland Poague.
"Beardsley's *Aesthetics* and Film Criticism."
"The Cleavage Plane of André Bazin."
"The Problem of Film Genre."
"Semiology, Human Nature, and John Ford."
"Hitchcock and the Ethics of Vision."
"Auteurism: Theory as against Policy."
"Intentionality, Authorship, and Film Criticism."
"History/Cinema/Criticism."
"Film Interpretation: Theory and Practice."
"Toward a Cartesian Aesthetics."
IN: Film Criticism

926 Cagney, James.
"I *Never* Said, 'You Dirty Rat'."
IN: Bedside Hollywood

927 Cagney, James.
"The Ham Instinct ..."
IN: Celebrity Articles ...

928 *Cahiers du Cinéma*.
"Cinema, Ideology, Politics (for Poretta-Terme)."
IN: Cahiers du Cinéma: 1969-1972

929 *Cahiers du Cinéma*.
"A Collective Text."
IN: Sternberg

930 *Cahiers du Cinéma*.
[Excerpts.]
IN: Theories of Authorship

931 *Cahiers du Cinéma*, collective editorial statement
(*Cahiers du Cinéma, Cinéthique, Tel Quel*).
"Cinema, Literature, Politics."
IN: Cahiers du Cinéma: 1969-1972

932 *Cahiers du Cinéma*, collective text.
"Josef von Sternberg's *Morocco*."
IN: Cahiers du Cinéma: 1969-1972

933 *Cahiers du Cinéma*, editors.
"John Ford's *Young Mr. Lincoln*."
IN: Film Theory and Criticism /2 ed
Film Theory and Criticism /3 ed
Narrative, Apparatus, Ideology
Movies and Methods: An Anthology
Screen Reader 1

934 *Cahiers du Cinéma*.
"Twenty Years of French Cinema: The Best French
Films since the Liberation."
IN: Cahiers du Cinéma, 1960-1968

935 *Cahiers du Cinéma*, editorial.
"The Langlos Affair."
"The Estates General of the French Cinema."
"Editorial Changes in *Cahiers*."
IN: Cahiers du Cinéma, 1960-1968

936 *Cahiers du Cinéma*, editorial.
"Russia in the 20s (1)."
"Japanese Cinema (1)."
"Politics and Ideological Class Struggle."
IN: Cahiers du Cinéma: 1969-1972

937 Cain, James M.
"James M. Cain: Tough Guy." [Interview by Peter
Brunette and Gerald Peary.]
IN: Backstory

938 Caine, Michael.
"Michael Caine." [Interview by Judith Crist.]
IN: Take 22

939 Callenbach, Ernest.
"Seeing Style in Film (With Some Notes on *Red
Desert*)."
IN: The Compleat Guide to Film Study

940 Callenbach, Ernest.
"Classics Revisited: *The Gold Rush*."
IN: The Classic Cinema

941 Callenbach, Ernest.
"Gdansk Journal: September 1980."
IN: Politics, Art and Commitment ...

942 Callenbach, Ernest.
"The Movie Industry and the Film Culture."
IN: Film: Readings in the Mass Media

943 Cameron, Evan William.
"Walter Reisch."
IN: Dictionary of Literary Biography /v. 44

944 Cameron, Evan William.
"*Citizen Kane*: The Influence of Radio Drama on
Cinematic Design."

IN: Sound and the Cinema

945 Cameron, Ian.
"Frank Tashlin & the New World."
"Suspense and Meaning." [RE: Hitchcock.]
"Films, Directors and Critics."
"The Darwinian World of Claude Chabrol."
"The Mechanics of Suspense." [RE: Hitchcock.]
"Bonjour Tristesse."
"Judex."
"Now About These Women."
IN: Movie Reader

946 Cameron, Ian.
"L'Avventura."
IN: Great Film Directors

947 Cameron, Ian.
"Films, Directors and Critics." [NOTE: An excerpt from
Movie.]
IN: Theories of Authorship

948 Cameron, Ian.
"Nagisa Oshima."
IN: Second Wave

949 Cameron, Ian and Richard Jeffery.
"The Universal Hitchcock."
IN: A Hitchcock Reader
Movie Reader

**950 Cameron, Ian, Jim Hillier, V.F. Perkins, Michael
Walker and Robin Wood.**
"The Return of *Movie*: A Discussion." [NOTE: An
excerpt from *Movie.*]
IN: Theories of Authorship

Cameron, Ian. SEE: Perkins, V.F.

951 Cameron, Kate.
"Vivid Action-Movie at the Paramount." [RE:
Geronimo, 1930.]
IN: The American West on Film

952 Campbell, Edward D.C., Jr.
"'Burn, Mandingo, Burn': The Plantation South in Film,
1958-1978."
IN: The South and Film

953 Campbell, Mary B.
"Biological Alchemy and the Films of David
Cronenberg."
IN: Planks of Reason

954 Campbell, Ramsey.
"The Quality of Terror."
IN: Cut!: Horror Writers ...

955 Campbell, Russell.
"Radical Cinema in the 1930s: The Film and Photo
League."
IN: Jump Cut

956 Campbell, Russell.
"Radical Documentary in the United States,
1930-1942."
IN: Show Us Life

957 Campbell, Russell.
"The Grapes of Wrath [novel by] John Steinbeck.
Trampling Out the Vintage: Sour Grapes."
IN: The Modern American Novel ...

958 Camper, Fred.
"1966-1967 (*Samadhi; Film in Which There Appear
Sprocket Holes, Edge Lettering, Dirt Particles, Etc.;
Castro Street; Notes on the Circus; Lapis;
Wavelength*)."
IN: A History of the American Avant-Garde Cinema

959 Camper, Fred.
"Sound and Silence in Narrative and Nonnarrative
Cinema."
IN: Film Sound

960 Camper, Fred.
"Disputed Passage."
IN: Movies and Methods: An Anthology

Camper, Fred. SEE: Landow, George.

961 Canby, Vincent.
"Amarcord."
"King of Hearts."
"One Flew Over the Cuckoo's Nest."
"Playtime."
"Putney Swope."
"Trash."
"Laurel and Hardy."
IN: Movie Comedy

962 Canby, Vincent.
"That Obscure Object of Desire: Buñuel's Triumph,
Bertolucci's Flop."
IN: The World of Luis Buñuel

963 Canby, Vincent.
"Character Actors vs. Stars: The Distinction Is Fading."
"Sophia Loren and Marcello Mastroianni."
"Teleperforming vs. Screen Acting: Sally Field."
"The Performer vs. the Role: Catherine Deneuve and
James Mason."
IN: The Movie Star: The National ...

964 Canby, Vincent.
"The power of the *Times* critic ..."
IN: The Cineaste Interviews

965 Canby, Vincent.
"Violence and Beauty Mesh in *Wild Bunch.*"
IN: The American West on Film

966 Candelaria, Cordelia.
"Social Equity in Film Criticism."
IN: Chicano Cinema

967 Canemaker, John.
"A Day with J.R. Bray."
"Vlad Tytla: Animation's Michelangelo."
"Winsor McCay."
IN: The American Animated Cartoon

968 Canham, Kingsley.
"Michael Curtiz."

"Raoul Walsh."
"Henry Hathaway."
IN: The Hollywood Professionals /v. 1

969 Canham, Kingsley.
"Lewis Milestone."
IN: The Hollywood Professionals /v. 2

970 Canham, Kingsley.
"John Cromwell."
"Mervyn LeRoy."
IN: The Hollywood Professionals /v. 5

971 Cannon, David.
"A Struggling Young Actor."
IN: Hollywood Speaks!

972 Cantor, Eddie.
"Comics and the War."
"I Like to Remember."
"The Unknown Soldier Speaks."
IN: The Best of Rob Wagner's Script

973 Canudo, Ricciotto.
"The Birth of a Sixth Art."
"Reflections on the Seventh Art."
IN: French Film Theory and Criticism /v. 1

974 Canudo, Ricciotto.
"Another View of *Nanook*."
IN: The Documentary Tradition /1 ed
The Documentary Tradition /2 ed

975 Capote, Truman.
"The Writer and Motion Pictures."
IN: Authors on Film

976 Capra, Frank.
"Breaking Hollywood's 'Pattern of Sameness'."
IN: Hollywood Directors 1941-1976

977 Capra, Frank.
"Frank Capra." [Interview by Richard Schickel.]
IN: The Men Who Made the Movies

978 Capra, Frank.
"Reminiscence and Reflection: à Director."
IN: Sound and the Cinema

979 Capra, Frank.
"The Gag Man."
IN: Hollywood Directors 1914-1940

980 Capra, Frank.
"*Why We Fight*."
IN: Propaganda on Film

981 Capriles, Oswaldo.
"*The Milky Way*."
IN: The World of Luis Buñuel

982 Card, James.
"Confessions of a *Casablanca* Cultist: An Enthusiast Meets the Myth and Its Flaws."
IN: The Cult Film Experience

983 Card, James.
"Influences of the Danish Film."

"Shooting Off-the-Set."
"Silent-Film Speed."
"The Films of Mary Pickford."
"The Screen's First Tragedienne: Asta Nielsen."
"The Silent Films of Cecil B. DeMille."
IN: Image on the Art ...

984 Card, James.
"The Historical Motion-Picture Collections at George Eastman House."
IN: A Technological History ...

Card, James. SEE: Brooks, Louise.

985 Cardullo, Bert.
"Pride of the Working Class: *Room at the Top* Reconsidered."
"*Way Down East*: Play and Film."
"*Der Letzte Mann* Gets the Last Laugh: F.W. Murnau's Comic Vision."
"The Dream Structure of *Some Like It Hot*."
"The Symbolism of *Hiroshima, mon amour*."
"Take Comfort, Take Caution: Tragedy and Homily in *Day of Wrath*."
"The Circumstance of the East, the Fate of the West: Notes, Mostly on *The Seven Samurai*."
"The Art of *Shoeshine*."
"Re-viewing *The Rain People*."
"Expressionism and the Real *Cabinet of Dr. Caligari*."
"Expressionism and *Nosferatu*."
"Expressionism and *L'avventura*."
"Bresson's *Une femme douce*: A New Reading."
"The Film Style of Federico Fellini: *The Nights of Cabiria* as Paradigm."
"Style and Meaning in *Shoot the Piano Player*."
"The Space in the Distance: A Study of Robert Altman's *Nashville*."
"The Fall of Béatrice, the Salvation of Pomme: Simultaneity and Stillness in Goretta's *Lacemaker*."
IN: Indelible Images

986 Cardullo, Bert.
"The Real Fascination of *Citizen Kane*."
IN: Before His Eyes
Indelible Images

987 Care, Ross B.
"Threads of Melody: The Evolution of a Major Film Score—Walt Disney's *Bambi*."
IN: Wonderful Inventions

988 Carewe, Edwin.
"Directorial Training."
IN: Hollywood Directors 1914-1940

989 Carey, G.
"The Long, Long Road to Brenda Patimkin."
IN: The Black Man on Film

990 Carey, Gary.
"George Cukor."
"Greta Garbo."
"Jacques Demy."
"Vincente Minnelli and the 1940s Musical."
IN: Cinema: A Critical Dictionary

991 Carey, Gary.
"Notes on the Shooting Script."
IN: The Citizen Kane Book

992 Carey, Gary.
"Prehistory: Anita Loos."
IN: The Hollywood Screenwriters

993 Carey, John.
"Conventions and Meaning in Film."
IN: Film/Culture: Explorations ...

994 Carhall, H.K.
"*The Sentimental Bloke*."
IN: An Australian Film Reader

995 Carlino, Lewis John.
"Lewis John Carlino." [Interview by William Froug.]
IN: The Screenwriter Looks ...

996 Carlson, Jerry W.
"*Washington Square* [novel by] Henry James. *Washington Square* and *The Heiress*: Comparing Artistic Forms."
IN: The Classic American Novel ...

997 Cárlson, Terry.
"*Antônio das Mortes*."
IN: Brazilian Cinema

998 Carmines, Al.
"Keep the Camp Fires Burning."
IN: The Image Maker

999 Carné, Marcel.
"Cinema and the World."
"When Will the Cinema Go Down into the Street?"
IN: French Film Theory and Criticism /v. 2

1000 Carpenter, Edmund.
"The New Languages."
IN: Perspectives on the Study of Film

1001 Carpenter, John.
"John Carpenter." [Interview by Stanley Wiater.]
IN: Dark Visions

1002 Carr, Jay.
"*Dreamchild*."
"*Heart Like a Wheel*."
"*The Dead*."
IN: Produced and Abandoned

1003 Carr, William H.A.
"The Star-Crossed."
"Roscoe (Fatty) Arbuckle: A Party in 'Frisco."
"William Desmond Taylor: Who Killed the Mystery Man?"
"Paul Bern: Why Did Jean Harlow's Husband Die?"
"Thelma Todd: The Wrong Time for Death."
"Mary Astor: The Trouble with Diaries."
"Errol Flynn: The Moon through a Porthole."
"Charlie Chaplin: Blood Won't Tell."
"Lupe Velez: She Didn't Believe in Marriage."
"Ingrid Bergman: The Saint Was a Woman."
"Lana Turner: Death of a Playmate."
"Marilyn Monroe: Death and the Kennedy Connection."
"Judy [Garland], Liz [Taylor], Frances [Farmer], and Jayne [Mansfield]: The Insecurities of Stardom."
"Bruce Lee and James Dean: How Cults Are Born."
"Sharon Tate: Sex, Satanism, and Sacrifice."
IN: Hollywood Tragedy

1004 Carrico, J. Paul.
"Film and the Teaching of English."
IN: Films Deliver

1005 Carrière, Jean-Claude.
"The Buñuel Mystery."
IN: The World of Luis Buñuel

1006 Carril, M. Martinez.
"Ingmars Ansikte." [RE: Ingmar Bergman.]
IN: Focus on The Seventh Seal

1007 Carringer, Robert L.
"Film Studies at the University of Illinois at Urbana-Champaign."
IN: Film Study in the Undergraduate Curriculum

1008 Carroll, Kent E.
"Film and Revolution: Interview with the Dziga-Vertov Group."
IN: Focus on Godard

1009 Carroll, Noël.
"[From:] *Philosophical Problems of Classical Film Theory*: The Specificity Thesis."
IN: Film Theory and Criticism /4 ed

1010 Carroll, Noël.
"[From:] *Mystifying Movies*: Jean-Louis Baudry and 'The Apparatus'."
IN: Film Theory and Criticism /4 ed

1011 Carroll, Noel.
"*Vanity Fair* [novel by] W.M. Thackeray; *Becky Sharp* [film by] Rouben Mamoulian. Becky Sharp Takes Over."
IN: The English Novel and the Movies

1012 Carroll, Noël.
"*King Kong*: Ape and Essence."
IN: Planks of Reason

1013 Carroll, Noël.
"Back to Basics." [RE: genre.]
IN: American Media

1014 Carroll, Noël.
"Buster Keaton, *The General*, and Visible Intelligibility."
IN: Close Viewings

1015 Carroll, Noël.
"Keaton: Film Acting as Action."
IN: Making Visible the Invisible

1016 Carroll, Noël.
"Lang and Pabst: Paradigms of Early Sound Practice."
IN: Film Sound

1017 Carroll, Noël.
"Notes on the Sight Gag."
IN: Comedy/Cinema/Theory

1018 **Carroll, Noël.**
"The Moral Ecology of Melodrama: The Family Plot and *Magnificent Obsession*."
IN: Imitations of Life

1019 **Carroll, Noël and Patrick.**
"Notes on Movie Music."
IN: The Cinematic Text

Carroll, Raymond L. SEE: Lichty, Lawrence W.

1020 **Carroll, Willard.**
"John Michael Hayes."
IN: Dictionary of Literary Biography /v. 26

1021 **Carstairs, John Paddy.**
"The Technical Advisor ..."
IN: Celebrity Articles ...

1022 **Carter, Everett.**
"Cultural History Written with Lightning: The Significance of *The Birth of a Nation*."
IN: Hollywood as Historian
Focus on The Birth of a Nation

1023 **Carter, Hodding.**
"Mississippi Movie."
IN: Ideas on Film

1024 **Carunungan, Celso Al.**
"Early Years of Philippine Movies."
IN: Readings in Philippine Cinema

1025 **Casaus, Victor.**
"*Las Hurdes: Land Without Bread*."
IN: The World of Luis Buñuel

Cash, Jim. SEE: Epps, Jack, Jr.

1026 **Casper, Joseph Andrew.**
"*The Little Prince* [novel by] Antoine de Saint Exupéry. I Never Met a Rose: Stanley Donen and *The Little Prince*."
IN: Children's Novels and the Movies

1027 **Cassady, Ralph, Jr.**
"Monopoly in Motion Picture Production and Distribution: 1908-1915."
IN: The American Movie Industry

1028 **Cassavetes, John.**
"John Cassavetes." [Interview by Joseph Gelmis.]
IN: The Film Director as Superstar

1028a **Cassavetes, John**
"John Cassavetes." [Interview by Anthony Loeb.]
IN: Filmmakers in Conversation

1029 **Cassavetes, John.**
"What's Wrong with Hollywood."
IN: The Movies: An American Idiom

1030 **Cassavetes, John and Gena Rowlands.**
"John Cassavetes and Gena Rowlands." [Interview by Charles Higham.]
IN: Celebrity Circus

1031 **Cassill, R.V.**
"In the Central Blue."
IN: Man and the Movies

1032 **Cassou, Jean.**
"From Avant-Garde to Popular Front."
IN: French Film Theory and Criticism /v. 2

1033 **Castello, Giulio Cesare.**
"Italian Silent Cinema."
IN: Cinema: A Critical Dictionary

1034 **Castro, David and Jerry Stoll.**
"Profile of Art in Revolution." [RE: politics.]
IN: Perspectives on the Study of Film

1035 **Casty, Alan.**
"Griffith and the Expressiveness of Editing."
IN: The First Film Makers

1036 **Casty, Alan.**
"The Existential Art of the New Film."
IN: The Image Maker

1037 **Casty, Alan.**
"The Films of D.W. Griffith: A Style for the Times."
IN: Imitations of Life

1038 **Cates, Gilbert.**
"*I Never Sang for My Father*." [NOTE: Mr. Cates' name is misprinted as "Gates" in the article.]
IN: Directors in Action

1039 **Caughie, John.**
"Broadcasting and Cinema: 1: Converging Histories."
IN: All Our Yesterdays

1040 **Caughie, John.**
"Representing Scotland: New Questions for Scottish Cinema."
IN: From Limelight to Satellite

1041 **Cavalcanti, Alberto.**
"Comedies and Cartoons."
IN: Footnotes to the Film

1042 **Cavalcanti, Alberto.**
"Sound in Films."
IN: Film Sound

1043 **Cavalcanti, Alberto.**
"The Sound Film."
IN: The Emergence of Film Art /1 ed
The Emergence of Film Art /2 ed

1044 **Cavalcanti, Alberto.**
"The Neorealist Movement in England."
IN: French Film Theory and Criticism /v. 2

1045 **Cavander, Kenneth.**
"Interview with Harold Pinter and Clive Donner."
IN: Focus on Film and Theatre

1046 **Cavell, Stanley.**
"Cons and Pros: *The Lady Eve*."
"Knowledge as Transgression: *It Happened One Night*."
"Leopards in Connecticut: *Bringing Up Baby*."

"The Importance of Importance: *The Philadelphia Story*."
"Counterfeiting Happiness: *His Girl Friday*."
"The Courting of Marriage: *Adam's Rib*."
"The Same and Different: *The Awful Truth*."
    IN: Pursuits of Happiness

1047   **Cavell, Stanley.**
"[From:] *The World Viewed*: Photograph and Screen."
"[From:] *The World Viewed*: Audience, Actor, Star."
    IN: Film Theory and Criticism /2 ed
        Film Theory and Criticism /3 ed
        Film Theory and Criticism /4 ed

1048   **Cavell, Stanley.**
"[From:] *The World Viewed*: Ideas of Origin."
"[From:] *The World Viewed*: Types; Cycles as Genres."
    IN: Film Theory and Criticism /1 ed
        Film Theory and Criticism /2 ed
        Film Theory and Criticism /3 ed
        Film Theory and Criticism /4 ed

1049   **Cavell, Stanley.**
"An Afterimage—On Makavejev and Bergman."
    IN: Film and Dream

1050   **Cavell, Stanley.**
"Psychoanalysis and Cinema: The Melodrama of the Unknown Woman." [RE: *Letter from an Unknown Woman*.]
    IN: Images in Our Souls

1051   **Cavell, Stanley.**
"*North by Northwest*."
    IN: A Hitchcock Reader

1052   **Cavens, Fred.**
"Sword Play in the Movies."
    IN: Celebrity Articles ...

1053   **Cawelti, John G.**
"*Bonnie and Clyde*: Tradition and Transformation."
"The Artistic Power of *Bonnie and Clyde*."
    IN: Focus on Bonnie and Clyde

1054   **Cawelti, John G.**
"Reflections on the New Western Films: The Jewish Cowboy, The Black Avenger, and the Return of the Vanishing American." [NOTE: Also called "Reflections on the New Western Films."]
    IN: The Pretend Indians
        Focus on The Western

1055   **Cawelti, John G.**
"Savagery, Civilization and the Western Hero."
    IN: Focus on The Western

1056   **Cawelti, John G.**
"*Chinatown* and Generic Transformation in Recent American Films."
    IN: Film Genre Reader
        Film Theory and Criticism /2 ed
        Film Theory and Criticism /3 ed
        Film Theory and Criticism /4 ed

1057   **Cawelti, John.**
"The Evolution of Social Melodrama."
    IN: Imitations of Life

1058   **Cawley, Leo.**
"The War about the War: Vietnam Films and American Myth."
    IN: From Hanoi to Hollywood

1059   **Cawston, Richard.**
"*Royal Family*." [Interview by Alan Rosenthal.]
    IN: The New Documentary in Action

1060   **Cawston, Richard.**
"Richard Cawston." [Interview by G. Roy Levin.]
    IN: Documentary Explorations

1061   **Cayrol, Jean.**
"*Night and Fog* (*Nuit et Brouillard*: The script for Alain Resnais' film)."
    IN: Film: Book 2

1062   **Cazals, Felipe.**
"Felipe Cazals." [Interview by Beatrice Reyes Nevares.]
    IN: The Mexican Cinema

Ceccettini, Philip Alan. SEE: Whittemore, Don

1063   **Cecchetti, Giovanni.**
"The Poetry of the Past and the Poetry of the Present."
    IN: Italian Cinema

1064   **Cendrars, Blaise.**
"On *The Cabinet of Dr. Caligari*."
"The Modern: A New Art, the Cinema."
    IN: French Film Theory and Criticism /v. 1

1065   **Cha, Theresa Hak Kyung.**
"Commentaire."
    IN: Apparatus

1066   **Chabot, Jean.**
"Jean-Pierre Lefebvre."
    IN: Second Wave

1067   **Chabrol, Claude.**
"Claude Chabrol." [Interview by Andrew Sarris.]
    IN: Interviews with Film Directors

1068   **Chabrol, Claude.**
"Evolution of the Thriller."
"Serious Things." [RE: *Rear Window*.]
    IN: Cahiers du Cinéma, The 1950s

1069   **Chabrol, Claude.**
"Little Themes."
    IN: The New Wave: Critical Landmarks

1070   **Chabrol, Claude, Jacques Doniol-Valcroze, Jean-Luc Godard, Pierre Kast, Luc Moullet, Jacques Rivette, François Truffaut.**
"Questions about American Cinema: A Discussion."
    IN: Cahiers du Cinéma, 1960-1968

Chabrol, Claude. SEE: Rohmer, Eric.

1071 **Chalfen, Richard.**
"Home Movies as Cultural Documents."
IN: Film/Culture: Explorations ...

1072 **Cham, Mbye-Baboucar.**
"Film Production in West Africa."
IN: Film and Politics in the Third World

1073 **Champlin, Charles.**
"*Fat City.*"
"*Payday.*"
IN: Produced and Abandoned

1074 **Champlin, Charles.**
"*The Odd Couple.*"
"*Beat the Devil.*"
IN: Movie Comedy

1075 **Champlin, Charles.**
"Falstaff in King Hollywood's Court: An Interview
Concerning *The Other Side of the Wind*."
IN: Focus on Orson Welles

1076 **Champlin, Charles.**
"Can TV Save the Films?"
IN: The Movies: An American Idiom

1077 **Chanan, Michael.**
"Economic Conditions of Early Cinema."
IN: Early Cinema ...

1078 **Chanan, Michael.**
"Introduction: The Historical Background; the Roots of
Economic Imperialism in Chile; the Formation of
Cinema in Chile."
IN: Chilean Cinema

1079 **Chanan, Michael.**
"Rediscovering Documentary: Cultural Context and
Intentionality."
IN: The Social Documentary ...

1080 **Chanan, Michael.**
"The Emergence of an Industry."
IN: British Cinema History

1081 **Chandler, Raymond.**
"Oscar Night in Hollywood."
IN: Sight and Sound

1082 **Chandler, Raymond.**
"Notebooks on *Strangers on a Train*."
IN: Focus on Hitchcock

Changas, Estelle. SEE: Loveland, Kay; SEE: Farber, Stephen.

1083 **Chaplin, Charles.**
"Can Art Be Popular?"
IN: Hollywood Directors 1914-1940

1084 **Chaplin, Charles.**
"Charles Chaplin." [Interview by Andrew Sarris.]
IN: Interviews with Film Directors

1085 **Chaplin, Charles.**
"Directing My First Film."
IN: Film Makers on Film Making

1086 **Chaplin, Charles.**
"Experiment in the Dark."
"Give Us More Bombs over Berlin."
"Rhythm."
"Charlie Chaplin's First Story."
"Nocturne."
"The Fool."
"A Salute to Russia."
IN: The Best of Rob Wagner's Script

1087 **Chaplin, Charles.**
"The Tramp."
IN: Bedside Hollywood

1088 **Chaplin, Charlie.**
"Acting-Directing Apprenticeship with Mack Sennett."
"A Rejection of the Talkies."
"Creating the Role of Dr. Body in *Casey's Court Circus*."
"Development of the Comic Story and the Tramp Character."
"What People Laugh At."
IN: Focus on Chaplin

1089 **Chapman, Jay.**
"Two Aspects of the City--Cavalcanti and Ruttmann."
[RE: *Rien que les heures*; *Berlin*.]
IN: The Documentary Tradition /1 ed
The Documentary Tradition /2 ed

1090 **Chapman, Michael.**
"Michael Chapman." [Interview by Dennis Schaefer
and Larry Salvato.]
IN: Masters of Light

1091 **Chappell, Fred.**
"Twenty-Six Propositions about Skin Flicks."
IN: Man and the Movies

1092 **Chase, Doris.**
"Doris Chase." [Interview by Lynn Fieldman Miller.]
IN: The Hand That Holds the Camera

1093 **Chatman, Seymour.**
"What Novels Can Do That Films Can't (and Vice Versa)."
IN: Film Theory and Criticism /4 ed

1094 **Chavance, Louis.**
"The Case of Josef von Sternberg."
IN: Sternberg

1095 **Chavance, Louis.**
"The Cinema in the Service of the Popular Front."
IN: French Film Theory and Criticism /v. 2

1096 **Chayefsky, Paddy.**
"Paddy Chayefsky." [Interviewed by John Brady.]
IN: The Craft of the Screenwriter

1097 **Chen Kaige and Zhang Yimou.**
"Chen Kaige and Zhang Yimou." [Interview by George
S. Semsel.]
IN: Chinese Film

"'See You in Thailand': America and the Third World
    (Featuring *Missing*; *Under Fire*; *The Killing Fields*;
    and *Salvador*)."
"'Do We Get to Win This Time?': The New Patriotism
    (Featuring *Red Dawn*; *Rambo*; *Protocol*; *Power*,
    and *Platoon*)."
    IN: Reel Politics

1117 **Christians, Clifford G. and Kim B. Rotzoll.**
"Ethical Issues in the Film Industry."
    IN: Current Research in Film /v. 2

1118 **Christie, Ian.**
"Blimp, Churchill and the State." [RE: *The Life and
    Death of Colonel Blimp*.]
"Chronicle." [RE: Michael Powell and Emeric
    Pressburger.]
"The Scandal of *Peeping Tom*."
    IN: Powell, Pressburger and Others

1119 **Christie, Ian.**
"Down to Earth: *Aelita* Relocated."
    IN: Inside the Film Factory

1120 **Christie, Ian.**
"From Willie the Whale to *Ivan the Terrible*."
    IN: Eisenstein at Ninety

1121 **Christie, Ian.**
"Making Sense of Early Soviet Sound."
    IN: Inside the Film Factory

Christie, Ian. SEE: Taylor, Richard.

1122 **Churchill, Robert.**
"The Unauthorized Reproduction of Educational
    Audiovisual Materials--Golden Egg Productions:
    The Goose Cries 'Foul'."
    IN: Fair Use and Free Inquiry

1123 **Churchill, Winston.**
"Everybody's Language."
    IN: Focus on Chaplin

1124 **Chytilová, Vera.**
"Vera Chytilová." [Interview by Antonín J. Liehm.]
    IN: Closely Watched Films

1125 **Ciment, Michel.**
"Glauber Rocha."
"Ruy Guerra."
    IN: Second Wave

1126 **Ciment, Michel.**
"The Odyssey of Stanley Kubrick: (Part 3:) Toward
    the Infinite–*2001*."
    IN: Focus on The Science Fiction Film

1127 **Cimino, Michael.**
"Michael Cimino." [Interview by John Andrew
    Gallagher.]
    IN: Film Directors on Directing

Cinethique. SEE: Cahiers du Cinema.

1128 **Circuit Court of Appeals, Second Circuit.**
"Edison v. American Mutoscope Company."
    IN: The Movies in Our Midst

1129 **Cirillo, Albert R.**
"The Art of Franco Zeffirelli and Shakespeare's
    Romeo and Juliet."
    IN: Film and Literature: Contrasts ...

1130 **Citron, Michelle.**
"Comic Critique: The Films of Jan Oxenberg."
    IN: Jump Cut

1131 **Citron, Michelle.**
"Films of Jan Oxenberg: Comic Critique."
    IN: Films for Women

1132 **Citron, Michelle.**
"Michelle Citron." [Interview by Lynn Fieldman Miller.]
    IN: The Hand That Holds the Camera

1133 **Citron, Michelle.**
"Women's Film Production: Going Mainstream."
    IN: Female Spectators

1134 **Citron, Michelle and Ellen Seiter.**
"The Perils of Feminist Film Teaching."
    IN: Jump Cut

Citron, Michelle. SEE: Becker, Edith.

1135 **Clair, Jean.**
"The Road to Damascus: *Blow-Up*."
    IN: Focus on Blow-Up

1136 **Clair, René.**
"*Coeur fidèle*."
"*La Roue*."
"Pure Cinema and Commercial Cinema."
"Rhythm."
    IN: French Film Theory and Criticism /v. 1

1137 **Clair, René.**
"*Le Million*."
"Film Authors Don't Need You."
"Talkie versus Talkie."
    IN: French Film Theory and Criticism /v. 2

1138 **Clair, René.**
"How Films Are Made."
    IN: Film: An Anthology

1139 **Clair, René.**
"René Clair to Tay Garnett: On Filmmaking."
    IN: Rediscovering French Film

1140 **Clair, René.**
"René Clair." [Interview by Charles T. Samuels.]
    IN: Encountering Directors

1141 **Clair, René.**
"The Art of Sound."
    IN: Film Sound
        Film: A Montage of Theories

1142 **Clancy, William P.**
"The Catholic as Philistine."
    IN: The Movies in Our Midst

1143 **Clandfield, David.**
"*Stagecoach*."
    IN: Western Movies

1144 Clarens, Carlos.
"*Gone with the Wind*."
"Cecil B. DeMille."
"Mae West."
"Marlene Dietrich."
"Paul Leni."
"Rex Ingram."
    IN: <u>Cinema: A Critical Dictionary</u>

1145 Clark, Dennis J.
"The Irish in the Movies: A Tradition of Permanent
    Blur."
    IN: <u>Ethnic Images ...</u>

1146 Clark, Dennis and William J. Lynch.
"Hollywood and Hibernia: The Irish in the Movies."
    IN: <u>The Kaleidoscopic Lens</u>

1147 Clark, Leslie.
"*Breakfast at Tiffany's* [novel by] Truman Capote.
    Brunch on Moon River."
    IN: <u>The Modern American Novel ...</u>

1148 Clark, Leslie.
"Charles MacArthur."
    IN: <u>Dictionary of Literary Biography /v. 44</u>

1149 Clark, Paul.
"The Sinification of Cinema: The Foreignness of Film
    in China."
    IN: <u>Cinema and Cultural Identity</u>

1150 Clark, Paul.
"Two Hundred Flowers on China's Screens."
    IN: <u>Perspectives on Chinese Cinema</u>

1151 Clark, Randall.
"Ben Hecht."
"Stirling Silliphant."
    IN: <u>Dictionary of Literary Biography /v. 26</u>

1152 Clark, Randall.
"Frank Tashlin."
"Joseph L. Mankiewicz."
"Walter Hill."
    IN: <u>Dictionary of Literary Biography /v. 44</u>

1153 Clark, Susan.
"Susan Clark." [Interview by Rex Reed.]
    IN: <u>Travolta to Keaton</u>

1154 Clark, Walter Van Tilburg and Lemar Trotti.
"Two Views of Heroism." [RE: *The Ox-Box Incident*.]
    IN: <u>The American West on Film</u>

1155 Clarke, A.C.
"*When Worlds Collide*."
    IN: <u>Focus on The Science Fiction Film</u>

Clarke, Jane. SEE: Nicolson, Annabel.

1156 Clarke, Robert.
"Robert Clarke." [An interview.]
    IN: <u>Interviews with B ...</u>

Clarke, Shirley. SEE: De Hirsch, Storm.

1157 Clavir, Judith.
"Black Spookery: *Blackula, Dracula A.D. 1972*."
    IN: <u>Film in Society</u>

1158 Clegg, Cyndia.
"The Problem of Realizing Medieval Romance in Film:
    John Boorman's *Excalibur*."
    IN: <u>Shadows of the Magic Lamp</u>

1159 Clemens, Sarah.
"And Now, This Brief Commercial Message: Sex Sells
    Fantasy!"
    IN: <u>Eros in the Mind's Eye</u>

1160 Clément, René.
"The Situation of the Serious Filmmaker."
    IN: <u>Film: Book 1</u>

1161 Clifton, Charles H.
"Making an Old Thing New: Kurosawa's Film
    Adaptation of Shakespeare's *Macbeth*." [RE:
    Throne of Blood.]
    IN: <u>Ideas of Order in Literature & Film</u>

1162 Clover, Carol J.
"Her Body, Himself: Gender in the Slasher Film."
    IN: <u>Fantasy and the Cinema</u>

1163 Clurman, Harold.
"Flaherty's *Louisiana Story*."
    IN: <u>The Documentary Tradition /1 ed</u>
        <u>The Documentary Tradition /2 ed</u>

1164 Coates, Anne V.
"Anne V. Coates." [Interview by Vincent LoBrutto.]
    IN: <u>Selected Takes</u>

1165 Coates, Paul.
"The Story of the Lost Reflection."
"Cinema, Symbolism and the *Gesamtkunstwerk*."
"The Breakdown of Narrative in Contemporary Film."
"Cinema and Self-Reference."
"Fragments of a Theory (Notes on Colour; Film and
    Dream; Subtitle/Voice-over; Dubbing; Montage;
    Narrative and Stardom in European and American
    Film; A Brief Phenomenology of the Western;
    Television and Film; The Art of Forgetting; The
    Filmic Image as a Portmanteau Word)."
"The Detective's Long Goodbye and the Reign of
    Terror."
"In the Realm of the Senses: 'Eroticism',
    'Pornography' and Beyond."
"Realist and Non-Realist Film."
"A Note on the Auteur Theory."
"The Indirections of Robert Altman."
"No Face, No Name and No Number: Antonioni."
"Bertolucci: The Uses of Division."
"Buñuel: A Dialectic of Views."
"Coppola, or the Ambiguities of Technology."
"Notes on Godard."
"Werner Herzog: The Prophetic Present."
"Hermetic Propaganda: Francesco Rosi."
"Tarkovsky: Through a Glass Darkly."
"François Truffaut: The Once-Wild Child."
"Skolimowski: Rituals and Romance."

"The Epic Political Theatre of Andrzej Wajda: From *Man of Marble* to *Danton*."
"Zanussi: 'Who is my Neighbour?'."
    IN: <u>The Story of the Lost Reflection</u>

1166 **Coates, Paul.**
"Exile and Identity: [Krzysztof] Kieslowski and His Contemporaries."
    IN: <u>Before the Wall Came Down</u>

1167 **Cobb, Irvin S.**
"Out of the Frying Pan into the Hollywood."
    IN: <u>Celebrity Articles ...</u>

1168 **Cobleigh, Rolfe.**
"A Propaganda Film." [RE: *Birth of a Nation*.]
    IN: <u>The First Film Makers</u>

1169 **Cobleigh, Rolfe.**
"Why I Oppose *The Birth of a Nation*."
    IN: <u>Focus on The Birth of a Nation</u>

1170 **Cobos, Juan, Miguel Rubio and J.A. Pruneda.**
"A Trip to Don Quixoteland: Conversations with Orson Welles."
    IN: <u>Focus on Citizen Kane</u>

1171 **Coburn, Bob.**
"Bob Coburn." [Interview by John Kobal.]
    IN: <u>People Will Talk</u>

1171a **Cochrane, J. Scott.**
"*The Wizard of Oz* and Other Mythic Rites of Passage."
    IN: <u>Image and Likeness</u>

1172 **Cochrane, Robert H.**
"Advertising Motion Pictures."
    IN: <u>The Story of the Films</u>

1173 **Cocks, Jay.**
"*The Three Musketeers*."
"*Traffic*."
    IN: <u>Movie Comedy</u>

1174 **Cocteau, Jean.**
"Carte Blanche."
    IN: <u>French Film Theory and Criticism /v. 1</u>

1175 **Cocteau, Jean.**
"*Le Sang d'un poète*."
    IN: <u>French Film Theory and Criticism /v. 2</u>

1176 **Cocteau, Jean.**
"Cocteau on the Film."
    IN: <u>Film: An Anthology</u>

1177 **Cocteau, Jean.**
"Dialogues with Cocteau, with André Fraigneau."
    IN: <u>Film Makers on Film Making</u>

1178 **Cocteau, Jean.**
"Encounter with Chaplin."
    IN: <u>Authors on Film</u>

1179 **Cocteau, Jean.**
"Storytelling in Silence."
    IN: <u>Rediscovering French Film</u>

1179a **Cocteau, Jean.**
"Theatre and Cinema."
"On Tragedy."
"A Wonderful and Dangerous Weapon in a Poet's Hands."
"Film as a Medium for Poetry."
"Good Luck to *Cinémonde*."
"Presentation."
"Poetry and Films."
"Poetry in Cinematography."
"Beauty in Cinematography."
"On the Venice Biennale."
"On the *Film Maudit*."
"What we can Learn from Festivals."
"Cannes."
"Science and Poetry."
"Sound Civilization."
"In Praise of 16mm."
"Great Sixteen."
"Brigitte Bardot."
"André Bazin."
"Jacques Becker."
"Robert Bresson."
"Charlie Chaplin."
"James Dean."
"Cecil B. De Mille."
"Marlene Dietrich."
"S.M. Eisenstein."
"Jean Epstein."
"Joë Hamman."
"Laurel and Hardy."
"Marcel Marceau."
"Jean-Pierre Melville."
"Gérard Philippe."
"François Reichenbach."
"Jean Renoir."
"Jiri Trnka."
"Orson Welles."
"Robert Wiene."
"Poetry and the Public."
"The Origins of Films."
"Continuation of a Retrospective."
"End of a Retrospective." [RE: *Ben-Hur*, 1925.]
"*Bonjour Paris* (Jean Image)."
"*Le Diable au Corps* (Claude Autant-Lara)."
"*Jules et Jim* (François Truffaut)."
"*Le Mystère Picasso* (Henri-Georges Clouzot)."
"*Les Noces de Sable*."
"*Othello* (Sergei Yutkevich)."
"*The Passion of Joan of Arc* (Carl Dreyer)."
"*Pickpocket* (Robert Bresson)."
"*Jigokumon* (Teinosuki Kinugasa)" [RE: *Gate of Hell*.]
"*Le Sang des Bêtes* (Georges Franju)."
"*Une Si Jolie Petite Plage* (Yves Allegret)."
"*Bicycle Thief* (Vittorio De Sica)."
"*Les Yeux Sans Visage* (Georges Franju)."
"Hollywood."
"Japanese Cinema."
"The Myth of Woman."

"Actors."
"Serge Lido and Dance."
"The Genius of Our Workers."
"For G.M. Film."
"Nothing Good is Achieved Without Love..."
"*Le Sang d'un poète*."
"*La Belle et la Bête*."
"*L'Aigle à deux têtes*."
"*Les Parents terribles*."
"Yvonne de Bray on Screen."
"*Orphée*."
"*Le Testament d'Orphée*."
"Dates."
"*La Voix Humaine*."
"*Ruy Blas*."
"*L'Eternel retour*."
"*La Princesse de Clèves*."
"*Orphée* [an unpublished synopsis]."
"An Episode from 'The Life of Coriolanus, or It Goes
    Without Saying' [an unpublished synopsis]."
"*Coriolan* [an unpublished synopsis]."
"*Pas de Chance* [an unpublished synopsis]."
"*The Gaslight*: A Farcical Comedy [an unpublished
    synopsis]."
"*La Ville Maudite* [an unpublished synopsis]."
"La Venus D'Ille (From a Story by Mérimée) [an
    unpublished synopsis]."
    IN: The Art of Cinema

1180   **Code, Grant.**
       "The Art of Kipps."
       IN: Hound & Horn

1181   **Coffee, Lenore.**
       "Lenore Coffee: Easy Smiler, Easy Weeper."
       [Interview by Pat McGilligan.]
       IN: Backstory

1182   **Cogley, John.**
       "HUAC: The Mass Hearings." [NOTE: Also called
       "The Mass Hearings."]
       IN: The American Film Industry
           The American Film Industry /rev ed

1183   **Cogley, John.**
       "Report on Blacklisting."
       IN: The Movies in Our Midst

1184   **Cohen, Abraham.**
       "Using Films--Practical Considerations."
       IN: Films Deliver

1185   **Cohen, Joan.**
       "The International Tournée of Animation-- Talking with
       Prescott Wright."
       IN: The American Animated Cartoon

1185a **Cohen, Keith.**
       "Capacities of Cinema: Thoughts, Dreams, and
       Repetition."
       "The Word, the Image."
       "Rules of the Game and the Question of
       Verisimilitude."
       "Innovation, Avant-garde."

"Art, Ideology, Taste."
    IN: Writing in a Film Age

1186   **Cohen, Keith.**
       "*An American Tragedy* [novel by] Theodore Dreiser.
       Eisenstein's Subversive Adaptation."
       IN: The Classic American Novel ...

1187   **Cohen, Larry.**
       "Larry Cohen." [Interview by Stanley Wiater.]
       IN: Dark Visions

1188   **Cohen, Larry.**
       "The New Audience: From Andy Hardy to Arlo
       Guthrie."
       IN: The Compleat Guide to Film Study

1189   **Cohen, Richard.**
       "*Hurry Tomorrow* [Interview with] Richard Cohen."
       IN: The Documentary Conscience

1190   **Coldicutt, K.J.**
       "*Turksib*--Building a Railroad."
       IN: The Documentary Tradition /1 ed
           The Documentary Tradition /2 ed

1191   **Cole, Jack.**
       "Jack Cole." [Interview by John Kobal.]
       IN: People Will Talk

1192   **Coles, Robert.**
       "Hollywood's New Social Criticism."
       IN: Film in Society

1193   **Colette.**
       "A Short Manual for an Aspiring Scenario Writer."
       IN: Women and the Cinema

1194   **Colette.**
       "Film Criticism: *Mater Dolorosa*."
       "Cinema: *The Cheat*."
       IN: French Film Theory and Criticism /v. 1

1195   **Colina, Enrique.**
       "The Film Critic on Prime Time." [RE: Cuba.]
       IN: Cinema and Social Change ...

1196   **Colla, Richard.**
       "*Zig Zag*."
       IN: Directors in Action

1197   **Collective (of Brazilian filmmakers).**
       "*The Luz e Ação* Manifesto."
       IN: Brazilian Cinema

1198   **Collet, Jean.**
       "*Les Carabiniers*."
       "An Audacious Experiment: The Sound Track of *Vivre
       sa vie*."
       "No Questions Asked: Conversation with Jean-Luc
       Godard on *Bande à part*."
       IN: Focus on Godard

1199   **Collier, John.**
       "Censorship and the National Board."
       IN: The Movies in Our Midst

1200   **Collier, Peter.**
       "*Bonnie and Clyde*."

IN: <u>Focus on Bonnie and Clyde</u>

1201 Collins, James M.
"The Musical."
IN: <u>Handbook of American Film Genres</u>

1202 Collins, Jim.
"Toward Defining a Matrix of the Musical Comedy: The Place of the Spectator Within the Textual Mechanisms."
IN: <u>Genre: The Musical</u>

1203 Collins, Nancy A.
"The Place of Dreams."
IN: <u>Cut!: Horror Writers ...</u>

1204 Collins, Richard.
"Genre: A Reply to Ed Buscombe."
IN: <u>Movies and Methods: An Anthology</u>

1205 Combs, Richard.
"Henry King."
"John Cassavetes."
"King Vidor."
"Marco Bellocchio."
"Mauritz Stiller."
"Sidney Lumet."
"Walerian Borowczyk."
"Werner Herzog."
"William Wellman."
IN: <u>Cinema: A Critical Dictionary</u>

1206 Combs, Richard.
"The Eyes of Texas: Terrence Malick's *Days of Heaven*."
IN: <u>Sight and Sound</u>

1207 Combs, Richard.
"Westerns."
IN: <u>Anatomy of the Movies</u>

1208 Combs, Richard.
"*Ulzana's Raid*."
IN: <u>The Pretend Indians</u>

1209 Comden, Betty and Adolph Green.
"Betty Comden and Adolph Green: Almost Improvisation." [Interview by Tina Daniell and Patrick McGilligan.]
IN: <u>Backstory 2</u>

1210 Comito, Terry.
"*Touch of Evil*."
IN: <u>Focus on Orson Welles</u>

1211 Communication Experience, The.
"A New Kind of Writing: Basic Skills Revisited and Revised."
IN: <u>Perspectives on the Study of Film</u>

1212 Comolli, Jean-Louis.
"Polemic: Lelouch, or the Clear Conscience."
"The Ironical Howard Hawks."
"Notes on the New Spectator."
"A Morality of Economics."
"Postscript: *Hour of the Wolf*."
IN: <u>Cahiers du Cinéma, 1960-1968</u>

1213 Comolli, Jean-Louis.
"Technique and Ideology: Camera, Perspective, Depth of Field."
IN: <u>Movies and Methods /v. 2</u>
<u>Cahiers du Cinéma: 1969-1972</u>

1214 Comolli, Jean-Louis.
"Technique and Ideology: Camera, Perspective, Depth of Field (Parts 3 and 4)."
IN: <u>Narrative, Apparatus, Ideology</u>

1215 Comolli, Jean-Louis.
"Machines of the Visible."
IN: <u>Film Theory and Criticism /3 ed</u>
<u>The Cinematic Apparatus</u>

1216 Comolli, Jean-Louis.
"Film/Politics (2): *L'Aveu*: 15 Propositions."
IN: <u>Cahiers du Cinéma: 1969-1972</u>

1217 Comolli, Jean-Louis.
"*Anticipation*."
IN: <u>Focus on Godard</u>

1218 Comolli, Jean-Louis.
"Signposts on the Trail." [RE: John Ford.]
IN: <u>Theories of Authorship</u>

1219 Comolli, Jean-Louis.
"Discussion (of Jeanne Thomas Allen, 'The Industrial Context of Film Technology: Standardisation and Patents')."
IN: <u>The Cinematic Apparatus</u>

1220 Comolli, Jean-Louis.
"The Love of Renoir."
IN: <u>Renoir on Renoir</u>

1221 Comolli, Jean-Louis and André S. Labarthe.
"*Bonnie and Clyde*: An Interview with Arthur Penn."
IN: <u>Focus on Bonnie and Clyde</u>

1222 Comolli, Jean-Louis and François Géré.
"Two Fictions Concerning Hate."
IN: <u>Fritz Lang: The Image ...</u>

1223 Comolli, Jean-Louis, Jean Domarchi, Jean-André Fieschi, Pierre Kast, André S. Labarthe, Claude Ollier, Jacques Rivette and François Weyergans.
"The Misfortunes of *Muriel*."
IN: <u>Cahiers du Cinéma, 1960-1968</u>

1224 Comolli, Jean-Louis, Jean-André Fieschi, Gérard Guégan, Michel Mardore, Claude Ollier, André Téchiné.
"Twenty Years On: A Discussion about American Cinema and the *politique des auteurs*."
IN: <u>Cahiers du Cinéma, 1960-1968</u>

1225 Comolli, Jean-Louis, Peter Wollen, Douglas Gomery.
"Discussion (of Mary Ann Doane, 'Ideology and the Practice of Sound Editing and Mixing')."
IN: <u>The Cinematic Apparatus</u>

1226 Comolli, Jean-Louis and Jean Narboni.
"Cinema/Ideology/Criticism."

IN: Cahiers du Cinéma: 1969-1972
    Movies and Methods
    Film Theory and Criticism /4 ed

1227 Comolli, Jean-Louis and Jean Narboni.
"Cinema/Ideology/Criticism (1)."
"Cinema/Ideology/Criticism (2)."
"Cinema/Ideology/Criticism (2) Continued."
    IN: Screen Reader 1

Comolli, Jean-Louis. SEE: Pierre, Sylvie; SEE: Truffaut, François; SEE: Godard, Jean-Luc; SEE: Mulvey, Laura; SEE: Oudart, Jean-Pierre; SEE: Rohmer, Eric; SEE: Bonitzer, Pascal.

1228 Conant, Michael.
"Bankers and Theaters."
    IN: The First Tycoons

1229 Conant, Michael.
"The Impact of the Paramount Decrees."
    IN: The American Film Industry

1230 Conant, Michael.
"The Paramount Case and Its Legal Background."
    IN: The Movies in Our Midst

1231 Conant, Michael.
"The Paramount Decrees Reconsidered."
    IN: The American Film Industry /rev ed

1232 Concoff, Gary O.
"Foreign Tax Incentives and Government Subsidies."
    IN: The Movie Business Book

1233 Cone, Fairfax M.
"What's Bad for TV Is Worse for Advertising."
    IN: Sight, Sound, and Society

Conger, Syndy M. SEE: Welsch, Janice R.

1234 Conley, Tom.
"The Filmic Icon: *Boudu sauvé des eaux*."
"The Law of the Letter: *Scarlet Street*."
"Dummies Revived: *Manpower*."
"The Nether Eye: *Objective Burma!*."
"Facts and Figures of History: *Paisan*."
"The Human Alphabet: *La bête humaine*."
"Decoding Film Noir: *The Killers* [1944], *High Sierra*, and *White Heat*."
    IN: Film Hieroglyphs

1235 Conley, Tom.
"Documentary Surrealism: On *Land without Bread*."
    IN: Dada and Surrealist Film

1236 Conner, Bruce.
"Bruce Conner." [Interview by Scott MacDonald.]
    IN: A Critical Cinema

1237 Connolly, Keith.
"Social Realism."
    IN: The New Australian Cinema

1238 Conrad, Randall.
"'A Magnificent and Dangerous Weapon': The Politics of Luis Buñuel's Later Films."
    IN: The World of Luis Buñuel

1239 Conrad, Randall.
"Luis Buñuel: An Integral Vision of Reality."
    IN: The Emergence of Film Art /2 ed

1240 Conrad, Tony.
"A Few Remarks Before I Begin."
    IN: The Avant-Garde Film

1241 Conroy, Hilary.
"Concerning the Asian-American Experience."
    IN: Ethnic Images ...

1241a Coogan, Jack.
"Comic Rhythm, Ambiguity, and Hope in *City Lights*."
    IN: Image and Likeness

1242 Cook, David A.
"Some Structural Approaches to Cinema: A Survey of Models."
    IN: Cinema Examined

1243 Cook, Jim.
"*The Ship That Died of Shame*."
    IN: All Our Yesterdays

1244 Cook, Page.
"*Bonnie and Clyde*."
    IN: Focus on Bonnie and Clyde

1245 Cook, Page.
"Film Music as Noise."
    IN: Film and the Liberal Arts

1246 Cook, Pam.
"*Mandy*: Daughters of Transition."
    IN: All Our Yesterdays

1247 Cook, Pam.
"Approaching the Work of Dorothy Arzner."
    IN: Feminism and Film Theory
        Sexual Stratagems

1248 Cook, Pam.
"Duplicity in *Mildred Pierce*."
    IN: Women in Film Noir

1249 Cook, Pam.
"Melodrama and the Woman's Picture."
    IN: Imitations of Life

1250 Cook, Pam.
"Reflections on Eros: *An Epic Poem*."
    IN: Films for Women

1251 Cook, Pam.
"The Point of Self-Expression in Avant-Garde Film."
    IN: Theories of Authorship

1252 Cook, Pam and Claire Johnston.
"The Place of Woman in the Cinema of Raoul Walsh."
    IN: Feminism and Film Theory
        Movies and Methods /v. 2
        Issues in Feminist Film Criticism

1253 Cook, Pam (editor) with James Donald, Christine Gledhill, Sheila Johnston, Paul Kerr, Annette

Kuhn, Andy Medhurst, Geoffrey Nowell-Smith, Jane Root and Terry Stapes.
"American Film Industry."
"Technology."
"National Cinemas and Film Movements."
"Stars."
"History of Genre Criticism."
"The Western."
"Melodrama."
"The Gangster/Crime Film."
"Film Noir."
"The Horror Film."
"The Musical."
"Authorship in Art Cinema."
"For a New French Cinema: The 'politique des auteurs'."
"The Auteur Theory."
"Auteur Theory and British Cinema."
"Structuralism and Auteur Study."
"Auteur Study after Structuralism."
"Early Cinema."
"The Classic Narrative System."
"Alternative Narrative System."
"Bazin."
"Metz."
"Lévi-Strauss."
"Propp."
"Barthes."
"Narrative and Audience."
IN: The Cinema Book

Cook, Patsy L. SEE: Palmgreen, Philip.

1254 **Cooke, Alistair (editor).**
Modern Times." [Collected comments.]
"Alistair Cooke." [Collected film capsules.]
IN: Garbo and the Night Watchmen

1255 **Cooke, Alistair.**
"Films of the Quarter."
IN: Sight and Sound

1256 **Cooke, Alistair.**
"The Critic in Film History."
IN: Footnotes to the Film

1257 **Cooper, Jackie.**
"Coming of Age in Hollywood."
IN: Bedside Hollywood

1258 **Cooper, John C.**
"The Image of Man in the Recent Cinema."
IN: Celluloid and Symbol

1259 **Cooper, Margaret.**
"The Challenge of Radical Film Distribution: Conversations with Toronto's DEC Films Collective."
IN: Show Us Life

1260 **Cooper, Scott.**
"The Study of Third Cinema in the United States: A Reaffirmation."
IN: Questions of Third Cinema

1261 **Copjec, Joan.**
"*India Song/Son nom de Venise dans Calcutta desert*: The Compulsion of Repeat."
IN: Feminism and Film Theory

1261a **Coppola, Francis.**
"Francis Coppola." [Interview by David Breskin.]
IN: Inner Views

1262 **Coppola, Francis Ford.**
"The Director."
IN: Movie People

1263 **Coppola, Francis Ford.**
"Francis Ford Coppola." [Interview by Joseph Gelmis.]
IN: The Film Director as Superstar

1264 **Coppola, Francis Ford.**
"Francis Ford Coppola." [Interview by Charles Higham.]
IN: Celebrity Circus

1265 **Corbusier, Le.**
"Spirit of Truth."
IN: French Film Theory and Criticism *v. 2*

1266 **Cordasco, Francesco.**
"Images of Puerto Ricans in American Film and Television."
IN: Ethnic Images ...

1267 **Corkin, Stanley.**
"Hemingway, Film, and U.S. Culture: *In Our Time* and *The Birth of a Nation*."
IN: A Moving Picture Feast

1268 **Corliss, Richard.**
"Ben Hecht."
"Preston Sturges."
"Norman Krasna."
"Frank Tashlin."
"George Axelrod."
"Peter Stone."
"Howard Koch."
"Borden Chase."
"Abraham Polonsky."
"Billy Wilder."
"Samson Raphaelson."
"Nunnally Johnson."
"Ernest Lehman."
"Betty Comden and Adolph Green."
"Garson Kanin (and Ruth Gordon)."
"Robert Riskin."
"Dudley Nichols."
"Joseph L. Mankiewicz."
"Herman J. Mankiewicz."
"Dalton Trumbo."
"Jules Furthman."
"Sidney Buchman."
"Casey Robinson."
"Morrie Ryskind."
"Edwin Justus Mayer."
"Delmer Daves."
"Charles Lederer."

"Charles Brackett."
"Frank S. Nugent."
"Ring Lardner, Jr."
"Terry Southern."
"Erich Segal."
"Buck Henry."
"Jules Feiffer."
"David Newman and Robert Benton."
    IN: <u>Talking Pictures: Screenwriters ...</u>

1269 **Corliss, Richard.**
"*The Front Page* and *His Girl Friday*."
"*Trouble in Paradise*."
"*Some Like It Hot*."
"Billy Wilder."
"Paul Mazursky."
    IN: <u>Movie Comedy</u>

1270 **Corliss, Richard.**
"Abraham Polonsky."
"American Cinema of the 70s."
"American Screenwriters."
"Joseph L. Mankiewicz."
"John Frankenheimer."
"Richard Lester."
"Robert Flaherty."
"Sergio Leone."
"Stanley Donen."
    IN: <u>Cinema: A Critical Dictionary</u>

1271 **Corliss, Richard.**
"Ben Hecht."
"Dalton Trumbo."
"New Breed from New York." [RE: screenwriters.]
"The Hollywood Screenwriters."
    IN: <u>The Hollywood Screenwriters</u>

1272 **Corliss, Richard.**
"Barbara Stanwyck."
"Greta Garbo."
"Gene Kelly."
"Vanessa Redgrave."
    IN: <u>The Movie Star: The National ...</u>

1273 **Corliss, Richard.**
"Notes on a Screenwriter's Theory, 1973–Introduction
    to *Talking Pictures*."
    IN: <u>Awake in the Dark</u>

1274 **Corliss, Richard.**
"Robert Flaherty: The Man in the Iron Myth."
    IN: <u>Nonfiction Film Theory and Criticism</u>
        <u>Great Film Directors</u>

1275 **Corliss, Richard.**
"The Hollywood Screenwriter."
    IN: <u>Film Theory and Criticism /1 ed</u>
        <u>Film Theory and Criticism /2 ed</u>
        <u>Film Theory and Criticism /3 ed</u>
        <u>Film Theory and Criticism /4 ed</u>

1276 **Corliss, Richard.**
"Writing in Silence."
    IN: <u>The First Film Makers</u>

1277 **Corman, Gene.**
"Gene Corman." [An interview.]
    IN: <u>Interviews with B ...</u>

1278 **Corman, Roger.**
"Roger Corman." [Interview by Stanley Wiater.]
    IN: <u>Dark Visions</u>

1279 **Corman, Roger.**
"Roger Corman." [Interview by Joseph Gelmis.]
    IN: <u>The Film Director as Superstar</u>

1280 **Corman, Roger.**
"The Young Filmmakers."
    IN: <u>Hollywood Directors 1941-1976</u>

1280a **Corman, Roger.**
"Filmgroup."
    IN: <u>The New Poverty Row</u>

1281 **Cornell, Joseph.**
"'Enchanted Wanderer': Excerpts from a Journey
    Album for Hedy Lamarr."
    IN: <u>The Shadow and Its Shadow</u>

1282 **Cornell, Joseph.**
"Monsieur Phot." [RE: *Monsieur Phot.*]
    IN: <u>The Avant-Garde Film</u>

1283 **Cornwell, Regina.**
"Maya Deren and Germaine Dulac: Activists of the
    Avant-Garde."
    IN: <u>Sexual Stratagems</u>

1284 **Cornwell, Regina.**
"Paul Sharits: Illusion and Object."
    IN: <u>Movies and Methods: An Anthology</u>

1285 **Cornwell, Regina.**
"[On] Joyce Wieland."
    IN: <u>Structural Film Anthology</u>

1286 **Corrigan, Philip.**
"Film Entertainment as Ideology and Pleasure:
    Towards a History of Audiences."
    IN: <u>British Cinema History</u>

1287 **Corrigan, Timothy.**
"A History, A Cinema: Hollywood, Audience Codes,
    and the New German Cinema."
"Wenders's *Kings of the Road*: The Voyage from
    Desire to Language."
"Transformations in Fassbinder's *Bitter Tears of Petra
    von Kant*."
"Types of History: Schlöndorff's *Coup de Gràce*."
"The Semantics of Security in Kluge's *Strongman
    Ferdinand*."
"The Original Tradition: Hypnotic Space in Herzog's
    The Mystery of Kaspar Hauser."
"The Exorcism of the Image: Syberberg's *Hitler, A
    Film from Germany*."
"Other Courses in Time."
    IN: <u>New German Film: The Displaced Image</u>

1288 **Corrigan, Timothy.**
"The Tension of Translation: Handke's *The
    Left-Handed Woman*."

IN: German Film and Literature

1289 Corrigan, Timothy.
"Producing Herzog: From a Body of Images."
IN: The Films of Werner Herzog

1290 Corrigan, Timothy.
"Film and the Culture of the Cult."
IN: The Cult Film Experience

Cort, David. SEE: Shamberg, Michael.

1291 Cortázar, Julio.
"*Blow-Up*." [RE: the short story.]
IN: Focus on Blow-Up

1292 Cortázar, Julio.
"Lucas, his Friends." [RE: *Un tal Lucas*.]
"Statement on Jorge Cedrón."
IN: Argentine Cinema

1293 Cortes, Carlos E.
"Chicanas in Film: History of an Image."
IN: Chicano Cinema

1294 Cortes, Carlos.
"Challenges of Using Film and Television as
Socio-Cultural Documents to Teach History."
IN: Image as Artifact

1295 Cortez, Stanley.
"Stanley Cortez." [Interviews by Charles Higham.]
IN: Hollywood Cameramen

1296 Costa-Gavras, Constantin.
"A film is like a match, you can make a big fire or
nothing at all ..."
"*Missing*."
"More and more of our films will be political ..."
IN: The Cineaste Interviews

1297 Costabile, Rita.
"*Far from the Madding Crowd* [novel by] Thomas
Hardy; *Far from the Madding Crowd* [film by] John
Schlesinger. Hardy in Soft Focus."
IN: The English Novel and the Movies

1298 Costard, Hellmuth.
"A Call to Revolt: On *Particularly Noteworthy* and
Chronicle of Anna Magdalena Bach."
IN: West German Filmmakers on Film

1299 Costello, Donald P.
"*Pygmalion*."
IN: Film and Literature: Contrasts ...

1300 Coultass, Clive.
"British Cinema and the Reality of War."
IN: Britain and the Cinema ...

1301 Coultass, Clive.
"Film Preservation: the Archives."
IN: The Historian and Film

1302 Cournot, Michel.
"A Leap into Emptiness: Interview with Suzanne
Schiffmann, Continuity Girl for *Alphaville*."
IN: Focus on Godard

1303 Coursodon, Jean-Pierre.
"Frank Borzage."
"John Brahm."
"Edward L. Cahn."
"Frank Capra."
"Charles Chaplin."
"George Cukor."
"Delmer Daves."
"William Dieterle."
"John Ford."
"Norman Foster."
"Tay Garnett."
"Byron Haskin."
"Henry Hathaway."
"Howard Hawks."
"Stuart Heisler."
"Alfred Hitchcock."
"John Huston."
"Fritz Lang."
"Joseph H. Lewis."
"Ernst Lubitsch."
"Rouben Mamoulian."
"Anthony Mann."
"Leo McCarey."
"Lewis Milestone."
"Otto Preminger."
"Vincent Sherman."
"Robert Siodmak."
"Douglas Sirk."
"Josef von Sternberg."
"George Stevens."
"Preston Sturges."
"Raoul Walsh."
"Billy Wilder."
"William Wyler."
IN: American Directors /v. 1

1304 Coursodon, Jean-Pierre.
"Robert Aldrich."
"Woody Allen."
"Laslo Benedek."
"William Castle."
"Jules Dassin."
"Edward Dmytryk."
"Stanley Donen."
"Gordon Douglas."
"Richard Fleischer."
"John Frankenheimer."
"Hugo Fregonese."
"Samuel Fuller."
"Elia Kazan."
"Gene Kelly."
"Stanley Kubrick."
"Jerry Lewis."
"Joseph Losey."
"Sidney Lumet."
"Vincente Minnelli."
"Robert Parrish."
"Sam Peckinpah."
"Arthur Penn."

"Sydney Pollack."
"Richard Quine."
"Nicholas Ray."
"Steven Spielberg."
"John Sturges."
"Frank Tashlin."
"Don Weis."
"Orson Welles."
"Robert Wise."
    IN: American Directors /v. 2

1305 **Cousins, Norman.**
"The Free Ride."
    IN: Film and Society

1306 **Covington, F.**
"The Negro Invades Hollywood."
    IN: The Black Man on Film

1307 **Cowen, Paul S.**
"A Social-Cognitive Approach to Ethnicity in Films."
    IN: Unspeakable Images

1308 **Cowie, Elizabeth.**
"The Popular Film as a Progressive Text--a
Discussion of *Coma*." [NOTE: Also called "A
Discussion of *Coma*."]
    IN: Feminism and Film Theory
         Films for Women

1309 **Cowie, Peter (editor).**
"Lindsay Anderson."
"Michelangelo Antonioni."
"Ingmar Bergman."
"Bernardo Bertolucci."
"Sergey Bondarchuk."
"Robert Bresson."
"Richard Brooks."
"Luis Buñuel."
"Claude Chabrol."
"Jacques Demy."
"Jörn Donner."
"Mark Donskoy."
"Federico Fellini."
"Miloš Forman."
"Georges Franju."
"John Frankenheimer."
"Bert Haanstra."
"Alfred Hitchcock."
"Kon Ichikawa."
"Joris Ivens."
"Miklós Jancsó."
"Elia Kazan."
"Grigori Kozintsev."
"Stanley Kubrick."
"Akira Kurosawa."
"Joseph Losey."
"Sidney Lumet."
"Dušan Makavejev."
"Louis Malle."
"Jean-Pierre Melville."
"Jan Nemec."
"Nagisa Oshima."

"Pier Paolo Pasolini."
"Arthur Penn."
"Roman Polanski."
"Satyajit Ray."
"Alain Resnais."
"Eric Rohmer."
"Francesco Rosi."
"John Schlesinger."
"Evald Schorm."
"Jerzy Skolimowski."
"Jacques Tati."
"Leopoldo Torre Nilsson."
"Jan Troell."
"François Truffaut."
"Luchino Visconti."
"Andrzej Wajda."
"Orson Welles."
"Bo Widerberg."
    IN: 50 Major Film-Makers

1310 **Cowie, Peter.**
"*Pandora's Box*."
"*The Crowd*."
"Asta Nielsen--A Star in Her Own Light."
"Louis Delluc—Critic and Craftsman."
"Scandinavia and Germany--Silents of the North."
"Victor Sjöström and Mauritz Stiller —Sweden's Silent
Masters."
    IN: Movies of the Silent Years

1311 **Cowie, Peter.**
"Bergman's *Passion*: Dream and Reality."
    IN: Film and Dream

1312 **Cowie, Peter.**
"Ingmar Bergman: The Middle Period."
    IN: Focus on The Seventh Seal

1313 **Cowie, Peter.**
"Milieu and Texture in *The Seventh Seal*."
    IN: The Classic Cinema

1314 **Cowie, Peter.**
"The Study of Persecution: *The Trial*."
    IN: Focus on Citizen Kane

1315 **Cowie, Peter.**
"The Study of a Colossus: *Citizen Kane*." [NOTE:
Also called "The Study of a Colossus."]
    IN: The Emergence of Film Art /1 ed
         The Emergence of Film Art /2 ed
         Focus on Citizen Kane

1316 **Cox, Harvey G., Jr.**
"The Purpose of the Grotesque in Fellini's Films."
    IN: Celluloid and Symbol

1317 **Cozarinsky, Edgardo.**
"*Días de odio*."
"*Hombre de la esquina rosada*."
"*Invasión*."
"*Emma Zunz*."
"*Strategia del ragno*."
"*Les autres*."

"*Los orilleros* and *El muerto / Cacique Bandeira*."
"*Splits*."
"*Ghazal, A Intrusa* and *Oraingoz izen gabe*."
    IN: Borges in/and/on Film

1318 **Cozarinsky, Edgardo.**
"Alberto Lattuada."
"Per Lindberg."
"Joseph Losey."
"G.W. Pabst."
"Glauber Rocha."
"Robert Rossen."
"Alf Sjöberg."
"George Stevens."
"Raoul Walsh."
"Bo Widerberg and Swedish Cinema Since 1960."
"American Film Noir."
"Marco Ferreri."
    IN: Cinema: A Critical Dictionary

1319 **Cozarinsky, Edgardo.**
"Foreign Filmmakers in France."
    IN: Rediscovering French Film

1320 **Cozarinsky, Edgardo.**
"Partial Enchantments of Narrative: Borges in/and/on Film."
    IN: Argentine Cinema

1321 **Crabe, James.**
"James Crabe." [Interview by Kris Malkiewicz.]
    IN: Film Lighting

1322 **Crabtree, J.I.**
"The Motion Picture Laboratory."
    IN: A Technological History ...

1323 **Cranny-Francis, Anne.**
"Feminist Futures: A Generic Study."
    IN: Alien Zone

1324 **Craven, Wes.**
"Wes Craven." [Interview by Stanley Wiater.]
    IN: Dark Visions

1325 **Crawford, Joan.**
"Joan Crawford." [Interview by John Kobal.]
    IN: People Will Talk

1326 **Crawford, Merritt.**
"William Kennedy Laurie Dickson: Movie Pioneer."
    IN: The Movies in Our Midst

1327 **Crawford, Merritt.**
"Pioneer Experiments of Eugene Lauste in Recording Sound."
"Some Accomplishments of Eugene Augustin Lauste, Pioneer Sound-Film Inventor."
    IN: A Technological History ...

1328 **Crawley, Budge, Fletcher Markle, and Gerald Pratley.**
"I Wish I Didn't Have to Shoot the Picture: An Interview with Alfred Hitchcock."
    IN: Focus on Hitchcock

1329 **Creed, Barbara.**
"Gynesis, Postmodernism and the Science Fiction Horror Film."
"*Alien* and the Monstrous-Feminine."
    IN: Alien Zone

1330 **Creed, Barbara.**
"Horror and the Monstrous-Feminine: An Imaginary Abjection."
    IN: Fantasy and the Cinema

1330a **Cremonini, Giorgio.**
"Gag and Narration in Chaplin's Cinema at the Transition from Short to Full-Length Movies."
    IN: Charlie Chaplin

1331 **Crespo, Osvaldo Sanchez.**
"The Perspective of the Present: Cuban History, Cuban Filmmaking [*The Last Supper* by Tomas Gutierrez Alea]."
"The Perspective of the Present: Cuban History, Cuban Filmmaking [*One Way or Another* by Sara Gomez]."
    IN: Reviewing Histories

1332 **Cripps, Thomas R.**
"The Death of Rastus: Negroes in American Films Since 1945."
    IN: The Movies: An American Idiom

1333 **Cripps, Thomas R.**
"The Reaction of the Negro to the Motion Picture *Birth of a Nation*."
    IN: Focus on The Birth of a Nation

1334 **Cripps, Thomas.**
"'Race Movies' as Voices of the Black Bourgeoisie: *The Scar of Shame*."
    IN: American History/American Film

1335 **Cripps, Thomas.**
"*Casablanca, Tennessee Johnson* and *The Negro Soldier*: Hollywood Liberals and World War II."
    IN: Feature Films as History

1336 **Cripps, Thomas.**
"*Sweet Sweetback's Baadasssss Song* and the Changing Politics of Genre Film."
    IN: Close Viewings

1337 **Cripps, Thomas.**
"Black Film as Genre."
"*The Scar of Shame*."
"*The St. Louis Blues*."
"*The Blood of Jesus*."
"*The Negro Soldier*."
"*Nothing But a Man*."
"*Sweet Sweetback's Baadasssss Song*."
"Criticism and Scholarship."
    IN: Black Film as Genre

1338 **Cripps, Thomas.**
"Black Stereotypes on Film."
    IN: Ethnic Images ...

1339 **Cripps, Thomas.**
"Racial Ambiguities in American Propaganda Movies."
IN: Film & Radio Propaganda ...

1340 **Cripps, Thomas.**
"The Dark Spot in the Kaleidoscope: Black Images in
American Film."
IN: The Kaleidoscopic Lens

1341 **Cripps, Thomas.**
"The Year of *The Birth of a Nation*."
IN: The First Film Makers

1342 **Cripps, Thomas.**
"The Death of Rastus: Negroes in American Films
Since 1945."
IN: The Black Man on Film

1343 **Cripps, Thomas.**
"The Moving Image as Social History: Stalking the
Paper Trail."
IN: Image as Artifact

1344 **Cripps, Thomas and David Culbert.**
"*The Negro Soldier*: Film Propaganda in Black and
White."
IN: Hollywood as Historian

1345 *Crisis, The.*
"Fighting Race Calumny." [RE: *The Birth of a Nation*.]
"NAACP v. The Birth of a Nation."
"Still Fighting the Film." [RE: *The Birth of a Nation*.]
IN: The Black Man on Film

1346 **Crisp, C.G.**
"*The 400 Blows*: From Scenario to Film."
IN: Great Film Directors

1347 **Crist, Judith.**
"*Bound for Glory*."
"*Buffalo Bill and the Indians*."
"*The Long Goodbye*."
IN: Produced and Abandoned

1348 **Crist, Judith.**
"*Cat Ballou*."
"*Dr. Strangelove*."
"*Monsieur Verdoux* and *Nothing but the Best*."
"*Seduced and Abandoned*."
"*A Thousand Clowns*."
"*W.C. Fields*."
IN: Movie Comedy

1349 **Crist, Judith.**
"*Jack Lemmon*."
"*Judy Garland*."
"*Katharine Hepburn*."
IN: The Movie Star: The National ...

1350 **Crist, Judith.**
"Movies: Morals, Violence, Sex—Anything Goes."
IN: Film: Readings in the Mass Media

1351 **Crist, Judith.**
"Rossif's *To Die in Madrid*."

IN: The Documentary Tradition /1 ed
The Documentary Tradition /2 ed

1352 **Crist, Judith.**
"The Great Dozen: A Critique." [RE: Western.]
IN: Directors in Action

1353 **Crivello, Kirk.**
"Gail Russell."
"Sharon Tate."
"Barbara Payton."
"Inger Stevens."
"Carol Landis."
"Barbara Bates."
"Natalie Wood."
"Suzan Ball."
"Jean Seberg."
"Susan Peters."
"Gia Scala."
"Jayne Mansfield."
"Marilyn Monroe."
IN: Fallen Angels

1354 **Croce, Arlene.**
"Dance in Film."
IN: Cinema: A Critical Dictionary

1355 **Croce, Arlene.**
"Invisible to the Naked Eye." [RE: *Blow-up*; *Rear
Window*.]
IN: The Film

1356 **Croce, Arlene.**
"*The 400 Blows*: A Review."
IN: Great Film Directors

Croft, Jeremy. SEE: Pronay, Nicholas.

1357 **Cromwell, John.**
"The Voice Behind the Megaphone."
IN: Hollywood Directors 1914-1940

1358 **Cronenberg, David.**
"David Cronenberg." [Interview by Stanley Wiater.]
IN: Dark Visions

1358a **Cronenberg, David.**
"David Cronenberg." [Interview by David Breskin.]
IN: Inner Views

1359 **Cronenweth, Jordan.**
"Jordan Cronenweth." [Interview by Kris Malkiewicz.]
IN: Film Lighting

1360 **Crosby, Bing.**
"'The Ears Are Wingy'."
IN: Bedside Hollywood

1361 **Crosby, John.**
"Macabre Merriment."
IN: Focus on Hitchcock

1362 **Crosman, Henrietta.**
"Now Am I Hollywood ..."
IN: Celebrity Articles ...

1363 Crow, James Francis.
"Lorentz's *The Fight for Life*."
IN: The Documentary Tradition /1 ed
The Documentary Tradition /2 ed

1364 Crowdus, Gary.
"*Harlan County, U.S.A.*"
IN: The Documentary Tradition /2 ed

1365 Crowdus, Gary and Dan Georgakas.
"History Is the Theme of All My Films: An Interview with Emile de Antonio."
IN: New Challenges for Documentary

Crowdus, G. SEE: Kalishman, H; SEE: Broullon, R.

1366 Crowther, Bosley.
"Movies and Censorship."
IN: The Movies: An American Idiom

1367 Crowther, Bosley.
"[From:] Movies and Censorship."
IN: Film and Society

1368 Crowther, Bosley.
"*Shoot the Piano Player*."
IN: Focus on Shoot the Piano Player

1369 Crowther, Bosley.
"*Citizen Kane*."
IN: Focus on Citizen Kane

1370 Crowther, Bosley.
"*Henry V* [1944]."
IN: Focus on Shakespearean Films

1371 Crowther, Bosley.
"*The Seventh Seal*."
IN: Focus on The Seventh Seal

1372 Crowther, Bosley.
"*Rashomon*."
IN: Focus on Rashomon

1373 Crowther, Bosley.
"*Bonnie and Clyde*."
IN: Focus on Bonnie and Clyde

1374 Crowther, Bosley.
"Cousteau's *The Silent World*."
IN: The Documentary Tradition /1 ed
The Documentary Tradition /2 ed

1375 Crowther, Bosley.
"Cleaving the Color Line."
"The Significance of Sidney." [RE: Sidney Poitier.]
IN: The Black Man on Film

1376 Crowther, Bosley.
"Loew Buys a Studio."
"Marcus Loew Is Willing."
"The Saga of *Ben Hur* [1925]."
IN: The First Tycoons

1377 Crowther, Bosley.
"The Movies."
IN: The Movies in Our Midst

1378 Crowther, Bosley.
"Tales Out of School." [RE: *The Graduate*.]
IN: Film: Readings in the Mass Media

1379 Crowther, Bosley.
"*The Mortal Storm*."
"*The Great Dictator*."
"*The Ramparts We Watch*."
"*Wake Island*."
"*Bataan*."
"*I Was a Communist for the FBI*."
"Adrift in *Lifeboat*."
IN: Propaganda on Film

1380 Cruickshank, Art.
"Combining Animation with Live Action."
IN: The ASC Treasury ...

1381 Cruikshank, Sally.
"Sally Cruikshank [on Animation]." [Interview by David Chell.]
IN: Moviemakers at Work

1382 Cruse, H.
"The Crisis of the Negro Intellectual [excerpt]."
IN: The Black Man on Film

1383 Cruse, Harold.
"Purblind Slant on Africa."
IN: Africa on Film

1384 Cruz, Andres Cristobal.
"Remembrance of Movies Past."
IN: Readings in Philippine Cinema

1385 Cukier, Dan A. and Jo Gryn.
"A Conversation with François Truffaut."
IN: Focus on Shoot the Piano Player

1386 Cukor, George.
"George Cukor." [Interview by Richard Schickel.]
IN: The Men Who Made the Movies

1387 Cukor, George.
"George Cukor." [Talking to Richard Overstreet.]
IN: Hollywood Voices

1388 Cukor, George.
"George Cukor."
IN: The Celluloid Muse

1389 Cukor, George.
"George Cukor." [Interview by Andrew Sarris.]
IN: Interviews with Film Directors

1390 Cukor, George.
"The Director."
IN: Hollywood Directors 1914-1940
Behind the Screen

1391 Culbert, David (editor).
The Documents:
"Senate Investigation of Hollywood, 1941."
"Army Inspector General's Investigation of Hollywood, 1942."
"Truman Committee's Investigation of Hollywood, 1943."

"Final Report of Inspector General, 1943; Fight with Truman Committee."
"Testimony of Independent Producers."
"Testimony of Hollywood Moguls."
"Testimony Revealing Cronyism, Including Darryl Zanuck."
"Military Production of Training and Morale Films, Including Capra's *Why We Fight* Series."
IN: Film and Propaganda in America /v. 2

1392 **Culbert, David (editor).**
The Documents:
"Defining Wartime Propaganda and Morale."
"The Capra *Why We Fight* Series."
"John Huston's *San Pietro*."
"Distribution and Utilization of Films in Wartime."
IN: Film and Propaganda in America /v. 3

1393 **Culbert, David.**
"Our Awkward Ally: *Mission to Moscow*."
IN: American History/American Film

1394 **Culbert, David.**
"*Why We Fight*: Social Engineering for a Democratic Society at War."
IN: Film & Radio Propaganda ...

Culbert, David. SEE: Cripps, Thomas.

1395 **Culkin, John M.**
"Films Deliver."
"The Teacher and the Theater Owner."
IN: Films Deliver

1396 **Culkin, John M.**
"I Was a Teen-age Movie Teacher."
IN: Sight, Sound, and Society

1397 **Cumbow, Robert C.**
"Prometheus: The Scientist and His Creations."
"Survivors: The Day After Doomsday."
IN: Omni's Screen Flights ...

1398 **cummings, e.e.**
"Miracles and Dreams." [RE: Krazy Kat]
IN: The American Animated Cartoon

1399 **Cunha, Richard E. and Arthur A. Jacobs.**
"Richard E. Cunha and Arthur A. Jacobs." [An interview.]
IN: Interviews with B ...

1400 **Cunningham, Stuart.**
"Hollywood Genres, Australian Movies."
IN: An Australian Film Reader

1401 **Curran, Trisha.**
"*Of Human Bondage* [novel by] W. Somerset Maugham; *Of Human Bondage* [films by] John Cromwell and Ken Hughes. Variations on a Theme."
IN: The English Novel and the Movies

1402 **Curran, Trisha.**
"*Gone with the Wind*: An American Tragedy."
IN: The South and Film

1403 **Currie, Barton W.**
"The Nickel Madness." [RE: Nickelodeon.]
IN: The Movies in Our Midst

1404 **Currie, Hector.**
"Encounter with Essence: The Schematic Image."
"The Schematized Vision of Josef von Sternberg in *Blonde Venus*."
"Fritz Lang's *M*: Symbol of Transformation."
"The 'Heights of Abstraction' in Antonioni: *L'Avventura*."
"Metaphysic in the Marketplace: Orson Welles' *Touch of Evil*."
"Godard Moving in Crystal—*Weekend*."
IN: Cinema Drama Schema

1405 **Curtin, Judge John T.**
"The Unauthorized Reproduction of Educational Audiovisual Materials--Preliminary Injunction Against Board of Cooperative Educational Service (BOCES)."
IN: Fair Use and Free Inquiry

1406 **Curtin, Philip D.**
"Investigating Africa's Past."
"The Promise and the Terror of a Tropical Environment."
IN: Africa on Film

Curtis, David. SEE: Hammond, Roger.

1407 **Curtiz, Michael.**
"Talent Shortage Is Causing Two-Year Production Delay."
IN: Hollywood Directors 1941-1976

1408 **Cushman, Robert.**
"Mary Pickford at Biograph: Legend and Legacy."
IN: The American Film Heritage

1409 **Custen, George F.**
"Talking About Film."
IN: Film/Culture: Explorations ...

1410 **Cutts, Graham.**
"*Indonesia Calling* and Joris Ivens."
IN: An Australian Film Reader

1411 **Cvetkovich, Ann.**
"Postmodern *Vertigo*: The Sexual Politics of Allusion in De Palma's *Body Double*."
IN: Hitchcock's Re-Released Films

1412 **da Cunha, Uma (editor).**
"G. Aravindan (*Kanchana Sita*)."
"Shyam Benegal (*Manthan* [and] *Bhumika*)."
"Basu Chatterji (*Sara Akash*)."
"Rabindra Dharmaraj (*Chakra*)."
"Ritwik Ghatak (*Ajantrik*)."
"Adoor Gopalakrishnan (*Kodiyettam*)."
"Girish Karnad (*Kaadu* [and] *Ondanondu Kaladalli*)."
"Girish Kasaravalli (*Ghatashraddha*)."
"Awtar Kaul (*27 Down*)."
"Mani Kaul (*Uski Roti*)."
"Ketan Mehta (*Bhavni Bhavai*)."

"Saeed Mirza (*Albert Pinto Ko Gussa Kyon Aata Hai*)."
"Govind Nihalani (*Aakrosh*)."
"Ramdas Phutane (*Sarvasakshi*)."
"Pattabhi Rama Reddy (*Samskara*)."
"M.S. Sathyu (*Garm Hava*)."
"Mrinal Sen (*Bhuvan Shome* [and] *Aakaler Sandhaney*)."
"Kumar Shahani (*Maya Darpan*)."
"Surinder Suri (*Rikki Tikki Tavi*)."
"Bansi Chandragupta."
IN: Film India

1413 **Dadoun, Roger.**
"*Metropolis*: Mother-City--'Mittler'."
IN: Close Encounters

1414 **Dadoun, Roger.**
"Fetishism in the Horror Film."
IN: Fantasy and the Cinema

1415 **Dagle, Joan.**
"Narrative Discourse in Film and Fiction: The Question of the Present Tense."
IN: Narrative Strategies

1416 **Dagrón, Alfonso Gumucio.**
"A Product of Circumstances: Reflections of a Media Activist."
IN: Cinema and Social Change ...

1417 **Dagron, Alfonso Gumucio.**
"The Cinema of Jorge Sanjinés."
IN: Film and Politics in the Third World

1418 **Dagron, Alfonso Gumucio.**
"Reflections of a Media Activist."
IN: Forbidden Films

1419 **Dagron, Alfonso Gumucio.**
"Argentina: A Huge Case of Censorship."
IN: Argentine Cinema

1420 **Dahl, Gustavo.**
"Embrafilme: Present Problems and Future Possibilities."
IN: Brazilian Cinema

1421 **Dalle Vacche, Angela.**
"Representation, Spectacle, Performance in Bernardo Bertolucci's *The Conformist*."
IN: Making Visible the Invisible

1422 **Dalrymple, Ian.**
"The Crown Film Unit, 1940-43."
IN: Propaganda, Politics and Film

1423 **Dalton, [Susan] Elizabeth.**
"Women at Work: Warners in the 1930s."
IN: Women and the Cinema

1424 **Dalton, Susan Elizabeth.**
"Bugs and Daffy Go to War."
IN: The American Animated Cartoon

1425 **Damico, James.**
"Ingrid from Lorraine to Stromboli: Analyzing the Public's Perception of a Film Star." [RE: Ingrid Bergman.]

IN: Star Texts
Movies as Artifacts

1426 **Damico, James.**
"William K. Howard."
IN: Cinema: A Critical Dictionary

1427 **Danek, Oldrich.**
"Oldrich Danek." [Interview by Antonín J. Liehm.]
IN: Closely Watched Films

1428 **Daney, Serge and Jean-Pierre Oudart.**
"Work, Reading, Pleasure."
"The Name of the Author (on the 'place' of *Death in Venice*)."
IN: Cahiers du Cinéma: 1969-1972

Daney, Serge. SEE: Bonitzer, Pascal.

1428a **Daniel, Dennis.**
"Eco-Horrors and Biohazards."
IN: The Deep Red Horror Handbook

1429 **Daniel, František.**
"The Czech Difference."
IN: Politics, Art and Commitment ...

1430 **Daniels, Gordon.**
"Japanese Domestic Radio and Cinema Propaganda, 1937-1945: an Overview."
IN: Film & Radio Propaganda ...

1431 **Daniels, William.**
"William Daniels." [Interviews by Charles Higham.]
IN: Hollywood Cameramen

1432 **Dardis, Tom.**
"F. Scott Fitzgerald: What Do You Do When There's Nothing to Do?"
"William Faulkner: 'They're Gonna Pay Me Saturday, They're Gonna Pay Me Saturday'."
"Nathanael West: The Scavenger of the Back Lots."
"Aldous Huxley: The Man Who Knew Too Much Goes West."
"James Agee: The Man Who Loved the Movies."
IN: Some Time in the Sun

1433 **Daroy, Petronilo Bn.**
"Social Significance and the Filipino Cinema."
IN: Readings in Philippine Cinema

1434 **Darrach, Henry Bradford, Jr.**
"A Religion of Film."
IN: Film and Society

1435 **Darretta, Gian-Lorenzo.**
"Vittorio De Sica's Vision of Cycles." [RE: *The Bicycle Thief.*]
IN: The Classic Cinema

1436 **Dates, Jannette.**
"Thoughts on Black Stereotypes in Television."
IN: Ethnic Images ...

1437 **Daudelin, Robert.**
"Gilles Groulx."
IN: Second Wave

1466 de Cordova, Richard.
"From Lumière to Pathé: The Break-Up of
Perspectival Space."
IN: Early Cinema ...

1467 de Cordova, Richard.
"Genre and Performance: An Overview."
IN: Star Texts
Film Genre Reader

1468 de Cordova, Richard.
"A Case of Mistaken Legitimacy: Class and
Generational Difference in Three Family
Melodramas." [RE: *Home from the Hill*; *Splendor in
the Grass*; *Written on the Wind.*]
IN: Home Is Where the Heart Is

1468a de Cordova, Richard.
"The Emergence of the Star System in America."
IN: Stardom

1469 de Cordova, Richard and Edward Lowry.
"Enunciation and the Production of Horror in *White
Zombie.*"
IN: Planks of Reason

1470 de Gourmont, Rémy.
"Epilogues: Cinematograph."
IN: French Film Theory and Criticism /v. 1

1471 De Grazia, Edward and Roger K. Newman.
"*The Birth of a Nation*—and of Censorship."
"The Rise of Self-Regulation."
"The Struggle for Control of the Screen."
"World War II and the Postwar Years."
"Sacrilege and the Supreme Court."
"The Era of Constitutionalization."
"Protection Amidst Turbulence."
"Decentralization of Censorship of the Screen."
"1908-1919 (*The James Boys in Missouri*; *Night
Riders*; *The Birth of a Nation*; *The Ordeal*;
Willard-Johnson Boxing Match; *Birth Control*; *The
Hand That Rocks the Cradle*; *The Sex Lure*; *The
Spirit of '76*; *The Spy*; *The Easy Way*; *The Brand*;
Fit to Win)."
"1920-1939 (*Newsreels*; *The Naked Truth*; *Alibi*; *The
Road to Ruin*; *Ecstasy*; *The Youth of Maxim*; *Spain
in Flames*; *Tomorrow's Children*; *The Birth of a
Baby*; *Professor Mamlock*; *Remous*)."
"1940-1959 (*Victory in the West*; *The Outlaw*; *Amok*;
Mom and Dad; *Curley*; *The Miracle*; *La Ronde*;
Latuko; *M*; *Miss Julie*; *Pinky*; *The Moon Is Blue*;
Native Son; *Baby Doll*; *The Game of Love*; *The
Garden of Eden*; *The Man with the Golden Arm*;
Wild Weed; *Lady Chatterley's Lover*; *Naked
Amazon*; *And God Created Woman*; *The Anatomy
of a Murder*; *Desire Under the Elms*; *Don Juan*;
The Lovers; *Never on Sunday*; *The Connection*;
The Virgin Spring; *Women of the World*; *Bachelor
Tom Peeping*; *491*; *Have Figure Will Travel*; *Lorna*;
Revenge at Daybreak; *A Stranger Knocks*; *The
Twilight Girls*; *The Bedford Incident*; *Bunny Lake Is
Missing*; *The Dirty Girls*; *The Unsatisfied*; *Un Chant
d'Amour*; *This Picture Is Censored*; *Viva Maria*; *A
Woman's Urge*; *Body of a Female*; *I, a Woman*; *I*

Am Curious–Yellow; *Mondo Freudo*; *Rent-a-Girl*;
Alimony Lovers; *Carmen, Baby*; *The Female*; *The
Fox*; *Therese and Isabelle*; *Titicut Follies*; *The
Wicked Die Slow*; *Angelique in Black Leather*; *Blue
Movie*; *Candy*; *The Language of Love*; *Odd
Triangle*; *Pattern of Evil*; *Yellow Bird*)."
"1970-1981 (*The Collection*; *The Libertine*; *The Secret
Sex Lives of Romeo and Juliet*; *Starlet*; *The Vixen*;
Where Eagles Dare; *Without a Stitch*; *Woodstock*;
The Art of Marriage; *Cindy and Donna*; *Computer
Game*; *It All Came Out in the End*; *The Killing of
Sister George*; *Lysistrata*; *Magic Mirror*;
Pornography in Denmark; *Sexual Freedom in
Denmark*; *Carnal Knowledge*; *Cry Uncle*; *Deep
Throat*; *Sinderella*; *Behind the Green Door*; *The
Exorcist*; *The Last Picture Show*; *Last Tango in
Paris*; *The Newcomers*; *Class of '74*; *School Girl*;
Stewardesses; *The Devil in Miss Jones*; *Gun
Runners*; *I Am Sandra*; *Naked Came the Stranger*;
Caligula; *Emmanuelle*)."
IN: Banned Films

1472 De Havilland, Olivia.
"The Dream that Never Died." [RE: *Gone With the
Wind.*]
IN: The Movies: An American Idiom

1473 De Hirsch, Storm and Shirley Clarke.
"A Conversation."
IN: Women and the Cinema

de Kieffer, Robert. SEE: Johnson, Lamar.

1474 De Landa, Manuel.
"Manuel DeLanda." [Interview by Scott MacDonald.]
IN: A Critical Cinema

1475 De Landa, Manuel.
"Wittgenstein at the Movies."
IN: Cinema Histories, Cinema Practices

1476 de Lauretis, Teresa.
"Imaging."
"Snow on the Oedipal Stage." [RE: *Presents.*]
"Desire in Narrative."
"Semiotics and Experience."
IN: Alice Doesn't

1477 de Lauretis, Teresa.
"The Technology of Gender."
"Fellini's 9-1/2."
"Strategies of Coherence: Narrative Cinema, Feminist
Poetics, and Yvonne Rainer."
IN: Technologies of Gender

1478 de Lauretis, Teresa.
"Semiotics, Theory, and Social Practice: A Critical
History of Italian Semiotics."
IN: Explorations in Film Theory

1479 de Lauretis, Teresa.
"From a Dream of Woman."
IN: Cinema and Language

1480 de Lauretis, Teresa.
"Now and Nowhere: Roeg's *Bad Timing.*"

"Randall Duell." [An interview.]
"Jack Martin Smith." [An interview.]
"Vincente Minnelli." [An interview.]
"Joseph Ruttenberg." [An interview.]
    IN: <u>Dance in the Hollywood Musical</u>

1506 **Delamater, Jerome.**
"Ritual, Realism and Abstraction: Performance in the
    Musical."
    IN: <u>Making Visible the Invisible</u>

1507 **Delamater, Jerome.**
"Peforming Arts: The Musical."
    IN: <u>American Film Genres /1 ed</u>

1508 **Delgaudio, Sybil.**
"Seduced and Reduced: Female Animal Characters in
    Some Warners' Cartoons."
    IN: <u>The American Animated Cartoon</u>

1508a **Delgaudio, Sybil.**
"Columbia and the Counterculture: Trilogy of Defeat."
    IN: <u>Columbia Pictures</u>

1509 **Delluc, Louis.**
"Antoine at Work." [RE: André Antoine.]
"Beauty in the Cinema."
"Cadence."
"Cinema: *The Cold Deck*."
"Cinema: *The Outlaw and His Wife*."
"From Orestes to Rio Jim."
"Notes to Myself: *La Dixième Symphonie*."
"Prologue."
"The Crowd."
    IN: <u>French Film Theory and Criticism /v. 1</u>

1510 **Delluc, Louis.**
"Max Linder's and Elsie Codd's Views on the Working
    Method."
"Impressions of Two Early Comedy Films."
    IN: <u>Focus on Chaplin</u>

1511 **Delmas, Jean.**
"Buñuel, Citizen of Mexico."
    IN: <u>The World of Luis Buñuel</u>

1512 **Deloria, V., Jr.**
"Stereotyping."
    IN: <u>The Black Man on Film</u>

1512a **Demme, Jonathan.**
"Demme on Demme."
    IN: <u>Projections: A Forum ...</u>

1513 **Demonsablon, Philippe.**
"The Imperious Dialectic of Fritz Lang."
    IN: <u>Fritz Lang: The Image ...</u>

1514 **Demos, Gary.**
"Gary Demos [on Computer Graphics]." [Interview by
    David Chell.]
    IN: <u>Moviemakers at Work</u>

1515 **Dempsey, Michael.**
"James Poe, An Interview."
    IN: <u>The Hollywood Screenwriters</u>

1516 **Denby, David.**
"*Over the Edge*."
"*The Late Show*."
"*The Bounty*."
"*River's Edge*."
    IN: <u>Produced and Abandoned</u>

1517 **Denby, David.**
"Documenting America." [RE: Frederick Wiseman.]
    IN: <u>The Documentary Tradition /1 ed</u>
          <u>The Documentary Tradition /2 ed</u>
          <u>Nonfiction Film Theory and Criticism</u>

1518 **Denby, David.**
"Stolen Privacy: Coppola's *The Conversation*."
    IN: <u>Sight and Sound</u>

1519 **Dench, Ernest Alfred.**
"The Dangers of Employing Redskins as Movie
    Actors."
    IN: <u>The Pretend Indians</u>

1520 **DeNitto, Dennis and William Herman.**
"*The Last Laugh*."
"*The Gold Rush*."
"*M*."
"*Grand Illusion*."
"*The Rules of the Game*."
"*Beauty and the Beast*."
"*Rashomon*."
"*La Ronde*."
"*The Seventh Seal*."
"*Wild Strawberries*."
"*Ashes and Diamonds*."
"*L'Avventura*."
"*Il Posto*."
"*Jules and Jim*."
    IN: <u>Film and the Critical Eye</u>

1521 **DeNitto, Dennis.**
"*Sons and Lovers* [novel by] D.H. Lawrence; *Sons
    and Lovers* [film by] Jack Cardiff. All Passion
    Spent."
    IN: <u>The English Novel and the Movies</u>

1522 **Denne, John D.**
"Society and the Monster."
    IN: <u>Focus on The Horror Film</u>
          <u>Conflict and Control in the Cinema</u>

1523 **Denove, Thomas.**
"Thomas Denove." [Interview by Kris Malkiewicz.]
    IN: <u>Film Lighting</u>

1524 **Denton, Clive.**
"Henry King."
    IN: <u>The Hollywood Professionals /v. 2</u>

1525 **Denton, Clive.**
"King Vidor."
    IN: <u>The Hollywood Professionals /v. 5</u>

1526 **Denton, James F.**
"The Red Man Plays Indian."
    IN: <u>The Pretend Indians</u>

1527 **Depue, Oscar B.**
"My First Fifty Years in Motion Pictures."
IN: A Technological History ...

1528 **Omitted.**

1529 **Deren, Maya.**
"A Letter to James Card."
IN: Women and the Cinema

1530 **Deren, Maya.**
"An Anagram of Ideas on Art, Form and Film."
IN: The Art of Cinema
Apparatus

1531 **Deren, Maya.**
"Cinema as an Art Form."
IN: A Casebook on Film
Introduction to the Art of the Movies

1532 **Deren, Maya.**
"Cinematography: The Creative Use of Reality."
IN: The Avant-Garde Film
The Art of Cinema
Film Theory and Criticism /3 ed
Film Theory and Criticism /4 ed

1533 **Deren, Maya.**
"Tempo and Tension."
IN: The Movies as Medium

1534 **Deren, Maya.**
"The Camera as a Creative Medium."
IN: Art in Cinema

1535 **Deren, Maya, Arthur Miller, Dylan Thomas, Parker Tyler, Willard Maas.**
"Poetry and the Film: A Symposium."
IN: Film Culture Reader
Film And/As Literature

1536 **Dermody, Susan.**
"Action and Adventure."
IN: The New Australian Cinema

1537 **Derry, Charles.**
"More Dark Dreams: Some Notes on the Recent Horror Film."
IN: American Horrors

1538 **Dervin, Daniel.**
"A Psychotechnology of the Cinema."
"Oz; or, Over the Rainbow and Under the Twister: the Primal Scene as Movie; the Movie as Primal Scene." [RE: *Wizard of Oz.*]
"Antonioni: *Blow-up* and Beyond."
"Ingmar Bergman: From Spider-God to Spider Artist."
"Creativity versus Collaboration in Three American Movies." [RE: *Hustle; Alice Doesn't Live Here Anymore; Little Big Man.*]
"Conditions into Conventions: The Genres of Comedy and Science Fiction."
"Splitting and Its Variants in Four Films plus *10.*" [RE: *Five Easy Pieces; Interiors; Wifemistress; Despair.*]
"Cinema and the Three Worlds of Experience."
IN: Through a Freudian Lens Deeply

1539 **Dervin, Daniel.**
"Primal Conditions and Conventions: The Genre of Science Fiction."
IN: Alien Zone

1540 **Deryan, Bedros.**
"Icons of a Free Man Who Once Had A Camera." [RE: Sergei Paradjanov.]
IN: Forbidden Films

1541 **Deschanel, Caleb.**
"Caleb Deschanel." [Interview by Kris Malkiewicz.]
IN: Film Lighting

1542 **Desmarais, James.**
"George Seaton."
IN: Dictionary of Literary Biography /v. 44

1543 **Desnos, Robert.**
"*Fantômas, Les Vampires, Les Mystères de New York.*"
"Dream and Cinema."
IN: French Film Theory and Criticism /v. 1

1544 **Desnos, Robert.**
"Avant-Garde Cinema."
IN: The Shadow and Its Shadow
French Film Theory and Criticism /v. 1

1545 **Desnos, Robert.**
"Eroticism."
"Picture Palaces."
IN: The Shadow and Its Shadow

1546 **Desnos, Robert and Man Ray.**
"Scenario for *L'Etoile de mer.*"
IN: Dada and Surrealist Film

1547 **Desser, David.**
"'Charlie Don't Surf': Race and Culture in the Vietnam War Films."
IN: Inventing Vietnam

1548 **Desser, David.**
"The Cinematic Melting Pot: Ethnicity, Jews, and Psychoanalysis."
IN: Unspeakable Images

Desser, David. SEE: Studlar, Gaylyn.

1549 **Deutelbaum, Marshall.**
"Structural Patterning in the Lumière Film."
IN: Film Before Griffith

1550 **Deutelbaum, Marshall.**
"*The Cheat.*"
IN: The Rivals of D.W. Griffith

1551 **Deutelbaum, Marshall.**
"'Rounds of Amusement': The Thaumatrope."
"Trial Balloons: *The Chamber Mystery.*"
"The Quiet Love Triangle of *Smouldering Fires.*"
"King Vidor's *The Crowd.*"
IN: Image on the Art ...

1552 **Deutelbaum, Marshall.**
"Finding the Right Man in *The Wrong Man.*"

IN: A Hitchcock Reader

1553 **Deutelbaum, Marshall and George C. Pratt.**
"Coming Attractions: American Movie Stills as
Photography."
IN: Image on the Art ...

1554 **Deutsch, Leonard J.**
"*Sounder* [novel by] William H. Armstrong. The
Named and the Unnamed."
IN: Children's Novels and the Movies

1555 **Dharap, B.V.**
"The Mythological or Taking Fatalism for Granted."
IN: Indian Cinema Superbazaar

1556 **Diakité, Madubuko.**
"The Films of Oscar Micheaux."
"The Films of Melvin Van Peebles."
"The Films of Ousmane Sembene."
IN: Film, Culture, and the Black Filmmaker

1557 **Diamant-Berger, Henri.**
"The Scenario."
"The Decoupage."
IN: French Film Theory and Criticism /v. 1

1558 **Diamond, I.A.L.**
"I.A.L. Diamond." [Interview by William Froug.]
IN: The Screenwriter Looks ...

Diamond, I.A.L. SEE: Wilder, Billy.

1559 **Diawara, Manthia.**
"Film in Anglophone Africa: A Brief Survey."
IN: Critical Perspectives on Black ...

1560 **Diawara, Manthia.**
"Oral Literature and African Film: Narratology in *Wend
Kuuni*."
IN: Questions of Third Cinema

1561 **Dick, Bernard F.**
"Samuel Ornitz: *Mazel Tov!* to the World."
"Lester Cole: Hollywood Red."
"John Howard Lawson: Hollywood Commissar."
"Herbert Biberman: The Salt That Lost Its Savor."
"Albert Maltz: Asking of Writers."
"Alvah Bessie: The Eternal Brigadier."
"Adrian Scott: A Decent Man."
"Edward Dmytryk: To Work, Perchance to Dream."
"Ring Lardner, Jr.: Radical Wit."
"Dalton Trumbo: The Bull That Broke the Blacklist."
IN: Radical Innocence

1562 **Dick, Bernard F.**
"Adaptation as Archaeology: *Fellini Satyricon* from the
'Novel' by Petronius."
IN: Modern European Filmmakers ...

1562a **Dick, Bernard F.**
"The History of Columbia, 1920-1991: From the
Brothers Cohn to Sony Corp."
"An Interview with Daniel Taradash: From Harvard to
Hollywood."
IN: Columbia Pictures

1563 **Dick, Vivienne.**
"Vivienne Dick." [Interview by Scott MacDonald.]
IN: A Critical Cinema

Dickerson, Bodie. SEE: Becker, Boris W.

1564 **Dickinson, Margaret.**
"The State and the Consolidation of Monopoly."
IN: British Cinema History

1565 **Dickinson, Thorold.**
"Films to Unite the Nations."
IN: Film: Book 2

1566 **Dickson, W.K.L.**
"A Brief History of the Kinetograph, the Kinetoscope,
and the Kineto-Phonograph."
IN: A Technological History ...

1567 **Dickson, W.K.L. and Antonia.**
"Edison's Invention of the Kineto-Phonograph."
IN: The Movies in Our Midst

1568 **Dickstein, Morris.**
"The Aesthetics of Fright."
IN: Planks of Reason

1569 **Diegues, Carlos.**
"Cinema Novo."
IN: Brazilian Cinema

1570 **Diegues, Carlos.**
"The Mind of Cinema Novo." [RE: Brazil.]
IN: Cinema and Social Change ...

1571 **Diegues, Carlos and Rui Guerra.**
"Popular Cinema and the State: Two Views."
IN: Brazilian Cinema

1572 **Diehl, Digby.**
"Paul Newman."
"Roger Corman."
IN: Directors in Action

1573 **Dieterle, William.**
"Thoughts About Directing."
IN: Hollywood Directors 1914-1940

1574 **Dieterle, William.**
"Europeans in Hollywood."
IN: Hollywood Directors 1941-1976

1575 **Dietz, Howard.**
"Public Relations."
IN: Behind the Screen

1576 **Dika, Vera.**
"Introduction: Methods for Classification and Analysis."
"*Halloween*: The Beginning of the Stalker Cycle."
"Paradigms: The Basic Elements of the Stalker
Formula."
"The Most Successful Recombinations: *Friday the
13th* and *Friday the 13th, Part 2*."
"The Films of the Stalker Cycle: *Prom Night*; *Terror
Train*; *Graduation Day*; *Happy Birthday to Me*; *Hell
Night*; *The Burning*."

"Conclusion: A Psychological and Sociological
   Evaluation."
   IN: Games of Terror

1577   **Dika, Vera.**
       "The Stalker Film, 1978-81."
       IN: American Horrors

1578   **Dillard, R.H.W.**
       "*Night of the Living Dead*: It's Not Like Just a Wind
          That's Passing Through."
       IN: American Horrors

1579   **Dillard, R.H.W.**
       "Even a Man Who Is Pure at Heart: Poetry and
          Danger in the Horror Film."
       IN: Man and the Movies

1580   **Dillard, R.H.W.**
       "The Pageantry of Death."
       IN: Focus on The Horror Film

1581   **Dimeo, Stephen.**
       "*Slaughterhouse-Five, or The Children's Crusade*
          [novel by] Kurt Vonnegut, Jr. Novel into Film: So It
          Goes."
       IN: The Modern American Novel ...

1582   **Disney, Walt.**
       "The Testimony of Walter E. Disney Before the House
          Committee on Un-American Activities."
       IN: The American Animated Cartoon

1583   **Dispenza, Joseph E.**
       "Making It Wholesome: The Owens Collection."
       IN: The American Film Heritage

1584   **Dissanayake, Wimal.**
       "Cultural Identity and Asian Cinema: An Introduction."
       "Art, Vision, and Culture: Satyajit Ray's Apu Trilogy
          Revisited."
       IN: Cinema and Cultural Identity

1585   **Dittmar, Linda.**
       "Larding the Text: Problems in Filming *The Old Man
          and the Sea*."
       IN: A Moving Picture Feast

1586   **Dittmar, Linda and Gene Michaud.**
       "America's Vietnam War Films: Marching Toward
          Denial."
       IN: From Hanoi to Hollywood

1587   **Dixon, Thomas.**
       "Fair Play for *The Birth of a Nation*."
       "Reply to the *New York Globe*." [RE: *Birth of a Nation*.]
       IN: Focus on The Birth of a Nation

1588   **Dixon, Wheeler Winston.**
       "Fitzgerald in Hollywood."
       "*The Great Gatsby*."
       "*Tender Is the Night*."
       "The Screenplays."
       "*The Last Tycoon*."
       "Adaptations."
       IN: The Cinematic Vision of F. Scott Fitzgerald

1589   **Dmytryk, Edward.**
       "The Director and the Editor."
       IN: Hollywood Directors 1941-1976

1590   **Doane, Mary Ann.**
       "*Caught* and *Rebecca*: The Inscription of Femininity
          as Absence."
       "Woman's Stake: Filming the Female Body."
       IN: Feminism and Film Theory

1591   **Doane, Mary Ann.**
       "Film and the Masquerade: Theorising the Female
          Spectator." [NOTE: Also called "Film and the
          Masquerade."]
       IN: Issues in Feminist Film Criticism
          Film Theory and Criticism /4 ed

1592   **Doane, Mary Ann.**
       "Ideology and the Practice of Sound Editing and
          Mixing." [SEE: Jean-Louis Comolli, "Discussion".]
       IN: The Cinematic Apparatus
          Film Sound

1593   **Doane, Mary Ann.**
       "Misrecognition and Identity."
       IN: Explorations in Film Theory

1594   **Doane, Mary Ann.**
       "Remembering Women: Psychical and Historical
          Constructions in Film Theory."
       IN: Psychoanalysis and Cinema

1595   **Doane, Mary Ann.**
       "The Film's Time and the Spectator's 'Space'."
       IN: Cinema and Language

1596   **Doane, Mary Ann.**
       "The 'Woman's Film': Possession and Address."
       IN: Re-vision
          Home Is Where the Heart Is

1597   **Doane, Mary Ann.**
       "The Voice in the Cinema: The Articulation of Body
          and Space."
       IN: Film Sound
          Narrative, Apparatus, Ideology
          Movies and Methods /v. 2

1598   **Doane, Mary Ann.**
       "The Erotic Barter: *Pandora's Box*."
       IN: The Films of G.W. Pabst

1599   **Doane, Mary Ann.**
       "The Moving Image: Pathos and the Maternal."
       IN: Imitations of Life

1600   **Doane, Mary Ann, Patricia Mellencamp and Linda
       Williams.**
       "Feminist Film Criticism: An Introduction."
       IN: Re-vision

1601   **Dodds, John C. and Morris B. Holbrook.**
       "What's an Oscar Worth? An Empirical Estimation of
          the Effects of Nominations and Awards on Movie
          Distribution and Revenues."
       IN: Current Research in Film /v. 4

1602 **Doherty, Thomas.**
"American Teenagers and Teenpics, 1955-1957: A Study of Exploitation Filmmaking."
IN: Current Research in Film /v. 2

1603 **Doherty, Thomas.**
"Witness to War: Oliver Stone, Ron Kovic, and *Born on the Fourth of July*."
IN: Inventing Vietnam

1604 **Domarchi, Jean.**
"Knife in the Wound." [RE: Marxism.]
IN: Cahiers du Cinéma, The 1950s

1605 **Domarchi, Jean, Jacques Doniol-Valcroze, Jean-Luc Godard, Pierre Kast, Jacques Rivette, Eric Rohmer.**
"Hiroshima, notre amour." [RE: *Hiroshima mon amour*.]
IN: Cahiers du Cinéma, The 1950s

Domarchi, Jean. SEE: Comolli, Jean-Louis.

1606 **Dominick, Joseph R.**
"Film Economics and Film Content: 1964-1983."
IN: Current Research in Film /v. 3

1607 **Domnick, Ottomar.**
"Freeing Oneself from Old Hat."
IN: West German Filmmakers on Film

1608 **Donald, James.**
"The Fantastic, the Sublime and the Popular; Or, What's at Stake in Vampire Films?"
IN: Fantasy and the Cinema

Donald, James. SEE: Cook, Pam.

1608a **Donaldson, Mara E.**
"Love and Duty in *Casablanca*."
IN: Image and Likeness

1609 **Donaldson, Peter S.**
"'Claiming from the Female': Gender and Representation in Laurence Olivier's *Henry V*."
"Olivier, Hamlet, and Freud." [RE: *Hamlet*.]
"Surface and Depth: *Throne of Blood* as Cinematic Allegory."
"Mirrors and M/Others: The Welles *Othello*."
"'Haply for I Am Black': Liz White's *Othello*."
"'Let Lips Do What Hands Do': Male Bonding, *Eros*, and Loss in Zeffirelli's *Romeo and Juliet*."
"Disseminating Shakespeare: Paternity and Text in Jean-Luc Godard's *King Lear*."
IN: Shakespearean Films/Shakespearean Directors

1610 **Donat, Robert.**
"Film Acting."
IN: Footnotes to the Film

Doniol-Valcroze, Jacques. SEE: Chabrol, Claude; SEE: Bazin, André; SEE: Domarchi, Jean.

1611 **Donnell, Ed.**
"Letters [of a Nebraska homesteader]."
IN: The American West on Film

1612 **Donner, Clive.**
"Clive Donner." [Interview by Andrew Sarris.]
IN: Interviews with Film Directors

1613 **Donner, Jorn.**
"The Role of Jöns in *The Seventh Seal*."
IN: The Classic Cinema

1614 **Door, John H.**
"Roger Corman."
IN: American Directors /v. 2

1615 **Dorcy, Michael M.**
"The Fine Art of Editing."
IN: Screen Experience

1616 **Dörfler, Goswin.**
"Josef von Sternberg's *Daughters of Vienna*."
IN: Sternberg

1617 **Dorfman, Dan.**
"The Raise of the Year from a 'Board of Robots'."
IN: The Movies in Our Midst

1618 **Dornfeld, Barry.**
"Dear America: Transparency, Authority, and Interpretation in a Vietnam War Documentary."
IN: From Hanoi to Hollywood

1619 **Dörrie, Doris.**
"Searching for Stories in a Gray Germany."
IN: West German Filmmakers on Film

1620 **Dorris, George E.**
"Griffith in Retrospect."
IN: Man and the Movies

1621 **Dort, Bernard.**
"Towards a Brechtian Criticism of Cinema."
IN: Cahiers du Cinéma, 1960-1968

1622 **Doss, Janet C.**
"Fellini's Demythologized World." [RE: *Satyricon*.]
IN: The Classic Cinema

1623 **Doublier, Francis.**
"Reminiscences of an Early Motion-Picture Operator." [RE: Lumieres.]
IN: Image on the Art ...

1624 **Douchet, Jean.**
"A Laboratory Art: *Blind Date*." [RE: Joseph Losey.]
IN: Cahiers du Cinéma, 1960-1968

1625 **Douchet, Jean.**
"Hitch and His Public." [NOTE: Also called "Hitch and His Audience."]
IN: A Hitchcock Reader
Cahiers du Cinéma, 1960-1968

1626 **Douglas, Jeanne Masson.**
"Seeking Copyright Clearances for an Audiovisual Center."
IN: Fair Use and Free Inquiry

1627 **Douglas, Kirk.**
"Kirk Douglas." [Interview by Charles Higham.]
IN: Celebrity Circus

1628 **Doumic, René.**
"Drama Review: The Cinema Age."
IN: <u>French Film Theory and Criticism</u> /v. 1

1629 **Dovzhenko, Alexander Petrovitch.**
"Beginnings--Sources."
IN: <u>Cinema in Revolution</u>

1630 **Dovzhenko, Alexander.**
"The Artist's Teacher and Friend."
IN: <u>The Film Factory</u>

1631 **Downer, Alan S.**
"The Monitor Image."
IN: <u>Man and the Movies</u>

1632 **Downey, Robert.**
"Robert Downey." [Interview by Joseph Gelmis.]
IN: <u>The Film Director as Superstar</u>

1633 **Downing, John D.H.**
"Four Films of Tomás Gutiérrez Alea."
IN: <u>Film and Politics in the Third World</u>

1634 **Doyle, Stuart.**
"A Trade Viewpoint."
IN: <u>An Australian Film Reader</u>

1635 **Draper, Ellen.**
"Finding a Language for Vietnam in the
Action-Adventure Genre."
IN: <u>Inventing Vietnam</u>

1636 **Dreiser, Theodore.**
"The Real Sins of Hollywood."
IN: <u>Authors on Film</u>

1637 **Dréville, Jean.**
"Documentary: The Soul of Cinema."
IN: <u>French Film Theory and Criticism</u> /v. 2

1638 **Drew, Bernard.**
"Burt Lancaster."
"Glenda Jackson."
"Gloria Swanson."
"Jill Clayburgh."
"Laurence Olivier."
IN: <u>The Movie Star: The National ...</u>

1639 **Drew, Bernard.**
"High Comedy in the Thirties."
IN: <u>Movie Comedy</u>

1640 **Drew, Robert L.**
"An Independent with the Networks."
IN: <u>New Challenges for Documentary</u>

Drew, Robert. SEE: Bachman, Gideon.

1641 **Dreyer, Carl Th.**
"Color and Color Films."
IN: <u>Film Makers on Film Making</u>
    <u>The Movies as Medium</u>

1642 **Dreyer, Carl Th.**
"Metaphysic of *Ordet*."
IN: <u>Film Culture Reader</u>

1643 **Dreyer, Carl.**
"Carl Dreyer." [Interview by Andrew Sarris.]
IN: <u>Interviews with Film Directors</u>

1644 **Dreyer, Carl.**
"The Situation of the Serious Filmmaker."
IN: <u>Film: Book 1</u>

1645 **Dreyer, Carl.**
"Thoughts on My Craft."
IN: <u>Film: A Montage of Theories</u>

1646 **Dreyfus, Jean-Paul.**
"*L'Age d'or*."
IN: <u>French Film Theory and Criticism</u> /v. 2

1647 **Dreyfuss, Richard and John Badham.**
"Richard Dreyfuss and John Badham." [Interview by
Judith Crist.]
IN: <u>Take 22</u>

1648 **Drinkwater, John.**
"The Trust Fight."
IN: <u>The First Tycoons</u>

1649 **Driscoll, John P.**
"Robert Buckner."
IN: <u>Dictionary of Literary Biography</u> /v. 26

1650 **Driscoll, John.**
"Laurence Stallings."
IN: <u>Dictionary of Literary Biography</u> /v. 44

1651 **Drobashenko, Sergei.**
"Soviet Documentary Film, 1917-40."
IN: <u>Propaganda, Politics and Film</u>

1652 **Drobashenko, Sergei and Peter Kenez.**
"Film Propaganda in the Soviet Union, 1941-1945:
Two Views."
IN: <u>Film & Radio Propaganda ...</u>

Drummond, Fred. SEE: Glaessner, Verina.

1653 **Du Cane, John.**
"[On] John Du Cane."
IN: <u>Structural Film Anthology</u>

Du Cane, John. SEE: Gidal, Peter.

1654 **Dubrovsky, Alexander.**
"The Soviet Cinema in Danger."
IN: <u>The Film Factory</u>

1655 **Duda, Matthew.**
"Chronology--Ingmar Bergman: His Life and Work."
IN: <u>Film and Dream</u>

1656 **Duffield, George C.**
"Diary [of a cattle drover]."
IN: <u>The American West on Film</u>

1657 **Duigan, Virginia.**
"Children's Films."
IN: <u>The New Australian Cinema</u>

1658 **Dulac, Germaine.**
"[From:] 'Visual and Anti-visual Films'."

"The Essence of the Cinema: The Visual Idea."
"The Avant-Garde Cinema."
   IN: The Avant-Garde Film

1659 Dulac, Germaine.
"Aesthetics, Obstacles, Integral *Cinégraphie*."
"The Expressive Techniques of the Cinema."
   IN: French Film Theory and Criticism /v. 1

1660 Dulles, Foster Rhea.
"The Role of Moving Pictures."
   IN: The Movies: An American Idiom

1661 Duncan, David.
"David Duncan." [An interview.]
   IN: Interviews with B ...

1662 Duncan, Robert W.
"*Hiroshima-Nagasaki--August, 1945*."
   IN: Nuclear War Films

1663 Dunford, Mike.
"[On] Mike Dunford."
   IN: Structural Film Anthology

1664 Dunn, Linwood G.
"Cinemagic of the Optical Printer."
"Technique of Optical Printing."
   IN: The ASC Treasury ...

1665 Dunne, Irene.
"Irene Dunne." [Interview by John Kobal.]
   IN: People Will Talk

1666 Dunne, Philip.
"'I'd Like You To Meet Our Writer,' They Mean 'That Menial'--" [RE: an interview.]
   IN: Blueprint on Babylon

1667 Dunne, Philip.
"Fascismo Americano."
   IN: The Best of Rob Wagner's Script

1668 Dunne, Philip.
"Philip Dunne: Fine Cabinetmaker." [Interview by Tina Daniell.]
   IN: Backstory

1669 Dunne, Philip.
"Philip Dunne." [Interview by Lee Server.]
   IN: Screenwriter: Words Become Pictures

1670 Dunne, Philip.
"The Documentary and Hollywood."
   IN: Nonfiction Film Theory and Criticism

1671 Duprez, June.
"June Duprez." [Interview by John Kobal.]
   IN: People Will Talk

1672 Duras, Marguerite.
"Green Eyes (*Les Yeux verts*): Selections."
   IN: Writing in a Film Age

1673 Durgnat, Raymond.
"*The Discreet Charm of the Bourgeoisie*."
"Style and Anti-Style."
   IN: The World of Luis Buñuel

1674 Durgnat, Raymond.
"*This Island Earth*: Villains and Heroes in Space."
   IN: Conflict and Control in the Cinema

1675 Durgnat, Raymond.
"Eyes without a Face."
   IN: Focus on The Horror Film

1676 Durgnat, Raymond.
"Epic, Epic, Epic, Epic, Epic."
   IN: Film Genre

1677 Durgnat, Raymond.
"Fantasy and Reality in *Belle de Jour*."
   IN: The Classic Cinema

1678 Durgnat, Raymond.
"Inside Norman Bates." [RE: *Psycho*.]
   IN: Great Film Directors
       Focus on Hitchcock

1679 Durgnat, Raymond.
"Michael Powell."
   IN: Movie Reader
       Powell, Pressburger and Others

1680 Durgnat, Raymond.
"Mute Poetry in the Commercial Cinema."
   IN: Crossroads to the Cinema

1681 Durgnat, Raymond.
"On *The Small Back Room*."
   IN: Powell, Pressburger and Others

1682 Durgnat, Raymond.
"Renoir and Realism: The Thirties."
   IN: Great Film Directors

1683 Durgnat, Raymond.
"Six Films of Josef von Sternberg."
   IN: Movies and Methods: An Anthology
       Movie Reader

1684 Durgnat, Raymond.
"The Impossible Takes a Little Longer."
   IN: Film and the Liberal Arts

1685 Durgnat, Raymond.
"The Strange Case of Alfred Hitchcock, Part Three."
   IN: Focus on Hitchcock

1686 Durgnat, Raymond.
"The Mongrel Muse."
   IN: Film And/As Literature
       Film and Literature

1687 Durgnat, Raymond.
"Ways of Melodrama."
   IN: Imitations of Life

1688 Durham, Philip C. and Everett L. Jones.
"The Negro Cowboys [excerpt]."
"The West As Fiction."
   IN: The American West on Film

1689 Durovicova, Natasa.
"Auditioning for America: Method, Madness and Banality in *Anna*."

IN: Before the Wall Came Down

1690 Durwood, Stanley H. and Joel H. Resnick.
"The Theatre Chain: American Multi-Cinema."
IN: The Movie Business Book

1691 Dusinberre, Deke.
"[On] Peter Gidal."
IN: Structural Film Anthology

1692 Dutta, Kavery.
"Kavery Dutta." [Interview by Lynn Fieldman Miller.]
IN: The Hand That Holds the Camera

1693 Dwan, Allan.
"Adaptations."
IN: Hollywood Directors 1914-1940

1694 Dworet, Laurence.
"Laurence Dworet." [Interview by William Froug.]
IN: The New Screenwriter Looks ...

1695 Dworkin, Martin S.
"The Lonely Night--Dramatic Power."
IN: The Documentary Tradition /1 ed
     The Documentary Tradition /2 ed

1696 Dyer, Peter John.
"Saturday Night and Sunday Morning."
IN: Sight and Sound

1697 Dyer, Peter John.
"The Seventh Seal."
IN: Focus on The Seventh Seal

1698 Dyer, Peter John.
"Sling the Lamps Low." [RE: Howard Hawks.]
IN: Focus on Howard Hawks

1699 Dyer, Richard.
"[From:] *Stars.*"
IN: Film Theory and Criticism /4 ed

1700 Dyer, Richard.
"Mahogany."
IN: Films for Women

1701 Dyer, Richard.
"Entertainment and Utopia."
IN: Movies and Methods /v. 2
     Genre: The Musical

1702 Dyer, Richard.
"Four Films of Lana Turner." [RE: *Ziegfeld Girl; The Postman Always Rings Twice; The Bad and the Beautiful; Imitation of Life.*] [NOTE: Also called "Lana: Four Films of Lana Turner."]
IN: Star Texts
     Imitations of Life

1703 Dyer, Richard.
"Monroe and Sexuality."
IN: Women and Film

1704 Dyer, Richard.
"Rejecting Straight Ideals: Gays in Film."
IN: Jump Cut

1705 Dyer, Richard.
"Resistance Through Charisma: Rita Hayworth and *Gilda.*"
IN: Women in Film Noir

1706 Dyer, Richard.
"Stars as Signs."
IN: Popular Television and Film

1707 Dyer, Richard.
"Stereotyping."
IN: Gays and Film
     Gays and Film /rev ed

1708 Dyer, Richard.
"The Role of Stereotypes."
IN: Images of Alcoholism

1708a Dyer, Richard.
"Charisma."
"A Star Is Born and the Construction of Authenticity."
IN: Stardom

1709 Dynia, Philip.
"Alfred Hitchcock and the Ghost of Thomas Hobbes."
IN: Cinema Examined

1710 Eagle, Herbert.
"Russian Formalist Film Theory: An Introduction."
IN: Russian Formalist Film Theory

1711 Eagle, Herbert.
"The Syntagmatic and Paradigmatic Axes in *Closely Watched Trains.*"
IN: Explorations in National Cinemas

1712 Eagle, Herbert.
"Yugoslav Marxist Humanism and the Films of Dušan Makavejev."
IN: Politics, Art and Commitment ...

1713 Earle, William.
"Revolt against Realism in the Films."
IN: Film Theory and Criticism /2 ed
     Film Theory and Criticism /3 ed

1714 Earnest, Olen J.
"Star Wars: A Case Study of Motion Picture Marketing."
IN: Current Research in Film /v. 1

1715 Eastman, Susan Tyler, David E. Bradbury, and Robert S. Nemes.
"Influences of Previews on Movie Viewers' Expectations."
IN: Current Research in Film /v. 1

1716 Eatherley, Gill.
"[On] Gill Eatherley."
IN: Structural Film Anthology

1717 Eaton, Mick.
"Television Situation Comedy."
IN: Popular Television and Film

1718 Eaton, Walter Prichard.
"A New Epoch in the Movies."
IN: The Movies in Our Midst

1719 Ebert, Roger.
"Russ Meyer: King of the Nudies."
"Joe Solomon: The Last of the Schlockmeisters."
IN: Kings of the Bs

1720 Ebert, Roger.
"*City Lights*."
"*Love Affair, or The Case of the Missing Switchboard Operator*."
"*The Firemen's Ball*."
"*The Great Dictator*."
"Fields vs. Chaplin."
IN: Movie Comedy

1721 Ebert, Roger.
"*High Hopes*."
"*Say Anything*."
"*The Mighty Quinn*."
IN: Produced and Abandoned

1722 Ebert, Roger.
"The Day that Marilyn Died; Robert Mitchum; Michael Caine; Mel Brooks; Walter Matthau."
"Jerry Lewis; Sylvester Stallone; Tony Curtis; Rodney Dangerfield."
"Groucho Marx; Lee Marvin; Lee Marvin II."
"Edy Williams; Lord Grade; John Wayne; Kirk Douglas; Sybil Danning."
"Werner Herzog; Clint Eastwood; Martin Scorsese; Ingmar Bergman; Orson Welles."
"Rainer Werner Fassbinder; Kris Kristofferson I; Kris Kristofferson II; Richard Harris; David Bowie; John Belushi; John Belushi II."
"Linn Ulmann; Charles Bronson; Muhammad Ali; William Hurt."
"Brooke Shields; Nastassja Kinski; Woody Allen."
"Bob and Ray; Matt Dillon; Diane Lane and Vincent Spano; Charles Chaplin; Ingrid Bergman."
"Burns and Matthau."
IN: A Kiss Is Still a Kiss

1723 Ebert, Roger and Gene Siskel.
"Gene Siskel and Roger Ebert Interview Martin Scorsese."
"Gene Siskel Interviews Steven Spielberg."
"Roger Ebert Interviews George Lucas."
IN: The Future of the Movies

1724 Eberwein, Robert T.
"Vachel Lindsay."
"Hugo Münsterberg."
"The Russian Contribution: Lev Kuleshov, V.I. Pudovkin; Sergei M. Eisenstein."
"Béla Balázs."
"Rudolf Arnheim."
"André Bazin."
"Siegfried Kracauer."
"The American Journalistic Contribution: James Agee, Robert Warshow, Pauline Kael, Stanley Kauffmann, Andrew Sarris."
"Feminist Criticism: Molly Haskell, Marjorie Rosen, Joan Mellen."

"Structuralist Criticism: Noël Burch, Christian Metz, Peter Wollen."
IN: A Viewer's Guide to Film Theory and Criticism

1725 Eberwein, Robert T.
"The Master Text of *Blow-Up*."
IN: Close Viewings

1726 Eckert, Charles W.
"The English Cine-Structuralists."
IN: Conflict and Control in the Cinema
Theories of Authorship

1727 Eckert, Charles W.
"Shall We Deport Lévi-Strauss?"
IN: Conflict and Control in the Cinema

1728 Eckert, Charles.
"Shirley Temple and the House of Rockefeller."
IN: Star Texts
Jump Cut
Stardom

1729 Eckert, Charles.
"The Anatomy of a Proletarian Film: Warner's *Marked Woman*."
IN: Movies and Methods /v. 2
Imitations of Life

1730 Eckert, Charles.
"The Carole Lombard in Macy's Window."
IN: Fabrications
Stardom

1731 Eckman, S., Jr.
"Distribution."
IN: Behind the Screen

1732 Eco, Umberto.
"Articulations of the Cinematic Code."
IN: Movies and Methods: An Anthology

1733 Eco, Umberto.
"On the Contribution of Film to Semiotics."
IN: Film Theory and Criticism /2 ed
Film Theory and Criticism /3 ed

1734 Eco, Umberto.
"*De interpretatione*; or, The Difficulty of Being Marco Polo: On the Occasion of Antonioni's China Film."
IN: New Challenges for Documentary

1735 Edelstein, David.
"*Weeds*."
"*Thy Kingdom Come, Thy Will Be Done*."
"*The Stepfather*."
IN: Produced and Abandoned

1736 Edgerton, Gary.
"Film and Radio."
IN: Film and the Arts in Symbiosis

1737 Edgerton, Gary.
"The Film Bureau Phenomenon In America: State and Municipal Advocacy of Contemporary Motion Picture and Television Production."
IN: Current Research in Film /v. 2

1738 Editorial, An.
"*The Birth of a Nation*."
  IN: <u>Focus on The Birth of a Nation</u>

1739 Edlund, Richard.
"Photographic Effects for *The Empire Strikes Back*."
  IN: <u>The ASC Treasury ...</u>

1740 Edouart, Farciot.
"History of Background Projection."
  IN: <u>The ASC Treasury ...</u>

1741 Edwards, Blake and Julie Andrews.
"Blake Edwards and Julie Andrews." [Interview by Judith Crist.]
  IN: <u>Take 22</u>

1742 Eells, George.
"Ginger Rogers: Survivor."
"Miriam Hopkins: The Maverick."
"Ruth Etting: The Box-Office Bait."
"Kay Francis: The Sellout."
"Loretta Young: The Manipulator."
"Irene Bentley: The Dropout."
  IN: <u>Ginger, Loretta and Irene Who?</u>

1743 Egea, José Luis.
"Buñuel Is Written with a Tilde and Is Seventy Years Old."
  IN: <u>The World of Luis Buñuel</u>

1744 Eguino, Antonio.
"Neorealism in Bolivia."
  IN: <u>Cinema and Social Change ...</u>

1745 Ehlers, Leigh A.
"*Carrie*: Book and Film."
  IN: <u>Ideas of Order in Literature & Film</u>

1746 Ehrenstein, David.
"Jack Smith."
"Ken Jacobs."
"Owen Land (George Landow)."
"Bruce Conner."
"David Brooks."
"Werner Schroeter."
"Philippe Garrel."
"Luc Moullet."
"Raul Ruiz."
"Warren Sonbert."
"Curt McDowell."
"Lizzie Borden."
"Sally Potter."
"Joel DeMott and Jeff Kreines."
"Laurence Jarvik."
"Orson Welles."
  IN: <u>Film: The Front Line 1984</u>

1747 Ehrenstein, David.
"No Story To Tell."
  IN: <u>The New American Cinema</u>

1748 Ehrlich, Evelyn.
"Frances Goodrich and Albert Hackett."
  IN: <u>Dictionary of Literary Biography /v. 26</u>

1749 Ehrlich, Evelyn.
"The Civil War in Early Film: Origin and Development of a Genre."
  IN: <u>The South and Film</u>

1750 Eidsvik, Charles.
"Dark Laughter: Buñuel's *Tristana* from the Novel by Benito Pérez Galdós."
  IN: <u>Modern European Filmmakers ...</u>

1751 Eidsvik, Charles.
"Mock Realism: The Comedy of Futility in Eastern Europe."
  IN: <u>Comedy/Cinema/Theory</u>

1752 Eidsvik, Charles.
"Soft Edges: The Art of Literature, the Medium of Film."
"Toward a 'Politique des Adaptations'."
  IN: <u>Film And/As Literature</u>

1753 Eikhenbaum, B.
"Problems of Cine-Stylistics."
  IN: <u>The Poetics of Cinema</u>

1754 Eisenschitz, Bernard.
"A Fickle Man, or Portrait of Boris Barnet as a Soviet Director."
  IN: <u>Inside the Film Factory</u>

1755 Eisenschitz, Bernard.
"Abel Gance."
"Jean Grémillon."
  IN: <u>Cinema: A Critical Dictionary</u>

1756 Eisenstein, Sergei M.
"The Unexpected."
"Methods of Montage."
"A Course in Treatment."
"Film Language."
"Film Form: New Problems."
"The Structure of the Film."
"Achievement."
"Notes from a Director's Laboratory."
  IN: <u>Film Form</u>

1757 Eisenstein, Sergei M.
"Word and Image."
"Synchronization of Senses."
"Color and Meaning."
"Form and Content: Practice."
"*Strike*, A Sequence."
"*An American Tragedy*, Reel 10."
"*Sutter's Gold*, Reel 4."
"First Outline of *Que Viva Mexico!*."
"*Ferghana Canal*, Reel 1."
  IN: <u>The Film Sense</u>

1758 Eisenstein, Sergei.
"The Eighth Art: On Expressionism, America and, of course, Chaplin." (Written with Sergei Yutkevich.)
"The Montage of Film Attractions."
"The Method of Making a Workers' Film."
"Constanta (Whither *The Battleship Potemkin*)."
"However Odd--Khokhlova!"

"Eisenstein on Eisenstein, the Director of *Potemkin*."
"Béla Forgets the Scissors." [RE: Béla Balázs.]
"The Two Skulls of Alexander the Great."
"The German Cinema: A Traveller's Impression."
"Give Us a State Plan."
"Literature and Cinema: Reply to a Questionnaire."
"What We Are Expecting from the Party Conference on Cinema."
"Our *October*: Beyond the Played and the Non-Played."
"For a Workers' Hit."
"An Unexpected Juncture."
"The Twelfth Year." (With Grigori Alexandrov.)
"The GTK Teaching and Research Workshops: A Conversation with the Leader of the Workshop, S.M. Eisenstein."
"Conversation with Eisenstein on Sound Cinema."
"The Form of the Script."
"*The Arsenal*."
"Beyond the Shot."
"Perspectives."
"The Principles of the New Russian Cinema."
"Rin-Tin-Tin Does His Tricks for Noted Russian Movie Man."
"Help Yourself!"
"In the Interests of Form."
"Through the Revolution to Art: Through Art to the Revolution."
"Pantagruel Will Be Born."
"To Your Posts!"
"Georges Méliès's Mistake."
"An Attack by Class Allies."
"For Elevated Ideological Content, for Film Culture!"
"On Fascism, German Cinema and Real Life: An Open Letter to the German Minister of Propaganda, Dr. Goebbels."
"'Eh!' On the Purity of Film Language."
"At Last!"
  IN: <u>S.M. Eisenstein: Selected Works /v. 1</u>

1759 Eisenstein, Sergei.
"How I Became a Film Director."
"The Twelve Apostles."
"Alexander Nevsky."
"True Ways of Invention (*Alexander Nevsky*)."
"Organic Unity and Pathos in the Composition of *Potemkin*."
"Montage in 1938."
"An American Tragedy."
"A Few Thoughts About Soviet Comedy."
"Wolves and Sheep (Directors and Actors)."
"Not Coloured, but in Colour."
"The Greatest Creative Honesty."
"The Birth of an Artist."
"Twenty-Five and Fifteen."
"P-R-K-F-V."
"Hello, Charlie!"
"The Dictator." [RE: *The Great Dictator*.]
  IN: <u>Notes of a Film Director</u>

1760 Eisenstein, Sergei.
"Organic Unity and *Pathos*."
"The Milk Separator and the Holy Grail."
"Twenty-two Supporting Columns."
"The Lion in Old Age."
"El Greco."
"Piranesi or the Flux of Form." [RE: Giovanni Batista Piranesi.]
"Examples of Ecstasy."
"The Gothic."
"Superconcreteness."
"On the Question of Suprahistory."
"The Kangaroo."
"Once Again on the Surface of Things."
"The Music of Landscape and the Fate of Montage Counterpoint at a New Stage."
  IN: <u>Nonindifferent Nature</u>

1761 Eisenstein, Sergei.
"A Personal Statement."
"The Method of Making Workers' Films."
"Soviet Cinema."
"The New Language of Cinema."
"Perspectives."
"GTK - GIK - VGIK; Past - Present - Future."
"Lessons from Literature."
"The Embodiment of a Myth."
"More Thoughts on Structure."
"Mr Lincoln by Mr Ford." [RE: *Young Mr. Lincoln*.]
"A Close-Up View."
"Problems of Composition."
  IN: <u>Film Essays and a Lecture</u>

1762 Eisenstein, Sergei.
"Dickens, Griffith, and the Film Today."
  IN: <u>The First Film Makers</u>
      <u>Film Form</u>
      <u>Film and the Liberal Arts</u>
      <u>Film And/As Literature</u>

1763 Eisenstein, Sergei.
"[From:] Dickens, Griffith, and the Film Today."
  IN: <u>Film Theory and Criticism /1 ed</u>
      <u>Film Theory and Criticism /2 ed</u>
      <u>Film Theory and Criticism /3 ed</u>
      <u>Film Theory and Criticism /4 ed</u>

1764 Eisenstein, Sergei.
"[From:] *Film Form*: A Dialectic Approach to Film Form." [NOTE: Also called "The Dramaturgy of Film Form (The Dialectical Approach to Film Form)."]
  IN: <u>Film Form</u>
      <u>Film Theory and Criticism /2 ed</u>
      <u>Film Theory and Criticism /3 ed</u>
      <u>Film Theory and Criticism /4 ed</u>
      <u>S.M. Eisenstein: Selected Works /v. 1</u>

1765 Eisenstein, Sergei.
"[From:] *Film Form*: The Cinematographic Principle and the Ideogram."
  IN: <u>Film Form</u>
      <u>Film Theory and Criticism /2 ed</u>
      <u>Film Theory and Criticism /3 ed</u>

1791 **Elkin, Frederick.**
"The Psychological Appeal for Children of the
    Hollywood B Western."
    IN: <u>Focus on The Western</u>

1792 **Elley, Derek.**
"Mai Zetterling: Free Fall."
    IN: <u>Sexual Stratagems</u>

1793 **Ellingsworth, Rosalind K.**
"Defunct Theater Was Once Grand."
    IN: <u>The Movies: An American Idiom</u>

1794 **Elliot, Ramey and Jack G. Shaheen.**
"*Ladybug, Ladybug*."
    IN: <u>Nuclear War Films</u>

1795 **Elliott, David.**
"Taking a Line for a Dance."
    IN: <u>Eisenstein at Ninety</u>

1796 **Ellis, Jack C.**
"Modes of Film."
    IN: <u>Film Study in Higher Education</u>

    Ellis, Jack C. SEE: MacCann, Richard Dyer.

1797 **Ellis, John.**
"Stars as a Cinematic Phenomenon."
    IN: <u>Star Texts</u>

1798 **Ellis, John.**
"[From:] *Visible Fictions*: Stars as a Cinematic
    Phenomenon." [NOTE: This is an abridged version
    of the extract reprinted in *Star Texts*.]
    IN: <u>Film Theory and Criticism /4 ed</u>

1799 **Ellis, John.**
"[From:] *Visible Fictions*: Broadcast TV as Sound and
    Image."
    IN: <u>Film Theory and Criticism /4 ed</u>

1800 **Ellis, John.**
"Watching Death at Work: An Analysis of *A Matter of
    Life and Death*."
    IN: <u>Powell, Pressburger and Others</u>

1801 **Ellis, Kate.**
"*Little Women* [novel by] Louisa May Alcott. Life with
    Marmee: Three Versions." [RE: *Little Women*,
    1933 and 1949.]
    IN: <u>The Classic American Novel ...</u>

1802 **Ellis, Kate and E. Ann Kaplan.**
"*Jane Eyre* [novel by] Charlotte Bronte; *Jane Eyre*
    [films by] Robert Stevenson and Delbert Mann.
    Feminism in Bronte's Novel and Its Film Versions."
    IN: <u>The English Novel and the Movies</u>

1803 **Ellison, Harlan.**
"Lurching Down Memory Lane with *It, Them, The
    Thing, Godzilla*, HAL 9000 ... That Whole Crowd:
    An Overview of the Science Fiction Cinema."
"*Outland*: Out of Its Mind But, Sadly, Not Out of Sight."
    IN: <u>Omni's Screen Flights ...</u>

1804 **Ellison, Harlan.**
"*The Train*."

"*Von Ryan's Express*."
"*Masquerade*."
"*Mickey One*."
"*The War Lord*."
"*The Battle of the Bulge*."
"*Juliet of the Spirits*."
"*You're a Big Boy Now!*"
"*Beau Geste*."
"*Up the Down Staircase*."
"*Rosemary's Baby*."
"*Les Carabiniers*."
"*Hard Contact*."
"Harlan Ellison's Handy Guide to *2001: A Space
    Odyssey*."
"*Joe*."
"*Silent Running*."
"A Sort of Interview with Peter Boyle."
"Luke Skywalker Is A Nerd And Darth Vader Sucks
    Runny Eggs."
"*Star Trek–The Motionless Picture*."
    IN: <u>Harlan Ellison's Watching</u>

1805 **Ellison, Mary.**
"Blacks in American Film."
    IN: <u>Cinema, Politics and Society in America</u>

1806 **Ellison, Ralph.**
"The Shadow and the Act."
    IN: <u>The Black Man on Film</u>

1807 **Ellsworth, Elizabeth.**
"Illicit Pleasures: Feminist Spectators and *Personal
    Best*."
    IN: <u>Issues in Feminist Film Criticism</u>

1808 **Ellul, Jacques.**
"Characteristics of Propaganda."
    IN: <u>Propaganda on Film</u>

1809 **Ellwood, D.W.**
"'Showing the World What It Owed to Britain': Foreign
    Policy and 'Cultural Propaganda', 1935-45."
    IN: <u>Propaganda, Politics and Film</u>

1810 **Ellwood, David.**
"Italy: the Regime, the Nation and the Film Industry,
    an Introduction." [RE: WWII.]
    IN: <u>Film & Radio Propaganda ...</u>

1811 **Elsaesser, Thomas.**
"From anti-illusionism to hyper-realism: Bertolt Brecht
    and contemporary film."
    IN: <u>Re-interpreting Brecht</u>

1812 **Elsaesser, Thomas.**
"Dada/Cinema?"
    IN: <u>Dada and Surrealist Film</u>

1813 **Elsaesser, Thomas.**
"Narrative Cinema and Audience-Oriented Aesthetics."
    IN: <u>Popular Television and Film</u>

1814 **Elsaesser, Thomas.**
"Tales of Sound and Fury: Observations on the
    Family Melodrama."

1841 **Epstein, Jean.**
"The Cinema Continues."
"*Photogénie* and the Imponderable."
IN: <u>French Film Theory and Criticism</u> /v. 2

1842 **Epstein, Jon.**
"Jon Epstein." [An interview.]
IN: <u>Producers on Producing</u>

1843 **Epstein, Julius J.**
"Julius J. Epstein: A King of Comedy." [Interview by Pat McGilligan.]
IN: <u>Backstory</u>

1844 **Epstein, Julius J.**
"Reminiscence and Reflection: à Screenwriter."
IN: <u>Sound and the Cinema</u>

1845 **Epstein, Leslie.**
"*The Movie on the Whorehouse Wall / The Devil in Miss Jones.*"
IN: <u>The Movie That Changed My Life</u>

1846 **Erdrich, Louise.**
"Z."
IN: <u>The Movie That Changed My Life</u>

1847 **Erens, Patricia.**
"Between Two Worlds: Jewish Images in American Film."
IN: <u>The Kaleidoscopic Lens</u>

1848 **Erens, Patricia.**
"Starring Shirley MacLaine ... In Defense of Stars: A Response." [RE: Response to Sarafina K. Bathrick.]
IN: <u>Jump Cut</u>

1849 **Erens, Patricia.**
"Towards a Feminist Aesthetic: Reflection - Revolution - Ritual."
IN: <u>Sexual Stratagems</u>

1850 **Erens, Patricia.**
"Women's Documentary Filmmaking: The Personal Is Political."
IN: <u>New Challenges for Documentary</u>

1851 **Erland, Jonathan.**
"Jonathan Erland [on Special Effects: Scientific and Technical Development]." [Interview by David Chell.]
IN: <u>Moviemakers at Work</u>

1852 **Ermolayev, G.**
"What Is Holding Up the Development of Soviet Cinema?"
IN: <u>The Film Factory</u>

1853 **Eskind, Andrew H.**
"*She Banked in Her Stockings; or, Robbed of Her All*: Mutoscopes Old and New."
IN: <u>Image on the Art ...</u>

1854 **Espinosa, Julio Garcia.**
"Theory and Practice of Film and Popular Culture in Cuba." [RE: Cuba.]
IN: <u>Cinema and Social Change ...</u>

1855 **Espinosa, Julio Garcia.**
"For an Imperfect Cinema." [RE: Cuba.]
IN: <u>Reviewing Histories</u>

1856 **Esrock, Ellen.**
"Literature and Philosophy as Narrative Writing."
IN: <u>Ideas of Order in Literature & Film</u>

1857 **Esselman, Kathryn C.**
"From Camelot to Monument Valley: Dramatic Origins of the Western Film."
IN: <u>Focus on The Western</u>

1858 **Essex, Harry J.**
"Harry J. Essex." [An interview.]
IN: <u>Interviews with B ...</u>

1859 **Esslin, Martin.**
"Some Reflections on Brecht and acting."
IN: <u>Re-interpreting Brecht</u>

1860 **Estevam, Carlos.**
"For a Popular Revolutionary Art."
IN: <u>Brazilian Cinema</u>

1861 **Estève, Michel.**
"*The Exterminating Angel*: No Exit from the Human Condition."
IN: <u>The World of Luis Buñuel</u>

1862 **Estrada, José.**
"José Estrada." [Interview by Beatrice Reyes Nevares.]
IN: <u>The Mexican Cinema</u>

1863 **Estrin, Allen.**
"Frank Capra."
"George Cukor."
"Clarence Brown."
IN: <u>The Hollywood Professionals</u> /v. 6

1864 **Estrin, Mark W.**
"*The Scarlet Letter* [novel by] Nathaniel Hawthorne. 'Triumphant Ignominy' on the Screen."
IN: <u>The Classic American Novel ...</u>

1865 **Eszterhas, Joe.**
"Joe Eszterhas." [Interview by William Froug.]
IN: <u>The New Screenwriter Looks ...</u>

1866 **Etulain, Richard W.**
"Cultural Origins of the Western."
IN: <u>Focus on The Western</u>

1867 **Etulain, Richard W.**
"Recent Interpretations of the Western Film: A Bibliographical Essay."
IN: <u>Western Films: A Brief History</u>

1868 **Evans, Chris.**
"Chris Evans [on Special Effects: Matte Painting]." [Interview by David Chell.]
IN: <u>Moviemakers at Work</u>

Evans, Peter William. SEE: Babington, Bruce.

1869 **Evans, Robert.**
"Confessions of a Kid Mogul."

IN: <u>Anatomy of the Movies</u>

1870 Evans, Robert.
"The Producer."
IN: <u>The Movie Business Book</u>

1870a Evans, Robert.
"Robert Evans, producer." [Interview by Constance
Nash and Virginia Oakey.]
IN: <u>The Screenwriter's Handbook</u>

1871 Evans, Walter.
"Monster Movies: A Sexual Theory."
IN: <u>Sexuality in the Movies</u>
<u>Planks of Reason</u>

1872 Everson, William K.
"The 'B' Western."
IN: <u>The American Film Heritage</u>

1873 Everson, William K.
"*The Italian.*"
IN: <u>The First Film Makers</u>

1874 Everson, William K.
"*Of Mice and Men* [novel by] John Steinbeck.
Thoughts on a Great Adaptation."
IN: <u>The Modern American Novel ...</u>

1875 Everson, William K.
"*Hell's Hinges.*"
IN: <u>The Rivals of D.W. Griffith</u>

1876 Everson, William K.
"William K. Howard."
IN: <u>Between Action and Cut</u>

1877 Everson, William K.
"Seventy Years of Westerns."
IN: <u>Crossroads to the Cinema</u>

1878 Everson, William K.
"*The Triumph of the Will.*"
IN: <u>The Documentary Tradition /1 ed</u>
<u>The Documentary Tradition /2 ed</u>

Everson, William K. SEE: Fenin, George N.

1879 Ewell, Tom.
"Tom Ewell." [Interview by Charles Higham.]
IN: <u>Celebrity Circus</u>

1880 Eyles, Allen.
"*The Covered Wagon.*"
IN: <u>Movies of the Silent Years</u>

1881 Eyles, Allen.
"*1984*: Orwell Compromised."
IN: <u>Omni's Screen Flights ...</u>

**1882 Faber, Ronald J., Thomas C. O'Guinn, and
Andrew P. Hardy.**
"Art Films in the Suburbs: A Comparison of Popular
and Art Film Audiences."
IN: <u>Current Research in Film /v. 4</u>

1883 Fadiman, William.
"Should American Films Be Subsidized?"

IN: <u>Film: Readings in the Mass Media</u>
<u>Sight, Sound, and Society</u>

1884 Fagan, Myron C.
"Documentation of the Red Stars in Hollywood."
IN: <u>The Movies in Our Midst</u>

1885 Fairlie, Henry.
"The Unreal World of Television."
IN: <u>Sight, Sound, and Society</u>

1886 Falk, Quentin.
"Movies in Production."
IN: <u>Anatomy of the Movies</u>

1887 Falk, Quentin.
"Strengths and Signposts."
IN: <u>British Cinema Now</u>

1888 Falsetto, Mario.
"The Mad and the Beautiful: A Look at Two
Performances in the Films of Stanley Kubrick."
IN: <u>Making Visible the Invisible</u>

1889 Fanne, Dominique.
"The Books of His Life." [RE: François Truffaut.]
"*Jules and Jim*: A Masculine Couple."
IN: <u>Great Film Directors</u>

1890 Faragoh, Francis Edwards.
"The Polychrome Typewriter." [RE: *Becky Sharp*.]
IN: <u>Celebrity Articles ...</u>

1891 Farber, Manny.
"*Rashomon.*"
IN: <u>Focus on Rashomon</u>

1892 Farber, Manny.
"*The Great Gatsby* [novel by] F. Scott Fitzgerarld.
East Egg on the Face: Gatsby 1949."
IN: <u>The Classic American Novel ...</u>

1893 Farber, Manny.
"Blame the Audience."
"Val Lewton: Unorthodox Artistry at RKO."
IN: <u>Kings of the Bs</u>

1894 Farber, Manny.
"Howard Hawks and the Action Film."
IN: <u>Great Film Directors</u>

1895 Farber, Manny.
"Howard Hawks."
IN: <u>Focus on Howard Hawks</u>

1896 Farber, Manny.
"One for the Ages—*Desert Victory*."
IN: <u>The Documentary Tradition /1 ed</u>
<u>The Documentary Tradition /2 ed</u>

1897 Farber, Manny.
"Saccharine Symphony—*Bambi*."
IN: <u>The American Animated Cartoon</u>

1898 Farber, Manny.
"The Decline of the Actor."
IN: <u>Awake in the Dark</u>

1899   **Farber, Manny.**
       "Underground Films." [RE: low-budget.]
           IN: Film: An Anthology
               Awake in the Dark

1900   **Farber, Manny.**
       "Val Lewton and the School of Shudders."
           IN: Focus on The Horror Film

1901   **Farber, Manny (with W.S. Poster).**
       "Preston Sturges: Success in the Movies."
           IN: Awake in the Dark

1902   **Farber, Stephen.**
       "The Magnificent Ambersons."
           IN: Focus on Orson Welles

1903   **Farber, Stephen.**
       "Billy Wilder."
           IN: American Directors /v. 1

1904   **Farber, Stephen.**
       "Paul Newman."
           IN: The Movie Star: The National ...

1905   **Farber, Stephen.**
       "The New American Gothic."
           IN: Focus on The Horror Film

1906   **Farber, Stephen.**
       "The Movie Rating Game."
           IN: The Movies in Our Midst

1907   **Farber, Stephen.**
       "A Man Called Horse and *Flap."*
           IN: The Pretend Indians

1908   **Farber, Steven [*sic*, Stephen].**
       "The Outlaws."
           IN: The Movies: An American Idiom

1909   **Farber, Stephen and Estelle Changas.**
       "The Graduate."
           IN: Film: Readings in the Mass Media
               A Casebook on Film

1910   **Fargier, Jean-Paul.**
       "Parenthesis or Indirect Route."
           IN: Screen Reader 1

1911   **Farias, Roberto.**
       "Toward a Common Market of Portuguese- and
           Spanish-Speaking Countries."
           IN: Brazilian Cinema

1912   **Farmer, Harcourt.**
       "Is the Charlie Chaplin Vogue Passing?"
           IN: Focus on Chaplin

       Farr, Raye. SEE: Kuchl, Jerome.

1913   **Farrell, James T.**
       "The Language of Hollywood."
           IN: Authors on Film

1914   **Farris, John.**
       "A User's Guide to Hollywood Horror (as told to Kelley
           Wilde)."

           IN: Cut!: Horror Writers ...

1915   **Fassbinder, Rainer Werner.**
       "Michael Curtiz--Anarchist in Hollywood? Unordered
           Thoughts about a Seemingly Paradoxical Idea."
       "The German Feature Film and Reality."
       "Public Statement Regarding *Garbage, the City, and
           Death."*
       "Talking about Oppression with Margit Carstensen."
       "Homage to Werner Schroeter."
           IN: West German Filmmakers on Film

1916   **Fassbinder, Rainer Werner.**
       "I let the audience feel and think ..."
           IN: The Cineaste Interviews

       Fassbinder, Rainer Werner. SEE: Brustellin, Alf.

1917   **Faulkner, William.**
       "The Writer and Motion Pictures."
       "My Hollywood Experience."
           IN: Authors on Film

1918   **Faure, Elie.**
       "The Art of Cineplastics."
           IN: Film: An Anthology
               French Film Theory and Criticism /v. 1

1919   **Faure, Elie.**
       "The Art of Cineplastics (excerpts)."
           IN: Art in Cinema

1920   **Favazza, Armando.**
       "Fellini: Analyst Without Portfolio."
           IN: Man and the Movies

1921   **Fechner, Eberhard.**
       "The Experience of History."
           IN: West German Filmmakers on Film

1922   **Fehr, Rudi.**
       "Rudi Fehr." [Interview by Vincent LoBrutto.]
           IN: Selected Takes

1923   **Fejos, Paul.**
       "Illusion on the Screen."
           IN: Hollywood Directors 1914-1940

1924   **Fekete, John.**
       "Culture, History, and Ambivalence: On the Subject of
           Walter Benjamin."
           IN: Explorations in Film Theory

1925   **Feldman, Ellen.**
       "1970-1972 (*Serene Velocity, The Riddle of Lumen,
           Endurance/Remembrance/Metamorphosis,
           Nostalgia*)."
           IN: A History of the American Avant-Garde Cinema

1926   **Feldman, Ellen.**
       "John Paxton."
           IN: Dictionary of Literary Biography /v. 44

1927   **Feldman, Seth.**
       "Footnote to Fact: The Docudrama."
           IN: Film Genre Reader

1928 **Feldman, Seth.**
"The Film Program at the University of Western Ontario."
IN: Film Study in the Undergraduate Curriculum

1929 **Feldman, Seth.**
"'Cinema Weekly' and 'Cinema Truth': Dziga Vertov and the Leninist Proportion."
IN: Show Us Life

1930 **Fell, John L.**
"Motive, Mischief, and Melodrama: The State of Film Narrative in 1907."
IN: Film Before Griffith

1931 **Fell, John L.**
"The Correspondents' Curse: Vadim's *Les Liaisons Dangereuses 1960* from the Novel by Pierre Choderlos de Laclos."
IN: Modern European Filmmakers ...

1931a **Fell, John L.**
"Cellulose Nitrate Roots: Popular Entertainments and the Birth of Film Narrative."
IN: Before Hollywood

1932 **Fellini, Federico.**
"An Interview by Gideon Bachmann."
IN: Film: Book 1

1933 **Fellini, Federico.**
"Preface to the Screen Treatment of *Satyricon*."
IN: The Classic Cinema
Federico Fellini

1934 **Fellini, Federico.**
"The Bitter Life–Of Money."
IN: Film Makers on Film Making

1935 **Fellini, Federico.**
"My Experiences as a Director."
"Fellini on Television: *A Director's Notebook* and *The Clowns*."
"*Amarcord*: The Fascism within Us: An Interview with Valerio Riva."
"*Casanova*: An Interview with Aldo Tassone."
IN: Federico Fellini

1936 **Fellini, Federico.**
"The Road Beyond Neorealism."
IN: Film: A Montage of Theories

1937 **Fellini, Federico.**
"Federico Fellini." [Interview by Charles T. Samuels.]
IN: Encountering Directors

1938 **Fellini, Federico.**
"Federico Fellini." [Interview by Andrew Sarris.]
IN: Interviews with Film Directors

1939 **Fellman, Nat D.**
"The Exhibitor."
IN: The Movie Business Book

1940 **Fenin, George N. and William K. Everson.**
"Contents and Moral Influence of the Western."
IN: Film and the Liberal Arts

1941 **Fenin, George N. and William K. Everson.**
"The Western: From Silents to Cinerama [excerpt]."
IN: The American West on Film

1942 **Ferguson, Otis.**
"*Citizen Kane*."
IN: Focus on Citizen Kane

1943 **Ferguson, Otis.**
"Artists Among the Flickers (*Three Songs About Lenin*)."
"Cagney: Great Guy."
"Life Goes to the Pictures."
IN: Awake in the Dark

1944 **Ferguson, Otis.**
"Before the Cameras Roll."
IN: Film Theory and Criticism /1 ed
Film Theory and Criticism /2 ed

1945 **Ferguson, Otis.**
"Otis Ferguson." [Collected film capsules.]
IN: Garbo and the Night Watchmen

1946 **Ferguson, Otis.**
"Welles and His Wonders."
IN: Great Film Directors

1947 **Fergusson [*sic*, Ferguson], Otis.**
"At Your Own Risk." [RE: *The Ramparts We Watch*.]
IN: Propaganda on Film

1948 **Ferlita, Ernest.**
"Film and the Quest for Meaning."
"Luis Buñuel."
"The Analogy of Action in Film."
IN: Religion in Film

1949 **Fernández, Emilio.**
"Emilio Fernández." [Interview by Beatrice Reyes Nevares.]
IN: The Mexican Cinema

1950 **Fernández, Henry.**
"From Cortàzar to Antonioni: Study of an Adaptation."
IN: Focus on Blow-Up

1951 **Ferrara, Abel.**
"Abel Ferrara." [Interview by John Andrew Gallagher.]
IN: Film Directors on Directing

1952 **Ferrara, Giuseppe.**
"Neo-Realism: Yesterday."
"Neo-Realism: Today."
IN: Springtime in Italy

1953 **Ferro, Marc.**
"Stalinist Ideology Seen through *Chapayev*."
"Conflict Within *The Third Man*."
"*Le grande illusion* and Its Receptions."
"Dissolves in *Jud Süss*."
"Interviews in the Works of Ophüls, Harris, and Sédouy."
"The 'Fait Divers' and the Writing of History in Fritz Lang's *M*."
IN: Cinema and History

1954 **Ferro, Marc.**
"The Fiction Film and Historical Analysis."
IN: The Historian and Film

1955 **Ferry, Jean.**
"Concerning *King Kong.*"
IN: The Shadow and Its Shadow

1956 **Fescourt, Henri and Jean-Louis Bouquet.**
"*Idea and Screen: Opinions on the Cinema*, vol. 1."
"*Idea and Screen: Opinions on the Cinema*, vol. 3."
IN: French Film Theory and Criticism /v. 1

1957 **Feuer, Jane.**
"*Daughter Rite*: Living with Our Pain and Love."
IN: Films for Women

1958 **Feuer, Jane.**
"Hollywood Musicals: Mass Art as Folk Art."
IN: Jump Cut

1959 **Feuer, Jane.**
"The Hollywood Musical: An Annotated Bibliography."
IN: Genre: The Musical

1960 **Feuer, Jane.**
"The Self-Reflective Musical and the Myth of
Entertainment." [NOTE: Also called "The
Self-Reflexive Musical and the Myth of
Entertainment."]
IN: Film Genre Reader
Genre: The Musical
Film Theory and Criticism /4 ed

1961 **Feuillade, Louis.**
"Introduction: *Barrabas* and *Les Deux Gamines.*"
"*Scènes de la vie telle qu'elle est.*"
IN: French Film Theory and Criticism /v. 1

1962 **Feyder, Jacques.**
"The Possibilities of a Broadened Art."
IN: French Film Theory and Criticism /v. 2
Rediscovering French Film

1963 **Feyder, Jacques.**
"Visual Transpositions."
IN: French Film Theory and Criticism /v. 1

1964 **Feyen, Sharon.**
"The Stage Play Adapted."
IN: Screen Experience

Feyen, Sharon. SEE: Byrne, Richard B.

1965 **Fiedler, Leslie.**
"What Shining Phantom: Writers and the Movies."
IN: Man and the Movies

1966 **Fiedler, Theodore.**
"Alexander Kluge: Mediating History and
Consciousness."
IN: New German Filmmakers

1967 **Fielding, Raymond.**
"Hale's Tours: Ultrarealism in the Pre-1910 Motion
Picture."
IN: Film Before Griffith

1968 **Fielding, Raymond E.**
"Norman O. Dawn: Pioneer Worker in Special Effects
Cinematography."
IN: A Technological History ...

1969 **Fielding, Raymond.**
"The Technological Antecedents of the Coming of
Sound: An Introduction."
IN: Sound and the Cinema

1970 **Fields, Verna.**
"The Editor."
IN: Filmmakers on Filmmaking /v. 1

1971 **Fieschi, Jean-André.**
"Harold Lloyd."
"F.W. Murnau."
"Lupu Pick and Carl Mayer."
"Jacques Rivette."
"Jean Rouch."
"Mack Sennett."
"Jean-Marie Straub."
"Jacques Tati."
"Dziga Vertov."
"*The Cabinet of Dr. Caligari.*"
"Luis Buñuel."
"Louis Delluc."
"Jean Epstein."
"Alfred Hitchcock: II."
IN: Cinema: A Critical Dictionary

1972 **Fieschi, Jean-André.**
"Neo-neo-realism: *Bandits of Orgosolo.*"
"The Falling Sickness: *Fists in the Pocket.*"
IN: Cahiers du Cinéma, 1960-1968

Fieschi, Jean-André. SEE: Comolli, Jean-Louis.

1973 *Film Comment.*
"Screenwriters Symposium: Harry Brown, Delmer
Daves, Philip Dunne, Howard Koch, Norman
Krasna, Arthur Laurents, Ernest Lehman, Ben
Maddow, John Paxton, Morrie Ryskind, Michael
Wilson, George Zuckerman."
IN: The Hollywood Screenwriters

1974 **Filmer, Paul.**
"Literary Criticism & the Mass Media, with Special
Reference to the Cinema."
IN: Conflict and Control in the Cinema

1975 **Finkelstein, Haim.**
"Dalí and *Un Chien andalou*: The Nature of a
Collaboration."
IN: Dada and Surrealist Film

1976 **Finler, Joel W.**
"Action-Adventure."
IN: Anatomy of the Movies

1977 **Finler, Joel W.**
"Reassessment: Stroheim as Stylist and Myth Maker."
IN: The First Film Makers

1978 **Finler, Joel.**
"*Ben-Hur* (1925)."

IN: Movies of the Silent Years

1979 Firestone, Bruce.
"A Man Named Sioux." [RE: William S. Hart.]
IN: The First Film Makers

1980 Firestone, Cinda.
"*Attica* [Interview with] Cinda Firestone."
IN: The Documentary Conscience

1981 Fischer, Edward.
"Film Criticism."
IN: Film Study in Higher Education

1982 Fischer, Lucy.
"Pre/Texts: An Introduction (*Fatima*; *Take Off*)."
"Mythic Discourse (*The Lady from Shanghai*; *Riddle of the Sphinx*)."
"The Lives of Performers: The Actress as Signifier (*Persona*; *The Girls*)."
"Kiss Me Deadly: Heterosexual Romance (*Letter from an Unknown Woman*; *Straight through the Heart*; *Recital*)."
"Shall We Dance? Woman and the Musical (*Dames*; *Dance, Girl, Dance*; *Strange Ditties*; *Primitive Movers*; *The Eighties*)."
"Sisters: The Divided Self (*A Stolen Life*; *Dark Mirror*; *Cobra Woman*; *The Bad Sister*; *Sisters, or The Balance of Happiness*)."
"Girl Groups: Female Friendship (*Rich and Famous*; *Girlfriends*)."
"Women in Love: The Theme of Lesbianism (*Sotto, Sotto*; *Lianna*)."
"Murder, She Wrote: Women Who Kill (*Violette*; *A Question of Silence*)."
"The Dialogic Text: An Epilogue (*The Man Who Envied Women*)."
IN: Shot/Countershot

1983 Fischer, Lucy.
"The Lady Vanishes: Women, Magic, and the Movies."
IN: Film Before Griffith

1984 Fischer, Lucy.
"*Applause*: The Visual and Acoustic Landscape."
IN: Film Sound
Sound and the Cinema

1985 Fischer, Lucy.
"*Enthusiasm*: From Kino-Eye to Radio-Eye."
IN: Film Sound

1986 Fischer, Lucy.
"*Sunset Boulevard*: Fading Stars."
IN: Women and Film

1987 Fischer, Lucy.
"1943-1948 (*Meshes of the Afternoon*, *Geography of the Body*, *Early Abstractions*, *Fireworks*, *A Study in Choreography for Camera*, *Mother's Day*)."
IN: A History of the American Avant-Garde Cinema

1988 Fischer, Lucy.
"Seduced and Abandoned: Recollection and Romance in *Letter from an Unknown Woman*."
IN: Issues in Feminist Film Criticism

1989 Fischer, Lucy.
"Sometimes I Feel Like a Motherless Child: Comedy and Matricide."
IN: Comedy/Cinema/Theory

1990 Fischer, Lucy.
"The Lives of Performers: The Actress as Signifier in Cinema."
IN: Making Visible the Invisible

1991 Fischer, Lucy.
"The Image of Woman as Image: The Optical Politics of *Dames*."
IN: Sexual Stratagems
Genre: The Musical

1992 Fischer, Lucy.
"The Desire to Desire: *Desperately Seeking Susan*."
IN: Close Viewings

1993 Fischer, Lucy and Marcia Landy.
"*Eyes of Laura Mars*: A Binocular Critique."
IN: American Horrors

1994 Fischinger, Oskar.
"My Statements Are in My Work."
IN: Art in Cinema

1995 Fishbein, Leslie.
"*The Snake Pit*: The Sexist Nature of Sanity."
IN: Hollywood as Historian

1996 Fisher, David.
"Two Premières: Disney and UPA."
IN: The American Animated Cartoon

1997 Fisher, Eddie.
"Lucky Liz."
IN: Bedside Hollywood

1998 Fisher, Jack.
"*Last Tango in Paris*: The Skull Beneath the Skin Flick."
IN: Sexuality in the Movies

1999 Fisher, Morgan.
"Morgan Fisher." [Interview by Scott MacDonald.]
IN: A Critical Cinema

1999a Fisher, Rhonda Lee and Seymour Fisher.
"Pretending the World Is Funny: Charlie Chaplin's Job as the Prototype Comic Personality."
IN: Charlie Chaplin

Fisher, Seymour. SEE: Fisher, Rhonda.

2000 Fiske, Minnie Maddern.
"The Art of Charles Chaplin."
IN: Focus on Chaplin

2001 Fitzgerald, F. Scott.
"Letter to His Daughter."
IN: Authors on Film

2002 Fitzgerald, Geraldine.
"Geraldine Fitzgerald." [Interview by Rex Reed.]
IN: Travolta to Keaton

2003 Fitzmaurice, George.
"The Art of Directing."
IN: Hollywood Directors 1914-1940

2004 Fitzpatrick, John.
"Richard Brooks."
"Fred Zinnemann."
IN: American Directors /v. 2

2005 Flaherty, Frances.
"Explorations." [RE: Robert Flaherty.]
IN: Film: Book 1

2006 Flaherty, Robert J.
"How I Filmed *Nanook of the North*."
IN: Film Makers on Film Making

2007 Flaherty, Robert.
"Filming Real People."
IN: The Documentary Tradition /1 ed
The Documentary Tradition /2 ed

2008 Flaherty, Robert.
"Nanook." [RE: *Nanook of the North*.]
IN: The Emergence of Film Art /1 ed
The Emergence of Film Art /2 ed

2009 Flaherty, Robert.
"Picture Making in the South Seas."
IN: Hollywood Directors 1914-1940

2010 Fleischer, Richard.
"Underwater Filmmaking."
IN: Hollywood Directors 1941-1976

2011 Fleming, Alice.
"Edwin S. Porter."
"D.W. Griffith."
"Mack Sennett."
"Cecil B. DeMille."
"Robert Flaherty."
"Ernst Lubitsch."
"Frank Capra."
"John Ford."
"Walt Disney."
"Alfred Hitchcock."
"Stanley Kubrick."
IN: The Moviemakers

2012 Fleming, John.
"Science Fiction."
"Special Effects."
"Stunts."
IN: Anatomy of the Movies

2013 Fleming, Michael and Roger Manvell.
"Society and Madness: 'The Family and Madness' (*Now, Voyager*; *A Woman Under the Influence*) and 'Institutionalization of the Mad' (*The Snake Pit*; *One Flew Over the Cuckoo's Nest*)."
"Possession as Madness (*Dr. Jekyll and Mr. Hyde* [1931]; *The Exorcist*)."
"Eros and Madness: 'The Struggle between Love and Aggression' (*Secrets of a Soul*; *Bad Timing: A Sensual Obsession*), 'The Love of Aggression' (*M*; *Straw Dogs*) and 'Violence Against Women'."

"Murder and Madness: 'Murder and Mothers' (*White Heat*) and 'From Motive to Motiveless Murder' (*Badlands*)."
"War and Madness: 'World War II' (*Twelve O'Clock High*) and 'The Vietnam War' (*The Deer Hunter*)."
"Drugs and Madness (*The Lost Weekend*; *The Rose*)."
"Paranoia and Madness: 'Sexuality and Paranoia' and 'Paranoia as Reality'."
"Sanity as Madness, Madness as Sanity (*You Can't Take It with You*; *King of Hearts*)."
"Madness and the Psychiatrist."
IN: Images of Madness

2014 Flinn, Tom.
"Three Faces of Film Noir: *Stranger on the Third Floor*, *Phantom Lady*, and *Criss Cross*."
IN: Kings of the Bs

2015 Flinn, Tom and John Davis.
"*The Sea Wolf* [novel by] Jack London. Warners' War of the Wolf."
IN: The Classic American Novel ...

Flinn, Tom. SEE: Hart, Nancy K.; SEE: Davis, John.

2016 Flitterman, Sandy.
"Woman, Desire and the Look: Feminism and the Enunciative Apparatus in Cinema."
IN: Theories of Authorship

2017 Omitted

2018 Flitterman-Lewis, Sandy.
"Germaine Dulac: First Feminist of the Avant-Garde."
"Dulac in Context: French Film Production in the Twenties."
"From Fantasy to Structure of the Fantasm: *The Smiling Mme Beudet* and *The Seashell and the Clergyman*."
"Marie Epstein: A Woman in the Shadows."
"Epstein in Context: French Film Production in the Thirties."
"Nursery/Rhymes: Primal Scenes in *La Maternelle*."
"Agnès Varda and the Woman Seen."
"Varda in Context: French Film Production in the Early Sixties--the New Wave."
"From *Déesse* to *Idée*: Cleo From 5 to 7."
"The 'Impossible Portrait' of Femininity: *Vagabond*."
IN: To Desire Differently

2019 Flitterman-Lewis, Sandy.
"'Poetry of the Unconscious': Circuits of Desire in Two Films by Germaine Dulac: *La Souriante Mme Beudet* and *La Coquille et le clergyman*."
IN: French Film: Texts and Contexts

2020 Flitterman-Lewis, Sandy.
"The Image and the Spark: Dulac and Artaud Reviewed."
IN: Dada and Surrealist Film

Flitterman-Lewis, Sandy. SEE: Flitterman, Sandy; SEE: Stam, Robert.

2021 **Florey, Robert.**
"Foreign Atmosphere for the American Screen."
IN: Hollywood Directors 1914-1940

2022 **Flynn, Charles.**
"The Schlock/Kitsch/Hack Movies."
IN: Kings of the Bs

2023 **Flynn, Charles and Todd McCarthy.**
"The Economic Imperative: Why Was the B Movie Necessary?"
"Roger Corman." [Interview.]
"Joseph Kane." [Interview.]
"Arthur Lubin." [Interview.]
IN: Kings of the Bs

Flynn, Charles. SEE: McCarthy, Todd.

2024 **Flynn, Errol.**
"In Like Flynn."
IN: Bedside Hollywood

2025 **Fofi, Goffredo.**
"The Cinema of the Popular Front in France (1934-38)."
IN: Screen Reader 1

Fogel, Vladimir. SEE: Pudovkin, Vsevolod.

2026 **Folks, Jeffrey J.**
"William Faulkner and the Silent Film."
IN: The South and Film

2027 **Folsom, James K.**
"*Shane* and *Hud*."
IN: Western Movies

2028 **Folsom, James K.**
"Westerns as Social and Political Alternatives."
IN: Focus on The Western

2029 **Fonda, Henry.**
"The Leading Man."
IN: Hollywood Speaks!

2030 **Fonda, Jane.**
"I prefer films that strengthen people ..."
IN: The Cineaste Interviews

2031 **Fonda, Peter.**
"Peter Fonda on *Easy Rider*, Interview."
IN: The Image Maker

2032 **Fondane, Benjamin.**
"From Silent to Talkie: The Rise and Fall of the Cinema."
IN: French Film Theory and Criticism *v. 2*

2033 **Fons, Jorge.**
"Jorge Fons." [Interview by Beatrice Reyes Nevares.]
IN: The Mexican Cinema

2034 **Fontaine, Joan.**
"Joan Fontaine." [Interview by John Kobal.]
IN: People Will Talk

2035 **Fontaine, Joan.**
"Money is Sexy."

IN: Bedside Hollywood

2036 **Foote, Cheryl J.**
"Changing Images of Women in the Western Film."
IN: Western Films: A Brief History

2037 **Foote, Horton.**
"*Tomorrow*: The Genesis of a Screenplay."
IN: Faulkner, Modernism, and Film

2038 **Foote, Horton.**
"Writing for Film."
IN: Film and Literature: A Comparative ...

2039 **Ford, Greg.**
"Mostly on *Rio Lobo*."
IN: Focus on Howard Hawks
Movies and Methods: An Anthology

2040 **Ford, Hugh.**
"Hemingway's Hollywood Paris."
IN: A Moving Picture Feast

2041 **Ford, John D.**
"An Interview with John and Faith Hubley."
IN: The American Animated Cartoon

2042 **Ford, John.**
"Burt Kennedy Interviews John Ford."
"John Ford on *Stagecoach*."
IN: Directors in Action

2043 **Ford, John.**
"John Ford." [Interview by Andrew Sarris.]
IN: Interviews with Film Directors

2044 **Ford, John.**
"Veteran Producer Muses."
IN: Hollywood Directors 1914-1940

2045 **Fordin, Hugh.**
"*The Wizard of Oz* and *Babes in Arms*."
"*Strike Up the Band; Little Nellie Kelly; Lady Be Good; Babes on Broadway;* and *Panama Hattie*."
"*For Me and My Gal; Cabin in the Sky; Du Barry Was a Lady; Best Foot Forward;* and *Girl Crazy*."
"*Meet Me in St. Louis*."
"*Ziegfeld Follies; The Clock; The Harvey Girls;* and *Yolanda and the Thief*."
"*Till the Clouds Roll By; Summer Holiday; St. Louis Woman; The Pirate;* and *Good News*."
"*Easter Parade; Words and Music; Take Me Out to the Ball Park; The Barkleys of Broadway;* and *Any Number Can Play*."
"*On the Town*."
"*Annie Get Your Gun; Crisis; Pagan Love Song;* and *Royal Wedding*."
"*An American in Paris* and *Show Boat*."
"*Singin' in the Rain* and *The Belle of New York*."
"*Invitation to the Dance*."
"*The Band Wagon*."
"*Brigadoon; It's Always Fair Weather; Kismet;* and *Silk Stockings*."
"*Gigi*."
"*The Subterraneans; Bells Are Ringing;* and *Light in the Piazza*."

"The Fall of the [Arthur Freed] Empire."
IN: The World of Entertainment!

2046 **Fordin, Hugh.**
"*On the Town.*"
IN: The Hollywood Film Industry

2047 **Foreman, Alexa.**
"Jeanie Macpherson."
IN: Dictionary of Literary Biography /v. 44

2048 **Foreman, Carl.**
"Confessions of a Frustrated Screenwriter."
IN: The Hollywood Screenwriters

2049 **Foreman, Walter C., Jr.**
"The Poor Player Struts Again: Fellini's *Toby Dammit*
and the End of the Actor."
IN: Explorations in National Cinemas

2050 **Forman, Denis.**
"Interview [with] Denis Forman." [Interview by Eva
Orbanz, Klaus Wildenhahn and Richard Woolley.]
IN: Journey To a Legend and Back

2051 **Forman, Helen.**
"The Non-Theatrical Distribution of Films by the
Ministry of Information."
IN: Propaganda, Politics and Film

2052 **Forman, Henry James.**
"Our Movie Made Children."
IN: The Movies in Our Midst

2053 **Forman, Miloš.**
"Miloš Forman." [Interview by Antonín J. Liehm.]
IN: Closely Watched Films

2054 **Forman, Milos.**
"Milos Forman." [Interview by Joseph Gelmis.]
IN: The Film Director as Superstar

2055 **Forster, E.M.**
"Mickey and Minnie."
IN: Authors on Film
The American Animated Cartoon

2056 **Forsythe, Robert.**
"Robert Forsythe." [Collected film capsules.]
IN: Garbo and the Night Watchmen

2057 *Fortune.*
"The Hays Office."
IN: The American Film Industry

2058 *Fortune.*
"Loew's, Inc."
"Metro-Goldwyn-Mayer."
IN: The American Film Industry
The American Film Industry /rev ed

Foschetti, Bernardo. SEE: Levine, Arthur.

2059 **Foucault, Michel.**
"Film and Popular Memory: An Interview with Michel
Foucault."
IN: Conflict and Control in the Cinema

2060 **Foucault, Michel.**
"What Is an Author [extract]."
IN: Theories of Authorship

2061 **Fowler, Roy A.**
"*Citizen Kane*: Background and a Critique."
IN: Focus on Citizen Kane

2062 **Fox, Beryl.**
"*The Mills of the Gods: Vietnam* [Interview with] Beryl
Fox."
IN: The Documentary Conscience

2063 **Fox, Joan.**
"The New Wave."
IN: The Film

Fox, Rebecca. SEE: Paul, David W.

2064 **Fox, William.**
"Reminiscences and Observations."
IN: The Story of the Films

2065 **FPA.**
"Plutarch Lights of History, No. 5: Charles Chaplin."
IN: The Movies in Our Midst

2066 **Fraga, Jorge.**
"Cuba's Latin American Weekly Newsreel: Cinematic
Language and Political Effectiveness."
IN: The Social Documentary ...

2067 **Fraker, Bill.**
"Bill Fraker." [Interview by Dennis Schaefer and Larry
Salvato.]
IN: Masters of Light

2068 **Frakes, Margaret.**
"Time Marches Back." [RE: *The Ramparts We Watch.*]
IN: Propaganda on Film

2069 **Frampton, Hollis.**
"Eadweard Muybridge: Fragments of a Tesseract."
"Film in the House of the Word."
"Incisions in History/Segments of Eternity."
"For a Metahistory of Film: Commonplace Notes and
Hypotheses."
"Notes on Composing in Film."
"Meditations Around Paul Strand."
"Impromptus on Edward Weston: Everything in Its
Place."
"The Withering Away of the State of the Art."
"A Stipulation of Terms from Maternal Hopi."
"Digressions on the Photographic Agony."
IN: Circles of Confusion

2070 **Frampton, Hollis.**
"A Pentagram For Conjuring the Narrative."
IN: The Avant-Garde Film
Circles of Confusion

2071 **Frampton, Hollis.**
"Hollis Frampton." [Interview by Scott MacDonald.]
IN: A Critical Cinema

2072 **Frampton, Hollis.**
"Lecture."

IN: <u>The Avant-Garde Film</u>

Frampton, Hollis. SEE: Gidal, Peter.

2073 **Francia, Luis.**
"Philippine Cinema: The Struggle Against Repression."
IN: <u>Film and Politics in the Third World</u>

Francovich, A. SEE: Broullon, R.

2074 **Franju, Georges.**
"Exhibitionism."
IN: <u>French Film Theory and Criticism</u> /v. 2

2075 **Franju, Georges.**
"Georges Franju." [Interview by G. Roy Levin.]
IN: <u>Documentary Explorations</u>

2076 **Franju, Georges.**
"The Style of Fritz Lang."
IN: <u>Great Film Directors</u>

2077 **Frank, Micheline Klagsbrun.**
"*Kiss of the Spiderwoman* [*sic*]."
IN: <u>Images in Our Souls</u>

2078 **Frank, Sam.**
"Charles Brackett."
"I.A.L. Diamond."
"Robert Riskin."
IN: <u>Dictionary of Literary Biography</u> /v. 26

2079 **Frank, Sam.**
"Paddy Chayefsky."
IN: <u>Dictionary of Literary Biography</u> /v. 44

2080 **Frankenheimer, John.**
"John Frankenheimer."
IN: <u>The Celluloid Muse</u>

2081 **Frankenheimer, John.**
"Criticism as Creation."
IN: <u>Hollywood Directors 1941-1976</u>

2082 **Frankfather, William.**
"Colin Higgins."
IN: <u>Dictionary of Literary Biography</u> /v. 26

2083 **Franklin, B.J.**
"Promotion and Release."
IN: <u>Anatomy of the Movies</u>

2084 **Franklin, H. Bruce.**
"Don't Look Where We're Going: Visions of the Future
in Science Fiction Films, 1970-1982." [NOTE: Also
called "Visions of the Future in Science Fiction
Films, 1970-1982."]
IN: <u>Shadows of the Magic Lamp</u>
<u>Alien Zone</u>

2085 **Franklin, James.**
"Introduction to the New West German Cinema from
Oberhausen to Hamburg."
"Alexander Kluge."
"Jean-Marie Straub/Danièle Huillet."
"Volker Schlöndorff."
"Werner Herzog."
"Rainer Werner Fassbinder."

"Wim Wenders."
"Hans-Jürgen Syberberg."
IN: <u>New German Cinema: From Oberhausen ...</u>

2086 **Franklin, Joe.**
"*Hell's Hinges.*"
IN: <u>The First Film Makers</u>

2087 **Frayling, Christopher.**
"The American Western and American Society."
IN: <u>Cinema, Politics and Society in America</u>

2088 **Frazier, Cliff.**
"Film and the Ghetto."
IN: <u>The Compleat Guide to Film Study</u>

2089 **Freccero, John.**
"*Blow-Up*: From the Word to the Image."
IN: <u>Focus on Blow-Up</u>
<u>Great Film Directors</u>

2090 **Free, William J.**
"*Fellini's I Clowns* and the Grotesque."
IN: <u>Federico Fellini</u>

2091 **Free, William J.**
"Aesthetic and Moral Value in *Bonnie and Clyde*."
IN: <u>Focus on Bonnie and Clyde</u>

2092 **Freed, Arthur.**
"Arthur Freed." [Interview by John Kobal.]
IN: <u>People Will Talk</u>

2093 **Freeman, Judi.**
"Léger's *Ballet mécanique*."
IN: <u>Dada and Surrealist Film</u>

2094 **Freericks, Bernard.**
"Sound Recording."
IN: <u>Hollywood Speaks!</u>

2095 **Fregoso, Rosa Linda.**
"*Seguín*: The Same Side of the Alamo."
IN: <u>Chicano Cinema</u>

2096 **French Surrealist Group, The.**
"Some Surrealist Advice."
"Data Towards the Irrational Enlargement of a Film:
Shanghai Gesture."
"Manifesto of the Surrealists Concerning *L'Age d'or*."
IN: <u>The Shadow and Its Shadow</u>

2097 **French, Brandon.**
"The Scarlet 'A': *Sunset Boulevard*."
"The Joys of Marriage: *The Quiet Man*."
"Some Pretty Natural Noises: *The Marrying Kind*."
"The Amiable Spouse: *Shane*."
"The Hard and the Soft: *From Here to Eternity*."
"A Night Without a Star: *The Country Girl*."
"The Eleven-Year Itch: *The Tender Trap*."
"Dogs Like Us: *Marty*."
"Oppression in Sheep's Clothing: *All That Heaven
Allows*."
"A Minimal Feast: *Picnic*."
"Brides of Christ: *Heaven Knows, Mr. Allyson* [and]
The Nun's Story."
"Androgyny, Anyone?: *Some Like It Hot*."

IN: On the Verge of Revolt

2098 **French, Brandon.**
"*Lolita* [novel by] Vladimir Nabokov. The Celluloid Lolita: A Not-So-Crazy Quilt."
IN: The Modern American Novel ...

2099 **French, Brandon.**
"*Moby Dick* [novel by] Herman Melville. Lost at Sea."
IN: The Classic American Novel ...

2100 **French, Philip.**
"*Performance*."
IN: Sight and Sound

2101 **French, Philip.**
"All the Better Books."
IN: Film and the Liberal Arts

2102 **French, Philip.**
"Richard Lester."
IN: The Emergence of Film Art /1 ed
The Emergence of Film Art /2 ed

2103 **French, Philip.**
"The Indian in the Western Movie."
IN: The Pretend Indians

2104 **French, Philip.**
"Violence in the Cinema."
IN: Sight, Sound, and Society
Crossroads to the Cinema

2104a **French, Todd.**
"Dario Argento: Myth & Murder."
IN: The Deep Red Horror Handbook

2105 **French, Warren.**
"'The Southern': Another Lost Cause?"
IN: The South and Film

2106 **Freyer, Ellen.**
"*Chronicle of a Summer*--Ten Years After."
IN: The Documentary Tradition /1 ed
The Documentary Tradition /2 ed

Friar, Natasha A. SEE: Friar, Ralph E.

2107 **Friar, Ralph E. and Natasha A. Friar.**
"White Man Speaks with Split Tongue, Forked Tongue, Tongue of Snake."
IN: The Pretend Indians

2108 **Fric, Martin.**
"Martin Fric." [Interview by Antonín J. Liehm.]
IN: Closely Watched Films

2109 **Fried, Debra.**
"The Men in *The Women*."
IN: Women and Film

2110 **Friedberg, Anne.**
"'A Properly Adjusted Window': Vision and Sanity in D.W. Griffith's 1908-1909 Biograph Films."
IN: Early Cinema ...

2111 **Friedberg, Anne.**
"A Denial of Difference: Theories of Cinematic Identification."

IN: Psychoanalysis and Cinema

2112 **Friedberg, Anne.**
"An *Unheimlich* Maneuver Between Psychoanalysis and the Cinema: *Secrets of a Soul*."
IN: The Films of G.W. Pabst

2113 **Friedenberg, Edgar Z.**
"Calling Dr. Spock!" [RE: *The Graduate*.]
IN: A Casebook on Film

2114 **Friedkin, William.**
"Anatomy of a Chase." [NOTE: Also called "The Chase."] [RE: *The French Connection*.]
IN: Directors in Action
Hollywood Directors 1941-1976

2114a **Friedkin, William.**
"William Friedkin." [Interview by Anthony Loeb.]
IN: Filmmakers in Conversation

2115 **Friedman, Ken.**
"[A History of Italian Cinema:] 1945-1951."
IN: Italian Cinema

2116 **Friedman, Lester D.**
"*Frankenstein* [novel by] Mary Shelley; *Frankenstein* [film by] by James Whale. The Blasted Tree."
IN: The English Novel and the Movies

2117 **Friedman, Lester D.**
"'Canyons of Nightmare': The Jewish Horror Film."
IN: Planks of Reason

2118 **Friedman, Lester D.**
"Celluloid Palimpsests: An Overview of Ethnicity and the American Film."
IN: Unspeakable Images

2119 **Friedman, Murray.**
"The Images of Jews in American Film."
IN: Ethnic Images ...

2120 **Friedman, Regine Mihal.**
"*Ecce Ingenium Teutonicum: Paracelsus*."
IN: The Films of G.W. Pabst

2120a **Friedrich, Su.**
"Su Friedrich." [Interview by Scott MacDonald.]
IN: A Critical Cinema 2

2121 **Friendly, Fred W.**
"The McCarthy Broadcast."
IN: New Challenges for Documentary

2122 **Frizler, Paul.**
"Hal Ashby."
IN: Close-Up: The Contemporary Director

2123 **Frohman, Daniel.**
"Edison Is Agreeable."
IN: The First Tycoons

2124 **Frolov, Diane.**
"Diane Frolov." [Interview by William Froug.]
IN: The New Screenwriter Looks ...

2124a **Fry, William F., Jr.**
"Charles Chaplin: An Embodiment of Paradox."

IN: Charlie Chaplin

2125 **Fuchs, Cynthia J.**
"'All the Animals Come Out at Night': Vietnam Meets
   Noir in *Taxi Driver*."
   IN: Inventing Vietnam

2126 **Fuchs, Daniel.**
"Writing for the Movies."
   IN: Film and the Liberal Arts

2127 **Fuegi, John.**
"On Brecht's 'Theory' of Film."
   IN: Ideas of Order in Literature & Film

2128 **Fuentes, Carlos.**
"The Discreet Charm of Luis Buñuel."
   IN: The World of Luis Buñuel
      Great Film Directors

2129 **Fuller, Dan.**
"*The Adventures of Tom Sawyer* [novel by] Mark
   Twain. Tom Sawyer: Saturday Matinee."
   IN: The Classic American Novel ...

2130 **Fuller, Graham.**
"Making Some Light: An Interview with Michael Mann."
   IN: Projections: A Forum ...

2131 **Fuller, Samuel.**
"Film Fiction: More Factual than Facts."
   IN: Projections: A Forum ...

2132 **Fuller, Samuel.**
"Samuel Fuller." [Interview by Eric Sherman and
   Martin Rubin.]
   IN: The Director's Event

2133 **Fuller, Samuel.**
"What Is a Film?"
   IN: Hollywood Directors 1941-1976

2134 **Fullerton, John.**
"AB Svenska Biografteatern: Aspects of Production,
   1912-1920." [RE: Sweden.]
   IN: Current Research in Film /v. 1

2135 **Fullerton, John.**
"Spatial and Temporal Articulation in Pre-Classical
   Swedish Film."
   IN: Early Cinema ...

2136 **Fulmer, Mike.**
"Mike Fulmer [on Special Effects: Miniatures]."
   [Interview by David Chell.]
   IN: Moviemakers at Work

2137 **Fulton, A.R.**
"Editing in *The Birth of a Nation*."
   IN: Focus on The Birth of a Nation

2138 **Fulton, A.R.**
"From Novel to Film."
   IN: Film And/As Literature

2139 **Fulton, A.R.**
"Montage in *Potemkin*."
   IN: The Classic Cinema

2140 **Fulton, A.R.**
"Naturalism: From *McTeague* to *Greed*."
   IN: The First Film Makers

2141 **Fulton, A.R.**
"The Machine." [RE: prehistory.]
   IN: The American Film Industry
      The American Film Industry /rev ed

2142 **Fulton, John P.**
"How We Made *The Invisible Man*."
   IN: The ASC Treasury ...

2143 **Fung, Richard.**
"Looking for My Penis: The Eroticized Asian in Gay
   Video Porn."
   IN: How Do I Look

2144 **Funt, Allen.**
"*What Do You Say to a Naked Lady?*" [Interview by
   Alan Rosenthal.]
   IN: The New Documentary in Action

2145 **Furhammar, Leif and Folke Isaksson.**
"World War I."
"Russia after the Revolution."
"Germany: the Red Front."
"Produced by Joseph Goebbels."
"The Spanish Civil War."
"Hollywood and the World."
"Britain: Democracy at War."
"Caesar Zavattini."
"Cinema Nôvo: Brazil before the Revolution."
"*New Babylon*." [RE: *Novij Vavilon*.]
"*Hitlerjunge Quex*."
"*Triumph of the Will*."
"*The Spanish Earth*."
"*Der Ewige Jude*." [RE: *The Eternal Jew*.]
"*Ohm Krüger*."
"*Mrs. Miniver*."
"*Vier Vidkun Quislings Hirdmenn*."
"*Det Brinner en Eld*." [RE: *A Fire Is Burning*.]
"*The Hitler Gang*."
"*The Battle of Stalingrad*."
"*Sänt Händer inte Här*." [RE: *The Silence*.]
"*Unos*." [RE: *The Hijacking*.]
"*Man on a String*."
"*Torn Curtain*."
"*Ordinary Fascism*."
"*The Green Berets*."
"Hanoi, Martes 13 Diz."
"*Che*."
"The Aesthetics of Propaganda."
"From Personality Cult to Apotheosis."
   IN: Politics and Film

Furhammar, L. SEE: Isaksson, F.

2146 **Fürstenau, Theo.**
"*The Seventh Seal*."
   IN: Focus on The Seventh Seal

2147 **Fusco, Coco.**
"A Black Avant-Garde?: Notes on Black Audio Film Collective and Sankofa."
"An Interview with Martina Attille and Isaac Julien of Sankofa Film/Video Collective."
"An Interview with Black Audio Film Collective: John Akomfrah, Lina Gopaul, Avril Johnson and Reece Auguiste."
IN: Young British and Black

2148 **Fusco, Coco.**
"Long Distance Filmmaking: An Interview with the Cine-Ojo Collective." [RE: Chile.]
"Public Access Media and the Information War: An Interview with the Radio Venceremos Collective." [RE: El Salvador.]
"Reconstructing Nicaragua: Creating National Cinema—An Interview with Jorge Denti and Frank Pineda."
"The Politics of Mothering: An Interview with Susana Muñoz and Lourdes Portillo on *Las Madres: The Mothers of the Plaza de Mayo*." [RE: Argentina.]
IN: Reviewing Histories

Gabbard, Glen O. SEE: Gabbard, Krin.

2149 **Gabbard, Krin and Glen O. Gabbard.**
"*Alien* and Melanie Klein's Night Music."
"*3 Women*: Robert Altman's Dream World."
IN: Psychiatry and the Cinema

2150 **Gaber, Samuel L.**
"Jews in American Film and Television."
IN: Ethnic Images ...

2151 **Gabler, Neal.**
"Adolph Zukor."
"Carl Laemmle."
"Louis B. Mayer."
"Warner Brothers."
"Harry Cohn."
IN: An Empire of Their Own

2152 **Gabriel, Haile.**
"Triangular Cinema, Breaking Toys, and Dinknesh vs Lucy."
IN: Questions of Third Cinema

2153 **Gabriel, Teshome H.**
"Xala: A Cinema of Wax and Gold." [RE: *Xala.*]
IN: Jump Cut

2154 **Gabriel, Teshome H.**
"Towards a Critical Theory of Third World Films."
IN: Questions of Third Cinema

2155 **Gabriel, Teshome H.**
"Thoughts on Nomadic Aesthetics and the Black Independent Cinema: Traces of a Journey."
IN: Critical Perspectives on Black ...

2156 **Gabrilovitch, Yevgeni Iosipovitch.**
"Adventures and Encounters of a Scenarist."
IN: Cinema in Revolution

2157 **Gadi, R.B.**
"An Afternoon with Kurosawa."
IN: Focus on Rashomon

2158 **Gaines, Jane.**
"*The Scar of Shame*: Skin Color and Caste in Black Silent Melodrama."
IN: Imitations of Life

2159 **Gaines, Jane.**
"Costume and Narrative: How Dress Tells the Woman's Story."
"Fabricating the Female Body."
IN: Fabrications

2160 **Gaines, Jane.**
"The Showgirl and the Wolf."
IN: Cinema Examined

2161 **Gaines, Jane.**
"White Privilege and Looking Relations: Race and Gender in Feminist Film Theory."
"Women and Representation: Can We Enjoy Alternative Pleasure?"
IN: Issues in Feminist Film Criticism

Gaines, Jane Marie. SEE: Herzog, Charlotte Cornelia.

2162 **Galanes, Adriana.**
"The Image of Puerto Ricans in American Film and Television: The Two Faces of the Stereotypes."
IN: Ethnic Images ...

2163 **Galindo, Alejandro.**
"Alejandro Galindo." [Interview by Beatrice Reyes Nevares.]
IN: The Mexican Cinema

2164 **Gallagher, John A.**
"Victor Fleming."
IN: Between Action and Cut

2165 **Gallagher, Tag.**
"*Straight Shooting*."
IN: The Rivals of D.W. Griffith

2166 **Gallagher, Tag.**
"Shoot-Out at the Genre Corral: Problems in the 'Evolution' of the Western."
IN: Film Genre Reader

2167 **Galvão, Maria Rita.**
"Vera Cruz: A Brazilian Hollywood."
IN: Brazilian Cinema

2168 **Gan, Alexei.**
"Recognition for the Cine-Eyes."
"The 'Left Front' and Cinema."
"The Cinematograph and Cinema."
"The Thirteenth Experiment."
"Two Paths."
IN: The Film Factory

2169 **Gance, Abel.**
"A Sixth Art."
"My Napoleon."

IN: French Film Theory and Criticism /v. 1

2170 **Gance, Abel.**
"Images of Yesterday, Voices of Tomorrow."
IN: French Film Theory and Criticism /v. 2

2171 **Gance, Abel.**
"The Era of the Image Has Arrived."
IN: Rediscovering French Film

2171a **Gandhy, Behroze and Rosie Thomas.**
"Three Indian Film Stars." [RE: India; Nargis Dutt;
Smita Patil; 'Fearless' Nadia.]
IN: Stardom

2172 **Gans, Herbert J.**
"The Disaster Film."
"The Sociological Film."
"The Creator-Audience Relationship in the Mass
Media."
IN: Conflict and Control in the Cinema

2173 **Gao Jun.**
"A Changed Director: Transcription of a Dialogue with
Zhang Junzhao."
IN: Perspectives on Chinese Cinema

2174 **Garbo, Greta.**
"Why I'm Called a Recluse."
IN: Women and the Cinema

2175 **Garcia, Jessie B.**
"The Golden Decade of Filipino Movies."
IN: Readings in Philippine Cinema

2176 **Gardner, Craig Shaw.**
"Blood and Laughter: The Humor in Horror Film."
IN: Cut!: Horror Writers ...

2177 **Gardner, Gerald (editor).**
"Adventures: *Casablanca*; *The Treasure of the Sierra
Madre*; *The African Queen*."
"Musicals: *42nd Street*; *The French Line*; *Pal Joey*;
Guys and Dolls; *High Society*; *Going My Way*."
"Westerns: *The Outlaw*; *Duel in the Sun*; *High Noon*."
"Crime: *The Maltese Falcon*; *The Postman Always
Rings Twice*; *Double Indemnity*; *Angels with Dirty
Faces*."
"War: *For Whom the Bell Tolls* [1943]; *From Here to
Eternity*; *A Farewell to Arms* [1957]."
"Monsters: *Dr. Jekyll and Mr. Hyde* [1941]; *The Bride
of Frankenstein*."
"Romances: *Ecstasy*; *Now, Voyager*; *Wuthering
Heights*; *The Letter*."
"Epics: *The Ten Commandments* [1956]; *Spartacus*."
"Thrillers: *Rebecca*; *Notorious*; *Strangers on a Train*;
Rear Window; *The Birds*."
"Comedies: *Ninotchka*; *Mr. Smith Goes to
Washington*; *Mr. Deeds Goes to Town*; *Topper*;
Here Comes Mr. Jordan; *Bedtime for Bonzo*."
"The Marx Brothers: *Monkey Business* [1931]; *A Night
at the Opera*; *A Day at the Races*."
"Chaplin: *Modern Times*; *The Great Dictator*;
Monsieur Verdoux."
"W.C. Fields: *The Bank Dick*; *Never Give a Sucker an
Even Break*."

"Mae West: *I'm No Angel*; *Klondike Annie*."
"Comedies from Broadway: *Born Yesterday*; *The Man
Who Came to Dinner*; *Life with Father*; *Pygmalion*."
"Dramas: *The Best Years of Our Lives*; *Sunset
Boulevard*; *A Place in the Sun*; *The Man with the
Golden Arm*; *The Bicycle Thief*; *Gentlemen's
Agreement*; *The Lost Weekend*; *Dr. Ehrlich's Magic
Bullet*; *King's Row*."
"Dramas from Broadway: *Tea and Sympathy*; *The
Children's Hour*; *Inherit the Wind*; *Golden Boy*;
Who's Afraid of Virginia Woolf?; *A Streetcar
Named Desire*."
"After the Hays Office."
"Appendix I: The Motion Picture Production Code."
"Appendix II: List of 'Don'ts' and 'Be Carefuls'."
"Appendix III: Reasons Supporting the Production
Code."
IN: The Censorship Papers

2178 **Gardner, Robert.**
"A Chronicle of the Human Experience--*Dead Birds*."
IN: The Documentary Tradition /1 ed
The Documentary Tradition /2 ed
Nonfiction Film Theory and Criticism

2179 **Garey, Norman H.**
"Elements of Feature Financing."
"The Entertainment Lawyer."
IN: The Movie Business Book

2180 **Garga, B.D.**
"The History: A Diachronic Perspective."
IN: Indian Cinema Superbazaar

2181 **Garis, Robert.**
"Watching Antonioni." [RE: *Blow-Up*.]
IN: A Casebook on Film

2182 **Garland, Beverly.**
"Beverly Garland." [An interview.]
IN: Interviews with B ...

2183 **Garlick, R.J.**
"External Appearances in *Rules of the Game*."
IN: The Classic Cinema

2184 **Garmes, Lee.**
"Lee Garmes." [Interviews by Charles Higham.]
IN: Hollywood Cameramen

2185 **Garmes, Lee.**
"Photography." [RE: cinematography.]
IN: Behind the Screen

2186 **Garnett, Tay.**
"There's Profit in Sharing Profits."
IN: Hollywood Directors 1914-1940

2187 **Garnett, Tony.**
"Interview [with] Tony Garnett." [Interview by Eva
Orbanz, Helmut Wietz and Klaus Wildenhahn.]
IN: Journey To a Legend and Back

2188 **Garnett, Tony and Kenneth Loach.**
"Tony Garnett and Kenneth Loach." [Interview by G.
Roy Levin.]
IN: Documentary Explorations

2189   **Garnham, Nicholas.**
"TV Documentary and Ideology."
   IN: Screen Reader 1

2189a   **Garrelts, George.**
"*Citizen Kane*: Descent into the Demonic."
   IN: Image and Likeness

2190   **Garrett, George.**
"'Don't Make Waves'." [RE: screenwriting.]
   IN: Film And/As Literature
        Man and the Movies

2191   **Garrick, John.**
"Hemingway and *The Spanish Earth*."
"Inventing from Knowledge: Some Notes toward a
    Remake of *For Whom the Bell Tolls*."
   IN: A Moving Picture Feast

2192   **Garton, Ray.**
"On Kids and *Cat People* [1942]."
   IN: Cut!: Horror Writers ...

2193   **Garza, Héctor.**
"*El grito de las madres dolorosas*."
   IN: Chicano Cinema

2194   **Gates, Henry Louis, Jr.**
"Guess Who's Not Coming to Dinner?" [RE: *Jungle
    Fever*.]
   IN: Five for Five

2195   **Gaudreault, André.**
"Film, Narrative, Narration: The Cinema of the
    Lumière Brothers."
"The Infringement of Copyright Laws and its Effects
    (1900-1906)."
"Detours in Film Narrative: The Development of
    Cross-Cutting."
"Showing and Telling: Image and Word in Early
    Cinema."
   IN: Early Cinema ...

2196   **Gaudreault, André.**
"Temporality and Narrative in Early Cinema,
    1895-1908."
   IN: Film Before Griffith

2196a   **Gaudreault, André.**
"Chaplin's Short Films: Between Narration and
    Monstration."
   IN: Charlie Chaplin

2197   **Gaumont, Leon.**
"Gaumont Chronochrome Process Described by the
    Inventor."
   IN: A Technological History ...

2198   **Gauthier, Guy.**
"Science Fiction's Museum of the Imagination."
   IN: Focus on The Science Fiction Film

2199   **Gay, Carol.**
"*Little Women* [novel by] Louisa May Alcott. *Little
    Women* at the Movies."
   IN: Children's Novels and the Movies

2200   **Geduld, Carolyn.**
"*Bonnie and Clyde*: Society vs. the Clan."
   IN: Renaissance of the Film
        Focus on Bonnie and Clyde

2201   **Geduld, Carolyn.**
"*Juliet of the Spirits*: Guido's Anima."
   IN: Federico Fellini

2202   **Geduld, Carolyn.**
"*Sister Carrie* [novel by] Theodore Dreiser. Wyler's
    Suburban Sister: *Carrie* 1952."
   IN: The Classic American Novel ...

2203   **Geduld, Harry M.**
"Return to Méliès: Reflections on the Science Fiction
    Film."
   IN: Focus on The Science Fiction Film

2204   **Geduld, Harry.**
"The Voice of Vitaphone."
   IN: The Movies in Our Midst

2205   **Gehr, Ernie.**
"Program Notes."
   IN: The Avant-Garde Film

2206   **Gehring, Wes D.**
"Background of the Comic Antihero."
"Screwball Comedy Within American Humor: Defining
    a Genre."
"Howard Hawks."
"Leo McCarey."
"Preston Sturges."
"Gregory La Cava."
"Cary Grant."
"Carole Lombard/Irene Dunne."
"Claudette Colbert/Katharine Hepburn/Jean Arthur."
"Melvyn Douglas/Fred MacMurray."
"The Screwball Genre and Comedy Theory."
   IN: Screwball Comedy

2207   **Gehring, Wes D.**
"Black Humor."
"Clown Comedy."
"Genre: Introduction."
"Parody."
"Populist Comedy."
"Screwball Comedy."
   IN: Handbook of American Film Genres

2207a   **Gehring, Wes D.**
"Chaplin's Film Pioneer Status in Black or Macabre
    Humor."
   IN: Charlie Chaplin

2208   **Geiger, Peter W.**
"The Bank and Feature Financing."
   IN: The Movie Business Book

2209   **Geisler, Michael.**
"The Battleground of Modernity: *Westfront 1918*."
   IN: The Films of G.W. Pabst

2209a   **Geisler, Michael E.**

2222 **Georgakas, Dan.**
"*A Man Called Horse*."
IN: <u>Western Movies</u>

2223 **Georgakas, Dan.**
"*Finally Got the News*: The Making of a Radical Documentary."
IN: <u>Show Us Life</u>

2224 **Georgakas, Dan.**
"Greece."
IN: <u>World Cinema Since 1945</u>

2225 **Georgakas, Dan.**
"They Have Not Spoken: American Indians in Film."
IN: <u>The Pretend Indians</u>

2226 **Georgakas, Dan and Lenny Rubenstein.**
"'I Prefer Films that Strengthen People': An Interview with Jane Fonda." [NOTE: Also called "Interview with Jane Fonda."]
IN: <u>Conflict and Control in the Cinema</u>
<u>Women and the Cinema</u>

Georgakas, Dan. SEE: Crowdus, Gary.

2227 **George, Nelson.**
"*Do the Right Thing*: Film and Fury."
IN: <u>Five for Five</u>

2228 **Geraghty, Christine.**
"Three Women's Films."
IN: <u>Films for Women</u>

2229 **Geraghty, Christine.**
"Diana Dors."
IN: <u>All Our Yesterdays</u>

2230 **Gerassimov, Sergei Apollinarievitch.**
"Out of the Factory of the Eccentric Actor."
IN: <u>Cinema in Revolution</u>

Géré, François. SEE: Comolli, Jean-Louis.

2231 **Gere, Richard.**
"Richard Gere." [Interview by Rex Reed.]
IN: <u>Travolta to Keaton</u>

2232 **Germi, Pietro, Giuseppe De Santis and Luchino Visconti.**
"In Defense of Italian Cinema."
IN: <u>Springtime in Italy</u>

2233 **Gerould, Daniel.**
"Eisenstein's 'The Wise Man'."
IN: <u>Eisenstein at Ninety</u>

2234 **Gerould, Daniel.**
"Russian Formalist Theories of Melodrama."
IN: <u>Imitations of Life</u>

2235 **Gerstein, Evelyn.**
"English Documentary Films."
IN: <u>The Documentary Tradition /1 ed</u>
<u>The Documentary Tradition /2 ed</u>

2236 **Gerstein, Evelyn.**
"Russia's Film Wizard." [RE: Sergei Eisenstein.]

IN: <u>Introduction to the Art of the Movies</u>

2237 **Gessner, Robert.**
"Movies About Us."
IN: <u>The Documentary Tradition /1 ed</u>
<u>The Documentary Tradition /2 ed</u>

2238 **Gessner, Robert.**
"The Obligatory Scene in *The Seventh Seal*."
IN: <u>Focus on The Seventh Seal</u>

2239 **Gessner, Robert.**
"The Faces of Time."
IN: <u>The Movies as Medium</u>

2240 **Getino, Octavio.**
"Some Notes on the Concept of a 'Third Cinema'."
IN: <u>Argentine Cinema</u>

Getino, Octavio. SEE: Solanas, Fernando.

2241 **Ghali, Noureddine.**
"An Interview with Sembene Ousmane."
IN: <u>Film and Politics in the Third World</u>

2242 **Ghelli, Nino.**
"*Rashomon*."
IN: <u>Focus on Rashomon</u>

2243 **Giannetti, Louis D.**
"Godard's *Masculine-Feminine*: The Cinematic Essay."
"The Aesthetics of the Mobile Camera."
"Cinematic Metaphors."
"*Alice's Restaurant* and the Tradition of the Plotless Film."
IN: <u>Godard and Others</u>

2244 **Giannetti, Louis.**
"Introduction: Art, Industry, Audience."
"The Fountainhead: The Cinema of D.W. Griffith."
"The Little Fellow: The Cinema of Charles Chaplin."
"The Poetics of Space: The Cinema of Buster Keaton."
"The Way of the World: The Cinema of Ernst Lubitsch."
"The Individualist Mystique: The Cinema of Frank Capra."
"Leaves of Grass: The Cinema of John Ford."
"The Cult of Personality: The Cinema of Howard Hawks."
"The Tradition of Quality: The Cinema of William Wyler."
"Maschinenwerk: The Cinema of Fritz Lang."
"Roughing It: The Cinema of John Huston."
"Paradise Lost: The Cinema of Orson Welles."
"Cinema of the Absurd: The Cinema of Alfred Hitchcock."
"Hustling: The Cinema of Billy Wilder."
"America America: The Cinema of Elia Kazan."
"Films of Conscience: The Cinema of Fred Zinnemann."
"Coming Apart: The Cinema of Arthur Penn."
"Gray Matter: The Cinema of Stanley Kubrick."
"The Thrill of Discovery: The Cinema of Robert Altman."
IN: <u>Masters of the American Cinema</u>

2245 **Giannini, Attilio H.**
"The First Loans."
IN: The First Tycoons

2246 **Giannini, Attilio H.**
"Financial Aspects."
IN: The Story of the Films

2247 **Gibbons, Cedric.**
"The Art Director."
IN: Behind the Screen

2248 **Gid, Raymond.**
"Saul Bass."
IN: The Emergence of Film Art /1 ed
The Emergence of Film Art /2 ed

2249 **Gidal, Peter.**
"Technology and Ideology in/through/and
Avant-Garde Film: An Instance." [SEE: Laura
Mulvey, et al., "Discussion".]
IN: The Cinematic Apparatus

2250 **Gidal, Peter.**
"Theory and Definition of Structural/Materialist Film."
"[On] David Crosswaite."
"[On] Roger Hammond."
IN: Structural Film Anthology

2251 **Gidal, Peter and Hollis Frampton.**
"[On] Hollis Frampton."
IN: Structural Film Anthology

2252 **Gidal, Peter, Gordon Gow and Jonas Mekas.**
"[On] Malcolm LeGrice."
IN: Structural Film Anthology

2253 **Gidal, Peter, John Du Cane and William Raban.**
"[On] William Raban."
IN: Structural Film Anthology

**Gidal, Peter. SEE: Sharits, Paul; SEE: Mulvey,
Laura; SEE: Hartog, Simon.**

2254 **Giddings, Robert, Keith Selby and Chris Wensley.**
"The Literature/Screen Debate: an Overview."
"The Re-creation of the Past."
"The Classic Serial Tradition."
"The Classic Novel: *Great Expectations*."
"The Screening of *Great Expectations*."
"Case Study: The Dramatization of *Vanity Fair*."
"Case Study: The Production of *Vanity Fair*."
"The Transmission and Critical Reception of *Vanity
Fair*."
IN: Screening the Novel: The Theory ...

2255 **Giddis, Diane.**
"The Divided Woman: Bree Daniels in *Klute*."
IN: Women and the Cinema
Movies and Methods: An Anthology

2256 **Gide, Andre.**
"*Nosferatu*."
IN: Authors on Film

2257 **Gifford, Denis.**
"Fitz: The Old Man of the Screen." [RE: Lewin
Fitzhamon.]
IN: All Our Yesterdays

2258 **Gilbert, Bruce.**
"Hollywood's progressive producer ..."
IN: The Cineaste Interviews

2259 **Gilbert, Craig.**
"Reflections on *An American Family, I*."
"Reflections on *An American Family, II*."
IN: New Challenges for Documentary

2260 **Gilbert, Morris.**
"Paris Cinema Chatter."
IN: Sternberg

2261 **Giler, David.**
"David Giler." [Interview by William Froug.]
IN: The Screenwriter Looks ...

2262 **Giles, Dennis.**
"Conditions of Pleasure in Horror Cinema."
IN: Planks of Reason

2263 **Giles, Dennis.**
"Pornographic Space: The Other Place."
IN: Film: Historical-Theoretical ...

2264 **Giles, Dennis.**
"Show-making." [RE: sexuality.]
IN: Genre: The Musical

2265 **Giles, Dennis.**
"The Tao in *Woman in the Dunes*."
IN: Renaissance of the Film

2266 **Giles, Paul.**
"The Cinema of Catholicism: John Ford and Robert
Altman."
IN: Unspeakable Images

2267 **Gill, Brendan.**
"The Future of Film."
IN: Film: Readings in the Mass Media

2268 **Gillain, Anne.**
"The Script of Delinquency: François Truffaut's *Les
400 coups*."
IN: French Film: Texts and Contexts

2269 **Gillam, Barry.**
"Clarence Brown."
"Henry King."
IN: American Directors /v. 1

2270 **Gillam, Barry.**
"Budd Boetticher."
IN: American Directors /v. 2

2271 **Gillespie, Arnold 'Buddy'.**
"Special Visual Effects."
IN: Hollywood Speaks!

2272 **Gillet [*sic*, Gillett], John.**
"The Survivors."
IN: The Movies: An American Idiom

2273   Gillet[t], John.
"Michael Curtiz."
"Benjamin Christensen."
"Boris Barnet."
"Busby Berkeley and American Musicals of the 30s."
"Douglas Fairbanks and Mary Pickford."
"Gregory La Cava."
"Herbert Brenon."
"Ivan Mozhukhin."
"Kon Ichikawa."
"Mark Donskoi."
"Mitchell Leisen."
"Raymond Griffith and Clarence Badger."
"Teinosuke Kinugasa."
"Vincent Sherman."
  IN: <u>Cinema: A Critical Dictionary</u>

2274   Gillett, John.
"Japan--An Eye for Silence."
  IN: <u>Movies of the Silent Years</u>

2275   Gillett, John and James Blue.
"Keaton at Venice."
  IN: <u>Sight and Sound</u>

2276   Gilliatt, Penelope.
"Of Luis Buñuel."
"Of John Ford."
"Of Hitchcock."
"Of Satyajit Ray."
"The Decoy Fanatic: Henri Langlois."
"Old Master: Abel Gance."
"A Sense of Dream: Jeanne Moreau."
"The Urgent Whisper: Jean-Luc Godard."
"Guilty, With an Explanation: Woody Allen."
"*Love and Death*."
"*Annie Hall*."
"Her Own Best Disputant: Diane Keaton."
"*Interiors*."
"*Manhattan*."
"Roberto Rossellini."
"Retorts to *The Birth of a Nation*."
"Record of a Rascal Hunter." [RE: *I.F. Stone's Weekly*.]
"A Filmmaker's Meditation on America." [RE: *Hearts and Minds*.]
"'The Poor Don't Care What They Look Like'." [RE: *State of Siege*.]
"Notes on Reporting and Fiction."
"A Mind Pressed Against the Window." [RE: *A Woman at Her Window*.]
"Vivid Doldrums." [RE: *Swept Away*.]
"Church-Step Farce." [RE: *The Seduction of Mimi*.]
"Swiss Pride and Prejudice." [RE: *Charles Dead or Alive*.]
"A New Russian Classic." [RE: *A Slave of Love*.]
"Nabokov."
"Antonioni."
"Fellini."
"Fassbinder."
  IN: <u>Three-Quarter Face</u>

2277   Gilliatt, Penelope.
"Tati."
"Extinguished Salon." [RE: *The Exterminating Angel*.]
"Fellini Himself."
"The Golden Girl." [RE: Marilyn Monroe.]
"Woody Allen."
"A Good Night." [RE: *Ma Nuit Chez Maud*.]
"*Eroica*."
"Summer Judy Holliday."
"Beatrice Lillie, Elaine May."
"This Unpopular Century." [RE: *Desperate Characters*.]
"Cackle in Hell." [RE: *Laughter in the Dark*.]
"Godard's Folly of Soldiers." [RE: *Les Carabiniers*.]
"In the Thick of Europe." [RE: *Ashes and Diamonds*.]
"Polish Exile." [RE: Jerzy Skolimowski.]
"The Chaos of Cool." [RE: *Rosemary's Baby*.]
"Pinter."
"The Cleared Deck." [RE: *Life Upside Down*.]
"After Man." [RE: *2001, Dr. Strangelove*.]
"In Praise of Cowardice." [RE: *No More Excuses*.]
"Under Skin." [RE: *Petulia*.]
"Czech Wave."
"*A Report on the Party*."
"Dream of an Outrun Man." [RE: *The Joke*.]
"Chaplin on the Set." [RE: *A Countess from Hong Kong*.]
"*A Countess from Hong Kong* on the Screen."
"Funny in Need of Help." [RE: Mae West.]
"Harold Lloyd."
"The Vaudeville Infant." [RE: *The Cracksman*.]
"9-Million-Worth of Scrap-Yard Comedy." [RE: *It's a Mad, Mad, Mad, Mad World*.]
"Norman Wisdom."
"Demolishing Comedy." [RE: *Robin and the Seven Hoods*.]
"The Trouble with Dither." [RE: *The Man from the Diners' Club*.]
"Telling It Like It Isn't." [RE: *Don't Raise the Bridge, Lower the River*.]
"Nether Villainy." [RE: *You Only Live Twice*.]
"The Silents' Code." [RE: *Thirty Years of Fun*.]
"Birth-Pill Farce." [RE: *Prudence and the Pill*.]
"Feydeau, Move Over." [RE: *Pound, Up in the Cellar*.]
"Leading Back to Renoir." [RE: *Alice's Restaurant*.]
"The Divan Comedy." [RE: *Only Two Can Play*.]
"A Pox on Dying." [RE: *Hugs and Kisses*.]
"A Fairy Tale of New York." [RE: *Breakfast at Tiffany's*.]
"In the Best Bedrooms." [RE: Philippe de Broca.]
"A Movie, a Jug of Wine, a Loaf of Bread and What Was the Other Thing?" [RE: *Tu Seras Terriblement Gentille*.]
"Back to the Trees." [RE: *Hi, Mom!*]
"Could-Haves." [RE: *Entertaining Mr. Sloane*.]
"Bergman as a Comedian of Manners." [RE: *The Devil's Eye*.]
"The Bungling Detective." [RE: *Inspector Clouseau*.]
"Underling Spies." [RE: *The Spy with a Cold Nose, Casino Royale*.]

"Unemployable Maigret." [RE: *The Pink Panther.*]
"Snub by Computer." [RE: *Hot Millions.*]
"Feeling in the Wrong Is Wrong." [RE: *Goodbye, Columbus.*]
"To W.C. Fields, Dyspeptic Mumbler, Who Invented His Own Way Out."
"Billy Wilder's Thin Ice."
"The Most Dangerous Ground." [RE: *Watermelon Man.*]
"Mukel Swink." [RE: *Putney Swope.*]
"And We'll Be Back after This Message." [RE: *And Now for Something Completely Different.*]
"Carrying-On." [RE: the *Carry On* series.]
"Bad to Worse." [RE: *Don't Lose Your Head.*]
"Ophuls Restored." [RE: *Lola Montès.*]
"Shakespeare in Italy." [RE: Franco Zeffirelli.]
"Czech at Home." [RE: *Intimate Lighting.*]
"Czech in America." [RE: *Taking Off.*]
"*8-1/2.*"
"Bergman."
    IN: Unholy Fools

2278   **Gilliatt, Penelope.**
"Le Grand Monsieur de Deux Guerres, Libéré par Lui-même."
"Salute to Mayhem: *Boudu Sauvé des Eaux.*"
"Locked Out of a Golden Circle: *Toni.*"
"Boon Nights: *Le Crime de Monsieur Lange.*"
"Plight of a King: *La Marseillaise.*"
"Heredity: *La Bête Humaine.*"
"Acting: *Eléna et les Hommes.*"
"Pagan: *Le Déjeuner sur l'Herbe.*"
"Pax: *Le Caporal Epinglé.*"
"The Compere of the Game: *Le Petit Théâtre de Jean Renoir.*"
    IN: Jean Renoir: Essays ...

2279   **Gilliat [*sic*, Gilliatt], Penelope.**
"*See You at Mao* and *Pravda.*"
    IN: Focus on Godard

2280   **Gilliatt, Penelope.**
"*A Hard Day's Night.*" [NOTE: Also called "Beatles in Their Own Right."]
"Harry Langdon." [NOTE: Also called "Langdon."]
"Buster Keaton."
"*The Philadelphia Story.*" [NOTE: Also called "A Last Drop of the Hard Stuff."]
    IN: Unholy Fools
        Movie Comedy

2281   **Gilliatt, Penelope.**
"Flophouse: *Les Bas Fonds.*" [NOTE: Also called "Renoir's Flophouse."]
"Renoir: Le Meneur de Jeu."
    IN: Unholy Fools
        Jean Renoir: Essays...

2282   **Gilliatt, Penelope.**
"Game Without Umpire: *La Règle du Jeu.*" [NOTE: Also called "Renoir: Games Without Umpires."]
    IN: Movie Comedy
        Jean Renoir: Essays...

2283   **Gilliatt, Penelope.**
"*My Uncle.*"
"Marriage Comedies."
    IN: Movie Comedy

2284   **Gilliatt, Penelope.**
"Langdon."
    IN: Awake in the Dark
        Unholy Fools

2285   **Gilliatt, Penelope.**
"Charles Chaplin."
"W.C. Fields."
"Marilyn Monroe."
"Jeanne Moreau."
    IN: The Movie Star: The National ...

2286   **Gilman, Owen W., Jr.**
"Vietnam, Chaos, and the Dark Art of Improvisation."
    IN: Inventing Vietnam

2287   **Gilman, Richard.**
"And Nothing--with Precision."
    IN: Focus on Film and Theatre

2287a   **Gilpin, Kris.**
"Profile: Sam Raimi."
"Profile: H.G. Lewis."
"Profile: Tobe Hooper."
"Profile: Sean S. Cunningham."
"Profile: Mary Woronov."
"Profile: Fred Olen Ray."
"Profile: Lynn Lowry."
"Profile: Nicholas Worth."
    IN: The Deep Red Horror Handbook

2288   **Giral, Sergio.**
"Cuban Cinema and the Afro-Cuban Heritage."
    IN: Film and Politics in the Third World

2289   **Gish, Dorothy.**
"Dorothy Gish." [Interview by John Kobal.]
    IN: People Will Talk

2290   **Gish, Lillian.**
"Fade-Out."
"Griffith the Man."
    IN: Focus on D.W. Griffith

2291   **Gish, Lillian.**
"Griffith at Work." [RE: *Intolerance.*]
    IN: The Classic Cinema

2292   **Gish, Lillian.**
"Planning *The Birth of a Nation.*"
    IN: The First Film Makers

2293   **Gish, Lillian.**
"Screen."
    IN: The Best of Rob Wagner's Script

2294   **Gish, Lillian.**
"The Birth of *The Birth of a Nation.*"
    IN: Bedside Hollywood

2295   **Gish, Lillian.**
"The Making of *The Birth of a Nation.*"

IN: <u>Focus on The Birth of a Nation</u>

2296 **Gitlin, Todd.**
"Phantom India."
IN: <u>New Challenges for Documentary</u>

2297 **Gitlin, Todd.**
"The Medium: The Big Picture."
IN: <u>Seeing Through Movies</u>

2298 **Giuliano, Bruce.**
"The Family in Italy: Its Influence on the 'arte del vivere'."
IN: <u>Italian Cinema</u>

2299 **Glaessner, Verina and Fred Drummond.**
"[On] Fred Drummond."
IN: <u>Structural Film Anthology</u>

2300 **Glasser, Marc.**
"Dialog in Film and Fiction."
IN: <u>Explorations in National Cinemas</u>

2301 **Glassman, Marc.**
"To Stop Brothers Killing Brothers: An Interview with Tufan Gunar."
"The Documents in De's Case."
IN: <u>Forbidden Films</u>

2302 **Glazer, Benjamin.**
"The Photoplay with Sound and Voice."
IN: <u>Introduction to the Photoplay</u>

2303 **Gleber, Anke.**
"Masochism and Wartime Melodrama: *Komödianten*."
IN: <u>The Films of G.W. Pabst</u>

2304 **Gledhill, Christine.**
"Pleasurable Negotiations."
IN: <u>Female Spectators</u>

2305 **Gledhill, Christine.**
"The Melodramatic Field: An Investigation."
IN: <u>Home Is Where the Heart Is</u>

2306 **Gledhill, Christine.**
"A Contemporary Film Noir and Feminist Criticism."
"*Klute 2*: Feminism and *Klute*."
IN: <u>Women in Film Noir</u>

2307 **Gledhill, Christine.**
"Recent Developments in Feminist Criticism."
IN: <u>Film Theory and Criticism /3 ed</u>
<u>Film Theory and Criticism /4 ed</u>

2308 **Gledhill, Christine.**
"Developments in Feminist Film Criticism." [NOTE: A condensed and revised version of "Recent Developments in Feminist Film Criticism."]
IN: <u>Re-vision</u>

2308a **Gledhill, Christine.**
"Signs of Melodrama."
IN: <u>Stardom</u>

Gledhill, Christine. SEE: Cook, Pam.

2309 **Gleiberman, Owen.**
"*The Last Temptation of Christ*."

"*The Lonely Passion of Judith Hearn*."
IN: <u>Produced and Abandoned</u>

2310 **Glickenhaus, James.**
"James Glickenhaus." [Interview by John Andrew Gallagher.]
IN: <u>Film Directors on Directing</u>

2311 **Glut, Donald F.**
"When the Wolf Man Prowls."
"The Dual Horror of Dr. Jekyll."
"The Invisible Man and Co."
"The Curse of the Mummy."
"Quasimodo of Notre Dame."
"The Phantoms of the Opera."
"The Creature—Monster of the Fifties."
"His Majesty, King Kong."
"Godzilla, the New King."
IN: <u>Classic Movie Monsters</u>

2312 **Godard, Jean-Luc.**
"Early Texts (1950-1952)."
"Return to Criticism and First Short Films (August 1956-January 1958)."
"Struggle on Two Fronts: *Arts* and *Cahiers du Cinéma* (February-December 1958)."
"The Year of *A Bout de Souffle* (January–July 1959)."
"Marginal Notes While Filming (August 1959-August 1967)."
IN: <u>Godard on Godard</u>

2313 **Godard, Jean-Luc.**
"Beyond the Stars." [RE: *Bitter Victory*.]
"Nothing but Cinema." [RE: *Hot Blood*.]
"Sufficient Evidence." [RE: *Sait-on jamais*.]
"*Les 400 Coups*."
IN: <u>Cahiers du Cinéma, The 1950s</u>

2314 **Godard, Jean-Luc.**
"From Critic to Film-Maker." [Interview.]
"Struggling on Two Fronts." [Interview with Jacques Bontemps, Jean-Louis Comolli, Michel Delahaye, Jean Narboni.]
IN: <u>Cahiers du Cinéma, 1960-1968</u>

2315 **Godard, Jean-Luc.**
"Jean-Luc Godard." [Interview by Andrew Sarris.]
IN: <u>Interviews with Film Directors</u>

2316 **Godard, Jean-Luc.**
"Review of Astruc's *Une Vie*."
IN: <u>The New Wave: Critical Landmarks</u>

2317 **Godard, Jean-Luc.**
"The Art of the Director: Godard Interviews Antonioni."
IN: <u>Film and the Liberal Arts</u>

2318 **Godard, Jean-Luc and Fernando Solanas.**
"Godard on Solanas/Solanas on Godard--An Interview."
IN: <u>Reviewing Histories</u>

Godard, Jean-Luc. SEE: Chabrol, Claude; SEE: Domarchi, Jean.

2350 **Gomery, Douglas.**
"*Tobacco Road* [novel by] Erskine Caldwell. Three
Roads Taken: The Novel, the Play, and the Film."
IN: The Modern American Novel ...

2351 **Gomery, Douglas.**
"Building a Movie Theater Giant: The Rise of Cineplex
Odeon."
IN: Hollywood in the Age of Television

2352 **Gomery, Douglas.**
"Economic Struggle and Hollywood Imperialism:
Europe Converts to Sound."
IN: Film Sound

2353 **Gomery, Douglas.**
"Hollywood's Business."
IN: American Media

2354 **Gomery, Douglas.**
"Hollywood Converts to Sound: Chaos or Order?"
IN: Sound and the Cinema

2355 **Gomery, Douglas.**
"Problems in Film History: How Fox Innovated Sound."
IN: Hollywood as Historian

2356 **Gomery, Douglas.**
"Structuring the Moving Picture Image: The Classic
Hollywood Narrative."
IN: The Art of Moving Shadows

2357 **Gomery, Douglas.**
"The Movies Become Big Business: Publix Theatres
and the Chain-Store Strategy."
IN: The American Movie Industry
Cinema Examined

2358 **Gomery, Douglas.**
"The 'Warner-Vitaphone Peril': The American Film
Industry Reacts to the Innovation of Sound."
"Hollywood, the National Recovery Administration,
and the Question of Monopoly Power."
IN: The American Movie Industry

2359 **Gomery, Douglas.**
"The Coming of Sound: Technological Change in the
American Film Industry."
IN: Film Sound
The American Film Industry /rev ed

2360 **Gomery, Douglas.**
"The Economics of Film: What Is the Method?"
IN: Film/Culture: Explorations ...

2361 **Gomery, Douglas.**
"The Hollywood Studio System: 1930-49."
"Paramount."
"Loew's and Metro-Goldwyn-Mayer."
"20th Century-Fox."
"Warner Bros."
"Radio-Keith-Orpheum."
"Universal."
"Columbia."
IN: The Hollywood Studio System

2362 **Gomery, Douglas.**
"The Picture Palace: Economic Sense or Hollywood
Nonsense?"
IN: The Hollywood Film Industry

2363 **Gomery, Douglas.**
"The Theater: If You've Seen One, You've Seen the
Mall."
IN: Seeing Through Movies

2364 **Gomery, Douglas.**
"Toward a History of Film Exhibition: The Case of the
Picture Palace."
IN: Film: Historical-Theoretical ...

2365 **Gomery, Douglas.**
"Towards an Economic History of the Cinema: The
Coming of Sound to Hollywood."
IN: The Cinematic Apparatus

2366 **Gomery, Douglas.**
"Warner Bros. Innovates Sound: A Business History."
IN: The Movies in Our Midst

2367 **Gomery, Douglas.**
"Writing the History of the American Film Industry:
Warner Brothers and Sound."
IN: Movies and Methods /v. 2

2368 **Gomery, Douglas.**
"*The Singing Fool*."
IN: Close Viewings

Gomery, Douglas. SEE: Comolli, Jean-Louis.

2369 **Gomes, Paulo Emílio Salles.**
"Cinema: A Trajectory within Underdevelopment."
IN: Brazilian Cinema

2370 **Gomez, Joseph A.**
"*Women in Love* [novel by] D.H. Lawrence; *Women in
Love* [film by] Ken Russell. Russell's Images of
Lawrence's Vision."
IN: The English Novel and the Movies

2371 **Gomez, Joseph A.**
"Film in the English Department: The Wayne State
Version."
IN: Film Study in the Undergraduate Curriculum

2371a **Gong, Stephen.**
"Saving Early Cinema."
IN: Before Hollywood

2372 **Gontarski, S.E.**
"*The Virgin and the Gypsy* [novel by] D.H. Lawrence;
The Virgin and the Gypsy [film by] Christopher
Miles. An English Watercolor."
IN: The English Novel and the Movies

2373 **Goodlad, J.S.R.**
"The Function of Popular Drama."
IN: Conflict and Control in the Cinema

2374 **Goodman, Ezra.**
"Movement in Movies."
IN: The Movies as Medium

2375   **Goodman, Paul.**
"Designing Pacifist Films."
IN: Film: Book 2

2376   **Goodman, Paul.**
"Griffith and the Technical Innovations."
IN: Great Film Directors

2377   **Goodman, Paul.**
"Preliminary Topics in Defining Cinema."
IN: Introduction to the Art of the Movies

2378   **Goodrich, Frances and Albert Hackett.**
"Frances Goodrich and Albert Hackett:
Perfectionists." [Interview by Mark Rowland.]
IN: Backstory

2378a **Goodsell, Greg.**
"The Unwatchables."
"Hope I Die 'Fore I Get Old." [RE: *Don't Go Near the Park*.]
IN: The Deep Red Horror Handbook

2379   **Goodson, Mark.**
"Mark Goodson." [An interview.]
IN: Producers on Producing

2380   **Goodwin, James.**
"*The Secret Agent* [novel by] Joseph Conrad;
Sabotage [film by] Alfred Hitchcock. Conrad and
Hitchcock: Secret Shares."
IN: The English Novel and the Movies

2381   **Goodwin, James.**
"Clifford Odets."
"John Huston."
IN: Dictionary of Literary Biography /v. 26

2382   **Goodwin, Michael.**
"Heinlein on Film: *Destination Moon*."
IN: Omni's Screen Flights ...

2383   **Gorbman, Claudia.**
"Music as Salvation: Notes on Fellini and Rota." [RE:
The Nights of Cabiria; Nino Rota.]
IN: Federico Fellini

2384   **Gorbman, Claudia.**
"Narratological Perspectives on Film Music."
"Classical Hollywood Practice: The Model of Max
Steiner."
"Vigo/Jaubert: *Zéro de conduite* and Problems of
Methodology."
"Music and Sound Space in *Sous les toits de Paris*."
"Anempathy: *Hangover Square*."
IN: Unheard Melodies: Narrative Film Music

2385   **Gordon, Andrew.**
"The Power of the Force: Sex in the *Star Wars*
Trilogy."
IN: Eros in the Mind's Eye

2386   **Gordon, Bette.**
"*Variety*: The Pleasure in Looking."
IN: Issues in Feminist Film Criticism

2387   **Gordon, David.**
"Why the Movie Majors Are Major."
IN: The American Film Industry

2388   **Gordon, Henry Stephen.**
"D.W. Griffith Recalls the Making of *The Birth of a Nation*."
IN: Focus on The Birth of a Nation

2389   **Gordon, Linda.**
"Union Maids: Working-Class Heroines." [RE: *Union Maids*.]
IN: Jump Cut

2390   **Gordon, Richard.**
"Richard Gordon." [An interview.]
IN: Interviews with B ...

2391   **Gordon, Stuart.**
"Stuart Gordon." [Interview by Stanley Wiater.]
IN: Dark Visions

2392   **Gordon, Stuart.**
"Stuart Gordon." [Interview by John Andrew Gallagher.]
IN: Film Directors on Directing

       Gordon, Thomas F. SEE: Austin, Bruce A.

2393   **Gorky, Maxim.**
"The Kingdom of Shadows."
IN: Authors on Film

2394   **Gorky, Maxim.**
"The Lumière Cinematograph (extracts)."
IN: The Film Factory

2395   **Gorman, Ed.**
"Several Hundred Words About Wes Craven."
IN: Cut!: Horror Writers ...

2396   **Gormley, Charlie.**
"The Impact of Channel Four."
IN: From Limelight to Satellite

2397   **Gottesman, Ronald.**
"*Citizen Kane*: Past Present, and Future."
IN: Focus on Citizen Kane

2398   **Gottesman, Ronald.**
"Orson Welles: Obedient Servant and Disobedient
Master."
IN: Focus on Orson Welles

2399   **Gottheim, Larry.**
"Larry Gottheim." [Interview by Scott MacDonald.]
IN: A Critical Cinema

2400   **Gottlieb, Sidney.**
"*The Day of the Locust* [novel by] Nathanael West.
The Madding Crowd in the Movies."
IN: The Modern American Novel ...

2401   **Goudal, Jean.**
"Surrealism and Cinema."
IN: The Shadow and Its Shadow
French Film Theory and Criticism /v. 1

2402 **Gould, Heywood.**
"Jean-Luc Godard and the Sensibility of the Sixties."
IN: The Image Maker

2403 **Gould, Jack.**
"Forgotten Clues to the TV Crisis."
IN: Film and Society

2404 **Gould, Michael.**
"The Surrealist Sensibility (Breton; Duchamps; Dali; Ernst; Chirico; Gaudi; Magritte; Delvaux; Bronzino; Leonardo; *trompe-l'oeil*; Cocteau; Tyler; Durgnat; Weinberg; *Un chien andalou*; *L'age d'or*, *Rear Window*; *Psycho*; *The Ten Commandments*; *The Greatest Story Ever Told*; *Blood and Sand*; *Viridiana*; *Sherlock, Jr.*; *The Scarlet Empress*; *Ivan the Terrible*; *The Bride of Frankenstein*; *Spellbound*)."
"Luis Buñuel (*Un chien andalou*; *L'age d'or*, *Los olvidados*)."
"Josef von Sternberg (*The Scarlet Empress*; *The Devil Is a Woman*)."
"Alfred Hitchcock (*Psycho*; *North by Northwest*; *Vertigo*; *The Birds*)."
"Samuel Fuller (*The Naked Kiss*; *Shock Corridor*, *Underworld U.S.A.*; *Shark*)."
"Animated Film (*Betty Boop*; *Fantasia*; *Bambi*; *Sleeping Beauty*)."
"The Artist-Inventor (Edison; Warhol; Snow; *Wavelength*; *La région centrale*)."
IN: Surrealism and the Cinema

2405 **Gould, Timothy.**
"Stanley Cavell and the Plight of the Ordinary."
IN: Images in Our Souls

2406 **Goulding, Daniel J.**
"Yugoslav Film in the Post-Tito Era."
IN: Post New Wave Cinema ...

2407 **Goulding, Daniel.**
"The Films of Dusan Makavejev: Between East and West."
IN: Before the Wall Came Down

2408 **Goulding, Edmund.**
"The Talkers in Close-Up."
IN: Hollywood Directors 1914-1940

2409 **Goulet, Robert G.**
"Life With(out) Father: The Ideological Masculine in *Rope* and Other Hitchcock Films."
IN: Hitchcock's Re-Released Films

2410 **Gow, Gordon.**
"The Fifties."
IN: Hollywood 1920-1970

Gow, Gordon. SEE: Gidal, Peter.

2411 **Gozlan, Gérard.**
"In Praise of André Bazin."
"In Praise of André Bazin (second extract)."
IN: The New Wave: Critical Landmarks

2412 **Grady, Billy.**
"Casting."
IN: Behind the Screen

2413 **Graef, Roger.**
"*Decisions* [Interview with] Roger Graef."
IN: The Documentary Conscience

2414 **Graham, Allison.**
"Journey to the Center of the Fifties: The Cult of Banality."
IN: The Cult Film Experience

2415 **Graham, Allison.**
"'The Fallen Wonder of the World': Brian De Palma's Horror Films."
IN: American Horrors

2416 **Graham, Don B.**
"Audie Murphy: Kid With a Gun."
IN: Shooting Stars

2417 **Graham, Don.**
"*High Noon*."
"*The Great Northfield Minnesota Raid*."
IN: Western Movies

Graham, Don. SEE: Pilkington, William T.

2418 **Grant, Barry K.**
"Science Fiction Double Feature: Ideology in the Cult Film."
IN: The Cult Film Experience

2419 **Grant, Barry K.**
"Tradition and the Individual Talent: Poetry in the Genre Film."
IN: Narrative Strategies

2420 **Grant, Barry Keith.**
"Notes on Experience and the Teaching of Film: Brock University."
IN: Film Study in the Undergraduate Curriculum

2421 **Grant, Barry Keith.**
"Experience and Meaning in Genre Films."
IN: Film Genre Reader

2422 **Grant, Charles L.**
"Black-and-White, in Color."
IN: Cut!: Horror Writers ...

2423 **Grant, Marcus.**
"The Alcoholic as Hero."
IN: Images of Alcoholism

2424 **Granville, Bonita.**
"Bonita Granville & Lassie." [Interview by Rex Reed.]
IN: Travolta to Keaton

2425 **Grau, Robert.**
"Help from Overseas."
"The Growth of Universal."
IN: The First Tycoons

2426 **Gray, Hugh.**
"Film Aesthetics."
IN: Film Study in Higher Education

Green, Adolph. SEE: Comden, Betty.

2427   **Green, Fitzhugh.**
"A Soldier Falls." [RE: Sam Warner; coming of sound.]
    IN: <u>The Movies in Our Midst</u>

2428   **Green, Gary L.**
"The Author Behind the Author: George Cukor and the Adaptation of *The Philadelphia Story*."
    IN: <u>Film and Literature: A Comparative ...</u>

2429   **Green, Ian.**
"Ealing: In the Comedy Frame."
    IN: <u>British Cinema History</u>

2430   **Green, J. Ronald.**
"Film and Not-for-Profit Media Institutions."
    IN: <u>Film/Culture: Explorations ...</u>

2431   **Green, John.**
"Music Composer and Conductor."
    IN: <u>Hollywood Speaks!</u>

2432   **Greenberg, Harvey R.**
"*The Wizard of Oz*--Little Girl Lost--And Found."
"*The Treasure of the Sierra Madre*--There's Success Phobia in Them Thar Hills!"
"*The Maltese Falcon*--Even Paranoids Have Enemies."
"*Casablanca*--If It's So Schmaltzy, Why Am I Weeping?"
"*Psycho*--The Apes at the Windows."
"*8-1/2*--The Declensions of Silence."
"The Rags of Time--Ingmar Bergman's *Wild Strawberries*."
"Horror and Science Fiction--The Sleep of Reason."
"The Sleep of Reason--II."
"The Sleep of Reason--III."
    IN: <u>The Movies on Your Mind</u>

2433   **Greenberg, Harvey R., M.D.**
"Reimagining the Gargoyle: Psychoanalytic Notes on *Alien*."
    IN: <u>Close Encounters</u>

2434   **Greenberg, Jerry.**
"Jerry Greenberg." [Interview by Vincent LoBrutto.]
    IN: <u>Selected Takes</u>

2435   **Greenberg, Joel.**
"Walter Lang."
    IN: <u>Close Up: The Contract Director</u>

Greenberg, Joel. SEE: Higham, Charles.

2436   **Greene, Graham.**
"Graham Greene." [Collected film capsules.]
    IN: <u>Garbo and the Night Watchmen</u>

2437   **Greene, Graham.**
"Subjects and Stories."
    IN: <u>Footnotes to the Film</u>

2438   **Greene, Graham.**
"Three Reviews." [RE: *A Midsummer Night's Dream* (1935); *Romeo and Juliet* (1935); *Modern Times*.]
    IN: <u>Authors on Film</u>

2439   **Greene, Naomi.**
"Coppola, Cimino: The Operatics of History."
    IN: <u>Imitations of Life</u>

2440   **Greene, Ward.**
"*The Birth of a Nation*."
    IN: <u>Focus on The Birth of a Nation</u>

2441   **Greene, Wesley H.**
"Midwest Takes the Lead."
    IN: <u>Ideas on Film</u>

2442   **Greenspan, Roger.**
"*La Ronde*."
"*Carnal Knowledge*."
"*Stolen Kisses*."
"*Bananas*."
    IN: <u>Movie Comedy</u>

2443   **Greenspun, Roger.**
"'Elective Affinities'," [RE: *Jules and Jim*.]
    IN: <u>The Film</u>

2444   **Greenspun, Roger.**
"*Weekend*."
"*One Plus One*."
    IN: <u>Focus on Godard</u>

2445   **Greenspun, Roger.**
"Great Escapes: Four Films by Renoir." [RE: *Le Crime de Monsieur Lange*; *La Chienne*; *The Golden Coach*; *French CanCan*.]
    IN: <u>Rediscovering French Film</u>

2446   **Greenspun, Roger.**
"Through the Looking Glass." [RE: *Shoot the Piano Player*.]
    IN: <u>Focus on Shoot the Piano Player</u>
        <u>Renaissance of the Film</u>

2447   **Greig, Donald.**
"The Sexual Differentiation of the Hitchcock Text."
    IN: <u>Fantasy and the Cinema</u>

2448   **Grémillon, Jean.**
"French Realism."
    IN: <u>Rediscovering French Film</u>

2449   **Grenier, Richard.**
"The True Child: George Lucas and the *Star Wars* Series."
"The Uniforms That Guard: Kipling, Orwell, and Australia's *Breaker Morant*."
"Bolshevism as the Politics of Intent: Warren Beatty's *Reds*."
"Is It a Cuddly Universe? Spielberg's *E.T.* and Scott's *Blade Runner*."
"Fassbinder, Germany, and the Bloomingdale's Factor."
"The Gandhi Nobody Knows." [RE: *Gandhi*.]
"The Hard Left and the Soft: Hollywood Tests Its Radical Limits."
"The Feminization of Henry James: Vanessa Redgrave and *The Bostonians*."
"The Clint Eastwood Phenomenon: How He Became the World's Favorite Movie Star."

"Treason Chic: Britain Acclaims Its Traitors." [RE: *The Little Drummer Girl.*]

"Eddie Murphy in Post-Racist America."

"The 'Auteur' Cult: Truffaut and What France's Nouvelle Vague Was All About."

"Hitler's Favorite Baroness: The Dinesen-Streep *Out of Africa.*"

"Virtue in an Unknown Land: Argentina's *Official Story.*"

"Sex and the Military Man: Laclos's *Liaisons Dangereuses.*" [RE: the stage play.]

"Cry Fraud: Attenborough's *Cry Freedom.*"

"Splendor and the Beijing Party Line: Bertolucci's *The Last Emperor.*"

"From Russia with Angst: *The Burglar.*"

"Fidel and Vanity Fair Get Married: The Havana Film Festival."

"Eggs for the Soviet Omelette: The Russian Avant-Garde of the 1920s."

"The Ruckus over Jesus: Scorsese's *The Last Temptation of Christ.*"

"PBS at the Bat: Nestor Almendros's *Nobody Listened.*"

"The Film Director as Nazi: Ingmar Bergman."

"The Romance of Cocaine: *Tequila Sunrise.*"

"The Politics of Sentimentality: Charlie Chaplin."

"Heavy Thinking in the Afternoon: Oprah Winfrey and Shirley MacLaine."

"Mad Manichaeanism: Summer Blockbuster Movies." [RE: summer 1990.]

"Whose Vietnam? Brian de Palma's *Casualties of War.*"

"The Year of the Orgasmic Woman: *When Harry Met Sally.*"

"Treason Redux: Le Carré's *Russia House.*" [RE: the book.]

"Madame Butterfly's Revenge: *M. Butterfly* on Broadway."

"The FBI, the KKK, and a Sartrean Marxist: Costa Gavras's *Betrayed.*"

"Britain's Loony Left: *Letter to Brezhnev.*"

"The Sneaky Side of Pacifism: Spielberg's *Empire of the Sun.*"

"Can Jesus Save Madonna? 'Like a Prayer'." [RE: record album.]

"Culture's Mega-Stalinist: Brecht and *The Three Penny Opera.*" [RE: the play, with Sting.]

"A Broadway Flop Goes Downmarket: CBS's *A Pack of Lies.*"

"Jane Fonda Saves Mexico: Carlos Fuentes's *Old Gringo.*"

"Was Shakespeare Alienated? Branagh's Anti-War *Henry V.*"
   IN: <u>Capturing the Culture</u>

2450   **Grenville, John.**
"The Historian as Film-maker II."
   IN: <u>The Historian and Film</u>

2451   **Grierson, John.**
"The Logic of Comedy."
"Directors of the Thirties."
"Hollywood Looks at Life."

"The Russian Example."
"*Drifters.*"
"Creative Use of Sound."
"The E.M.B. Film Unit."
"Summary and Survey: 1935."
"Films and the Community."
"A Scottish Experiment."
"Battle for Authenticity."
"Metropolitan."
"Searchlight on Democracy."
"Education and the New Order."
"Education and Total Effort."
"Propaganda and Education."
"The Library in an International World."
"Films and the I.L.O."
"The Challenge of Peace."
"Report from America."
"Documentary: The Bright Example."
"Edinburgh and the Documentary Idea."
"Progress and Prospect."
"The Malaise of Disillusionment."
"Documentary: A World Perspective."
"Learning from Television."
"A Mind for the Future."
   IN: <u>Grierson on Documentary</u>

2452   **Grierson, John.**
"On Criticism."
"New York 1925-6."
"The Coming of the Talkies."
"What I Look For."
"The Logic of Comedy."
"The Master Craftsmen."
"Hollywood Looks at Life."
"The Cinema of Ideas."
"Hitchcock, Asquith and the English Cinema."
"From France and Germany."
"The Russian Cinema."
"Garbo, Dietrich, Mae West and Co."
"From Para Handy to Picasso."
"Robert Flaherty."
"Sergei Eisenstein."
"Charles Chaplin."
   IN: <u>Grierson on the Movies</u>

2453   **Grierson, John.**
"First Principles of Documentary."
   IN: <u>Nonfiction Film Theory and Criticism</u>
       <u>Film: A Montage of Theories</u>
       <u>Grierson on Documentary</u>

2454   **Grierson, John.**
"Flaherty."
   IN: <u>Great Film Directors</u>
       <u>Grierson on Documentary</u>

2455   **Grierson, John.**
"The Nature of Propaganda."
   IN: <u>Propaganda on Film</u>
       <u>Nonfiction Film Theory and Criticism</u>
       <u>Grierson on Documentary</u>

2479 **Griffith, Richard and Arthur Mayer.**
"The Men Who Owned the Business."
   IN: The First Tycoons

2480 **Griffith, Richard and Arthur Mayer.**
"[From:] Epilogue."
   IN: Film and Society

2481 **Grignaffini, Giovanna.**
"Female Identity and Italian Cinema of the 1950s."
   IN: Off Screen

2482 **Grigor, Murray.**
"Whiskey Galore!"
   IN: From Limelight to Satellite

2483 **Grigsby, Michael.**
"Interview [with] Michael Grigsby." [Interview by Eva Orbanz, Helmut Wietz and Klaus Wildenhahn.]
   IN: Journey To a Legend and Back

2484 **Grinde, Nick.**
"Pictures for Peanuts."
   IN: Hollywood Directors 1941-1976

2485 **Grindon, Leger.**
"Risorgimento History and Screen Spectacle: Visconti's *Senso*."
   IN: Resisting Images

2486 **Grogg, Sam L., Jr., and John G. Nachbar.**
"Movies and Audiences: A Reasonable Approach for American Film Criticism."
   IN: Movies as Artifacts

2487 **Gromada, Thaddeus V.**
"The Image of Poles in American Film and Television."
   IN: Ethnic Images ...

2488 **Gromaire, Marcel.**
"A Painter's Ideas about the Cinema."
   IN: French Film Theory and Criticism /v. 1

2489 **Grönlund, Enrique and Moylan C. Mills.**
"*Dona Flor and Her Two Husbands*: A Tale of Sensuality, Sustenance, and Spirits."
   IN: Film and Literature: A Comparative ...

2490 **Grosbard, Ulu.**
"Ulu Grosbard." [Interview by John Andrew Gallagher.]
   IN: Film Directors on Directing

2491 **Gross, Larry.**
"The Ethics of (Mis)representation."
   IN: Image Ethics

2492 **Gross, Larry, John Stuart Katz, and Jay Ruby.**
"Introduction: A Moral Pause."
   IN: Image Ethics

2493 **Grosser, David.**
"'We Aren't on the Wrong Side, We Are the Wrong Side': Peter Davis Targets (American) *Hearts and Minds*."
   IN: From Hanoi to Hollywood

2494 **Grumman, Lee.**
"Lee Grumman, American Actress." [Interview by George S. Semsel.]
   IN: Chinese Film

2495 **Grunberg, Slowomir.**
"A Polish Filmmaker in the United States."
   IN: Before the Wall Came Down

Gryn, Jo. SEE: Cukier, Dan A.

2496 **Guback, Thomas H.**
"Film As International Business: The Role of American Multinationals."
   IN: The American Movie Industry

2497 **Guback, Thomas H.**
"Hollywood's International Market."
   IN: The American Film Industry
       The American Film Industry /rev ed

2498 **Guback, Thomas.**
"Government Financial Support to the Film Industry in the United States."
   IN: Current Research in Film /v. 3

2499 **Guback, Thomas.**
"Non-Market Factors in the International Distribution of American Films."
   IN: Current Research in Film /v. 1

2500 **Guback, Thomas.**
"Shaping the Film Business in Postwar Germany: The Role of the US Film Industry and the US State."
   IN: The Hollywood Film Industry

Guégan, Gérard. SEE: Comolli, Jean-Louis.

Guerra, Rui. SEE: Diegues, Carlos.

2501 **Guerrero, Amadis Ma.**
"Gerardo de Leon: A Master Film-Maker Speaks Out."
   IN: Readings in Philippine Cinema

2502 **Guerrero, Rafael Ma.**
"Tagalog Movies: A New Understanding."
"Lino Brocka: Dramatic Sense, Documentary Aspirations."
   IN: Readings in Philippine Cinema

2503 **Guitry, Sacha.**
"For the Theater and Against the Cinema."
   IN: French Film Theory and Criticism /v. 2

2504 **Gujral, I.K.**
"I.K. Gujral." [Interview.]
   IN: Indian Cinema Superbazaar

2505 **Gulzar.**
"Gulzar." [Interview.]
   IN: Indian Cinema Superbazaar

2506 **Gunning, Tom.**
"An Unseen Energy Swallows Space: The Space in Early Film and Its Relation to American Avant-Garde Film."
   IN: Film Before Griffith

2507 Gunning, Tom.
"Non-Continuity, Continuity, Discontinuity: A Theory of Genres in Early Films."
"The Cinema of Attractions: Early Film, its Spectator and the Avant-Garde."
"Weaving a Narrative: Style and Economic Background in Griffith's Biograph Films."
"'Primitive' Cinema: A Frame-Up? Or, The Trick's on Us."
IN: <u>Early Cinema ...</u>

2508 Gunning, Tom.
"Weaving the Narrative." [RE: D.W. Griffith; NOTE: This is an abridged version of the essay in *Early Cinema*.]
IN: <u>The First Film Makers</u>

2509 Gunton, Sharon R. (compiler and editor).
"Woody Allen."
"Robert Altman."
"Ingmar Bergman."
"Bernardo Bertolucci."
"Robert Bresson."
"Tod Browning."
"Luis Buñuel."
"Frank Capra."
"Claude Chabrol."
"Charles Chaplin."
"Michael Cimino."
"Shirley Clarke."
"Jean Cocteau."
"Francis Ford Coppola."
"Maya Deren."
"Carl Theodor Dreyer."
"Federico Fellini."
"John Ford."
"Werner Herzog."
"Alfred Hitchcock."
"Elia Kazan."
"Stanley Kubrick."
"Akira Kurosawa."
"George Lucas."
"Rouben Mamoulian."
"Elaine May."
"Albert and David Maysles."
"Yasujiro Ozu."
"Gordon Parks."
"Roman Polanski."
"Satyajit Ray."
"Alain Resnais."
"Leni Riefenstahl."
"Eric Rohmer."
"Ken Russell."
"Agnès Varda."
"Luchino Visconti."
"Andrzej Wajda."
"Lina Wertmüller."
IN: <u>Contemporary Literary ... /v. 16</u>

2510 Gunton, Sharon R. (compiler and editor).
"Lindsay Anderson."

"Michelangelo Antonioni."
"John Cassavetes."
"René Clair."
"Brian De Palma."
"Vittorio De Sica."
"Marguerite Duras."
"Rainer Werner Fassbinder."
"Bob Fosse."
"Jean-Luc Godard."
"John Huston."
"Kon Ichikawa."
"Buster Keaton."
"Fritz Lang."
"Richard Lester."
"Laurence Olivier."
"Nagisa Oshima."
"Pier Paolo Pasolini."
"Sam Peckinpah."
"Jean Renoir."
"Carlos Saura."
"Martin Scorsese."
"Joan Micklin Silver."
"Jerzy Skolimowski."
"Steven Spielberg."
"Josef von Sternberg."
"François Truffaut."
"Melvin Van Peebles."
"Andy Warhol."
"Peter Weir."
"Orson Welles."
"Billy Wilder."
"Frederick Wiseman."
IN: <u>Contemporary Literary ... /v. 20</u>

2511 Gupta, Chidananda Das.
"The 'New' Cinema: A Wave or a Future?"
IN: <u>Indian Cinema Superbazaar</u>

2512 Gupta, Chidananda Das.
"The Painted Face of Politics: The Actor Politicians of South India."
IN: <u>Cinema and Cultural Identity</u>

2513 Gupta, Udayan.
"New Visions in Indian Cinema."
IN: <u>Film and Politics in the Third World</u>

2514 Gustafson, Robert.
"Film and Labor: What the Credits Mean."
IN: <u>Film/Culture: Explorations ...</u>

2515 Gustafson, Robert.
"'What's Happening to Our Pix Biz?' From Warner Bros. to Warner Communications Inc." [and] "Supplement: Warner Communications' International Operations."
IN: <u>The American Film Industry /rev ed</u>

2516 Guy-Blaché, Alice.
"Woman's Place in Photoplay Production."
IN: <u>Hollywood Directors 1914-1940</u>

2517 Guzmán, Patricio.
"Politics and the Documentary in People's Chile."

IN: Cinema and Social Change ...

2518 **Guzmán, Patricio and Julianne Burton.**
"Politics and the Documentary in People's Chile." [RE: *Battle for Chile*.]
IN: Film and Politics in the Third World

2519 **Guzzetti, Alfred.**
"Christian Metz and the Semiology of the Cinema."
IN: Film Theory and Criticism /2 ed
Film Theory and Criticism /3 ed

2520 **Gvozdev, Alexei.**
"A New Triumph for Soviet Cinema (*The Battleship Potemkin* and the 'Theatrical October')."
IN: The Film Factory

2521 **Haber, Bill and Rowland Perkins.**
"Bill Haber and Rowland Perkins." [Interview by William Froug.]
IN: The New Screenwriter Looks ...

2522 **Habley, Henry.**
"Industrially Sponsored Films: Telephone Film Distribution."
IN: Ideas on Film

2523 **Hacker, Jonathan and David Price.**
"Lindsay Anderson."
"Sir Richard Attenborough."
"Bill Forsyth."
"Stephen Frears."
"Peter Greenaway."
"Derek Jarman."
"Kenneth Loach."
"Alan Parker."
"Nicholas Roeg."
"John Schlesinger."
IN: Take 10

Hackett, Albert. SEE: Goodrich, Frances.

2524 **Hackett, Francis.**
"*The Kid*."
IN: Focus on Chaplin

2525 **Hackett, Francis.**
"Brotherly Love." [RE: D.W. Griffith.]
IN: The First Film Makers
Focus on The Birth of a Nation

2526 **Haddock, William.**
"William Haddock: The Director."
IN: The Real Tinsel

2527 **Hagan, John.**
"Cinema and the Romantic Tradition."
IN: Film Before Griffith

2528 **Hagan, John.**
"Ben Maddow."
IN: Dictionary of Literary Biography /v. 44

2529 **Hagen, William M.**
"*Apocalypse Now*: Joseph Conrad and the Television War."
IN: Hollywood as Historian

2530 **Haggard, H. Rider.**
"[From:] *King Solomon's Mines*."
IN: Africa on Film

2531 **Haines, Fred.**
"Art in Court: City of Angels vs. *Scorpio Rising*."
IN: The Movies in Our Midst

2532 **Haines, Harry W.**
"'They Were Called and They Went': The Political Rehabilitation of the Vietnam Veteran."
IN: From Hanoi to Hollywood

Haislip, William. SEE: Patrick, Robert.

2532a **Hake, Sabine.**
"Lubitsch's Period Films as Palimpsest: On *Passion* and *Deception*."
IN: Framing the Past

2533 **Halberstadt, Ira.**
"An Interview with Fred Wiseman."
IN: Nonfiction Film Theory and Criticism

2534 **Hall, Ben M.**
"The Strand Theatre."
IN: The First Tycoons

2535 **Hall, Conrad.**
"Conrad Hall." [Interview by Dennis Schaefer and Larry Salvato.]
IN: Masters of Light

2536 **Hall, Conrad.**
"Conrad Hall." [Interview by Kris Malkiewicz.]
IN: Film Lighting

2536a **Hall, Conrad.**
"Interview with Conrad Hall." [Interview by Leonard Maltin.]
IN: The Art of the Cinematographer

2537 **Hall, James and Jack G. Shaheen.**
"*To Die, To Live*."
IN: Nuclear War Films

2538 **Hall, Ken.**
"Strategies for an Industry–Television and Co-production."
IN: An Australian Film Reader

2539 **Hall, Mark.**
"*The Day the Earth Caught Fire*."
IN: Nuclear War Films

2540 **Hall, Melissa Mia.**
"Love Kills: Another Look at *Fatal Attraction*."
IN: Cut!: Horror Writers ...

2541 **Hall, Mordaunt.**
"The Vitaphone."
IN: The Movies in Our Midst

2542 **Hall, Stuart.**
"Media Power: The Double Bind."
IN: New Challenges for Documentary

2543 Hall, William.
"John Schlesinger."
"Richard Lester."
     IN: <u>Directors in Action</u>

2544 Halliday, Jon.
"Douglas Sirk."
"Max Ophuls."
     IN: <u>Cinema: A Critical Dictionary</u>

2545 Halliwell, Leslie.
"The Dread of Dracula."
"The Fear of Frankenstein."
"The Menace of the Mummy."
"A Note on Zombies and the Assorted Undead."
     IN: <u>The Dead That Walk</u>

2546 Halliwell, Leslie.
"Very Merry Men: *The Adventures of Robin Hood*."
"Life Upon the Wicked Stage: *All About Eve*."
"The Devil to Pay: *All That Money Can Buy*."
"The Leisen Touch: *Arise, My Love*."
"A Show That Is Really a Show Sends You Out in a
     Kind of a Glow: *The Band Wagon*."
"Down These Dark Streets a Man Must Go: *The Big
     Sleep*."
"Medium Rare: *Blithe Spirit*."
"They Called Her Wicked Lola: *The Blue Angel*."
"My Only Weakness: *The Bride of Frankenstein*."
"Passion on Platform Four: *Brief Encounter*."
"He Just Went Gay: *Bringing Up Baby*."
"Everybody Went to Rick's: *Casablanca*."
"The Body-in-the-Library Syndrome: *The Cat and the
     Canary* [1939]."
"I'll Bet You Five You're Not Alive if You Don't Know
     His Name: *Citizen Kane*."
"Is the Pellet with the Poison in the Flagon with the
     Dragon or the Chalice from the Palace?: *The Court
     Jester*."
"Unfamiliar Haunts: *Dead of Night*."
"Welcome to Bottleneck: *Destry Rides Again*."
"Alter Ego: *Dr. Jekyll and Mr. Hyde* [1931]."
"Just Wait Till He Gets Through with It: *Duck Soup*."
"Hat, Cane and Baggy Pants: *Easy Street* and *A
     Dog's Life*."
"A Musical Education: *Fantasia*."
"A Rendezvous with La Duchesse de Guermantes:
     Father Brown."
"Ze Roo-bees: *Gaslight* [1940]."
"A Fine Romance: *The Gay Divorcee* and *Top Hat*."
"Golden Silence: *The General*."
"Vintage Run: *Genevieve*."
"Hate Is an Exciting Emotion: *Gilda*."
"Ashley and Melanie and Scarlett and Rhett: *Gone
     with the Wind*."
"Californy Er Bust: *The Grapes of Wrath*."
"The Least Unlikely Person: *Green for Danger*."
"The Trail of the White Rabbit: *Harvey*."
"Anything Can Happen and It Probably Will:
     Hellzapoppin."
"Cry God for Larry: *Henry the Fifth*."
"Sons of Bitches: *His Girl Friday*."

"Quick, Watson, the Rathbone: *The Hound of the
     Baskervilles*."
"Films I Love to Hate: *House of Dracula*."
"California French: *I Married a Witch*."
"Encounters of Too Close of a Kind: *Invasion of the
     Body Snatchers*."
"Give That Boy a Spotlight: *The Jolson Story*."
"Never Trust Elderly Men on Ships: *Journey into Fear*
     and *Across the Pacific*."
"Eighth Wonder of the World: *King Kong* [1933]."
"Through Lace Curtains, Darkly: *King's Row*."
"Days of Steam and Spying: *The Lady Vanishes*."
"London Suburban: *The Lavender Hill Mob* and
     Passport to Pimlico."
"Moon over Malaya: *The Letter*."
"The Other Side of the Mountain: *Lost Horizon*."
"The Son of a Gun Is Nothing But a Tailor: *Love Me
     Tonight*."
"The Stuff That Dreams Are Made Of: *The Maltese
     Falcon*."
"What Closes Saturday Night: *The Man in the White
     Suit*."
"Old Parties: *The Man Who Came to Dinner*."
"A Distinct Smell of Fried Onions: *A Matter of Life and
     Death*."
"Et Voilà!: *Le Million*."
"On a Clear Day You Can See the Catskills: *Mr.
     Blandings Builds His Dream House*."
"The Best of All Possible Worlds: *Mr. Smith Goes to
     Washington*."
"Things That Go Arggggh: *The Mummy's Hand*."
"For Your Added Entertainment: *Mysterious Mr. Moto*
     and *Charlie Chan at the Opera*."
"Shaggy Face Story: *The Mystery of the Wax
     Museum*."
"Lady, Ever See a Man Looks Like This?: *The Naked
     City*."
"The Old Man in the Bright Nightgown: *Never Give a
     Sucker an Even Break*."
"And Two Hard-Boiled Eggs: *A Night at the Opera*
     and elsewhere."
"Alfred Hitchcock Re-Presents: *North By Northwest*."
"Faster! Faster!: *Occupe-Toi D'Amélie*."
"Joe the Cockeyed Miller: *Oh Mr. Porter*."
"Bats in the Belfry: *The Old Dark House*."
"The Very Dickens: *Oliver Twist* and *Great
     Expectations*."
"L'Oiseau Chante Avec Ses Doigts: *Orphée*."
"A Horse in the Bedroom: *The Palm Beach Story*."
"Mac the Night Watchman Is a Prince Among Men:
     The Philadelphia Story."
"All the Cat's Fault: *The Picture of Dorian Gray*."
"Experiment with Time: *Portrait of Jennie*."
"The Thalberg Style: *Pride and Prejudice*."
"Before the Lights Went Out: *The Prisoner of Zenda*."
"It Begins with a B: *Pygmalion*."
"The Art of Adaptation: *Quartet*."
"Skeleton in the Cupboard: *Rebecca*."
"Gotta Dance, Gotta Dance: *The Red Shoes*."
"The Devil of an Actor: *Rembrandt*, *Henry VIII* and
     The Hunchback of Notre Dame [1939]."

"Open Up That Golden Gate: *San Francisco*."
"Shame of a Nation: *Scarface* and *Little Caesar*."
"Regency Buck: *The Scarlet Pimpernel*."
"Seaside Postcard: *Sing As We Go*."
"Fit as a Fiddle and Ready to Dance: *Singin' in the Rain*."
"Our Dear Old Friends: *Sons of the Desert*."
"Figures in the Landscape: *Stagecoach* [1939]."
"Just Plain Folks: *Star Spangled Rhythm*."
"With a Little Bit of Sex: *Sullivan's Travels*."
"Something to Look Down On: *Sunset Boulevard* and *Ace in the Hole*."
"Our Eyes Have Seen Great Wonders: *The Thief of Baghdad* [1940]."
"A Cocktail Before Murder: *The Thin Man*."
"Prophet with Honour: *Things to Come*."
"No More Waltzes from Vienna: *The Third Man*."
"Innocence Is Running for Your Life: *The Thirty-Nine Steps*."
"Just the Perfect Blendship: *The Three Musketeers* and *Abbott and Costello Meet Frankenstein*."
"Midland and Scottish: *The Titfield Thunderbolt* and *Whisky Galore*."
"It'll Get a Terrific Laugh: *To Be or Not to Be*."
"Cosmo Topper, Alfalfa Switzer, and David Wark Griffith: *Topper Returns*."
"Night, Youth, Paris and the Moon: *Trouble in Paradise*."
"Let Right Be Done: *Twelve Angry Men*."
"On the Trail of the Lonesome Pine: *Way Out West*."
"Pie in the Sky: *The Wizard of Oz* and *The Blue Bird*."
   IN: Halliwell's Hundred

2547 **Halprin, Sara.**
"A Wives' Tale: Rewriting Working-Class History ... In Review: Voices and Visions."
   IN: Jump Cut

    Halprin, Sara. SEE: Steven, Peter.

2548 **Halsey, Richard.**
"Richard Halsey." [Interview by Vincent LoBrutto.]
   IN: Selected Takes

2549 **Halsey, Stuart & Co.**
"The Motion Picture Industry as a Basis for Bond Financing."
   IN: The American Film Industry
      The American Film Industry /rev ed

2550 **Hames, Peter.**
"Ján Kadár and Elmar Klos."
"Ladislav Helge."
"*Desire*--Vojtech Jansny."
"*Sunshine in a Net*--Stefan Uher."
"František Vláčil."
"Karel Kachyna."
"*The Cry*--Jaromil Jireš."
"Evald Schorm."
"Hynek Bocan."
"Miloš Forman."
"Jaroslav Papoušek."
"Ivan Passer."

"Pavel Jurácek."
"Jirí Menzel."
"Jan Nemec."
"Vera Chytilová."
"*Valerie and Her Week of Wonders*--Jaromil Jireš."
"Juraj Jakubisko."
"Juraj Herz."
   IN: The Czechoslovak New Wave

2551 **Hames, Peter.**
"Czechoslovakia: After the Spring."
   IN: Post New Wave Cinema ...

2552 **Hamill, Pete.**
"A Scene from *Doc*."
   IN: The American West on Film

2553 **Hamilton, Guy.**
"Guy Hamilton." [Interview by Judith Crist.]
   IN: Take 22

2554 **Hamilton, James Shelley.**
"What Is a Motion Picture?"
   IN: Introduction to the Art of the Movies

2555 **Hamilton, William.**
"Bergman and Polanski on the Death of God."
   IN: Celluloid and Symbol

2556 **Hammen, Scott.**
"*The Birth of a Nation*."
"*Intolerance*."
"*Way Down East*."
"*Orphans of the Storm*."
"*Isn't Life Wonderful*."
"*Sherlock, Jr.*."
"*The Navigator*."
"*The General*."
"*The Gold Rush*."
"*Modern Times*."
"*Sunrise*."
"*Nanook of the North*."
"*The Land*."
"*Louisiana Story*."
"*Potemkin*."
"*October*."
"*Man With a Movie Camera*."
"*Zero for Conduct*."
"*The Italian Straw Hat*."
"*A Nous la Liberte*."
"*La Chienne*."
"*Boudou Saved from Drowning*."
"*Toni*."
"*The Crime of M. Lange*."
"*A Day in the Country*."
"*The Lower Depths*."
"*The Grand Illusion*."
"*La Marseillaise*."
"*La Bete Humaine*."
"*The Rules of the Game*."
"*Metropolis*."
"*M*."
"*You Only Live Once*."

"*The Blue Angel.*"
"*Anna Christie.*"
"*Susan Lennox, Her Fall and Rise.*"
"*Mata Hari.*"
"*Grand Hotel.*"
"*Queen Christina.*"
"*The Painted Veil.*"
"*Camille.*"
"*Conquest.*"
"*Trouble in Paradise.*"
"*Ninotchka.*"
"*She Done Him Wrong.*"
"*The Thirty-Nine Steps.*"
"*The Lady Vanishes.*"
"*Shadow of a Doubt.*"
"*Notorious.*"
"*The Wrong Man.*"
"*North by Northwest.*"
"*Duck Soup.*"
"*My Favorite Wife.*"
"*Bringing Up Baby.*"
"*Only Angels Have Wings.*"
"*His Girl Friday.*"
"*The Big Sleep.*"
"*I Was a Male War Bride.*"
"*Monkey Business.*"
"*Gunga Din.*"
"*Penny Serenade.*"
"*Judge Priest.*"
"*Young Mr. Lincoln.*"
"*Drums Along the Mohawk.*"
"*The Grapes of Wrath.*"
"*My Darling Clementine.*"
"*Mr. Roberts.*"
"*The Lady Eve.*"
"*The Ox-Bow Incident.*"
"*Daisy Kenyon.*"
"*It Happened One Night.*"
"*Prelude to War.*"
"*It's a Wonderful Life.*"
"*The Maltese Falcon.*"
"*Across the Pacific.*"
"*Report from the Aleutians.*"
"*The Battle of San Pietro.*"
"*The Treasure of the Sierra Madre.*"
"*Key Largo.*"
"*We Were Strangers.*"
"*The Asphalt Jungle.*"
"*The Red Badge of Courage.*"
"*The African Queen.*"
"*Beat the Devil.*"
"*Citizen Kane.*"
"*The Magnificent Ambersons.*"
"*Lady from Shanghai.*"
"*Touch of Evil.*"
"*The Third Man.*"
"*Day of Wrath.*"
"*Ossessione.*"
"*La Terre Trema.*"
"*Open City.*"

"*Paisan.*"
"*Voyage to Italy.*"
"*The Rise of Louis XIV.*"
"*Shoeshine.*"
"*Bicycle Thieves.*"
"*Miracle in Milan.*"
"*Umberto D.*"
"*Bitter Rice.*"
"*The Path of Hope.*"
"*La Dolce Vita.*"
"*8-1/2.*"
"*Sunset Boulevard.*"
"*Smiles of a Summer Night.*"
"*Viridiana.*"
"*Belle de Jour.*"
"*The Red Desert.*"
"*Une Femme Douce.*"
"*Breathless.*"
"*The 400 Blows.*"
"*Shoot the Piano Player.*"
"*Jules and Jim.*"
"*The Soft Skin.*"
"*Fahrenheit 451.*"
"*The Bride Wore Black.*"
"*Stolen Kisses.*"
"*The Wild Child.*"
"*Bed and Board.*"
"*Two English Girls.*"
"*Day for Night.*"
　　IN: <u>Film Notes</u>

2557　**Hammond, Paul.**
"Off at a Tangent."
　　IN: <u>The Shadow and Its Shadow</u>

2558　**Hammond, Roger and David Curtis.**
"[On] Mike Leggett."
　　IN: <u>Structural Film Anthology</u>

2559　**Hammons, Earle W.**
"Short Reels and Educational Subjects."
　　IN: <u>The Story of the Films</u>

2560　**Hamner, Earl, Jr.**
"Earl Hamner, Jr." [An interview.]
　　IN: <u>Producers on Producing</u>

2561　**Hampton, Benjamin B.**
"J. Stuart Blackton."
"The Rise of First National."
"William Fox Improves His Position."
　　IN: <u>The First Tycoons</u>

2562　**Handelman, Janet.**
"*The Selling of the Pentagon.*"
　　IN: <u>The Documentary Tradition /2 ed</u>

2563　**Handke, Peter.**
"Theatre and Film: The Misery of Comparison."
　　IN: <u>Focus on Film and Theatre</u>

2564　**Handler, Mario.**
"Starting from Scratch: Artisanship and Agitprop."
　　[RE: Uruguay.]

IN: <u>Cinema and Social Change ...</u>

2565 Handley, Charles W.
"History of Motion-Picture Studio Lighting."
  IN: <u>A Technological History ...</u>

2566 Handling, Piers.
"Canada."
  IN: <u>World Cinema Since 1945</u>

2567 Handzo, Stephen.
"Under Capracorn." [RE: Frank Capra.]
  IN: <u>Great Film Directors</u>

2568 Hanhardt, John G.
"Chronology 1943-1972."
  IN: <u>A History of the American Avant-Garde Cinema</u>

2569 Hani, Susumu.
"Susumu Hani." [Interview by Joan Mellen.]
  IN: <u>Voices from the Japanese Cinema</u>

2569a Hanisch, Michael.
"The Chaplin Reception in Germany."
  IN: <u>Charlie Chaplin</u>

2570 Hanlon, Lindley P.
"1963-1966 (*Scorpio Rising*; *Fire of Waters*; *Window*; *The Flicker*)."
  IN: <u>A History of the American Avant-Garde Cinema</u>

2571 Hanlon, Lindley.
"*Lady Chatterly's Lover* [novel by] D.H. Lawrence; *Lady Chatterly's Lover* [film by] Marc Allegret. Sensuality and Simplification."
  IN: <u>The English Novel and the Movies</u>

2572 Hanlon, Lindley.
"Sound in Bresson's *Mouchette*."
  IN: <u>Film Sound</u>

2573 Hanlon, Lindley.
"The 'Seen' and the 'Said': Bresson's *Une Femme Douce* from the Story 'The Gentle Creature' by Fyodor Dostoevsky."
  IN: <u>Modern European Filmmakers ...</u>

2574 Hansen, Miriam.
"Early Cinema—Whose Public Sphere?"
  IN: <u>Early Cinema ...</u>

2575 Hansen, Miriam.
"Pleasure, Ambivalence, Identification: Valentino and Female Spectatorship."
  IN: <u>Star Texts</u>
    <u>Stardom</u>

2576 Hansen, Miriam.
"Space of History, Language of Time: Kluge's *Yesterday Girl*."
  IN: <u>German Film and Literature</u>

2577 Hanson, Karen.
"Being Doubted, Being Assured." [RE: Stanley Cavell.]
  IN: <u>Images in Our Souls</u>

2578 Haralovich, Mary Beth.
"Film Advertising, the Film Industry and the Pin-up: The Industry's Accommodations to Social Forces in the 1940s."
  IN: <u>Current Research in Film /v. 1</u>

2579 Haralovich, Mary Beth.
"*All That Heaven Allows*: Color, Narrative Space, and Melodrama."
  IN: <u>Close Viewings</u>

2580 Harcourt, Peter.
"In Defense of Film History."
  IN: <u>Perspectives on the Study of Film</u>

2581 Harcourt, Peter.
"Adaptation Through Inversion: Wenders's *Wrong Movement* Freely Based on *Wilhelm Meister's Apprenticeship* by Johann Wolfgang Goethe."
  IN: <u>Modern European Filmmakers ...</u>

2582 Harcourt, Peter.
"Introduction: A Note on Film Criticism."
"The Reality of Sergei Eisenstein."
"A Flight from Passion: Images of Uncertainty in the Work of Jean Renoir."
"Luis Buñuel: Spaniard and Surrealist."
"The Troubled Pilgrimage of Ingmar Bergman."
"The Secret Life of Federico Fellini."
"Godard le fou: a Glimpse of the Struggle between Love and Politics in the Work of Jean-Luc Godard."
  IN: <u>Six European Directors</u>

2583 Harcourt, Peter.
"The Secret Life of Federico Fellini."
  IN: <u>Federico Fellini</u>

2584 Harding, Ann.
"Unique and Extraordinary ..."
  IN: <u>Celebrity Articles ...</u>

2585 Hardison, O.B.
"The Rhetoric of Hitchcock's Thrillers."
  IN: <u>Man and the Movies</u>
    <u>Film and the Liberal Arts</u>

Hardy, Andrew P. SEE: Faber, Ronald J.

2586 Hardy, Gene.
"*The Hobbit* [novel by] J.R.R. Tolkien. More Than a Magic Ring."
  IN: <u>Children's Novels and the Movies</u>

2587 Hardy, H. Forsyth.
"British Documentaries in the War."
  IN: <u>The Documentary Tradition /1 ed</u>
    <u>The Documentary Tradition /2 ed</u>
    <u>Nonfiction Film Theory and Criticism</u>

2588 Hardy, Forsyth.
"Censorship and Film Societies."
  IN: <u>Footnotes to the Film</u>

2589 Hare, Harlow.
"*The Birth of a Nation*."
  IN: <u>Focus on The Birth of a Nation</u>

2590 **Hark, Ina Rae.**
"Revalidating Patriarchy: Why Hitchcock Remade *The Man Who Knew Too Much*."
IN: <u>Hitchcock's Re-Released Films</u>

2591 **Harman, Gilbert.**
"Eco-location."
"Semiotics and the Cinema: Metz and Wollen."
IN: <u>Film Theory and Criticism /2 ed</u>

2592 **Harmetz, Aljean.**
"Mary Pickford--America's [Gothic] Sweetheart."
"Cocaine and Hollywood."
"Ms. Rona: Don't Call Her a Gossip." [RE: Rona Barrett.]
"What Price Glory at Columbia."
"Jack Nicholson—Odd Man Out."
"Hollywood's Hot New Screen Writer." [RE: Lawrence Kasdan.]
"Jessica Lange--Film Star Whose Future Is Here."
"Rating the Ratings."
"Astaire at 80."
"The $110,000 Blunder, or the Man Who Couldn't Work Miracles." [RE: Barry Jagoda.]
"ReCooping: The Rise and Fall and Rise of a Child Star." [RE: Jackie Cooper.]
"Peckinpah: 'Man Was a Killer Long Before He Served God'."
"The Dime-Store Way to Make Movies." [RE: Samuel Z. Arkoff.]
"How Hollywood Decides If a Film Is a Hit."
"Reap the Wilder Wind." [RE: Billy Wilder.]
"Fonda at Forty." [RE: Jane Fonda.]
"Video Wars: Hollywood's Corporate Rollerderby."
"The Man with No Name Is a Big Name Now." [RE: Clint Eastwood.]
"How a Hollywood Rumor Was Born, Flourished, and Died."
"Barbara Stanwyck: Still a Golden Girl."
"Martin Ritt: Survivor Extraordinaire."
"The Anatomy of the Sneak Preview."
"Today's Hottest Movie Stars." [RE: *Star Wars*.]
"From A(dolph) to Z(ukor)."
"The Great and Powerful Wizard of Lucasfilm." [RE: George Lucas.]
IN: <u>Rolling Breaks</u>

2593 **Harper, Sue.**
"Historical Pleasures: Gainsborough Costume Melodrama."
IN: <u>Home Is Where the Heart Is</u>

2594 **Harper, Sue.**
"The Representation of Women in British Feature Films, 1939-45."
IN: <u>Britain and the Cinema ...</u>

2595 **Harrie, Ivar.**
"Ingmar Bergman Wants to be the Kaj Munk of Sweden."
IN: <u>Focus on The Seventh Seal</u>

2596 **Harrington, Curtis.**
"*Rashomon* and the Japanese Cinema."
IN: <u>Focus on Rashomon</u>

2597 **Harrington, Curtis.**
"Ghoulies and Ghosties."
IN: <u>Focus on The Horror Film</u>

2598 **Harrington, John.**
"*Wuthering Heights* [novel by] Emily Bronte; *Wuthering Heights* [film by] William Wyler. Wyler as Auteur."
IN: <u>The English Novel and the Movies</u>

2599 **Harris, Hilary.**
"Thoughts on Movement."
IN: <u>The Movies as Medium</u>

2600 **Harris, Jack H.**
"Jack H. Harris." [An interview.]
IN: <u>Interviews with B ...</u>

2600a **Harris, Neil.**
"A Subversive Form."
IN: <u>Before Hollywood</u>

2601 **Harris, Thomas J.**
"*12 Angry Men*."
"*Witness for the Prosecution*."
"*I Want to Live!*."
"*Compulsion*."
"*Anatomy of a Murder*."
"*Inherit the Wind*."
"*Judgment at Nuremberg*."
"*The Verdict*."
IN: <u>Courtroom's Finest Hour ...</u>

2601a **Harris, Thomas.**
"The Building of Popular Images: Grace Kelly and Marilyn Monroe."
IN: <u>Stardom</u>

2602 **Harrison, Carey.**
"*Blow-Up*."
IN: <u>Focus on Blow-Up</u>

2603 **Harrison, Carey.**
"*The Taming of the Shrew* [1966]."
IN: <u>Focus on Shakespearean Films</u>

2604 **Harrison, Harry.**
"A Cannibalized Novel Becomes *Soylent Green*."
IN: <u>Omni's Screen Flights ...</u>

2605 **Harrison, Louis Reeves.**
"*The Squaw Man*."
IN: <u>The First Tycoons</u>

2606 **Harrison, Tony.**
"Losing Touch."
IN: <u>Projections: A Forum ...</u>

2607 **Harrisson, Tom.**
"Films and the Home Front--the Evaluation of Their Effectiveness by 'Mass-Observation'."
IN: <u>Propaganda, Politics and Film</u>

2608 **Harsh, Donna J.**
"*The Lion, the Witch, and the Wardrobe* [novel by]
C.S. Lewis. Aslan in Filmland: The Animation of
Narnia."
IN: Children's Novels and the Movies

2609 **Hart, Henry.**
"*The Seventh Seal.*"
IN: Focus on The Seventh Seal

2610 **Hart, Henry.**
"*Rashomon.*"
IN: Introduction to the Art of the Movies

2611 **Hart, Nancy K.**
"Edward Dmytryk."
IN: Close Up: The Contract Director

2612 **Hart, Nancy K.**
"Frank Capra."
IN: Close-Up: The Hollywood Director

2613 **Hart, Nancy K. and Tom Flinn.**
"William Dieterle."
IN: Close Up: The Contract Director

2614 **Hart, Richard.**
"Richard Hart." [Interview by Kris Malkiewicz.]
IN: Film Lighting

2615 **Hart, William S.**
"Living Your Character."
IN: Hollywood Directors 1914-1940

2616 **Hart, William S.**
"Working for Ince."
IN: The First Film Makers

2617 **Hartley, Hal.**
"Knowing Is Not Enough."
"Surviving Desire."
IN: Projections: A Forum ...

2618 **Hartman, Geoffrey H.**
"Between the Acts: Jeanne Moreau's *Lumière*."
"The Dubious Charm of M. Truffaut."
"Plenty of Nothing: Hitchcock's *North by Northwest*."
IN: Easy Pieces

2619 **Hartman, Geoffrey.**
"*The Exterminating Angel.*"
IN: The Movie That Changed My Life

2620 **Hartman, Michael.**
"Sydney Boehm."
IN: Dictionary of Literary Biography /v. 44

2621 **Hartog, Simon.**
"State Protection of a Beleaguered Industry."
IN: British Cinema History

2622 **Hartog, Simon, Annette Michelson, Peter Gidal
and Michael Snow.**
"[On] Michael Snow."
IN: Structural Film Anthology

2623 **Hartung, Philip T.**
"The Future of Film."
IN: Film: Readings in the Mass Media

2624 **Harvey, Anthony.**
"Anthony Harvey." [Interview by John Andrew
Gallagher.]
IN: Film Directors on Directing

2625 **Harvey, James.**
"Lubitsch: The Naughty Operetta."
"Lubitsch: A 'Serious' Film."
"Lubitsch: Comedies Without Music."
"Frank Capra."
"Powell and Loy."
"Astaire and Rogers."
"Carole Lombard."
"Irene Dunne."
"Leo McCarey."
"Cary Grant."
"Ginger Rogers."
"Claudette Colbert."
"Jean Arthur."
"Lubitsch in the Late Thirties."
"George Stevens."
"Howard Hawks."
"Lubitsch in the Forties."
"Sturges: 'Genius at Work'."
"Sturges: American Success."
"Sturges: The Stanwyck Films."
"Sturges: The McCrea Films."
"Sturges: The Eddie Bracken Films."
"Sturges: A Black Comedy."
"Interview with Irene Dunne."
IN: Romantic Comedy

2626 **Harvey, Stephen.**
"Autant-Lara's *Douce*."
IN: Rediscovering French Film

2627 **Harvey, Stephen.**
"Fred Astaire."
"Ingrid Bergman."
"Joan Crawford."
IN: The Movie Star: The National ...

2628 **Harvey, Sylvia.**
"An Introduction to *The Song of the Shirt*."
IN: Films for Women

2629 **Harvey, Sylvia.**
"The 'Other Cinema' in Britain: Unfinished Business in
Oppositional and Independent Film, 1929-1984."
IN: All Our Yesterdays

2630 **Harvey, Sylvia.**
"Woman's Place: The Absent Family of Film Noir."
IN: Women in Film Noir

Harvey, Sylvia. SEE: Blanchard, Simon.

Harvill, Jerry G. SEE: Palmgreen, Philip.

2631 **Harwin, Judith and Shirley Otto.**
"Women, Alcohol and the Screen."
IN: Images of Alcoholism

2632 **Haskell, Molly.**
"[From:] *From Reverence to Rape*: The Woman's Film."
IN: Film Theory and Criticism /2 ed

2633 **Haskell, Molly.**
"From Reverence to Rape: The Treatment of Women in the Movies."
IN: Star Texts

2634 **Haskell, Molly.**
"[From:] *From Reverence to Rape*: Female Stars of the 1940s."
IN: Film Theory and Criticism /4 ed

2635 **Haskell, Molly.**
"*Man's Favorite Sport?* (Revisited)."
IN: Focus on Howard Hawks

2636 **Haskell, Molly.**
"*Madame de*: A Musical Passage."
"Lina Wertmüller: Swept Away on a Wave of Sexism."
IN: Sexual Stratagems

2637 **Haskell, Molly.**
"*One Flew Over the Cuckoo's Nest* [novel by] Ken Kesey. Kesey Cured: Forman's Sweet Insanity."
IN: The Modern American Novel ...

2638 **Haskell, Molly.**
"*Sleeper*."
"*The Heartbreak Kid*."
"Marriage Cukor Style."
"Women and the Silent Comedians."
IN: Movie Comedy

2639 **Haskell, Molly.**
"Are Women Directors Different?"
"Liv Ullmann: The Goddess as Ordinary Woman."
IN: Women and the Cinema

2640 **Haskell, Molly.**
"Burt Reynolds."
"Gould vs. Redford vs. Nicholson: The Absurdist as Box-Office Draw."
"Gregory Peck."
"Jodie Foster and Tatum O'Neal."
"Doris Day."
IN: The Movie Star: The National ...

2641 **Haskell, Molly.**
"Eric Rohmer."
"Howard Hawks."
IN: Cinema: A Critical Dictionary

2642 **Haskell, Molly.**
"Film criticism and feminism ..."
IN: The Cineaste Interviews

2643 **Haskell, Molly.**
"Ideological Criticism: The Uses and Abuses of a Feminist Approach to Film."
IN: Ideas of Order in Literature & Film

2644 **Haskell, Molly.**
"Marlon Brando."

IN: Awake in the Dark

2645 **Haskell, Molly.**
"Three Documentaries." [RE: *Johnny Cash*; *A Married Couple*; *Other Voices*.]
IN: The Documentary Tradition /1 ed
The Documentary Tradition /2 ed

2646 **Hathaway, Henry.**
"Henry Hathaway." [Interview by John Kobal.]
IN: People Will Talk

2646a **Hatt, Harold.**
"*Notorious*: Penance as a Paradigm of Redemption."
IN: Image and Likeness

2647 **Haugmard, Louis.**
"The 'Aesthetic' of the Cinematograph."
IN: French Film Theory and Criticism /v. 1

2648 **Hauser, Arnold.**
"Space and Time in the Film."
IN: Film: A Montage of Theories

2649 **Hauser, Arnold.**
"Surrealistic Art and the Film."
IN: Film and the Liberal Arts

2650 **Hauser, Arnold.**
"The Film Age."
IN: A Casebook on Film
Film: An Anthology
Conflict and Control in the Cinema

2651 **Havetta, Elo.**
"Elo Havetta." [Interview by Antonín J. Liehm.]
IN: Closely Watched Films

2652 **Hawes, Stanley.**
"Grierson in Australia."
IN: An Australian Film Reader

2653 **Hawks, Howard.**
"Howard Hawks." [Interview by John Kobal.]
IN: People Will Talk

2654 **Hawks, Howard.**
"Howard Hawks." [Interview by Richard Schickel.]
IN: The Men Who Made the Movies

2655 **Hawks, Howard.**
"Howard Hawks." [Interview by Andrew Sarris.]
IN: Interviews with Film Directors

2656 **Hawn, Goldie.**
"Goldie Hawn." [Interview by Rex Reed.]
IN: Travolta to Keaton

2657 **Haworth, Bryan.**
"Film in the Classroom."
IN: The Historian and Film

2658 **Hayakawa, S.I.**
"Television and the American Negro."
IN: Sight, Sound, and Society

2659 **Haydon, Tom.**
"*The British Empire* [Interview with] Tom Haydon."
IN: The Documentary Conscience

2660 **Hayes, John Michael.**
""You Go And Talk With Cary—Delay, Delay, Til It's Too Late'--" [RE: an interview.]
IN: Blueprint on Babylon

2661 **Hays, Will H.**
"Supervision from Within."
IN: The Story of the Films

2662 **Hays, Will H.**
"The Motion Picture Industry."
IN: The Movies in Our Midst

2663 **Hayward, Susan.**
"Gender Politics--Cocteau's Belle Is Not that Bête: Jean Cocteau's *La Belle et la Bête*."
"Beyond the gaze and into *femme-filmécriture*: Agnès Varda's *Sans toit ni loi*."
IN: French Film: Texts and Contexts

2664 **Hazam, Lou.**
"Documentaries and Dollars."
IN: The Documentary Tradition /1 ed
The Documentary Tradition /2 ed

2665 **Head, Edith.**
"Costume Design."
IN: Hollywood Speaks!

2666 **Head, Edith.**
"The Costume Designer."
IN: Filmmakers on Filmmaking /v. 2

2667 **Heath, Stephen.**
"*Jaws*, Ideology and Film Theory."
IN: Popular Television and Film
Movies and Methods /v. 2

2668 **Heath, Stephen.**
"Comment on 'The Idea of Authorship'."
IN: Theories of Authorship

2669 **Heath, Stephen.**
"Language, Sight and Sound."
IN: Cinema and Language

2670 **Heath, Stephen.**
"Narrative Space."
IN: Narrative, Apparatus, Ideology

2671 **Heath, Stephen.**
"Questions of Property: Film and Nationhood."
"The Turn of the Subject."
IN: Explorations in Film Theory

2672 **Heath, Stephen.**
"The Cinematic Apparatus: Technology as Historical and Cultural Form."
IN: The Cinematic Apparatus

2673 **Hecht, Ben.**
"A Child of the Century."
IN: The Movies in Our Midst

2674 **Hecht, Ben.**
"Elegy for Wonderland."
IN: The Movies: An American Idiom

2675 **Hecht, Ben.**
"Enter, the Movies."
IN: Film: An Anthology

2676 **Hecht, Ben.**
"The Common Man."
IN: The Best of Rob Wagner's Script

2677 **Hecht, Chandra.**
"Total Institutions on Celluloid: Wiseman Films."
IN: Film in Society

2678 **Heck-Rabi, Louise.**
"Alice Guy-Blache: Photoplay Pioneer."
"Germaine Dulac: Mother of Surrealism."
"Lois Weber: Moralist Moviemaker."
"Dorothy Arzner: An Image of Independence."
"Leni Riefenstahl: A Crystal Grotto."
"Muriel Box: 'Let Me Entertain You'."
"Maya Deren: Delicate Magician of Film."
"Ida Lupino: Daring the Family Tradition."
"Mai Zetterling: The Uncompromiser."
"Shirley Clarke: Reality Rendered."
"Agnes Varda: From an Underground River."
IN: Women Filmmakers

2679 **Hedges, Inez.**
"Breaking the Frame: *Zazie* and Film Language."
"Film Writing and the Poetics of Silence."
"Forms of Representation in *La Nuit de Varennes*."
"Truffaut and Cocteau: Representations of Orpheus."
"Mediated Vision: Women's Subjectivity."
"Women and Film Space."
"Scripting Children's Minds: *E.T.* and *The Wizard of Oz*."
"The Myth of the Perfect Woman: Cinema as Machine Célibataire." [RE: Catherine Deneuve.]
IN: Breaking the Frame

2680 **Hedges, Inez.**
"Constellated Visions: Robert Desnos's and Man Ray's *L'Etoile de mer*."
IN: Dada and Surrealist Film

Hedges, Inez. SEE: Metz, Christian.

2681 **Heim, Alan.**
"Alan Heim." [Interview by Vincent LoBrutto.]
IN: Selected Takes

2682 **Hein, Birgit.**
"Some Notes about Our Film Work."
IN: West German Filmmakers on Film

2683 **Hein, Birgit.**
"[On] Birgit and Wilhelm Hein."
IN: Structural Film Anthology

2684 **Heinlein, Robert A.**
"Shooting *Destination Moon*."
IN: Focus on The Science Fiction Film

2685 **Heldreth, Leonard G.**
"The Beast Within: Sexuality and Metamorphosis in Horror Films."

IN: Eros in the Mind's Eye

2686 Helge, Ladislav.
"Ladislav Helge." [Interview by Antonín J. Liehm.]
IN: Closely Watched Films

2687 Heller, Franklin.
"Mel Brooks."
IN: Directors in Action

2688 Heller, Joseph.
"*Catch-22* [novel by] Joseph Heller. A Discussion with Joseph Heller."
IN: The Modern American Novel ...

2689 Hellmann, John.
"Vietnam and the Hollywood Genre Film: Inversions of American Mythology in *The Deer Hunter* and *Apocalypse Now*."
"Rambo's Vietnam and Kennedy's New Frontier."
IN: Inventing Vietnam

Helm, David M. SEE: Palmgreen, Philip.

2690 Helprin, Morris.
"The Making of *Que viva Mexico!*."
IN: The Documentary Tradition /1 ed
The Documentary Tradition /2 ed

2691 Hemingway, Ernest.
"A Tribute to Mamma from Papa Hemingway (On Marlene Dietrich)."
IN: Authors on Film

2692 Hemmeter, Thomas.
"Twisted Writing: *Rope* as an Experimental Film."
IN: Hitchcock's Re-Released Films

2693 Hemmeter, Thomas and Kevin W. Sweeney.
"Marriage as Moral Community: Cinematic Critiques of Hemingway's *To Have and Have Not*."
IN: A Moving Picture Feast

2694 Hemming, Roy.
"Harold Arlen."
"Irving Berlin."
"George Gershwin."
"Jerome Kern."
"Jimmy McHugh."
"Cole Porter."
"Ralph Rainger."
"Richard Rodgers."
"Harry Warren."
"Richard Whiting."
IN: The Melody Lingers On

2695 Hemple, Amy.
"*3 Women*."
IN: The Movie That Changed My Life

2696 Hemsing, Albert.
"Labor and the Film."
IN: Ideas on Film

2697 Henabery, Joseph.
"*Intolerance*."
IN: The First Film Makers

2698 Henderson, Archibald.
"Table-Talk of G.B.S.: The Drama, the Theatre and the Films."
IN: Focus on Film and Theatre

2699 Henderson, Brian.
"The Structure of Bazin's Thought."
"*Godard on Godard*: Notes for a Reading."
"Metz: *Essais I* and Film Theory."
"Segmentation."
"Film Semiotics as Semiotics."
IN: A Critique of Film Theory

2700 Henderson, Brian.
"Critique of Cine-Structuralism (Part I)."
IN: Theories of Authorship

2701 Henderson, Brian.
"Critique of Cine-Structuralism."
IN: Conflict and Control in the Cinema
A Critique of Film Theory

2702 Henderson, Brian.
"*The Searchers*: An American Dilemma."
IN: Movies and Methods /v. 2

2703 Henderson, Brian.
"Cartoon and Narrative in the Films of Frank Tashlin and Preston Sturges."
IN: Comedy/Cinema/Theory

2704 Henderson, Brian.
"Romantic Comedy Today: Semi-Tough or Impossible?"
IN: Film Genre Reader

2705 Henderson, Brian.
"Toward a Non-Bourgeois Camera Style." [RE: Godard's late films.]
IN: Film Theory and Criticism /2 ed
A Critique of Film Theory
Movies and Methods: An Anthology

2706 Henderson, Brian.
"The Long Take."
"Two Types of Film Theory." [RE: Eisenstein and Bazin.]
IN: Movies and Methods: An Anthology
A Critique of Film Theory

2707 Henderson, Brian.
"*Targets*: An Unshielding Darkness."
IN: Focus on The Horror Film

2708 Henderson, Lisa.
"Access and Consent in Public Photography."
IN: Image Ethics

2709 Henderson, Randell.
"Assistant Director."
IN: Hollywood Speaks!

2710 Henderson, Robert M.
"Biograph."
IN: The First Tycoons

2711 **Hendricks, Gordon.**
"The Kinetoscope: Fall Motion Picture Production."
IN: Film Before Griffith

2712 **Hendricks, Gordon (cataloguer).**
"A Collection of Edison Films."
IN: Image on the Art ...

2713 **Hendricks, Gordon.**
"The History of the Kinetoscope."
IN: The American Film Industry
The American Film Industry /rev ed

2714 **Hennebelle, Guy.**
"Cinema Djidid."
IN: Algerian Cinema

2715 **Hennebelle, Guy.**
"French Radical Documentary After May 1968."
IN: Show Us Life

2716 **Henning-Jensen, Bjarne.**
"The Situation of the Serious Filmmaker."
IN: Film: Book 1

Henreid, Paul. SEE: Reiner, Carl.

2717 **Henry, Buck.**
"Buck Henry." [Interview by William Froug.]
IN: The Screenwriter Looks ...

2717a **Henry, Buck.**
"Buck Henry." [Interview by Anthony Loeb.]
IN: Filmmakers in Conversation

2718 **Henry, Michael.**
"Brian DePalma."
IN: American Directors /v. 2

2719 **Henry, Ralph L.**
"The Cultural Influence of the 'Talkies'."
IN: The Movies in Our Midst

2720 **Henstell, Bruce.**
"*Here Comes Mr. Jordan*: From Script to Screen."
IN: The American Film Heritage

2721 **Hepburn, Audrey.**
"The Costume Makes the Actors: A Personal View."
IN: Fashion in Film

2722 **Hepburn, Katharine.**
"Katharine Hepburn." [Interview by John Kobal.]
IN: People Will Talk

2723 **Hepburn, Katharine.**
"Katharine Hepburn." [Interview by Charles Higham.]
IN: Celebrity Circus

2724 **Hepworth, Cecil.**
"Those Were the Days."
IN: Film Makers on Film Making

2725 **Herbst, Helmut.**
"New German Cinema, 1962-83: A View from Hamburg."
IN: West German Filmmakers on Film

2726 **Herman, Gerald.**
"Documentary, Newsreel, and Television News as Factual Resources in the History Classroom."
IN: Image as Artifact

Herman, Peter J. SEE: Ayer, Douglas.

Herman, William. SEE: DeNitto, Dennis.

2727 **Hernandez, Andres R.**
"Filmmaking and Politics, The Cuban Experience."
IN: Conflict and Control in the Cinema

2728 **Hernando, Mario A.**
"Ishmael Bernal: Merging Art and Commercialism."
IN: Readings in Philippine Cinema

2729 **Herold, Don.**
"Don Herold." [Collected film capsules.]
IN: Garbo and the Night Watchmen

2730 **Herold, Don.**
"Los Angeles--A Pain in the Neck to New York."
IN: The Best of Rob Wagner's Script

2731 **Herring, Billie Grace.**
"Library and Learning Resources: How Will Copyright Apply?"
IN: Fair Use and Free Inquiry

2732 **Herring, Robert.**
"Film Imagery: Seastrom."
IN: Hollywood Destinies

2733 **Herring, Robert.**
"Robert Herring." [Collected film capsules.]
IN: Garbo and the Night Watchmen

2734 **Herrmann, Bernard.**
"Score for a Film."
IN: Focus on Citizen Kane

2735 **Herrmann, Bernard.**
"Reminiscence and Reflection: à Composer."
IN: Sound and the Cinema

2736 **Herzog, Charlotte.**
"'Powder Puff' Promotion: The Fashion Show-in-the-Film."
IN: Fabrications

2736a **Herzog, Charlotte Cornelia and Jane Marie Gaines.**
"'Puffed Sleeves Before Tea-Time': Joan Crawford, Adrian and Women Audiences."
IN: Stardom

2737 **Herzog, Werner.**
"Tribute to Lotte Eisner."
IN: West German Filmmakers on Film

2738 **Herzstein, Robert E.**
"Newsfilm and Documentary as Sources for Factual Information."
IN: Image as Artifact

2739 **Hess, John.**
"Collective Experience, Synthetic Forms: El Salvador's Radio Venceremos."

2766 **Hill, Elbert R.**
"*A Hero Ain't Nothin' But A Sandwich* [novel by] Alice Childress. *A Hero* for the Movies."
IN: Children's Novels and the Movies

2767 **Hill, Geoffrey.**
"From Cave Shadows to the Silver Screen: The Wisdom of Cinemyth."
"From Formalism to Cinemasophia: Film Analysis."
"*The Sailor Who Fell from Grace with the Sea*: The Religion of the Nietzschean Samurai Warriors."
"*The Seventh Seal*: A Morality Play of the Feminine Principle."
"*It's a Wonderful Life*: Saint George and the Dragon."
"*Insignificance*: The Destruction of Universal Significance."
"*A Year of the Quiet Sun*: Amazing Grace."
"*Shane*: The Ambivalent, Violent Prince of Peace."
"*Babette's Feast* and *The Cook, the Thief, His Wife and Her Lover*: Two Stories of Redemptive Ritual Sacrifice."
"*Little Shop of Horrors*: The Battle between Heaven and Earth."
"*The Trip to Bountiful*: Paradise Regained."
"*The Graduate*: The Terrible Mother from the Black Lagoon."
"*Blue Velvet*: Embracing the Shadow."
"*Santa Sangre*: The Bloody Alchemy of the Soul."
"*Rumble Fish*: The Motorcycle Messiah."
"*Taxi Driver*: The Mad Messiah of Historic Christian Art."
"*Repo Man*: A Prophet of Time Travel."
"*Field of Dreams*: Seeing the Invisible."
IN: Illuminating Shadows

2768 **Hill, John.**
"Working Class Realism and Sexual Reaction: Some Theses on the British 'New Wave'."
IN: British Cinema History

2769 **Hill, Pamela.**
"Pamela Hill." [An interview.]
IN: Producers on Producing

2770 **Hill, Steven P.**
"A Quantitative View of Soviet Cinema."
IN: Cinema Examined

2771 **Hillier, Jim.**
"French Cinema."
"American Cinema."
"Italian Cinema."
"Criticism."
"CinemaScope."
IN: Cahiers du Cinéma, The 1950s

2772 **Hillier, Jim.**
"[American Cinema:] The Apotheosis of *mise en scène*."
"*Cahiers du Cinéma* in the 1960s."
"Re-thinking and Re-making French cinema."
"Re-thinking American Cinema."
"Re-thinking the Function of Cinema and Criticism."
IN: Cahiers du Cinéma, 1960-1968

2773 **Hillier, Jim.**
"Arthur Penn."
IN: Focus on Bonnie and Clyde

2774 **Hillier, Jim.**
"Humphrey Jennings."
IN: Studies in Documentary

Hillier, Jim. SEE: Cameron, Ian.

2775 **Hillmer, Melanie.**
"The Cinema in the Wardrobe: A Stroll through Seven Decades."
IN: Fashion in Film

2776 **Hilmes, Michele.**
"Pay Television: Breaking the Broadcast Bottleneck."
IN: Hollywood in the Age of Television

2777 **Hinde, John.**
"*Barry McKenzie* and *Alvin*, Ten Years Later."
IN: An Australian Film Reader

2778 **Hinds, Nanda and Rick Berman.**
"[A History of Italian Cinema:] 1927-1943."
IN: Italian Cinema

2779 **Hines, Kay.**
"Three Sequences from *Blow-Up*: A Shot Analysis."
IN: Focus on Blow-Up

2780 **Hinojosa, Rolando.**
"*I Am Joaquín*: Relationships Between the Text and the Film."
IN: Chicano Cinema

2781 **Hinson, Hal.**
"*Hamburger Hill*."
"*The Dressmaker*."
"*The Adventures of Baron Munchhausen*."
"*The Good Mother*."
IN: Produced and Abandoned

2782 **Hirano, Kyoko.**
"*The Japanese Tragedy*: Film Censorship and the American Occupation."
IN: Resisting Images

2783 **Hirano, Kyoko.**
"Japan."
IN: World Cinema Since 1945

2784 **Hirsch, Foster.**
"*Midnight Cowboy*."
IN: Sexuality in the Movies

2785 **Hirsch, Tina.**
"Tina Hirsch." [Interview by Vincent LoBrutto.]
IN: Selected Takes

2786 **Hitchcock, Alfred.**
"Direction."
IN: Film: Readings in the Mass Media
Footnotes to the Film
Film: A Montage of Theories
Focus on Hitchcock

2787 Hitchcock, Alfred.
"Production Methods Compared."
IN: <u>Hollywood Directors 1941-1976</u>

2788 Hitchcock, Alfred.
"My Own Methods."
IN: <u>Sight and Sound</u>

2789 Hitchcock, Alfred.
"Pete Martin Calls on Hitchcock."
IN: <u>Film Makers on Film Making</u>

2790 Hitchcock, Alfred.
"Alfred Hitchcock." [Interview by Richard Schickel.]
IN: <u>The Men Who Made the Movies</u>

2791 Hitchcock, Alfred.
"Alfred Hitchcock."
IN: <u>The Celluloid Muse</u>

2792 Hitchcock, Alfred.
"Alfred Hitchcock." [Interview by Charles Higham.]
IN: <u>Celebrity Circus</u>

2793 Hitchcock, Alfred.
"Rear Window."
IN: <u>Focus on Hitchcock</u>

2794 Hitchcock, Alfred.
"Alfred Hitchcock." [Interview by Charles T. Samuels.]
IN: <u>Encountering Directors</u>

2795 Hitchcock, Alfred.
"Alfred Hitchcock." [Interview by Andrew Sarris.]
IN: <u>Interviews with Film Directors</u>

2796 Hitchcock, Henry-Russell, Jr.
"Periodical Reviews: Movie Magazines [1928]."
IN: <u>Hound & Horn</u>

2797 Hitchens, Gordon.
"On Abraham Polonsky."
IN: <u>The Image Maker</u>

2798 Hjertén, Hanserik.
"The Seventh Seal."
IN: <u>Focus on The Seventh Seal</u>

2799 Hoberman, J.
"Smorgasbord."
"The Company of Wolves."
"Under the Cherry Moon."
IN: <u>Produced and Abandoned</u>

2800 Hoberman, J.
"A Face to the *Shtetl*: Soviet Yiddish Cinema, 1924-36."
IN: <u>Inside the Film Factory</u>

2801 Hobson, Allan.
"Dream Image and Substrate: Bergman's Films and the Psychology of Sleep."
IN: <u>Film and Dream</u>

2802 Hobson, Harold.
"Secret of Success."
IN: <u>Film and Society</u>

2803 Hodeir, André.
"The Marx Brothers."
IN: <u>Cinema: A Critical Dictionary</u>

2804 Hodgens, Richard.
"A Brief, Tragical History of the Science Fiction Film."
IN: <u>Focus on The Science Fiction Film</u>

2805 Hodsdon, Barrett.
"The Avant-garde Impulse and Australian Narrative: *Palm Beach* in context."
IN: <u>An Australian Film Reader</u>

2806 Hofsess, John.
"Claude Jutra."
"Alan King."
"Don Shebib."
"Jack Darcus."
"Graeme Ferguson."
"Frank Vitale."
"William Fruet."
"Paul Almond."
"Denys Arcand."
"Pierre Berton."
IN: <u>Inner Views</u>

2807 Hogan, David J.
"Lugosi, Lee, and the Vampire Lovers."
"High Priestess of Horror: Barbara Steele."
"Hitch."
"The Ironic Universe of Roger Corman."
"Prince of Perversity: Edward D. Wood, Jr."
"The Spawn of Herschell Gordon Lewis."
IN: <u>Dark Romance</u>

2808 Hogan, John V.L.
"The Early Days of Television."
IN: <u>A Technological History ...</u>

2809 Hogenkamp, Bert.
"The Workers' Film Movement in Britain, 1929-39."
IN: <u>Propaganda, Politics and Film</u>

2810 Hogenkamp, Bert.
"Workers' Newsreels in Germany, the Netherlands, and Japan During the Twenties and Thirties."
IN: <u>Show Us Life</u>

2811 Hoggard, Lynn.
"Writing with the Ink of Light: Jean Cocteau's *Beauty and the Beast*."
IN: <u>Film and Literature: A Comparative ...</u>

2812 Hoggatt, John P.
"Four Days in November."
IN: <u>The Documentary Tradition /1 ed</u>
       <u>The Documentary Tradition /2 ed</u>

2812a Hohr, Hal.
"Interview with Hal Hohr." [Interview by Leonard Maltin.]
IN: <u>The Art of the Cinematographer</u>

Holbrook, Morris B. SEE: Dodds, John C.

2813 **Holder, Nancy.**
"Why *The Haunting* Is So Damn Scary."
IN: Cut!: Horror Writers ...

2814 **Holender, Adam.**
"Adam Holender." [Interview by Kris Malkiewicz.]
IN: Film Lighting

2815 **Holland, Norman A [*sic*, N].**
"Meaning and Defense."
IN: Film And/As Literature

2816 **Holland, Norman N.**
"The Follies Fellini." [RE: *La Dolce Vita*.]
IN: Renaissance of the Film

2817 **Holland, Norman N.**
"*The Seventh Seal*: The Film as Iconography."
IN: Renaissance of the Film
The Classic Cinema

2818 **Holland, Norman N.**
"Movies You Are Not Supposed To Dig."
IN: Sight, Sound, and Society

2819 **Holloway, Ronald.**
"Bulgaria: The Cinema of Poetics."
IN: Post New Wave Cinema ...

2820 **Holloway, Ronald.**
"The Short Film in Eastern Europe: Art and Politics of Cartoon and Puppets."
IN: Politics, Art and Commitment ...

2821 **Hollyman, Burnes St. Patrick.**
"The First Picture Shows: Austin, Texas, 1894-1913."
"Alexander Black's Picture Plays, 1893-1894."
IN: Film Before Griffith

2822 **Holmes, John Clellon.**
"A Decade of Coming Attractions."
IN: The Movies: An American Idiom

2823 **Holte, Jim.**
"Pilgrims in Space: Puritan Ideology and the American Science Fiction Film."
IN: Eros in the Mind's Eye

2824 **Homans, Peter.**
"Puritanism Revisited: An Analysis of the Contemporary Screen-Image Western."
IN: Focus on The Western

2825 **Hondo, Abid Med.**
"The Cinema of Exile."
IN: Film and Politics in the Third World

2826 **Hood, Stuart.**
"A Cool Look at the Legend." [RE: British Free Cinema.]
IN: Journey To a Legend and Back

2827 **Hood, Stuart.**
"John Grierson and the Documentary Film Movement."
IN: British Cinema History

2828 **Höök, Marianne.**
"Ingmar Bergman: Craftsman and Visionary."
IN: Focus on The Seventh Seal

2829 **Hopkins, Arthur.**
"Hollywood Takes over the Theatre."
IN: Celebrity Articles ...

2830 **Hopkins, Miriam.**
"Miriam Hopkins." [Interview by John Kobal.]
IN: People Will Talk

2831 **Hopper, Dennis.**
"Dennis Hopper." [Interview by John Andrew Gallagher.]
IN: Film Directors on Directing

2832 **Horak, Jan-Christopher.**
"*The Last of the Mohicans* [novel by] James Fenimore Cooper. Maurice Tourneur's Tragic Romance."
IN: The Classic American Novel ...

2833 **Horak, Jan-Christopher.**
"Postwar Traumas in Klaren's *Wozzeck*."
IN: German Film and Literature

2834 **Horak, Jan-Christopher.**
"The Pre-Hollywood Lubitsch."
"Southern Landscapes of the Mind's Eye: Griffith's *The White Rose*."
IN: Image on the Art ...

2835 **Horak, Jan-Christopher.**
"W.H. or the Mysteries of Walking in Ice."
IN: The Films of Werner Herzog

2836 **Horak, Jan-Christopher.**
"Pabst in Hollywood: *A Modern Hero*."
IN: The Films of G.W. Pabst

2836a **Horak, Jan-Christopher.**
"Eros, Thanatos, and the Will to Myth: Prussian Films in German Cinema."
IN: Framing the Past

2837 **Horikawa, Herbert.**
"Psychological Implications of the Asian Stereotypes in the Media."
IN: Ethnic Images ...

2838 **Horn, Camilla.**
"Camilla Horn." [Interview by John Kobal.]
IN: People Will Talk

2839 **Horne, James.**
"James Horne's Own Story."
IN: Hollywood Directors 1914-1940

2840 **Horner, Harry.**
"The Production Designer."
IN: Filmmakers on Filmmaking /v. 2

2841 **Horner, William R.**
"Bad as They Come: Jack Elam, Neville Brand, Lee Van Cleef."
"The Rednecks: Bo Hopkins, Luke Askew, Bill McKinney."
"Inspector Callahan's Nemesis: Andrew Robinson."
"Hell on Horseback: Robert Donner, L.Q. Jones, Strother Martin."

IN: Bad at the Bijou

2842 **Horowitz, Alan S.**
"Woody Allen."
IN: Dictionary of Literary Biography /v. 44

2843 **Horowitz, Irving Louis.**
"*The Discreet Charm of the Bourgeoisie*." [NOTE:
Also called "Buñuel's Bourgeoisie."]
IN: Film in Society
The World of Luis Buñuel

2844 **Horrigan, William.**
"Just About Krazy." [RE: Krazy Kat.]
IN: The American Animated Cartoon

2845 **Horrigan, William.**
"*A Farewell to Arms* [novel by] Ernest Hemingway.
Dying Without Death: Borzage's *A Farewell to
Arms* [1932]."
IN: The Classic American Novel ...

2846 **Horton, Andrew.**
"Filmmaking in the Middle: From Belgrade to Beverly
Hills."
IN: Before the Wall Came Down

2847 **Horton, Andrew.**
"Growing Up Absurd: Malle's *Zazie dans le Métro*
from the Novel by Raymond Queneau."
IN: Modern European Filmmakers ...

2848 **Horton, Andrew.**
"The Mouse Who Wanted to F--k a Cow: Cinematic
Carnival Laughter in Dusan Makavejev's Films."
IN: Comedy/Cinema/Theory

2849 **Horton, Andrew.**
"Wim Wenders' *Alice in the Cities*: Song of the Open
Road."
IN: Ideas of Order in Literature & Film

2850 **Horton, Edward Everett.**
"Edward Everett Hornton [*sic*, Horton]: The Player."
IN: The Real Tinsel

2851 **Horvath, Imre.**
"Imre Horvath." [An interview.]
IN: Producers on Producing

2852 **Horwitz, Margaret M.**
"*The Birds*: A Mother's Love."
IN: A Hitchcock Reader

2853 **Hostetler, John A. and Donald B. Kraybill.**
"Hollywood Markets the Amish." [RE: *Witness*.] - ?
IN: Image Ethics

2854 **Houston, Beverle.**
"Film Studies at Pitzer College, Claremont."
IN: Film Study in the Undergraduate Curriculum

2855 **Houston, Beverle.**
"The Manifestation of Self in *The Silence*."
IN: Film and Dream

2856 **Houston, Beverle and Marsha Kinder.**
"Self Explanation and Survival in *Persona* and *The
Ritual*: The Way In--drawing on the depth
psychology of Sigmund Freud and C.G. Jung."
"Sex and Politics in *Weekend*; *Sweet Movie*; and
Seven Beauties: The Way Out--drawing on
Marxism and Feminism."
"Experience and Behavior in *Red Desert* and *Une
Femme Douce*: A View from Inside Out—drawing
on the behaviorism of B.F. Skinner and R.D. Laing."
"Subject and Object in *Last Year at Marienbad* and
The Exterminating Angel: A Mutual
Creation--drawing on the phenomenological
criticism of Alain Robbe-Grillet and Jean-Paul
Sartre."
"The One and the Many in *El Topo*; *2001: A Space
Odyssey*; and *Zardoz*: Archetypal Journeys Beyond
the Self--drawing on Northrop Frye's archetypal
criticism."
"Cultural and Cinematic Codes in *The Man Who Fell
To Earth* and *Walkabout*: Insiders and Outsiders in
the Films of Nicolas Roeg—drawing on the
structuralism of Claude Levi-Strauss and Roland
Barthes and the cinesemiology of Christian Metz."
IN: Self and Cinema

Houston, Beverle. SEE: Kinder, Marsha.

2857 **Houston, Penelope.**
"The Critical Question."
IN: A Casebook on Film
Sight and Sound

2858 **Houston, Penelope.**
"The Great Blank Page." [RE: Buster Keaton.]
IN: Great Film Directors

2859 **Houston, Penelope.**
"Uncommitted Artists?"
IN: Focus on Shoot the Piano Player

2860 **Houston, Penelope.**
"Preston Sturges."
"Michelangelo Antonioni."
"Orson Welles."
"Alfred Hitchcock: I."
IN: Cinema: A Critical Dictionary

2861 **Houston, Penelope.**
"Preston Sturges."
"*Grierson on the Movies*.
"Cannes '76.""
IN: Sight and Sound

2862 **Houston, Penelope.**
"The Movie-Makers." [RE: Ingmar Bergman.]
IN: Focus on The Seventh Seal

2863 **Houston, Penelope.**
"Towards a New Cinema."
IN: Film: A Montage of Theories

2864 **Hovde, Ellen.**
"*Grey Gardens* [Interview with] Ellen Hovde."
IN: The Documentary Conscience

2865 **Hoveyda, Fereydoun.**
"Nicholas Ray's Reply: *Party Girl*."
"Sunspots."
"Self-Criticism."
"*Cinéma vérité*, or Fantastic Realism."
IN: Cahiers du Cinéma, 1960-1968

2866 **Hoveyda, Fereydoun.**
"The First Person Plural." [RE: *Les 400 Coups*.]
IN: Cahiers du Cinéma, The 1950s

Hoveyda, Fereydoun. SEE: Rohmer, Eric.

2867 **Howard, Cy.**
"*Lovers and Other Strangers*."
IN: Directors in Action

2868 **Howard, Leslie.**
"The Actor - I."
IN: Behind the Screen

2869 **Howard, Leslie.**
"The Theatre Is the Only True Actor's Medium."
IN: Celebrity Articles ...

2870 **Howard, William K.**
"Filming in Astoria."
IN: Hollywood Directors 1914-1940

2871 **Howe, James Wong.**
"Director of Photography."
IN: Hollywood Speaks!

2872 **Howe, James Wong.**
"Electric Shadows."
IN: The Best of Rob Wagner's Script

2873 **Howe, James Wong.**
"James Wong Howe." [Interviews by Charles Higham.]
IN: Hollywood Cameramen

2874 **Howe, James Wong.**
"James Wong Howe." [Interview by Kris Malkiewicz.]
IN: Film Lighting

2875 **Howe, James Wong.**
"The Cinematographer."
IN: Filmmakers on Filmmaking /v. 1

2876 **Howe, James Wong.**
"The Approach to Create: James Wong Howe."
[Interview by George C. Pratt.]
IN: Image on the Art ...

2877 **Howells, W.D.**
"Editor's Easy Chair."
IN: Authors on Film

2878 **Huaco, George A.**
"German Expressionism."
"Italian Neorealism."
IN: The Sociology of Film Art

2879 **Huaco, George A.**
"Soviet Expressive Realism."
IN: Conflict and Control in the Cinema
The Sociology of Film Art

2880 **Hubácek, Miroslav.**
"Miroslav Hubácek." [Interview by Antonín J. Liehm.]
IN: Closely Watched Films

2881 **Huddleston, Eugene L.**
"Mae West."
IN: Dictionary of Literary Biography /v. 44

2882 **Huettig, Mae D.**
"Economic Control of the Motion Picture Industry."
IN: The American Film Industry /rev ed

2883 **Huettig, Mae D.**
"The Battle for Theaters."
IN: The First Tycoons

2884 **Huettig, Mae D.**
"The Motion Picture Industry Today."
IN: The American Film Industry
The Movies in Our Midst

2885 **Huff, Theodore.**
"Hollywood's Predecessor: Fort Lee, N.J."
IN: The First Film Makers

Huffman, John L. SEE: Trauth, Denise M.

2886 **Huggins, Roy.**
"Roy Huggins." [An interview.]
IN: Producers on Producing

2887 **Huggins, Roy.**
"[From:] The Bloodshot Eye."
IN: Film and Society

2888 **Hughes, Emmett John.**
"M.G.M.: War Among the Lion Tamers."
IN: The Movies in Our Midst

2889 **Hughes, John and Brett Levy.**
"The Waterside Workers' Federation Film Unit,
1953-1958: An Interview with Norma Disher, Keith
Gow and Jock Levy."
IN: An Australian Film Reader

2890 **Hughes, Robert.**
"Murder / A 'big problem'."
IN: Film: Book 2

2891 **Hughes, William.**
"Howard Koch."
IN: Dictionary of Literary Biography /v. 26

2892 **Hughes, William.**
"The Evaluation of Film as Evidence."
IN: The Historian and Film

2893 **Huillet, Danièle.**
"Notes on Gregory's Work Journal." [RE: Gregory
Woods' "A Work Journal of ..."]
IN: Apparatus

2894 **Huillet, Danièle and Jean-Marie Straub.**
"Every Revolution Is a Throw of the Dice."
IN: Apparatus

Huillet, Daniele. SEE: Straub, Jean-Marie.

2895 **Hull, David Stewart.**
"1933: The Subversion of the Film Industry."
IN: Propaganda on Film

2896 **Humphrey, Hal.**
"Fabian Sole Survivor of 'Bus Stop' Pileup."
IN: Film and Society

2897 **Humphries, Reynold.**
"*The Woman in the Window*: Home Sweet Home."
"*House by the River*: Pinups and Hangups."
"*Secret beyond the Door*: Romance in a Low Key."
"SutureSelf."
IN: Fritz Lang: Genre and ...

2898 **Hunt, Barbara.**
"Modes of Definition: Running Order Through Chaos."
IN: Ideas of Order in Literature & Film

2899 **Hunt, Leon.**
"*The Student of Prague*: Division and Codification of Space."
IN: Early Cinema ...

2900 **Hunter, Alan.**
"Bill Forsyth: The Imperfect Anarchist."
IN: From Limelight to Satellite

2901 **Hunter, Ian.**
"Corsetway to Heaven: Looking Back to Hanging Rock." [RE: *Picnic at Hanging Rock*.]
IN: An Australian Film Reader

Hunter, Tim. SEE: Thompson, Richard.

2902 **Huot, Robert.**
"Robert Huot." [Interview by Scott MacDonald.]
IN: A Critical Cinema

2903 **Hurd, Gale Ann.**
"Gale Ann Hurd." [Interview by Stanley Wiater.]
IN: Dark Visions

2904 **Hurd, Geoffrey.**
"Parodying Genre: The Case of *Gangsters*."
"The Television Presentation of the Police."
IN: Popular Television and Film

2905 **Hurley, Neil P.**
"Alfred Hitchcock."
"Charles Chaplin."
"Cinematic Transfigurations of Jesus."
"Lina Wertmüller."
IN: Religion in Film

2905a **Hurley, Neil P., S.J.**
"*On the Waterfront*: Rebirth of a 'Contenduh'."
IN: Image and Likeness

2906 **Hurrell, George.**
"George Hurrell." [Interview by John Kobal.]
IN: People Will Talk

2907 **Hurt, James.**
"Introduction: Film/Theatre/Film/Theatre/Film."
IN: Focus on Film and Theatre

2908 **Hurwitz, Edith.**
"Sonya Levien."
IN: Dictionary of Literary Biography /v. 44

2909 **Hurwitz, Leo T.**
"The Revolutionary Film--Next Step."
IN: The Documentary Tradition /1 ed
The Documentary Tradition /2 ed

2910 **Huss, Roy.**
"Film Form as a Mirror of the Self: Merging and Symbiosis in Larry Peerce's *A Separate Peace* and Michal Bat-Adam's *Each Other*."
"Film Images as Symbols of Alienation: Kinesics and Proxemics in Frank Perry's *David and Lisa* and Zenzo Matsuyama's *Happiness of Us Alone*."
IN: The Mindscapes of Art

2911 **Huss, Roy.**
"Vampire's Progress: *Dracula* from Novel to Film via Broadway."
"Almost Eve: The Creation Scene in *The Bride of Frankenstein*."
IN: Focus on The Horror Film

2912 **Huss, Roy and Norman Silverstein.**
"Film Study: Shot Orientation for the Literary Minded."
IN: The Compleat Guide to Film Study

2913 **Huss, Roy and Norman Silverstein.**
"Tone and Point of View."
IN: Film and Literature: Contrasts ...

2914 **Huston, John.**
"*Let There Be Light I* The script."
"The Courage of the Men."
IN: Film: Book 2

2915 **Huston, John.**
"John Huston." [Talking to Gideon Bachmann.]
IN: Hollywood Voices

2916 **Huston, John.**
"John Huston." [Interview by Andrew Sarris.]
IN: Interviews with Film Directors

2917 **Huston, John.**
"Picture Partners."
IN: Hollywood Directors 1941-1976

2918 **Hutchings, Peter.**
"*Frenzy*: A Return to Britain."
IN: All Our Yesterdays

2919 **Hutchison, David.**
"Flickering Light: Some Scottish Silent Films."
IN: From Limelight to Satellite

2920 **Hutton, Anne.**
"Black Australia and Film: Only if it Makes Money."
IN: An Australian Film Reader

2921 **Hutton, Lauren.**
"Lauren Hutton." [Interview by Rex Reed.]
IN: Travolta to Keaton

2922 **Huxley, Aldous.**
"Education on the Nonverbal Level."

IN: Perspectives on the Study of Film

2923 **Huxley, Aldous.**
"Silence Is Golden." [RE: coming of sound.]
IN: The Movies in Our Midst
Authors on Film

2924 **Hyams, Joe.**
"[From:] What Should We Do About the Crisis in
Movie Morals?: The Answer: 'Graded' Films."
IN: Film and Society

2925 **Hyde, Thomas.**
"The Moral Universe of Hitchcock's *Spellbound.*"
IN: A Hitchcock Reader

2926 **Hyman, Timothy.**
"*8-1/2* as an Anatomy of Melancholy."
IN: Federico Fellini

**Ibarra, Carlos Vicente. SEE: Vazquez, Emilio
Rodriguez.**

2927 **Ichikawa, Kon.**
"Kon Ichikawa." [Interview by Joan Mellen.]
IN: Voices from the Japanese Cinema

2928 **Iden, Peter.**
"The Impact-Maker."
IN: Fassbinder

2929 **Ignatieva, Nina.**
"Society and Individual in Soviet Films."
IN: Crossroads to the Cinema

2930 **Ihering, Herbert.**
"*The Blue Angel* and *An American Tragedy.*"
IN: Sternberg

2931 **Iimura, Taka.**
"Taka Iimura." [Interview by Scott MacDonald.]
IN: A Critical Cinema

2932 **Ilal, Ersan.**
"On Turkish Cinema."
IN: Film and Politics in the Third World

Iljon, Jeannette. SEE: Nicolson, Annabel.

2933 **Imai, Tadashi.**
"Tadashi Imai." [Interview by Joan Mellen.]
IN: Voices from the Japanese Cinema

2934 **Ince, Thomas H.**
"The Early Days at Kay Bee."
IN: Hollywood Directors 1914-1940

2935 **Ince, Thomas H.**
"The Challenge for the Motion Picture Producer."
IN: The First Film Makers

2936 ***Independent, The.***
"The Birth of a New Art."
IN: Introduction to the Art of the Movies

2936a **Inge, M. Thomas.**
"Charlie Chaplin and the Comic Strips."
IN: Charlie Chaplin

2937 **Inglis, Ruth A.**
"Freedom of the Movies."
IN: The Movies in Our Midst

2938 **Inglis, Ruth A.**
"Self-Regulation in Operation." [RE: Production Code.]
IN: The American Film Industry /rev ed

2939 **Ingram, Rex.**
"Directing the Picture."
IN: Hollywood Directors 1914-1940

2940 **Insdorf, Annette and Sharon Goodman.**
"*Tom Jones* [novel by] Henry Fielding; *Tom Jones*
[film by] Tony Richardson. A Whisper and a Wink."
IN: The English Novel and the Movies

2941 **Iros, Ernst.**
"Expansion of the German and Austrian Film."
IN: Experiment in the Film

2942 **Irwin, Will.**
"The Low Spot."
"Waiting at the Theatre."
IN: The First Tycoons

2943 **Isaac, Alberto.**
"Alberto Isaac." [Interview by Beatrice Reyes
Nevares.]
IN: The Mexican Cinema

2944 **Isaacs, Neil D.**
"The Triumph of Artifice: Antonioni's *Blow-Up* from the
Short Story by Julio Cortázar."
IN: Modern European Filmmakers ...

2945 **Isaksson, F. and L. Furhammar.**
"*The Green Berets.*"
"The First Person Plural."
IN: Conflict and Control in the Cinema

Isaksson, Folke. SEE: Furhammar, Leif.

2946 **Isenberg, Michael T.**
"The Great War Viewed from the Twenties: *The Big
Parade.*"
IN: American History/American Film

2947 **Isherwood, Christopher.**
"Christopher Isherwood." [Interview by Charles
Higham.]
IN: Celebrity Circus

2948 **Ishioka, Eiko.**
"Eiko Ishioka [on Production Design]." [Interview by
David Chell.]
IN: Moviemakers at Work

2949 ***Iskusstvo kino*, Editorial.**
"The Fascist Cur Eradicated."
IN: The Film Factory

2950 **Issari, M. Ali and Doris A. Paul.**
"What is Cinéma Vérité?"
"Dziga Vertov."
"Robert Flaherty."
"Neo-Realism."

"Nouvelle Vague."
"The Free Cinema."
"Television."
"Jean Rouch: The French School."
"Richard Leacock: The American School."
"Differences in Approach."
"Other Pioneers and Practitioners: Mario Ruspoli,
    Jacques Rozier, Chris Marker, Albert Maysles,
    William C. Jersey, Jr., and other American
    practitioners."
"Equipment."
"The End or the Way?"
    IN: What is Cinéma Vérité?

2951 **Ito, Daisuke.**
"Daisuke Ito." [Interview by Joan Mellen.]
    IN: Voices from the Japanese Cinema

2952 **Ivens, Joris.**
"A Camera Approach to Reality."
    IN: Celebrity Articles ...

2953 **Ivens, Joris.**
"Reflections on the Avant-Garde Documentary."
    IN: French Film Theory and Criticism /v. 2

2954 **Ivens, Joris.**
"Spain and *The Spanish Earth*."
    IN: Nonfiction Film Theory and Criticism

2955 **Ivens, Joris.**
"The Making of *Rain*."
    IN: The Documentary Tradition /1 ed
        The Documentary Tradition /2 ed

2956 **Iwasaki, Akira.**
"Kurosawa and His Work."
    IN: Great Film Directors
        Focus on Rashomon

2957 **Jabor, Arnaldo.**
"Jack Valenti's Brazilian Agenda."
    IN: Brazilian Cinema

2958 **Jacchia, Paolo.**
"Drama and Lesson of the Defeated."
    IN: Focus on Rashomon

2959 **Jackson, Anne and Eli Wallach.**
"Anne Jackson and Eli Wallach." [Interview by Judith
    Crist.]
    IN: Take 22

Jackson, Arthur. SEE: Taylor, John Russell.

2960 **Jackson, Martin A.**
"The Uncertain Peace: *The Best Years of Our Lives*."
    IN: American History/American Film

2961 **Jacob, Gilles.**
"Atonal Cinema for Zombies."
    IN: Focus on Godard

2962 **Jacob-Arzooni, Gloria.**
"*Salah Shabbati*."
"*Siege*."
"*I Am a Jerusalemite*."

"*I Love You, Rosa*."
"*Peeping Toms*."
"*Salomonico*."
    IN: The Israeli Film

2963 **Jacobowitz, Florence and Lori Spring.**
"Unspoken and Unsolved: *Tell Me a Riddle*."
    IN: Issues in Feminist Film Criticism

Jacobs, Arthur A. SEE: Cunha, Richard E.

2964 **Jacobs, Diane.**
"John Cassavetes."
"Robert Altman."
"Francis Ford Coppola."
"Martin Scorsese."
"Paul Mazursky."
    IN: Hollywood Renaissance

2965 **Jacobs, Diane.**
"*Heart of Darkness* [novel by] Joseph Conrad;
    Apocalypse Now [film by] Francis Coppola.
    Coppola Films Conrad in Vietnam."
    IN: The English Novel and the Movies

2966 **Jacobs, Diane.**
"Francis Ford Coppola."
    IN: American Directors /v. 2

2967 **Jacobs, Lea.**
"Censorship and the Fallen Woman Cycle."
    IN: Home Is Where the Heart Is

2968 **Jacobs, Lewis (editor).**
"*Collected comments by*: Lindsay Anderson,
    Michelangelo Antonioni, Ingmar Bergman, Stan
    Brakhage, Luis Buñuel, Jean Cocteau, Carl Dreyer,
    Federico Fellini, John Ford, Jean-Luc Godard,
    Alfred Hitchcock, John Huston, Elia Kazan, Stanley
    Kubrick, Akiro Kurosawa, Fritz Lang, Richard
    Lester, Joseph Losey, Sidney Lumet, Len Lye,
    Jonas Mekas, Satyajit Ray, Sir Carol Reed, Jean
    Renoir, Alain Resnais, Tony Richardson, Josef von
    Sternberg, George Stevens, François Truffaut,
    Dziga Vertov, King Vidor, Andrezej Wajda, Orson
    Welles, Billy Wilder, William Wyler, Fred
    Zinnemann."
    IN: The Movies as Medium

2969 **Jacobs, Lewis.**
"The Raw Material."
"The Meaningful Image."
"Movement: Real and Cinematic."
"The Expression of Time and Space."
"The Mobility of Color."
"Sound as Speech, Noise, Music."
    IN: The Movies as Medium

2970 **Jacobs, Lewis.**
"Documentary Becomes Engaged and Vérité."
"From Innovation to Involvement." [RE: documentary.]
"New Trend in British Documentary--Free Cinema."
"The Military Experience and After."
"The Turn Toward Conservatism."
"The Feel of a New Genre." [RE: documentary.]

IN: The Documentary Tradition /1 ed
The Documentary Tradition /2 ed

2971 Jacobs, Lewis.
"D.W. Griffith: *The Birth of a Nation*."
IN: Focus on The Birth of a Nation

2972 Jacobs, Lewis.
"*Intolerance*."
IN: Focus on D.W. Griffith

2973 Jacobs, Lewis.
"Avant-Garde Production in America."
IN: Experiment in the Film

2974 Jacobs, Lewis.
"D.W. Griffith." [NOTE: Also called "D.W. Griffith: New Discoveries."]
IN: Film: An Anthology
The Emergence of Film Art /1 ed
The Emergence of Film Art /2 ed

2975 Jacobs, Lewis.
"Edwin S. Porter and the Editing Principle."
"Georges Méliès: Artificially Arranged Scenes."
IN: The Emergence of Film Art /1 ed
The Emergence of Film Art /2 ed

2976 Jacobs, Lewis.
"Films of the Postwar Decade." [RE: WWI.]
"World War II and the American Film."
IN: The Movies: An American Idiom

2977 Jacobs, Lewis.
"From Political Activism to Women's Consciousness."
IN: The Documentary Tradition /2 ed

2978 Jacobs, Lewis.
"Griffith Leaves Biograph."
IN: The First Film Makers

2979 Jacobs, Lewis.
"Movies in the World War." [RE: WWI.]
IN: The Movies in Our Midst

2980 Jacobs, Lewis.
"Technique in *Intolerance*."
IN: The Classic Cinema

2981 Jacobs, Lewis.
"*The Birth of a Nation*."
IN: The Black Man on Film

2982 Jacobson, Laurie.
"Ramon Novarro."
"William Desmond Taylor."
"D.W. Griffith."
"Wallace Reid."
"Jim Thorpe."
"Clara Bow."
"Mack Sennett."
"Peg Entwistle."
"Bela Lugosi."
"Russ Columbo."
"Thelma Todd."
"Jean Harlow."
"F. Scott Fitzgerald."
"Robert Walker."
"Carl 'Alfalfa' Switzer."
"Albert Dekker."
"Aldous Huxley."
"Ernie Kovacs."
"Dorothy Dandridge."
"George Reeves."
"Sal Mineo."
"Marilyn Monroe."
"Lenny Bruce."
"Sam Cooke."
"Inger Stevens."
"Janis Joplin."
"Sharon Tate."
"Freddie Prinze."
"Natalie Wood."
"John Belushi."
"Marvin Gaye."
IN: The Tragic and Mysterious Deaths ...

2983 Jacoby, Irving and Robert Anderson.
"Scenario for Psychiatry."
IN: Ideas on Film

2984 Jaffe, Ira S.
"Fighting Words: *City Lights*, *Modern Times*, and *The Great Dictator*."
IN: Hollywood as Historian

2985 Jahier, Valéry.
"*L'Atalante*."
"*Toni*."
"*Angèle*."
"Prologue to a Cinema."
IN: French Film Theory and Criticism /v. 2

2986 Jahrous, Donald A.
"Building Miniatures."
IN: The ASC Treasury ...

2987 Jakobson, Roman.
"Is the Cinema in Decline?"
IN: Russian Formalist Film Theory

2988 Jakubisko, Juraj.
"Juraj Jakubisko." [Interview by Antonín J. Liehm.]
IN: Closely Watched Films

2989 James, David E.
"Documenting the Vietnam War."
IN: From Hanoi to Hollywood

2990 Jameson, Fredric.
"Reification and Utopia in Mass Culture."
"*Diva* and French Socialism."
"'In the destructive element immerse': Hans-Jürgen Syberberg and Cultural Revolution."
"Historicism in *The Shining*."
"Allegorizing Hitchcock."
"On Magic Realism in Film."
"The Existence of Italy."
IN: Signatures of the Visible

2991 **Jameson, Fredric.**
"Class and Allegory in Contemporary Mass Culture:
Dog Day Afternoon as a Politcal Film."
IN: Movies and Methods /v. 2
Signatures of the Visible

2992 **Jameson, Richard T.**
"The Right Stuff."
"George Stevens: A Filmmaker's Journey."
"Strange Invaders."
IN: Produced and Abandoned

2993 **Jameson, Richard T.**
"Lewis Milestone."
IN: Cinema: A Critical Dictionary

2994 **Jameson, Richard T.**
"An Infinity of Mirrors."
IN: Focus on Orson Welles

2995 **Jancso, Miklos.**
"Miklos Jancso." [Interviewed by Tibor Hirsch.]
IN: The Image Maker

2996 **Jarvie, I.C.**
"The Present State & Structure of Capitalist
Production."
IN: Conflict and Control in the Cinema

2997 **Jarvie, Ian C.**
"Stars and Ethnicity: Hollywood and the United
States, 1932-51."
IN: Unspeakable Images

2998 **Jarvie, Ian.**
"Suppressing Controversial Films: From *Objective
Burma* to *Monty Python's Life of Brian*."
IN: Current Research in Film /v. 1

2999 **Jarvie, Ian.**
"The Social Experience of Movies."
IN: Film/Culture: Explorations ...

3000 **Jasny, Vojtech.**
"Vojtech Jasny." [Interview by Antonín J. Liehm.]
IN: Closely Watched Films

3001 **Jasset, Victorin.**
"An Essay on Mise-en-scène in Cinematography."
IN: French Film Theory and Criticism /v. 1

3002 **Jaubert, Maurice.**
"Music on the Screen."
IN: Footnotes to the Film

3003 **Jaubert, Maurice.**
"Music in the Film."
IN: Rediscovering French Film

3004 **Jaubert, Maurice.**
"The Cinema: Music."
IN: French Film Theory and Criticism /v. 2

3005 **Jay, Anthony.**
"Royal Family." [Interview by Alan Rosenthal.]
"The Future Came Yesterday." [Interview by Alan
Rosenthal.]
IN: The New Documentary in Action

3006 **Jayamanne, Laleen.**
"Speaking of 'Ceylon', a Clash of Cultures."
IN: Questions of Third Cinema

Jayamanne, Laleen. SEE: Sayer, Sally.

3007 **Jeancolas, Jean-Pierre.**
"Beneath the Despair, the Show Goes On: Marcel
Carné's *Les Enfants du Paradis*."
IN: French Film: Texts and Contexts

3008 **Jeanson, Henri.**
"Jean Renoir."
IN: French Film Theory and Criticism /v. 2

Jeffery, Richard. SEE: Cameron, Ian.

3009 **Jeffords, Susan.**
"Reproducing Fathers: Gender and the Vietnam War
in U.S. Culture."
IN: From Hanoi to Hollywood

3010 **Jenkins, Bruce L.**
"Hollis Frampton's *Autumnal Equinox*: A Modernist
Film and its Pictoral Past."
IN: Film: Historical-Theoretical ...

3011 **Jenkins, C. Francis.**
"History of the Motion Picture."
IN: A Technological History ...

3012 **Jenkins, Henry, III.**
"*Star Trek* Rerun, Reread, Rewritten: Fan Writing as
Textual Poaching."
IN: Close Encounters

3013 **Jenkins, Stephen.**
"Fritz Lang: A Documentary Record."
"Lang: Fear and Desire."
IN: Fritz Lang: The Image ...

3014 **Jenkins, Steve.**
"A Critical Impasse."
IN: British Cinema Now

3015 **Jennings, J. Devereaux.**
"Photographing Miniatures."
IN: The ASC Treasury ...

3016 **Jennings, Wade.**
"Fantasy."
IN: Handbook of American Film Genres

3017 **Jennings, Wade.**
"The Star as Cult Icon: Judy Garland."
IN: The Cult Film Experience

3018 **Jensen, A.G.**
"The Evolution of Modern Television."
IN: A Technological History ...

3019 **Jensen, Monika.**
"The Role of the Filmmaker: An Interview with
Ousmane Sembene."
IN: Conflict and Control in the Cinema

3020 **Jensen, Paul.**
"Dudley Nichols."

IN: The Hollywood Screenwriters

3021 **Jensen, Paul.**
"Encounters with Sound." [RE: *M*.]
IN: The Classic Cinema

3022 **Jenson, Robert W.**
"Film, Preaching, and Meaning."
IN: Celluloid and Symbol

3023 **Jeter, Ida.**
"The Collapse of the Federated Motion Picture Crafts:
A Case Study of Class Collaboration in the Motion
Picture Industry."
IN: The Hollywood Film Industry

3024 **Jeter, Ida.**
"*Jezebel* and the Emergence of the Hollywood
Tradition of a Decadent South."
IN: The South and Film

3025 **Jireš, Jaromil.**
"Jaromil Jireš." [Interview by Antonín J. Liehm.]
IN: Closely Watched Films

3026 **Jires, Jaromil.**
"Jaromil Jires." [Interviewed by Jules Cohen.]
IN: The Image Maker

3027 **Johnson, Albert.**
"*Bonnie and Clyde*."
IN: Focus on Bonnie and Clyde

3028 **Johnson, Charles.**
"One Meaning of *Mo' Better Blues*."
IN: Five for Five

3029 **Johnson, Ian.**
"Merely Players." [RE: Shakespeare.]
IN: Focus on Shakespearean Films

3030 **Johnson, Lamar and Robert de Kieffer.**
"If You Want To Get Across an Idea."
IN: Ideas on Film

3031 **Johnson, Millard.**
"Early Days in Australia."
IN: An Australian Film Reader

3032 **Johnson, Nunnally.**
"Nunnally Johnson." [Interview by William Froug.]
IN: The Screenwriter Looks ...

3033 **Johnson, Randal.**
"Joaquim Pedro de Andrade: The Poet of Satire."
"Carlos Diegues: *Alegoria, Alegria*."
"Ruy Guerra: Radical Critique."
"Glauber Rocha: Apocalypse and Resurrection."
"Nelson Pereira dos Santos: Toward a Popular
Cinema."
IN: Cinema Novo x 5

3034 **Johnson, Randal and Robert Stam.**
"The Cinema of Hunger: Nelson Pereira dos Santos's
Vidas Secas."
"*São Bernardo*: Property and the Personality."
"Carnivalesque Celebration in *Xica da Silva*."
"Cinema Novo and Cannibalism: *Macunaíma*."

"*Lesson of Love*."
IN: Brazilian Cinema

3035 **Johnson, Vlda T.**
"The Films of Andrei Konchalovsky."
IN: Before the Wall Came Down

3036 **Johnson, William.**
"*Balthazar*."
"*Marnie*."
IN: Renaissance of the Film

3037 **Johnson, William.**
"Coming to Terms with Color."
IN: The Movies as Medium

3038 **Johnson, William.**
"Introduction: Journey into Science Fiction."
IN: Focus on The Science Fiction Film

3039 **Johnson, William.**
"Orson Welles: Of Time and Loss."
IN: Focus on Citizen Kane

3040 **Johnston, Alva.**
"The Great Goldwyn."
IN: Film: An Anthology

3041 **Johnston, Claire.**
"*Double Indemnity*."
IN: Women in Film Noir

3042 **Johnston, Claire.**
"Dorothy Arzner: Critical Strategies."
IN: Feminism and Film Theory

3043 **Johnston, Claire.**
"Femininity and the Masquerade: *Anne of the Indies*."
IN: Psychoanalysis and Cinema

3044 **Johnston, Claire.**
"Myths of Women in the Cinema."
IN: Women and the Cinema

3045 **Johnston, Claire.**
"Towards a Feminist Film Practice: Some Theses."
IN: Movies and Methods /v. 2

3046 **Johnston, Claire.**
"Women's Cinema as Counter-Cinema."
IN: Sexual Stratagems
Movies and Methods: An Anthology

3047 **Johnstone [*sic*, Johnston], Claire.**
"*Maeve*."
IN: Films for Women

3048 **Johnston, Claire and Paul Willemen.**
"Brecht in Britain: *The Nightcleaners* and the
Independent Political Film."
IN: Show Us Life

Johnston, Claire. SEE: Cook, Pam.

3049 **Johnston, Eric.**
"[From:] Hollywood: America's Travelling Salesman."
IN: Film and Society

IN: <u>Movies as Artifacts</u>
<u>Film Before Griffith</u>

3076 **Jowett, Garth S.**
"They Taught It at the Movies: Films as Models for Learned Sexual Behavior."
IN: <u>Film/Culture: Explorations ...</u>

3077 **Jowett, Garth.**
"Bullets, Beer and the Hays Office: *Public Enemy*."
IN: <u>American History/American Film</u>

3078 **Juhnke, Janet.**
"*The Wonderful Wizard of Oz* [novel by] L. Frank Baum. A Kansan's View." [RE: *The Wizard of Oz*.]
IN: <u>The Classic American Novel ...</u>

3079 **Juliani, Richard N.**
"The Image of the Italian in American Film and Television."
IN: <u>Ethnic Images ...</u>

3080 **Juovitz, Dalia.**
"Anemic Vision in Duchamps: Cinema as Readymade."
IN: <u>Dada and Surrealist Film</u>

3081 **Jurácek, Pavel.**
"Pavel Jurácek." [Interview by Antonín J. Liehm.]
IN: <u>Closely Watched Films</u>

3082 **Kachyna, Karel.**
"Karel Kachyna." [Interview by Antonín J. Liehm.]
IN: <u>Closely Watched Films</u>

3083 **Kadár, Jan.**
"Jan Kadár." [Interview by Antonín J. Liehm.]
IN: <u>Closely Watched Films</u>

3084 **Kael, Pauline.**
"Raising Kane." [RE: *Citizen Kane*.]
IN: <u>Great Film Directors</u>
<u>The Citizen Kane Book</u>

3085 **Kael, Pauline.**
"... from 'Raising Kane'." [RE: *Citizen Kane*.]
IN: <u>The Classic Cinema</u>

3086 **Kael, Pauline.**
"Circles and Squares." [NOTE: Also called "Circles and Squares: Joys and Sarris."]
IN: <u>Film Theory and Criticism /1 ed</u>
<u>Film Theory and Criticism /2 ed</u>
<u>Film Theory and Criticism /3 ed</u>
<u>Perspectives on the Study of Film</u>
<u>Awake in the Dark</u>

3087 **Kael, Pauline.**
"*Bonnie and Clyde*."
IN: <u>A Casebook on Film</u>
<u>Awake in the Dark</u>

3088 **Kael, Pauline.**
"Notes on the Nihilist Poetry of Sam Peckinpah."
"Three Program Notes." [RE: *All About Eve*; *My Little Chickadee*; *Ecstasy*.]
IN: <u>Awake in the Dark</u>

3089 **Kael, Pauline.**
"*Boudu Saved from Drowning*."
"*Miracle in Milan*."
"*Morgan!* and *Georgy Girl*."
"*Shoot the Piano Player*."
"*Smiles of a Summer Night*."
"*The Graduate*."
"*The Golden Coach*."
"*The Knack* and *Help!*."
"*Weekend*."
"*Zazie*."
"Against Spoofing."
"Three Alec Guinness Comedies."
IN: <u>Movie Comedy</u>

3090 **Kael, Pauline.**
"*Lolita*."
IN: <u>The Film</u>

3091 **Kael, Pauline.**
"*Melvin and Howard*."
"*Pennies from Heaven*."
"*Casualties of War*."
"*The Border*."
"*Utu*."
IN: <u>Produced and Abandoned</u>

3092 **Kael, Pauline.**
"A Dreamlike Requiem Mass for a Nation's Lost Honour."
IN: <u>An Australian Film Reader</u>

3093 **Kael, Pauline.**
"Americana: *Tell Them Willie Boy Is Here*."
IN: <u>The Pretend Indians</u>

3094 **Kael, Pauline.**
"Are Movies Going to Pieces?"
IN: <u>Film: A Montage of Theories</u>

3095 **Kael, Pauline.**
"Fantasies of the Art-House Audience."
"On the Future of Movies [1974]."
IN: <u>The Movies in Our Midst</u>

3096 **Kael, Pauline.**
"It's Only a Movie."
IN: <u>Film Study in Higher Education</u>

3097 **Kael, Pauline.**
"Lillian Gish and Mae Marsh."
"Marlon Brando and James Dean."
"Richard Pryor."
"Sidney Poitier."
IN: <u>The Movie Star: The National ...</u>

3098 **Kael, Pauline.**
"Morality Plays Right and Left." [RE: *Night People*; *Salt of the Earth*.]
IN: <u>Propaganda on Film</u>

3099 **Kael, Pauline.**
"Movies on Television."
IN: <u>Film and the Liberal Arts</u>
<u>Crossroads to the Cinema</u>

3100 **Kael, Pauline.**
"Movies, the Desperate Art."
  IN: <u>Film: An Anthology</u>
      <u>Film: Readings in the Mass Media</u>

3101 **Kael, Pauline.**
"Movie Brutalists."
  IN: <u>The Emergence of Film Art /1 ed</u>
      <u>The Emergence of Film Art /2 ed</u>

3102 **Kael, Pauline.**
"Saddle Sore." [RE: *El Dorado*; *The War Wagon*; *The Way West*.]
  IN: <u>The American West on Film</u>

3103 **Kael, Pauline.**
"Saintliness." [RE: *Simon of the Desert*.]
  IN: <u>The World of Luis Buñuel</u>

3104 **Kael, Pauline.**
"The Concealed Art of Carol Reed."
  IN: <u>Film and Literature: Contrasts ...</u>

3105 **Kael, Pauline.**
"Three Films [of Alfred Hitchcock]." [RE: *The 39 Steps*; *Spellbound*; *Strangers on a Train*.]
  IN: <u>Focus on Hitchcock</u>

3106 **Kael, Pauline.**
"Youth Is Beauty." [RE: *Masculine Feminine*.]
  IN: <u>Renaissance of the Film</u>

3107 **Kael, Pauline.**
"A Great Folly." [RE: D.W. Griffith.]
"*Shoot the Piano Player* and *Jules and Jim*."
  IN: <u>Great Film Directors</u>

3108 **Kael, Pauline.**
"*Shoot the Piano Player*." [NOTE: This is an abbreviated version of the previous entry.]
  IN: <u>Focus on Shoot the Piano Player</u>
      <u>Movie Comedy</u>

3109 **Kaes, Anton.**
"History, Fiction, Memory: Fassbinder's *The Marriage of Maria Braun*."
  IN: <u>German Film and Literature</u>

3109a **Kaes, Anton.**
"History and Film: Public Memory in the Age of Electronic Dissemination."
  IN: <u>Framing the Past</u>

3110 **Kagan, Norman.**
"Michelangelo Antonioni: *Zabriskie Point*."
"John Boorman: *Point Blank*."
"Jacques Demy: *The Model Shop*."
"Milos Forman: *Taking Off*."
"Jean-Luc Godard: *Made in U.S.A.*."
"John Schlesinger: *Midnight Cowboy*."
"Agnes Varda: *Lions Love*."
  IN: <u>Greenhorns</u>

3111 **Kahn, Gordon.**
"Hollywood on Trial." [RE: HUAC.]
  IN: <u>The Movies in Our Midst</u>

3112 **Kahn, Michael.**
"Michael Kahn." [Interview by Vincent LoBrutto.]
  IN: <u>Selected Takes</u>

3113 **Kahn, Richard.**
"Motion Picture Marketing."
  IN: <u>The Movie Business Book</u>

3114 **Kakar, Sudhir.**
"The Cinema as Collective Fantasy."
  IN: <u>Indian Cinema Superbazaar</u>

3115 **Kalishman, H. and G. Crowdus.**
"'A Film is Like a Match: You Can Make a Big Fire or Nothing at All': An Interview with Costa-Gavras."
  IN: <u>Conflict and Control in the Cinema</u>

3115a **Kalmar, Ivan.**
"Chaplin: The Little Jew and *The Great Dictator*."
  IN: <u>Charlie Chaplin</u>

3116 **Kalmus, H.T.**
"Technicolor Adventures in Cinemaland."
  IN: <u>A Technological History ...</u>

3117 **Kalmus, Natalie M.**
"Colour."
  IN: <u>Behind the Screen</u>

3118 **Kaminsky, Stuart M.**
"Variations on a Major Genre: The Big Caper Film."
  IN: <u>American Film Genres /1 ed</u>

3119 **Kaminsky, Stuart M.**
"Narrative Time in Sergio Leone's *Once Upon a Time in America*." [NOTE: Also called "The Individual Film: *Once Upon a Time in America* as Narrative Model."]
  IN: <u>American Film Genres /2 ed</u>
      <u>The Cinematic Text</u>

3120 **Kaminsky, Stuart M.**
"What Is Film Genre?" [NOTE: Only slight changes to /2e.]
  IN: <u>American Film Genres /1 ed</u>
      <u>American Film Genres /2 ed</u>

3121 **Kaminsky, Stuart M.**
"The Individual Film: *Little Caesar* as Prototype." [NOTE: Also called "*Little Caesar* and the Gangster Film."]
  IN: <u>American Film Genres /1 ed</u>
      <u>American Film Genres /2 ed</u>

3122 **Kaminsky, Stuart M.**
"Comparative Forms: The Samurai Film and the Western."
  IN: <u>American Film Genres /1 ed</u>
      <u>American Film Genres /2 ed</u>

3123 **Kaminsky, Stuart M.**
"Historical Perspective: The White-Hot Violence of the 1970s." [NOTE: Also called "Contemporary Problems: The White-Hot Violence of the 1970s"; only slight changes to /2e.]
  IN: <u>American Film Genres /1 ed</u>
      <u>American Film Genres /2 ed</u>

3124 **Kaminsky, Stuart M.**
"Psychological Perspective: Horror and Science Fiction." [NOTE: Also called "Psychological Considerations: Horror and Science Fiction"; only slight changes to /2e.]
IN: <u>American Film Genres /1 ed</u>
<u>American Film Genres /2 ed</u>

3125 **Kaminsky, Stuart M.**
"Social Perspective: Comedy and Social Change." [NOTE: Also called "History and Social Change: Comedy and Individual Expression"; only slight changes to /2e.]
IN: <u>American Film Genres /1 ed</u>
<u>American Film Genres /2 ed</u>

3126 **Kaminsky, Stuart M.**
"The Genre Director: The Films of Donald Siegel." [NOTE: Only slight changes to /2e.]
IN: <u>American Film Genres /1 ed</u>
<u>American Film Genres /2 ed</u>

3127 **Kaminsky, Stuart M.**
"The Genre Director: Character Types in the Films of John Ford." [NOTE: Only slight changes to /2e.]
IN: <u>American Film Genres /1 ed</u>
<u>American Film Genres /2 ed</u>

3128 **Kaminsky, Stuart M.**
"Comparative Forms: The Kung Fu Film and the Dance Musical."
IN: <u>American Film Genres /2 ed</u>

3129 **Kaminsky, Stuart M.**
"The Genre Director: The Grotesque West of Sergio Leone."
IN: <u>American Film Genres /2 ed</u>

3130 **Kaminsky, Stuart M.**
"*Treasure of the Sierra Madre* [novel by] B. Traven. Gold Hat, Gold Fever, Silver Screen." [NOTE: Also called "Literary Adaptation: *The Treasure of the Sierra Madre*--Novel into Film"; only slight differences.]
IN: <u>American Film Genres /2 ed</u>
<u>The Modern American Novel ...</u>

3131 **Kaminsky, Stuart M.**
"Kung Fu Film as Ghetto Myth."
IN: <u>Movies as Artifacts</u>

3132 **Kaminsky, Stuart.**
"Literary Adaptation: 'The Killers'--Hemingway, Film Noir, and the Terror of Daylight." [RE: 1946 and 1964 versions.]
IN: <u>A Moving Picture Feast</u>
<u>American Film Genres /1 ed</u>
<u>American Film Genres /2 ed</u>

Kane, Bruce. SEE: Reiser, Joel.

3133 **Kane, Kathryn.**
"The World War II Combat Film."
IN: <u>Handbook of American Film Genres</u>

3134 **Kané, Pascal.**
"Re-reading Hollywood Cinema: *Sylvia Scarlett*."
IN: <u>Cahiers du Cinéma: 1969-1972</u>

3135 **Kanfer, Stefan.**
"John Wayne as the Last Hero."
IN: <u>Conflict and Control in the Cinema</u>

3136 **Kanin, Fay.**
"Fay Kanin." [Interview by William Froug.]
IN: <u>The New Screenwriter Looks ...</u>

3137 **Kanin, Garson.**
"Garson Kanin: Self-Expression." [Interview by Patrick McGilligan.]
IN: <u>Backstory 2</u>

3138 **Kanjo, Eugene.**
"Hemingway's Cinematic Style."
IN: <u>A Moving Picture Feast</u>

3139 **Kann, Maurice.**
"Hollywood and Britain—Three Thousand Miles Apart."
IN: <u>Footnotes to the Film</u>

3140 **Kanter, Hal.**
"No Great Pride In Being A Member Of A Family—" [RE: an interview.]
IN: <u>Blueprint on Babylon</u>

3141 **Kantor, Bernard R., Irwin R. Blacker, and Anne Kramer.**
"Interview with Elia Kazan."
IN: <u>Focus on Film and Theatre</u>

3142 **Kaplan, Carola.**
"Reginald Rose."
IN: <u>Dictionary of Literary Biography /v. 26</u>

3143 **Kaplan, E. Ann.**
"Is the Gaze Male?"
"Patriarchy and the Male Gaze in Cukor's *Camille*."
"Fetishism and the Repression of Motherhood in Von Sternberg's *Blonde Venus*."
"The Struggle for Control Over the Female Discourse and Female Sexuality in Welles's *Lady from Shanghai*."
"Forms of Phallic Domination in the Contemporary Hollywood Film: Brooks's *Looking for Mr. Goodbar*."
"The Avant-Gardes in Europe and the USA."
"Silence as Female Resistance in Marguerite Duras's *Nathalie Granger*."
"Female Politics in the Symbolic Realm: Von Trotta's *Marianne and Juliane* (*The German Sisters*)."
"The American Experimental Woman's Film: Yvonne Rainer's *Lives of Performers* and *Film about a Woman Who...*"
"The Realist Debate in the Feminist Film: A Historical Overview of Theories and Strategies in Realism and the Avant-Garde Theory Film."
"The Avant-Garde Theory Film: Three Case Studies from Britain and the USA: *Sigmund Freud's Dora*, *Thriller*, Mulvey/Wollen's *Amy!*."
"Mothers and Daughters in Two Recent Women's Films: Mulvey/Wollen's *Riddles of the Sphinx* and Michelle Citron's *Daughter-Rite*."
"The Woman Director in the Third World: Sara Gomez's *One Way or Another*."

"The Future of the Independent Feminist Film:
Strategies of Production, Exhibition, and
Distribution in the USA."
IN: Women and Film: Both Sides of the Camera

3144   **Kaplan, E. Ann.**
"*The House of the Seven Gables* [novel by] Nathaniel
Hawthorne. Hawthorne's 'Fancy Pictures' on Film."
IN: The Classic American Novel ...

3145   **Kaplan, E. Ann.**
"Discourses of Terrorism, Feminism, and the Family
in von Trotta's *Marianne and Juliane*."
IN: Women and Film

3146   **Kaplan, E. Ann.**
"Feminist Film Criticism: Current Issues and
Problems."
IN: The Cinematic Text

3147   **Kaplan, E. Ann.**
"From Plato's Cave to Freud's Screen."
"Motherhood and Representation: From Postwar
Freudian Figurations to Postmodernism."
IN: Psychoanalysis and Cinema

3148   **Kaplan, E. Ann.**
"Interview with British Cine-Feminists."
IN: Women and the Cinema

3149   **Kaplan, E. Ann.**
"Mothering, Feminism and Representation: The
Maternal in Melodrama and the Woman's Film
1910-40."
IN: Home Is Where the Heart Is

3150   **Kaplan, E. Ann.**
"Problematising Cross-cultural Analysis: The Case of
Women in the Recent Chinese Cinema."
IN: Perspectives on Chinese Cinema

3151   **Kaplan, E. Ann.**
"Theory and Practice of the Realist Documentary
Form in *Harlan County, U.S.A.*"
IN: Show Us Life

3152   **Kaplan, E. Ann.**
"Theories and Strategies of the Feminist
Documentary."
IN: New Challenges for Documentary

3153   **Kaplan, E. Ann.**
"The Search for the Mother/Land in
Sanders-Brahms's *Germany, Pale Mother*."
IN: German Film and Literature

3154   **Kaplan, E. Ann.**
"The Case of the Missing Mother: Maternal Issues in
Vidor's *Stella Dallas*."
IN: Issues in Feminist Film Criticism

3155   **Kaplan, E. Ann.**
"The Place of Women in Fritz Lang's *The Blue
Gardenia*."
IN: Women in Film Noir

3156   **Kaplan, E. Ann.**
"Whose Imaginary? The Television Apparatus, the
Female Body and Textual Strategies in Select
Rock Videos on MTV."
IN: Female Spectators

Kaplan, E. Ann. SEE: Ellis, Kate.

3157   **Kaplan, Nelly.**
"At the Warrior's Table."
IN: The Shadow and Its Shadow

3158   **Kapoor, Shashi.**
"Shashi Kapoor." [Interview.]
IN: Indian Cinema Superbazaar

3159   **Kapur, Geeta.**
"Articulating the Self into History: Ritwik Ghatak's
Jukti takko ar gappo."
IN: Questions of Third Cinema

3160   **Karanjia, B.K.**
"The Star System: 'Another Kind of Nonsense,
Another Profound Humanitiy'."
IN: Indian Cinema Superbazaar

3161   **Karetnikova, Inga.**
"The Beginning of Screenwriting: *Nosferatu, a
Symphony of Horror*."
"Script Composition: *La Strada*."
"Opening, Climax, Resolution: *The Servant*."
"Character Development: *The Godfather*."
"The Construction of Suspense: *Notorious*."
"Transforming Literature into Cinematic Space and
Time: *Rashomon*."
"Details, Motifs, and the Director's Commentaries:
Viridiana."
"Screen Dialogue: *Bicycle Thieves*."
"The Screenplay as a Model for Literature: *Kiss of the
Spider Woman*."
IN: How Scripts Are Made

3162   **Karloff, Boris.**
"Cricket in California ..."
IN: Celebrity Articles ...

3163   **Karmen, Roman.**
"Soviet Documentary."
IN: Experiment in the Film

3164   **Karnad, Girish.**
"Girish Karnad." [Interview.]
IN: Indian Cinema Superbazaar

3165   **Karr, Kathleen.**
"Early Animation: The Movement Begins."
"Hooray for Providence, Wilkes-Barre, Saranac
Lake--and Hollywood."
"Oz Lives!" [RE: *His Majesty, the Scarecrow; The
Magic Cloak of Oz; The New Wizard of Oz*.]
IN: The American Film Heritage

3166   **Karr, Lawrence F.**
"The Movies Learn to Talk."
IN: The American Film Heritage

3167 **Karr, Lawrence F.**
"The American Film Institute and the Library of
Congress."
IN: Wonderful Inventions

3168 **Karriker, Alexandra Heidl.**
"Patterns of Spirituality in Tarkovsky's Later Films."
IN: Before the Wall Came Down

3169 **Karsunke, Yaak.**
"History of Anti-Teater: The Beginnings."
IN: Fassbinder

3170 **Kas, Pierre.**
"*Shoot the Piano Player.*"
IN: Focus on Shoot the Piano Player

3171 **Kass, Judith.**
"Don Siegel."
IN: The Hollywood Professionals /v. 4

3172 **Kast, Pierre.**
"Don't Play with Fire." [RE: *The Day the Earth Stood
Still.*]
IN: Focus on The Science Fiction Film

3173 **Kast, Pierre.**
"Flattering the Fuzz: Some Remarks on Dandyism
and the Practice of Cinema."
IN: Cahiers du Cinéma, The 1950s

**Kast, Pierre. SEE: Comolli, Jean-Louis; SEE:
Chabrol, Claude; SEE: Bazin, André; SEE:
Delahaye, Michel; SEE: Domarchi, Jean.**

3174 **Katz, John Stuart.**
"Interaction and Film Study."
IN: Perspectives on the Study of Film

3175 **Katz, John Stuart and Judith Milstein Katz.**
"Ethics and the Perception of Ethics in
Autobiographical Film."
IN: Image Ethics

Katz, John Stuart. SEE: Gross, Larry.

Katz, Judith Milstein. SEE: Katz, John Stuart.

3176 **Katz, Samuel.**
"Theatre Management."
IN: The Story of the Films

3177 **Kauffmann, Stanley.**
"The Film Generation." [NOTE: Also called "The Film
Generation: Celebration and Concern."]
IN: Film: Readings in the Mass Media
Film and Literature
The Emergence of Film Art /1 ed
The Emergence of Film Art /2 ed

3178 **Kauffmann, Stanley.**
"*Shoot the Piano Player.*"
IN: Focus on Shoot the Piano Player

3179 **Kauffmann, Stanley.**
"Cum Laude." [RE: *The Graduate.*]
IN: A Casebook on Film

3180 **Kauffmann, Stanley.**
"*La Notte.*"
IN: Awake in the Dark

3181 **Kauffmann, Stanley.**
"Allan King's *Warrendale.*"
IN: The Documentary Tradition /1 ed
The Documentary Tradition /2 ed

3182 **Kauffmann, Stanley.**
"The Achievement of *The Red Desert.*"
IN: The Classic Cinema

3183 **Kauffmann, Stanley.**
"Films and the Future."
IN: Perspectives on the Study of Film

3184 **Kauffmann, Stanley.**
"The Artist Advances." [RE: *The Red Desert.*]
IN: Renaissance of the Film

3185 **Kauffmann, Stanley.**
"A Year with *Blow-Up*: Some Notes."
IN: Focus on Blow-Up

3186 **Kauffmann, Stanley.**
"The Future of Film."
IN: Film: Readings in the Mass Media

3187 **Kauffmann, Stanley.**
"Notes on Theatre-and-Film."
IN: Focus on Film and Theatre

3188 **Kauffmann, Stanley.**
"*Persona.*"
"*Potemkin.*"
"*The Story of Adèle H..*"
IN: Great Film Directors

3189 **Kauffmann, Stanley.**
"*The Sound and the Fury* [novel by] William Faulkner.
Signifying Nothing?"
IN: The Classic American Novel ...

3190 **Kaufman, Boris.**
"Jean Vigo's *A propos de Nice.*"
IN: The Documentary Tradition /1 ed
The Documentary Tradition /2 ed

3191 **Kaul, Mani.**
"Mani Kaul." [Interview.]
"Towards a Cinematic Object."
IN: Indian Cinema Superbazaar

3192 **Kavanagh, James H.**
"Feminism, Humanism and Science in *Alien.*"
IN: Alien Zone

3193 **Kawakita, Mme. Kashiko.**
"Mme. Kashiko Kawakita." [Interview by Joan Mellen.]
IN: Voices from the Japanese Cinema

3194 **Kawin, Bruce F.**
"Children of the Light."
IN: Film Genre Reader
Shadows of the Magic Lamp

3195 Kawin, Bruce F.
"*The Funhouse* and *The Howling*."
 IN: American Horrors

3196 Kawin, Bruce.
"After Midnight."
 IN: The Cult Film Experience

3197 Kawin, Bruce.
"The Mummy's Pool."
 IN: Film Theory and Criticism /3 ed
 Film Theory and Criticism /4 ed
 Planks of Reason

3198 Kawin, Bruce.
"The Montage Element in Faulkner's Fiction."
"Faulkner's Film Career: The Years with Hawks."
 IN: Faulkner, Modernism, and Film

3199 Kawin, Bruce.
"William Faulkner."
 IN: Dictionary of Literary Biography /v. 44

3200 Kay, Karyn.
"*Part-Time Work of a Domestic Slave*, or Putting the
 Screws to Screwball Comedy."
 IN: Women and the Cinema

3201 Kay, Karyn.
"Sisters of the Night." [RE: *Marked Woman*.]
 IN: Movies and Methods: An Anthology

3202 Kay, Karyn.
"*A Very Curious Girl*."
 IN: Sexual Stratagems

3203 Kay, Karyn and Gerald Peary.
"Dorothy Arzner's *Dance, Girl, Dance*."
"Interview with Dorothy Arzner."
 IN: Women and the Cinema

3204 Kayser, Hans Christopher.
"The Monocle as Symbol of German Arrogance in the
 American Media."
 IN: Ethnic Images ...

3205 Kazan, Elia.
"Introduction to *A Face in the Crowd*."
 IN: Hollywood Directors 1941-1976

3206 Kazan, Elia.
"The Situation of the Serious Filmmaker."
 IN: Film: Book 1

3207 Kazanskij, B. [Kazansky, B.]
"The Nature of Cinema."
 IN: Russian Formalist Film Theory
 The Poetics of Cinema

3208 Keane, Marian E.
"A Closer Look at Scopophilia: Mulvey, Hitchcock,
 and *Vertigo*."
 IN: A Hitchcock Reader

3209 Keane, Marian.
"The Great Profile: How Do We Know the Actor from
 the Acting."
 IN: Making Visible the Invisible

3210 Kearns, Edward A.
"Greene's Fictional Treatment: An Experiment in
 Storytelling." [RE: *The Third Man*.]
 IN: Film and Literature: A Comparative ...

3211 Keaton, Buster.
"'Anything Can Happen--and Generally Did': Buster
 Keaton on His Silent-Film Career." [Interview by
 George C. Pratt.]
 IN: Image on the Art ...

3212 Keaton, Buster.
"Buster Keaton." [Interview by Andrew Sarris.]
 IN: Interviews with Film Directors

3213 Keaton, Buster.
"Why I Never Smile."
 IN: Hollywood Directors 1914-1940

3214 Keaton, Diane.
"Diane Keaton." [Interview by Rex Reed.]
 IN: Travolta to Keaton

3215 Kehr, Dave.
"*After Hours*."
"*Lost in America*."
"*Love Streams*."
 IN: Produced and Abandoned

3216 Kehr, Dave.
"Clint Eastwood."
"Travolta vs. Winkler: Transfers from Other Media."
 IN: The Movie Star: The National ...

3217 Keisman, Michael.
"'Frankly, My Dear, I Don't Give a Damn'."
 IN: The Compleat Guide to Film Study

3218 Keller, Gary D.
"*Ballad of an Unsung Hero*."
"The Image of the Chicano in Mexican, United States,
 and Chicano Cinema: An Overview."
 IN: Chicano Cinema

3219 Keller, Marthe.
"Marthe Keller." [Interview by Rex Reed.]
 IN: Travolta to Keaton

3219a Kelley, William and Earl Wallace.
"William Kelley, Earl Wallace." [Interview by Syd Field.]
 IN: Selling a Screenplay

3220 Kellner, Douglas.
"Television Research and Fair Use."
 IN: Fair Use and Free Inquiry

Kellner, Douglas. SEE: Ryan, Michael.

3221 Kellogg, Edward W.
"History of Sound Motion Pictures."
 IN: A Technological History ...

3222 Kelly, Gene.
"Gene Kelly." [Interview by Charles Higham.]
 IN: Celebrity Circus

3223 Kelly, Gene.
"Some Notes for Young Dancers."

IN: Hollywood Directors 1941-1976

3224 Kelly, Keith.
"Abraham Polonsky."
IN: Dictionary of Literary Biography /v. 26

3225 Kelly, Robert.
"On *The Art of Vision*."
"The Image of the Body."
IN: Film Culture Reader

3226 Kelly, Tanita C.
"Robert Bloch."
IN: Dictionary of Literary Biography /v. 44

3227 Kelly, Tanita C.
"Wendell Mayes."
IN: Dictionary of Literary Biography /v. 26

3228 Kelman, Ken.
"Naturalism Transcended (von Stroheim's *Greed*)."
"Perspective Reperceived (Brakhage's *Anticipation of the Night*)."
"The Anti-Information Film (Connor's *Report*)."
"The Films of Jean Vigo: A life."
"The Other Side of Realism (Bunuel's *Un Chien Andalou, L'Age D'Or, Land without Bread*)."
"The Quintessential Documentary (Agee, Levitt, and Loeb's *In the Street*)."
"The Structure of Fate (Bresson's *Pickpocket*)."
IN: The Essential Cinema /v. 1

3229 Kelman, Ken.
"Anticipations of the Light."
IN: The New American Cinema

3230 Kelman, Ken.
"Classic Plastics (and Total Tectonics)."
"Dreyer."
"Smith Myth." [RE: Jack Smith.]
IN: Film Culture Reader

3231 Kelman, Ken.
"The Reality of New Cinema."
IN: The New American Cinema
Film: Readings in the Mass Media

3232 Kelman, Ken.
"*Vampyr* and *Gertrud*."
IN: Great Film Directors

3233 Kendall, Elizabeth.
"Capra and Stanwyck: *Ladies of Leisure*."
"Capra and Colbert: *It Happened One Night*."
"Romantic Comedy Settles In."
"Stevens and Hepburn: *Alice Adams*."
"Stevens and Rogers: *Swing Time*."
"Capra and Arthur: *Mr. Deeds Goes to Town*."
"La Cava and Lombard: *My Man Godfrey*."
"La Cava, Rogers, and Hepburn: *Stage Door*."
"McCarey and Dunne: *The Awful Truth*."
"McCarey, Stevens, and Dunne: *Love Affair* and *Penny Serenade*."
"Sturges, Stanwyck, and Colbert: *The Lady Eve* and *The Palm Beach Story*."
IN: The Runaway Bride

Kenez, Peter. SEE: Drobashenko, Sergei.

3234 Kennedy, Joseph P.
"General Introduction to the Course."
IN: The Story of the Films

3235 Kennedy, Margaret.
"The Mechanized Muse."
IN: Film: An Anthology

3236 Kennedy, X.J.
"Who Killed King Kong?"
IN: Focus on The Horror Film

3237 Kenner, Hugh.
"Faulkner and the Avant-Garde."
IN: Faulkner, Modernism, and Film

3238 Kent, Roberta.
"Exploiting Book-Publishing Rights."
IN: The Movie Business Book

3239 Kent, Sidney R.
"Distributing the Product."
IN: The Story of the Films

3240 Kephart, Edwin T.
"Stewart Stern."
IN: Dictionary of Literary Biography /v. 26

3241 Kepley, Vance, Jr.
"From 'Frontal Lobes' to the 'Bob-and-Bob' Show: NBC Management and Programming Strategies, 1949-65."
IN: Hollywood in the Age of Television

3242 Kepley, Vance, Jr.
"The Evolution of Eisenstein's *Old and New*."
IN: Cinema Examined

3243 Kepley, Vance, Jr.
"Cinema and Everyday Life: Soviet Worker Clubs of the 1920s."
IN: Resisting Images

3244 Kepley, Vance, Jr.
"*Intolerance* and the Soviets: A Historical Investigation."
"The Origins of Soviet Cinema: A Study in Industry Development."
IN: Inside the Film Factory

3245 Kermode, Frank.
"Shakespeare in the Movies."
IN: Film Theory and Criticism /1 ed

3246 Kernan, Margot.
"Radical Image: Revolutionary Film."
IN: Conflict and Control in the Cinema

3247 Kerouac, Jack.
"*Nosferatu*."
IN: Authors on Film
Film and the Liberal Arts

3248 Kerr, Paul.
"Out of What Past? Notes on the B *film noir*."
IN: The Hollywood Film Industry

3249   **Kerr, Paul.**
"Stars and Stardom."
IN: <u>Anatomy of the Movies</u>

Kerr, Paul. SEE: Cook, Pam.

3250   **Kerr, Walter.**
"The Lineage of *Limelight*."
IN: <u>Focus on Chaplin</u>

3251   **Kerr, Walter.**
"The Movies Are Better Than the Theater."
IN: <u>Film: Readings in the Mass Media</u>

3252   **Keshena, Rita.**
"The Role of the American Indians in Motion Pictures."
IN: <u>The Pretend Indians</u>

3252a   **Ketcham, Charles B.**
"*One Flew Over the Cuckoo's Nest*: A Salvific Drama
of Liberation."
IN: <u>Image and Likeness</u>

3253   **Keyerleber, Joseph.**
"*On the Beach*."
IN: <u>Nuclear War Films</u>

3254   **Keyes, A.A.**
"Copyright and Fair Dealing in Canada."
IN: <u>Fair Use and Free Inquiry</u>

3255   **Keyser, Lester J.**
"*A Christmas Carol* [novel by] Charles Dickens; *A
Christmas Carol* [film by] Brian Desmond Hurst. A
Scrooge for All Seasons."
IN: <u>The English Novel and the Movies</u>

3256   **Keyser, Lester.**
"Sex in the Contemporary European Film."
IN: <u>Sexuality in the Movies</u>

3256a   **Keyser, Les.**
"*Taxi Driver*: Bringing Home the War." [RE: Vietnam.]
IN: <u>Columbia Pictures</u>

3257   **Khan, Feroz.**
"Feroz Khan." [Interview.]
IN: <u>Indian Cinema Superbazaar</u>

3258   **Kidd, Charles.**
"The Barrymore Dynasty."
"The Bennett Sisters and Gloria Swanson."
"The Fairbanks Dynasty."
"The Norma Shearer Family Circle."
"Howard Hawks and Mary Astor."
"Alan Ladd and Family."
"The Cansino Dynasty: Rita Hayworth."
"Ginger Rogers and Husbands."
"Marion Davies and Sisters."
"The Lasky, Goldwyn and Warner Dynasties."
"Tyrone Power: Ancestry and Family."
"Humphrey Bogart and Lauren Bacall."
"Gloria Grahame: Ancestry and Family."
"Richard Greene: Ancestry and Family."
"Elizabeth Taylor's Family Circle."
IN: <u>Debrett Goes to Hollywood</u>

3259   **Kidney, Peggy.**
"Bertolucci's Adaptation of *The Conformist*: A Study of
the Function of the Flashbacks in the Narrative
Strategy of the Film."
IN: <u>Film and Literature: A Comparative ...</u>

3260   **Kies, Cosette.**
"The CBS-Vanderbilt Litigation: Taping the Evening
News."
IN: <u>Fair Use and Free Inquiry</u>

3261   **Kilbourne, Don.**
"Herman Mankiewicz."
"Julius and Philip Epstein."
IN: <u>Dictionary of Literary Biography /v. 26</u>

3262   **Kilgore, John.**
"Sexuality and Identity in *The Rocky Horror Picture
Show*."
IN: <u>Eros in the Mind's Eye</u>

3263   **Kindem, Gorham.**
"Hollywood's Movie Star System: An Historical
Overview."
"Hollywood's Conversion to Color: The Technological,
Economic, and Aesthetic Factors."
"The Demise of Kinemacolor."
IN: <u>The American Movie Industry</u>

3264   **Kindem, Gorham.**
"Southern Exposure: *Kudzu* and *It's Grits*."
IN: <u>The South and Film</u>

3265   **Kindem, Gorham and Charles Teddlie.**
"Film Effects and Ethnicity."
IN: <u>Film/Culture: Explorations ...</u>

3266   **Kinder, Marsha.**
"*Tent of Miracles*."
IN: <u>Brazilian Cinema</u>

3267   **Kinder, Marsha.**
"A Thrice-Told Tale: Godard's *Le Mépris* from the
Novel *A Ghost at Noon* by Alberto Moravia."
IN: <u>Modern European Filmmakers ...</u>

3268   **Kinder, Marsha.**
"Antonioni in Transit."
IN: <u>Focus on Blow-Up</u>

3269   **Kinder, Marsha.**
"Reflections on 'Jeanne Dielman'."
IN: <u>Sexual Stratagems</u>

3270   **Kinder, Marsha.**
"The Penetrating Dream Style of Ingmar Bergman."
IN: <u>Film and Dream</u>

3271   **Kinder, Marsha and Beverle Houston.**
"Edwin S. Porter."
"D.W. Griffith: *Birth of a Nation*."
"*Battleship Potemkin*."
"The Expressionist Film: *The Cabinet of Dr. Caligari*."
"The Realist Film: *The Last Laugh, The Love of
Jeanne Ney*."
"*Ballet Mécanique, Un Chien Andalou, The Passion of
Joan of Arc*."

"*Blackmail, M.*"
"*The Rules of the Game, Citizen Kane.*"
"*2001: A Space Odyssey.*"
"*Nanook of the North, Land without Bread, Mosori Monika.*"
"*Triumph of the Will, Listen to Britain, Night and Fog.*"
"*Monterey Pop, Woodstock, Gimme Shelter.*"
"Roberto Rossellini: *Open City, The Rise of Louis XIV.*"
"Luchino Visconti: *La Terra Trema, The Damned.*"
"François Truffaut: *The 400 Blows, Shoot the Piano Player, Jules et Jim, The Wild Child.*"
"Alain Resnais: *Hiroshima, mon amour, Muriel, or the Time of a Return.*"
"Jean-Luc Godard: *Breathless, A Married Woman: Fragments of a Film, La Chinoise.*"
"*Faces, Nude Restaurant, Trash.*"
"*8-1/2, Blow-Up, Contempt, The Immortal Story, Hour of the Wolf.*"
"*Woman in the Dunes.*"
"*The Shooting, Bonnie and Clyde, Rosemary's Baby.*"
"*Satyricon, La Dolce Vita, The Clowns.*"
"*The Battle of Algiers, Z, Zabriskie Point, The Conformist.*"
IN: <u>Close-Up: A Critical ...</u>

3272 **Kinder, Marsha and Beverle Houston.**
"Bertolucci and the Dance of Danger."
IN: <u>Sight and Sound</u>

3273 **Kinder, Marsha and Beverle Houston.**
"Seeing Is Believing: *The Exorcist* and *Don't Look Now.*"
IN: <u>American Horrors</u>

3274 **Kinder, Marsha and Beverle Houston.**
"A Film from Fellini's Mythology." [RE: *Satyricon.*]
IN: <u>The Classic Cinema</u>

3275 **Kinder, Marsha and Chick Strand.**
"Film Studies at Occidental College."
IN: <u>Film Study in the Undergraduate Curriculum</u>

Kinder, Marsha. SEE: Houston, Beverle.

3276 **King, Allan.**
"*A Married Couple.*" [Interview by Alan Rosenthal.]
IN: <u>The New Documentary in Action</u>

3277 **King, Barry.**
"Articulating Stardom."
IN: <u>Star Texts</u>
<u>Stardom</u>

3278 **King, Barry.**
"Stardom as an Occupation."
IN: <u>The Hollywood Film Industry</u>

King, Gayle. SEE: Straubhaar, Joseph Dean.

3279 **King, Henry.**
"No End of Stars."
IN: <u>Hollywood Directors 1941-1976</u>

3280 **King, John.**
"Argentina, Uruguay, Paraguay: Recent Decades."

"Brazil: Cinema Novo to TV Globo."
"Mexico: Inside the Industrial Labyrinth."
"Cuba: Revolutionary Projections."
"Chilean Cinema in Revolution and Exile."
"Andean Images: Bolivia, Ecuador and Peru."
"Colombia and Venezuela: Cinema and the State."
"Central America and the Caribbean: Movies in Big Brother's Backyard."
IN: <u>Magical Reels</u>

3281 **King, Kenneth.**
"23 Toward Re:Programming *Nature* with Mirrors: Film, Theater &."
IN: <u>The New American Cinema</u>

3282 **King, Larry L.**
"The Battle of Popcorn Bay."
IN: <u>Crossroads to the Cinema</u>

3283 **King, Norman.**
"History and Actuality: Abel Gance's *Napoléon vu par Abel Gance.*"
"Eye for *Irony*: Eric Rohmer's *Ma nuit chez Maud.*"
IN: <u>French Film: Texts and Contexts</u>

3284 **King, Roger.**
"Drinking and Drunkenness in *Crossroads* and *Coronation Street.*" [RE: British television.]
IN: <u>Images of Alcoholism</u>

3285 **King, Stephen.**
"The Modern American Horror Movie--Text and Subtext."
"The Horror Movie as Junk Food."
"The Glass Teat, or, This Monster Was Brought to You by Gainesburgers."
"Horror Fiction."
"The Last Waltz--Horror and Morality, Horror and Magic."
IN: <u>Stephen King's Danse Macabre</u>

3286 **Kingsley, Dorothy.**
"Dorothy Kingsley: The Fixer." [Interview by Patrick McGilligan.]
IN: <u>Backstory 2</u>

3287 **Kinnear, G.C.**
"Ingmar Bergman, Master of Illusion."
IN: <u>Man and the Movies</u>

3288 **Kinney, Judy Lee.**
"*Gardens of Stone, Platoon,* and *Hamburger Hill*: Ritual and Remembrance."
IN: <u>Inventing Vietnam</u>

3289 ***Kino i zhizn,* editorial.**
"Film Work and the Mass Audience."
"Is There a Soviet Sound Cinema?"
IN: <u>The Film Factory</u>

3290 **Kintner, Robert E.**
"Broadcasting and the News."
IN: <u>Sight, Sound, and Society</u>

3291 **Kirihara, Don.**
"Kabuki, Cinema and Mizoguchi Kenji."
IN: <u>Cinema and Language</u>

3292 Kirihara, Donald.
"Sound in *Les Vacances de Monsieur Hulot*."
IN: <u>Close Viewings</u>

3293 Kirshon, Vladimir.
"Literature, Theatre and Cinema (extract)."
IN: <u>The Film Factory</u>

3294 Kirstein, Lincoln.
"James Cagney and the American Hero."
IN: <u>Hound & Horn</u>

3295 Kitses, Jim.
"Anthony Mann: the Overreacher."
"Budd Boetticher: the Rules of the Game."
"Sam Peckinpah: the Savage Eye."
IN: <u>Horizons West</u>

3296 Kitses, Jim.
"Authorship and Genre: Notes on the Western."
IN: <u>Horizons West</u>
   <u>Conflict and Control in the Cinema</u>

3297 Kitses, Jim.
"Borden Chase, An Interview."
IN: <u>The Hollywood Screenwriters</u>

3298 Kitses, Jim.
"The Western: Ideology and Archetype."
IN: <u>Focus on The Western</u>

Klaidman, Stephen. SEE: Beauchamp, Thomas.

3299 Klapp, Orrin.
"Heroes, Villains and Fools, as Agents of Social
   Control."
IN: <u>Conflict and Control in the Cinema</u>

3300 Klaprat, Cathy.
"The Star as Market Strategy: Bette Davis in Another
   Light."
IN: <u>The American Film Industry /rev ed</u>

3301 Klawans, Stuart.
"Colorization: Rose-Tinted Spectacles."
IN: <u>Seeing Through Movies</u>

3302 Kleiman, Evan.
"[A History of Italian Cinema:] The 60's and 70's."
IN: <u>Italian Cinema</u>

Kleiman, Evan. SEE: Suckow, Sherrie.

3303 Kleiman, Naum.
"Eisenstein's Graphic Work."
IN: <u>Eisenstein at Ninety</u>

3304 Klein, I.
"On Mighty Mouse."
IN: <u>The American Animated Cartoon</u>

Klein, James. SEE: Reichert, Julia.

3305 Klein, Michael.
"*Barry Lyndon* [novel by] W.M. Thackeray; [film by]
   Stanley Kubrick. Narrative and Discourse in
   Kubrick's Modern Tragedy."
IN: <u>The English Novel and the Movies</u>

3306 Klein, Michael.
"*Miss Lonelyhearts* [novel by] Nathanael West. Miss
   L. Gets Married."
IN: <u>The Modern American Novel ...</u>

3307 Klein, Michael.
"Historical Memory, Film, and the Vietnam Era."
IN: <u>From Hanoi to Hollywood</u>

3308 Klein, Michael.
"Strick's Adaptation of Joyce's *Portrait of the Artist*:
   Discourse and Containing Discourse."
IN: <u>Narrative Strategies</u>

3309 Klein, Michael.
"The Twilight of Romanticism: *Adele H.*"
IN: <u>Women and the Cinema</u>

3310 Klein, Michael.
"The Literary Sophistication of François Truffaut."
IN: <u>The Emergence of Film Art /1 ed</u>
   <u>The Emergence of Film Art /2 ed</u>
   <u>Film And/As Literature</u>

3311 Kleinhans, Chuck.
"*Marilyn Times Five*."
IN: <u>Women and the Cinema</u>

3312 Kleinhans, Chuck.
"*Two or Three Things I Know About Her*: Godard's
   Analysis of Women in Capitalist Society."
IN: <u>Sexual Stratagems</u>

3313 Kleinhans, Chuck.
"Forms, Politics, Makers and Context: Basic Issues
   for a Theory of Radical Political Documentary."
IN: <u>Show Us Life</u>

3314 Kleinhans, Chuck.
"Notes on Melodrama and the Family under
   Capitalism."
IN: <u>Imitations of Life</u>

3315 Kleinhans, Chuck.
"Working-Class Film Heroes: Junior Johnson, Evel
   Knievel and the Film Audience." [RE: *The Last
   American Hero*; *Evel Knievel*.]
IN: <u>Jump Cut</u>

**Kleinhans, Chuck. SEE: Steven, Peter; SEE:
Waugh, Tom.**

3316 Kline, Herbert.
"Films Without Make-Believe."
IN: <u>The Documentary Tradition /1 ed</u>
   <u>The Documentary Tradition /2 ed</u>

3317 Kline, Richard.
"Richard Kline." [Interview by Kris Malkiewicz.]
IN: <u>Film Lighting</u>

3318 Kline, T. Jefferson.
"The Absent Presence: Stendhal in *Prima della
   rivoluzione*."
"Doubling *The Double*: *Partner* as Imitation and
   Oppression."

"The Villa Borges: Labyrinths in *The Spider's Stratagem*."
"The Unconforming *Conformist*."
"'A Turgid, Unreal Past, in Certain Measure True': *Last Tango in Paris*."
"Doppia della rivoluzione: *Novecento* and the Play of Repetions as Revolution."
"'... Perforce to Dream': Oneiric Projection and Protection in *Luna*."
   IN: Bertolucci's Dream Loom

3319 **Kline, T. Jefferson.**
"The Unconformist: Bertolucci's *The Conformist* from the Novel by Alberto Moravia."
   IN: Modern European Filmmakers ...

3320 **Klinger, Barbara.**
"Cinema/Ideology/Criticism."
   IN: Film Genre Reader

3321 **Klinger, Barbara.**
"*Psycho*: The Institutionalization of Female Sexuality."
   IN: A Hitchcock Reader

3322 **Kluge, Alexander.**
"Word and Film."
   IN: Writing in a Film Age

3323 **Kluge, Alexander.**
"Pact with a Dead Man."
"Theses about the New Media."
"The Spectator as Entrepreneur."
"The Early Days of the Ulm Institute for Film Design."
"Utopian Cinema."
"What Do the 'Oberhauseners' Want?"
   IN: West German Filmmakers on Film

Kluge, Alexander. SEE: Brustellin, Alf.

3324 **Klugherz, Daniel.**
"Documentary—Where's the Wonder?"
   IN: The Documentary Tradition /1 ed
        The Documentary Tradition /2 ed

3325 **Knapp, Steven and Barry L. Sherman.**
"Motion Picture Attendance: A Market Segmentation Approach."
   IN: Current Research in Film /v. 2

3326 **Knight, Arthur.**
"*Gold of Naples*."
"*Tom Jones*."
"Ernst Lubitsch."
"René Clair."
   IN: Movie Comedy

3327 **Knight, Arthur.**
"An Approach to Film History."
   IN: Film Study in Higher Education

3328 **Knight, Arthur.**
"Arthur Knight: The Critic."
   IN: The Real Tinsel

3329 **Knight, Arthur.**
"Engaging the Eye-Minded."
   IN: Film: Readings in the Mass Media

3330 **Knight, Arthur.**
"Experimental Film."
   IN: Ideas on Film

3331 **Knight, Arthur.**
"For Eggheads Only?"
   IN: Film and Society
        Film: Book 1

3332 **Knight, Arthur.**
"Marcel Ophuls's *The Sorrow and the Pity*."
   IN: The Documentary Tradition /2 ed

3333 **Knight, Arthur.**
"Sweden's Arne Sucksdorff."
   IN: The Documentary Tradition /1 ed
        The Documentary Tradition /2 ed

3334 **Knight, Arthur.**
"The Father of Film Technique." [RE: D.W. Griffith.]
"*The Birth of a Nation*."
   IN: The First Film Makers

3335 **Knight, Arthur.**
"The Eucalyptic Dream."
   IN: The Movies: An American Idiom

3336 **Knight, Arthur.**
"The Movies Learn to Talk: Ernst Lubitsch, René Clair, and Rouben Mamoulian."
   IN: Film Sound

3337 **Knight, Arthur.**
"The Course of Italian Neorealism."
   IN: The Emergence of Film Art /1 ed
        The Emergence of Film Art /2 ed

3338 **Knight, Arthur.**
"The Future of Film."
   IN: Film: Readings in the Mass Media

3339 **Knight, Arthur.**
"Three Encounters with *Blow-Up*."
   IN: Focus on Blow-Up

3340 **Knight, Arthur.**
"*Citizen Kane* Revisited."
   IN: Directors in Action
        Focus on Citizen Kane

3341 **Knight, Arthur.**
"*Stagecoach* Revisited."
   IN: Directors in Action

3342 **Knight, Eric W.**
"Letter on Levaco's Introduction." [RE: Ron Levaco's "Kuleshov and Semiology".]
   IN: Screen Reader 1

3343 **Knock, Thomas J.**
"History with Lightning: The Forgotten Film *Wilson*."
   IN: Hollywood as Historian

3344 **Knowlton, Marianne H.**
"'Soldier's Home': A Space Between."
   IN: A Moving Picture Feast

3345   Knox, Alexander.
"Acting and Behaving."
IN: <u>Film: A Montage of Theories</u>

3346   Knox, Donald.
"[From:] *The Magic Factory*: The *American in Paris* Ballet."
IN: <u>Film Theory and Criticism /3 ed</u>

3347   Kobal, John.
"Clara Bow—the 'It' Girl."
IN: <u>Movies of the Silent Years</u>

3348   Kobayashi, Masaki.
"Masaki Kobayashi." [Interview by Joan Mellen.]
IN: <u>Voices from the Japanese Cinema</u>

3349   Koch, Gertrud.
"Blindness as Insight: Visions of the Unseen in *Land of Silence and Darkness*."
IN: <u>The Films of Werner Herzog</u>

3350   Koch, Gertrud.
"The Stairway to Exile: *High and Low*."
IN: <u>The Films of G.W. Pabst</u>

3351   Koch, Gertrude.
"Between Two Worlds: von Sternberg's *The Blue Angel*."
IN: <u>German Film and Literature</u>

3352   Koch, Howard W.
"Howard W. Koch." [An interview.]
IN: <u>Interviews with B ...</u>

3353   Koch, Howard.
"Script to Screen with Max Ophuls."
IN: <u>The Hollywood Screenwriters</u>

3354   Koch, Stephen.
"Andy Warhol's Silence."
IN: <u>The Avant-Garde Film</u>

3355   Koch, Stephen.
"*Blow-Job* and Pornography."
IN: <u>Movies and Methods: An Anthology</u>

3356   Kolker, Robert Phillip.
"Bloody Liberations, Bloody Declines: Arthur Penn."
"Tectonics of the Mechanical Man: Stanley Kubrick."
"Leave the Gun. Take the Cannoli: Francis Ford Coppola."
"Expressions of the Street: Martin Scorsese."
"Radical Surfaces: Robert Altman."
IN: <u>A Cinema of Loneliness</u>

3357   Kolker, Robert Phillip.
"Woman as Genre."
IN: <u>Women and Film</u>

Komarov, Sergei. SEE: Pudovkin, Vsevolod.

3358   Konigsberg, Ira.
"Cinema of Entrapment: Rivette's *La Religieuse* from the Novel by Denis Diderot."
IN: <u>Modern European Filmmakers ...</u>

3359   Kopit, Arthur.
"*Indians* [excerpt]."
IN: <u>The American West on Film</u>

3360   Kopple, Barbara and Hart Perry.
"*Harlan County, USA* [Interviews with] Barbara Kopple and Hart Perry."
IN: <u>The Documentary Conscience</u>

3361   Korda, Alexander.
"British Films: To-day and To-morrow."
IN: <u>Footnotes to the Film</u>

3362   Kort, Melissa Sue.
"'Shadows of the Substance': Women Screenwriters in the 1930s."
IN: <u>Women and Film</u>

3363   Korte, Walter F., Jr.
"Marxism and Formalism in the Films of Luchino Visconti."
IN: <u>Cinema Examined</u>

3364   Korte, Walter.
"*Vaghe stelle dell'orsa ...*: Recent Work of a Neglected Master."
IN: <u>Man and the Movies</u>

3365   Koster, Henry.
"Directing in CinemaScope."
IN: <u>Hollywood Directors 1941-1976</u>

3366   Koszarski, Diane Kaiser.
"Gdansk Macabre."
IN: <u>Politics, Art and Commitment ...</u>

3367   Koszarski, Diane.
"C. Gardner Sullivan."
IN: <u>Dictionary of Literary Biography /v. 26
    The First Film Makers</u>

3368   Koszarski, Richard.
"*Greed*."
IN: <u>Movies of the Silent Years</u>

3369   Koszarski, Richard.
"The Years Have Not Been Kind to Lois Weber."
IN: <u>Women and the Cinema</u>

3370   Koszarski, Richard.
"The Men with the Movie Cameras."
IN: <u>Film Theory and Criticism /1 ed
    Film Theory and Criticism /2 ed</u>

3371   Koszarski, Richard.
"*The Gun Woman*."
"Introduction: The Film Scene in 1913-18."
"*Behind the Screen, The Rink* [and] *The Immigrant*."
"*The Gangsters and The Girl*."
"*Rumplestiltskin*."
"*The Blue Bird*."
"Lost Films."
IN: <u>The Rivals of D.W. Griffith</u>

3372   Koszarski, Richard.
"Jules Furthman."
IN: <u>The Hollywood Screenwriters</u>

3373 Koszarski, Richard.
"Clarence Brown."
"Rowland Brown."
"E.A. Dupont."
"Maurice Tourneur."
"Harry Langdon."
IN: Cinema: A Critical Dictionary

3373a Koszarski, Richard.
"Offscreen Spaces: Images of Early Cinema
Production and Exhibition."
IN: Before Hollywood

3374 Kotcheff, Ted.
"Ted Kotcheff." [Interview by John Andrew Gallagher.]
IN: Film Directors on Directing

3375 Kott, Jan.
"Shakespeare--Cruel and True."
IN: Film and the Liberal Arts

3376 Kovács, Katherine Singer.
"George[s] Méliès and the *Féerie*."
IN: Film Before Griffith

3377 Kovács, Katherine Singer.
"Luis Buñuel and Pierre Louÿs: Two Visions of
Obscure Objects."
IN: Cinema Examined

3378 Kovacs, Laszlo.
"Laszlo Kovacs." [Interview by Dennis Schaefer and
Larry Salvato.]
IN: Masters of Light

3379 Kovács, Steven.
"Robert Desnos: The Visionary as Critic."
"Dada Comes in at Intermission: Picabia and René
Clair on *Entr'acte*."
"An American in Paris: Man Ray as Filmmaker."
"What the Surrealist Film Might Have Been: Artaud
and the Cinema."
"The Fulfillment of Surrealist Hopes: Dali and Buñuel
Appear."
IN: From Enchantment to Rage

3380 Kowalski, Bernard L.
"Bernard L. Kowalski." [An interview.]
IN: Interviews with B ...

3381 Kozintsev, Grigori and Leonid Trauberg.
"*The Youth of Maxim* (extracts)."
IN: The Film Factory

3382 Kozintsev, Grigori Mikhailovitch [G.M.].
"A Child of the Revolution." [RE: Soviet silent cinema.]
IN: Conflict and Control in the Cinema
Cinema in Revolution

**3383 Kozintsev, Grigori, Leonid Trauberg, Sergei
Yutkevich and Georgi Kryzhitsky.**
"Eccentrism."
IN: The Film Factory

3384 Kozlenko, William.
"The Animated Cartoon and Walt Disney."

IN: The Emergence of Film Art /1 ed
The Emergence of Film Art /2 ed

3385 Kozloff, Max.
"*The Blow-Up*."
IN: Focus on Blow-Up

3386 Kracauer, Siegfried.
"[From:] *Theory of Film*: The Establishment of
Physical Existence."
IN: Film Theory and Criticism /1 ed
Film Theory and Criticism /2 ed
Film Theory and Criticism /3 ed
Film Theory and Criticism /4 ed

3387 Kracauer, Siegfried.
"[From:] *Theory of Film*: Basic Concepts."
IN: Film Theory and Criticism /1 ed
Film Theory and Criticism /2 ed
Film Theory and Criticism /3 ed
Film Theory and Criticism /4 ed

3388 Kracauer, Siegfried.
"[From:] *Theory of Film*: The Spectator."
IN: Film Theory and Criticism /1 ed
Film: Book 1

3389 Kracauer, Siegfried.
"Theory of Film [excerpt]."
IN: Film: A Montage of Theories

3390 Kracauer, Siegfried.
"[From:] *From Caligari to Hitler: The Cabinet of Dr.
Caligari*." [NOTE: Also called "*Caligari*".]
IN: Film Theory and Criticism /4 ed
Film: An Anthology

3391 Kracauer, Siegfried.
"The Making of *Caligari*." [NOTE: This is an
abbreviated version of the piece in previous entry.]
"Murderer Among Us." [RE: *M*.]
IN: The Classic Cinema

3392 Kracauer, Siegfried.
"Jean Vigo."
IN: Introduction to the Art of the Movies

3393 Kracauer, Siegfried.
"*The Blue Angel*."
IN: Sternberg

3394 Kracauer, Siegfried.
"National Types as Hollywood Presents Them."
IN: The Movies: An American Idiom

3395 Kracauer, Siegfried.
"Dialogue and Sound."
IN: Film Sound

3396 Kracauer, Siegfried.
"Cross-Section Films."
IN: The Documentary Tradition /1 ed
The Documentary Tradition /2 ed

3397 Kracauer, Siegfried.
"[From:] Propaganda and the Nazi War Film."
IN: Film and Society

3398 Kracauer, Siegfried.
"*Metropolis* and *M*."
    IN: Great Film Directors

3399 Kracauer, Sigfried.
"The German Horror Film: The Case of Dr. Caligari."
    IN: Conflict and Control in the Cinema

3400 Král, Petr.
"Larry Semon's Message."
    IN: The Shadow and Its Shadow

Kramer, Anne. SEE: Kantor, Bernard R.

3401 Kramer, Stanley.
"*On the Beach*: A Renewed Interest."
    IN: Omni's Screen Flights ...

3402 Krams, Arthur.
"Set Decorator."
    IN: Hollywood Speaks!

3403 Krasna, Norman.
"Norman Krasna: The Woolworth's Touch." [Interview by Pat McGilligan.]
    IN: Backstory

Kraybill, Donald B. SEE: Hostetler, John A.

3404 Krejcik, Jiri.
"Jirí Krejcik." [Interview by Antonín J. Liehm.]
    IN: Closely Watched Films

3405 Kress, Harold.
"Harold Kress." [Interview by Vincent LoBrutto.]
    IN: Selected Takes

3406 Kreuger, Miles (editor).
"The *Jazz Singer*."
"*The Broadway Melody*."
"*The Love Parade*."
"*All Quiet on the Western Front*."
"*Grand Hotel*."
"*Dinner at Eight*."
"*Captains Courageous*."
"*The Good Earth*."
"*Lost Horizon*."
"*Gone with the Wind*."
"*The Great Dictator*."
"*Citizen Kane*."
    IN: Souvenir Programs

3407 Krieger, Martin Theo.
"Finding a Home in Berlin."
    IN: West German Filmmakers on Film

3408 Kristeva, Julia.
"Ellipsis on Dread and the Specular Seduction."
    IN: Narrative, Apparatus, Ideology

3409 Kristl, Vlado.
"Application for Film Subsidy."
    IN: West German Filmmakers on Film

3410 Kroll, Jack.
"James Cagney."
"Jane Fonda."
"John Wayne."
"Robert De Niro."
"Woody Allen."
    IN: The Movie Star: The National ...

3411 Krška, Václav.
"Václav Krška." [Interview by Antonín J. Liehm.]
    IN: Closely Watched Films

3412 Krumbachová, Ester.
"Ester Krumbachová." [Interview by Antonín J. Liehm.]
    IN: Closely Watched Films

Kryzhitsky, Georgi SEE: Kozintsev, Grigori.

3413 Kubelka, Peter.
"The Theory of Metrical Film."
    IN: The Avant-Garde Film

3414 Kubrick, Stanley.
"Stanley Kubrick." [Interview by Joseph Gelmis.]
    IN: The Film Director as Superstar

3415 Kubrick, Stanley.
"Words and Movies."
    IN: Hollywood Directors 1941-1976

3416 Kucera, Jaroslav.
"Jaroslav Kucera." [Interview by Antonín J. Liehm.]
    IN: Closely Watched Films

3417 Kuchar, George.
"George Kuchar." [Interview by Scott MacDonald.]
    IN: A Critical Cinema

3418 Kuchl, Jerome, John Pett, Susan McConachy and Raye Farr.
"*The World at War* [Interviews with] Jerome Kuchl, Associate Producer; John Pett, Director; Susan McConachy, Researcher; Raye Farr, Film Research."
    IN: The Documentary Conscience

3419 Kuehl, Jerry.
"History on the Public Screen II."
    IN: The Historian and Film
        New Challenges for Documentary

3420 Kuehl, Jerry.
"Truth Claims."
    IN: New Challenges for Documentary

3421 Kuhn, Anna K.
"Rainer Werner Fassbinder: The Alienated Vision."
    IN: New German Filmmakers

3422 Kuhn, Annette.
"Cultural Theory and Science Fiction Cinema."
    IN: Alien Zone

3423 Kuhn, Annette.
"Hollywood and the New Women's Cinema."
    IN: Films for Women

3424 Kuhn, Annette.
"Textual Politics."
    IN: Issues in Feminist Film Criticism

3425 **Kuhn, Annette.**
"Women's Genres: Melodrama, Soap Opera and
Theory."
IN: Home Is Where the Heart Is

3426 **Kuhn, Annette [with Frances Borzello, Jill Pack
and Cassandra Wedd].**
"Living Dolls and 'Real Women'." [RE: feminism.]
"Lawless Seeing." [RE: pornography.]
"Sexual Disguise and Cinema."
"*The Big Sleep*: Censorship, Film Text and Sexuality."
"A Moral Subject: The VD Propaganda Feature."
IN: The Power of the Image

Kuhn, Annette. SEE: Cook, Pam.

3427 **Kuhns, William.**
"Can Teachers Liberate Commercial TV."
IN: Films Deliver

3428 **Kuiper, John B.**
"The Growth of a Film Director—D.W. Griffith."
IN: Wonderful Inventions

3429 **Kuleshov, Lev.**
"Americanitis."
"The Question of the Film Repertory."
"Handiwork."
"Will ... Tenacity ... Eye."
"Why I Am Not Working."
"David Griffith and Charlie Chaplin."
"The Rehearsal Method."
"Our First Experiences."
"Address to the Union of Soviet Film Workers."
"The Principles of Montage."
"In Maloi Gnezdnikovsky Lane."
"On the Red Front."
IN: Kuleshov on Film

3430 **Kuleshov, Lev.**
"Art, Contemporary Life and Cinema."
"Americanism."
"Chamber Cinema."
"Cinema as the Fixing of Theatrical Action."
"The Tasks of the Artist in Cinema."
"'Art' Cinema."
"*Mr. West*." [RE: *The Extraordinary Adventures of Mr.
West in the Land of the Bolsheviks*.]
IN: The Film Factory

3431 **Kuleshov, Lev (prepared by Ron Levaco).**
"Kuleshov and Semiology: Selections from Lev
Kuleshov's *Art of the Cinema*."
IN: Screen Reader 1

3432 **Kuleshov, Lev Vladimirovitch.**
"The Origins of Montage."
IN: Cinema in Revolution

3433 **Kuleshov, Lev.**
"The Art of Cinema."
IN: The Film Factory
Kuleshov on Film

3434 **Kuleshov, Lev.**
"The Training of the Actor."
IN: Star Texts

3435 **Kuney, Jack.**
"*Dubrovnik Festival*." [Interview by Alan Rosenthal.]
IN: The New Documentary in Action

3436 **Kuntz, Jonathan.**
"Norman Panama and Melvin Frank."
IN: Dictionary of Literary Biography /v. 26

3437 **Kuntzel, Thierry.**
"Le Défilement: A View in Closeup." [RE: *Appetite of a
Bird*.]
IN: Apparatus

3438 **Kunzle, David.**
"Hogarth Piracies and the Origin of Visual Copyright."
IN: Fair Use and Free Inquiry

3439 **Kupferberg, Audrey.**
"Ernest Vajda."
IN: Dictionary of Literary Biography /v. 44

3440 **Kurosawa, Akira.**
"Akira Kurosawa." [Interview by Joan Mellen.]
IN: Voices from the Japanese Cinema

3441 **Kurosawa, Akira.**
"Akira Kurosawa." [Interview by Andrew Sarris.]
IN: Interviews with Film Directors

3442 **Kurosawa, Akira.**
"Japan's Poet Laureate on Film."
IN: Film Makers on Film Making

3443 **Kusielewicz, Eugene.**
"Questions About the Polish Image in American Film
and Television."
IN: Ethnic Images ...

3444 **Kustow, Michael.**
"*Hamlet* [1964]."
IN: Focus on Shakespearean Films

3445 **Kustow, Michael.**
"Chris Marker's *Le Joli Mai*."
IN: The Documentary Tradition /1 ed
The Documentary Tradition /2 ed

3446 **Kwapy, William.**
"Literary Adaptations."
IN: Screen Experience

3447 **Kwok and M.C. Quiquemelle.**
"Chinese Cinema and Realism."
IN: Film and Politics in the Third World

3448 **Kwok Wah Lau, Jenny.**
"A Cultural Interpretation of the Popular Cinema of
China and Hong Kong."
IN: Perspectives on Chinese Cinema

3449 **Kyrou, Ado.**
"*L'Age D'Or*."
"Monsters." [RE: *Nazarin*.]
IN: The World of Luis Buñuel

3450 Kyrou, Ado.
"Science and Fiction."
IN: Focus on The Science Fiction Film

3451 Kyrou, Ado.
"The Fantastic--The Marvellous."
"Eroticism [equals] Love."
"The Film and I."
"The Marvellous is Popular."
IN: The Shadow and Its Shadow

3452 L'Amour, Louis.
"Shanghai, Not Without Gestures."
"Show Me the Way to Go Home."
"The Outlaw Rides Again."
IN: The Best of Rob Wagner's Script

3453 L'Herbier, Marcel.
"Hermes and Silence."
IN: French Film Theory and Criticism /v. 1

3454 La Place, Maria.
"Producing and Consuming the Woman's Film:
Discursive Struggle in *Now, Voyager*."
IN: Home Is Where the Heart Is

3455 La Rochelle, Réal.
"Committed Documentary in Quebec: A Still-Birth?"
IN: Show Us Life

3456 La Rocque, Rod.
"Rod La Rocque: The Player."
IN: The Real Tinsel

3457 La Valley, Albert J.
"Traditions of Trickery: The Role of Special Effects in
the Science Fiction Film."
IN: Shadows of the Magic Lamp

3458 La Valley, Albert J.
"*Dodsworth* [novel by] Sinclair Lewis. The Virtues of
Unfaithfulness."
IN: The Classic American Novel ...

3459 Laban, Lawrence F.
"*Joseph Andrews* [novel by] Henry Fielding; *Joseph
Andrews* [film by] Tony Richardson. Visualizing
Fielding's Point of View."
IN: The English Novel and the Movies

3460 Labarthe, André S.
"The Purest Vision: *Les Bonnes Femmes*."
"Marienbad Year Zero." [RE: *Last Year at Marienbad*.]
"Pagnol."
IN: Cahiers du Cinéma, 1960-1968

Labarthe, André S. SEE: Comolli, Jean-Louis.

3461 Lacaba, Jose F.
"Movies, Critics, and the 'Bakya' Crowd."
"Notes on 'Bakya': Being an Apologia of Sorts for
Filipino Masscult."
IN: Readings in Philippine Cinema

3462 Lacassin, Francis.
"Out of Oblivion: Alice Guy Blaché."
IN: Sexual Stratagems

Lacy, Madison. SEE: Marshall, Melba.

3463 Laemmle, Carl.
"The Business of Motion Pictures."
IN: The American Film Industry

3464 Laemmle, Robert.
"The Independent Exhibitor."
IN: The Movie Business Book

3465 Lafargue, André.
"Working with a Friend." [RE: Charles Chaplin.]
IN: Essays on Chaplin

3466 Lafferty, William.
"Feature Films on Prime-Time Television."
IN: Hollywood in the Age of Television

3467 Lafferty, William.
"Film and Television."
IN: Film and the Arts in Symbiosis

3468 Lagny, Michel.
"The Fleeting Gaze: Jean Renoir's *La Bête humaine*."
IN: French Film: Texts and Contexts

3469 Lahiri, Monojit.
"The Commercial: The Dawn of a Golden Period?"
IN: Indian Cinema Superbazaar

3470 Laiter, Salomón.
"Salomón Laiter." [Interview by Beatrice Reyes
Nevares.]
IN: The Mexican Cinema

3471 Lake, Veronica.
"You've Got to Have a Gimmick."
IN: Bedside Hollywood

3472 Lambert, Gavin.
"*Romeo and Juliet* [1954]."
IN: Focus on Shakespearean Films

3473 Lambert, Gavin.
"Sight and Sound."
IN: Film: A Montage of Theories

3474 Lambert, Gavin.
"Stroheim: He Didn't Really Belong to America."
IN: The First Film Makers

3475 Lambert, Gavin.
"Who Wants True?" [RE: aesthetics.]
"*Paths of Glory*."
IN: Sight and Sound

3476 Lambert, Gavin.
"*Un condamné à mort s'est échappé*: A Review."
IN: Great Film Directors

3477 Lancaster, Burt.
"Burt Lancaster." [Interview by Judith Crist.]
IN: Take 22

3478 Lancaster, Burt.
"Burt Lancaster." [Interview by Rex Reed.]
IN: Travolta to Keaton

3479 **Landow, George and Fred Camper.**
"[On] George Landow."
IN: Structural Film Anthology

3480 **Landry, Lionel.**
"Caligarism or the Theater's Revenge."
"*El Dorado* [1921]."
IN: French Film Theory and Criticism /v. 1

3481 **Landy, Marcia.**
"The Family Melodrama in the Italian Cinema, 1929-1943."
IN: Imitations of Life

Landy, Marcia. SEE: Fischer, Lucy.

3482 **Lang, Fritz.**
"Fritz Lang: The Director."
IN: The Real Tinsel

3483 **Lang, Fritz.**
"Fritz Lang."
IN: The Celluloid Muse

3484 **Lang, Fritz.**
"Fritz Lang." [Interview by Andrew Sarris.]
IN: Interviews with Film Directors

3485 **Lang, Fritz.**
"Happily Ever After."
IN: Film Makers on Film Making

3486 **Lang, Fritz.**
"The Freedom of the Screen."
IN: Hollywood Directors 1941-1976

3487 **Lang, Robert.**
"Melodrama and the 'Ways of the World'."
"Tragedy, Melodrama, and the 'Moral Occult'."
"Spectacle and Narrative."
"Address."
"Genre."
"D.W. Griffith ... The Victorian Heritage: *Way Down East*."
"D.W. Griffith ... The Loom of Fate: *The Mother and the Law*."
"D.W. Griffith ... 'The Tragic Dead End of Victorian American Culture': *Broken Blossoms*."
"King Vidor ... Melodrama and Identity in Mass Society: *The Crowd*."
"King Vidor ... 'I don't want to be like me ... but like the people in the movie!': *Stella Dallas*."
"King Vidor ... From the Wrong Side of the Tracks: *Ruby Gentry*."
"King Vidor ... Vidor and the Social Discourse: Provisional Conclusions."
"Vincente Minnelli ... What a Woman Really Wants, or What She Really Means: *Madame Bovary*."
"Vincente Minnelli ... Coming Home: *Some Came Running*."
"Vincente Minnelli ... To Be a Man: *Home from the Hill*."
"Vincente Minnelli ... Minnelli and Melodrama: Provisional Conclusions."
"Affects and Ideals: An Afterword."

IN: American Film Melodrama

3488 **Langdon, Harry.**
"The Serious Side of Comedy Making."
IN: Hollywood Directors 1914-1940

3489 **Langer, Susanne.**
"A Note on the Film."
IN: Film: A Montage of Theories
Film: An Anthology

3490 **Langlois, Henri.**
"*Les Bas-Fonds*."
IN: French Film Theory and Criticism /v. 2

3491 **Langlois, Henri.**
"French Cinema: Origins."
"German Cinema: Its Origins and Its Masters of the 20s."
IN: Cinema: A Critical Dictionary

3492 **Langlois, Henri.**
"The Modernity of Howard Hawks."
IN: Focus on Howard Hawks

3493 **Langlois, Walter G.**
"Malraux's *Sierra de Teruel*."
IN: Wonderful Inventions

3494 **Lankes, L.R.**
"Historical Sketch of Television's Progress."
IN: A Technological History ...

3495 **Lansdale, Joe R.**
"A Hard-on for Horror: Low-Budget Excitement."
IN: Cut!: Horror Writers ...

3496 **Lant, Antonia.**
"The Female Spy: Gender, Nationality, and War in *I See a Dark Stranger*."
IN: Resisting Images

3497 **Lapsansky, E. Jones.**
"Distorted Reflections: Thoughts on Afro-Americans and American Visual Imagery."
IN: Ethnic Images ...

3498 **Lardner, Ring, Jr.**
"Ring Lardner, Jr." [Interview by William Froug.]
IN: The Screenwriter Looks ...

3499 **Larkin, Alile Sharon.**
"Black Women Film-makers Defining Ourselves: Feminism in Our Own Voice."
IN: Female Spectators

3500 **Larsson, Donald F.**
"The Camera Eye: 'Cinematic' Narrative in *U.S.A.* and *Gravity's Rainbow*."
IN: Ideas of Order in Literature & Film

3501 **Larue, Johanne and Carole Zucker.**
"James Dean: The Pose of Reality? *East of Eden* and the Method Performance."
IN: Making Visible the Invisible

3502 **Lary, N. M.**
"Shklovsky and Dostoevsky as Demons of Darkness / *House of the Dead*: A Dossier."

"Roshal's Socialist Realist Myth / Shklovsky and
   Eisenstein on the New Myths."
"Ermler's Pure Art of the Party Line / Shklovsky and
   Eisenstein on Ermler."
"Eisenstein's Cinema of Cruelty."
"Ivan Pyriev: Struggles of a Jouneyman."
"Gambles with(in) Socialist Realism / Kozintzev on the
   Inadequacies of the Ruling Model."
"Kulidzhanov's Urbane Dangers."
"Kozintsev: The Retrospective View / Demonological."
"The Tragic Universe of Eisenstein's *Ivan the Terrible*."
"Eisenstein's Notes for a 'Chapter on Dostoevsky'."
   IN: Dostoevsky and Soviet Film

3503   **Laskos, Andrew.**
"The Hollywood Majors."
   IN: Anatomy of the Movies

3504   **Lasky, Jesse L.**
"Cruzing Over the Santa Fe Trail."
"So We Combined."
"The Power and the Glory."
"*The Squaw Man*."
   IN: The First Tycoons

3505   **Lasky, Jesse L.**
"Is a Screen Test Necessary?"
   IN: Celebrity Articles ...

3506   **Lasky, Jesse L.**
"Production Problems."
   IN: The Story of the Films
        The First Tycoons

3507   **Lassally, Walter.**
"Communication and the Creative Process."
   IN: Sight, Sound, and Society

Lassie. SEE: Granville, Bonita.

3508   **Latham, Michael.**
"*The Man Alive Reports* [Interview with] Michael
   Latham."
   IN: The Documentary Conscience

3509   **Lathrop, George Parsons.**
"Edison's Kinetograph."
   IN: The Movies in Our Midst

3510   **Lathrop, Philip.**
"Philip Lathrop." [Interview by Kris Malkiewicz.]
   IN: Film Lighting

3510a **Lauder, Robert E.**
"*It's a Wonderful Life*: Divine Benevolence and Love
   of Neighbor."
   IN: Image and Likeness

3511   **Laufer, Joseph M.**
"Television in the Seventies: Planting the Seeds of
   Change for Puerto Rican Images."
   IN: Ethnic Images ...

3512   **Laughlin, Karen.**
"Brechtian theory and American feminist theatre."
   IN: Re-interpreting Brecht

3513   **Laura, Ernesto G.**
"*Invasion of the Body Snatchers*."
   IN: Focus on The Science Fiction Film

3514   **Laurence, Frank M.**
"Hemingway on Movies: *The Old Man and the Sea*."
"Screen Romance: *A Farewell to Arms* [1932; 1958]."
"Action Adventure: *To Have and Have Not*."
"Hemingway Entertainment in the Hollywood Style."
"Hemingway Censored."
"Story, Movie, Film: *The Killers* [1946 and 1964]."
"Hemingway's Cinematic Style."
"The Hemingway Hero as Hollywood Star."
"The Ernest Hemingway Story."
   IN: Hemingway and the Movies

3515   **Laurence, Frank M.**
"Hollywood Publicity and Hemingway's Popular
   Reputation."
"Death in the Matinée: The Film Endings of
   Hemingway's Fiction."
"*The Sun Also Rises*: The NBC Version."
   IN: A Moving Picture Feast

3516   **Laurents, Arthur.**
"Arthur Laurents: Emotional Reality." [Interview by
   Patrick McGilligan.]
   IN: Backstory 2

3517   **Lavery, David.**
"Gnosticism and the Cult Film."
   IN: The Cult Film Experience

3518   **Lawder, Standish D.**
"Modern Painters Discover the Cinema."
"Film as Modern Art: Picasso, Survage, Kandinsky,
   Schönberg."
"The Abstract Film: Richter, Eggeling, and Ruttmann."
"Léger and the Film."
"La Roue, Cendrars and Gance."
"Léger, L'Herbier, and L'Inhumaine."
"*Ballet Mécanique*."
"Dulac and Seeber."
"The Avant-Garde Film and Its Public."
   IN: The Cubist Cinema

3519   **Lawder, Standish D.**
"Eisenstein and Constructivism (*Strike*; *Potemkin*)."
   IN: The Essential Cinema /v. 1
        Great Film Directors

3520   **Lawrence, Amy.**
"The Pleasures of Echo: The 'Problem' of the
   Speaking Woman."
"Constructing a Woman's Speech: Words and Images
   (*Miss Thompson* [1921]; *Rain* [1921]; *Sadie
   Thompson* [1928])."
"Constructing a Woman's Speech: Sound Film (*Rain*
   [1932])."
"The Problem of the Speaking Woman (*The Spiral
   Staircase* [1946]; *Blackmail* [1929]; *Notorious*
   [1946]; *Sorry, Wrong Number* [1948])."
"Recuperating Woman's Speech (*Miss Sadie
   Thompson* [1953]; *Sunset Boulevard* [1950])."

"Women and the Authorial Voice: Disembodied Desire (*To Kill a Mockingbird* [1962])."
IN: Echo and Narcissus

3521 **Lawrence, Catalina.**
"Script Supervisor."
IN: Hollywood Speaks!

3522 **Lawrence, Florence.**
"Growing Up with the Movies."
IN: The Movies in Our Midst

3523 **Lawrence, Floyd B.**
"*The Missouri Breaks.*"
IN: Western Movies

3524 **Lawrence, John Shelton.**
"Copyright Law, Fair Use, and the Academy: An Introduction."
"Donald Duck v. Chilean Socialism: A Fair Use Exchange."
"The Administration of Copyrighted Imagery: Walt Disney Productions."
IN: Fair Use and Free Inquiry

3525 **Lawrence, John Shelton and Bernard Timberg.**
"Conclusions: Scholars, Media, and the Law in the 1980s."
IN: Fair Use and Free Inquiry

3526 **Lawson, John Howard.**
"Premise and Progression in *The Gold Rush.*"
IN: The Classic Cinema

3527 **Lawson, John Howard.**
"Concerning Critics and Criticism ..."
IN: Celebrity Articles ...

3528 **Lawson, John Howard.**
"The Decline of Hollywood."
IN: The Movies: An American Idiom

3529 **Lawson, John Howard.**
"Camera and Microphone."
IN: The Emergence of Film Art /1 ed
The Emergence of Film Art /2 ed

3530 **Lawson, John Howard.**
"Time and Space."
IN: The Movies as Medium

3531 **Lawson, John Howard.**
"Organizing the Screen Writers Guild."
IN: The Cineaste Interviews

3532 **Lawson, John Howard.**
"Our Film and Theirs: *Grapes of Wrath* and *Bonnie and Clyde.*"
IN: Focus on Bonnie and Clyde

3533 **Lawson, Steve.**
"For Valor: The Career of Ingmar Bergman."
IN: Before His Eyes

3534 **Lawson, Sylvia.**
"*Serious Undertakings.*"
"Australian Film, 1969."
"Not for the Likes of Us."

IN: An Australian Film Reader

3535 **Lawson, Sylvia.**
"Good Taste at Hanging Rock." [RE: *Picnic at Hanging Rock.*]
IN: Conflict and Control in the Cinema

3536 **Lawton, Anna M.**
"Dziga Vertov: A Futurist with a Movie Camera."
IN: Explorations in National Cinemas

3537 **Lawton, Anna.**
"Toward a New Openness in Soviet Cinema, 1976-1987."
IN: Post New Wave Cinema ...

3538 **Lawton, Ben.**
"Literary Trends."
"Socio-Political Trends."
IN: Italian Cinema

3539 **Lawton, Ben.**
"The Storyteller's Art: Pasolini's *Decameron* from *The Decameron* by Giovanni Boccaccio."
IN: Modern European Filmmakers ...

Lawton, Ben. SEE: Rossi, Patrizio.

3540 **Lawton, Harry.**
"Italian Cinema in the Sixties: The Political Revival; Trends and Major Directors."
IN: Italian Cinema

3541 **Layton, Lynne.**
"Peter Lilienthal: Decisions Before Twelve."
IN: New German Filmmakers

3542 **Lazarus, Paul N.**
"Distribution: A Disorderly Dissertation."
IN: The Movie Business Book

3543 **Le Borg, Reginald.**
"Reginald LeBorg." [An interview.]
IN: Interviews with B ...

3544 **Le Duc, Don R.**
"The Common Market Film Industry: Beyond Law and Economics."
IN: The American Movie Industry

3545 **Le Fanu, Mark.**
"Bob Rafelson."
"Michael Ritchie."
IN: American Directors /v. 2

Le Grice, Malcolm. SEE: LeGrice, Malcolm.

Le Roy, Mervyn. SEE: LeRoy, Mervyn.

3546 **Leab, Daniel J.**
"Deutschland, USA: German Images in American Film."
IN: The Kaleidoscopic Lens

3547 **Leab, Daniel J.**
"The Blue Collar Ethnic in Bicentennial America: *Rocky.*"
IN: American History/American Film

3548 **Leab, Daniel.**
"Goethe or Attila? The Celluloid German."
IN: <u>Ethnic Images ...</u>

3549 **Leab, Daniel.**
"The Moving Image as Interpreter of History: Telling the Dancer from the Dance."
IN: <u>Image as Artifact</u>

3550 **Leach, Jim.**
"Hideousness and Beauty: a Reading of Tarkovsky's *The Sacrifice*."
IN: <u>Before the Wall Came Down</u>

3551 **Leach, Jim.**
"The Body Snatchers: Genre and Canadian Cinema."
IN: <u>Film Genre Reader</u>

3552 **Leach, Jim.**
"The Screwball Comedy."
IN: <u>Film Genre</u>

3553 **Leacock, Richard.**
"For an Uncontrolled Cinema."
IN: <u>Film Culture Reader</u>

3554 **Leacock, Richard.**
"Richard Leacock." [Interview by G. Roy Levin.]
IN: <u>Documentary Explorations</u>

Leacock, Richard. SEE: Bachman, Gideon.

3555 **Leaming, Barbara.**
"*Merchant of Four Seasons*: Structures of Alienation."
IN: <u>The Emergence of Film Art /2 ed</u>

3556 **Lean, David.**
"David Lean." [Interview by Andrew Sarris.]
IN: <u>Interviews with Film Directors</u>

3557 **Lean, David.**
"The Situation of the Serious Filmmaker."
IN: <u>Film: Book 1</u>

Lean, David. SEE: Anderson, Lindsay.

3558 **Lean, Tangye.**
"*Citizen Kane*."
IN: <u>Focus on Citizen Kane</u>

3559 **Lear, Norman.**
"The Studio Executive."
IN: <u>Filmmakers on Filmmaking /v. 2</u>

3560 **Leblanc, Gérard.**
"Direction."
IN: <u>Screen Reader 1</u>

3561 **Ledeen, Michael A.**
"*Amarcord*."
IN: <u>Film in Society</u>

3562 **Lederer, Richard.**
"Management: New Rules of the Game."
IN: <u>The Movie Business Book</u>

Lederman, Susan J. SEE: Nichols, Bill.

Lee, Christopher T. SEE: Adamson, Joseph.

3563 **Lee, David D.**
"Appalachia on Film: The Making of *Sergeant York*."
IN: <u>The South and Film</u>

3564 **Lee, Leo Ou-Fan.**
"The Tradition of Modern Chinese Cinema: Some Preliminary Explorations and Hypotheses."
IN: <u>Perspectives on Chinese Cinema</u>

3565 **Lee, Patricia-Ann.**
"Teaching Film and Television as Interpreters of History."
IN: <u>Image as Artifact</u>

3566 **Lee, Rohama.**
"Canada Carries On."
IN: <u>The Documentary Tradition /1 ed</u>
<u>The Documentary Tradition /2 ed</u>

3566a **Lee, Spike.**
"Spike Lee." [Interview by David Breskin.]
IN: <u>Inner Views</u>

Leece, Mary Pat. SEE: Nicolson, Annabel.

3567 **Leenhardt, Roger.**
"Cinematic Rhythm."
"More on *The Informer* and *La Bandera*."
"On Opening a School for Spectators."
"*La Marseillaise*."
IN: <u>French Film Theory and Criticism /v. 2</u>

Leenhardt, Roger. SEE: Bazin, André.

3568 *Lef Ring, The.*
"Comrades! A Clash of Views!" [RE: *The Eleventh Hour*.]
IN: <u>The Film Factory</u>

3569 **Leff, Leonard J.**
"*Aguirre, The Wrath of God*."
"*All Quiet on the Western Front*."
"*Annie Hall*."
"*L'Avventura*."
"*Battleship Potemkin*."
"*Bicycle Thieves*."
"*The Birth of a Nation*."
"*The Blue Angel*."
"*Bonnie and Clyde*."
"*Breathless*."
"*Cabaret*."
"*The Cabinet of Dr. Caligari*."
"*Casablanca*."
"*Chinatown*."
"*Citizen Kane*."
"*Le Crime de Monsieur Lange*."
"*Dr. Strangelove, Or How I Learned to Stop Worrying and Love the Bomb*."
"*Easy Rider*."
"*8-1/2*."
"*The General*."
"*The Godfather*."

"The Godfather, Part II."
"The Gold Rush."
"Gone with the Wind."
"The Grapes of Wrath."
"High Noon."
"Hiroshima Mon Amour."
"Invasion of the Body Snatchers."
"It Happened One Night."
"Jules and Jim."
"King Kong."
"The Lady Eve."
"The Last Laugh."
"Last Tango in Paris."
"M."
"The Magnificent Ambersons."
"The Maltese Falcon."
"The Marriage of Maria Braun."
"Metropolis."
"Mr. Smith Goes to Washington."
"Modern Times."
"Nashville."
"North by Northwest."
"On the Waterfront."
"One Flew Over the Cuckoo's Nest."
"La Passion de Jeanne D'Arc."
"Persona."
"Psycho."
"The Public Enemy."
"Rashomon."
"Rebel Without a Cause."
"Red River."
"Rules of the Game."
"The Searchers."
"The Seventh Seal."
"Singin' in the Rain."
"Stagecoach."
"Sunset Boulevard."
"2001: A Space Odyssey."
"Ugetsu Monogartari."
"Umberto D."
"Viridiana."
"Viva Zapata!."
"Way Down East."
"The Wild Bunch."
"Written on the Wind."
"Wuthering Heights."
    IN: <u>Film Plots</u> /v. 1

3570   **Leff, Leonard J.**
"All That Heaven Allows."
"Amadeus."
"Apocalypse Now."
"Atlantic City."
"Being There."
"The Big Sleep."
"The Birds."
"Blackmail."
"Body Heat."
"Broken Blossoms."
"City Lights."

"A Clockwork Orange."
"Closely Watched Trains."
"Crossfire."
"The Discreet Charm of the Bourgeoisie."
"Duck Soup."
"The 400 Blows."
"Frenzy."
"Grand Illusion."
"Letter from an Unknown Woman."
"Mildred Pierce."
"Mr. Hulot's Holiday."
"Mother."
"My Darling Clementine."
"Ninotchka."
"Nosferatu: A Symphony of Horror."
"Notorious."
"Los Olvidados."
"Pandora's Box."
"The Paradine Case."
"Pather Panchali."
"Rear Window."
"Rebecca."
"The Rocking Horse Winner."
"Sabotage."
"Scarface."
"Shane."
"Some Like It Hot."
"Spellbound."
"Stolen Kisses."
"La Strada."
"Strangers on a Train."
"A Streetcar Named Desire."
"Taxi Driver."
"The Third Man."
"The 39 Steps."
"Tootsie."
"The Treasure of the Sierra Madre."
"Vertigo."
"Wild Strawberries."
    IN: <u>Film Plots</u> /v. 2

3571   **Leff, Leonard J.**
"A Test of American Film Censorship: *Who's Afraid of Virginia Woolf?*."
    IN: <u>Hollywood as Historian</u>
         <u>Cinema Examined</u>

3572   **Leff, Leonard J.**
"Hitchcock at Metro."
    IN: <u>A Hitchcock Reader</u>

3573   **Leff, Leonard J. and Jerold L. Simmons.**
"Welcome Will Hays!"
"'You Can Be Had'."
"Welcome Joe Breen."
"Dead End."
"Gone with the Wind."
"The Outlaw and *The Postman Always Rings Twice."*
"The Bicycle Thief."
"Detective Story and *A Streetcar Named Desire."*
"The Moon Is Blue and *The French Line."*

"*Lolita*."
"*Who's Afraid of Virginia Woolf?*"
 IN: The Dame in the Kimono

3574 **Léger, Fernand.**
"A New Realism--The Object."
 IN: Introduction to the Art of the Movies

3575 **Léger, Fernand.**
"*La Roue*: Its Plastic Quality."
"Painting and Cinema."
 IN: French Film Theory and Criticism /v. 1

3576 **Léger, Susan H.**
"Marguerite Duras's Cinematic Spaces."
 IN: Women and Film

3577 **Legrand, Gérard.**
"Elixir of Potboiler and Unlabelled Love Potions."
 IN: The Shadow and Its Shadow

3578 **LeGrice, Malcolm.**
"Abstract Film and Beyond."
"[On] Kurt Kren."
"[On] Tony Conrad."
 IN: Structural Film Anthology

3579 **LeGrice, Malcolm.**
"Problematizing the Spectator's Placement in Film."
 IN: Cinema and Language

3580 **Lehman, Ernest.**
"Ernest Lehman." [Interviewed by John Brady.]
 IN: The Craft of the Screenwriter

3580a **Lehman, Ernest.**
"Ernest Lehman, screenwriter-producer-director."
 [Interview by Constance Nash and Virginia Oakey.]
 IN: The Screenwriter's Handbook

3581 **Lehman, Peter.**
"Penis-size Jokes and Their Relation to Hollywood's
 Unconscious."
 IN: Comedy/Cinema/Theory

3582 **Lehman, Peter.**
"Texas 1868 / America 1956: *The Searchers*."
 IN: Close Viewings

3583 **Lehman, Peter.**
"The Avant-Garde: Power, Change, and the Power to
 Change."
 IN: Cinema Histories, Cinema Practices

3584 **Leigh, Janet.**
"*Psycho*: What to Wear in the Shower?"
 IN: Bedside Hollywood

3585 **Leighton, Dr. J.A.**
"The Photoplay and Aesthetic Culture of the World."
 IN: Introduction to the Photoplay

3586 **Leitch, Thomas M.**
"Self and World at Paramount."
 IN: Hitchcock's Re-Released Films

3587 **Leiterman, Douglas.**
"*One More River* [Interview with] Douglas Leiterman."

 IN: The Documentary Conscience

3588 **Leiterman, Richard.**
"*A Married Couple*." [Interview by Alan Rosenthal.]
 IN: The New Documentary in Action

Leites, Nathan. SEE: Wolfenstein, Martha.

3589 **Leiva, Agustin Aragon.**
"Eisenstein's Film on Mexico." [RE: *Que viva Mexico!*]
 IN: The Documentary Tradition /1 ed
     The Documentary Tradition /2 ed

3590 **Lellis, George.**
"Bertolt Brecht."
"Cahiers du Cinéma."
"Groupe Dziga-Vertov."
"Pascal Bonitzer."
"Jean-Louis Comolli."
"Costa-Gavras."
"Jean-Marie Straub."
"Robert Kramer."
"*Tout va bien*."
"*Coup pour coup*."
"*Trop tot, Trop tard*."
 IN: Bertolt Brecht ...

3591 **Lellis, George.**
"A Dissenting View of Milos Forman's *Amadeus*."
 IN: Before the Wall Came Down

3592 **Lellis, George and H. Philip Bolton.**
"*Pride and Prejudice* [novel by] Jane Austen; *Pride
 and Prejudice* [film by] Robert Z. Leonard. Pride
 but No Prejudice."
 IN: The English Novel and the Movies

3593 **Lemaitre, Henri.**
"Shakespeare, the Imaginary Cinema and the
 Pre-cinema."
 IN: Focus on Shakespearean Films

3594 **Lemkin, Jonathan.**
"Archetypal Landscape and *Jaws*."
 IN: Planks of Reason

3595 **Lemmon, Jack.**
"Jack Lemmon." [Interview by Rex Reed.]
 IN: Travolta to Keaton

3596 **Lenburg, Jeff.**
"Friz Freleng."
"Ub Iwerks."
"Chuck Jones."
"Hanna and Barbera."
"Bob Clampett."
"Tex Avery."
"Walter Lantz."
"Dave Fleischer."
 IN: The Great Cartoon Directors

3597 **Lenfest, David S.**
"*I Am Curious Yellow*: A Practical Education."
 IN: Sexuality in the Movies

Lenglet, Philippe. SEE: Vasudev, Aruna.

3598 **Lenihan, John H.**
"Classics and Social Commentary: Postwar Westerns, 1946-1960."
IN: Western Films: A Brief History

3599 **Lenihan, John H.**
"The Western Heroism of Randolph Scott."
IN: Shooting Stars

3600 **Lenin, Vladimir.**
"Art Belongs to the People. Conversation with Clara Zetkin."
"Directive on Cinema Affairs."
IN: The Film Factory

3601 **Lenne, Gérard.**
"Monster and Victim: Women in the Horror Movie."
IN: Sexual Stratagems

3602 **Lennig, Arthur.**
"Lumière, Méliès, Porter."
"D.W. Griffith."
"*The Birth of a Nation.*"
"*The Mother and the Law.*"
"*Intolerance.*"
"*Broken Blossoms.*"
"*Way Down East.*"
"*Isn't Life Wonderful.*"
"*Civilization.*"
"*Tol'able David.*"
"*Dancing Mothers.*"
"*Douglas Fairbanks.*"
"*The Mystery of the Leaping Fish.*"
"*Reaching for the Moon.*"
"*Wild and Woolly.*"
"*The Mollycoddle.*"
"*The Mark of Zorro.*"
"*Robin Hood.*"
"*The Thief of Bagdad.*"
"*Mr. Robinson Crusoe.*"
"*Seventh Heaven.*"
"*A Woman of the World.*"
"*The Son of the Sheik.*"
"*Robert Flaherty.*"
"*Erich von Stroheim.*"
"*Blind Husbands.*"
"*Merry-Go-Round.*"
"*Greed.*"
"*The Wedding March.*"
"*Queen Kelly.*"
"*The Treasure of Arne.*"
"*The Phantom Chariot.*"
"The German Film." [RE: Weimar Germany.]
"*The Cabinet of Dr. Caligari.*"
"Fritz Lang."
"*The Nibelungen (Siegfried* and *Kriemhilde's Revenge).*"
"*Warning Shadows.*"
"*Der Letzte Mann (The Last Laugh).*"
"The Soviet Film." [RE: Socialist Realism.]
"Sergei Eisenstein."
"*Strike.*"

"*October.*"
"*Thunder Over Mexico.*"
"*Pudovkin.*"
"*Mechanics of the Brain.*"
"*Mother.*"
"*The End of St. Petersburg.*"
"*Dovzhenko.*"
"*Zvenigora.*"
"*Arsenal.*"
"*Earth.*"
"*Bed and Sofa.*"
"*The Ghost that Never Returns.*"
"Abel Gance."
"*La Roue.*"
"*Napoleon.*"
"*Fragment of an Empire.*"
IN: The Silent Voice: The Golden Age ...

3603 **Lennig, Arthur.**
"*The Birth of a Nation.*"
"*Orphans of the Storm.*"
"*America.*"
"*Isn't Life Wonderful.*"
"*Civilization.*"
"Erich Von Stroheim."
"*Greed.*"
"*A Woman of the World.*"
"*The Son of the Sheik.*"
"Robert Flaherty."
"*Nanook of the North.*"
"*Moana.*"
"The Swedish Cinema."
"*The Treasure of Arne.*"
"*The Phantom Chariot.*"
"Dovzhenko."
"*Zvenigora.*"
"*Arsenal.*"
"Pudovkin."
"*Mechanics of the Brain.*"
"*The End of St. Petersburg.*"
"Fritz Lang."
"*Dr. Mabuse Der Spieler.*"
"*Spione.*"
"A Note on *The Cabinet of Dr. Caligari.*"
"A Note on *Der Letzte Mann (The Last Laugh).*"
"A Note on *Siegfried.*"
IN: The Silent Voice: A Sequel

3604 **Lennig, Arthur.**
"*The Wedding March.*"
"An Unconventional Masterpiece." [RE: *Broken Blossoms.*]
IN: The First Film Makers

3605 **Lennig, Arthur.**
"*Thomas Graal's Best Child.*"
IN: The Rivals of D.W. Griffith

3606 **Lennig, Arthur.**
"A History of Censorship of the American Film."
IN: Sexuality in the Movies

3630 **Levee, M.C.**
"The Commercial Requirements." [RE: the photoplay.]
IN: Introduction to the Photoplay

3631 **Lévi-Strauss, Claude.**
"The Structural Study of Myth [extract]."
IN: Theories of Authorship

3632 **Levin, Meyer.**
"Meyer Levin." [Collected film capsules.]
IN: Garbo and the Night Watchmen

3633 **Levin, Meyer.**
"*Tuesday Brown.*"
IN: Introduction to the Art of the Movies

3634 **Levine, Arthur, Bernardo Foschetti and Susan Reisman.**
"[A History of Italian Cinema:] 1896-1929."
IN: Italian Cinema

3635 **Levine, Joseph E.**
"The Producer."
IN: Filmmakers on Filmmaking /v. 2

3636 **Levine, Scott.**
"Charles Lederer."
IN: Dictionary of Literary Biography /v. 26

3637 **Levinson, Andre.**
"The Nature of the Cinema."
IN: Introduction to the Art of the Movies

Levy, Brett. SEE: Hughes, John.

3638 **Levy, David.**
"Edison Sales Policy and the Continuous Action Film, 1904-1906."
IN: Film Before Griffith

3639 **Lévy, Jean.**
"*King Kong.*"
IN: French Film Theory and Criticism /v. 2

3640 **Levy, Len.**
"Len Levy." [An interview.]
IN: Producers on Producing

3641 **Lewalski, Barbara K.**
"Federico Fellini's *Purgatorio.*" [RE: *8-1/2.*]
IN: Federico Fellini

3642 **Lewin, Albert.**
"Albert Lewin: The Executive."
IN: The Real Tinsel

3643 **Lewin, Albert.**
"'Peccavi!' The True Confession of a Movie Producer."
IN: Hollywood Directors 1941-1976

3644 **Lewington, Mike.**
"Alcohol and the Movies: An Overview."
IN: Images of Alcoholism

3645 **Lewis, George H.**
"Culture, Kubrick, and *Barry Lyndon.*"
IN: Film in Society

3646 **Lewis, Grover.**
"Splendor in the Short-Grass: The Filming of *The Last Picture Show.*"
"Roaring Around with Robert Redford: I."
"The Jeaning of Barbra Streisand."
"Up in Fat City with Stacy Keach and John Huston." [RE: *Fat City.*]
"The Hollywood Film to End All: On the Set of *Play It As It Lays.*"
"John Cassavetes Goes for the Edge."
"Roaring Around with Robert Redford: II."
"Sam Peckinpah in Mexico: Over-learning with *El Jefe.*" [RE: *The Getaway.*]
"Lee Marvin's Great, Goddamned Moments of the Big Kavoom."
"Crusin' for Burgers with Paul Newman."
"One Step Over the Fucked-up Line with Robert Mitchum."
IN: Academy All the Way

3647 **Lewis, Jerry.**
"A Handsome Man and a Monkey."
IN: Bedside Hollywood

3648 **Lewis, Jerry.**
"Jerry Lewis." [Interview by Charles Higham.]
IN: Celebrity Circus

3648a **Lewis, Leon.**
"Fellini: The Psychology of the Self."
"Humphrey Bogart: Hard Guy Means Well."
"John Ford and Liberty Valance."
"The Ship Sinks."
"War Movies."
"The Frog Jumps At Six."
"James Bond."
"Some Men of Our Time."
"Tony Quinn the Greek." [RE: *Zorba the Greek.*]
"*Shoot the Piano Player.*"
"The Way of Sport."
"*To Die in Madrid.*"
"Olmi and Risi."
IN: Landscapes of Contemporary Cinema

3648b **Lewis, Leon and William David Sherman.**
"The Emotional Intensity of Sidney Lumet."
"The New American Cinema."
"Mobled Queen Is Good."
IN: Landscapes of Contemporary Cinema

3649 **Lewis, R.**
"'Cabin' Picture Called Insult."
IN: The Black Man on Film

3650 **Lewis, Roger.**
"The Producer."
IN: Movie People

3651 **Leyda, Jay.**
"*The Italian.*"
IN: The Rivals of D.W. Griffith

3652 **Leyda, Jay.**
"Esther Schub."

IN: Sexual Stratagems

3653   **Leyda, Jay.**
"The Art and Death of D.W. Griffith."
IN: Focus on D.W. Griffith

3654   **Leyda, Jay.**
"The Work of Pudovkin."
IN: Introduction to the Art of the Movies

3655   **Leyda, Jay.**
"Theory into Practice." [RE: *Potemkin*.]
IN: The Classic Cinema

Leyda, Jay. SEE: Meyers, Sidney.

3656   **Li Jie.**
"Xie Jin's Era Should End."
IN: Chinese Film Theory

3657   **Lichty, Lawrence W.**
"'Vietnam: A Television History': Media Research and
Some Comments."
IN: New Challenges for Documentary

3658   **Lichty, Lawrence W. and Raymond L. Carroll.**
"Fragments of War: *Platoon*."
IN: American History/American Film

3659   **Liebman, Max.**
"Max Liebman." [An interview.]
IN: Producers on Producing

3660   **Liebman, Stuart.**
"*Un Chien andalou*: The Talking Cure."
IN: Dada and Surrealist Film

3661   **Liebman, Stuart.**
"1949-1958 (*The Lead Shoes*; *Bells of Atlantis*; *The
Wonder Ring*; *Bridges-Go-Round*; *A Movie*;
Recreation; *Anticipations of the Night*)."
IN: A History of the American Avant-Garde Cinema

3662   **Liehm, Antonín J.**
"Miloš Forman: the Style and the Man."
IN: Politics, Art and Commitment ...

3663   **Liehm, Antonin.**
"*That Obscure Object of Desire*: An Appreciation
(Buñuel At Seventy-Seven--Or--L'Amour Fou Fifty
Years Later)."
IN: The World of Luis Buñuel

3664   **Liehm, Antonin.**
"On Jaromil Jires."
IN: The Image Maker

Liehm, A.J. SEE: Liehm, Mira; SEE: Liehm, D.

3665   **Liehm, D. and A.J.**
"Czechoslovak Cinema of the 60s."
IN: Cinema: A Critical Dictionary

3666   **Liehm, Mira and A.J.**
"Miklós Jancsó and Post-War Hungarian Cinema."
"Roman Polansky [*sic*, Polanski], Jerzy Skolimowski
and the Polish Emigrés."
"Polish Cinema Since the War."
IN: Cinema: A Critical Dictionary

3667   **Lightman, Herb A.**
"Filming *2001: A Space Odyssey*."
IN: Focus on The Science Fiction Film

3668   **Lightman, Herbert A.**
"The Subjective Camera."
IN: The Movies as Medium

3669   **Lincoln, Freeman.**
"The Comeback of the Movies."
IN: The American Film Industry

3670   **Linden, George W.**
"The Storied World."
IN: Film And/As Literature
Film and Literature

3671   **Linden, George W.**
"*Dr. Strangelove, Or: How I Learned to Stop Worrying
and Love the Bomb*."
IN: Nuclear War Films

3672   **Linder, Carl.**
"Notes for *The Devil Is Dead*."
IN: The New American Cinema

3673   **Linderman, Deborah.**
"Cinematic Abreaction: Tourneur's *Cat People*."
IN: Psychoanalysis and Cinema

3674   **Linderman, Deborah.**
"Uncoded Images in the Heterogeneous Text."
IN: Narrative, Apparatus, Ideology

3675   **Lindgren, Ernest.**
"Editing: Basic Principles."
IN: Crossroads to the Cinema

Lindsay, Lois. SEE: Marshall, Melba.

3676   **Lindsay, Vachel.**
"Sculpture-in-Motion."
IN: Film: A Montage of Theories

3677   **Lindsay, Vachel.**
"The Intimate Photoplay."
IN: The Movies in Our Midst

3678   **Lindsay, Vachel.**
"The Picture of Crowd Splendor."
IN: Introduction to the Art of the Movies

3679   **Lindsay, Vachel.**
"Thirty Differences Between the Photoplays and the
Stage."
IN: Focus on Film and Theatre
Awake in the Dark

3680   **Linton, James M.**
"The Nature of the Viewing Experience: The Missing
Variable in the Effects Equation."
IN: Film/Culture: Explorations ...

3681   **Linton, James M. and Joseph A. Petrovich.**
"The Application of the Consumer Information
Acquisition Approach to Movie Selection: An
Exploratory Study."
IN: Current Research in Film /v. 4

3682 **Lipkin, Steve.**
"The New Wave and the Post-War Film Economy."
IN: Current Research in Film /v. 2

3683 **Lipkin, Steven N.**
"Melodrama."
IN: Handbook of American Film Genres

3684 **Lippe, Richard.**
"The Horror of *Martin*."
"*Full Circle*: A Circle of Deception."
IN: American Nightmare

3685 **Lish, Gordon.**
"The Stag Film."
IN: The Movie That Changed My Life

3686 **Litle, Michael.**
"The Sound Track of *The Rules of the Game*."
IN: Film Sound

3687 **Litman, Barry R.**
"The Economics of the Television Market for
Theatrical Movies."
IN: The American Movie Industry

3688 **Litman, Barry.**
"Network Oligopoly Power: An Economic Analysis."
IN: Hollywood in the Age of Television

3689 **Littin, Miguel.**
"Film in Allende's Chile."
IN: The Cineaste Interviews

3690 **Littin, Miguel.**
"Interview with Miguel Littin."
IN: Chilean Cinema

3691 **Littleton, Carol.**
"Carol Littleton." [Interview by Vincent LoBrutto.]
IN: Selected Takes

3692 **Littleton, Carol.**
"Carol Littleton [on Editing]." [Interview by David
Chell.]
IN: Moviemakers at Work

3693 **Litwak, Mark.**
"'Welcome to Hollywood'."
"The Rise of CAA." [RE: Creative Artists Agency.]
"The New Power Brokers."
"Inside the Studios."
"Studio Business."
"What's Commercial."
"Breaking In, Moving Up, Holding On."
"Deal-Making."
"Writers."
"Directors."
"Actors and Stars."
"Producers."
"Marketing."
"Distribution and Exhibition."
"Independent Filmmaking."
"Sex, Drugs and Creative Accounting."
"Hollywood Journalism."
"Conclusion."

IN: Reel Power

3694 **Liu Zhuang.**
"Liu Zhuang, Composer." [Interview by George S.
Semsel.]
IN: Chinese Film

3695 **Lloyd, Harold.**
"A Laugh, A Scream and a Laugh."
IN: Bedside Hollywood

3696 **Lloyd, Harold.**
"Mind Over Matter: Harold Lloyd Reminisces."
[Interview by George C. Pratt.]
IN: Image on the Art ...

3697 **Lloyd, Harold.**
"The Hardships of Fun Making."
IN: Hollywood Directors 1914-1940

3698 **Lloyd, Ronald.**
"The Dream-Makers."
"John Ford."
"Orson Welles."
"Howard Hawks."
"Alfred Hitchcock."
"Arthur Penn."
"Stanley Kubrick."
"The New Directors."
IN: American Film Directors

Loach, Kenneth. SEE: Garnett, Tony.

3699 **Loader, Jayne.**
"*Jeanne Dielman*: Death in Installments."
IN: Movies and Methods /v. 2

3700 **Lockerbie, Ian.**
"Pictures in Small Country: The Scottish Film
Production Fund."
IN: From Limelight to Satellite

3701 **Lockhart, Gene.**
"Little Orson Annie."
"The Mikado–1942."
IN: The Best of Rob Wagner's Script

3702 **Lodge, Jack.**
"*Blue Jeans*."
IN: The Rivals of D.W. Griffith

3703 **Lodge, Jack.**
"Gösta Berlings Saga." [RE: *The Atonement of Gösta
Berling*.]
"*Napoleon*."
"*Sparrows*."
"*The Immigrant*."
"*The Lodger*."
"Abel Gance–Resting in Peace."
"Alias Harold Lloyd."
"Carl Theodor Dreyer--In Search of the Spiritual Self."
"End of the Silents."
"Mary Pickford--America's Sweetheart."
"Rudolph Valentino."
"The Avenging Spirit of Feuillade."
"The Griffith Girls."

IN: <u>Movies of the Silent Years</u>

3704   **Loevinger, Lee.**
"The FCC and Program Regulation."
IN: <u>Sight, Sound, and Society</u>

3705   **Loew, Marcus.**
"The Motion Picture and Vaudeville."
IN: <u>The Story of the Films</u>

3706   **Logan, Joshua.**
"My Invasion of Marseilles." [RE: *Fanny*.]
IN: <u>Hollywood Directors 1941-1976</u>

3707   **Lombardo, Lou.**
"Lou Lombardo." [Interview by Vincent LoBrutto.]
IN: <u>Selected Takes</u>

3708   **London, Jack.**
"The Message of Motion Pictures."
IN: <u>Authors on Film</u>

3709   **Londoner, David J.**
"The Changing Economics of Entertainment." [RE: television.]
IN: <u>The American Film Industry /rev ed</u>

3710   **Loos, Anita.**
"Anita Loos." [Interview by John Kobal.]
IN: <u>People Will Talk</u>

3711   **Loos, Anita.**
"Anita Loos: The Writer."
IN: <u>The Real Tinsel</u>

3712   **Loos, Anita.**
"What Killed Jean Harlow."
IN: <u>Bedside Hollywood</u>

3713   **Lopate, Phillip.**
"*Diary of a Country Priest*."
IN: <u>The Movie That Changed My Life</u>

3714   **López, Ana M.**
"An 'Other' History: The New Latin American Cinema."
IN: <u>Resisting Images</u>

3715   **López, Ana M.**
"Are All Latins from Manhattan?: Hollywood, Ethnography, and Cultural Colonialism."
IN: <u>Unspeakable Images</u>

3716   **Lopez, Ana M.**
"At the Limits of Documentary: Hypertextual Transformation and the New Latin American Cinema."
"*The Battle of Chile*: Documentary, Political Process, and Representation."
IN: <u>The Social Documentary ...</u>

3717   **Lopez, Ana.**
"The Melodrama in Latin America: Films, Telenovelas, and the Currency of a Popular Form."
IN: <u>Imitations of Life</u>

3718   **Loren, Sophia.**
"Sophia Loren." [Interview by Rex Reed.]
IN: <u>Travolta to Keaton</u>

3719   **Lorentz, Pare.**
"*The Ramparts We Watch*."
IN: <u>The Documentary Tradition /1 ed</u>
<u>The Documentary Tradition /2 ed</u>

3720   **Losano, Wayne A.**
"The Sex Genre: Tradition and Modern Variations on the Flesh Film."
IN: <u>Sexuality in the Movies</u>

3721   **Losey, Joseph.**
"Joseph Losey (with Nicholas Ray)." [Interview by Andrew Sarris.]
IN: <u>Interviews with Film Directors</u>

3722   **Losey, Joseph and Nicholas Ray.**
"Joseph Losey and Nicholas Ray." [Talking to Penelope Houston and John Gillett.]
IN: <u>Hollywood Voices</u>

3723   **Losey, Mary.**
"Joris Ivens's *Power and the Land*."
IN: <u>The Documentary Tradition /1 ed</u>
<u>The Documentary Tradition /2 ed</u>

3724   **Losey, Mary.**
"More Seeing, Less Selling."
IN: <u>Ideas on Film</u>

3725   **Löthwall, Lars-Olof.**
"Ingmar Bergman and the Black Death."
IN: <u>Focus on The Seventh Seal</u>

3726   **Lotman, Jurij.**
"[From:] *Semiotics of Cinema*: The Illusion of Reality."
IN: <u>Film Theory and Criticism /2 ed</u>

3727   **Lottman, Evan.**
"Evan Lottman." [Interview by Vincent LoBrutto.]
IN: <u>Selected Takes</u>

3728   **Loughney, Patrick G.**
"In the Beginning Was the Word: Six Pre-Griffith Motion Picture Scenarios."
IN: <u>Early Cinema ...</u>

3729   **Loughney, Patrick G.**
"*From the Manger to the Cross*: The First American Film Spectacular."
IN: <u>Wonderful Inventions</u>

3730   **Loughney, Patrick.**
"Still Images in Motion: The Influence of Photography on Motion Pictures in the Early Silent Period."
IN: <u>The Art of Moving Shadows</u>

3731   **Louis, Jean.**
"Jean Louis." [Interview by John Kobal.]
IN: <u>People Will Talk</u>

3732   **Lourdeaux, Lee.**
"Irish and Italian Immigrants and the Movies."
"Irish and Italian Immigrants Stereotypes in the 1920s."
"John Ford and the Landscapes of Irish America."
"Frank Capra and His Italian Vision of America."
"Francis Coppola and Ethnic Double Vision."

"Martin Scorsese in Little Italy and Greater Manhattan."
IN: Italian and Irish Filmmakers ...

3733 **Loveland, Kay and Estelle Changas.**
"Eleanor Perry, An Interview."
IN: The Hollywood Screenwriters

3734 **Lovell, Alan.**
"Free Cinema."
"The Documentary Film Movement: John Grierson."
IN: Studies in Documentary

3735 **Lovell, Alan.**
"The Western."
IN: Movies and Methods: An Anthology

3736 **Lovell, Terry.**
"The Social System of the Cinema."
IN: Conflict and Control in the Cinema

3737 **Lövgren, Håkan.**
"Trauma and Ecstasy."
IN: Eisenstein at Ninety

3738 **Low, Rachel.**
"England Expects ... the British Film Industry 1910-1929."
IN: Movies of the Silent Years

3739 **Lowe, Philip M.**
"Refreshment Sales and Theatre Profits."
IN: The Movie Business Book

3740 **Lowry, Edward.**
"Edwin J. Hadley: Traveling Film Exhibitor."
IN: Film Before Griffith

Lowry, Edward. SEE: de Cordova, Richard.

3741 **Lowry, F.C.**
"The University Extension Film Library's Role."
IN: Ideas on Film

3742 **Lubitsch, Ernst.**
"A Tribute from a Great Director to a 'Great Actor'."
[RE: Will Rogers.]
IN: The Best of Rob Wagner's Script

3743 **Lubitsch, Ernst.**
"Ernst Lubitsch." [Interview by Andrew Sarris.]
IN: Interviews with Film Directors

3744 **Lubitsch, Ernst.**
"Film Directing."
IN: Hollywood Directors 1914-1940

3745 **Lucas, Blake.**
"*Lady of the Pavements.*"
"Infinite Shadings of Human Emotion."
IN: The First Film Makers

3746 **Lucas, Blake.**
"Borden Chase."
"James Edward Grant."
IN: Dictionary of Literary Biography /v. 26

3747 **Luchting, Wolfgang A.**
"*Hiroshima, Mon Amour*, Time, and Proust."

IN: Renaissance of the Film

3748 **Ludwig, William.**
"William Ludwig." [Interview by Lee Server.]
IN: Screenwriter: Words Become Pictures

3749 **Lugo, Marvin D.**
"*Barry Lyndon*: Kubrick on the Rules of the Game."
IN: Explorations in National Cinemas

3750 **Luhr, William.**
"*David Copperfield* [novel by] Charles Dickens; *David Copperfield* [film by] George Cukor. Dickens's Narrative, Hollywood's Vignettes."
IN: The English Novel and the Movies

3751 **Luhr, William.**
"The Function of Narrative in Literature and Film: Some Issues."
IN: Ideas of Order in Literature & Film

3752 **Luhr, William.**
"Tracking *The Maltese Falcon*: Classical Hollywood Narration and Sam Spade."
IN: Close Viewings

3753 **Lumbera, Bienvenido.**
"Problems in Philippine Film History."
IN: Readings in Philippine Cinema

3754 **Lumet, Sidney.**
"The Director."
IN: Movie People

3755 **Lumière, Louis.**
"The Last Interview, with Georges Sadoul."
IN: Film Makers on Film Making

3756 **Lumière, Louis.**
"The Lumière Cinematograph."
IN: A Technological History ...

3757 **Lunacharsky, Anatoli.**
"The Tasks of the State Cinema in the RSFSR." [RE: Russian Soviet Federated Socialist Republic.]
"Conversation with Lenin. I: Of all the Arts ..."
"Conversation with Lenin. II: Newsreel and Fiction Film."
"Revolutionary Ideology and Cinema—Theses."
"Cinema--the Greatest of the Arts."
"Speech to Film Workers."
"Review of *October*."
"Synopsis of a Report on the Tasks of Dramaturgy (extract)."
IN: The Film Factory

3758 **Lund, Daniel Manny.**
"Writing Film History: The Struggle for Synthesis."
IN: Film/Culture: Explorations ...

3759 **Luo Yijun.**
"A Review of Part IV of Shao Mujun's Article 'Summary of Casual Thinking on Film Aesthetics'."
IN: Chinese Film Theory

3760 **Lupino, Ida.**
"Ida Lupino." [Interview by John Kobal.]
IN: People Will Talk

3761 **Lupino, Ida.**
"Me, Mother Directress."
IN: Hollywood Directors 1941-1976

3761a **Lusted, David.**
"The Glut of the Personality."
IN: Stardom

3762 **Lye, Len.**
"The Man Who Was Colorblind."
IN: The Emergence of Film Art /1 ed
The Emergence of Film Art /2 ed

3762a **Lynch, David.**
"David Lynch." [Interview by David Breskin.]
IN: Inner Views

3763 **Lynch, William F.**
"Counterrevolution in the Movies."
IN: Celluloid and Symbol

Lynch, William J. SEE: Clark, Dennis.

3764 **Lynd, Ralph A.**
"Billy the Kid." [*Billy the Kid*, 1930.]
IN: The American West on Film

3765 **Lyne, Adrian.**
"Adrian Lyne." [Interview by John Andrew Gallagher.]
IN: Film Directors on Directing

3766 **Lynn, James.**
"Introduction: Feminist Film Theory (The Problems of Women in Film)."
IN: Women and Film

3767 **Lynn, Kane W.**
"Hemisphere Pictures."
IN: The New Poverty Row

3768 **Lyon, Elisabeth.**
"The Cinema of Lov V. Stein."
IN: Fantasy and the Cinema

3769 **Lyons, Timothy J.**
"The Idea in *The Gold Rush*: A Study of Chaplin's Use of the Comic Technique of Pathos-Humor."
IN: Focus on Chaplin

3770 **Lyotard, Jean Francois.**
"Acinema."
IN: Narrative, Apparatus, Ideology

3771 **Ma Ning.**
"Notes on the New Filmmakers."
IN: Chinese Film

3772 **Ma Qiang.**
"The Chinese Film in the 1980s: Art and Industry."
IN: Cinema and Cultural Identity

Maas, Willard. SEE: Deren, Maya.

3773 **MacBean, James Roy.**
"Politics, Poetry, and the Language of Signs in *Made in USA*."
"*Weekend*, or The Self-Critical Cinema of Cruelty."

"*Le Gai Savoir*. Critique Plus Auto-Critique du Critique."
"*One Plus One*, or The Praxis of History."
"'See You at Mao': Godard's Revolutionary *British Sounds*."
"Godard and Rocha at the Crossroads of *Wind from the East*."
"Godard/Gorin/The Dziga Vertov Group: Film and Dialectics in *Pravada*, *Struggle in Italy*, and *Vladimir and Rosa*."
"*Tout Va Bien* and *Letter to Jane*: The Role of the Intellectual in the Revolution."
"*La Hora de los Hornos*: 'Let Them See Nothing but Flames!'"
"The *Ice*-man Cometh No More: He Gave His Balls to the Revolution."
"Sex and Politics: Wilhelm Reich, World Revolution, and Makavejev's *WR: The Mysteries of the Organism*."
"The Working Class Goes Directly to Heaven, Without Passing Go: Or, The Name of the Game Is Still Monopoly." [RE: *The Working Class Goes Directly to Heaven*.]
"Contra Semiology: A Critical Reading of Metz."
"The Ideological Situation of Post-Bazin Film Criticism."
IN: Film and Revolution

3774 **MacBean, James Roy.**
"Rossellini's Materialist Mise-en-Scène of *La Prise de pouvoir par Louis XIV*."
IN: Great Film Directors
Film and Revolution

3775 **MacBean, James Roy.**
"Politics and Poetry in *Two or Three Things I Know About Her* and *La Chinoise*." [NOTE: Also called "Politics and Poetry in Two Recent Films by Godard."]
IN: Conflict and Control in the Cinema
Film and Revolution
The Emergence of Film Art /2 ed

3776 **MacBean, James Roy.**
"*Two Laws* from Australia, One White, One Black."
IN: New Challenges for Documentary

3777 **MacBean, James Roy.**
"*The Sorrow and the Pity*: France and Her Political Myths."
IN: New Challenges for Documentary
Film and Revolution

3778 **MacBean, James Roy.**
"*Vent d'Est* or Godard and Rocha at the Crossroads."
IN: Movies and Methods: An Anthology

3779 **MacCabe, Colin.**
"Realism and the Cinema: Notes on Some Brechtian Theses."
IN: Popular Television and Film

3780 **MacCabe, Colin.**
"Theory and Film: Principles of Realism and Pleasure."
IN: Narrative, Apparatus, Ideology
Film Theory and Criticism /4 ed

3781 **MacCann, Richard Dyer.**
"The Problem Film in America."
"[From:] Hollywood Faces the World."
IN: <u>Film and Society</u>

3782 **MacCann, Richard Dyer.**
"World War II–Armed Forces Documentary."
IN: <u>The Documentary Tradition /1 ed</u>
<u>The Documentary Tradition /2 ed</u>
<u>Nonfiction Film Theory and Criticism</u>

3783 **MacCann, Richard Dyer.**
"The End of the Assembly Line."
IN: <u>The Movies: An American Idiom</u>

3784 **MacCann, Richard Dyer.**
"Film and Foreign Policy: The USIA, 1962-1967."
IN: <u>Nonfiction Film Theory and Criticism</u>

3785 **MacCann, Richard Dyer.**
"Hollywood Faces the World."
IN: <u>The Movies in Our Midst</u>

3786 **Macdonald, Dwight.**
"D.W. Griffith, or Genius American Style."
"*Ivan the Terrible, Part II.*"
IN: <u>Great Film Directors</u>

3787 **Macdonald, Dwight.**
"*8-1/2*: Fellini's Obvious Masterpiece."
"*The Greatest Story Ever Told.*"
IN: <u>Awake in the Dark</u>

3788 **Macdonald, Dwight.**
"Notes on Hollywood Directors." [RE: Griffith; [King]
Vidor; Mamoulian; Lubitsch; [Henry] King; von
Stroheim; von Sternberg; LeRoy.]
IN: <u>Introduction to the Art of the Movies</u>

3789 **Macdonald, Dwight.**
"Objections to the New American Cinema."
IN: <u>The New American Cinema</u>

3790 **Macdonald, Dwight.**
"*Hamlet* [1964]."
IN: <u>Focus on Shakespearean Films</u>

3791 **Macdonald, Dwight.**
"Eisenstein, Pudovkin and Others."
IN: <u>The Emergence of Film Art /1 ed</u>
<u>The Emergence of Film Art /2 ed</u>

3792 **Macdonald, Dwight.**
"Our Elizabethan Movies." [RE: film and literature.]
IN: <u>Film and the Liberal Arts</u>

3793 **Macdonald, Gus.**
"Fiction Friction."
IN: <u>From Limelight to Satellite</u>

3794 **MacDonald, Ruth K.**
"*Toby Tyler* [novel by] James Otis Kaler.
Mouseketeer in the Center Ring."
IN: <u>Children's Novels and the Movies</u>

3795 **MacDonald, Stephen.**
"*Woodstock*–One for the Money."

IN: <u>The Documentary Tradition /1 ed</u>
<u>The Documentary Tradition /2 ed</u>

3796 **MacDougall, David.**
"Beyond Observational Cinema."
IN: <u>Movies and Methods /v. 2</u>

3797 **MacDougall, David.**
"Prospects of the Ethnographic Film."
IN: <u>Movies and Methods: An Anthology</u>

3798 **MacDougall, Ranald.**
"'I Tooled Off Into The Night, Never To Return'--" [RE:
an interview.]
IN: <u>Blueprint on Babylon</u>

3799 **Mace, Kevin.**
"Charles Bennett."
"Curt Siodmak."
"John Lee Mahin."
IN: <u>Dictionary of Literary Biography /v. 44</u>

3800 **Mace, Nigel.**
"British Historical Epics in the Second World War."
IN: <u>Britain and the Cinema ...</u>

3801 **MacFadden, Patrick.**
"Remarks on the Polish Session."
IN: <u>Before the Wall Came Down</u>

3802 **Macgowan, Kenneth.**
"Film in the University."
IN: <u>Ideas on Film</u>

3803 **Macgowan, Kenneth.**
"The Triangle of Griffith, Ince, and Sennett."
"The Coming of the Feature Film."
IN: <u>The First Tycoons</u>

3804 **MacGowan [*sic*, Macgowan], Kenneth.**
"On the Screen."
IN: <u>Introduction to the Art of the Movies</u>

3805 **Macgowan, Kenneth.**
"Color over Hollywood." [RE: *Becky Sharp*.]
IN: <u>Celebrity Articles ...</u>

3806 **Macgowan, Kenneth.**
"The Producer Explains." [RE: *Lifeboat*.]
"*Hearts of the World*."
IN: <u>Propaganda on Film</u>

3807 **Macherey, Pierre.**
"Literary Analysis: The Tomb of Structures [extract]."
IN: <u>Theories of Authorship</u>

3808 **Maciel, David R.**
"Visions of the Other Mexico: Chicanos and
Undocumented Workers in Mexican Cinema,
1954-1982."
IN: <u>Chicano Cinema</u>

3809 **Maciunas, George.**
"On 'Structural Film' (by P. Adams Sitney)." [SEE: P.
Adams Sitney, "Structural Film".]
IN: <u>Film Culture Reader</u>

3810 **Mackenzie, Aeneas.**
"Leonardo of the Lenses."

IN: <u>Sternberg</u>

Mackie, Fiona. SEE: Bishop, Rod.

3811 **Macklin, F. Anthony.**
"Dark Pilgrim: The Vision of Ingmar Bergman in *The Silence*."
IN: <u>Renaissance of the Film</u>

3812 **Macklin, F.A.**
"*Blow-Up*."
IN: <u>Focus on Blow-Up</u>

3813 **Macksey, Richard.**
"Francis Ford Coppola."
IN: <u>Dictionary of Literary Biography /v. 44</u>

3814 **MacLaine, Shirley.**
"Jackpot."
IN: <u>Bedside Hollywood</u>

3815 **MacLiammóir, Mícheál.**
"[From:] Put Money in Thy Purse." [RE: *Othello*, 1951.]
IN: <u>Focus on Shakespearean Films</u>

3816 **MacMahon, Henry.**
"The Art of the Movies."
IN: <u>Introduction to the Art of the Movies</u>

3817 **MacPherson, William.**
"For the Future: The Science Fiction Film in the Classroom."
IN: <u>The Compleat Guide to Film Study</u>

3818 **MacQueen, Scott.**
"*The Bat*: Thrice Told." [RE: also *The Bat Whispers*.]
IN: <u>The Cinema of Adventure, Romance & Terror</u>

3819 **MacQueen, Scott.**
"Roland West."
IN: <u>Between Action and Cut</u>

3820 **Maddison, John.**
"Experiment in the Scientific Film."
IN: <u>Experiment in the Film</u>

3821 **Maddow, Ben.**
"Ben Maddow: The Invisible Man." [Interview by Patrick McGilligan.]
IN: <u>Backstory 2</u>

3822 **Madson, Roy Paul (editor).**
"The Producer, with Robert Watts."
"The Screenwriter, with Norman Corwin."
"Adaptation, with Craig Noel."
"Production Design, with Dean Tavoularis."
"The Director, with Mark Rydell."
"The Players, with Paul Newman."
"Comedy and Humor, with Jack Lemmon."
"The Cinematographer, with Vilmos Zsigmond."
"The Editor, with Peter Zinner."
"The Sound Designer, with Walter Murch."
"Visual Effects, with Artists of Lucasfilm."
"Animation, with Art Scott of Hanna-Barbera."
IN: <u>Working Cinema</u>

Magee, Rosemary. SEE: Becker, Boris W.

Magretta, Joan. SEE: Magretta, William R.

3823 **Magretta, William R.**
"Reading the Writerly Film: Fassbinder's *Effi Briest* from the Novel by Theodor Fontane."
IN: <u>Modern European Filmmakers ...</u>

3824 **Magretta, William R. and Joan Magretta.**
"Story and Discourse: Schlöndorff & von Trotta's *The Lost Honor of Katharina Blum* from the Novel by Heinrich Böll."
"Private 'I': Tavernier's *The Clockmaker* from the Novel *The Clockmaker of Everton* by Georges Simenon."
IN: <u>Modern European Filmmakers ...</u>

3825 **Mahin, John Lee.**
"'The Biggest Ears I've Ever Seen, But He Reeks With Animal Magnetism'—" [RE: an interview.]
IN: <u>Blueprint on Babylon</u>

3826 **Mahin, John Lee.**
"John Lee Mahin: Team Player." [Interview by Todd McCarthy and Joseph McBride.]
IN: <u>Backstory</u>

3827 **Mahoney, Dennis F.**
"A Recast Goethe: Günther's *Lotte in Weimar*."
IN: <u>German Film and Literature</u>

3828 **Maibaum, Richard.**
"Richard Maibaum: A Pretense of Seriousness." [Interview by Pat McGilligan.]
IN: <u>Backstory</u>

3829 **Mailer, Norman.**
"*The Naked and the Dead* [novel by] Norman Mailer. Naked Before the Camera."
IN: <u>The Modern American Novel ...</u>

3830 **Mailer, Norman.**
"Norman Mailer." [Interview by Joseph Gelmis.]
IN: <u>The Film Director as Superstar</u>

3831 **Mainwaring, Daniel.**
"Daniel Mainwaring: Americana." [Interview by Tom Flinn.]
IN: <u>Backstory 2</u>

3832 **Maio, Kathi.**
"*Desert Bloom*."
"*The Stepfather*."
"*Housekeeping*."
"*The Color Purple*."
"*Wish You Were Here*."
"*Steetwise* and *Seventeen*."
"*Adventures in Babysitting*."
"*Wildcats*."
"*Who's That Girl*."
"Whoopi Goldberg's Comedies."
"*Hello Again*."
"*Dirty Dancing* and *Maid to Order*."
"*Desert Hearts*."
"*Desperately Seeking Susan*."
"*Satisfaction*."

"*Bright Lights, Big City*, and *High Tide*."
"*I've Heard the Mermaids Singing*."
"*The Allnighter*."
"*Outrageous Fortune*."
"*Crimes of the Heart*."
"*Working Girls*."
"*Witches of Eastwick*."
"*Steaming*."
"*Heartburn*."
"*Compromising Positions*."
"*Jewel of the Nile*."
"*Peggy Sue Got Married*."
"*Black Widow*."
"*Jagged Edge*."
"*The Big Easy*."
"*Fatal Attraction* and *Someone to Watch Over Me*."
  IN: Feminist in the Dark

3833 **Maio, Kathi.**
"*Pretty Woman*."
"*Earth Girls are Easy*."
"*Ghost*."
"*White Palace / Tune in Tomorrow*."
"*Chances Are / See You in the Morning / Skin Deep*."
"*A World Apart*."
"*Shag*."
"*A Dry White Season*."
"*Bagdad Cafe*."
"*Beaches*."
"*Working Girl*."
"*Mystic Pizza*."
"*Steel Magnolias*."
"*Blue Steel / Impulse*."
"*The Good Mother / The Accused*."
"*Shame*."
"*She-Devil*."
"*Heathers*."
"*Men Don't Leave*."
"*Look Who's Talking / Immediate Family*."
"*Postcards from the Edge*."
"*Mermaids*."
"*Another Woman*."
"*Betsy's Wedding*."
"*Strapless*."
"*Cookie*."
"*Driving Miss Daisy / Stella / Stanley and Iris / Where the Heart Is*."
  IN: Popcorn and Sexual Politics

3834 **Makavejev, Dušan.**
"An Investigation—Bergman's Non-Verbal Sequences: Sources of a Dream Film Experiment."
  IN: Film and Dream

3835 **Makavejev, Dusan.**
"Let's put the life back in political life ..."
  IN: The Cineaste Interviews

3836 **Makolkina, Anna.**
"A Nostalgic Vision of Tarkovsky's *Nostalgia*."
  IN: Before the Wall Came Down

3837 **Maland, Charles J.**
"America and Hollywood, 1936-1941."
"Chaplin: The Tramp Turns Social."
"John Ford: The Historical Films of 1939."
"John Ford: The Family and the Modern World."
"Frank Capra: Filmmaking and Commitment."
"Frank Capra and the American Way."
"Orson Welles: American Maverick."
"Films, Filmmakers, and Culture."
  IN: American Visions

3838 **Maland, Charles J.**
"The Social Problem Film."
  IN: Handbook of American Film Genres

3839 **Maland, Charles.**
"*Dr. Strangelove*: Nightmare Comedy and the Ideology of Liberal Consensus."
  IN: Hollywood as Historian

3840 **Maland, Charles.**
"*Agee: A Film*."
  IN: The South and Film

3840a **Maland, Charles.**
"Frank Capra at Columbia: Necessity and Invention."
  IN: Columbia Pictures

3841 **Malcolm, Derek.**
"*The Milky Way*."
  IN: The World of Luis Buñuel

3842 **Maldoror, Sarah.**
"On *Sambizanga*."
  IN: Women and the Cinema

3843 **Malkames, Don G.**
"Early Projector Mechanisms."
  IN: A Technological History ...

3844 **Malm, Linda.**
"Elaine May."
  IN: Dictionary of Literary Biography /v. 44

3845 **Malmberg, Tarmo.**
"Traditional Finnish Cinema: An Historical Overview."
  IN: Cinema in Finland

3846 **Malraux, André.**
"A Sketch of the Rhetoric of the Sound Film."
  IN: Film and the Liberal Arts

3847 **Maltby, Richard.**
"Made for Each Other: The Melodrama of Hollywood and the House Committee on Un-American Activities, 1947."
"The Political Economy of Hollywood: The Studio System."
  IN: Cinema, Politics and Society in America

3848 **Maltin, Leonard.**
"Charlie Chaplin."
"Mabel Normand."
"Fatty Arbuckle."
"Buster Keaton."
"Harold Lloyd."

"Harry Langdon."
"Charley Chase."
"Raymond Griffith."
"Marie Dressler."
"Laurel & Hardy."
"Will Rogers."
"Joe E. Brown."
"The Marx Brothers."
"W.C. Fields."
"Mae West."
"The Three Stooges."
"Abbott & Costello."
"Bob Hope."
"Danny Kaye."
"Red Skelton."
"Jerry Lewis."
"Woody Allen."
    IN: The Great Movie Comedians

3849 **Maltin, Leonard.**
"Hal Roach" [RE: the studio.]
"Columbia Pictures."
"RKO."
"Educational Pictures."
"MGM."
"Paramount."
"Mack Sennett." [RE: the studio.]
"Warner Brothers." [RE: the studio.]
"Our Gang."
"Laurel and Hardy."
"Charley Chase."
"Harry Langdon."
"The Boy Friends."
"W.C. Fields."
"Thelma Todd–ZaSu Pitts."
"Thelma Todd–Patsy Kelly."
"Andy Clyde."
"Edgar Kennedy."
"The Three Stooges."
"The Pete Smith Specialties."
"Buster Keaton."
"Crime Does Not Pay."
"Robert Benchley."
"Screen Snapshots."
"John Nesbitt's Passing Parade."
"Joe McDoakes."
    IN: The Great Movie Shorts

3850 **Maltin, Leonard.**
"Laurel and Hardy."
"Clark and McCullough."
"Wheeler and Woolsey."
"The Marx Brothers."
"Thelma Todd and ZaSu Pitts."
"Thelma Todd and Patsy Kelly."
"Burns and Allen."
"The Three Stooges."
"The Ritz Brothers."
"Olsen and Johnson."
"Abbott and Costello."
"Martin and Lewis."

"Other Teams: Moran and Mack; Smith and Dale; The
Wiere Brothers; Mitchell and Durant; Fibber McGee
and Molly; Brown and Carney; Noonan and
Mitchell; Rowan and Martin."
    IN: Movie Comedy Teams

3851 **Maltin, Leonard.**
"Walt Disney."
"Max Fleischer."
"Paul Terry and Terrytoons."
"Walter Lantz."
"Ub Iwerks."
"The Van Beuren Studio."
"Columbia: Charles Mintz and Screen Gems."
"Warner Bros."
"MGM"
"Paramount/Famous Studios."
"UPA."
    IN: Of Mice and Magic

3852 **Maltin, Leonard.**
"Don Siegel."
    IN: Directors in Action

3853 **Maltin, Leonard.**
"Film: The Personal Experience."
    IN: The Compleat Guide to Film Study

3854 **Maltin, Leonard.**
"George Stevens."
    IN: Directors in Action

3855 **Maltin, Leonard.**
"The RKO Shorts."
"The Hal Roach Shorts."
    IN: The American Film Heritage

3855a **Maltin, Leonard.**
"A Survey of Hollywood Cinematography."
    IN: The Art of the Cinematographer

3856 **Mamber, Stephen.**
"Cinema Verite: Definitions and Backgrounds."
"Drew Associates."
"Direct Cinema and the Crisis Structure."
"The Maysles Brothers."
"D.A. Pennebaker."
"Richard Leacock."
"Frederick Wiseman."
    IN: Cinema Verite in America

3857 **Mamber, Stephen.**
"In Search of Radical Metacinema."
    IN: Comedy/Cinema/Theory

3858 **Mambrino, Jean.**
"The Seventh Seal."
    IN: Focus on The Seventh Seal

3859 **Mamoulian, Rouben.**
"Some Problems in the Direction of Color Pictures."
    IN: Hollywood Directors 1914-1940

3860 **Mamoulian, Rouben.**
"Controlling Color for Dramatic Effect."
    IN: Hollywood Directors 1941-1976

3861 **Mamoulian, Rouben.**
"Rouben Mamoulian." [Interview by Andrew Sarris.]
[NOTE: Also called "Rouben Mamoulian ... Talking
to Andrew Sarris."]
    IN: Interviews with Film Directors
        Hollywood Voices

3862 **Mamoulian, Rouben.**
"Will Talking Pictures Become 'Talking Paintings'."
[RE: *Becky Sharp.*]
    IN: Celebrity Articles ...

3863 **Mamoulian, Rouben.**
"Rouben Mamoulian."
    IN: The Celluloid Muse

3864 **Mamoulian, Rouben.**
"Reminiscence and Reflection: Director."
    IN: Sound and the Cinema

3865 **Manceaux, Michèle.**
"Learning Not to Be Bitter: Interview with Jean-Luc
Godard on *Le petit soldat.*"
"A Movie Is a Movie: Interview with Jean-Luc Godard
on *Une Femme est une femme.*"
    IN: Focus on Godard

3866 **Manchel, Frank.**
"The Dandy: Max Linder."
"The Comedy King of the Pioneers: Mack Sennett."
"The Master Clown: Charles Chaplin."
"The Human Mop: Buster Keaton."
"The Glass Comic: Harold Lloyd."
"The Last of the Great Clowns: Harry Langdon."
    IN: Yesterday's Clowns

3867 **Manchel, Frank.**
"The Immortal Brats: Stan Laurel and Oliver Hardy."
"The Noblest Fraud: W.C. Fields."
"The Funniest Bad Girl: Mae West."
"The Lunatic Clowns: The Marx Brothers."
    IN: The Talking Clowns

3868 **Manchel, Frank.**
"The Archetypal American."
    IN: The Compleat Guide to Film Study

3869 **Mancini, Elaine.**
"Belgium."
    IN: World Cinema Since 1945

3870 **Mancini, Marc.**
"The Sound Designer."
    IN: Film Sound

3871 **Mandel, Loring.**
"Before Sinai, There Was Eden."
    IN: Sight, Sound, and Society

3872 **Mandell, Paul.**
"Enigma of *The Black Cat.*"
    IN: The Cinema of Adventure, Romance & Terror

3873 **Mangolte, Babette.**
"Babette Mangolte." [Interview by Scott MacDonald.]
    IN: A Critical Cinema

3874 **Mankiewicz, Herman J. and Orson Welles.**
"The Shooting Script."
    IN: The Citizen Kane Book

3875 **Manley, Nellie.**
"Hairstyling."
    IN: Hollywood Speaks!

3876 **Mann, Anthony.**
"Empire Demolition."
    IN: Hollywood Directors 1941-1976

3876a **Mann, Delbert.**
"Delbert Mann, director-producer." [Interview by
Constance Nash and Virginia Oakey.]
    IN: The Screenwriter's Handbook

3877 **Mann, Denise.**
"The Spectacularization of Everyday Life: Recycling
Hollywood Stars and Fans in Early Television
Variety Shows."
    IN: Star Texts

3878 **Mann, Heinrich.**
"*The Blue Angel* Is Shown to Me."
"On *The Blue Angel*: Heinrich Mann to Karl Lemke."
    IN: Authors on Film

3879 **Mann, Thomas.**
"On the Film."
    IN: Authors on Film

3880 **Mannes, Marya.**
"The Hot Documentary."
    IN: The Documentary Tradition /1 ed
        The Documentary Tradition /2 ed

3881 **Mansfield, Joseph.**
"*The Wet Parade* [novel by] Upton Sinclair. Que Viva
Prohibition."
    IN: The Modern American Novel ...

3882 **Manvell, Roger.**
"Shakespeare: from the Open Stage to the Screen."
"Shakespeare and the Silent Film."
"The Arrival of Sound: the First Phase of Adaptation
(*The Taming of the Shrew* [1929], *A Midsummer
Night's Dream* [1935], *Romeo and Juliet* [1936], *As
You Like It* [1936])."
"Laurence Olivier and the Filming of Shakespeare
(*Henry V* [1944], *Hamlet* [1948], *Richard III* [1955])."
"Shakespeare by Orson Welles (*Macbeth* [1948],
Othello [1952], *Chimes at Midnight* [1965])."
"The Russian Adaptations: Yutkevitch and Kozintsev
(*Othello* [1955], *Hamlet* [1964], *King Lear*
[1970-71])."
"The Adaptations of *Julius Caesar* (*Julius Caesar*
[1953], *Julius Caesar* [1969])."
"The Italians and Shakespeare: Castellani and
Zeffirelli (*Romeo and Juliet* [1954], *Romeo and
Juliet* [1968], *The Taming of the Shrew* [1966])."
"Akira Kurosawa's *Macbeth, The Castle of the
Spider's Web* [1957]."
"Theatre into Film (*Macbeth* [1960], *The Winter's Tale*
[1966], *Othello* [1965], *A Midsummer Night's
Dream* [1969], *Hamlet* [1969])."

"Peter Brook's Film of *King Lear* [1970]."
IN: Shakespeare and the Film

3883 **Manvell, Roger.**
"Stage Play and Screenplay: Forms and Principles."
"*Pygmalion* (Play by Bernard Shaw; film by Anthony Asquith and Leslie Howard)."
"*Electra* (Play by Euripides; film by Michael Cacoyannis)."
"*Three Sisters* (Play by Anton Checkhov; film, S. Samsonov)."
"*Long Day's Journey into Night* (Play by Eugene O'Neill; film by Sidney Lumet)."
"*A Streetcar Named Desire* (Play by Tennessee Williams; film by Elia Kazan)."
"Shakespeare on Film: The Public Theater of Shakespeare's Time and the Cinema; *Henry V* (film by Laurence Olivier); *Macbeth* (film by Roman Polanski); *A Midsummer Night's Dream* (film by Peter Hall); *Hamlet* (film by Grigori Kozintsev, Laurence Olivier, Tony Richardson); *Macbeth* (film by Akira Kurosawa)."
"*Miss Julie* (Play by August Strindberg; film by Alf Sjöberg)."
"*The Caretaker* (Play by Harold Pinter; film by Clive Donner)."
"*Who's Afraid of Virginia Woolf?* (Play by Edward Albee; film by Mike Nichols)."
"*The Marat-Sade* (Play by Peter Weiss; film by Peter Brook)."
"The American Film Theatre."
"Film and Theater: The Views of Allardyce Nicoll and André Bazin."
IN: Theatre and Film

3884 **Manvell, Roger.**
"*Monsieur Verdoux*."
IN: Focus on Chaplin

3885 **Manvell, Roger.**
"Experiment in the Film."
IN: Experiment in the Film

3886 **Manvell, Roger.**
"Psychological Intensity in *The Passion of Joan of Arc*."
IN: The Classic Cinema

3887 **Manvell, Roger.**
"Ufa—Pride of Germany."
IN: Movies of the Silent Years

3888 **Manvell, Roger.**
"[From:] The Cinema and Society."
IN: Film and Society

Manvell, Roger. SEE: Fleming, Michael.

3889 **March, Frederic.**
"So You're Going to Tahiti, Eh?"
IN: Celebrity Articles ...

3890 **Marchetti, Gina.**
"Ethnicity, the Cinema, and Cultural Studies."
IN: Unspeakable Images

3891 **Marchetti, Gina.**
"Subcultural Studies and the Film Audience: Rethinking the Film Viewing Context."
IN: Current Research in Film /v. 2

3892 **Marco, Paul.**
"Paul Marco." [An interview.]
IN: Interviews with B ...

3893 **Marcorelles, Louis.**
"The Leacock Experiment."
IN: Cahiers du Cinéma, 1960-1968

3894 **Marcorelles, Louis.**
"Improvisation in Film-Acting: An Interview with Albert Finney and Mary Ure."
IN: Focus on Shoot the Piano Player

3895 **Marcorelles, Louis.**
"Ford of the Movies."
IN: Theories of Authorship

3896 **Marcus, Fred H.**
"Film and Fiction: *An Occurrence at Owl Creek Bridge*."
IN: Film and Literature: Contrasts ...

3897 **Marcus, Fred H. and Paul Zall.**
"*Catch-22*: Is Film Fidelity an Asset?"
IN: Film and Literature: Contrasts ...

Marcus, Fred H. SEE: Birdsall, Eric R.

3898 **Marcus, Millicent.**
"Rossellini's *Open City*: The Founding."
"De Sica's *Bicycle Thief*: Casting Shadows on the Visionary City."
"De Santis's *Bitter Rice*: A Neorealist Hybrid."
"De Sica's *Umberto D*: Dark Victory for Neorealism."
"Comencini's *Bread, Love, and Fantasy*: Consumable Realism."
"Fellini's *La strada*: Transcending Neorealism."
"Visconti's *Senso*: The Risorgimento According to Gramsci." [RE: Antonio Gramsci.]
"Antonioni's *Red Desert*: Abstraction as the Guiding Idea."
"Olmi's *Il posto*: Discrediting the Economic Miracle."
"Germi's *Seduced and Abandoned*: Inside the Honor Code."
"Pasolini's *Teorema*: The Halfway Revolution."
"Petri's *Investigation of a Citizen above Suspicion*: Power as Pathology."
"Bertolucci's *The Conformist*: A Morals Charge."
"Wertmuller's *Love and Anarchy*: The High Price of Commitment."
"Rosi's *Christ Stopped at Eboli*: A Tale of Two Italies."
"The Taviani Brothers' *Night of the Shooting Stars*: Ambivalent Tribute to Neorealism."
"Scola's *We All Loved Each Other So Much*: An Epilogue."
IN: Italian Film in the Light of Neorealism

Mardore, Michel. SEE: Comolli, Jean-Louis.

3899 **Margolis, Harriet.**
"'Nur Schauspieler': Spectacular Politics, *Mephisto*, and *Good*."
IN: Film and Literature: A Comparative ...

3900 **Margulies, Michael D..**
"Michael D. Margulies." [Interview by Kris Malkiewicz.]
IN: Film Lighting

3901 **Marie, Michel.**
"'Let's sing it one more time': René Clair's *Sous les toits de Paris*."
"'It really makes you sick!': Jean-Luc Godard's *A bout de souffle*."
IN: French Film: Texts and Contexts

3902 **Marien, Marcel.**
"Another Kind of Cinema."
IN: The Shadow and Its Shadow

3903 **Marion, Frances.**
"The Scenario Writing."
IN: Behind the Screen

3904 **Markel, Lester.**
"A Program for Public-TV."
IN: Sight, Sound, and Society

3905 **Markfield, Wallace.**
"The Dark Geography of W.C. Fields."
"'Play it Again, Sam'—And Again."
IN: The Movies: An American Idiom

Markle, Fletcher. SEE: Crawley, Budge.

3906 **Markopoulos, Gregory.**
"Three Filmmakers (Andy Meyer, Charles Boultenhouse, Storm De Hirsch)."
IN: The New American Cinema

3907 **Marks, John.**
"John Marks." [Collected film capsules.]
IN: Garbo and the Night Watchmen

3908 **Marks, Richard.**
"Richard Marks." [Interview by Vincent LoBrutto.]
IN: Selected Takes

3909 **Marsden, Michael T.**
"Savior in the Saddle: The Sagebrush Testament."
IN: Focus on The Western

3910 **Marsden, Michael T.**
"The Rise of the Western Movie: From Sagebrush to Screen."
IN: Western Films: A Brief History

3911 **Marsden, Michael T.**
"Western Films: America's Secularized Religion."
IN: Movies as Artifacts

3912 **Marsh, Mae.**
"Mae Marsh: The Player."
IN: The Real Tinsel

3913 **Marshall, Herbert.**
"Vsevolod Pudovkin."
"Dziga Vertov."
"Alexander Dovzhenko."
"Sergei Eisenstein."
IN: Masters of the Soviet Cinema

3914 **Marshall, Melba.**
"Melba Marshall/Lois Lindsay/Madison Lacy." [Interview by John Kobal.]
IN: People Will Talk

3915 **Marshall, Stuart.**
"The Contemporary Political Use of Gay History: The Third Reich."
IN: How Do I Look

3916 **Martin, Adrian.**
"Fantasy."
IN: The New Australian Cinema

3917 **Martin, Adrian.**
"What is This Thing Called 'The Super-8 Phenomenon'?"
IN: An Australian Film Reader

3918 **Martin, Angela.**
"Chantal Akerman's Films: Notes on the Issues Raised for Feminism."
IN: Films for Women

3919 **Martin, Ernest F.**
"Five."
IN: Nuclear War Films

3919a **Martin, John.**
"Olde Worlde Horrors."
IN: The Deep Red Horror Handbook

3920 **Martin, John and Donna L. Van Bodegraven.**
"Mythical Patterns in Jorge Amado's *Gabriela--Clove and Cinnamon* and Bruno Barreto's Film *Gabriela*."
IN: Film and Literature: A Comparative ...

3921 **Martin, Marcel.**
"Shoot the Piano Player."
IN: Focus on Shoot the Piano Player

3922 **Martin, Marcel.**
"The Priest and The Man." [RE: *Nazarin*.]
IN: The World of Luis Buñuel

3923 **Martin, Olga J.**
"The Legion of Decency Campaign."
IN: The Movies in Our Midst

3924 **Martin, P.T.**
"The 'Silent Pictures' Era in the Philippines."
IN: Readings in Philippine Cinema

3925 **Martineau, Barbara Halpern.**
"Talking About our Lives and Experiences: Some Thoughts about Feminism, Documentary, and 'Talking Heads'."
IN: Show Us Life

3926 **Martineau, Barbara Halpern.**
"Documenting the Patriarchy: *Chinatown*."
IN: Women and the Cinema

3957 **Matthews, Glenn E. and Raife G. Tarkington.**
"Early History of Amateur Motion-Picture Film."
IN: A Technological History ...

3958 **Matthews, J.H.**
"*Duck Soup*."
"*King Kong*."
"*Peter Ibbetson*."
"*Dark Passage*."
"*Pandora and the Flying Dutchman*."
"*The Night of the Hunter*."
"*The Last Remake of Beau Geste*."
IN: Surrealism and American Feature Films

3959 **Mauerhofer, Hugo.**
"Psychology of Film Experience."
IN: The Art of Cinema
Film: A Montage of Theories

3960 **Maugham, W. Somerset.**
"On Writing for the Films."
IN: Authors on Film

3961 **Mauriac, Claude.**
"*Masculin-Féminin*."
IN: Focus on Godard

3962 **May, John R.**
"Federico Fellini."
"Francis Coppola."
"The Demonic in American Cinema."
"Visual Story and the Religious Interpretation of Film."
IN: Religion in Film

3962a **May, John R.**
"*The Godfather* Films: Birth of a Don, Death of a
Family."
IN: Image and Likeness

3963 **May, Lary.**
"The Backdrop: Victorian America and Amusements."
"Through a Lens Darkly: The Decline of Progress."
"Rescuing the Family: Urban Progressivism and
Modern Leisure."
"Apocalyptic Cinema: D.W. Griffith and the Aesthetics
of Reform."
"Revitalization: Douglas Fairbanks, Mary Pickford,
and the New Personality, 1914-1918."
"You Are the Star: The Evolution of the Theater
Palace, 1908-1929."
"The New Frontier: 'Hollywood,' 1914-1920."
"Politics Dissolved: Cecil B. DeMille and the
Consumer Ideal, 1918-1929."
IN: Screening Out the Past

3964 **May, Richard P.**
"Sample Exhibition Contract."
IN: The Movie Business Book

3965 **Mayakovsky, Vladimir.**
"Theatre, Cinema, Futurism."
"The Destruction of 'Theatre' by Cinema as a Sign of
the Resurrection of Theatrical Art."
"The Relationship Between Contemporary Theatre
and Cinema and Art."
"Cinema and Cinema."
"Help!"
"Speech in Debate on 'The Paths and Policy of
Sovkino'."
"On Cinema."
IN: The Film Factory

3966 **Mayakovsky, Vladimir.**
"Two Mayakovsky Scenarios."
IN: Screen Reader 1

3967 **Mayer, Arthur L.**
"Documentary Dilemma."
IN: Ideas on Film

3968 **Mayer, Arthur L.**
"The Origins of United Artists."
IN: The First Tycoons

3969 **Mayer, Arthur.**
"Arthur Mayer: The Publicity Director."
IN: The Real Tinsel

3970 **Mayer, Arthur.**
"Growing Pains of a Shrinking Industry."
IN: The Movies: An American Idiom

Mayer, Arthur. SEE: Griffith, Richard.

3971 **Mayer, Geoff.**
"Comedy."
IN: The New Australian Cinema

3972 **Mayer, Michael F.**
"The Exhibition License."
IN: The Movie Business Book

3973 **Mayer, Roger L.**
"Studio Operations."
IN: The Movie Business Book

3974 **Mayersberg, Paul.**
"Carmen and Bess." [RE: *Carmen Jones*; *Porgy and
Bess*.]
"Contamination." [RE: *The Damned*.]
"From *Laura* to *Angel Face*." [RE: Preminger.]
"*Vanina Vanini*."
"*The Trial of Joan of Arc*."
"*Paris nous appartient*."
"*Freaks*."
IN: Movie Reader

3975 **Mayersberg, Paul.**
"Passage to Hollywood."
IN: Sight, Sound, and Society

Mayersberg, Paul. SEE: Perkins, V.F.

3976 **Maynard, Richard.**
"Films and Paperbacks in Social Studies."
IN: Films Deliver

3977 **Mayne, Judith.**
"The Woman Question and the Soviet Silent Film."
"*Strike* and Displaced Vision."
"*Mother* and Son."
"*Bed and Sofa* and the Edge of Domesticity."

"*Fragment of an Empire* and the Woman in the
   Window."
    IN: Kino and the Woman Question

3978 **Mayne, Judith.**
"*Man with a Movie Camera* and Woman's Work."
    IN: Explorations in Film Theory
      Kino and the Woman's Question

3979 **Mayne, Judith.**
"Dracula in the Twilight: Murnau's *Nosferatu*."
    IN: German Film and Literature

3980 **Mayne, Judith.**
"Fassbinder's *Ali: Fear Eats the Soul* and
   Spectatorship."
    IN: Close Viewings

3981 **Mayne, Judith.**
"Female Narration, Women's Cinema: Helke Sander's
   The All-Round Reduced Personality/Redupers."
    IN: Issues in Feminist Film Criticism

3982 **Mayne, Judith.**
"Herzog, Murnau, and the Vampire." [RE: *Nosferatu*.]
    IN: The Films of Werner Herzog

3983 **Mayne, Judith.**
"Lesbian Looks: Dorothy Arzner and Female
   Authorship."
    IN: How Do I Look

3984 **Mayne, Judith.**
"Mediation, the Novelistic, and Film Narrative."
    IN: Narrative Strategies

3985 **Mayne, Judith.**
"The Female Audience and the Feminist Critic."
    IN: Women and Film

3986 **Mayne, Judith.**
"The Woman at the Keyhole: Women's Cinema and
   Feminist Criticism."
    IN: Re-vision

3986a **Mayne, Judith.**
"Uncovering the Female Body."
    IN: Before Hollywood

3987 **Maysles, Albert.**
"*Salesman*." [Interview by Alan Rosenthal.]
    IN: The New Documentary in Action

3988 **Maysles, Albert and David.**
"Albert and David Maysles." [Interview by G. Roy
   Levin.]
    IN: Documentary Explorations

Maysles, David. SEE: Maysles, Albert.

3989 **Mazzella, Anthony J.**
"Author, Auteur: Reading *Rear Window* from Woolrich
   to Hitchcock."
    IN: Hitchcock's Re-Released Films

3990 **McArthur, Colin.**
"Genre."
"Development."

"Background."
"Fritz Lang."
"John Huston."
"Jules Dassin."
"Robert Siodmak."
"Elia Kazan."
"Nicholas Ray."
"Samuel Fuller."
"Don Siegel."
"Jean-Pierre Melville."
    IN: Underworld U.S.A.

3991 **McArthur, Colin.**
"The Iconography of the Gangster Film."
    IN: Film Genre
      Underworld U.S.A.

3992 **McArthur, Colin.**
"Historical Drama."
    IN: Popular Television and Film

3993 **McArthur, Colin.**
"Scotland and Cinema: The Iniquity of the Fathers."
    IN: Scotch Reels

3994 **McArthur, Colin.**
"The Rises and Falls of the Edinburgh International
   Film Festival."
    IN: From Limelight to Satellite

3995 **McBride, Jim.**
"Jim McBride." [Interview by Joseph Gelmis.]
    IN: The Film Director as Superstar

3996 **McBride, Joseph.**
"*Chimes at Midnight*."
"Welles Before *Kane*."
    IN: Focus on Orson Welles

3997 **McBride, Joseph.**
"The Director as Superstar." [RE: *Fellini: A Director's
   Notebook*.]
    IN: Federico Fellini

3998 **McBride, Joseph and Michael Wilmington.**
"The Noble Outlaw." [RE: John Ford.]
    IN: Great Film Directors

3999 **McCaffrey, Donald W.**
"An Evaluation of Chaplin's Silent Comedy Films,
   1916-36."
"*City Lights* and *Modern Times*: Skirmishes with
   Romance, Pathos, and Social Significance."
    IN: Focus on Chaplin

4000 **McCall, Anthony.**
"Two Statements."
    IN: The Avant-Garde Film

4000a **McCall, Anthony.**
"Anthony McCall." [Interview by Scott MacDonald.]
    IN: A Critical Cinema 2

4001 **McCall, Mary C., Jr.**
"My Name Isn't Costello."
    IN: Celebrity Articles ...

4002 **McCambridge, Mercedes.**
"Mercedes McCambridge." [Interview by Charles Higham.]
IN: Celebrity Circus

4003 **McCarten, John.**
"*Rashomon*."
IN: Focus on Rashomon

4004 **McCarthy, Mary.**
"A Prince of Shreds and Patches." [RE: *Hamlet*, 1948.]
IN: Focus on Shakespearean Films

4005 **McCarthy, Todd.**
"*The Delinquents*."
IN: Kings of the Bs

4006 **McCarthy, Todd.**
"William A. Wellman."
IN: American Directors /v. 1

4007 **McCarthy, Todd and Charles Flynn.**
"Herschell Gordon Lewis." [Interview.]
"Albert Zugsmith." [Interview.]
IN: Kings of the Bs

4008 **McCarthy, Todd and Richard Thompson.**
"Phil Karlson." [Interview.]
IN: Kings of the Bs

McCarthy, Todd. SEE: Flynn, Charles.

4009 **McCleery, Albert.**
"The Pioneer Television Producer."
IN: Hollywood Speaks!

4010 **McCloud, George E.**
"*Consuelo ¿Quiénes Somos?*."
IN: Chicano Cinema

4011 **McClure, Arthur F.**
"Censor the Movies!"
IN: The Movies: An American Idiom

4012 **McClure, Arthur F. and Alfred E. Twomey.**
"Character People: Faces from the Past."
IN: The Movies: An American Idiom

4013 **McClure, Michael.**
"Defense of Jayne Mansfield."
IN: Film Culture Reader

McConachy, Susan. SEE: Kuchl, Jerome.

4014 **McConnell, Frank D.**
"Leopards and History: The Problem of Film Genre."
IN: Film Genre

4015 **McConnell, Frank D.**
"We Are Not Alone."
IN: American Media

4016 **McConnell, Frank D.**
"Song of Innocence: *The Creature from the Black Lagoon*."
IN: Movies as Artifacts

4017 **McConnell, Frank.**
"Born in Fire: The Ontology of the Monster."
IN: Shadows of the Magic Lamp

4018 **McConnell, Frank.**
"Rough Beasts Slouching."
IN: Focus on The Horror Film

4019 **McConnell, Robert L.**
"The Genesis and Ideology of *Gabriel over the White House*."
IN: Cinema Examined

4020 **McCormick, Richard W.**
"The Body versus the Head: Peter Schneider's *Lenz*."
"The Other Begins to Speak: Karin Struck's *Class Love*."
"Postmodern Pessimism? Botho Strauss's *Devotion*."
"The Writer in Film: *Wrong Move* by Peter Handke and Wim Wenders."
"Women's Discourse and the German Past: *Germany, Pale Mother* by Helma Sanders-Brahms."
"Re-Presenting History: *The Subjective Factor* by Helke Sander."
IN: Politics of the Self

4021 **McCormick, Ruth.**
"Women's Liberation Cinema."
IN: The Documentary Tradition /2 ed

4022 **McCormick, Ruth.**
"*Swept Away*."
"Notes on Women's Liberation Cinema." [NOTE: This is a revised version "Women's Liberation Cinema."]
IN: Women and the Cinema

4023 **McCormick, Ruth.**
"Alf Brustellin and Bernhard Sinkel: A Uniquely Utopian Aura."
IN: New German Filmmakers

4024 **McCormick, Ruth.**
"Fassbinder's Reality: An Imitation of Life."
IN: Imitations of Life
Fassbinder

McCormick, Ruth. SEE: Scheib-Rothbart, Ingrid.

4025 **McCrea, Joel.**
"Joel McCrea." [Interview by John Kobal.]
IN: People Will Talk

4026 **McCreadie, Marsha.**
"*New Yorker* Niceties: Pauline Kael and Penelope Gilliatt."
"The Europeans: Bryher, C.A. Lejeune, Lotte Eisner, Penelope Houston, and Jan Dawson."
"The Feminists: Molly Haskell, Marjorie Rosen, Joan Mellen, and Laura Mulvey."
"The Reviewers: Judith Crist, Dilys Powell, Renata Adler, and Janet Maslin."
"The Theorists: Susan Sontag, Annette Michelson, Maya Deren, Hortense Powdermaker, and Claude-Edmonde Magny."
"Iris Barry: Historian and All-Round Critic."

"The Culture Critics: Diana Trilling, Simone de
Beauvoir, Joan Didion, and Nora Sayre."
"The Writer's View: Colette, Louise Bogan, Virginia
Woolf, Dorothy Richardson, Marianne Moore, H.D.,
and Anais Nin."
IN: Women on Film

4027 McCullough, John B.
"Joseph T. Tykociner: Pioneer in Sound Recording."
IN: A Technological History ...

4028 McDonald, Archie P.
"John Wayne: Hero of the Western."
IN: Western Films: A Brief History
Shooting Stars

4029 McDonald, Keiko I.
"The Dialectic of Light and Darkness in Kurosawa's
Rashomon."
"Sand, Man, and Symbols: Teshigahara's *The
Woman in the Dunes*."
"Giri, Ninjo, and Fatalism: Image Pattern and
Thematic Conflict in Shinoda's *Double Suicide*."
"Images of Son and Superhero in Kurosawa's *Red
Beard*."
"Character Types and Psychological Revelation in
Ichikawa's *The Harp of Burma*."
"Atmosphere and Thematic Conflict in Mizoguchi's
Ugetsu."
"Freedom of Imagination in Oshima's *Death by
Hanging*."
"The Phantasmagorical World of Kurosawa's *The
Throne of Blood*."
"Time, Sex, and Politics in Yoshinda's *Ero plus
Massacre*."
"A Basic Narrative Mode in Yasujiro Ozu's *Tokyo
Story*."
"Kinoshita and the Gift of Tears: *Twenty-four Eyes*."
"The Viewer's View of Ichikawa's *Odd Obsession*."
IN: Cinema East

4030 McDonald, Keiko.
"Japan."
IN: The Asian Film Industry

4031 McDonald, Marianne.
"Pasolini's *Medea*: The Lesson of the Grain."
"Dassin's *Dream of Passion*: Ancient Theater/Modern
Tragedy."
"Dassin's *Phaedra*: Fireworks and Death Among the
Jet Set."
"Cacoyannis and Euripides' *Iphigenia at Aulis*: A New
Heroism."
"Victor/Victim: A Dialectic--Cacoyannis' *The Trojan
Women*."
"Cacoyannis' *Electra*: All in the Family."
IN: Euripides in Cinema

4032 McDonald, Neil.
"Australia."
IN: World Cinema Since 1945

4033 McDonald, T. Liam.
"The Horror of Hammer: The House That Blood Built."
IN: Cut!: Horror Writers ...

4034 McDougal, Stuart Y.
"Adaptation: The Metamorphic Art."
"The Craft of Film: *Citizen Kane*."
"Plot and Structure: *The Grapes of Wrath*; *The
Thirty-Nine Steps*; *The Member of the Wedding*; *A
Doll's House*."
"Character: *The Treasure of the Sierra Madre*;
Macbeth; *Jules and Jim*."
"Point of View: *The Innocents*; *The Collector*;
Rashomon."
"The World of Inner Experience: *The Loneliness of a
Long-Distance Runner*; *The Stranger*; *Blow-up*."
"Figurative Discourse: *The Throne of Blood*; *The
Fallen Idol*; *Women in Love*."
"Symbol and Allegory: *The Rocking-Horse Winner*;
Stagecoach; *Fellini Satyricon*."
"Time: *An Occurrence at Owl Creek Bridge*; *Miss
Julie*; *High Noon*."
IN: Made Into Movies

4035 McDougal, Stuart Y.
"Adaptation of an Auteur: Truffaut's *Jules et Jim* from
the Novel by Henri-Pierre Roché."
IN: Modern European Filmmakers ...

4036 McDowell, Michael.
"Michael McDowell." [Interview by Stanley Wiater.]
IN: Dark Visions

4036a McElwee, Ross.
"Ross McElwee." [Interview by Scott MacDonald.]
IN: A Critical Cinema 2

4037 McFarlane, Brian.
"From Page to Screen."
"*Wake in Fright*."
"*Picnic at Hanging Rock*."
"*The Getting of Wisdom*."
"*The Mango Tree*."
"*The Chant of Jimmie Blacksmith*."
"*My Brilliant Career*."
"*Monkey Grip*."
"*The Year of Living Dangerously*."
"*The Night the Prowler*."
"Martin Boyd on Television: Lucinda Brayford and
Outbreak of Love."
IN: Words and Images

4038 McFarlane, Brian.
"A Literary Cinema? British Films and British Novels."
IN: All Our Yesterdays

4039 McFarlane, Brian.
"Horror and Suspense."
IN: The New Australian Cinema

4040 McGann, Kevin.
"*The Fountainhead* [novel by] Ayn Rand. Ayn Rand in
the Stockyard of the Spirit."
IN: The Modern American Novel ...

4041 McGilligan, Patrick.
"Dede Allen."
IN: Women and the Cinema

4042 McGilligan, Patrick.
"*The Human Comedy* [novel by] William Saroyan. Mr.
Saroyan's Thoroughly American Movie."
IN: The Modern American Novel ...

4043 McGilligan, Patrick.
"Robert Clampett."
"A Talk with Ralph Bakshi."
IN: The American Animated Cartoon

4044 McGillis, Roderick.
"*Alice's Adventures in Wonderland* [novel by] Lewis
Carroll. Novelty and Roman Cement: Two
Versions of *Alice*."
IN: Children's Novels and the Movies

4045 McGillivray, David.
"Failures."
IN: Anatomy of the Movies

4046 McGuinness, P.P.
"Peter Weir's Hauntingly Beautiful Film Makes the
Film World Sit Up." [RE: *Picnic at Hanging Rock*.]
IN: An Australian Film Reader

4047 McGuinness, Richard.
"*Carnal Knowledge*."
IN: Sexuality in the Movies

4048 McGuire, Dorothy.
"Dorothy McGuire." [Interview by Rex Reed.]
IN: Travolta to Keaton

4049 McIntosh, Ned.
"*The Birth of a Nation*."
IN: Focus on The Birth of a Nation

4050 McKay, Craig.
"Craig McKay." [Interview by Vincent LoBrutto.]
IN: Selected Takes

4051 McKee, Sister Katherine.
"Film Aesthetics in the Curriculum."
IN: The Compleat Guide to Film Study

4052 McLaren, Norman.
"*Neighbours* and *Pas de Deux*." [Interview by Alan
Rosenthal.]
IN: The New Documentary in Action

4053 McLaren, Norman.
"Living with *Neighbours*."
IN: Film: Book 2

4054 McLaughlin, James.
"All in the Family: Alfred Hitchcock's *Shadow of a
Doubt*."
IN: A Hitchcock Reader

4055 McLuhan, Marshall.
"Movies: The Reel World."
IN: Film and the Liberal Arts
Film: Readings in the Mass Media
Film And/As Literature
Crossroads to the Cinema

4056 McLuhan, Marshall.
"Classrooms Without Walls."

IN: Perspectives on the Study of Film

4057 McMillan, Terry.
"*The Wizard of Oz*."
IN: The Movie That Changed My Life

4058 McMillan, Terry.
"Thoughts on *She's Gotta Have It*."
IN: Five for Five

4059 McMullen, Jay.
"Jay McMullen." [An interview.]
IN: Producers on Producing

4060 McMurtry, Larry.
"No Clue: Or Learning to Write for the Movies."
"The Hired Pen."
"The Deadline Syndrome."
"The Telephone Booth Screenwriter."
"The Fun of It All."
"*All the President's Men*, *Seven Beauties*, History,
Innocence, Guilt, Redemption, and the Star
System."
"The Screenplay as Non-Book: A Consideration."
"Pencils West: Or a Theory for the Shoot-'Em-Up."
"'Mary Hartman, Mary Hartman' and the Movie-Less
Novelists."
"O Ragged Time Knit Up Thy Ravell'd Sleave."
"The Situation in Criticism: Reviewers, Critics,
Professors."
"Character, the Tube, and the Death of Movies."
"The Disappearance of Love."
"Woody Allen, Keith Carradine, Lily Tomlin, and the
Disappearance of Grace."
"The Last Picture Shows."
"The Seasons of L.A."
"The Last Movie Column."
"The Last Picture Show: A Last Word."
"Approaching Cheyenne ... Leaving Lumet. Oh,
Pshaw!"
"Moving-Tripping: My Own Rotten Film Festival."
"A Walk in Pasadena with Di-Annie and Mary Alice."
IN: Film Flam

4061 McMurtry, Larry.
"Cowboys, Movies, Myths, and Cadillacs: Realism in
the Western."
IN: Man and the Movies
The American West on Film

4061a McNamara, Brooks.
"Scene Design and the Early Film."
IN: Before Hollywood

4062 McNiven, Roger.
"Gregory La Cava."
"Jacques Tourneur."
IN: American Directors /v. 1

4063 McPherson, Robin.
"Declarations of Independence."
IN: From Limelight to Satellite

4064 McRobbie, Angela.
"*Fame*, *Flashdance*, and Fantasies of Achievement."

IN: Fabrications

4065   Mead, Syd.
"Designing the Future."
IN: Omni's Screen Flights ...

4066   Mead, Taylor.
"The Movies Are a Revolution."
IN: The New American Cinema

Med Hondo, Abid. SEE: Hondo, Abid Med.

4067   Medhurst, Andy.
"Dirk Bogarde."
"Music Hall and British Cinema."
IN: All Our Yesterdays

4068   Medhurst, Andy.
"Notes on Recent Gay Film Criticism."
IN: Gays and Film /rev ed

Medhurst, Andy. SEE: Cook, Pam.

4069   Medved, Harry and Michael.
"*Intolerance*."
"*Quo Vadis?*"
"*Noah's Ark*."
"*Cain and Mabel*."
"*Underwater!*"
"*The Conqueror*."
"*Scipio Africanus*."
"*Kolberg*."
"*Hello Everbody!*"
"*Sincerely Yours*."
"*Hotel Imperial*."
"*Darling Lili*."
"*Cleopatra* [1963]."
"*Boom*."
"*The Only Game in Town*."
"*Doctor Dolittle*."
"*The Blue Bird*."
"*The Greatest Story Ever Told*."
"*Mohammad: Messenger of God*."
"*Paint Your Wagon*."
"*Can't Stop the Music*."
"*Heaven's Gate*."
"*Inchon*."
IN: The Hollywood Hall of Shame

4070   Medvedkin, Alexander.
"Interview with Alexander Medvedkin."
IN: Inside the Film Factory

4071   Meeker, Hubert.
"*Blow-Up*."
IN: Renaissance of the Film
Focus on Blow-Up

4072   Mees, C.E. Kenneth.
"History of Professional Black-and-White
Motion-Picture Film."
IN: A Technological History ...

4073   Megaw, Ruth.
"American Influence on Australian Cinema
Management, 1896-1923."
IN: An Australian Film Reader

4074   Meisel, Myron.
"Allan Dwan."
"John Cromwell."
IN: American Directors /v. 1

4075   Meisel, Myron.
"Blake Edwards."
"John Cassavetes."
IN: American Directors /v. 2

4076   Meisel, Myron.
"Edgar G. Ulmer: The Primacy of the Visual."
"Joseph H. Lewis: Tourist in the Asylum."
IN: Kings of the Bs

4077   Mekas, Jonas.
"*Ordet*."
IN: Renaissance of the Film

4078   Mekas, Jonas.
"Experiment in the Fifties."
IN: Film: Book 1

4079   Mekas, Jonas.
"Film Happenings."
"Free Cinema and the New Wave."
IN: The Emergence of Film Art /1 ed
The Emergence of Film Art /2 ed

4080   Mekas, Jonas.
"Interview with Peter Kubelka."
"Notes on Some New Movies and Happiness."
"The Experimental Film in America."
"A Call for a New Generation of Film-Makers."
IN: Film Culture Reader

4081   Mekas, Jonas.
"Movie Journal."
IN: Perspectives on the Study of Film

4082   Mekas, Jonas.
"Notes on the New American Cinema."
IN: Film: A Montage of Theories
Film Culture Reader

4083   Mekas, Jonas.
"The Diary Film." [RE: *Reminiscences of a Journey to
Lithuania*.]
IN: The Avant-Garde Film

4084   Mekas, Jonas.
"The Other Direction."
IN: Film And/As Literature
The Movies as Medium

4085   Mekas, Jonas.
"Where Are We--the Underground?"
IN: The New American Cinema
Film: Readings in the Mass Media

4086   Mekas, Jonas.
"[On] Peter Kubelka."

IN: Structural Film Anthology

4086a Mekas, Jonas.
"Jonas Mekas." [Interview by Scott MacDonald.]
IN: A Critical Cinema 2

Mekas, Jonas. SEE: Gidal, Peter.

4087 Melandri, Lea.
"Ecstasy, Coldness, and the Sadness Which Is
Freedom."
IN: Off Screen

4088 Melchiori, Paola.
"Women's Cinema: A Look at Female Identity."
IN: Off Screen

4089 Melchiot, Ib J.
"Ib J. Melchiot." [An interview.]
IN: Interviews with B ...

4090 Méliès, Georges.
"Cinematographic Views."
IN: French Film Theory and Criticism /v. 1

4091 Mellen, Joan.
"*The Phantom of Liberty*: Further Investigations Into
The Discreet Charm of the Bourgeoisie."
"An Overview of Buñuel's Career."
"*Tristana*."
IN: The World of Luis Buñuel

4092 Mellen, Joan.
"[From:] *Women and Their Sexuality in the New Film*:
The Mae West Nobody Knows."
IN: Film Theory and Criticism /3 ed
Film Theory and Criticism /4 ed

4093 Mellen, Joan.
"On Lina Wertmuller."
IN: Film in Society

4094 Mellen, Joan.
"Welcoming the Future."
IN: Omni's Screen Flights ...

4095 Mellencamp, Patricia.
"The Sexual Economics of *Gold Diggers of 1933*."
IN: Close Viewings

4096 Mellencamp, Patricia.
"Spectacle and Spectator: Looking Through the
American Musical Comedy."
IN: Explorations in Film Theory

4097 Mellencamp, Patricia.
"Jokes and Their Relation to the Marx Brothers."
IN: Cinema and Language

4098 Mellencamp, Patricia.
"Uncanny Feminism: The Exquisite Corpses of
Cecelia Condit."
IN: Fantasy and the Cinema

4099 Mellencamp, Patricia.
"Situation Comedy, Feminism, and Freud: Discourses
of Gracie and Lucy." [RE: Gracie Allen; Lucille Ball.]
IN: Star Texts

Mellencamp, Patricia. SEE: Doane, Mary Ann.

4100 Melling, P.H.
"The Mind of the Mob: Hollywood and Popular Culture
in the 1930s."
IN: Cinema, Politics and Society in America

4101 Mencken, H.L.
"Appendix for Moronia."
"Appendix from Moronia: Valentino."
IN: Authors on Film

4102 Mencken, H.L.
"Interlude in the Socratic Manner."
IN: The Movies in Our Midst

4103 Mencken, H.L.
"The Movies."
IN: Film: Readings in the Mass Media

4104 Mendelson, Lois and Bill Simon.
"[On] Ken Jacobs."
IN: Structural Film Anthology

4105 Mengers, Sue.
"The Agent."
IN: Filmmakers on Filmmaking /v. 1

4106 Menges, Chris.
"Chris Menges [on Cinematography]." [Interview by
David Chell.]
IN: Moviemakers at Work

4107 Menzel, Jirí.
"Jirí Menzel." [Interview by Antonín J. Liehm.]
IN: Closely Watched Films

4108 Menzies, William Cameron.
"Pictorial Beauty in the Photoplay."
IN: Introduction to the Photoplay
Hollywood Directors 1914-1940

4109 Mercer, Kobena.
"Diaspora Culture and the Dialogic Imagination: The
Aesthetics of Black Independent Film in Britain."
IN: Critical Perspectives on Black ...

4110 Mercer, Kobena.
"Skin Head Sex Thing: Racial Difference and the
Homoerotic Imaginary."
IN: How Do I Look

4110a Mercer, Kobena.
"Monster Metaphors—Notes of Michael Jackson's
Thriller." [RE: LP record and music video.]
IN: Stardom

4111 Mercier, Pierre.
"*Rashomon*."
IN: Focus on Rashomon

4112 Merck, Mandy.
"*Lianna* and the Lesbians of Art Cinema."
IN: Films for Women

4113 Mercken-Spaas, Godelieve.
"Narrative Levels in Alain Tanner's *La Salamandre*."
IN: Explorations in National Cinemas

IN: <u>Omni's Screen Flights ...</u>

4140 Meyer, Richard J.
"The Films of David Wark Griffith: The Development
of Themes and Techniques in Forty-two of His
Films."
IN: <u>Focus on D.W. Griffith</u>
<u>Great Film Directors</u>

4141 Meyer, Russ.
"The Low-Budget Producer."
IN: <u>The Movie Business Book</u>

4142 Meyer, William R.
"*Tumbleweeds.*"
"*Hit the Saddle.*"
"*Stagecoach.*"
"*Jesse James.*"
"*Drums Along the Mohawk.*"
"*The Westerner.*"
"*They Died with Their Boots On.*"
"*The Ox-Bow Incident.*"
"*Duel in the Sun.*"
"*Red River.*"
"*Fort Apache.*"
"*Broken Arrow.*"
"*The Gunfighter.*"
"*High Noon.*"
"*Shane.*"
"*Johnny Guitar.*"
"*The Man from Laramie.*"
"*The Tall T.*"
"*Rio Bravo.*"
"*The Magnificent Seven.*"
"*The Misfits.*"
"*Ride the High Country.*"
"*Hud.*"
"*For a Few Dollars More.*"
"*The Professionals.*"
"*El Dorado.*"
"*True Grit.*"
"*The Wild Bunch.*"
"*Butch Cassidy and the Sundance Kid.*"
"*McCabe and Mrs. Miller.*"
IN: <u>The Making of the Great Westerns</u>

4143 Meyer, William.
"War in Short."
IN: <u>Nuclear War Films</u>

4144 Meyerhold, Vsevolod.
"The Cinefication of Theatre."
"On Cinema."
IN: <u>The Film Factory</u>

4145 Meyers, Sidney and Jay Leyda.
"Joris Ivens--Artist in Documentary."
IN: <u>The Documentary Tradition /1 ed</u>
<u>The Documentary Tradition /2 ed</u>

4146 Meyers, Sidney.
"An Event--*The Wave.*" [RE: *Redes.*]
IN: <u>The Documentary Tradition /1 ed</u>
<u>The Documentary Tradition /2 ed</u>

4147 Meyers, Sidney.
"The Situation of the Serious Filmmaker."
IN: <u>Film: Book 1</u>

4148 Michaels, Leonard.
"*Gilda.*"
IN: <u>The Movie That Changed My Life</u>

4149 Michalczyk, John J.
"Jean Cocteau."
"Sacha Guitry."
"Marcel Pagnol."
"Jean Giono."
"André Malraux."
"Alain Robbe-Grillet."
"Marguerite Duras."
IN: <u>The French Literary Filmmakers</u>

4150 Michalczyk, John J.
"Francesco Rosi: The Dialectical Cinema."
"Pier Paolo Pasolini: The Epical-Religious Cinema of
Political Sexuality."
"Bernardo Bertolucci: The Strategy of a Freudian
Marxist."
"Marco Bellocchio: An Autobiographical Leap into the
Political Beyond."
"Gillo Pontecorvo: At the Perilous Crossroads of
History."
"Elio Petri: A Kafkaesque Moralist (Often) above
Suspicion."
"Lina Wertmuller: The Politics of Sexuality."
IN: <u>The Italian Political Filmmakers</u>

4151 Michaczyk [*sic*, Michalczyk], John J.
"Costa Gavras's *Missing*: A Legal and Political
Battlefield."
IN: <u>Current Research in Film /v. 3</u>

4152 Michalek, Boleslaw.
"Andrzej Wajda's Vision of One Country's Past and
Present."
IN: <u>Politics, Art and Commitment ...</u>

Michaud, Gene. SEE: Dittmar, Linda.

4153 Michel, Martin.
"National Screen Service."
IN: <u>The Movie Business Book</u>

4154 Michel, Sonya.
"Feminism, Film, and Public History."
IN: <u>Issues in Feminist Film Criticism</u>

4155 Michel, Walter S.
"In Memoriam of Dimitri Kiranov, a Neglected Master."
IN: <u>Film Culture Reader</u>

4156 Michelson, Annette.
"From Magician to Epistemologist (Vertov's *The Man
with the Movie Camera*)."
IN: <u>The Essential Cinema /v. 1</u>

4157 Michelson, Annette.
"Film and the Radical Aspiration."
IN: <u>Film Theory and Criticism /1 ed</u>
<u>Film Theory and Criticism /2 ed</u>

4182 Miller, Robert E.
"The Canadian Feature Film Conundrum: 1894-1967."
    IN: Current Research in Film /v. 4

4183 Miller, Warren.
"Progress in Documentary."
    IN: The Documentary Tradition /1 ed
        The Documentary Tradition /2 ed

4184 Millichap, Joseph R.
"Of Mice and Men."
"The Grapes of Wrath."
"The Forgotten Village."
"Tortilla Flat."
"The Moon Is Down."
"Lifeboat."
"A Medal for Benny."
"The Pearl."
"The Red Pony."
"Viva Zapata!."
"East of Eden."
"The Wayward Bus."
"Flight."
"Cannery Row."
    IN: Steinbeck and Film

4185 Millichap, Joseph R.
"Harry Brown."
"Horton Foote."
    IN: Dictionary of Literary Biography /v. 26

4186 Millichap, Joseph.
"Lonne Elder III."
"Calder Willingham."
    IN: Dictionary of Literary Biography /v. 44

4187 Millner, Sherry.
"Third World Newsreel: Interview with Christine Choy."
    IN: Jump Cut

Mills, Moylan C. SEE: Gronlund, Enrique.

4188 Milne, Tom.
"Carl Theodor Dreyer: The Early Works."
"Georges Franju."
"Jacques Becker."
"Jean Renoir: from 1939."
"Jean-Pierre Melville."
"Lev Kuleshov."
"Rouben Mamoulian."
"Thomas Harper Ince."
"Victor Sjöström."
"Vittorio Cottafavi, Riccardo Freda and Mario Bava."
    IN: Cinema: A Critical Dictionary

4189 Milne, Tom.
"Commentary."
    IN: Godard on Godard

4190 Milne, Tom.
"Horror."
    IN: Anatomy of the Movies

4191 Milne, Tom.
"Jean-Luc Godard, ou la Raison Ardente."
    IN: Focus on Godard

4192 Milne, Tom.
"Rohmer's Siege Perilous."
"Flavour of Green Tea Over Rice."
    IN: Sight and Sound

4193 Milne, Tom.
"The Two Chambermaids." [RE: Le Journal d'Un Femme de Chambre, 1946 and 1964.]
    IN: The World of Luis Buñuel

4194 Milne, Tom.
"The World Beyond." [RE: Luis Buñuel.]
    IN: The Classic Cinema
        Great Film Directors

4195 Milne, Tom.
"Buffalo Bill and the Indians."
    IN: The Pretend Indians

4196 Minami, Hiroshi.
"Copyright in Japan."
    IN: Fair Use and Free Inquiry

4197 Minh-ha, Trinh T.
"Outside In Inside Out."
    IN: Questions of Third Cinema

4197a Minh-ha, Trinh T.
"Trinh T. Minh-ha." [Interview by Scott MacDonald.]
    IN: A Critical Cinema 2

4198 Minnelli, Liza.
"Liza Minnelli." [Interview by Rex Reed.]
    IN: Travolta to Keaton

4199 Minnelli, Vincente.
"Vincente Minnelli."
    IN: The Celluloid Muse

4200 Minnelli, Vincente.
"Vincente Minnelli." [Interview by Richard Schickel.]
    IN: The Men Who Made the Movies

4201 Minter, Mary Miles.
"Mary Miles Minter." [Interview by Charles Higham.]
    IN: Celebrity Circus

4201a Mintz, Lawrence E.
"Comedy and Pathos in City Lights."
    IN: Charlie Chaplin

4202 Mintz, Penny.
"Orson Welles's Use of Sound."
    IN: Film Sound

4203 Miscuglio, Annabella.
"An Affectionate and Irreverent Account of Eighty Years of Women's Cinema in Italy."
    IN: Off Screen

4204 Mitchell, Edward.
"Apes and Essences: Some Sources of Significance in the American Gangster Film."
    IN: Film Genre Reader

4205 Mitchell, George J.
"All Quiet on the Western Front [1930]."

IN: The Cinema of Adventure, Romance & Terror

4206 Mitchell, George.
"The Consolidation of the American Film Industry, 1915-1920."
IN: Explorations in Film Theory

4207 Mitchell, Stanley.
"Marinetti and Mayakovsky: Futurism, Fascism, Communism."
IN: Screen Reader 1

4208 Mitrani, Nora.
"Intention and Surprise."
IN: The Shadow and Its Shadow

4209 Mitry, Jean.
"The Concreteness of Ince's Films."
IN: The First Film Makers

4210 Mix, Tom.
"A Problem in Chivalry."
IN: The Best of Rob Wagner's Script

4211 Mixajlov, E. and A. Moskvin.
"The Role of the Cinematographer in the Creation of a Film."
IN: Russian Formalist Film Theory

4212 Mo Zhong.
"A Reader's Letter That Will Make People Think."
IN: Perspectives on Chinese Cinema

4213 Mocki, Ali.
"Reflections on the Algerian Cinema."
IN: Algerian Cinema

4214 Moctezuma, Juan López.
"Juan López Moctezuma." [Interview by Beatrice Reyes Nevares.]
IN: The Mexican Cinema

4215 Modleski, Tania.
"Rape vs. Mans/laughter: *Blackmail*."
"Male Hysteria and the 'Order of Things': *Murder!*"
"Woman and the Labyrinth: *Rebecca*."
"The Woman Who Was Known Too Much: *Notorious*."
"The Master's Dollhouse: *Rear Window*."
"Femininity by Design: *Vertigo*."
"Rituals of Defilement: *Frenzy*."
"Afterward: Hitchcock's Daughters."
IN: The Women Who Knew Too Much

4216 Modleski, Tania.
"Hitchcock, Feminism, and the Patriarchal Unconscious."
IN: Issues in Feminist Film Criticism

4217 Modleski, Tania.
"The Search for Tomorrow in Today's Soap Operas." [RE: television.]
IN: Imitations of Life

4218 Modleski, Tania.
"Time and Desire in the Woman's Film."
IN: Home Is Where the Heart Is
Film Theory and Criticism /4 ed

4219 Mogno, Dario.
"Trieste: The First Science Fiction Festival."
IN: Focus on The Science Fiction Film

4220 Mohr, Hal.
"Camera on the Move: An Interview with Hal Mohr."
[Interview by George C. Pratt.]
IN: Image on the Art ...

4221 Mohr, Hal.
"Hal Mohr: The Cameraman."
IN: The Real Tinsel

4222 Mohr, Hal.
"Reminiscence and Reflection: à Cinematographer."
IN: Sound and the Cinema

4223 Möhrmann, Renate.
"The influence of Brecht on women's cinema in West Germany."
IN: Re-interpreting Brecht

4224 Moley, Raymond.
"Mr. Forman Goes to Town." [SEE: Henry James Forman, "Our Movie Made Children".]
"The Birth of the Production Code."
IN: The Movies in Our Midst

4225 Moloney, Mick.
"Stereotypes in the Media: The Irish-American Case."
IN: Ethnic Images ...

4225a Molyneaux, Gerard.
"*Modern Times* and the American Culture of the 1930's."
IN: Charlie Chaplin

4226 Monaco, James.
"The Camera Writes."
"Truffaut: The Antoine Doinel Cycle."
"Truffaut: The Statement of Genres."
"Truffaut: The Explosion of Genres."
"Truffaut: Intimate Politics."
"Godard: Women and the Outsider."
"Godard: Modes of Discourse."
"Godard: A Season in Hell (Icy Poetry)."
"Godard: Returning to Zero (Picture and Act)."
"Godard: Theory and Practice (The Dziga-Vertov Period)."
"Chabrol: Films Noirs in Color."
"Rohmer: Moral Tales (The Art of Courtly Love)."
"Rivette: The Process of Narrative."
IN: The New Wave: Truffaut, Godard ...

4227 Monaco, James.
"Jean Eustache."
"Kenneth Loach."
"Krzysztof Zanussi."
"Louis Malle."
"Marguerite Duras."
"Swiss Cinema."
"American Documentary Since 1960."
"François Truffaut."
IN: Cinema: A Critical Dictionary

4228 **Monaco, Paul.**
"Realism, Italian Style."
"The First Crest of the New Wave."
"The Bitburg Syndrome."
"Memory without Pain." [RE: U.S. 1970s.]
IN: Ribbons in Time

4229 **Monaco, Paul.**
"Movies and National Consciousness: Germany and France in the 1920s."
IN: Feature Films as History

4230 **Monegal, Emir Rodriguez.**
"Alberto Cavalcanti."
IN: Nonfiction Film Theory and Criticism

4231 **Monroe, Marilyn.**
"A Gentleman From Center Field." [RE: Joe DiMaggio.]
IN: Bedside Hollywood

4232 **Montagu, Ivor.**
"Rhythm."
IN: The Movies as Medium

4233 **Montague, Ivor.**
"German Film Trade under National Socialism."
IN: Celebrity Articles ...

4234 **Monte, Joseph L.**
"Correcting the Image of the Italian in American Film and Television."
IN: Ethnic Images ...

4235 **Monteleone, Thomas F.**
"A Double Feature and a Cartoon for 35 Cents."
IN: Cut!: Horror Writers ...

4236 **Montgomery, John.**
"A Brief Overall View."
IN: Focus on Chaplin

4237 ***Monthly Film Guide.***
"*School in the Mailbox.*"
IN: An Australian Film Reader

4238 **Monti, Adriana.**
"Introduction to the Script of the Film *Scuola senza fine.*"
IN: Off Screen

4239 **Moonjean, Hank.**
"Associate Producer."
IN: Hollywood Speaks!

4240 **Moore, Colleen.**
"Colleen Moore." [Interview by John Kobal.]
IN: People Will Talk

4241 **Moore, James.**
"Billy Wilder."
"Dalton Trumbo."
"John Balderston."
IN: Dictionary of Literary Biography /v. 26

4242 **Moore, James.**
"Paul Mazursky."
IN: Dictionary of Literary Biography /v. 44

4243 **Moore, Roger.**
"Roger Moore." [Interview by Rex Reed.]
IN: Travolta to Keaton

4244 **Moore, Suzanne.**
"Here's Looking at You, Kid!"
IN: The Female Gaze

4245 **Moorehead, Agnes.**
"The Character Player."
IN: Hollywood Speaks!

4246 **Morales, Alejandro.**
"Expanding the Meaning of Chicano Cinema: *Yo soy chicano, Raíces de sangre, Seguín.*"
IN: Chicano Cinema

4247 **Morales, Sylvia.**
"Chicano-Produced Celluloid Mujeres."
IN: Chicano Cinema

4248 **Moran, Albert.**
"From the Tropics to the Snow: The Commonwealth Film Unit in the 1960s."
"A State Government Business Venture: The South Australian Film Corporation."
IN: An Australian Film Reader

4249 **Moravia, Alberto.**
"Dreaming up Petronius." [RE: *Fellini Satyricon.*]
IN: Federico Fellini

4250 **Moravia, Alberto.**
"For Whom Do We Write?"
IN: Springtime in Italy

4251 **Mordden, Ethan.**
"Florence Lawrence."
"Theda Bara."
"Mae Murray."
"Geraldine Farrar."
"Betty Bronson."
"ZaSu Pitts."
"Nazimova."
"Colleen Moore."
"Clara Bow."
"Gloria Swanson."
"Mary Pickford."
"Lillian Gish."
"Janet Gaynor."
"Norma Shearer."
"Greta Garbo."
"Joan Crawford."
"Ruth Chatterton."
"Ann Harding."
"Helen Hayes."
"Lynn Fontanne."
"Jeanette MacDonald."
"Myrna Loy."
"Irene Dunne."
"Margaret Dumont."
"Greer Garson."
"Marlene Dietrich."

"Jean Harlow."
"Mae West."
"Marie Dressler."
"Carole Lombard."
"Marion Davies."
"Lucille Ball."
"Gracie Allen."
"Eve Arden."
"Katharine Hepburn."
"Glenda Farrell."
"Joan Blondell."
"Rosalind Russell."
"Alice Faye."
"Barbara Stanwyck."
"Bette Davis."
"Shirley Temple."
"Deanna Durbin."
"Judy Garland."
"Elizabeth Taylor."
"Rita Hayworth."
"Betty Grable."
"Ava Gardner."
"Marilyn Monroe."
"Jayne Mansfield."
"Kim Novak."
"Judy Holliday."
"Audrey Hepburn."
"Madeline Kahn."
"Miss Piggy."
"Lily Tomlin."
"Goldie Hawn."
"Doris Day."
"Julie Andrews."
"Barbra Streisand."
"Liza Minnelli."
"Bernadette Peters."
"Ingrid Bergman."
"Raquel Welch."
"Bo Derek."
"Sally Kellerman."
"Diane Keaton."
"Jane Fonda."
"Meryl Streep."
    IN: Movie Star: A Look at ...

4252   **Mordden, Ethan.**
"Paramount: The Sophisticate."
"Metro-Goldwyn-Mayer: The Supreme."
"Small Studios: The Independent."
"Warner Brothers: The Slicker."
"Fox: The Rube."
"RKO: The New Yorker."
"Universal: The Old Monster."
    IN: The Hollywood Studios

4252a **Morey, Ann-Janine.**
"*High Noon*: On the Uncertainty of Certainty."
    IN: Image and Likeness

4253   **Morgenstern, Joseph.**
"Two Views." [RE: *Bonnie and Clyde*.]

    IN: A Casebook on Film

4254   **Morgenstern, Joseph.**
"History Right in the Face." [RE: *In the Year of the Pig*.]
    IN: The Documentary Tradition /1 ed
        The Documentary Tradition /2 ed

4255   **Morgenstern, Joseph.**
"Summa Cum Laude." [RE: *The Graduate*.]
"The Future of Film."
    IN: Film: Readings in the Mass Media

4256   **Morin, E. and C. Bremond.**
"An International Survey of the Film Hero."
    IN: Conflict and Control in the Cinema

4257   **Morlion, Felix A.**
"The Philosophical Basis of Neo-Realism."
    IN: Springtime in Italy

4258   **Morris, Chester.**
"Brother, Can You Spare a Dime?"
    IN: Celebrity Articles ...

4259   **Morris, Chris.**
"Roger Corman: The Schlemiel as Outlaw."
    IN: Kings of the Bs

4260   **Morris, George.**
"Charlton Heston."
"Errol Flynn."
"Henry Fonda."
    IN: The Movie Star: The National ...

4261   **Morris, Meaghan.**
"Personal Relationships and Sexuality."
"They Made a Film and Nobody Came."
    IN: The New Australian Cinema

4261a **Morris, Michael Thomas, O.P.**
"*Sunset Boulevard*: Twilight of the Gods."
    IN: Image and Likeness

4262   **Morris, Neil.**
"The Uses of History / Eastern Europe."
    IN: Film: Book 2

4263   **Morris, Peter.**
"Images of Canada."
    IN: Film Before Griffith

4264   **Morrisett, Anne.**
"Sweden: Paradise and Paradox."
    IN: Conflict and Control in the Cinema

4265   **Morrison, Chester.**
"3-D: High, Wide, and Handsome."
    IN: The Movies in Our Midst

4266   **Morrison, George.**
"The French Avant-Garde."
    IN: The Emergence of Film Art /1 ed
        The Emergence of Film Art /2 ed

4267   **Morrison, Nan.**
"Buck Henry."
    IN: Dictionary of Literary Biography /v. 26

4268 Morsberger, Robert E.
"'That Hemingway Kind of Love': Macomber in the
   Movies."
   IN: A Moving Picture Feast

4269 Morse, Margaret.
"Paradoxes of Realism: The Rise of Film in the Train
   of the Novel."
   IN: Explorations in Film Theory

4270 Morse, Susan E.
"Susan E. Morse." [Interview by Vincent LoBrutto.]
   IN: Selected Takes

4271 Mosier, John.
"Hungary."
   IN: World Cinema Since 1945

4272 Moskowitz, Ken.
"Media Events, Cool Media, and *Medium Cool*."
   IN: Explorations in National Cinemas

4273 Moskowitz, Suree.
"Some Observations on the Images of
   Asian-Americans in American Popular Visual
   Media."
   IN: Ethnic Images ...

Moskvin, A. SEE: Mikhailov, E.

4274 Motion Picture Association of America.
"Reasons Underlying the General Principles [of The
   Motion Picture Production Code]."
   IN: Film and Society

4275 Motion Picture Association of America.
"Industry Economic Review and Audience Profile."
   IN: The Movie Business Book

4276 Motion Picture Association of America.
"Rating Code."
   IN: Film: Readings in the Mass Media

**4277 Motion Picture Producers and Distributors of
America.**
"The Don'ts and Be Carefuls."
"The Motion Picture Production Code of 1930."
   IN: The Movies in Our Midst

4278 Mottram, Eric.
"Blood on the Nash Ambassador: Cars in American
   Film."
   IN: Cinema, Politics and Society in America

4279 Mottram, Ron.
"*The Mysterious X*."
   IN: The Rivals of D.W. Griffith

4280 Mottram, Ron.
"American Sound Films, 1926-1930."
   IN: Film Sound

4281 Moullet, Luc.
"Sam Fuller: In Marlowe's Footsteps."
   IN: Cahiers du Cinéma, The 1950s

4282 Moullet, Luc.
"Jean-Luc Godard."

   IN: Cahiers du Cinéma, 1960-1968

4283 Moullet, Luc.
"Saint Janet."
   IN: Sternberg

4284 Moullet, Luc, André Bazin, Jacques Rivette.
"Exchanges about Kurosawa and Mizoguchi."
   IN: Cahiers du Cinéma, The 1950s

Moullet, Luc. SEE: Chabrol, Claude.

4285 Mourlet, Michel.
"Fritz Lang's Trajectory."
   IN: Fritz Lang: The Image ...

4286 Mourlet, Michel.
"In Defence of Violence."
   IN: Stardom
       Cahiers du Cinéma, 1960-1968

4286a Mourlet, Michel.
"The Beauty of Knowledge: Joseph Losey."
   IN: Cahiers du Cinéma, 1960-1968

4287 Moussinac, Léon.
"The Condition of International Cinema."
   IN: French Film Theory and Criticism /v. 2

4288 Moussinac, Léon.
"Cinema: Social Expression."
"Eisenstein."
"The Question of the 'Avant-Garde' Film."
"Technique and the Future."
"Cinema: *Broken Blossoms*."
"Cinema: *Fièvre, L'Atlantide, El Dorado*."
"On Cinegraphic Rhythm."
   IN: French Film Theory and Criticism /v. 1

4288a Mouton, Janice.
"*The Last Emperor*: A Subject-in-the-Making."
   IN: Columbia Pictures

4289 "Movie Makers" [John Grierson].
"*Stark Love* and *Moana*."
   IN: The Documentary Tradition /1 ed
       The Documentary Tradition /2 ed

4290 *Moving Picture World, The*.
"*The Birth of a Nation*."
   IN: Focus on The Birth of a Nation

4291 *Moving Picture World*.
"The Nickelodeon."
   IN: The First Tycoons

4292 *Moving Picture World*.
"*The Bargain*."
   IN: The First Film Makers

4293 Moynahan, Julian.
"*Great Expectations* [novel by] Charles Dickens;
   Great Expectations [film by] David Lean. Seeing
   the Book, Reading the Movie."
   IN: The English Novel and the Movies

4294 Mpoyi-Buatu, Th.
"Sembene Ousmane's *Ceddo* & Med Hondo's *West Indies*."
IN: Film and Politics in the Third World

4295 Mraz, John.
"Santiago Alvarez: From Dramatic Form to Direct Cinema."
IN: The Social Documentary ...

4296 Muir, Anne Ross.
"The Status of Women Working in Film."
IN: The Female Gaze

4297 Mukherjee, Bharati.
"*Love Me or Leave Me*."
IN: The Movie That Changed My Life

4298 Mullin, Michael.
"Orson Welles' *Macbeth*: Script and Screen."
IN: Focus on Orson Welles

4299 Mulvey, Laura.
"The Spectacle is Vulnerable: Miss World 1970." [Co-written with Margarita Jimenez.]
"Fears, Fantasies and the Male Unconscious[,] or 'You Don't Know What is Happening, Do You Mr. Jones?'"
"Fassbinder and Sirk."
"Images of Women, Images of Sexuality: Some Films by J.L. Godard." [Co-written with Colin MacCabe.]
"Melodrama Inside and Outside the Home."
"Frida Kahlo and Tina Modotti." [Co-written with Peter Wollen.]
"Film, Feminism and the Avant-Garde."
"Dialogue with Spectatorship: Barbara Kruger and Victor Burgin."
"'Magnificent Obsession': An Introduction to the Work of Five Photographers."
"Impending Time: Mary Kelly's *Corpus*."
"Changes: Thoughts on Myth, Narrative and Historical Experience."
"The Oedipus Myth: Beyond the Riddles of the Sphinx."
IN: Visual and Other Pleasures

4300 Mulvey, Laura.
"Visual Pleasure and Narrative Cinema." [NOTE: Also called "Film and Visual Pleasure."]
IN: Feminism and Film Theory
Movies and Methods /v. 2
Popular Television and Film
Women and the Cinema
Narrative, Apparatus, Ideology
Issues in Feminist Film Criticism
Film Theory and Criticism /3 ed
Film Theory and Criticism /4 ed
Visual and Other Pleasures

4301 Mulvey, Laura.
"Afterthoughts on 'Visual Pleasure and Narrative Cinema' inspired by *Duel in the Sun*." [NOTE: Also called "Afterthoughts on 'Visual Pleasure and Narrative Cinema'."]

IN: Psychoanalysis and Cinema
Feminism and Film Theory
Visual and Other Pleasures

4302 Mulvey, Laura.
"Notes on Sirk and Melodrama."
IN: Home Is Where the Heart Is
Visual and Other Pleasures

4302a Mulvey, Laura.
"Laura Mulvey (on *Riddles of the Sphinx*)."
IN: A Critical Cinema 2

4303 Mulvey, Laura, Christian Metz, Sandy Flitterman, Jean-Louis Comolli, Maureen Turim and Peter Gidal.
"Discussion (of Peter Gidal, 'Technology and Ideology in/through/and Avant-Garde Film: An Instance')."
IN: The Cinematic Apparatus

4304 Munerato, Elice and Maria Helena Darcy de Oliveira.
"When Women Film."
IN: Brazilian Cinema

4305 Munn, Michael.
"From Shoot-outs in the West to Arbuckle in Court."
"William Desmond Taylor: The All-star Murder Mystery."
"Thomas Ince: M-m-m-m-Murder?"
"Paul Kelly: Convicted Killer."
"Thelma Todd: The Ice Cream Blonde."
"Bugsy Siegel: George Raft's Blue-eyed Buddy."
"Lana Turner's Tragic Valentine."
"Murder at the Alamo."
"Los Angeles Police File: Marilyn Monroe—Murder."
"Ramon Novarro: The Halloween Murder."
"The Sharon Tate Massacre."
"Bruce Lee: A Macabre Romantic Notion?"
"Sal Mineo: The Switchblade Kid."
"Gig Young: Game of Death."
"Murder in Hollywood."
IN: The Hollywood Murder Casebook

4306 Muñoz, Carlos, Jr.
"*The Unwanted*."
IN: Chicano Cinema

4307 Munro, Caroline.
"Caroline Munro." [Interview by Stanley Wiater.]
IN: Dark Visions

4308 Münsterberg, Hugo.
"[From:] *The Film: A Psychological Study*: The Means of the Photoplay."
IN: Film Theory and Criticism /1 ed
Film Theory and Criticism /2 ed
Film Theory and Criticism /3 ed
Film Theory and Criticism /4 ed
Film And/As Literature

4309 Muren, Dennis.
"Dennis Muren [on Special Effects: Visual Effects]." [Interview by David Chell.]
IN: Moviemakers at Work

4310 Murnau, F.W.
"Films of the Future."
IN: Hollywood Directors 1914-1940

4311 Murphy, A.D.
"Distribution and Exhibition: An Overview."
IN: The Movie Business Book

4312 Murphy, Brian.
"Monster Movies: They Came from Beneath the
Fifties."
IN: Movies as Artifacts
Crossroads to the Cinema

4313 Murphy, J.J.
"J.J. Murphy." [Interview by Scott MacDonald.]
IN: A Critical Cinema

4314 Murphy, Jeanette.
"*A Question of Silence*."
IN: Films for Women

4315 Murphy, Kathleen.
"*Belle de jour*."
IN: Women and the Cinema

4316 Murphy, Kathleen.
"*Daisy Miller* [novel by] Henry James. An
International Episode."
IN: The Classic American Novel ...

Murphy, Pat. SEE: Nicolson, Annabel.

4317 Murphy, Richard.
"That's When The So-Called Semi-Documentary
Tradition Began--" [RE: an interview.]
IN: Blueprint on Babylon

4318 Murphy, Robert.
"Rank's Attempt on the American Market, 1944-9."
IN: British Cinema History

4319 Murphy, Robert.
"Riff-raff: British Cinema and the Underworld."
"Under the Shadow of Hollywood."
IN: All Our Yesterdays

4320 Murphy, Robert.
"The British Film Industry: Audiences and Producers."
IN: Britain and the Cinema ...

4321 Murphy, Robert.
"Three Companies: Boyd's Co., HandMade and
Goldcrest."
IN: British Cinema Now

4322 Murray, Bruce.
"An Introduction to the Commercial Film Industry in
Germany from 1895 to 1933."
IN: Film and Politics in the Weimar Republic

4323 Murray, Edward.
"Dramatists, Novelists, and the Motion Pictures."
"George Bernard Shaw and Luigi Pirandello."
"Stage and Screen--Some Basic Distinctions."
"Eugene O'Neill, Expressionism, and Film."
"Mixed-Media--from Bertolt Brecht to Happenings."

"Tennessee Williams--after *The Celluloid Brassiere*."
"Gertrude Stein."
"Arthur Miller--*Death of a Salesman*, *The Misfits*, and
After the Fall."
"The Theater of the Absurd and Film--Eugene
Ionesco and Samuel Beckett."
"Critique of the Cinematic Drama and Present Trends."
"Thomas Mann and Franz Kafka."
"Page and Screen--Some Basic Distinctions."
"Theodore Dreiser in 'Hooeyland'."
"The Stream-of-Consciousness Novel and Film,
I--James Joyce."
"The Stream-of-Consciousness Novel and Film,
II--Virginia Woolf."
"The Stream-of-Consciousness Novel and Film,
III--William Faulkner."
"John Dos Passos and the Camera-Eye--*Manhattan
Transfer* and *U.S.A.*."
"F. Scott Fitzgerald, Hollywood, and *The Last Tycoon*."
"Nathanael West--The Pictorial Eye in Locust-Land."
"Thomas Wolfe and Robert Penn Warren."
"Ernest Hemingway--Cinematic Structure in Fiction
and Problems in Adaptation."
"Graham Greene and the Silver Screen."
"John Steinbeck, Point of View, and Film."
"Jean-Paul Sartre and Henry Miller."
"Alain Robbe-Grillet, the New Novel, and the New
Cinema."
"Critique of the Cinematic Novel and Present Trends."
IN: The Cinematic Imagination

4324 Murray, Edward.
"*Potemkin*."
"*Citizen Kane*."
"*The Bicycle Thief*."
"*Ikiru*."
"*La Strada*."
"*On the Waterfront*."
"*Wild Strawberries*."
"*The 400 Blows*."
"*L'Avventura*."
"*Bonnie and Clyde*."
IN: Ten Film Classics

4325 Murray, Edward.
"*La Strada*." [NOTE: A slightly abridged version of the
essay in *Ten Film Classics*.]
IN: Federico Fellini

4326 Murray, Lawrence L.
"Hollywood, Nihilism, and the Youth Culture of the
Sixties: *Bonnie and Clyde*."
IN: American History/American Film

4327 Murray, William.
"The Return of Busby Berkeley."
IN: The Movies: An American Idiom

4328 Muse, Clarence.
"When a Negro Sings a Song ..."
IN: Celebrity Articles ...

4329 Museum of Modern Art.
"*Triumph of the Will*--An Outline."

IN: <u>Propaganda on Film</u>

4330 Musser, Charles.
"The American Vitagraph, 1897-1901: Survival and
   Success in a Competitive Industry."
   IN: <u>Film Before Griffith</u>

4331 Musser, Charles.
"Ethnicity, Role-playing, and American Film Comedy:
   From *Chinese Laundry Scene* to *Whoopee*
   (1894-1930)."
   IN: <u>Unspeakable Images</u>

4332 Musser, Charles.
"The Travel Genre in 1903-1904: Moving Towards
   Fictional Narrative."
"The Nickelodeon Era Begins: Establishing the
   Framework for Hollywood's Mode of
   Representation."
   IN: <u>Early Cinema ...</u>

4333 Musser, Charles.
"Work, Ideology, and Chaplin's Tramp."
   IN: <u>Resisting Images</u>

4333a Musser, Charles.
"The Changing Status of the Film Actor."
   IN: <u>Before Hollywood</u>

4334 Mussman, Toby.
"Marcel Duchamps's *Anemic Cinema*."
"The Images of Robert Whitman."
   IN: <u>The New American Cinema</u>

4335 Muybridge, Eadweard.
"The Attitudes of Animals in Motion."
   IN: <u>The Movies in Our Midst</u>

4336 Myers, John Bernard.
"A Letter to Gregory Battcock."
   IN: <u>The New American Cinema</u>

4337 Myers, Kurtz.
"European Film Festival."
   IN: <u>Ideas on Film</u>

4338 Myers, Peter S.
"The Studio as Distributor."
   IN: <u>The Movie Business Book</u>

4339 Myles, Lynda.
"The Movie Brats and Beyond."
   IN: <u>Anatomy of the Movies</u>

Myles, Lynda. SEE: Pye, Michael.

4340 *Na literaturnom postu*, editorial.
"For the Reconstruction of Soviet Cinema."
   IN: <u>The Film Factory</u>

4341 Nachbar, Jack.
"*Ulzana's Raid*."
   IN: <u>Western Movies</u>

4342 Nachbar, Jack.
"Film Noir."
   IN: <u>Handbook of American Film Genres</u>

4343 Nachbar, Jack.
"Horses, Harmony, Hope and Hormones: Western
   Movies, 1930-1946."
   IN: <u>Western Films: A Brief History</u>

4344 Nachbar, Jack.
"Riding Shotgun: The Scattered Formula in
   Contemporary Western Movies."
   IN: <u>Focus on The Western</u>

4345 Nachbar, Jack.
"The Interdisciplinary Film Studies Program at
   Bowling Green State University."
   IN: <u>Film Study in the Undergraduate Curriculum</u>

Nachbar, John G. SEE: Grogg, Sam L.

4346 Nadeau, Robert L.
"*The Old Man and the Sea* [novel by] Ernest
   Hemingway. Film and Mythic Heroism: Sturges's
   Old Man."
   IN: <u>The Modern American Novel ...</u>

4347 Nadeau, Robert L.
"*Billy Budd* [novel by] Herman Melville. Melville's
   Sailor in the Sixties."
   IN: <u>The Classic American Novel ...</u>

Nadotti, Maria. SEE: Bruno, Giuliana.

4348 Naficy, Hamid.
"Mediawork's Representation of the Other: The Case
   of Iran."
   IN: <u>Questions of Third Cinema</u>

4349 Nagel, Conrad.
"Conrad Nagel: The Player."
   IN: <u>The Real Tinsel</u>

4350 Nagel, Conrad.
"The Actor's Art."
   IN: <u>Introduction to the Photoplay</u>

4351 Naha, Ed.
"The Inner Search for Spock: An Interview with
   Leonard Nimoy."
"Cautionary Fables: An Interview with Roger Corman."
   IN: <u>Omni's Screen Flights ...</u>

4352 Narath, Albert.
"Oskar Messter and his Work."
   IN: <u>A Technological History ...</u>

4353 Narboni, Jean.
"Against the Clock: *Red Line 7000*."
"Towards Impertinence."
   IN: <u>Cahiers du Cinéma, 1960-1968</u>

4354 Narboni, Jean.
"Casting Out the Eights: John Ford's *Seven Women*."
   IN: <u>Theories of Authorship</u>

4355 Narboni, Jean.
"Vicarious Power."
   IN: <u>Cahiers du Cinéma: 1969-1972</u>

4356 Narboni, Jean, Sylvie Pierre and Jacques Rivette.
"Montage."

IN: Cahiers du Cinéma: 1969-1972

Narboni, Jean. SEE: Oudart, Jean-Pierre; SEE: Comolli, Jean-Louis; SEE: Delahaye, Michel; SEE: Aumont, Jacques; SEE: Bonitzer, Pascal; SEE: Truffaut, François; SEE: Godard, Jean-Luc.

4357 **Nardone, Mark.**
"Robert McKimson Interviewed."
IN: The American Animated Cartoon

4358 **Naremore, James.**
"Lillian Gish in *True Heart Susie*."
"Charles Chaplin in *The Gold Rush*."
"Marlene Dietrich in *Morocco*."
"James Cagney in *Angels with Dirty Faces*."
"Katharine Hepburn in *Holiday*."
"Marlon Brando in *On the Waterfront*."
"Cary Grant in *North by Northwest*."
"*Rear Window*."
"*The King of Comedy*."
IN: Acting in the Cinema

4359 **Naremore, James.**
"Expressive Coherence and the 'Acted Image'."
IN: The Cinematic Text

4360 **Naremore, James.**
"Style and Theme in *The Lady from Shanghai*."
IN: Focus on Orson Welles

4361 **Naremore, James.**
"The Performance Frame."
IN: Star Texts

4362 **Nargis.**
"Nargis." [Interview.]
IN: Indian Cinema Superbazaar

4363 **Narushima, Toichiro.**
"Toichiro Narushima." [Interview by Joan Mellen.]
IN: Voices from the Japanese Cinema

4364 **Nash, Paul.**
"The Colour Film."
IN: Footnotes to the Film

4365 **Nathan, George Jean.**
"A Reaction to the Praise Given Chaplin's Artistry."
IN: Focus on Chaplin

4366 **Nathan, George Jean.**
"Notes on the Movies." [RE: coming of sound.]
IN: The Movies in Our Midst

4367 **Nathan, Robert.**
"A Novelist Looks at Hollywood."
IN: Film: A Montage of Theories

National Association for the Advancement of Colored People. SEE: Boston Branch, National Association for the Advancement of Colored People.

4368 **National Board of Review.**
"State Censorship of Motion Pictures."
IN: The Movies in Our Midst

4369 **Neale, Stephen.**
"Genre and Cinema."
IN: Popular Television and Film

4370 **Neale, Stephen.**
"Issues of Difference: *Alien* and *Blade Runner*."
IN: Fantasy and the Cinema

4371 **Neale, Steve.**
"*Halloween*: Suspense, Aggression and the Look."
IN: Planks of Reason

4372 **Neale, Steve.**
"Notes and Questions on Political Cinema: from *Hour of the Furnaces* to *Ici et ailleurs*."
IN: Show Us Life

4373 **Neale, Steve.**
"'You've Got To Be Fucking Kidding!' Knowledge, Belief and Judgement in Science Fiction."
IN: Alien Zone

4374 **Negulesco, Jean.**
"Jean Negulesco."
IN: The Celluloid Muse

4375 **Neilan, Marshall.**
"Acting for the Screen: The Six Great Essentials."
IN: Hollywood Directors 1914-1940

4376 **Nekes, Werner.**
"What Really Happens between the Frames."
IN: West German Filmmakers on Film

4377 **Nelson, Joyce.**
"*Mildred Pierce* Reconsidered."
IN: Movies and Methods /v. 2

4378 **Nelson, Mark W.**
"*The Decision to Drop the Bomb*."
IN: Nuclear War Films

4379 **Nelson, Richard Alan.**
"Before Laurel: Oliver Hardy and the Vim Company, A Studio Biography."
IN: Current Research in Film /v. 2

4380 **Nelson, Robert.**
"Robert Nelson." [Interview by Scott MacDonald.]
IN: A Critical Cinema

4381 **Nemec, Jan.**
"Jan Nemec." [Interview by Antonín J. Liehm.]
IN: Closely Watched Films

4382 **Nemes, Károly.**
"Socialism and Film."
"Soviet Film."
"Hungarian Film."
"Polish Film."
"Andrzej Munk."
"Jerzy Kawalerowicz."
"Andrzej Wajda."
"Czechoslovak Film."
"Yugoslav Film."
IN: Films of Commitment: Socialist Cinema in Eastern Europe

Nemes, Robert S. SEE: Eastman, Susan Tyler.

4383   **Nemeskürty, István.**
"In the Beginning, 1896-1911."
IN: Film Before Griffith

4384   **Neve, Brian.**
"The 1950s: The Case of Elia Kazan and *On the Waterfront*."
IN: Cinema, Politics and Society in America

4385   **Neveux, Georges.**
"The Tunnel 1930-1940."
IN: French Film Theory and Criticism /v. 2

4386   **Nevins, Francis M., Jr.**
"William Witney."
IN: Close Up: The Contract Director

4387   **New American Cinema Group.**
"The First Statement of the New American Cinema Group."
IN: Film Culture Reader

4388   ***New York Independent, The.***
"The Drama of the People."
IN: Introduction to the Art of the Movies

4389   ***New York Times.***
"Pennsylvania Ban on 'Ramparts' Film." [RE: *The Ramparts We Watch*.]
"Ramparts Ban Upheld." [RE: *The Ramparts We Watch*.]
"War Vividly Seen in Griffith Film." [RE: *Hearts of the World*, 1918.]
IN: Propaganda on Film

4390   ***New York Times.***
"*Stanley and Livingstone*."
"An Impressive Jungle Melodrama." [RE: *King Solomon's Mines*.]
"Bwana Metro Makes a Piksha." [RE: *Bwana Devil*.]
"Tarzan, the Ape Man."
IN: Africa on Film

4391   ***New York World.***
"Warners Ready to Defend Selves Against Kuhn." [*Confessions of a Nazi Spy*; Fritz Kuhn.]
IN: Propaganda on Film

4392   **Newhall, Beaumont.**
"The Horse in Gallop." [RE: E. Muybridge.]
"Muybridge and the First Motion Picture: The Horse in the History of the Movies."
IN: Image on the Art ...

4393   **Newhart, Bob.**
"June Allyson Never Kicked Anyone in the Shins."
IN: The Movies: An American Idiom

4394   **Newman, Chris.**
"Chris Newman [on Sound: Production Recording]." [Interview by David Chell.]
IN: Moviemakers at Work

4395   **Newman, Paul.**
"Paul Newman." [Interview by Charles Higham.]

IN: Celebrity Circus

4396   **Newman, Paul and Joanne Woodward.**
"Paul Newman and Joanne Woodward." [Interview by Judith Crist.]
IN: Take 22

Newman, Roger K. SEE: De Grazia, Edward.

4397   **Newman, Walter Brown.**
"Walter Brown Newman." [Interview by William Froug.]
IN: The Screenwriter Looks ...

4398   **Newsom, Jon.**
"'A Sound Idea': Music for Animated Film."
"David Raksin: A Composer in Hollywood."
IN: Wonderful Inventions

4399   **Newton, Judith.**
"Feminism and Anxiety in *Alien*."
IN: Alien Zone

4400   **Niblo, Fred.**
"Americanizing the American Pictures."
IN: Hollywood Directors 1914-1940

4401   **Nichols, Bill.**
"Art and the Perceptual Process."
"The Analysis of Representational Images."
"The Cinema: Movement, Narrative, and Paradox."
"*Blonde Venus*: Playing with Performance."
"For *The Birds*."
"The Documentary Film and Principles of Exposition."
"Frederick Wiseman's Documentaries: Theory and Structure."
"Documentary, Criticism, and the Ethnographic Film."
IN: Ideology and the Image

4402   **Nichols, Bill.**
"Ideological and Marxist Criticism: Towards a Metahermeneutics."
IN: The Cinematic Text

4403   **Nichols, Bill.**
"Introducing Film Study in an Undergraduate Context: Queen's University."
IN: Film Study in the Undergraduate Curriculum

4404   **Nichols, Bill.**
"Newsreel, 1967-1972: Film and Revolution."
IN: Show Us Life

4405   **Nichols, Bill.**
"Style, Grammar, and the Movies."
IN: Movies and Methods: An Anthology

4406   **Nichols, Bill.**
"The Voice of Documentary."
IN: Movies and Methods /v. 2
New Challenges for Documentary

4407   **Nichols, Bill and Susan J. Lederman.**
"Flicker and Motion in Film."
IN: The Cinematic Apparatus

4408   **Nichols, Dudley.**
"Death of a Critic." [RE: Henry James.]
IN: Introduction to the Art of the Movies

4409 **Nichols, Dudley.**
"The Writer and the Film."
　IN: Film: Readings in the Mass Media
　　Film: A Montage of Theories
　　Film And/As Literature
　　A Casebook on Film

4410 **Nichols, Mike.**
"Mike Nichols." [Interview by Joseph Gelmis.]
　IN: The Film Director as Superstar

4411 **Nicoll, Allardyce.**
"Film Reality: The Cinema and the Theater." [NOTE:
Also called "Film and Theatre."]
　IN: Film: An Anthology
　　Focus on Shakespearean Films
　　Film And/As Literature
　　Focus on Film and Theatre
　　Film and Literature
　　Film: A Montage of Theories

4412 **Nicoll, Allardyce.**
"[From:] Shakespeare and the Cinema."
　IN: Film and Society

4413 **Nicolson, Annabel, Felicity Sparrow, Jane Clarke,
Jeannette Iljon, Lis Rhodes, Mary Pat Leece, Pat
Murphy, Susan Stein.**
"Woman and the Formal Film."
　IN: Films for Women

4414 **Nielsen, Elizabeth.**
"Handmaidens of the Glamour Culture: Costumers in
the Hollywood Studio System."
　IN: Fabrications

4415 **Niemeyer, G. Charles, Ph.D.**
"David Wark Griffith: In Retrospect, 1965."
　IN: Focus on D.W. Griffith

4416 **Niver, Kemp R.**
"Paper Prints of Early Motion Pictures."
　IN: Film Before Griffith

4417 **Niver, Kemp R.**
"From Film to Paper to Film."
　IN: Wonderful Inventions

4418 **Nixon, Agnes.**
"Agnes Nixon." [An interview.]
　IN: Producers on Producing

4419 **Nizhny, Vladimir.**
"Directorial Solution."
"Mise-en-Scène."
"Break-up into Shots."
"Mise-en-Shot."
　IN: Lessons with Eisenstein

4420 **Noble, Andrew.**
"Bill Douglas's Trilogy." [RE: *My Childhood*; *My Ain
Folk*; *My Way Home*.]
　IN: From Limelight to Satellite

4421 **Noble, Peter.**
"The Negro in *The Birth of a Nation*."
　IN: Focus on The Birth of a Nation

4422 **Noble, Thom.**
"Thom Noble [on Editing]." [Interview by David Chell.]
　IN: Moviemakers at Work

4423 **Nodelman, Perry.**
"*Treasure Island* [novel by] Robert Louis Stevenson.
Searching for *Treasure Island*."
　IN: Children's Novels and the Movies

4424 **Noden, Martin.**
"Film and Painting."
　IN: Film and the Arts in Symbiosis

4425 **Nolan, Jack Edmund.**
"Hitchcock's TV Films."
　IN: Focus on Hitchcock

4426 **Nolan, William F.**
"William F. Nolan." [Interview by Stanley Wiater.]
　IN: Dark Visions

4427 **Norden, Martin F.**
"Business and Love in the Post-Reconstruction South:
Warner Brothers' *Bright Leaf*."
　IN: The South and Film

4428 **Norden, Martin F.**
"Portrait of a Disabled Vietnam Veteran: Alex Cutter
of *Cutter's Way*."
　IN: From Hanoi to Hollywood

4429 **Norden, Martin F.**
"Sexual References in James Whale's *Bride of
Frankenstein*
　IN: Eros in the Mind's Eye

4430 **Norden, Martin F. and Kim Wolfson.**
"Cultural Influences on Film Interpretation among
Chinese and American Students."
　IN: Current Research in Film /v. 2

4430a **Noren, Andrew.**
"Andrew Noren." [Interview by Scott MacDonald.]
　IN: A Critical Cinema 2

4431 **Norman, Barry.**
"The Coming of Sound."
"The Studio System."
"Hollwood and Sex."
"Hollywood Goes to War." [RE: World War II.]
"Hollywood and Crime."
"Hollywood and Politics."
"The 'B' Movie."
"The Western."
"The Decline of the Studios."
"Hollywood Now."
　IN: Talking Pictures

4432 **Norman, Barry.**
"Clark Gable."
"Errol Flynn."
"Spencer Tracy."
"Gary Cooper."
"Humphrey Bogart."
"Joan Crawford."
"Ronald Colman."

"Historical Analysis, Stage Two: Four Frameworks for
Historical Inquiry."
"Historical Analysis, Stage One: Gathering
Information on the Contents, Production, and
Reception of a Moving Image Document."
IN: Image as Artifact

4457 O'Dell, Paul.
"The Modern Story in *Intolerance*."
IN: The Classic Cinema

4458 O'Dell, Paul.
"The Simplicity of True Greatness."
IN: Focus on D.W. Griffith

4459 Odets, Clifford.
"The Transient Olympian: The Psychology of the Male
Movie Star."
IN: Sight, Sound, and Society

4460 O'Doherty, Brian.
"Bruce Conner and His Films."
IN: The New American Cinema

4461 Odom, Keith C.
"*The Railway Children* [novel by] E. Nesbit. Children,
Daffodils, and Railways."
IN: Children's Novels and the Movies

4462 O'Donnell, Victoria.
"The Southern Woman as Time-Binder in Film."
IN: The South and Film

4463 Oehling, Richard A.
"The Yellow Menace: Asian Images in American Film."
IN: The Kaleidoscopic Lens

4464 Oehling, Richard A.
"The German-Americans, Germany, and the
American Media."
IN: Ethnic Images ...

4465 Oekonomidis, Demetrius.
"The Freedom To Quote According To German Law."
IN: Fair Use and Free Inquiry

4466 Ogle, Patrick L.
"Technological and Aesthetic Influences upon the
Development of Deep Focus Cinematography in
the United States."
IN: Screen Reader 1
Movies and Methods /v. 2

4467 Oglesbee, Frank W.
"*The World, the Flesh, and the Devil*."
IN: Nuclear War Films

4468 O'Grady, Gerald.
"The Preparation of Teachers of Media."
IN: Perspectives on the Study of Film

O'Guinn, Thomas C. SEE: Faber, Ronald J.

4469 O'Hara, John.
"*Citizen Kane*."
IN: Focus on Citizen Kane

4470 O'Higgins, Harvey.
"Charlie Chaplin's Art."

IN: The Movies in Our Midst

4471 Ohlin, Peter.
"Film as Word: Questions of Language and
Documentary Realism."
IN: Explorations in Film Theory

4472 Olcott, Sidney.
"The Present and the Future of Film."
IN: Hollywood Directors 1914-1940

4473 O'Leary, Liam.
"Rex Ingram—Pageant-Master."
IN: Movies of the Silent Years

4474 Oler, Harriet L.
"Copyright Law and the Fair Use of Visual Images."
IN: Fair Use and Free Inquiry

4475 Olhovich, Sergio.
"Sergio Olhovich." [Interview by Beatrice Reyes
Nevares.]
IN: The Mexican Cinema

4476 Olin, Joyce.
"Frances Marion."
IN: Dictionary of Literary Biography /v. 44

4477 Olin, Joyce.
"Ring Lardner, Jr."
IN: Dictionary of Literary Biography /v. 26

4478 Olivier, Laurence.
"The Prince and the Showgirl." [RE: Marilyn Monroe.]
IN: Bedside Hollywood

4479 Ollier, Claude.
"A King in New York." [RE: *King Kong*, 1933.]
IN: Focus on The Horror Film
Cahiers du Cinéma, 1960-1968

4480 Ollier, Claude.
"Josef von Sternberg."
IN: Cinema: A Critical Dictionary

Ollier, Claude. SEE: Comolli, Jean-Louis.

4481 Olmi, Ermanno.
"Ermanno Olmi." [Interview by Charles T. Samuels.]
IN: Encountering Directors

4482 Oms, Marcel.
"Josef von Sternberg."
IN: Sternberg

4483 Ong, Walter J.
"Wired for Sound: Teaching, Communications, and
Technological Culture."
IN: Sight, Sound, and Society

4484 Onipede, Oladipo.
"Hollywood's Holy War Against Africa."
IN: Africa on Film

4485 Ono, Yoko.
"On Yoko Ono."
IN: Women and the Cinema

4485a Ono, Yoko.

"Yoko Ono." [Interview by Scott MacDonald.]
IN: A Critical Cinema 2

4486 Onosko, Tom.
"Mathemagicians: Computer Moviemakers of the 1980s and Beyond."
IN: Omni's Screen Flights ...

4487 Ophuls, Max.
"Max Ophuls." [Interview by Andrew Sarris.]
IN: Interviews with Film Directors

4488 O'Pray, Michael.
"Surrealism, Fantasy and the Grotesque: The Cinema of Jan Svankmajer."
IN: Fantasy and the Cinema

4489 Ord, Priscilla A.
"*From the Mixed-Up Files on Mrs. Basil E. Frankweiler* [novel by] E.L. Konigsburg. Different on the Inside Where It Counts."
IN: Children's Novels and the Movies

4490 O'Regan, Tom.
"*The Man from Snowy River* and Australian Popular Culture."
"Documentary in Controversy."
IN: An Australian Film Reader

4491 Orr, Christopher.
"Closure and Containment: Marylee Hadley in *Written on the Wind*."
IN: Imitations of Life

4492 Ortmayer, Roger.
"Fellini's Film Journey."
IN: Three European Directors

4493 Ortmayer, Roger.
"Film Criticism as Process."
IN: The Image Maker

Osborn, Elodie. SEE: Osborn, Robert.

4494 Osborn, Robert and Elodie.
"Who Cut the Comedy?"
IN: Film: Book 1

4495 Osheroff, Abe.
"*Dreams and Nightmares* [Interview with] Abe Osheroff."
IN: The Documentary Conscience

4496 Oshima, Nagisa.
"Nagisa Oshima." [Interview by Joan Mellen.]
IN: Voices from the Japanese Cinema

4497 Oswald, Laura.
"Discourse/Figure: The Inscription of the Subject in Surrealist Film."
IN: Cinema and Language

4498 Othman, Frederick C.
"War in the World of Make Believe." [RE: WWII.]
IN: The Movies in Our Midst

4499 Ottinger, Ulrike.
"The Pressure to Make Genre Films: About the Endangered *Autorenkino*."

IN: West German Filmmakers on Film

Otto, Shirley. SEE: Harwin, Judith.

4500 Oudart, Jean-Pierre.
"Conclusion to the *Cahiers du Cinéma* editors' 'John Ford's *Young Mr. Lincoln*' [extract]."
"The Absent Field of the Author."
IN: Theories of Authorship

4501 Oudart, Jean-Pierre.
"Cinema and Suture."
"Word Play, Master Play."
"The Reality Effect."
"Notes for a Theory of Representation."
"A Lacking Discourse."
IN: Cahiers du Cinéma: 1969-1972

4502 Oudart, Jean-Pierre, Jean Narboni and Jean-Louis Comolli.
"Readings of Jancsó: Yesterday and Today."
IN: Cahiers du Cinéma: 1969-1972

Oudart, Jean-Pierre. SEE: Daney, Serge; SEE: Aumont, Jacques; SEE: Bonitzer, Pascal.

4503 Oumano, Ellen.
"Profiles: Chantal Akerman, Nestor Almendros, Robert Altman, Emile de Antonio, Bernardo Bertolucci, Claude Chabrol, Jacques Demy, R.W. Fassbinder, Milos Forman, Jean-Luc Godard, Perry Henzel, Henry Jaglom, Benoit Jacquot, Barbara Kopple, Sidney Lumet, Dusan Makavejev, Al Maysles, Philip Messina, Ermanno Olmi, Elio Petri, Michael Powell, Mark Rappaport, Eric Rohmer, George Romero, Jean Rouch, Werner Schroeter, Martin Scorsese, Joan Micklin Silver, Raphael D. Silver, Jean-Marie Straub, André Techine, Lina Wertmuller, Billy Williams, Yves Yersin, Krzysztof Zanussi."
"Cinematography: Godard, Scorsese, Rohmer, Almendros, Williams, Rouch, Olmi, Altman, Fassbinder, Wertmuller, Akerman, Techine, Romero, Jacquot, Straub, Chabrol, Makavejev."
"Sound: Rouch, Jacquot, Schroeter, Yersin, Techine, Fassbinder, Makavejev, Altman, Jaglom, Forman, Godard, de Antonio."
"The Actor: Godard, Rappaport, Altman, Petri, Makavejev, Demy, Olmi, Forman, Jaglom, Rouch, Romero, the Silvers."
"Structure and Rhythm: Rappaport, Romero, Makavejev, Techine, Straub, Yersin, de Antonio, Scorsese, Godard."
"Film and Reality: Olmi, Almendros, Rohmer, Bertolucci, Demy, Jacquot, Jaglom, Makavejev, Techine, Zanussi, Straub, Henzel, Fassbinder, Romero, Kopple, Schroeter, Rappaport, de Antonio, Rouch, Maysles, Godard, Scorsese, Chabrol."
"The Process—Writing, Shooting, and Editing the Film: Godard, Jaglom, Demy, Romero, Lumet, Jacquot, Olmi, Makavejev, Rouch, Maysles, de Antonio, Fassbinder, Powell, Straub, Forman, Rappaport, Scorsese."

"The Viewer: Olmi, Makavejev, Bertolucci, Schroeter, Henzel, de Antonio, Jaglom, Maysles, Wertmuller, Straub, Chabrol, Petri, Akerman, Lumet, Altman, Godard."
"Film and Society: Maysles, Rouch, Schroeter, de Antonio, Zanussi, Henzel, Bertolucci, Wertmuller, Olmi, Scorsese."
"Movie Business--Production, Distribution, and Exhibition: de Antonio, Petri, Romero, Scorsese, Olmi, Akerman, Demy, Powell, Altman, Messina, Kopple, Rappaport, Jaglom, the Silvers."
IN: Film Form: 35 Top Filmmakers ...

4504 **Oxenhandler, Neal.**
"The Distancing Perspective in *Satyricon*."
IN: The Classic Cinema

4505 **Page, Geraldine.**
"Geraldine Page." [Interview by Rex Reed.]
IN: Travolta to Keaton

4506 **Pagnol, Marcel.**
"Cinematurgy of Paris."
"The Talkie Offers the Writer New Resources."
IN: French Film Theory and Criticism /v. 2

4507 **Pagnol, Maurice.**
"The Talking Film."
IN: Rediscovering French Film

4508 **Paine, Frank.**
"Sound Mixing and *Apocalypse Now*: An Interview with Walter Murch."
IN: Film Sound

4509 **Pajaczkowska, Claire.**
"'Liberté! Egalité! Paternité!': Jean-Luc Godard's and Anne-Marie Miéville's *Sauve qui peut (la vie)*."
IN: French Film: Texts and Contexts

4510 **Pajaczkowska, Claire.**
"Images and Pornography."
IN: Explorations in Film Theory

4511 **Palmer, Christopher.**
"Max Steiner: Birth of an Era."
"Erich Wolfgang Korngold."
"Alfred Newman."
"Franz Waxman."
"Dimitri Tiomkin."
"Roy Webb."
"Miklós Rózsa."
"Bernard Herrmann."
"Alex North, Elmer Bernstein and Leonard Rosenman: End of an Era."
IN: The Composer in Hollywood

4512 **Palmer, Jerry.**
"James Bond: The Deviant Behind the Consensus."
IN: Conflict and Control in the Cinema

4513 **Palmer, Barton.**
"Frank Nugent."
IN: Dictionary of Literary Biography /v. 44

4514 **Palmer, R. Barton.**
"Methos and Mimesis in *Theory of Film*: Kracauer's Realism Re-examined."
"Bakhtinian Translinguistics and Film Criticism: The Dialogical Image?"
IN: The Cinematic Text

4515 **Palmer, William J.**
"Movie Villains: The Seventies."
"*Blow-Up*: The Game with No Balls."
"*Blow-Up* Meets Richard Nixon."
"*Chinatown*: A World of Inscrutable Reality."
"The Vietnam War Films."
"The Forgotten Vietnam War Film." [RE: *Go Tell the Spartans*.]
"Superimposed Realities: The Visual/Verbal Themes in *Apocalypse Now*."
"The Australian War Films."
IN: The Films of the Seventies: A Social History

4516 **Palmgreen, Philip, Patsy L. Cook, Jerry G. Harvill, and David M. Helm.**
"The Motivational Framework of Moviegoing: Uses and Avoidances of Theatrical Films."
IN: Current Research in Film /v. 4

4517 **Palmieri, Rory.**
"*Straw Dogs*: Sam Peckinpah and the Classical Western Narrative."
IN: The Cinematic Text

4518 **Palombo, Stanley R.**
"Hitchcock's *Vertigo*: The Dream Function in Film."
IN: Images in Our Souls

4519 **Pan, Hermes.**
"Hermes Pan." [Interview by John Kobal.]
IN: People Will Talk

4520 **Panofsky, Erwin.**
"Style and Medium in the Motion Pictures."
IN: Film Theory and Criticism /1 ed
Film Theory and Criticism /2 ed
Film Theory and Criticism /3 ed
Film Theory and Criticism /4 ed
Awake in the Dark
Film: An Anthology
Perspectives on the Study of Film
A Casebook on Film
Film And/As Literature

4521 **Panofsky, Erwin.**
"On Movies."
IN: Film and the Liberal Arts

4522 **Papaleo, Joseph.**
"Ethnic Pictures and Ethnic Fate: The Media Image of Italian-Americans."
IN: Ethnic Images ...

4523 **Papoušek, Jaroslav.**
"Jaroslav Papoušek." [Interview by Antonín J. Liehm.]
IN: Closely Watched Films

4524 **Paran, Janice.**
"My Keaton."

Paul, Doris A. SEE: Issari, M. Ali.

4555 **Paul, Robert W.**
"Kinematographic Experiences."
IN: A Technological History ...

4556 **Paul, William.**
"Charles Chaplin and the Annals of Anality."
IN: Comedy/Cinema/Theory

4557 **Pauly, Thomas H.**
"*Gone with the Wind* and *The Grapes of Wrath* as
Hollywood Histories of the Depression."
IN: Movies as Artifacts

4558 **Paxton, John.**
"The Greeks Had Another Word For It,
Meaning--Exaltation--" [RE: an interview.]
IN: Blueprint on Babylon

4559 **Payne, Robert.**
"Charlie Chaplin: Portrait of a Moralist."
IN: Film: An Anthology

4560 **Payne, Robert.**
"The Frozen Hills." [RE: *The Gold Rush.*]
IN: The Classic Cinema

4561 **Pearson, Gabriel and Eric Rhode.**
"Cinema of Appearance."
IN: Focus on Shoot the Piano Player
Sight and Sound

4562 **Pearson, Gabriel and Eric Rhode.**
"Screened Culture--Letter from Venice." [RE: *Hamlet*,
1964.]
IN: Focus on Shakespearean Films

4563 **Pearson, Roberta E.**
"'O'er Step not the Modesty of Nature': A Semiotic
Approach to Acting in the Griffith Biographs."
IN: Making Visible the Invisible

Pearson, Roberta. SEE: Stam, Robert.

4564 **Peary, Dannis.**
"Stephanie Rothman: R-Rated Feminist."
IN: Women and the Cinema

4565 **Peary, Danny.**
"Directing *Mad Max* and *The Road Warrior*. An
Interview with George Miller."
"Directing *Alien* and *Blade Runner*. An Interview with
Ridley Scott."
"Playing Ripley in *Alien*: An Interview with Sigourney
Weaver."
"When Men and Machines Go Wrong: An Interview
with Michael Crichton."
"*Flash Gordon* and *Buck Rogers*: An Interview with
Buster Crabbe."
IN: Omni's Screen Flights ...

4566 **Peary, Danny.**
"Reminiscing with Walter Lantz."
IN: The American Animated Cartoon

4567 **Peary, Gerald.**
"Alice Guy Blaché: Czarina of the Silent Screen."
IN: Women and the Cinema

4568 **Peary, Gerald.**
"Fast Cars and Women." [RE: Howard Hawks.]
IN: Focus on Howard Hawks

4569 **Peary, Gerald.**
"Hollywood in Yugoslavia."
IN: Before the Wall Came Down

4570 **Peary, Gerald.**
"*Fahrenheit 451*: From Novel to Film."
IN: Omni's Screen Flights ...

4571 **Peary, Gerald.**
"*Little Caesar* [novel by] W.R. Burnett. Rico Rising:
Little Caesar Takes Over the Screen."
IN: The Classic American Novel ...

Peary, Gerald. SEE: Kay, Karyn.

4572 **Pechter, William S.**
"The Ballad and the Source." [RE: *The Virgin Spring.*]
IN: Renaissance of the Film

4573 **Pechter, William S.**
"John Ford: A Persistence of Vision."
"*American Madness.*"
"Welles After *Kane.*"
IN: Great Film Directors

4574 **Pechter, William S.**
"*M*A*S*H.*"
"*Love and Anarchy.*"
"Why We Laugh at Buñuel."
"Frank Capra."
IN: Movie Comedy

4575 **Pechter, William S.**
"Cagney vs. Allen vs. Brooks: On the Indispensability
of the Performer." [RE: Woody Allen; Mel Brooks.]
IN: The Movie Star: The National ...

4576 **Peck, Richard E.**
"Films, Television, and Tennis."
IN: Man and the Movies

4577 **Peckham, Linda.**
"Not Speaking with Language/Speaking with No
Language: Leslie Thornton's *Adynata.*"
IN: Psychoanalysis and Cinema

4578 **Peckinpah, Sam.**
"Sam Peckinpah." [Interview by Andrew Sarris.]
IN: Interviews with Film Directors

4579 **Peña, Richard.**
"After *Barren Lives*: The Legacy of Cinema Novo--An
Interview with Nelson Pereira Dos Santos." [RE:
Brazil.]
"Images of Exile: Two Films by Raoul Ruiz." [RE:
Hypothesis of the Stolen Painting and *Of Great
Events and Ordinary People.*]
IN: Reviewing Histories

4580 Peña, Richard.
"*How Tasty Was My Little Frenchman.*"
    IN: Brazilian Cinema

4581 Pendakur, Manjunath.
"Internationalization of the Canadian Film Industry."
    IN: Current Research in Film /v. 4

4582 Pendakur, Manjunath.
"Cultural Dependency in Canada's Feature Film Industry."
    IN: The American Movie Industry

4583 Pendakur, Manjunath.
"Canadian Feature Films in the Chicago Theatrical Market, 1978-1981: Economic Relations and Some Public Policy Questions."
    IN: Current Research in Film /v. 2

4584 Pendakur, Manjunath.
"India."
    IN: The Asian Film Industry

4585 Pendo, Stephen.
"*Farewell, My Lovely: Murder, My Sweet.*"
"*The Big Sleep.*"
"*The Lady in the Lake: Lady in the Lake.*"
"*The High Window: The Brasher Doubloon.*"
"*The Little Sister: Marlowe.*"
"*The Long Goodbye.*"
"*Farewell, My Lovely.*"
    IN: Raymond Chandler on Screen

4586 Penley, Constance.
"Time Travel, Primal Scene and the Critical Dystopia."
    IN: Alien Zone
        Fantasy and the Cinema
        Close Encounters

4587 Penley, Constance.
"The Avant-Garde and Its Imaginary."
    IN: Movies and Methods /v. 2

4588 Penley, Constance.
"*Cries and Whispers.*"
    IN: Movies and Methods: An Anthology

4589 Penley, Constance and Janet Bergstrom.
"The Avant-Garde: History and Theories."
    IN: Movies and Methods /v. 2

4590 Penn, Arthur.
"*Bonnie and Clyde*: Private Morality and Public Violence."
    IN: Hollywood Directors 1941-1976

4591 Penn, Arthur.
"Arthur Penn." [Interview by Eric Sherman and Martin Rubin.]
    IN: The Director's Event

4592 Penn, Arthur.
"Arthur Penn." [Interview by Joseph Gelmis.]
    IN: The Film Director as Superstar

4593 Pennebaker, D.A.
"D.A. Pennebaker." [Interview by G. Roy Levin.]

    IN: Documentary Explorations

4594 Pennebaker, Don Alan.
"*Don't Look Back* and *Monterey Pop.*" [Interview by Alan Rosenthal.]
    IN: The New Documentary in Action

Pennebaker, D.A. SEE: Bachman, Gideon.

4595 Pennington, Renée.
"Jules Furthman."
    IN: Dictionary of Literary Biography /v. 26

4596 Perelman, S.J.
"Vintage Swine." [RE: von Stroheim.]
    IN: The First Film Makers

4597 Perez, Michel.
"Jekyll and Hyde and the Cruel Cinema."
"The Puritan Despair."
    IN: Focus on The Horror Film

4598 Perisic, Zoran.
"The Zoptic Technique."
    IN: The ASC Treasury ...

4599 Perkins, Gil.
"Gil Perkins: The Stuntman."
    IN: The Real Tinsel

Perkins, Rowland. SEE: Haber, Bill.

4599a Perkins, Tessa.
"The Politics of 'Jane Fonda'."
    IN: Stardom

4600 Perkins, V.F.
"*Hatari!*"
"Hawks' Comedies."
"The British Cinema."
"Why Preminger?"
"*Rope.*"
    IN: Movie Reader

4601 Perkins, V.F.
"[From:] *Film as Film*: Form and Discipline."
    IN: Film Theory and Criticism /2 ed
        Film Theory and Criticism /3 ed
        Film Theory and Criticism /4 ed

4602 Perkins, V.F.
"A Critical History of Early Film Theory."
    IN: Movies and Methods: An Anthology

4603 Perkins, V.F.
"The Cinema of Nicholas Ray."
    IN: Movies and Methods: An Anthology
        Movie Reader

4604 Perkins, V.F.
"*Cheyenne Autumn.*"
    IN: The Pretend Indians

4605 Perkins, V.F, Paul Mayersberg, Ian Cameron.
"Movie Differences: A Discussion."
    IN: Movie Reader

Perkins, V.F. SEE: Cameron, Ian.

4606 **Perlmutter, Ruth.**
"The Sweetening of America: The Image of the Jew in Film."
IN: <u>Ethnic Images ...</u>

4607 **Perlmutter, Ruth.**
"Woody Allen's *Zelig*: An American Jewish Parody."
IN: <u>Comedy/Cinema/Theory</u>

4608 **Perrin, Nat.**
"Nat Perrin." [Interview by Lee Server.]
IN: <u>Screenwriter: Words Become Pictures</u>

Perry, Hart. SEE: Kopple, Barbara.

4609 **Perry, Laurie Loomis.**
"A Survey of Leftist Film Activity in the Weimar Republic."
IN: <u>Film and Politics in the Weimar Republic</u>

4610 **Perry, Ted.**
"Alessandro Blasetti."
"Francesco Rosi."
"Vittorio De Sica."
IN: <u>Cinema: A Critical Dictionary</u>

4611 **Perry, Ted.**
"On *8-1/2*."
IN: <u>Great Film Directors</u>

4612 **Perry, Ted.**
"The Seventh Art as Sixth Sense."
IN: <u>Perspectives on the Study of Film</u>

4613 **Pertsov, Viktor.**
"Literature and Cinema."
IN: <u>The Film Factory</u>

4614 **Petersen, Wolfgang.**
"Some Thoughts about Ernst."
IN: <u>West German Filmmakers on Film</u>

Peterson, L.S. SEE: Place, J.A.

4615 **Peterson, Richard A.**
"*Nashville* and America in One Dimension."
IN: <u>Film in Society</u>

4616 **Peterson, Sidney.**
"A Note on Comedy in Experimental Film."
IN: <u>Film Culture Reader</u>

4617 **Peterson, Sidney.**
"Cine Dance."
"Two Notes." [RE: *The Cage*; *Mr. Frenhofer and the Minotaur*.]
IN: <u>The Avant-Garde Film</u>

4618 **Petley, Julian.**
"*The Passion of Joan of Arc*."
IN: <u>Movies of the Silent Years</u>

4619 **Petley, Julian.**
"Cinema and State."
"The Lost Continent."
IN: <u>All Our Yesterdays</u>

4620 **Petley, Julian.**
"Reaching for the Stars."
IN: <u>British Cinema Now</u>

4621 **Petri, Elio.**
"Cinema is not for an elite, but for the masses ..."
IN: <u>The Cineaste Interviews</u>

4622 **Petric, Vlada.**
"A Theoretical-Historical Survey: Film and Dreams."
"Bergman's Cinematic Treatment of Psychopathic Phenomena."
IN: <u>Film and Dream</u>

4623 **Petric, Vlada.**
"*The Outlaw and His Wife*."
IN: <u>The Rivals of D.W. Griffith</u>

4624 **Petric, Vlada.**
"David Wark Griffith."
"Vsevolod Pudovkin."
IN: <u>Cinema: A Critical Dictionary</u>

4625 **Petric, Vlada.**
"Esther Shub: Film as a Historical Discourse."
IN: <u>Show Us Life</u>

4625a **Petrie, Dan, Jr.**
"Dan Petrie, Jr." [Interview by Syd Field.]
IN: <u>Selling a Screenplay</u>

4626 **Petrie, Graham.**
"'The Ogre who proves to be a pigmy': The Reception of Foreign Films in American, 1920-1927."
"F.W. Murnau: 'The German Genius of the Films.'"
"'In the Lubitsch Manner'."
"Victor Sjöström: 'The Greatest Director in the World."
"'They are a sad-looking people, these Swedes': Mauritz Stiller and Others."
IN: <u>Hollywood Destinies</u>

4627 **Petrie, Graham.**
"Miklós Jancsó: Decline and Fall?"
IN: <u>Politics, Art and Commitment ...</u>

4628 **Petrie, Graham.**
"On *Shoot the Piano Player*."
IN: <u>Focus on Shoot the Piano Player</u>

4629 **Petro, Patrice.**
"Film Censorship and the Female Spectator: *The Joyless Street*."
IN: <u>The Films of G.W. Pabst</u>

4630 **Petro, Patrice.**
"Rematerializing the Vanishing 'Lady': Feminism, Hitchcock, and Interpretation." [RE: *The Lady Vanishes*.]
IN: <u>A Hitchcock Reader</u>

4631 **Petrov-Bytov, Pavel.**
"We Have No Soviet Cinema."
IN: <u>The Film Factory</u>

Petrovich, Joseph A. SEE: Linton, James M.

Pett, John. SEE: Kuchi, Jerome.

Bridge; *Travels With My Aunt*)."

"Our Man in Vienna: Graham Greene's Film Adaptation of his Entertainments (The Three with Carol Reed: *The Fallen Idol*; *The Third Man*; *Our Man in Havana*; [and] *Loser Takes All*)."

"The Man Within: Adaptations of Greene's Serious Fiction by Other Screenwriters (*The Man Within/The Smugglers*; *The Fugitive*; *The Heart of the Matter*; *The End of the Affair*; *The Quiet American*)."

"Brown is not Greene: Greene's Film Adaptations of his Serious Fiction (*Brighton Rock*; *The Comedians*)."
IN: Graham Greene

4643 Phillips, Gene D.
"Novelist versus Screenwriter: The Case for Casey Robinson's Adaptations of Hemingway's Fiction."
IN: A Moving Picture Feast

4644 Phillips, Gene D.
"Paul Newman: Anti-Hero of the Alienated Generation."
IN: Movies as Artifacts

4645 Phillips, Gene D.
"The Boys on the Bandwagon: Homosexuality in the Movies."
IN: Sexuality in the Movies

4645a Phillips, Gene D.
"*Lawrence of Arabia*, 1962, 1989: 'It Looks *Damn* Good'."
IN: Columbia Pictures

4646 Phillips, Jayne Anne.
"*Premature Burial*."
IN: The Movie That Changed My Life

4647 Phillips, Joseph D.
"Film Conglomerate Blockbusters: International Appeal and Product Homogenization."
IN: The American Movie Industry

4648 Phillips, Klaus.
"Reinhard Hauff: A Cinema of Darwinism."
IN: New German Filmmakers

4649 Phoenix, River.
"My Director and I."
IN: Projections: A Forum ...

4650 Pichel, Irving.
"Seeing with the Camera." [NOTE: Also called "Change of Camera Viewpoint."]
IN: A Casebook on Film
Hollywood Directors 1941-1976
The Movies as Medium

4651 Pick, Zuzana M.
"Chilean Documentary: Continuity and Disjunction."
IN: The Social Documentary ...

4652 Picker, David V.
"The Film Company as Financier-Distributor."
IN: The Movie Business Book

4653 Picker, David.
"The Distributor."
IN: Movie People

4654 Picker, Jimmy.
"Jimmy Picker [on Animation]." [Interview by David Chell.]
IN: Moviemakers at Work

4655 Pickford, Mary.
"Mary Pickford." [Interview by Charles Higham.]
IN: Celebrity Circus

4656 Pickowicz, Paul G.
"Cinema and Revolution in China."
IN: Conflict and Control in the Cinema

4657 *Picture Show.*
"Our Own Screen Dramas."
IN: An Australian Film Reader

4658 Piekarski, Vicki.
"Sydney Pollack."
IN: Close-Up: The Contemporary Director

4659 Pierce, Lucy France.
"The Nickelodeon."
IN: The Movies in Our Midst

4660 Pierre, Sylvie and Jean-Louis Comolli.
"Two Faces of *Faces*."
IN: Cahiers du Cinéma, 1960-1968

Pierre, Sylvie. SEE: Narboni, Jean.

4661 Pike, Andrew.
"The Past: Boom and Bust."
IN: The New Australian Cinema

4662 Pilar, Santiago A.
"The Early Movies."
IN: Readings in Philippine Cinema

4663 Pilkington, William T.
"*Fort Apache*."
IN: Western Movies

4664 Pilkington, William T. and Don Graham.
"Introduction: A Fistful of Westerns."
IN: Western Movies

4665 Pincus, Ed.
"Ed Pincus." [Interview by G. Roy Levin.]
IN: Documentary Explorations

4666 Pines, Jim.
"*The Birth of a Nation*."
IN: Movies of the Silent Years

4667 Pines, Jim.
"The Cultural Context of Black British Cinema."
IN: Critical Perspectives on Black ...

4668 Piotrovskij, A.
"Towards a Theory of Cine-Genres." [NOTE: Also called "Towards a Theory of Film Genres."]
IN: Russian Formalist Film Theory
The Poetics of Cinema

IN: The Image Maker

4698 **Polonsky, Abraham.**
"Abraham Polonsky." [Interview by Eric Sherman and
     Martin Rubin.]
     IN: The Director's Event

4699 **Polonsky, Abraham.**
"Abraham Polonsky." [In correspondence with William
     Pechter.]
     IN: Hollywood Voices

4700 **Pommer, Erich.**
"The Origin of *Dr. Caligari*."
     IN: Art in Cinema

4701 **Ponkie.**
"Clothes Make the Man ... Especially in Hollywood."
     IN: Fashion in Film

4702 **Pontecorvo, Gillo.**
"Political terrorism in 'Ogro' ..."
"Using the contradictions of the system ..."
     IN: The Cineaste Interviews

4703 **Pontecorvo, Lisa.**
"Film Resources."
     IN: The Historian and Film

4704 **Popov, Alexei.**
"The Relationships Between Cinema and Theatre."
     IN: The Film Factory

4705 **Porte, Pierre.**
"Pure Cinema."
     IN: French Film Theory and Criticism /v. 1

4706 **Porter, Edwin S.**
"Evolution of the Motion Picture."
     IN: Hollywood Directors 1914-1940
          Film Makers on Film Making

4707 **Porter, Vincent.**
"The Context of Creativity: Ealing Studios and
     Hammer Films."
     IN: British Cinema History

4708 **Portuges, Catherine.**
"Between Worlds: Re-Placing Hungarian Cinema."
     IN: Before the Wall Came Down

      Poster, W.S. SEE: Farber, Manny.

4709 **Potamkin, Harry Alan.**
"Grierson's *Drifters*."
     IN: The Documentary Tradition /1 ed
          The Documentary Tradition /2 ed

4710 **Potamkin, Harry Alan.**
"The Future Cinema: Notes for a Study."
     IN: Introduction to the Art of the Movies

4711 **Potamkin, Harry Alan.**
"*The Passion of Jeanne D'Arc*."
     IN: The Emergence of Film Art /1 ed
          The Emergence of Film Art /2 ed
          Awake in the Dark

4712 **Potamkin, Harry Alan.**
"Eisenstein and the Theory of Cinema."
"A Proposal for a School of the Motion Picture."
"Pabst and the Social Film."
"Pudovkin and the Revolutionary Film."
     IN: Hound & Horn

4713 **Poteet, G. Howard.**
"Film as Language: Its Introduction into a High School
     Curriculum."
     IN: The Compleat Guide to Film Study

4714 **Potter, Cherry.**
"From Montage to Story: *Persona*."
"What's Going On Out There In The World?: *Touch of
     Evil* and *The Lacemaker*."
"The Interior World: *Wild Strawberries*, *The
     Conformist* and *Kaos*."
"Metaphors and Archetypes: *For a Few Dollars More*
     and *Kaos*."
"The Beginning: *Midnight Cowboy* and *Viridiana*."
"The Development: *Midnight Cowboy* and *Viridiana*."
"The Ending: *Midnight Cowboy* and *Viridiana*."
"The Disruption of a Genre: *Heaven's Gate*."
"The Problem of the Woman Protagonist: *Les
     Rendez-vous d'Anna*."
"The Classic Form and Feminine Disruption: *Mirror*."
"*Persona* Revisited."
     IN: Image, Sound and Story

4715 **Powdermaker, Hortense.**
"Hollywood and the U.S.A."
     IN: The Movies in Our Midst

4716 **Powdermaker, Hortense.**
"The Front Office."
     IN: Conflict and Control in the Cinema

4717 **Powdermaker, Hortense.**
"[From:] Hollywood the Dream Factory."
     IN: Film and Society

4718 **Powell, David.**
"Experiencing Film with Sixth-Graders."
     IN: Films Deliver

4719 **Powell, Dilys.**
"*The Seventh Seal*."
     IN: Focus on The Seventh Seal

4720 **Powell, Dilys.**
"Comedy."
     IN: Anatomy of the Movies

4721 **Powell, Eleanor.**
"Eleanor Powell." [Interview by John Kobal.]
     IN: People Will Talk

4722 **Prakash, Sanjeev.**
"Music, Dance and the Popular Film: Indian
     Fantasies, Indian Repressions."
     IN: Indian Cinema Superbazaar

      Pratley, Gerald. SEE: Crawley, Budge.

4723 **Prats, A.J.**
"An Art of Joy, An Art of Life: The Plasticity and Narrative Methods of *The Clowns*."
IN: Explorations in National Cinemas

4724 **Prats, A.J.**
"The New Narration of Values: *Fellini: A Director's Notebook*."
"The Narrative Dilemma: *Seven Beauties*."
"To the Threshold of the New Narrative: *Blowup*."
"Plasticity and Narrative Methods: *The Clowns*."
IN: The Autonomous Image

4725 **Pratt, George C. (text and editor).**
"In the Beginning: 'A Magic Lantern Run Mad'."
"Georges Méliès and Edwin S. Porter."
"'This Line is a Klondike': The Nickelodeon."
"Griffith at Biograph (I): The Miraculous Year (1909)."
"Griffith at Biograph (II): More Experiments."
"Thunder on the Right (1909-1913): Griffith Leaves Biograph."
"Foreign Invasion (I): Films from France, Britain, Scandinavia, Austria, German, Italy, Russia."
"Films Fine and Foolish (1909-1918)."
"Thomas H. Ince."
"Mack Sennett and Charlie Chaplin."
"Outposts of the Cinema's Advance: *The Birth of a Nation* and *Intolerance*."
"A Good Girl and a Bad One: Mary Pickford and Theda Bara."
"Cecil B. DeMille."
"*Broken Blossoms*, and Some Griffith Films of the Twenties."
"Chaplin in the Twenties."
"The American Film, 1919-1924."
"Foreign Invasion (II): Ernst Lubitsch."
"Two Rebels: Erich von Stroheim and Robert J. Flaherty."
"Foreign Invasion (III): Films from Germany, France, Scandinavia."
"The American Film, 1925-1929."
"'Thunder Drum for All Four Horsemen': Presentation." [RE: exhibition.]
"The Experimental Film."
"Foreign Invasion (IV): Films from Russia; Films of Carl-Th. Dreyer."
IN: Spellbound in Darkness

4726 **Pratt, George C.**
"A Myth Is as Good as a Milestone."
"Firsting the Firsts." [RE: Eidoloscope.]
"In the Nick of Time: D.W. Griffith and the 'Last Minute Rescue'." [RE: Tom Mix, W.S. Hart.]
"Restoring the Context." [RE: *Greed*.]
"The Posse Is Ridin' Like Mad." [RE: Broncho Billy Anderson.]
"The Blonde Telegrapher: Blanche Sweet." [RE: *The Lonedale Operator*.]
"The Posse Is Still Ridin' Like Mad." [RE: Tom Mix and W.S. Hart.]
"'See Mr. Ince ...,'."
IN: Image on the Art ...

4727 **Pratt, George.**
"'No Magic, No Mystery, No Sleight of Hand'."
[NOTE: Also called "'No Magic, No Mystery, No Sleight of Hand': The First Ten Years of Motion Pictures in Rochester."]
IN: The American Film Industry
Image on the Art ...

4728 **Pratt, George.**
"Multiple Reel Films."
IN: The First Tycoons

Pratt, George C. SEE: Deutelbaum, Marshall.

4729 **Pratt, James.**
"Production Manager."
IN: Hollywood Speaks!

4730 ***Pravda*, editorial.**
"The Whole Country is Watching *Chapayev*."
IN: The Film Factory

4731 **Prawer, S.S.**
"Book into Film I: Mamoulian's *Dr. Jekyll and Mr. Hyde*."
"Book into Film II: Dreyer's *Vampyr*."
"The Iconography of the Terror-film: Wiene's *Caligari*."
IN: Caligari's Children

4732 **Preminger, Otto.**
"Otto Preminger." [Interview by Andrew Sarris.]
IN: Interviews with Film Directors

4733 **Preminger, Otto.**
"Otto Preminger." [Talking to Ian Cameron, Mark Shivas and Paul Mayersberg.]
IN: Hollywood Voices

4734 **Pressburger, Emeric.**
"The Early Life of a Screenwriter."
IN: Projections: A Forum ...

4735 **Prévost, Jean.**
"The Cinema: *Metropolis*."
IN: French Film Theory and Criticism /V. 1

Price, David. SEE: Hacker, Jonathan.

4736 **Price, John A.**
"The Stereotyping of North American Indians in Motion Pictures."
IN: The Pretend Indians

4737 **Price, Michael H. and George E. Turner.**
"Derring-do of *Bulldog Drummond* [1929]."
"*Hell Harbor*--A Sea of Troubles."
"The Black Art of *White Zombie* [1932]."
"Ironic Justice of *Crime Without Passion*."
IN: The Cinema of Adventure, Romance & Terror

4738 **Price, Vincent.**
"Vincent Price." [Interview by Stanley Wiater.]
IN: Dark Visions

4739 **Priestley, J.B.**
"The Mad Sad World."
IN: Film and the Liberal Arts

4740 **Prigozy, Ruth.**
"A Modern Pietà: De Sica's *Two Women* from the Novel by Alberto Moravia."
IN: Modern European Filmmakers ...

4740a **Prigozy, Ruth.**
"Judy Holliday: The Star and the Studio."
IN: Columbia Pictures

4741 **Production Code Administration.**
"Code Seal and Letter."
IN: The Movies in Our Midst

4742 *Proletarskoe kino*, **editorial.**
"What Does 'Proletarian Cinema' Mean?"
"We Are Continuing the Struggle."
IN: The Film Factory

4743 **Proletkino.**
"Quasi-Theses."
IN: The Film Factory

4744 **Pronay, Nicholas.**
"'The Land of Promise': The Projection of Peace Aims in Britain."
IN: Film & Radio Propaganda ...

4745 **Pronay, Nicholas.**
"The News Media at War."
"The Political Censorship of Films in Britain Between the Wars."
IN: Propaganda, Politics and Film

4746 **Pronay, Nicholas.**
"The Newsreels: The Illusion of Actuality."
IN: The Historian and Film

4747 **Pronay, Nicholas.**
"The First Reality: Film Censorship in Liberal England."
IN: Feature Films as History

4748 **Pronay, Nicholas and Jeremy Croft.**
"British Film Censorship and Propaganda Policy During the Second World War."
IN: British Cinema History

4749 **Prose, Francine.**
"*Seven Brides for Seven Brothers*."
IN: The Movie That Changed My Life

4750 **Prouse, Derek.**
"*Othello* [1955]."
IN: Focus on Shakespearean Films

4751 **Prümm, Karl.**
"Dark Shadows and a Pale Victory of Reason: *The Trial*."
IN: The Films of G.W. Pabst

Pruneda, J.A. SEE: Cobos, Juan.

4752 **Pryluck, Calvin.**
"Front Office, Box Office, and Artistic Freedom: An Aspect of the Film Industry 1945-1969
IN: Movies as Artifacts

4753 **Pryluck, Calvin.**
"Industrialization of Entertainment in the United States."
IN: Current Research in Film /v. 2

4754 **Pryluck, Calvin.**
"Ultimately We Are All Outsiders: The Ethics of Documentary Filming."
IN: New Challenges for Documentary

4755 **Pryor, Thomas M.**
"Films in the 'Truth Campaign'."
IN: The Documentary Tradition /1 ed
The Documentary Tradition /2 ed

4756 **Ptacek, Kathryn.**
"You Are What You Eat/Watch: Cannibalism in Movies."
IN: Cut!: Horror Writers ...

4757 **Pudovkin, Vsevolod.**
"On the Principle of Sound in Film."
"Conversation on Sound Film."
"S.M. Eisenstein (from *Potemkin* to *October*)."
"The Role of Sound Cinema."
"The Director and the Scriptwriter (extracts)."
"Dialogue in Film (extract)."
"The Internal and the External in an Actor's Training."
"*The Youth of Maxim*."
IN: The Film Factory

4758 **Pudovkin, Vsevolod.**
"[From:] *Film Technique* [On Editing]."
IN: Film Theory and Criticism /1 ed
Film Theory and Criticism /2 ed
Film Theory and Criticism /3 ed
Film Theory and Criticism /4 ed

4759 **Pudovkin, V.I.**
"[From:] *Film Technique and Film Acting*
IN: Film and Literature: Contrasts ...

4760 **Pudovkin, V.I.**
"Asynchronism as a Principle of Sound Film."
IN: Film Sound

4761 **Pudovkin, V.I.**
"Film Technique."
IN: Film: An Anthology

4762 **Pudovkin, V.I.**
"Film Acting."
IN: Star Texts

4763 **Pudovkin, V.I.**
"On Cinema Acting."
IN: A Casebook on Film

4764 **Pudovkin, V.I.**
"The Plastic Material."
IN: Film: A Montage of Theories

4765 **Pudovkin, Vsevolod Illarionovitch.**
"The Force of Poetry."
IN: Cinema in Revolution

4766 Pudovkin, Vsevolod, Leonid Obolensky, Sergei Komarov and Vladimir Fogel.
"Preface to Kuleshov's Book *The Art of Cinema*."
IN: The Film Factory

Pudovkin, Vsevolod. SEE: Eisenstein, Sergei.

4767 Puig, Manuel.
"How the Provincial Argentine Left Literature for the Movies, Thereby Discovering the Immense Potentials of the Novel."
IN: Writing in a Film Age

4768 Pulleine, Tim.
"John Gilbert--A Gentleman's Fate."
IN: Movies of the Silent Years

4769 Purves, Alan C.
"A Model for Curriculum Evaluation in Film."
IN: Perspectives on the Study of Film

4770 Putsch, Henry E.
"Student Filmmaking."
"Teaching with Shadows."
IN: Films Deliver

Putsch, Henry E. SEE: Sohn, David.

4771 Putterman, Barry.
"George Roy Hill."
"Irvin Kershner."
"Peter Bogdanovich."
IN: American Directors /v. 2

4772 Pye, Douglas.
"Genre and Movies [The Western]."
IN: Film Genre

4773 Pye, Douglas.
"The Western (Genre and Movie)." [NOTE: An excerpt of the essay "Genre and Movies."]
IN: Film Genre Reader

4774 Pyle, Ernie.
"[From:] The Movies."
IN: Film and Society

4775 Pym, John.
"Ireland—Two Nations."
IN: New Challenges for Documentary

4776 Pym, John.
"The Middle American Sky." [RE: *Close Encounters of the Third Kind*.]
IN: Sight and Sound

4777 Pyne, Daniel.
"Daniel Pyne." [Interview by William Froug.]
IN: The New Screenwriter Looks ...

4778 Quart, Barbara Koenig.
"Antecedents: Alice Guy-Blache, Germaine Dulac, Lois Weber, Dorothy Arzner, Ida Lupino, Lina Wertmuller."
"American Women Directors: Elaine May, Joan Micklin Silver, Claudia Weill, Susan Seidelman, Joyce Chopra, Martha Coolidge, Donna Deitch, Barbra Streisand, Goldie Hawn, and others."
"Western European Women Directors: Margarethe von Trotta, Doris Dörrie, Agnes Varda, Diane Kurys, Gunnel Lindblom, Marleen Gorris, and others."
"Eastern European Women Directors: Márta Mészáros, Larisa Shepitko, Vera Chytilová, Agnieszka Holland."
"Notes on Third World Women Directors: Euzhan Palcy, Lu Xiaoya, Zhang Nuanxin, Ann Hui, Sachiko Hidari, Aparna Sen, Prema Karanth, Maria Luisa Bemberg, Susana Amaral, and others."
IN: Women Directors

4779 Quart, Leonard.
"*The Deer Hunter*: The Superman in Vietnam."
IN: From Hanoi to Hollywood

4780 Quart, Leonard and Albert Auster.
"The Working Class Goes to Hollywood."
IN: Cinema, Politics and Society in America

4781 Quigley, Martin.
"[From:] Importance of the Entertainment Film."
IN: Film and Society

4782 Quigley, Martin.
"Decency in Motion Pictures."
IN: The Movies in Our Midst

4783 Quiquemelle, Marie-Claire.
"The Wan Brothers and Sixty Years of Animated Film in China."
IN: Perspectives on Chinese Cinema

Quiquemelle, M.C. SEE: Kwok.

4784 Quirk, James R.
"An Open Letter to D.W. Griffith."
IN: The First Film Makers

Raban, William. SEE: Gidal, Peter.

4785 Rabinovitz, Lauren.
"The Woman Filmmaker in the New York Avant-garde."
"The Meaning of the Avant-garde."
"Avant-garde Cinemas before World War II."
"Maya Deren and an American Avant-garde Cinema."
"Shirley Clarke and the Expansion of American Independent Cinema."
"Joyce Wieland and the Ascendancy of Structural Film."
"After the Avant-garde: Joyce Wieland and New Avant-gardes in the 1970s."
"Women Sneaking around Museums."
IN: Points of Resistence

4786 Radok, Alfred.
"Alfred Radok." [Interview by Antonín J. Liehm.]
IN: Closely Watched Films

4786a Rae, Graham.
"Trans-Atlantic Terror Trends."
IN: The Deep Red Horror Handbook

4787 **Raeburn, John.**
"The Gangster Film."
IN: <u>Handbook of American Film Genres</u>

4788 **Rafferty, Terrence.**
"*The Animated Art of the Brothers Quay.*"
"*Comfort and Joy.*"
"*Carnival of Souls.*"
"*Barbarosa.*"
"*Sign o' the Times.*"
IN: <u>Produced and Abandoned</u>

4789 **Raimi, Sam.**
"Sam Raimi." [Interview by Stanley Wiater.]
IN: <u>Dark Visions</u>

4790 **Raina, Raghunath.**
"The Context: A Socio-Cultural Anatomy."
IN: <u>Indian Cinema Superbazaar</u>

4791 **Rainer, Peter.**
"*A Cry in the Dark.*"
"*Cattle Annie and Little Britches.*"
"*Shoot the Moon.*"
"*Something Wild.*"
"*Streetwise.*"
IN: <u>Produced and Abandoned</u>

4792 **Rainer, Peter.**
"Dean vs. Pryor: Acting in the Seventies."
IN: <u>The Movie Star: The National ...</u>

Rainer, Tristine. SEE: Schneble, Sylvie.

4793 **Rainer, Yvonne.**
"Some Ruminations around the Cinematic Antidotes
to the Oedipal Net(les) while Playing with De
Lauraedipus Mulvey, or, He May Be Off Screen,
but..."
IN: <u>Psychoanalysis and Cinema</u>

4793a **Rainer, Yvonne.**
"Yvonne Rainer (on *Privilege*)." [Interview by Scott
MacDonald.]
IN: <u>A Critical Cinema 2</u>

4794 **Raizman, Yuli.**
"Seminar at VGIK (extracts)." [RE: All-Union State
Cinema Institute.]
IN: <u>The Film Factory</u>

4795 **Rajadhyaksha, Ashish.**
"Debating the Third Cinema."
IN: <u>Questions of Third Cinema</u>

4796 **Raksin, David.**
"Life with Charlie." [RE: Charlie Chaplin.]
IN: <u>Wonderful Inventions</u>

4797 **Ramain, Paul.**
"The Influence of Dream on the Cinema."
IN: <u>French Film Theory and Criticism /v. 1</u>

4798 **Ramirez, John.**
"Nicaraguan Reconstruction Documentary: Toward a
Theory and Praxis of Participatory Cinema and
Dialogic Address."

IN: <u>The Social Documentary ...</u>

4799 **Ramirez, John.**
"The Sandinista Documentary: A Historical
Contextualization."
IN: <u>Show Us Life</u>

4800 **Ramsaye, Terry.**
"The Rise and Place of the Motion Picture."
IN: <u>The Movies: An American Idiom</u>

4801 **Ramsaye, Terry.**
"[From:] The Rise and Place of the Motion Picture."
[NOTE: An abridged version of the material in *The
Movies: An American Idiom*.]
IN: <u>Film and Society</u>

4802 **Ramsaye, Terry.**
"First Night on Broadway."
IN: <u>Film: An Anthology</u>
<u>The First Tycoons</u>

4803 **Ramsaye, Terry.**
"Hodkinson and Paramount."
"Lasky Rents a Barn."
"The Screen Theatre Arrives."
IN: <u>The First Tycoons</u>

4804 **Ramsaye, Terry.**
"In the House of the Wizard." [RE: Thomas Edison.]
IN: <u>The Movies in Our Midst</u>

4805 **Ramsaye, Terry.**
"The Story Picture Is Born."
"The Discovery of California."
IN: <u>The First Film Makers</u>

4806 **Ramsaye, Terry.**
"[From:] Paul and the 'Time Machine'."
IN: <u>Focus on The Science Fiction Film</u>

4807 **Ramsden, J.A.**
"Baldwin and Film." [RE: Stanley Baldwin.]
IN: <u>Propaganda, Politics and Film</u>

4808 **Ramsden, John.**
"British Society in the Second World War."
IN: <u>Britain and the Cinema ...</u>

4809 **Ramsland, Katherine.**
"*Angel Heart*: The Journey to Self as the Ultimate
Horror."
IN: <u>Cut!: Horror Writers ...</u>

4810 **Randall, Richard S.**
"Freedom of Speech in a Mass Medium."
IN: <u>Film: Readings in the Mass Media</u>

4811 **Randall, Richard S.**
"Censorship: From *The Miracle* to *Deep Throat*."
IN: <u>The American Film Industry</u>
<u>The American Film Industry /rev ed</u>

Rankin, Aimee. SEE: Metz, Christian.

4812 **Ranucci, Karen with Julianne Burton.**
"On the Trail of Independent Video."
IN: <u>The Social Documentary ...</u>

4842 Rebhorn, Marlette.
"*Fort Apache*: The Indians and the New Yeoman Farmer."
"*Ragtime*: Pre-war America--Age of Innocence?"
"*Birth of a Nation*: Prejudice Triumphant."
"*Reds*: The Disillusionment of American Radicalism."
"*Sergeant York*: The Reluctant Great Crusader."
"*City Lights*: Urban Pressures and the Little Tramp."
"*Inherit the Wind*: Gimme' that Ol' Time America."
"*Scarface*: The Bureaucratization of Crime."
"*The Grapes of Wrath*: Happy Days Are Not Yet Here Again."
"*Top Hat*: Escapism and the American Dance."
"*Casablanca*: A Farewell To Isolationism."
"*Judgment at Nuremberg*: Justice or Revenge?"
"*Adam's Rib*: The Working Woman Learns Her Place."
"*Rebel Without a Cause*: 1950's--American Dream or American Nightmare?"
"*On the Waterfront*: The Gang's All Here."
"*Dr. Strangelove*: Laughing at Armageddon."
"*The Autobiography of Miss Jane Pittman*: Stride Towards Freedom."
"*Deer Hunter*: Hard Hats with Hard Choices."
"*All the President's Men*: It Can Happen Here."
"*Fort Apache, The Bronx*: The War on Poverty--and Poverty Won."
  IN: <u>Screening America: Using Hollywood Films ...</u>

4843 Rebolledo, Carlos.
"Buñuel and the Picaresque Novel."
  IN: <u>The World of Luis Buñuel</u>

4844 Reboux, Paul.
"*Les Croix de bois*."
  IN: <u>French Film Theory and Criticism /v. 2</u>

4845 Reddick, L.D.
"Educational Programs for the Improvement of Race Relations: Motion Pictures."
  IN: <u>The Black Man on Film</u>

4846 Reddy, John.
"The Living Legacy of Walt Disney."
  IN: <u>The Movies: An American Idiom</u>

4847 Reed, Carol.
"Carol Reed." [Interview by Charles T. Samuels.]
  IN: <u>Encountering Directors</u>

4848 Reed, Joseph.
"Subgenres in Horror Pictures: The Pentagram, Faust and Philoctetes."
  IN: <u>Planks of Reason</u>

4849 Reed, Rex.
"*Bob & Carol & Ted & Alice*."
"*Harold and Maude*."
"*M*A*S*H*."
  IN: <u>Movie Comedy</u>

4850 Reed, Rex.
"Bette Davis."
"Ruth Gordon."
"Jane Wyman."
"Ingrid Bergman."
"Myrna Loy."
"Uta Hagen."
"Simone Signoret."
"Patricia Neal."
"Zoe Caldwell."
"Oskar Werner."
"Colleen Dewhurst."
"Irene Papas."
"Paul Newman and Joanne Woodward."
"Joseph Losey."
"Omar Sharif."
"Albert Finney."
"Jean Seberg."
"Mart Crowley."
"Leslie Caron."
"Burt Bacharach."
"George Sanders."
"James Earl Jones."
"Oliver Reed."
"Jon Voight."
"Carol White."
"Leonard Whiting and Olivia Hussey."
"Patty Duke."
  IN: <u>Conversations in the Raw</u>

4851 Reed, Rex.
"Comden and Green."
"Las Vegas."
  IN: <u>Travolta to Keaton</u>

4852 Reed, Rex.
"Diane Keaton."
"George C. Scott."
"Giancarlo Giannini."
"Montgomery Clift."
  IN: <u>The Movie Star: The National ...</u>

4853 Reed, Rex.
"Michelangelo Antonioni."
"Barbra Streisand."
"Warren Beatty."
"Carson McCullers."
"Mike Nichols."
"Lucille Ball."
"Gower Champion."
"Ava Gardner."
"Sandy Dennis."
"Lotte Lenya."
"Shirley Knight."
"Robert Anderson."
"Angela Lansbury."
"Buster Keaton."
"Marianne Moore."
"James Mason."
"Dame Edith Evans."
"Melina Mercouri."
"Otto Preminger."
"Michael Crawford."
"Hayley Mills."
"Lynn Redgrave."

"Beryl Reid."
"Jean Paul Belmondo."
"George Peppard."
"Franco Corelli."
"Gwen Verdon."
"Geraldine Chaplin."
"Leslie Uggams."
"Bill Cosby."
"Peter Fonda."
"Marlene Dietrich."
    IN: <u>Do You Sleep in the Nude?</u>

4854 Reed, Rex.
"Pages From My Diary."
"Elizabeth Taylor."
"Sophia Loren."
"Audrey Hepburn."
"Sylvia Syms."
"Hildegard Knef."
"Louise Fletcher."
"Pearl Bailey."
"George Burns."
"Melina Mercouri."
"Martin Ritt."
"Lillian Hellman."
"Jacqueline Susann."
"Bette Davis."
"Mabel Mercer."
"Carol Channing."
"The Andrews Sisters."
"Ginger Rogers."
"Dody Goodman."
"Carroll Baker."
"Geraldine Fitzgerald."
"Walter Matthau."
"Alexis Smith."
"William Holden."
"Jimmy Coco."
"Robert Evans."
"Valerie Perrine."
"Glenda Jackson."
"Jeff Bridges."
"Diane Ladd."
"Marvin Hamlisch."
"Roy Scheider."
"Ellen Burstyn."
"Katherine Ross."
"Madeline Kahn."
"Genevieve Bujold."
"Giancarlo Giannini."
"David Bowie."
"Robert Redford."
    IN: <u>Valentines and Vitriol</u>

4855 Reed, Rex.
"Tennessee Williams."
"Marcello Mastroianni."
"Sally Kellerman."
"Merle Oberon."
"Kay Thompson."
"*Gone With the Wind* Hits the Stage."

"Bette Midler."
"Carrie Snodgress."
"Sylvia Miles."
"Joan Hackett."
"On Location: Cliff Robertson and Joel Grey."
"Troy Donahue."
"On Location: Sir Laurence Olivier and Michael Caine."
"George C. Scott."
"Elia Kazan."
"Richard Chamberlain."
"Alice Faye."
"Dorothy Malone."
"Doris Day."
"Carroll Baker."
"Tuesdáy Weld."
"Gloria Grahame."
"Joanne Woodward."
"Maggie Smith."
"On Location: Glenda Jackson."
"On Location: Liv Ullmann and Edward Albert."
"On Location: Ken Russell."
"Alfred Hitchcock."
"On Location: James Bond/Roger Moore."
"Peter Bogdanovich and Cybill Shepherd."
"Ann-Margaret."
"Jack Lemmon."
"Jack Nicholson."
"Adolph Zukor's 100th Birthday Party."
    IN: <u>People Are Crazy Here</u>

4856 Reeves, Geoffrey.
"Finding Shakespeare on Film: From an Interview with Peter Brook."
    IN: <u>Film Theory and Criticism /1 ed</u>
         <u>Focus on Shakespearean Films</u>

4856a Reggio, Godfrey.
"Godfrey Reggio." [Interview by Scott MacDonald.]
    IN: <u>A Critical Cinema 2</u>

4857 Reichert, Julia and James Klein.
"*Union Maids* [Interviews with] Julia Reichert and James Klein."
    IN: <u>The Documentary Conscience</u>

4858 Reid, Margaret.
"Has the Flapper Changed? (Interview with F. Scott Fitzgerald)."
    IN: <u>Authors on Film</u>

4859 Reiner, Carl and Paul Henreid.
"A Conversation with Carl Reiner and Paul Henreid."
    IN: <u>Directors in Action</u>

4860 Reiner, Robert.
"Keystone to Kojak: The Hollywood Cop."
    IN: <u>Cinema, Politics and Society in America</u>

4861 Reingold, Nathan.
"A Footnote to History: MGM Meets the Atomic Bomb." [RE: *The Beginning or the End.*]
    IN: <u>American Media</u>

4862 Reisch, Walter.
"Reminiscence and Reflection: à Screenwriter."

IN: <u>Sound and the Cinema</u>

4863 Reisch, Walter.
"Walter Reisch: The Tailor." [Interview by Joel Greenberg.]
IN: <u>Backstory 2</u>

4864 Reiser, Joel and Bruce Kane.
"Sam Peckinpah."
IN: <u>Directors in Action</u>

Reisman, Susan. SEE: Levine, Arthur.

4865 Reisz, Karel.
"Interview [with] Karel Reisz." [Interview by Eva Orbanz, Helmut Wietz and Klaus Wildenhahn.]
IN: <u>Journey To a Legend and Back</u>

4866 Reisz, Karel and Gavin Millar.
"The Technique of *Shoot the Piano Player*."
IN: <u>Focus on Shoot the Piano Player</u>

4867 Reitz, Edgar.
"Love of Cinema."
"The Camera Is Not a Clock."
"The Dream of a German Film House."
IN: <u>West German Filmmakers on Film</u>

4868 Rennahan, Ray.
"The New Technicolor Is No Mystery: An Interview." [RE: *Becky Sharp*.]
IN: <u>Celebrity Articles ...</u>

4869 Renoir, Jean.
"First Interview [in *Cahiers du cinéma*], by Jacques Rivette and François Truffaut."
"Second Interview [in *Cahiers du cinéma*], by Jacques Rivette and François Truffaut."
"Third Interview [in *Cahiers du cinéma*]: My Next Films, by Michel Delahaye and Jean-André Fieschi."
"Fourth Interview [in *Cahiers du cinéma*]: The Progression of Ideas, by Michel Delahaye and Jean Narboni."
"Jean Renoir Talks about His Art."
"Jean Renoir the Boss."
"The Search for Relativity."
"The Rule and Its Exception."
"Jean Renoir Presents Twenty of His Films [for Television]."
"Hollywood Conversations [from *Cahiers du cinéma*]."
IN: <u>Renoir on Renoir</u>

4870 Renoir, Jean.
"Chaplin among the Immortals."
IN: <u>Hollywood Directors 1941-1976</u>

4871 Renoir, Jean.
"Jean Renoir." [Interview by Andrew Sarris.]
IN: <u>Interviews with Film Directors</u>

4872 Renoir, Jean.
"Jean Renoir." [Interviewed by James D. Pasternak.]
IN: <u>The Image Maker</u>

4873 Renoir, Jean.
"Jean Renoir to Tay Garnett: On Filmmaking."

"Memories."
IN: <u>Rediscovering French Film</u>

4874 Renoir, Jean.
"Jean Renoir." [Interview by Charles T. Samuels.]
IN: <u>Encountering Directors</u>

4875 Renoir, Jean.
"No, M. Verdoux Has Not Killed Charlie Chaplin!"
IN: <u>Essays on Chaplin</u>

4876 Renoir, Jean.
"The Director."
IN: <u>Filmmakers on Filmmaking /v. 2</u>

4877 Renoir, Jean.
"The Photogenic Golden Calf."
"How I Give Life to My Characters."
IN: <u>French Film Theory and Criticism /v. 2</u>

4878 Renoir, Jean.
"The Situation of the Serious Filmmaker."
IN: <u>Film: Book 1</u>

Renoir, Jean. SEE: Anderson, Lindsay.

4879 Renold, Evelyn.
"The Contemporary Movie Rating System in America."
IN: <u>Sexuality in the Movies</u>

4880 Renov, Michael.
"*Leave Her to Heaven*: The Double Bind of the Post-War Woman."
IN: <u>Imitations of Life</u>

4881 Renov, Michael.
"Imaging the Other: Representations of Vietnam in Sixties Political Documentary."
IN: <u>From Hanoi to Hollywood</u>

4882 Rentschler, Eric.
"Germany."
IN: <u>World Cinema Since 1945</u>

4883 Rentschler, Eric.
"Herbert Achternbusch: Celebrating the Power of Creation."
"Hans W. Geissendörfer: A Precise Craftsman."
IN: <u>New German Filmmakers</u>

4884 Rentschler, Eric.
"Specularity and Spectacle in Schlöndorff's *Young Törless*."
"Terms of Dismemberment: The Body in/and/of Fassbinder's *Berlin Alexanderplatz*."
IN: <u>German Film and Literature</u>

4885 Rentschler, Eric.
"The Politics of Vision: Herzog's *Heart of Glass*."
IN: <u>The Films of Werner Herzog</u>

4886 Rentschler, Eric.
"The Problematic Pabst: An Auteur Directed by History."
IN: <u>The Films of G.W. Pabst</u>

4887 Resnais, Alain.
"*Hiroshima Mon Amour*."

4914 **Richards, Jeffrey.**
"*The Cabinet of Dr. Caligari.*"
"The Golden West."
"The Silent Films of John Ford."
"Douglas Fairbanks--Cutting a Dash."
IN: Movies of the Silent Years

4915 **Richards, Jeffrey.**
"Gracie Fields: Consensus Personified."
"George Formby: The Road from Wigan Pier."
"Jessie Matthews: The Dancing Divinity."
"The Romantic Adventurer: Robert Donat and Leslie Howard."
IN: The Age of the Dream Palace

4916 **Richards, Jeffrey.**
"National Identity in British Wartime Films."
IN: Britain and the Cinema ...

4917 **Richards, Jeffrey.**
"'Patriotism with Profit': British Imperial Cinema in the 1930s."
IN: British Cinema History

4918 **Richards, Jeffrey.**
"Imperial Images: The British Empire and Monarchy on Film."
"John Ford: The Folk Memory."
IN: Conflict and Control in the Cinema

4919 **Richards, Jeffrey.**
"Frank Capra and the Cinema of Populism."
IN: Movies and Methods: An Anthology

4920 **Richards, Jeffrey.**
"Paul Robeson: The Black Man as Film Hero."
IN: All Our Yesterdays

4921 **Richards, Jeffrey and Anthony Aldgate.**
"Feature Films and the Historian."
"The Sun Never Sets: *Sanders of the River*."
"The Age of Consensus: *South Riding*."
"Why We Fight: *A Canterbury Tale*."
"What a Difference a War Makes: *The Life and Death of Colonel Blimp*."
"Lest We Forget: *Fame is the Spur*."
"Old School Ties: *The Guinea Pig*."
"Cul-de-Sac England: *The Ladykillers*."
"Vicious Circles: *I'm All Right Jack*."
"The Seeds of Further Compromise: *Saturday Night and Sunday Morning*."
"The Revolt of the Young: *If ...*"
IN: British Cinema and Society

Richards, Jeffrey. SEE: Aldgate, Anthony.

4922 **Richardson, F.H.**
"What Happened in the Beginning."
IN: A Technological History ...

4923 **Richardson, Robert.**
"The Question of Order and Coherence in Poetry and Film."
IN: Film And/As Literature

4924 **Richardson, Robert.**
"Waste Lands: The Breakdown of Order." [RE: *La Dolce Vita*; T.S. Eliot.]
IN: Federico Fellini

4925 **Richardson, Robert.**
"Verbal and Visual Languages."
IN: Film and Literature: Contrasts ...

4926 **Richardson, Tony.**
"*The Seven Samurai.*"
IN: Sight and Sound
Great Film Directors

4927 **Richardson, Tony.**
"The Films of Luis Buñuel."
IN: The World of Luis Buñuel

4928 **Richardson, Tony.**
"The Two Worlds of the Cinema."
IN: Film Makers on Film Making

4929 **Richie, Donald.**
"'Mono No Aware'/Hiroshima in Film."
IN: Film: Book 2

4930 **Richie, Donald.**
"*Rashomon.*"
IN: Focus on Rashomon

4931 **Richie, Donald.**
"Dostoevsky With a Japanese Camera." [RE: Akira Kurosawa.]
IN: The Emergence of Film Art /1 ed
The Emergence of Film Art /2 ed

4932 **Richie, Donald.**
"Kenji Mizoguchi."
"Mikio Naruse."
"Yasujiro Ozu."
IN: Cinema: A Critical Dictionary

4933 **Richie, Donald.**
"Kurosawa's Camera and Style."
"*Seven Samurai.*"
IN: Great Film Directors

4934 **Richie, Donald.**
"The Moral Code of Luis Buñuel."
IN: The World of Luis Buñuel

4935 **Richie, Donald.**
"Viewing Japanese Film: Some Considerations."
IN: Cinema and Cultural Identity

4936 **Richter, Hans.**
"A History of the Avant-garde."
IN: Art in Cinema

4937 **Richter, Hans.**
"Avant-Garde Film in Germany."
IN: Experiment in the Film

4938 **Richter, Hans.**
"The Badly Trained Sensibility."
IN: The Avant-Garde Film

4966 **Roberts, William S.**
"'They Don't Want You Because You Write Stuff That's Serious'–" [RE: an interview.]
IN: Blueprint on Babylon

4966a **Robertson, Anne.**
"Anne Robertson." [Interview by Scott MacDonald.]
IN: A Critical Cinema 2

4967 **Robertson, Cliff.**
"Cliff Robertson." [Interview by Judith Crist.]
IN: Take 22

4968 **Robertson, Richard C.**
"Just Dreamin' Out Loud: The Westerns of Burt Lancaster."
IN: Shooting Stars

4969 **Robertson, Richard.**
"New Directions in Westerns of the 1960s and 70s."
IN: Western Films: A Brief History

4970 **Robinson, Casey.**
"Casey Robinson: Master Adaptor." [Interview by Joel Greenberg.]
IN: Backstory

4971 **Robinson, David.**
"*Judex*."
"*The Kid*."
"*The Gold Rush*."
"*The General*."
"Charles Chaplin--Sixty-Two Years a King."
"Laughter in the Dark."
"Lumière's Cinématographe."
"Mack Sennett's Comic Touch."
"Poster Art and Revolution." [RE: Bolshevik cinema.]
"The Enduring Craft of Henry King."
"The Living Image."
IN: Movies of the Silent Years

4972 **Robinson, David.**
"Buster Keaton."
"Georges Méliès."
"Grigori Kozintsev and Leonid Trauberg."
"Laurel and Hardy."
"Soviet Cinema Since the War."
"W.C. Fields."
IN: Cinema: A Critical Dictionary

4973 **Robinson, David.**
"'Thank God–I Am Still An Atheist': Luis Buñuel and *Viridiana*."
IN: The World of Luis Buñuel

4974 **Robinson, David.**
"The Twenties."
IN: Hollywood 1920-1970

4975 **Robinson, David.**
"'The Lighter People'." [RE: Laurel and Hardy.]
IN: Sight and Sound

4976 **Robinson, Edward G.**
"*Little Caesar*."
IN: Bedside Hollywood

4977 **Robinson, Edward G.**
"The Movies, the Actor, and the Public Morals."
IN: The Movies in Our Midst

4978 **Robinson, Edward G.**
"Edward G. Robinson." [Interview by Charles Higham.]
IN: Celebrity Circus

4979 **Robinson, Glen.**
"Mechanical Effects for *Logan's Run*."
IN: The ASC Treasury ...

4980 **Robinson, Hubbell.**
"What's New, Copycat?"
IN: Sight, Sound, and Society

4981 **Robinson, W.R.**
"The Movies, Too, Will Make You Free."
IN: Man and the Movies
Film And/As Literature

4982 **Robson, Mark.**
"Mark Robson."
IN: The Celluloid Muse

4983 **Rocha, Glauber.**
"An Esthetic of Hunger."
"From the Drought to the Palm Trees."
"The Tricontinental Filmmaker: That Is Called the Dawn."
IN: Brazilian Cinema

4984 **Rocha, Glauber.**
"Beginning at Zero: Notes on Cinema and Society."
IN: Conflict and Control in the Cinema

4985 **Rocha, Glauber.**
"Cinema Novo vs. cultural colonialism ..."
IN: The Cineaste Interviews

4986 **Rocha, Glauber.**
"Cinema Novo and the Dialectics of Popular Culture." [RE: Brazil.]
IN: Cinema and Social Change ...

4987 **Rocha, Glauber.**
"History of Cinema Novo." [RE: Brazil.]
IN: Reviewing Histories

4988 **Rock, Joe.**
"Joe Rock: The Executive."
IN: The Real Tinsel

4989 **Rodakiewicz, Henwar.**
"Treatment of Sound in *The City*."
IN: The Movies as Medium

4990 **Roddam, Franc.**
"Franc Roddam." [Interview by John Andrew Gallagher.]
IN: Film Directors on Directing

4991 **Roddick, Nick.**
"'If the United States spoke Spanish, we would have a film industry ...'."
IN: British Cinema Now

4992 Roddick, Nick.
"*I Was Born, But ....*"
IN: Movies of the Silent Years

4993 Roddick, Nick.
"Betty Comden and Adolph Green."
"Ernest Lehman."
IN: Dictionary of Literary Biography /v. 44

4994 Roddick, Nick.
"Edward Anhalt."
"Jay Presson Allen."
IN: Dictionary of Literary Biography /v. 26

4995 Roddick, Nick.
"New Audiences, New Films."
IN: British Cinema Now

4996 Rödl, Josef.
"In Search of the Lost *Heimat.*"
IN: West German Filmmakers on Film

4997 Rodowick, D.N.
"The Enemy Within: The Economy of Violence in *The Hills Have Eyes.*"
IN: Planks of Reason

4998 Rodowick, David N.
"Madness, Authority, and Ideology in the Domestic Melodrama of the 1950s."
IN: Imitations of Life
    Home Is Where the Heart Is

4999 Rodríguez, Ismael.
"Ismael Rodríguez." [Interview by Beatrice Reyes Nevares.]
IN: The Mexican Cinema

5000 Rodriguez, José.
"Epilogue by an Old Pupil."
IN: The Best of Rob Wagner's Script

Rodriguez, Marta. SEE: Silva, Jorge.

5001 Roemer, Michael.
"Chaplin: Charles and Charlie."
IN: Great Film Directors

5002 Roemer, Michael.
"The Surface of Reality."
IN: A Casebook on Film
    Perspectives on the Study of Film
    Film: A Montage of Theories
    Film and Literature

5003 Roemer, Michael.
"Views and Reviews: Bergman's *The Seventh Seal.*"
IN: Focus on The Seventh Seal

5004 Rogers, Fred.
"Fred Rogers." [An interview.]
IN: Producers on Producing

5005 Rohdie, Sam.
"*Gallipoli*, Peter Weir and an Australian Art Cinema."
"The Australian State, A National Cinema."
IN: An Australian Film Reader

5006 Rohdie, Sam.
"Avant-garde."
IN: The New Australian Cinema

5007 Rohdie, Sam.
"Totems and Movies."
IN: Movies and Methods: An Anthology

5008 Rohmer, Eric.
"Cinema, the Art of Space."
"For a Talking Cinema."
"The Romance Is Gone."
"Reflections on Color."
"The Classical Age of Film."
"Such Vanity is Painting."
"Isou *or* Things As They Are (Views of the Avant-Garde)."
"Of Three Films and a Certain School."
"Of Taste and Colors."
"The Taste for Beauty."
"Letter to a Critic (concerning my *Contes moraux* [Moral Tales])."
"Film and the Three Levels of Discourse: Indirect, Direct, and Hyperdirect."
"André Bazin's 'summa'."
"Lesson of a Failure: *Moby Dick* by John Huston."
"Explanation of a Vote: *South Pacific* by Joshua Logan."
"Faith and Mountains: *Les Etoiles de midi* by Marcel Ichac."
"The Photogenics of Sports: the Olympics in Rome."
"Roberto Rossellini: *Stromboli.*"
"Howard Hawks: *The Big Sky.*"
"Skimming Picasso: Henri-Georges Clouzot's *The Mystery of Picasso.*"
"A Twentieth Century Tale: Orson Welles's *Mr. Arkadin/Confidential Agent.*"
"Nicholas Ray: *Bigger Than Life.*"
"Luis Buñuel: *The Criminal Life of Archibaldo de la Cruz.*"
"The Art of Caricature: Frank Tashlin's *Will Success Spoil Rock Hunter?*"
"The Quintessence of the Genre: George Cukor's *Les Girls.*"
"Politics against Destiny: Joseph L. Mankiewicz's *The Quiet American.*"
"Ingmar Bergman's *Dreams.*"
"Alfred Hitchcock's *Vertigo.*"
"The American Renoir."
"*Paris Does Strange Things*: Venus and the Apes."
"Renoir's Youth."
"*The Little Theater of Jean Renoir.*"
IN: The Taste for Beauty

5009 Rohmer, Eric.
"Ajax or the Cid?" [RE: *Rebel without a Cause.*]
"Rediscovering America."
"The Cardinal Virtues of CinemaScope."
"The Land of Miracles." [RE: *Viaggio in Italia.*]
IN: Cahiers du Cinéma, The 1950s

5010 Rohmer, Eric.
"The Old and the New [Rohmer in interview with Jean-Claude Biette, Jacques Bontemps, Jean-Louis Comolli]."
IN: Cahiers du Cinéma, 1960-1968

5011 Rohmer, Eric.
"*A Countess from Hong Kong*."
IN: Essays on Chaplin

5012 Rohmer, Eric.
"With *The Seventh Seal* Bergman Offers Us His Faust."
IN: Focus on The Seventh Seal

5013 Rohmer, Eric and Claude Chabrol.
"*The Wrong Man*."
IN: Focus on Hitchcock

5014 Rohmer, Eric and François Truffaut, Fereydoun Hoveyda and Jacques Rivette.
"Interviews with Roberto Rossellini."
IN: Cahiers du Cinéma, The 1950s

Rohmer, Eric. SEE: Bazin, André; SEE: Domarchi, Jean.

Rohrer, Jennifer. SEE: Blumenthal, Jerry.

5015 Roizman, Owen.
"Owen Roizman." [Interview by Dennis Schaefer and Larry Salvato.]
IN: Masters of Light

5016 Rokotov, T.
"Why is *October* Difficult?"
IN: The Film Factory

5017 Rolf, Tom.
"Tom Rolf." [Interview by Vincent LoBrutto.]
IN: Selected Takes

5018 Rollins, Peter C.
"Ideology and Film Rhetoric: Three Documentaries of the New Deal Era (1936-1941)." [RE: *March of Time*; *The River*; *Native Land*.]
"Film, Television, and American Studies."
IN: Hollywood as Historian

5019 Rollins, Peter C.
"Will Rogers and the Relevance of Nostalgia: *Steamboat 'Round the Bend*."
IN: American History/American Film

5020 Rölvaag, O.E.
"Giants of the Earth [excerpt]."
IN: The American West on Film

5021 Romains, Jules.
"The Crowd at the Cinematograph."
IN: French Film Theory and Criticism /v. 1

5022 Romberg, Sigmund.
"What's Wrong with Musical Pictures?"
IN: The Best of Rob Wagner's Script

5023 Romero, Eddie.
"A Film Director Speaks Out."

"Film Censorship and Social Change."
"My Work and Myself."
IN: Readings in Philippine Cinema

5024 Romero, George A.
"George A. Romero." [Interview by Stanley Wiater.]
IN: Dark Visions

5025 Romm, Mikhail Ilyitch.
"The Second Generation."
IN: Cinema in Revolution

5026 Rondolino, Gianni.
"Italian Propaganda Films: 1940-1943."
IN: Film & Radio Propaganda ...

5027 Rong Weijing.
"On the Presentation of Nationalism through Film."
IN: Chinese Film Theory

5028 Room, Abram.
"Cinema and Theatre."
IN: The Film Factory

5029 Root, Jane.
"Distributing *A Question of Silence*—A Cautionary Tale."
IN: Films for Women

Root, Jane. SEE: Cook, Pam.

5030 Root, Wells.
"Wells Root." [Interview by Lee Server.]
IN: Screenwriter: Words Become Pictures

5031 Ropars-Wuilleumier, Marie-Claire.
"Form and Substance, or the Avatars of the Narrative."
IN: Focus on Godard

5032 Ropars-Wuilleumier, Marie-Claire.
"How History Begets Meaning: Alain Resnais' *Hiroshima mon amour*."
IN: French Film: Texts and Contexts

5033 Rosa, Joseph G.
"The Gunfighter Legend."
IN: The American West on Film

5034 Rose, Brian.
"From the Outdoors to Outer Space: The Motion Picture Industry in the 1970s."
IN: Movies as Artifacts

5035 Rose, Cynthia.
"Romance."
IN: Anatomy of the Movies

5036 Rose, Jacqueline.
"Paranoia and the Film System."
IN: Feminism and Film Theory

5037 Rose, Jacqueline.
"The Cinematic Apparatus: Problems in Current Theory."
IN: The Cinematic Apparatus

5038 Rosen, David and Peter Hamilton.
"*The Ballad of Gregorio Cortez*."
"*Cold Feet*."

5056 **Rosenthal, Stuart.**
"Tod Browning."
IN: The Hollywood Professionals /v. 4

5057 **Rosenthal, Stuart.**
"Spectacle: Magnifying the Personal Vision."
IN: Federico Fellini

5058 **Rosenwein, Andrea.**
"James Agee."
IN: Dictionary of Literary Biography /v. 26

5059 **Roshal, Grigori.**
"Soviet Film."
IN: Experiment in the Film

5060 **Rosi, Francesco.**
"The audience should not be just passive spectators ..."
IN: The Cineaste Interviews

Rosolato, Guy. SEE: Bellour, Raymond.

Ross, Helen. SEE: Ross, Lillian.

5061 **Ross, Lillian.**
"Everything Has Just Gone Zoom." [RE: *The Red Badge of Courage*.]
IN: Film: An Anthology

5062 **Ross, Lillian and Helen Ross.**
"The Player: Actors Talk About Film Acting."
IN: Focus on Film and Theatre

5063 **Ross, Murray.**
"Hollywood's Extras."
IN: The Movies in Our Midst

5064 **Ross, Steven J.**
"Cinema and Class Conflict: Labor, Capital, the State, and American Silent Film."
IN: Resisting Images

5065 **Ross, T.J.**
"*The Servant* as Sex Thriller."
IN: Renaissance of the Film

5066 **Ross, T.J.**
"Cool Times." [RE: Michelangelo Antonioni.]
IN: Focus on Blow-Up

5067 **Ross, T.J.**
"Gipsies and Gentlemen." [RE: film and literature.]
IN: Film and the Liberal Arts

5068 **Ross, T.J.**
"Polanski, *Repulsion*, and the New Mythology."
IN: Focus on The Horror Film

5069 **Ross, T.J.**
"The Cult Send-Up: *Beat the Devil* or Goodbye, *Casablanca*."
IN: The Cult Film Experience

5070 **Ross, T.J.**
"Western Approaches: A Note on Dialogue."
IN: Focus on The Western

5071 **Rossellini, Roberto.**
"Roberto Rossellini." [Interview by Andrew Sarris.]
IN: Interviews with Film Directors

5072 **Rossellini, Roberto.**
"A Few Words about Neo-Realism."
IN: Springtime in Italy

5073 **Rossellini, Roberto.**
"Marx, Freud and Jesus."
IN: The Cineaste Interviews

5074 **Rossen, Robert.**
"New Characters for the Screen."
IN: Hollywood Directors 1941-1976

5075 **Rossi, Patrizio and Ben Lawton.**
"Reality, Fantasy, and Fellini."
IN: Federico Fellini

5076 **Rossner, Judith.**
"*Our Vines Have Tender Grapes*."
IN: The Movie That Changed My Life

5076a **Rosson, Hal.**
"Interview with Hal Rosson." [Interview by Leonard Maltin.]
IN: The Art of the Cinematographer

5077 **Rosten, Leo C.**
"The Movie Colony."
IN: Film: An Anthology
    The Movies in Our Midst

5078 **Rosten, Leo.**
"[From:] Movies and Propaganda."
IN: Film and Society

5079 **Roth, Lane.**
"Film, Society and Ideas: *Nosferatu* and *Horror of Dracula*."
IN: Planks of Reason

5080 **Roth, Mark.**
"Some Warners Musicals and the Spirit of the New Deal."
IN: Genre: The Musical

5081 **Roth, Philip.**
"*The Sun Also Rises* [novel by] Ernest Hemingway. Photography Does Not a Movie Make."
IN: The Classic American Novel ...

5082 **Rotha, Paul.**
"Sixty Years of Cinema."
"Technique of the Art-Director."
"The Art-Director and the Film Script."
"A Painter Looks at Films."
"A Museum for the Cinema."
"Old Film Stills."
"The 'Unusual' Film Movement."
"History of the Screen."
"The Magnificence of Fairbanks."
"Korda (1)."
"Korda (2)."
"Eisenstein."

"Chaplin."
"Making *Contact*."
"Films and Other Visual Techniques in Education."
"Presenting the World to the World."
"*People to People*."
"*Earth*."
"*Private Life of Henry VIII*."
"*I Was a Spy*."
"*Hunted People*."
"*La Maternelle*."
"*Deserter*."
"*Queen Christina*."
"*Jew Süss*."
"*Sanders of the River*."
"*Man of Aran*."
"Neo-Realism: *Bicycle Thieves*."
"Dark Victory: *Intruder in the Dust*."
"Test Case: *The Chance of a Lifetime*."
"Too Hot to Handle: *Young Man of Music*."
"Made with Modesty (1): *The Quiet One*."
"Made with Modesty (2): *Jour de fete*."
"Living History: *The Golden Twenties*."
"The Writing on the Wall: *La Vie commence demain*."
"Beside the Seaside: *Sunday in August*."
"Into Battle: *A Walk in the Sun*."
"Love in Transit: *La Ronde*."
"Junk and Jefferson: *Born Yesterday*."
"Murder, My Sweet!: *Macbeth*."
"Full House: *Ace in the Hole*."
"Quartet in Vienna: *Four in a Jeep*."
"*Umberto D.*"
"*Moby Dick*."
"*Lust for Life*."
"*Il Bidone* (*The Swindlers*)."
"*On the Bowery*."
"Postscript: A Letter to The Times."
"Films of Fact and Fiction."
"Films of Fact and the Human Element."
"The British Case (1)."
"The British Case (2)."
"Documentary Is Neither Short Nor Long."
"Information Services and Documentary Film Makers."
"The British Case (3)."
"British Feature Films at the Venice Film Festival
    (1932-52)."
"The Government and the Film Industry."
"The Chance Before British Films."
"The Film Crisis."
"A Plan for British Films."
"A Policy for Films."
"By Guess and By God."
"Films and Dollars."
"Forgotten Lessons in Realism."
    IN: Rotha on the Film

5083   Rotha, Paul.
"Interview [with] Paul Rotha." [Interview by Eva
    Orbanz, Gisela Tuchtenhagen and Klaus
    Wildenhahn.]
    IN: Journey To a Legend and Back

5084   Rotha, Paul.
"Some Principles of Documentary."
    IN: Film: An Anthology
        Nonfiction Film Theory and Criticism

5085   Rotha, Paul.
"The German Film."
    IN: The Emergence of Film Art /1 ed
        The Emergence of Film Art /2 ed

5086   Rothman, Stephanie.
"A New Beginning on *Terminal Island*."
    IN: Omni's Screen Flights ...

5087   Rothman, William.
"Hollywood Reconsidered: Reflections on the
    Classical American Cinema."
"D.W. Griffith and the Birth of the Movies."
"*Judith of Bethulia*."
"True Heart Griffith." [RE: *True Heart Susie*.]
"The Ending of *City Lights*."
"*Red Dust*: The Erotic Screen Image."
"Howard Hawks and *Bringing Up Baby*."
"To Have and Have Not Adapted a Film from a
    Novel." [RE: *To Have and Have Not*.]
"The Filmmaker in the Film: Octave and the Rules of
    the Game." [RE: *Rules of the Game*.]
"*The River*."
"*North by Northwest*: Hitchcock's Monument to the
    Hitchcock Film."
"Alfred Guzzetti's *Family Portrait Sittings*."
    IN: The "I" of the Camera

5088   Rothman, William.
"*To Have and Have Not* [novel by] Ernest
    Hemingway. To Have and Have Not Adapted a
    Novel." [NOTE: A slighly revised version of the
    essay that appears in the previous entry.]
    IN: The Modern American Novel ...

5089   Rothman, William.
"Against 'The System of the Suture'."
    IN: Movies and Methods: An Anthology
        Film Theory and Criticism /4 ed

5090   Rothman, William.
"Alfred Hitchcock's *Murder!*: Theater, Authorship, and
    the Presence of the Camera."
    IN: A Hitchcock Reader

5091   Rothman, William.
"Virtue and Villainy in the Face of the Camera."
    [NOTE: Also called "Virtue and Villainy in the Face
    of the Camera: A Reading of *Stella Dallas*."]
    IN: Making Visible the Invisible
        The "I" of the Camera

5092   Rothman, William.
"*Vertigo*: The Unknown Woman in Hitchcock."
    IN: Images in Our Souls
        The "I" of the Camera

5093   Rothschild, Amalie.
"Amalie Rothschild." [Interview by Lynn Fieldman
    Miller.]
    IN: The Hand That Holds the Camera

5094 **Rothschild, Amalie.**
"*It Happens to Us* and *Nana, Mom and Me* [Interview with] Amalie Rothschild."
IN: The Documentary Conscience

5095 **Rotzoll, Kim B.**
"The Captive Audience: The Troubled Odyssey of Cinema Advertising."
IN: Current Research in Film /v. 3

Rotzoll, Kim B. SEE: Christians, Clifford G.

5096 **Rouch, Jean.**
"Jean Rouch." [Interview by G. Roy Levin.]
IN: Documentary Explorations

5097 **Roud, Richard.**
"Abram Room."
"Agnès Varda."
"Alain Resnais."
"Allan Dwan."
"Chris Marker."
"Jacques Feyder."
"Jean Renoir: to 1939."
"Jean-Marie Straub."
"Jean-Luc Godard."
"Leopoldo Torre Nilsson."
"Louis Feuillade and the Serial."
"Marcel Pagnol."
"Marcel Carné and Jacques Prévert."
"René Clément and Henri-Georges Clouzot."
"Robert Kramer."
"Robert Bresson."
"Sacha Guitry."
IN: Cinema: A Critical Dictionary

5098 **Roud, Richard.**
"*Juve vs. Fantomas*."
IN: The Rivals of D.W. Griffith

5099 **Roud, Richard.**
"*Le Gai Savoir*."
IN: Focus on Godard

5100 **Roud, Richard.**
"Jean Grémillon and *Gueule d'Amour*."
"Louis Feuillade and the Serial." [NOTE: An adapted version of the essay in *Cinema: A Critical Dictionary*.]
"Melville."
IN: Rediscovering French Film

5101 **Roud, Richard.**
"Minimal Cinema: *The Chronicle of Anna Magdalena Bach*."
IN: Sight and Sound

5102 **Roud, Richard.**
"The Early Work of Robert Bresson."
IN: The Film

5103 **Roud, Richard.**
"*The Red Desert*: The Triple Split."
IN: The Classic Cinema

5104 **Routt, William.**
"On the Expression of Colonialism in Early Australian Films—Charles Chauvel and Naive Cinema."
IN: An Australian Film Reader

5105 **Rowe, Carel.**
"Illuminating Lucifer." [RE: *Lucifer Rising*.]
IN: The Avant-Garde Film

5106 **Rowland, Richard.**
"Carl Dreyer's World." [RE: *The Passion of Joan of Arc*.]
IN: The Classic Cinema

5107 **Rowland, Richard.**
"*Miss Julie*."
IN: Renaissance of the Film

5108 **Rowlands, Gena.**
"Gena Rowlands." [Interview by Judith Crist.]
IN: Take 22

Rowlands, Gena. SEE: Cassavetes, John.

Roy, Sue. SEE: Taylor, Al.

5108a **Royot, Daniel.**
"Charlie in the Far North: The Tall Tale Element in *The Gold Rush*."
IN: Charlie Chaplin

5109 **Rubbo, Michael.**
"*Sad Song of Yellow Skin* and *Waiting for Fidel* [Interview with] Michael Rubbo."
IN: The Documentary Conscience

5110 **Rubenstein, Joshua.**
"World War II—Soviet Style."
IN: New Challenges for Documentary

Rubenstein, Lenny. SEE: Georgakas, Dan.

5111 **Rubenstein, Richard E.**
"Sputtering Fires of Black Revolution: *BURN!*."
IN: Film in Society

5112 **Rubey, Dan.**
"*Star Wars*: 'Not So Long Ago, Not So Far Away."
IN: Jump Cut

5113 **Rubin, Lillian, NAVA.**
"Commercial Film Dealers."
IN: Ideas on Film

5114 **Rubin, Martin.**
"The Voice of Silence: Sound Style in John Stahl's *Back Street*."
IN: Film Sound

5115 **Rubin, Steven J.**
"Bullets or Ballads (*A Walk in the Sun*)."
"The Lion Returns to War (*Battleground*)."
"A Fox's Gamble (*The Longest Day*)."
"Freedom Before the Darkness (*The Great Escape*)."
"A Change of Emphasis (*Twelve O'Clock High*)."
"The Great Adventure (*The Bridge on the River Kwai*)."
"A Difference in Style (*Hell Is for Heroes*)."

"The Final Synthesis (*Patton*)."
IN: Combat Films

5116 **Rubinstein, L.**
"'Irony is a Double-Edged Weapon': An Interview with Alain Tanner."
IN: Conflict and Control in the Cinema

Rubio, Miguel. SEE: Cobos, Juan.

5117 **Ruble, Raymond.**
"Dr. Freud Meets Dr. Frank N. Furter." [RE: *The Rocky Horror Picture Show*.]
IN: Eros in the Mind's Eye

5118 **Ruby, Jay.**
"The Ethics of Imagemaking; or, 'They're Going to Put Me in the Movies. They're Going to Make a Big Star Out of Me...'"
"The Image Mirrored: Reflexivity and the Documentary Film."
IN: New Challenges for Documentary

Ruby, Jay. SEE: Gross, Larry.

5119 **Rudman, Norman G.**
"Over-Budget Protection and the Completion Guarantee."
IN: The Movie Business Book

5120 **Ruiz, Raúl.**
"Between Institutions." [RE: Chile.]
IN: Cinema and Social Change ...

5121 **Ruiz, Raul.**
"Interview with Raul Ruiz."
IN: Chilean Cinema

5122 **Ruiz, Reynaldo.**
"*Borderlands*."
"*Cinco vidas*."
IN: Chicano Cinema

5122a **Rule, Philip C., S.J.**
"*The Grapes of Wrath*: The Poor You Always Have with You."
IN: Image and Likeness

5123 **Rumanian Surrealist Group, The.**
"Malombra, Dark Ring of Absolute Love."
IN: The Shadow and Its Shadow

5124 **Ruppersberg, Hugh.**
"The Alien Messiah."
IN: Alien Zone

5125 **Ruppert, Peter.**
"Audience Engagement in Wenders' *The American Friend* and Fassbinder's *Ali: Fear Eats the Soul*."
IN: Narrative Strategies

5126 **Ruppert, Peter.**
"Introduction: Recent Ideas of Narrative Order."
IN: Ideas of Order in Literature & Film

5127 **Rush, Christopher.**
"Venus Peter: From Pictures to Pictures."
IN: From Limelight to Satellite

5128 **Russell, Rosalind.**
"The Leading Lady."
IN: Hollywood Speaks!

5129 **Russell, Sharon A.**
"Semiotics and Lighting Codes."
IN: Film: Historical-Theoretical ...

5130 **Russell, Sharon.**
"The Witch in Film: Myth and Reality."
IN: Planks of Reason

5131 **Rutherford, Charles S.**
"A New Dog with an Old Trick: Archetypal Patterns in *Sounder*."
IN: Movies as Artifacts

5132 **Rutland, J.R.**
"State Censorship of Motion Pictures."
IN: The Movies in Our Midst

5133 **Ryan, Michael and Douglas Kellner.**
"Technophobia."
IN: Alien Zone

5134 **Ryan, Tom.**
"Historical Films."
IN: The New Australian Cinema

5135 **Ryan, Trevor.**
"'The New Road to Progress': The Use and Production of Films by the Labour Movement, 1929-39."
IN: British Cinema History

5136 **Rydell, Mark.**
"Mark Rydell." [Interview by John Andrew Gallagher.]
IN: Film Directors on Directing

5137 **Rydell, Mark.**
"Mark Rydell." [Interview by Judith Crist.]
IN: Take 22

5138 **Ryo, Namikawa.**
"Japanese Overseas Broadcasting: a Personal View."
IN: Film & Radio Propaganda ...

5139 **Saare, Arla.**
"*A Married Couple*." [Interview by Alan Rosenthal.]
IN: The New Documentary in Action

5140 **Saarinen, Aline.**
"Cartoons as Art."
IN: The Emergence of Film Art /1 ed
        The Emergence of Film Art /2 ed

5141 **Sabath, Barry.**
"Samson Raphaelson."
IN: Dictionary of Literary Biography /v. 44

5142 **Sadoul, Georges.**
"*Les Bas-Fonds*."
"A Masterpiece of Cinema: *La Bête humaine*."
"Apropos Several Recent Films."
"Setting and Society."
"The Cinémathèque française."
"*La Marseillaise*, a Popular Epic."

"*La Règle du jeu..*"
    IN: French Film Theory and Criticism /v. 2

5143 **Sadoul, Georges.**
"Grémillon's *Lumière d'Eté*
"Jacques Becker."
    IN: Rediscovering French Film

5144 **Sadoul, Georges.**
"The Renaissance of the French Cinema—Feyder, Renoir, Duvivier, Carné."
    IN: Film: An Anthology

5145 **Sadoul, Georges.**
"Two or Three Things about an Apartment Complex." [RE: *Two or Three Things I Know About Her.*]
    IN: Focus on Godard

5146 **Saks, Gene.**
"Well, How Do You Like Directing Movies?"
    IN: Hollywood Directors 1941-1976

5147 **Salachas, Gilbert.**
"The Ambiguity of Satire." [RE: Federico Fellini.]
    IN: Great Film Directors

5148 **Salachas, Gilbert.**
"Fellini's Imagery from *Variety Lights* to *Juliet of the Spirits*."
    IN: Federico Fellini

5149 **Salamon, Julie.**
"*Lodz Ghetto.*"
    IN: Produced and Abandoned

5150 **Saless, Sohrab Shahid.**
"Culture as Hard Currency or: Hollywood in Germany."
    IN: West German Filmmakers on Film

5151 **Salmane, Hala.**
"Historical Background."
"On Colonial Cinema."
"Structures of Algerian Cinema."
"The Birth of Algerian Cinema."
    IN: Algerian Cinema

5152 **Salt, Barry.**
"Old Film Theory, New Film Theory."
"The Interpretation of Films."
"French Film Theory into English."
"Practical Film Theory."
"Film Style and Technology: 1895-1900."
"Film Style and Technology: 1900-1906."
"Film Style and Technology: 1907-1913."
"Film Style and Technology: 1914-1919."
"Statistical Style Analysis of Motion Pictures--Part 1."
"Film Style and Technology: 1920-1926."
"Film Style and Technology: 1926-1929."
"Statistical Style Analysis of Motion Pictures--Part 2."
"Film Style and Technology in the Thirties."
"Film Style and Technology in the Forties."
"Film Style and Technology in the Fifties."
"Film Style and Technology in the Sixties."
"The Nineteen-Seventies."
"Stylistic Analysis of the Films of Max Ophuls."
    IN: Film Style and Technology

5153 **Salt, Barry.**
"The Early Development of Film Form."
    IN: Film Before Griffith

5154 **Salt, Barry.**
"Film Form 1900-1906." [NOTE: A variation on the chapter in *Film Style and Technology*.]
    IN: Early Cinema ...

5155 **Salt, Barry.**
"Film Style and Technology in the Thirties: Sound."
    IN: Film Sound

5156 **Salt, Barry.**
"Seeing Is Believing: Special Effects in the Early Years."
    IN: Movies of the Silent Years

5157 **Salt, Barry.**
"Statistical Analysis of Motion Pictures."
    IN: Movies and Methods /v. 2

5158 **Salt, Barry.**
"Sternberg's Heart Beats in Black and White."
    IN: Sternberg

5159 **Salter, James.**
"The Screenwriter."
    IN: Movie People

5160 **Sammon, Paul M.**
"Paul M. Sammon." [Interview by Stanley Wiater.]
    IN: Dark Visions

5161 **Sammon, Paul M.**
"The Salacious Gaze: Sex, the Erotic Trilogy and the Decline of David Lynch." [RE: *Blue Velvet*; *Wild at Heart*; *Twin Peaks* (the pilot).]
    IN: Cut!: Horror Writers ...

5162 **Samson, Jen.**
"The Film Society, 1925-1939." [RE: Great Britain.]
    IN: All Our Yesterdays

5163 **Samuels, Charles Thomas.**
"Carol Reed and the Novelistic Film."
"Jean Renoir and the Theatrical Film."
"Federico Fellini: Juxtaposition."
"Puppets: From Z to *Zabriskie Point*."
"Bresson's Gentleness."
"The Context of *A Clockwork Orange*."
"Hyphens of the Self." [RE: authorship; Hitchcock; Truffaut.]
"How Not to Film a Novel." [RE: *Fat City*; *Deliverance*.]
    IN: Mastering the Film ...

5164 **Samuels, Charles Thomas.**
"Hitchcock."
    IN: Great Film Directors
         Mastering the Film ...

5165 **Samuels, Charles Thomas.**
"Tampering With Reality." [RE: *The Discreet Charm of the Bourgeoisie*; *Cries and Whispers*.]
    IN: The World of Luis Buñuel
         Mastering the Film ...

5166 Samuels, Charles Thomas.
"The Blow-Up: Sorting Things Out." [RE: *Blow-Up*.]
IN: <u>Focus on Blow-Up</u>
<u>A Casebook on Film</u>
<u>Mastering the Film ...</u>

5167 Samuels, Charles Thomas.
"*Bonnie and Clyde*."
IN: <u>Focus on Bonnie and Clyde</u>
<u>A Casebook on Film</u>
<u>Mastering the Film and Other Essays</u>

5168 Samuels, Stuart.
"The Age of Conspiracy and Conformity: *Invasion of the Body Snatchers*."
IN: <u>American History/American Film</u>

5169 Samuels, Stuart.
"The Evolutionary Image of the Jew in American Film."
IN: <u>Ethnic Images ...</u>

5170 Samway, Patrick.
"The Art of the Movie Director."
IN: <u>Screen Experience</u>

5171 Sandburg, Carl.
"*The Cabinet of Dr. Caligari*."
"Says Chaplin Could Play Serious Drama."
IN: <u>Authors on Film</u>

5172 Sander, Helke.
"Feminism and Film."
"Men Are Responsible That Women Become Their Enemies: Tales of Rejection."
IN: <u>West German Filmmakers on Film</u>

5173 Sanders, Roy.
"The Short Film."
IN: <u>Screen Experience</u>

5174 Sanders, Terry.
"The Financing of Independent Feature Films."
IN: <u>Hollywood Directors 1941-1976</u>

5175 Sanders-Brahms, Helma.
"'New German Cinema, *jeune cinema allemand*, Good Night': A Day in Oberhausen, 1982."
"My Critics, My Films, and I."
IN: <u>West German Filmmakers on Film</u>

5176 Sandford, Jeremy.
"*Cathy Come Home*." [Interview by Alan Rosenthal.]
IN: <u>The New Documentary in Action</u>

5177 Sandford, Jeremy.
"*Cathy Come Home* and *Edna, the Inebriate Woman* [Interview with] Jeremy Sandford."
IN: <u>The Documentary Conscience</u>

5178 Sandford, John.
"Alexander Kluge."
"Jean-Marie Straub."
"Volker Schlöndorff."
"Werner Herzog."
"Rainer Werner Fassbinder."
"Wim Wenders."
"Hans Jürgen Syberberg."
IN: <u>The New German Cinema</u>

5179 Sandro, Paul.
"Signification in the Cinema."
IN: <u>Movies and Methods /v. 2</u>

5180 Sanford, Harry.
"Joseph Kane."
"Lesley Selander."
IN: <u>Close Up: The Contract Director</u>

5181 Sanjinés, Jorge.
"Revolutionary Cinema: The Bolivian Experience."
IN: <u>Cinema and Social Change ...</u>

5182 Sanjines, Jorge.
"Language and Popular Culture." [RE: Bolivia.]
IN: <u>Reviewing Histories</u>

5183 Santner, Eric L.
"Postwar / Post-Holocaust / Postmodern: Some Reflections on the Discourses of Mourning."
"Germany and the Tasks of Mourning in the Second and Third Generations."
"Screen Memories Made in Germany: Edgar Reitz's *Heimat* and the Question of Mourning."
"Allegories of Grieving: The Films of Hans Jürgen Syberberg."
IN: <u>Stranded Objects</u>

5183a Santner, Eric L.
"On the Difficulty of Saying 'We': The Historians' Debate and Edgar Reitz's *Heimat*."
IN: <u>Framing the Past</u>

5184 Santos, Nelson Pereira dos.
"Toward a Popular Cinema." [RE: Brazil.]
IN: <u>Cinema and Social Change ...</u>

5185 Sarandon, Susan.
"Susan Sarandon." [Interview by Rex Reed.]
IN: <u>Travolta to Keaton</u>

5185a Sargent, Alvin.
"Alvin Sargent." [Interview by Syd Field.]
IN: <u>Selling a Screenplay</u>

5186 Saroyan, William.
"Boy O Boy O Boy, O Boy."
"Crazy Hollywood."
"How to Be a Writer."
"Or Leave a Kiss Within the Cup."
"So He Died Laughing."
"The End of the World."
IN: <u>The Best of Rob Wagner's Script</u>

5187 Sarris, Andrew.
"Notes on the Auteur Theory in 1962."
IN: <u>Film Theory and Criticism /1 ed</u>
<u>Film Theory and Criticism /2 ed</u>
<u>Film Theory and Criticism /3 ed</u>
<u>Film Theory and Criticism /4 ed</u>
<u>Film Culture Reader</u>
<u>Perspectives on the Study of Film</u>
<u>Theories of Authorship</u>
<u>Film And/As Literature</u>

5188 **Sarris, Andrew.**
"Toward a Theory of Film History [Introduction to *The American Cinema*]."
IN: Awake in the Dark
Movies and Methods: An Anthology

5189 **Sarris, Andrew.**
"The Auteur Theory." [NOTE: An abridged version of "Toward a Theory of Film History."]
IN: Crossroads to the Cinema

5190 **Sarris, Andrew.**
"*Cabiria*."
"*The Seventh Seal*."
"*The Blue Angel* and *Morocco*."
"*Viridiana* and *Belle de Jour*."
IN: Great Film Directors

5191 **Sarris, Andrew.**
"*Citizen Kane*: The American Baroque."
IN: Focus on Citizen Kane
Film Culture Reader
Renaissance of the Film
Great Film Directors

5192 **Sarris, Andrew.**
"*Dr. Strangelove*."
"*The Graduate*."
"*The Producers*."
"Ernst Lubitsch."
"For Mel." [RE: Mel Brooks.]
"Hawksian Comedy."
"Preston Sturges."
"The Marx Brothers."
IN: Movie Comedy

5193 **Sarris, Andrew.**
"No Antoniennui." [RE: Michelangelo Antonioni.]
IN: Focus on Blow-Up
Great Film Directors
The Film

5194 **Sarris, Andrew.**
"*State of Siege*."
"John Ford: *The Grapes of Wrath*."
IN: Awake in the Dark

5195 **Sarris, Andrew.**
"*The Seventh Seal*."
IN: Focus on The Seventh Seal

5196 **Sarris, Andrew.**
"*The Birth of a Nation*, or White Power Back When."
IN: Focus on The Birth of a Nation

5197 **Sarris, Andrew.**
"A Movie Is a Movie Is a Movie Is a." [RE: Jean-Luc Godard.]
IN: The Emergence of Film Art /1 ed
The Emergence of Film Art /2 ed

5198 **Sarris, Andrew.**
"Actors vs. Directors: The Actor as Auteur."
"Humphrey Bogart."
"James Stewart."
"Jean-Paul Belmondo."
"Jean Gabin."
IN: The Movie Star: The National ...

5199 **Sarris, Andrew.**
"Beatitudes of B Pictures."
IN: Kings of the Bs

5200 **Sarris, Andrew.**
"Charles Chaplin."
"Ernst Lubitsch: American Period."
"Frank Borzage."
"John M. Stahl."
"Robert Aldrich."
"William Wyler."
IN: Cinema: A Critical Dictionary

5201 **Sarris, Andrew.**
"Confessions of a middle class film critic ..."
IN: The Cineaste Interviews

5202 **Sarris, Andrew.**
"Film Criticism from Blurbs to Belle Lettres."
IN: The Film

5203 **Sarris, Andrew.**
"Hitchcock."
IN: Focus on Hitchcock

5204 **Sarris, Andrew.**
"Illusions and Independents."
IN: Sight, Sound, and Society

5205 **Sarris, Andrew.**
"Preston Sturges."
IN: The Hollywood Screenwriters

5206 **Sarris, Andrew.**
"The Devil and the Nun: *Viridiana*."
IN: Renaissance of the Film

5207 **Sarris, Andrew.**
"The Fall and Rise of the Film Director."
IN: A Casebook on Film

5208 **Sarris, Andrew.**
"The Independent Cinema."
IN: The New American Cinema

5209 **Sarris, Andrew.**
"The Beauty of *Belle de Jour*."
IN: The World of Luis Buñuel
The Classic Cinema

5210 **Sarris, Andrew.**
"The World of Howard Hawks."
IN: Focus on Howard Hawks

5211 **Sarris, Andrew.**
"The Critic."
IN: Movie People

5212 **Sarris, Andrew.**
"The Ladies' Auxiliary, 1976."
IN: Women and the Cinema

5213 **Sarris, Andrew.**
"The Underground Film."
IN: The Image Maker

5214 Sarris, Andrew.
"The Future of Film."
IN: <u>Film: Readings in the Mass Media</u>

5215 Sarris, Andrew.
"*Stagecoach* in 1939 and in Retrospect."
IN: <u>Directors in Action</u>

5216 Sarris, Andrew.
"*The Searchers*."
IN: <u>Theories of Authorship</u>

5217 Sartre, Jean-Paul.
"Childhood Memories."
IN: <u>Authors on Film</u>

5218 Sathe, Vasant.
"Vasant Sathe." [Interview.]
IN: <u>Indian Cinema Superbazaar</u>

5219 Sato, Tadao.
"*Rashomon*."
IN: <u>Focus on Rashomon</u>

5219a Saunders, Thomas J.
"History in the Making: Weimar Cinema and National
    Identity."
IN: <u>Framing the Past</u>

5220 Sauvage, Pierre.
"Andrew L. Stone."
"David Butler."
"Edmund Goulding."
"George Marshall."
"Jack Conway."
"Lloyd Bacon."
"Norman Z. McLeod."
"Roy Del Ruth."
"Sam Wood."
"Victor Fleming."
    IN: <u>American Directors /v. 1</u>

5221 Sauvage, Pierre.
"Curtis Harrington."
"Joshua Logan."
"Ralph Nelson."
    IN: <u>American Directors /v. 2</u>

5222 Savada, Elias.
"Waldemar Young."
IN: <u>Dictionary of Literary Biography /v. 26</u>

5223 Savini, Tom.
"Tom Savini." [Interview by Stanley Wiater.]
IN: <u>Dark Visions</u>

5224 Saxton, Christine.
"The Collective Voice as Cultural Voice."
IN: <u>Imitations of Life</u>

5225 Sayer, Sally and Laleen Jayamanne.
"*Burning an Illusion*."
IN: <u>Films for Women</u>

5226 Sayers, Valerie.
"*Gone with the Wind*."
IN: <u>The Movie That Changed My Life</u>

5227 Sayles, John.
"Counterculture revisited ..."
IN: <u>The Cineaste Interviews</u>

5228 Sayles, John.
"*Battle Beyond the Stars*: Notes from a Tacky Galaxy."
IN: <u>Omni's Screen Flights ...</u>

5229 Sayre, Nora.
"Winning the Weepstakes: The Problems of American
    Sports Movies."
IN: <u>Film Genre</u>

5230 Schackel, Sandra Kay.
"Women in Western Films: The Civilizer, the Saloon
    Singer, and Their Modern Sister."
IN: <u>Shooting Stars</u>

5231 Schallert, Edwin.
"The Principles of Criticism."
IN: <u>Introduction to the Photoplay</u>

5232 Schary, Dore.
"Dore Schary: The Executive."
IN: <u>The Real Tinsel</u>

5233 Schary, Dore.
"Nigger: Saying Good-By [*sic*, -Bye]."
IN: <u>The Best of Rob Wagner's Script</u>

5234 Schary, Dore.
"Our Movie Mythology."
IN: <u>Crossroads to the Cinema</u>

5235 Schatz, Thomas.
"The Genius of the System."
"Film Genres and the Genre Film."
"The Western."
"The Gangster Film."
"The Hardboiled-Detective Film."
"The Screwball Comedy."
"The Musical."
IN: <u>Hollywood Genres</u>

5236 Schatz, Thomas.
"[From:] *The Genius of the System*: The Whole
    Equation of Pictures."
IN: <u>Film Theory and Criticism /4 ed</u>

5237 Schatz, Thomas G.
"New Directions in Film Genre Study (A Response to
    Charles F. Altman)."
IN: <u>Film: Historical-Theoretical ...</u>

5238 Schatz, Thomas.
"The Western."
IN: <u>Handbook of American Film Genres</u>

5239 Schatz, Thomas.
"The Structural Influence: New Directions in Film
    Genre."
IN: <u>Film Genre Reader</u>

5240 Schatz, Thomas.
"The Family Melodrama."
    IN: <u>Imitations of Life</u>
        <u>Hollywood Genres</u>

5241 **Scheffauer, Herman G.**
"The Vivifying of Space."
IN: Introduction to the Art of the Movies

5242 **Scheib, Ronnie.**
"Ida Lupino."
IN: American Directors /v. 2

5243 **Scheib, Ronnie.**
"Tex Arcana: The Cartoons of Tex Avery."
IN: The American Animated Cartoon

5244 **Scheib-Rothbart, Ingrid and Ruth McCormick.**
"Edgar Reitz: Liberating Humanity and Film."
IN: New German Filmmakers

5245 **Schein, Harry.**
"Bergman the Poet." [RE: Ingmar Bergman.]
IN: Focus on The Seventh Seal

5246 **Scheuer, Philip K.**
"Henry Hathaway."
IN: Directors in Action

5247 **Scheurer, Timothy E.**
"The Aesthetics of Form and Convention in the Movie Musical."
IN: Movies as Artifacts
Film Genre

5248 **Schickel, Richard.**
"Charles Chaplin."
"John Ford."
"Preston Sturges."
"Alfred Hitchcock."
"Stanley Kubrick."
"The Hollywood Ten."
"Ronald Reagan."
"Douglas Fairbanks, Sr."
"Harold Lloyd."
"Gary Cooper."
"James Cagney."
"Humphrey Bogart."
"Marlon Brando."
"Woody Allen."
IN: Schickel on Film

5249 **Schickel, Richard.**
"*Divorce American Style*."
"*Bob & Carol & Ted & Alice*."
"*Closely Watched Trains*."
"Mack Sennett."
"Harold Lloyd."
"A Chaplin Overview."
"The Marx Brothers."
"Ernst Lubitsch."
"*Lonesome Cowboys*."
"*Blazing Saddles*."
"*What's New Pussycat?*."
"*Alfie*."
IN: Movie Comedy

5250 **Schickel, Richard.**
"*Handle with Care*."

"*Go Tell the Spartans*."
"*Smash Palace*."
"*The Man with Two Brains*."
"*The Ballad of Cable Hogue*."
IN: Produced and Abandoned

5251 **Schickel, Richard.**
"John Barrymore."
"Gary Cooper."
"Douglas Fairbanks."
"Jean Harlow."
"Bob Hope."
"Elizabeth Taylor."
"Rudolph Valentino."
"Stars vs. Celebrities: The Deterioration of the Star System."
IN: The Movie Star: The National ...

5252 **Schickel, Richard.**
"The Futuristic Films of Stanley Kubrick."
IN: Omni's Screen Flights ...

5253 **Schickel, Richard.**
"Why Indians Can't Be Villains Any More."
IN: The Pretend Indians

5254 **Schickel, Richard.**
"Sorriest Spectacle--*The Titicut Follies*."
IN: The Documentary Tradition /1 ed
The Documentary Tradition /2 ed

5255 **Schickel, Richard.**
"Almost Purely Emotional." [RE: WWI.]
IN: The Movies: An American Idiom

5256 **Schickel, Richard.**
"*Way Down East*: Finances and Responses."
IN: The First Film Makers

5257 **Schickel, Richard.**
"The Movies Are Now High Art."
"The Future of Film."
IN: Film: Readings in the Mass Media

5258 **Schickel, Richard.**
"*Bonnie and Clyde*."
IN: Focus on Bonnie and Clyde

5259 **Schickel, Richard.**
"The Stars."
IN: Crossroads to the Cinema

5260 **Schiff, Stephen.**
"*Diner*."
"*The Chant of Jimmie Blacksmith*."
"*Best Boy*."
"*The Brood*."
"*By Design*."
IN: Produced and Abandoned

5261 **Schildt, Jurgen.**
"*The Seventh Seal*."
IN: Focus on The Seventh Seal

5262 **Schillaci, Anthony.**
"Film as Environment."

IN: Perspectives on the Study of Film
   Films Deliver
   Film: Readings in the Mass Media
   Crossroads to the Cinema
   Film and Literature

5263 Schillaci, Anthony.
"The Language of Images."
   IN: Films Deliver

5264 Schillaci, Anthony.
"Bergman's Vision of Good and Evil."
   IN: Celluloid and Symbol

Schillaci, Anthony. SEE: Sohn, David.

5265 Schillaci, Peter P.
"Luis Bunuel and the Death of God."
   IN: Three European Directors

5266 Schillaci, Peter.
"Film Is Environment."
   IN: The Image Maker

5267 Schilling, Niklaus.
"Cinema, Melodrama, and the World of Emotion."
   IN: West German Filmmakers on Film

5268 Schlesinger, Arthur, Jr.
"The Fiction of Fact—and the Fact of Fiction." [RE:
   The Face of War.]
      IN: The Documentary Tradition /1 ed
         The Documentary Tradition /2 ed

5269 Schlesinger, Arthur, Jr.
"When the Movies Really Counted."
   IN: The Movies in Our Midst

5270 Schlesinger, Arthur, Jr.
"How Drastically Has Television Changed Our
   Politics?"
   IN: Sight, Sound, and Society

5271 Schlesinger, John.
"John Schlesinger." [Interview by Rex Reed.]
   IN: Travolta to Keaton

5272 Schlesinger, Philip.
"Scotland, Europe and Identity."
   IN: From Limelight to Satellite

5273 Schlöndorff, Volker.
"A Dream."
"Zimmermann's Execution Directives."
"Rereading Kracauer's *From Caligari to Hitler.*"
"David Bennent and Oskar Mazerath."
   IN: West German Filmmakers on Film

5274 Schlossheimer, Michael.
"The Independent Studios."
"RKO Radio Pictures."
"Columbia Pictures."
"Universal Pictures."
"Warner Brothers Pictures."
"Metro-Goldwyn-Mayer Pictures."
"Twentieth-Century-Fox Pictures."
"Paramount Pictures."

"The Unknown Quantities."
   IN: The Films You Don't See ...

5275 Schlüpmann, Heide.
"The First German Art Film: Rye's *The Student of
   Prague.*"
   IN: German Film and Literature

5276 Schlüpmann, Heide.
"The Brothel as an Arcadian Space? *Diary of a Lost
   Girl.*"
   IN: The Films of G.W. Pabst

Schlöndorff, Volker. SEE: Brustellin, Alf.

5277 Schmidt, Arthur.
"Arthur Schmidt." [Interview by Vincent LoBrutto.]
   IN: Selected Takes

5278 Schmidt, Eckhart.
"'... Preferably Naked Girls'."
   IN: West German Filmmakers on Film

5279 Schmidt, Jan.
"Jan Schmidt." [Interview by Antonín J. Liehm.]
   IN: Closely Watched Films

5280 Schneble, Sylvie and Tristine Rainer.
"Financing and Foreign Distribution."
   IN: The Movie Business Book

5281 Schneemann, Carolee.
"Kenneth Anger's *Scorpio Rising.*"
   IN: Film Culture Reader

5282 Schneemann, Carolee.
"Carolee Schneemann." [Interview by Scott
   MacDonald.]
   IN: A Critical Cinema

5283 Schneider, Irving.
"The Shows of Violence."
   IN: Images in Our Souls

5284 Schoedsack, Ernest B.
"Warriors of the Desert."
   IN: Hollywood Directors 1914-1940

5285 Schoenecke, Michael K.
"William S. Hart: Authenticity and the West."
   IN: Shooting Stars

5286 Scholar, Nancy.
"*Maedchen in Uniform.*"
   IN: Sexual Stratagems

5287 Scholes, Robert.
"Narration and Narrativity in Film."
      IN: Film Theory and Criticism /2 ed
         Film Theory and Criticism /3 ed

5288 Schorm, Evald.
"Evald Schorm." [Interview by Antonín J. Liehm.]
   IN: Closely Watched Films

5289 Schrader, Paul.
"Paul Schrader." [Interviewed by John Brady.]
   IN: The Craft of the Screenwriter

5290 **Schrader, Paul.**
"Blue Collar."
IN: The Cineaste Interviews

5291 **Schrader, Paul.**
"Notes on *Film Noir*."
IN: Awake in the Dark
Film Genre Reader

5292 **Schrader, Paul.**
"Ozu."
"Bresson."
"Dreyer."
IN: Transcendental Style in Film

5293 **Schrader, Paul.**
"Paul Schrader." [Interview by Charles Higham.]
IN: Celebrity Circus

5294 **Schramm, Wilbur.**
"What TV Is Doing to Our Children."
IN: Sight, Sound, and Society

5295 **Schreger, Charles.**
"Altman, Dolby, and The Second Sound Revolution."
IN: Film Sound

5296 **Schulberg, Budd.**
"The screen playwright as author ..."
IN: The Cineaste Interviews

5297 **Schulman, Grace.**
"*Beauty and the Beast*."
IN: The Movie That Changed My Life

5298 **Schulte-Sasse, Linda.**
"Film Criticism in the Weimar Press."
IN: Film and Politics in the Weimar Republic

5298a **Schulte-Sasse, Linda.**
"Leni Riefenstahl's Feature Films and the Question of a Fascist Aesthetic."
IN: Framing the Past

5299 **Schultheiss, John.**
"The 'Eastern' Writer in Hollywood."
IN: Cinema Examined

5300 **Schulze, Laurie.**
"On the Muscle."
IN: Fabrications

5301 **Schulze, Laurie.**
"The Made-for-TV Movie: Industrial Practice, Cultural Form, Popular Reception."
IN: Hollywood in the Age of Television

5302 **Schumach, Murray.**
"The Hollywood Blacklist and the Hollywood Underground."
IN: The Movies: An American Idiom

5303 **Schuth, H. Wayne.**
"Jules Feiffer."
IN: Dictionary of Literary Biography /v. 44

5304 **Schuth, H. Wayne.**
"The Image of New Orleans on Film."
IN: The South and Film

5305 **Schuth, H. Wayne.**
"*Hiroshima, Mon Amour*."
IN: Nuclear War Films

5306 **Schutte, Wolfram.**
"Franz, Mieze, Reinhold, Death and the Devil: Rainer Werner Fassbinder's *Berlin Alexanderplatz*."
IN: Fassbinder

5307 **Schuursma, Rolf.**
"The Historian as Film-maker I."
IN: The Historian and Film

5308 **Schwartz, Nancy L.**
"*Alice Adams* [novel by] Booth Tarkington. From American Tragedy to Small-Town Dream-Come-True."
IN: The Classic American Novel ...

5309 **Schwartz, Ronald.**
"Alvaro del Amo."
"Jaime de Arminán."
"Juan Antonio Bardem."
"Luis García Berlanga."
"José Luis Borau."
"Jaime Camino."
"Fernando Colomo."
"Jaime Chavarrí."
"Antonio Drove."
"Victor Erice."
"Jose Luis Garci."
"Antonio Giménez-Rico."
"Manuel Gutiérrez Aragón."
"Pilar Miró."
"Pedro Olea."
"Basilio Martín Patino."
"Miguel Picazo."
"Antoni Ribas."
"Carlos Saura."
"Fernando Trueba."
"Iván Zulueta."
IN: Spanish Film Directors

5310 **Schwarz, Roberto.**
"Cinema and *The Guns*."
IN: Brazilian Cinema

5311 **Schwichtenberg, Cathy.**
"A Case Study of Film Antitrust Legislation: *R.D. Goldberg v. Tri-States Theatre Corporation*."
IN: Current Research in Film /v. 2

5312 **Scorsese, Martin.**
"Confessions of a Movie Brat."
IN: Anatomy of the Movies

5313 **Scot, Darrin.**
"Filming *The Time Machine*."
IN: Focus on The Science Fiction Film

5314 **Scott, Allan.**
"Allan Scott: A Nice Life." [Interview by Pat McGilligan.]
IN: Backstory

5315 Scott, Allan.
"Allan Scott." [Interview by Lee Server.]
IN: Screenwriter: Words Become Pictures

5316 Scott, E. Kilburn.
"Career of L.A.A. LePrince."
IN: A Technological History ...

5317 Scott, James F.
"*Blow-Up*: Antonioni and the Mod World."
IN: Focus on Blow-Up
A Casebook on Film

5318 Scott, James F.
"Film as an Academic Subject: Reservations and Reminders."
IN: The Compleat Guide to Film Study

5319 Scott, James F.
"Ingmar Bergman in the 1950s."
IN: Great Film Directors
Focus on The Seventh Seal

5320 Scott, James F.
"New Terms for Order: Network Style and Individual Experiment in American Documentary Film."
IN: Ideas of Order in Literature & Film

5321 Scott, Nathan A., Jr.
"The New Mystique of *L'Actuelle*: A View of Cinema in Its Relation to Our Period-Style."
IN: Man and the Movies

5322 Scullion, Adrienne Clare.
"Screening the Heyday: Scottish Cinema in the 1930s."
IN: From Limelight to Satellite

5323 Seaton, George.
"'Yes, But Not As Hard As Playing Comedy.' Then He Died—" [RE: an interview.]
IN: Blueprint on Babylon

5324 Seaton, George.
"One Track Mind on a Two Way Ticket."
IN: Hollywood Directors 1941-1976

5325 Seguin, Louis.
"*Viridiana* and the Critics."
"In Three Points ..." [RE: *Nazarin*.]
IN: The World of Luis Buñuel

5326 Seidelman, Susan.
"Susan Seidelman." [Interview by John Andrew Gallagher.]
IN: Film Directors on Directing

5327 Seidman, Barbara.
"'The Lady Doth Protest Too Much, Methinks': Jane Fonda, Feminism, and Hollywood."
IN: Women and Film

5328 Seigel, Gary.
"*Rabbit, Run* [novel by] John Updike. Rabbit Runs Down."
IN: The Modern American Novel ...

5329 Seiter, Ellen E.
"*Island of the Blue Dolphins* [novel by] Scott O'Dell. Survival Tale and Feminist Parable."
IN: Children's Novels and the Movies

5330 Seiter, Ellen.
"Men, Sex, and Money in Recent Family Melodrama." [RE: television.]
IN: Imitations of Life

5331 Seiter, Ellen.
"The Political is Personal: Margarethe von Trotta's *Marianne and Juliane*."
IN: Films for Women

Seiter, Ellen. SEE: Citron, Michelle.

5332 Seiter, Richard D.
"*Charlie and the Chocolate Factory* [novel by] Roald Dahl. The Bittersweet Journey from *Charlie* to *Willy Wonka*."
IN: Children's Novels and the Movies

Selby, Keith. SEE: Giddings, Robert.

5333 Seldes, Gilbert.
"An Early, Detailed Account of the Action in *The Pawnshop*."
IN: Focus on Chaplin

5334 Seldes, Gilbert.
"Disney and Others."
IN: Introduction to the Art of the Movies

5335 Seldes, Gilbert.
"Media Managers, Critics, and Audiences."
IN: Sight, Sound, and Society

5336 Seldes, Gilbert.
"Pare Lorentz's *The River*."
IN: The Documentary Tradition /1 ed
The Documentary Tradition /2 ed

5337 Seldes, Gilbert.
"S-e-x."
IN: Film: An Anthology

5338 Seldes, Gilbert.
"The Lovely Art: Magic."
IN: Film Theory and Criticism /1 ed
Film Theory and Criticism /2 ed

5339 Seldes, Gilbert.
"The Keystone the Builders Rejected."
IN: Awake in the Dark

5340 Seldes, Gilbert.
"The Movies in Peril."
"Talkies' Progress."
IN: The Movies in Our Midst

5341 Seldes, Gilbert.
"[From:] The Lovely Art: Sound."
IN: Film and Society

5342 Self, Robert T.
"Ritual Patterns in Western Film and Fiction."
IN: Narrative Strategies

5343 **Self, Robert T.**
"The Sounds of *M*A*S*H*."
IN: Close Viewings

5344 **Selig, Michael.**
"Boys Will Be Men: Oedipal Drama in *Coming Home*."
IN: From Hanoi to Hollywood

5345 **Selznick, Joyce.**
"The Casting Director."
IN: Filmmakers on Filmmaking /v. 2

5346 **Sembene, Ousmane.**
"Filmmakers have a great responsibility to our people ..."
IN: The Cineaste Interviews

5347 **Semple, Lorenzo, Jr.**
"A Screenwriter on Screenwriting."
IN: Anatomy of the Movies

5348 **Semprun, Jorge.**
"The truth is always revolutionary ..."
IN: The Cineaste Interviews

5349 **Semsel, George S.**
"China."
IN: The Asian Film Industry

5350 **Semsel, George S.**
"The End of an Era."
IN: Chinese Film

Seneca, Gail. SEE: Arbuthnot, Lucie.

5351 **Sennett, Max [*sic*, Mack].**
"How to Throw a Pie."
IN: Bedside Hollywood
Film Makers on Film Making

5352 **Sennett, Mack.**
"Cloud-Cuckoo Country."
IN: Film: A Montage of Theories

5353 **Sennett, Mack.**
"King of Comedy [excerpt]."
IN: Film: Readings in the Mass Media

5354 **Sennett, Mack.**
"The Psychology of Film Comedy."
IN: Hollywood Directors 1914-1940

5355 **Sennwald, Andre.**
"The Future of Color." [RE: *Becky Sharp*.]
IN: Introduction to the Art of the Movies

5356 **Serceau, Daniel.**
"Mizoguchi's Oppressed Women."
IN: Sexual Stratagems

5357 **Serceau, Daniel.**
"The Communist Party and *La Vie est à nous*: Documentary and Fiction, Poetics and Politics."
IN: Show Us Life

5358 **Sersen, Fred M.**
"Making Matte Shots."
IN: The ASC Treasury ...

5359 **Seton, Marie.**
"Basil Wright's *Song of Ceylon*."
"*Three Songs About Lenin*."
IN: The Documentary Tradition /1 ed
The Documentary Tradition /2 ed

5360 **Seubert, Emelia.**
"Native American Media in the United States: An Overview."
IN: Film and Politics in the Third World

5360a **Severson, Anne.**
"Anne Severson (on *Near the Big Chakra*)."
IN: A Critical Cinema 2

5361 **Sganzerla, Rogério.**
"Everybody's Woman."
IN: Brazilian Cinema

5362 **Shadoian, Jack.**
"The Golden Age: The 'Classic' Gangster Film (*Little Caesar* and *The Public Enemy*)."
"Dark Transformations: The Descent into Noir (*High Sierra* and *The Killers*)."
"The Genre's 'Enlightenment': The Stress and Strain for Affirmation (*Kiss of Death*; *Force of Evil* and *Gun Crazy*)."
"Going Gray and Going Crazy: Disequilibrium and Change at Midcentury (*D.O.A.* and *White Heat*)."
"Focus on Feeling: 'Seeing' Through the Fifties (*Pickup on South Street*; *99 River Street*; *The Phenix City Story*; *The Brothers Rico* and *Kiss Me Deadly*)."
"Contemporary Colorations: The Modernist Perspective (*Bonnie and Clyde*; *Point Blank*; *The Godfather*; *Godfather II* and After)."
IN: Dreams and Dead Ends

5362a **Shagan, Steve.**
"Steve Shagan." [Interview by Anthony Loeb.]
IN: Filmmakers in Conversation

5363 **Shahani, Kumar.**
"Kumar Shahani." [Interview.]
"Politics and Ideology: The Foundation of Bazaar Realism."
IN: Indian Cinema Superbazaar

5364 **Shaheen, Jack G.**
"*Panic in Year Zero*."
"*A Thousand Cranes: Children of Hiroshima*."
"*The War Game*."
"*Only the Strong*."
IN: Nuclear War Films

5365 **Shaheen, Jack G.**
"Perspectives on the Television Arab."
IN: Image Ethics

5366 **Shaheen, Jack G. and Richard Taylor.**
"*The Beginning of the End*."
"*Footnotes on the Atomic Age*."
IN: Nuclear War Films

Shaheen, Jack G. SEE: Hall, James; SEE: Elliot, Ramsey.

5367 **Shale, Richard.**
"Film and the Graphic Arts."
    IN: Film and the Arts in Symbiosis

5368 **Shales, Tom.**
"*Only Angels Have Wings.*"
"Antecedents of *Citizen Kane.*"
"Frank Capra."
"W.C. Fields."
"Warners Musicals—Busby and Beyond."
"*Broadway.*"
"*High Sierra.*"
"*Miss Lulu Bett.*"
"*The Mystery of the Wax Museum.*"
"*The Vanishing American.*"
"*The Emperor Jones.*"
"*The Last Flight.*"
    IN: The American Film Heritage

5369 **Shamberg, Michael and David Cort.**
"Michael Shamberg and David Cort." [Interview by G. Roy Levin.]
    IN: Documentary Explorations

5370 **Shamroy, Leon.**
"Leon Shamroy." [Interviews by Charles Higham.]
    IN: Hollywood Cameramen

5371 **Shand, John and Tony Wellington (editors).**
"Blank Page to Blueprint - The Writer."
"From Conception to Release - The Producer."
"Holding the Fort - The Production Manager."
"Efficiency Expert - The First Assistant Director."
"Art for Film's Sake - The Production Designer and the Art Director."
"The Director's Eyes - The Director of Photography."
"All Ears - The Sound Recordist."
"Cutting Remarks - The Continuity Person."
"Celluloid Sculptor - The Editor."
"Aural Architects - The Sound Editor and the Mixer."
"Of Vampires and Butterflies - The Director."
    IN: Don't Shoot the Best Boy!

5372 **Shantaram, V.**
"V. Shantaram." [Interview.]
    IN: Indian Cinema Superbazaar

5373 **Shao Mujun.**
"Chinese Films Amidst the Tide of Reform."
    IN: Cinema and Cultural Identity

5374 **Shao Mujun.**
"Summary of Casual Thinking on Film Aesthetics, Part IV."
"The Road of Innovation in Chinese Cinema."
    IN: Chinese Film Theory

5375 **Shapiro, Burton J.**
"Frank Borzage."
    IN: The American Film Heritage

Shapiro, Burton J. SEE: Parker, David L.

5376 **Shapiro, Mitchell E. and Thompson Biggers.**
"Emotion-Eliciting Qualities in the Motion Picture Viewing Situation and Audience Evaluations."
    IN: Current Research in Film /v. 3

Shapiro, Mitchell E. SEE: Williams, Wenmouth, Jr.

5377 **Sharff, Stefan.**
"*Notorious.*"
"*Family Plot.*"
"*Frenzy.*"
    IN: Alfred Hitchcock's High Vernacular

5378 **Sharif, Omar.**
"The Eternal Male."
    IN: Bedside Hollywood

5379 **Sharits, Paul.**
"[From:] 'Words Per Page'."
"Hearing:Seeing."
    IN: The Avant-Garde Film

5380 **Sharits, Paul.**
"A Cinematics Model for Film Studies in Higher Education: Center for Media Study/State University of New York at Buffalo."
    IN: Film Study in the Undergraduate Curriculum

5381 **Sharits, Paul and Peter Gidal.**
"[On] Paul Sharits."
    IN: Structural Film Anthology

5382 **Sharp, Roberta.**
"Richard Matheson."
    IN: Dictionary of Literary Biography /v. 44

5383 **Sharrett, Christopher.**
"The Idea of Apocalypse in *The Texas Chainsaw Massacre.*"
    IN: Planks of Reason

5384 **Shatnoff, Judith.**
"François Truffaut—The Anarchist Imagination."
    IN: Focus on Shoot the Piano Player

5385 **Shatzkin, Roger.**
"*The Big Sleep* [novel by] Raymond Chandler. Who Cares Who Killed Owen Taylor?"
    IN: The Modern American Novel ...

5386 **Shatzkin, Roger.**
"Disaster Epics: Cashing in on Vicarious Experience."
    IN: Film in Society

5387 **Shavelson, Melville.**
"'Slow Up, We Haven't Written The Next Scene!'--" [RE: an interview.]
    IN: Blueprint on Babylon

5388 **Shaw, G. Bernard.**
"On Cinema."
    IN: Authors on Film

5389 **Shaw, George Bernard.**
"[From:] The Cinema as a Moral Leveller."
    IN: Film and Society

5390 Shaw, Wini.
"Wini Shaw: The Player."
IN: The Real Tinsel

5391 Shearer, Douglas.
"Douglas Shearer: The Sound Director."
IN: The Real Tinsel

5392 Shearer, Douglas.
"Sound."
IN: Behind the Screen

5393 Sheckley, Robert.
"*The Seventh Victim* and *The 10th Victim*."
IN: Omni's Screen Flights ...

5394 Sheed, Wilfrid.
"The Future of Film."
IN: Film: Readings in the Mass Media

5395 Sheehan, Henry.
"*Near Dark*."
IN: Produced and Abandoned

5396 Sheldon, Caroline.
"Lesbians and Film: Some Thoughts."
IN: Gays and Film
Gays and Film /rev ed

5397 Sheldon, Sidney.
"A Universal Mind, And That Universal Mind Is All
Creativity--" [RE: an interview.]
IN: Blueprint on Babylon

5398 Shepard, David.
"Authenticating Films."
IN: Wonderful Inventions

5399 Shepard, David.
"Thomas Ince."
IN: The American Film Heritage

5400 Sheratsky, Rodney E.
"Freaking Around with Film."
IN: The Compleat Guide to Film Study

5401 Sheridan, Ann.
"Ann Sheridan." [Interview by John Kobal.]
IN: People Will Talk

Sherman, Barry L. SEE: Knapp, Steven.

5402 Sherman, Eric (compiler).
"[*Collected comments by:*] Perry Miller Adato, Robert
Aldrich, Robert Altman, Hal Ashby, Richard
Attenborough, Laslo Benedek, Pandro S. Berman,
Bernardo Bertolucci, Budd Boetticher, Peter
Bogdanovich, Sergei Bondarchuk, Frank Borzage,
Stan Brakhage, James Bridges, Frank Capra, John
Cassavetes, Charles Chaplin, Shirley Clarke,
Merian C. Cooper, Roger Corman, Costa-Gavras,
George Cukor, Jacques Demy, Brian De Palma,
Allan Dwan, Ed Emshwiller, Federico Fellini, John
Ford, Milos Forman, William Friedkin, Samuel
Fuller, D.W. Griffith, Curtis Harrington, Howard
Hawks, Alfred Hitchcock, John Huston, Peter
Hyams, Jan Kadar, Buster Keaton, Irvin Kershner,
Stanley Kramer, Steve Krantz, Stanley Kubrick,
Buzz Kulik, Fritz Lang, Richard Leacock, Barbara
Loden, Louis Malle, Rouben Mamoulian, Paul
Mazursky, Leo McCarey, Vincente Minnelli, Paul
Morrissey, Ronald Neame, Ralph Nelson, Jack
Nicholson, George Pal, Arthur Penn, Roman
Polanski, Abraham Polonsky, Nicholas Ray, Carl
Reiner, Jean Renoir, Tamás Rēnyi, Martin Ritt,
Roberto Rossellini, Franklin Schaffner, John
Schlesinger, George Seaton, Vincent Sherman,
Douglas Sirk, Vilgot Sjöman, Steven Spielberg,
Josef von Sternberg, George Stevens, Erich von
Stroheim, Bob Taylor, King Vidor, Raoul Walsh,
Andy Warhol, Jiri Weiss, Orson Welles, Haskell
Wexler, Crane Wilbur, Oscar Williams, Paul
Williams, Michael Winner, Fred Zinnemann."
IN: Directing the Film: Film Directors on Their Art

5403 Sherman, Eric.
"Abraham Polonsky."
"Joseph L. Mankiewicz."
IN: American Directors /v. 2

5404 Sherman, Eric.
"King Vidor."
IN: American Directors /v. 1

5405 Sherman, Sam.
"Independent-International Pictures."
IN: The New Poverty Row

5406 Sherman, Vincent.
"Vincent Sherman." [Interview by John Kobal.]
IN: People Will Talk

5406a Sherman, William David.
"Antonioni in the Psychedelic Sixties."
"Godard's Homeric Cinema/Lester's Anarchic
Cinema." [RE: Jean-Luc Godard; Richard Lester.]
"Orson Welles, Are You Listening?"
"Wood/Weld." [RE: Natalie Wood; Tuesday Weld.]
"Jerry Lewis: A Dissent."
"Huck Finn in the Whorehouse."
"Hitchcock's Fiftieth."
"*The Cincinnati Kid*."
"The Morphology of Morgan Delt."
"*The Collector*."
"Otto's Lost Bunny."
"*Repulsion*."
"One-Dimensional Cinema."
"Instant London."
"Felix Greene Goes on Holiday."
"The Proprioceptive Critic."
IN: Landscapes of Contemporary Cinema

Sherman, William David. SEE: Lewis, Leon.

5407 Sherwood, Richard (prepared by).
"Documents from *Lef*."
IN: Screen Reader 1

5408 Sherwood, Robert E.
"*The Pilgrim*."
IN: Focus on Chaplin

5409 **Sherwood, Robert E.**
"With All Due Respect to Mr. Huxley." [SEE: Aldous
     Huxley, "Silence Is Golden".]
"*Don Juan* and the Vitaphone."
     IN: The Movies in Our Midst

5410 **Sherwood, Robert.**
"Robert Flaherty's *Nanook of the North*."
     IN: The Documentary Tradition /1 ed
         The Documentary Tradition /2 ed

5411 **Shields, Winifred.**
"The Orpheum Goes--And Memories Hold the Light in
     Center Stage."
     IN: The Movies: An American Idiom

5412 **Shindo, Kaneto.**
"Kaneto Shindo." [Interview by Joan Mellen.]
     IN: Voices from the Japanese Cinema

5413 **Shinoda, Masahiro.**
"Masahiro Shinoda." [Interview by Joan Mellen.]
     IN: Voices from the Japanese Cinema

5414 **Shirley, Wayne D.**
"'A Bugle Call to Arms for National Defense!': Victor
     Herbert and His Score for *The Fall of a Nation*."
     IN: Wonderful Inventions

5415 **Shivas, Mark.**
"*Gentlemen Prefer Blondes*."
     IN: Movie Reader

Shklovsky, E. SEE: Brik, O.; SEE: Tretyakov, S.

5416 **Shklovsky, V.**
"Poetry and Prose in the Cinema."
     IN: The Poetics of Cinema
         The Film Factory

5417 **Shklovsky, Viktor.**
"The Semantics of Cinema."
"The Soviet School of Acting."
"Beware of Music."
"Literature and Cinema (extracts)."
"Where is Dziga Vertov Striding?"
"The Cine-Eyes and Intertitles."
"Sergei Eisenstein and 'Non-Played' Film."
"The Temperature of Cinema."
"The Film Factory (extracts)."
"Mistakes and Inventions."
"The Script Laboratory."
"Sound as a Semantic Sign."
"The Film Language of *New Babylon*."
     IN: The Film Factory

5418 **Shohat, Ella.**
"Ethnicities-in-Relation: Toward a Multicultural
     Reading of American Cinema."
     IN: Unspeakable Images

5419 **Shohat, Ella.**
"Israel."
     IN: World Cinema Since 1945

5420 **Shohat, Ella.**
"Master Narrative/Counter Readings: The Politics of
     Israeli Cinema."
     IN: Resisting Images

5421 **Sholem, Lee.**
"Lee Sholem." [An interview.]
     IN: Interviews with B ...

5422 **Shore, Dinah.**
"Dinah Shore." [Interview by Charles Higham.]
     IN: Celebrity Circus

5423 **Short, K.R.M.**
"Hollywood Fights Anti-Semitism, 1940-1945."
     IN: Film & Radio Propaganda ...

5424 **Short, K.R.M.**
"Feature Films as History."
"Hollywood Fights Anti-Semitism, 1945-1947."
     IN: Feature Films as History

5425 **Short, K.R.M.**
"Cinematic Support for the Anglo-American Détente,
     1939-43."
     IN: Britain and the Cinema ...

5426 **Short, Robert.**
"Religion in Outer Space."
"*2001: A Space Odyssey* and the Religion of Atheistic
     Humanism."
"Visions Drawing Closer to Christ: *Close Encounters
     of the Third Kind* and *Superman*."
"Closer Still to Christ: The *Star Wars* Saga, or 'The
     Gospel According to Saint Lucas'."
"*E.T.* and 'The Ache of Universal Love'--Closer to
     Christ Than Even the Churches Are?"
     IN: The Gospel from Outer Space

5427 **Shub, Esfir.**
"The Advent of Sound in Cinema."
"The Manufacture of Facts."
"This Work Cries Out." [RE: *October*.]
"We Do Not Deny the Element of Mastery."
     IN: The Film Factory

**Shub, Esfir. SEE: Pudovkin, Vsevolod; SEE:
Tretyakov, S.**

5428 **Shumyatsky, Boris.**
"A Cinema for the Millions (extracts)."
"The Role of the Producer."
"Perfecting Our Mastery."
"The Film *Bezhin Meadow*."
     IN: The Film Factory

5429 **Shutko, Kirill.**
"Preface [to] *Poetics of Cinema*."
     IN: The Film Factory
         The Poetics of Cinema

5430 **Siclier, Jacques.**
"The Psychology of the Spectator, or the 'Cinema of
     Vichy' Did Not Exist."
"The Great Arletty."
     IN: Rediscovering French Film

5431 **Sidney, George.**
"George Sidney." [Interview by Charles Higham.]
IN: <u>Celebrity Circus</u>

5432 **Sidney, George.**
"The Director's Art."
IN: <u>Hollywood Directors 1941-1976</u>

5433 **Siegel, Don.**
"Don Siegel." [Interview by Charles Higham.]
IN: <u>Celebrity Circus</u>

5434 **Siegel, Joel E.**
"Val Lewton."
IN: <u>The American Film Heritage</u>

5435 **Siegel, Joel.**
"I Found It at the Nudies: Jacques Demy's *Lola*, At Last."
IN: <u>Renaissance of the Film</u>

5436 **Siepmann, C.A.**
"Documentary Redefined."
IN: <u>Ideas on Film</u>

5437 **Siepmann, Charles.**
"Robert Flaherty: The Man & the Filmmaker."
IN: <u>Film: Book 1</u>

5438 **Sierek, Karl.**
"The Primal Scene of the Cinema: Four Fragments from *The Mistress of Atlantis*."
IN: <u>The Films of G.W. Pabst</u>

Sigelman, Carol K. SEE: Sigelman, Lee.

5439 **Sigelman, Lee and Carol K. Sigelman.**
"The Politics of Popular Culture: Campaign Cynicism & *The Candidate*."
IN: <u>Conflict and Control in the Cinema</u>

5440 ***Sight and Sound*, editorial.**
"The Front Page."
IN: <u>Sight and Sound</u>

5441 **Silber, Irwin.**
"*Serpico*."
IN: <u>Movies and Methods: An Anthology</u>

5442 **Silberman, Marc.**
"Kleist in the Third Reich: Ucicky's *The Broken Jug*."
"*Semper fidelis*: Staudte's *The Subject*."
IN: <u>German Film and Literature</u>

5443 **Silberman, Marc.**
"Late Pabst: *The Last Ten Days*."
IN: <u>The Films of G.W. Pabst</u>

5444 **Silberman, Marc.**
"Ula Stöckl: How Women See Themselves."
IN: <u>New German Filmmakers</u>

5444a **Silberman, Marc.**
"Imagining History: Weimar Images of the French Revolution."
IN: <u>Framing the Past</u>

5445 **Silet, Charles L.P.**
"Through a Woman's Eyes: Sexuality and Memory in *The [39] Steps*." [RE: *The 39 Steps*.]
IN: <u>A Hitchcock Reader</u>

Silet, Charles L.P. SEE: Bataille, Gretchen.

5446 **Silliphant, Stirling.**
"Stirling Silliphant." [Interview by William Froug.]
IN: <u>The Screenwriter Looks ...</u>

5447 **Sills, Milton.**
"The Actor's Part."
IN: <u>The Story of the Films</u>

5448 **Silva, Fred.**
"*The Red Badge of Courage* [novel by] Stephen Crane. Uncivil Battles and Civil Wars."
IN: <u>The Classic American Novel ...</u>

5449 **Silva, Jorge and Marta Rodriguez.**
"Cine-Sociology and Social Change." [RE: Colombia.]
IN: <u>Cinema and Social Change ...</u>

5450 **Silver, Alain and Elizabeth Ward.**
"Leigh Brackett."
IN: <u>Dictionary of Literary Biography /v. 26</u>

5451 **Silver, Charles.**
"*The Immortal Story*."
IN: <u>Focus on Orson Welles</u>

5452 **Silver, Isidore.**
"All in the Mafia Family: *The Godfather*."
IN: <u>Film in Society</u>

5453 **Silver, Joan Micklin.**
"Joan Micklin Silver." [Interview by John Andrew Gallagher.]
IN: <u>Film Directors on Directing</u>

5454 **Silver, Joan Micklin.**
"The Writer-Director."
IN: <u>The Movie Business Book</u>

5455 **Silver, Raphael D.**
"Independent Distribution: Midwest Films."
IN: <u>The Movie Business Book</u>

5456 **Silverberg, Robert.**
"The Way the Future Looks: *THX 1138* and *Blade Runner*."
IN: <u>Omni's Screen Flights ...</u>

5457 **Silverman, Joan L.**
"*The Birth of a Nation*: Prohibition Propaganda."
IN: <u>The South and Film</u>

5458 **Silverman, Kaja.**
"Suture [excerpts]."
IN: <u>Narrative, Apparatus, Ideology</u>

5459 **Silverman, Kaja.**
"[From:] *The Subject of Semiotics*: On Suture."
IN: <u>Film Theory and Criticism /4 ed</u>

5460 **Silverman, Kaja.**
"Dis-Embodying the Female Voice."

IN: <u>Re-vision</u>
<u>Issues in Feminist Film Criticism</u>

5461 Silverman, Kaja.
"Historical Trauma and Male Subjectivity."
IN: <u>Psychoanalysis and Cinema</u>

5462 Silverman, Michael.
"Italian Film and American Capital, 1947-1951."
IN: <u>Cinema Histories, Cinema Practices</u>

5463 Silverstein, Morton.
"*Eye On* [Interview with] Morton Silverstein."
IN: <u>The Documentary Conscience</u>

5464 Silverstein, Morton.
"*What Harvest for the Reaper?*." [Interview by Alan Rosenthal.]
IN: <u>The New Documentary in Action</u>

Silverstein, Norman. SEE: Huss, Roy.

5465 Silvertone, Matthew.
"Finding the Money."
IN: <u>British Cinema Now</u>

5466 Silvey, Robert J.
"Viewing: A Frame of Reference."
IN: <u>Sight, Sound, and Society</u>

Simmons, Jerold L. SEE: Leff, Leonard J.

Simon, Bill. SEE: Mendelson, Lois.

5467 Simon, John.
"*The Passion of Anna*."
IN: <u>Awake in the Dark</u>

5468 Simon, John.
"A Bit Overblown." [RE: *Blow-Up*.]
IN: <u>A Casebook on Film</u>

5469 Simon, John.
"A Critical Credo."
IN: <u>A Casebook on Film</u>
<u>Awake in the Dark</u>

5470 Simon, John.
"A Variety of Hells." [RE: *Salesman*.]
IN: <u>The Documentary Tradition /1 ed</u>
<u>The Documentary Tradition /2 ed</u>

5471 Simon, John.
"Fellini's *8-1/2* Fancy."
IN: <u>The Film</u>

5472 Simon, John.
"Ingmar Bergman and Insanity."
IN: <u>Film and Dream</u>

5473 Simon, John.
"Pearl Throwing Free Style." [RE: *Othello*, 1965.]
IN: <u>Focus on Shakespearean Films</u>

5474 Simon, John.
"The Future of Film."
IN: <u>Film: Readings in the Mass Media</u>

5475 Simon, John.
"Why Is the Co-Eatus Always Interruptus?" [RE: *The Discreet Charm of the Bourgeoisie*.]
IN: <u>The World of Luis Buñuel</u>

5476 Simon, Neil.
"Neil Simon." [Interviewed by John Brady.]
IN: <u>The Craft of the Screenwriter</u>

5477 Simon, William G.
"Hitchcock: The Languages of Madness."
IN: <u>Hitchcock's Re-Released Films</u>

5478 Simon, William.
"An Analysis of the Structure of *The Godfather, Part One*."
IN: <u>The Cinematic Text</u>

5479 Simonet, Thomas.
"Conglomerates and Content: Remakes, Sequels, and Series in the New Hollywood."
IN: <u>Current Research in Film /v. 3</u>

5480 Sinclair, Andrew.
"Great Britain."
IN: <u>World Cinema Since 1945</u>

5481 Sinclair, Upton.
"Music and the Drama--Under Epic ..."
IN: <u>Celebrity Articles ...</u>

5482 Sinclair, Upton.
"Nickelodeons and Common Shows."
"Over the Hill."
IN: <u>Authors on Film</u>

5483 Sinclair, Upton.
"Technocracy: The New Hope."
IN: <u>The Best of Rob Wagner's Script</u>

5484 Sinclair, Upton.
"[From:] The Movies and Political Propaganda."
IN: <u>Film and Society</u>

5485 Sindicato de la Industria Cinematográfica Argentina.
"Report on the State of Argentine Cinema."
IN: <u>Argentine Cinema</u>

5486 Singer, Alan.
"Comprehending Appearances: Werner Herzog's Ironic Sublime."
IN: <u>The Films of Werner Herzog</u>

5487 Singer, Aubrey.
"Television: Window or Culture on Reflection in the Glass?"
IN: <u>Sight, Sound, and Society</u>

5488 Singer, Marilyn.
"Introduction [to the American avant-garde]."
IN: <u>A History of the American Avant-Garde Cinema</u>

5489 Singer, Phyllis Z.
"Michael Wilson."
IN: <u>Dictionary of Literary Biography /v. 44</u>

5490 **Singh, Bikram.**
"The Commercial: Reality Disturbed."
IN: Indian Cinema Superbazaar

5491 **Singh, Madan Gopal.**
"Technique as an Ideological Weapon."
IN: Indian Cinema Superbazaar

Sinkel, Bernhard. SEE: Brustellin, Alf.

5492 **Sinyard, Neil.**
"'In My Mind's Eye': Shakespeare on the Screen."
"Historian of Fine Consciousness: Henry James and the Cinema."
"Another Fine Mess: D.H. Lawrence and Thomas Hardy on Film."
"Age of Doublethink: George Orwell and the Cinema."
"Pinter's *Go-Between*."
"The Camera Eye of James Agee."
"Kindred Spirits: Analogies between the Film and Literary Artists (Charles Dickens and Charlie Chaplin; Mark Twain and John Ford; Graham Greene and Alfred Hitchcock; Joseph Conrad and Orson Welles)."
"Adaptation as Criticism: Four Films (*Great Expectations*; *Death in Venice*; *Barry Lyndon*; *The French Lieutenant's Woman*)."
"Bio-Pics: The Literary Life on Film."
"Film and Theatre."
IN: Filming Literature

5493 **Siodmak, Curt.**
"Curt Siodmak." [An interview.]
IN: Interviews with B ...

5494 **Siodmak, Curt.**
"Curt Siodmak: The Idea Man." [Interview by Dennis Fischer.]
IN: Backstory 2

5495 **Siodmak, Curt.**
"Curt Siodmak." [Interview by Lee Server.]
IN: Screenwriter: Words Become Pictures

5496 **Siodmak, Robert.**
"Hoodlums: The Myth."
IN: Hollywood Directors 1941-1976

5497 **Sippy, G.P.**
"G.P. Sippy." [Interview.]
IN: Indian Cinema Superbazaar

5498 **Siska, William C.**
"The Art Film as a Genre (... *Night Moves* as an Example)."
"The Intellectual Milieu of the Art Film."
"Arthur Penn's *Mickey One*: Decoding the Modernist Allegory."
"Federico Fellini's *8-1/2*: The Personal Film."
"Open Texture in Jean-Luc Godard's *Pierrot le fou*."
"The Myth of Self-appropriation."
IN: Modernism in the Narrative Cinema

5499 **Siska, William C.**
"Formal Reflexivity in Dennis Hopper's *The Last Movie*."

IN: Explorations in National Cinemas
Modernism in the Narrative Cinema

5500 **Siska, William C.**
"The Art Film."
IN: Handbook of American Film Genres

5501 **Sitney, P. Adams.**
"The Instant of Love: Image and Title in Surrealist Cinema."
"Revolutionary Time: Image and Title in Soviet Cinema."
"Moments of Revelation: Dreyer's Anachronistic Modernity."
"Cinematography vs. the Cinema: Bresson's Figures."
"The Récit and the Figure: Blanchot's *Au moment voulu*."
"Saying 'Nothing': *Persona* as an Allegory of Psychoanalysis."
"The Sentiment of Doing Nothing: Stein's Autobiographies."
"Out via Nothing: Olson's Genealogy of the Proper Poem."
"Whoever Sees God Dies: Cinematic Epiphanies."
"Theology vs. Psychoanalysis: Landow's Wit."
IN: Modernist Montage

5502 **Sitney, P. Adams.**
"A Reader's Guide to the American Avant-Garde Film."
"Imagism in Four Avant-Garde Films." [RE: *Choreography for Camera*; *Eaux d'Artifice*; *Handwritten*; *Dog Star Man, Part 1*.]
"Interview with Stan Brakhage."
"Structural Film."
IN: Film Culture Reader

5503 **Sitney, P. Adams.**
"American Avant-Garde Cinema."
"Avant-Garde Animation: The Graphic Cinema."
"Alexander Dovzhenko."
"Dimitri Kirsanoff."
IN: Cinema: A Critical Dictionary

5504 **Sitney, P. Adams.**
"Autobiography in Avant-Garde Film."
IN: The Avant-Garde Film

5505 **Sitney, P. Adams.**
"Dovzhenko's Intellectual Montage (*Arsenal*)."
"Michael Snow's Cinema."
"The Rhetoric of Robert Bresson."
IN: The Essential Cinema /v. 1

5506 **Sitney, P. Adams.**
"Harry Smith Inverview."
IN: The New American Cinema
The Avant-Garde Film
Film Culture Reader

5507 **Skillman, Teri.**
"Songs of Hindi Films: Nature and Function."
IN: Cinema and Cultural Identity

5508 **Skipp, John and Craig Spector.**
"Death's Rich Pageantry, or Skipp & Spector's
      Handy-Dandy Splatterpunk Guide to the Horrors of
      Non-horror Film."
      IN: Cut!: Horror Writers ...

5509 **Sklar, Robert.**
"*Oh! Althusser!*: Historiography and the Rise of
      Cinema Studies."
      IN: Resisting Images

5510 **Sklar, Robert.**
"Empire to the West: *Red River*."
      IN: American History/American Film

5511 **Sklar, Robert.**
"Moving Image Media in Culture and Society:
      Paradigms for Historical Interpretation."
      IN: Image as Artifact

5512 **Sklar, Robert.**
"New Producing Companies."
      IN: The First Tycoons

5513 **Sklar, Robert.**
"Stanley Kubrick and the American Film Industry."
      IN: Current Research in Film /v. 4

5514 **Sklar, Robert.**
"The Making of Cultural Myths--Walt Disney."
      IN: The American Animated Cartoon

5515 **Sklarew, Bruce H.**
"Ingmar Bergman's *Cries and Whispers*: The
      Consequences of Preoedipal Developmental
      Disturbances."
      IN: Images in Our Souls

5516 **Skornia, Harry J.**
"National Jukebox or Educational Resource?"
      IN: Sight, Sound, and Society

5517 **Skrade, Carl.**
"Theology and Films."
      IN: Celluloid and Symbol

5518 **Skvorecky, Josef.**
"Czechoslovakia."
      IN: World Cinema Since 1945

5519 **Sky, Laura.**
"Laura Sky: The Process of Censorship (An Interview
      with Marc Glassman)."
      IN: Forbidden Films

5520 **Slade, Joseph W.**
"Recent Trends in Pornographic Films."
      IN: Film in Society

5521 **Slade, Joseph W.**
"The Porn Market and Porn Formulas: The Feature
      Film of the Seventies."
      IN: Movies as Artifacts

5522 **Slade, Ruth.**
"Stanley in the Congo." [RE: *Stanley and Livingstone*.]
      IN: Africa on Film

5523 **Slafer, Eugene.**
"A Conversation wth Bill Hanna."
      IN: The American Animated Cartoon

5524 **Slater, Thomas J.**
"*One Flew Over the Cuckoo's Nest*: A Tale of Two
      Decades."
      IN: Film and Literature: A Comparative ...

5525 **Slater, Thomas J.**
"Teaching Vietnam: The Politics of Documentary."
      IN: Inventing Vietnam

5526 **Slater, Thomas.**
"Anthony Veiller."
"Eleanor Perry."
"Isobel Lennart."
"Jo Swerling."
"June Mathis."
"Lenore J. Coffee."
      IN: Dictionary of Literary Biography /v. 44

5527 **Slavitt, David R.**
"Sexuality in Film: Reconsiderations after Seeing
      Cries and Whispers."
      IN: Sexuality in the Movies

5528 **Slavitt, David.**
"Critics and Criticism."
      IN: Man and the Movies

5529 **Slide, Anthony.**
"Lois Weber."
"Margery Wilson."
"Mrs. Wallace Reid."
"Frances Marion."
"Dorothy Arzner."
      IN: Early Women Directors

5530 **Slide, Anthony.**
"Mignon Anderson."
"Hobart Bosworth."
"Billie Rhodes."
"Kathlyn Williams."
"Elmer Clifton."
"Olga Petrova."
"Henry B. Walthall."
"Priscilla Bonner."
"Bebe Daniels and Ben Lyon."
"Jetta Goudal."
"Ralph Graves."
"Alice Terry."
"Adele Whitely Fletcher."
"Ruth Waterbury."
      IN: The Idols of Silence

5531 **Slide, Anthony.**
"The Evolution of the Film Star."
"Comediennes of the 'teens."
"Child Stars of the 'teens."
"Ethel Grandin."
"Forgotten Early Directors."
"Mr. Edison and the Edison Company."
"Katherine Anne Porter and the Movies."

The Thanhouser Company."
"The Paralta Company."
"The O'Kalems."
"Early Film Magazines: An Overview."
"The First Motion Picture Bibliography."
"Film History Can Also Be Fun."
    IN: Aspects of American Film ...

5532 **Slide, Anthony.**
"*Stella Maris.*"
    IN: The Rivals of D.W. Griffith

5533 **Slide, Anthony.**
"Alice Guy Blaché."
    IN: The First Film Makers
         Early Women Directors

5534 **Slide, Anthony.**
"John Monk Saunders."
    IN: Dictionary of Literary Biography /v. 26

5535 **Slide, Anthony.**
"Zoë Akins."
    IN: Dictionary of Literary Biography /v. 26

5536 **Slifer, Clarence.**
"Creating Special Effects for *GWTW.*"
    IN: The ASC Treasury ...

5537 **Sloan, William J.**
"The Documentary Film and the Negro."
    IN: The Documentary Tradition /1 ed
         The Documentary Tradition /2 ed

5538 **Slover, George.**
"Isolation and Make-Believe in *Blow-Up.*"
    IN: Focus on Blow-Up

5539 **Slusser, George.**
"Fantasy, Science Fiction, Mystery, Horror."
    IN: Shadows of the Magic Lamp

5540 **Small, Edward.**
"Film and Video Arts."
    IN: Film and the Arts in Symbiosis

5541 **Smihi, Moumen.**
"Moroccan Society as Mythology."
    IN: Film and Politics in the Third World

5542 **Smith, Albert E.**
"A Handshake with Harry Warner."
"It Was a Rugged Era."
"Vitagraph."
    IN: The First Tycoons

5543 **Smith, Conrad.**
"The Early History of Animation."
    IN: The American Animated Cartoon

5544 **Smith, Dian G.**
"D.W. Griffith."
"Charles Chaplin."
"Buster Keaton."
"John Ford."
"Frank Capra."
"Howard Hawks."

"Alfred Hitchcock."
"George Cukor."
"Orson Welles."
"John Huston."
    IN: Great American Directors

5545 **Smith, Dian G.**
"Woody Allen."
"Robert Altman."
"Mel Brooks."
"Francis Coppola."
"Brian De Palma."
"George Lucas."
"Paul Mazursky."
"Martin Scorsese."
"Steven Spielberg."
    IN: American Film Makers Today

5546 **Smith, Dick.**
"Dick Smith." [Interview by Stanley Wiater.]
    IN: Dark Visions

5547 **Smith, Fred Y.**
"Film Editor."
    IN: Hollywood Speaks!

5548 **Smith, Harry.**
"On *Mahagonny.*"
    IN: The Avant-Garde Film

5549 **Smith, Henry Nash.**
"The Western Hero in the Dime Novel."
    IN: The American West on Film

5550 **Smith, Jack.**
"Belated Appreciation of V.S."
    IN: Sternberg

5551 **Smith, Julian.**
"Innocence Preserved or Audie Murphy Died for Your
    Sins, America."
    IN: Movies as Artifacts

5552 **Smith, Maynard Tereba.**
"Lamar Trotti."
    IN: Dictionary of Literary Biography /v. 44

5553 **Smith, Ralph A.**
"Teaching Film as Significant Art."
    IN: Perspectives on the Study of Film

5554 **Smith, Richard.**
"Linda Lovelace: The Blue-ing of America."
    IN: The Movies in Our Midst

5555 **Smith, Sarah W.R.**
"*Finnegans Wake* [novel by] James Joyce; *Passages
    from Finnegans Wake* [film by] Mary Ellen Bute.
    The World Made Celluloid.*"
    IN: The English Novel and the Movies

5556 **Smoller, Sanford J.**
"*Babbitt* [novel by] Sinclair Lewis. The 'Booboisie'
    and Its Discontents."
    IN: The Classic American Novel ...

5557 Smyth, Rosaleen.
"Movies and Mandarins: the Official Film and British Colonial Africa."
IN: <u>British Cinema History</u>

5558 Snead, James A.
"Images of Blacks in Black Independent Films: A Brief Survey."
IN: <u>Critical Perspectives on Black ...</u>

5559 Snow, Michael.
"Notes on Films."
"Two Letters."
IN: <u>The Avant-Garde Film</u>

5559a Snow, Michael.
"Michael Snow." [Interview by Scott MacDonald.]
IN: <u>A Critical Cinema 2</u>

Snow, Michael. SEE: Hartog, Simon.

5560 Snyder, Allegra Fuller.
"Three Kinds of Dance Film."
IN: <u>Crossroads to the Cinema</u>

5561 Snyder, Stephen.
"Color, Growth, and Evolution in *Fellini Satyricon*."
IN: <u>Federico Fellini</u>

5562 Snyder, Wm. Stephen.
"Fellini's *The White Sheik*: Discovering the Story in the Medium."
IN: <u>Explorations in National Cinemas</u>

5563 Sobchack, Thomas.
"Genre Film: A Classical Experience."
IN: <u>Film Genre</u>
    <u>Film Genre Reader</u>

5564 Sobchack, Thomas.
"The Adventure Film."
IN: <u>Handbook of American Film Genres</u>

Sobchack, Thomas. SEE: Bywater, Tim.

5565 Sobchack, Vivian C.
"The Violent Dance: A Personal Memoir of Death in the Movies."
IN: <u>Movies as Artifacts</u>

5566 Sobchack, Vivian C.
"*The Grapes of Wrath*: Thematic Emphasis through Visual Style."
IN: <u>Hollywood as Historian</u>

5567 Sobchack, Vivian C.
"*No Lies*: Direct Cinema as Rape."
IN: <u>New Challenges for Documentary</u>

5568 Sobchack, Vivian.
"Bringing It All Back Home: Family Economy and Generic Exchange."
IN: <u>American Horrors</u>

5569 Sobchack, Vivian.
"Child/Alien/Father: Patriarchal Crisis and Generic Exchange."
IN: <u>Close Encounters</u>

5570 Sobchack, Vivian.
"Genre Film: Myth, Ritual, and Sociodrama."
IN: <u>Film/Culture: Explorations ...</u>

5571 Sobchack, Vivian.
"Postmodern Modes of Ethnicity."
IN: <u>Unspeakable Images</u>

5572 Sobchack, Vivian.
"Science Fiction."
IN: <u>Handbook of American Film Genres</u>

5573 Sobchack, Vivian.
"The Virginity of Astronauts: Sex and the Science Fiction Film."
IN: <u>Alien Zone</u>
    <u>Shadows of the Magic Lamp</u>

5574 Sochen, June.
"The New Woman and Twenties America: *Way Down East*."
IN: <u>American History/American Film</u>

5575 Sodowsky, Alice, Roland Sodowsky and Stephen Witte.
"The Epic World of *American Graffiti*."
IN: <u>Movies as Artifacts</u>

Sodowsky, Roland. SEE: Sodowsky, Alice.

5576 Sohn, David A.
"Films within the Curriculum."
"Finding Films."
IN: <u>Films Deliver</u>

5577 Sohn, David A., Henry E. Putsch, and Anthony Schillaci.
"A Teaching Unit of Films on War."
IN: <u>Films Deliver</u>

5578 Sokolov, Ippolit.
"The Legend of 'Left' Cinema."
"The Second Sound Film Programme."
IN: <u>The Film Factory</u>

5579 Solan, Peter.
"Peter Solan." [Interview by Antonín J. Liehm.]
IN: <u>Closely Watched Films</u>

5580 Solanas, Fernando and Octavio Getino.
"Toward a Third Cinema." [RE: Argentina.]
IN: <u>Reviewing Histories</u>
    <u>Movies and Methods: An Anthology</u>

Solanas, Fernando. SEE: Godard, Jean-Luc.

5581 Solás, Humberto.
"Every Point of Arrival Is a Point of Departure." [RE: Cuba.]
IN: <u>Cinema and Social Change ...</u>

5582 Solberg-Ladd, Helena.
"The View from the United States." [RE: Brazil.]
IN: <u>Cinema and Social Change ...</u>

5583 Solomon, Barbara H.
"Father and Son in De Sica's *The Bicycle Thief*."
IN: <u>The Classic Cinema</u>

5584 Solomon, Laurence.
"*What Harvest for the Reaper?* [Interview by Alan Rosenthal.]
   IN: The New Documentary in Action

5585 Solomon, Stanley J.
"The Western as Myth and Romance: *Stagecoach* (1939); *Winchester '73* (1950); *Shane* (1953); *Johnny Guitar* (1954); *The Searchers* (1956); *Comanche Station* (1960); *The Wild Bunch* (1969); *Butch Cassidy and The Sundance Kid* (1969)."
"Singing and Dancing: *Gold Diggers of 1933* (1933); *Top Hat* (1935); *Swing Time* (1936); *The Pirate* (1948); *Singin' in the Rain* (1952); *The Band Wagon* (1953); *Funny Girl* (1968); *Cabaret* (1972)."
"The Nightmare World: *King Kong* (1933); *The Bride of Frankenstein* (1935); *Invasion of the Body Snatchers* (1956); *Psycho* (1960); *The Birds* (1963); *Night of the Living Dead* (1968); *Rosemary's Baby* (1968); *The Exorcist* (1973)."
"The Life of Crime: *The Public Enemy* (1931); *Force of Evil* (1949); *White Heat* (1949); *Riot in Cell Block 11* (1954); *On the Waterfront* (1954); *Bonnie and Clyde* (1969); *The Godfather* (1972)."
"The Search for Clues: *The Maltese Falcon* (1941); *The Big Sleep* (1946); *Harper* (1966); *Bullitt* (1968); *Klute* (1971); *Dirty Harry* (1972); *Chinatown* (1974)."
"Wars Hot and Cold: *Hell's Angels* (1930); *Gone with the Wind* (1939); *To Be or Not To Be* (1942); *Casablanca* (1942); *Paths of Glory* (1957); *North by Northwest* (1959); *Dr. Strangelove, or How I Learned to Stop Worrying and Love the Bomb* (1963); *Patton* (1970)."
   IN: Beyond Formula

5586 Solomon, Stanley J.
"Aristotle in Twilight: American Film Narrative in the 1980s."
   IN: The Cinematic Text

5587 Solomon, Stanley J.
"Modern Uses of the Moving Camera."
   IN: The Movies as Medium

5588 Sontag, Susan.
"Spiritual Style in the Films of Robert Bresson."
"Godard's *Vivre Sa Vie*."
"Resnais' *Muriel*."
"A Note on Novels and Films."
   IN: Against Interpretation

5589 Sontag, Susan.
"Bergman's *Persona*."
"Godard."
   IN: Styles of Radical Will

5590 Sontag, Susan.
"Godard." [NOTE: Excerpted from "Godard" in the previous entry.]
"*Persona*: The Film in Depth." [NOTE: Excerpted and revised from "Bergman's *Persona*" in the previous entry.]
   IN: Great Film Directors

5591 Sontag, Susan.
"The Imagination of Disaster."
   IN: Film Theory and Criticism /1 ed
      Film Theory and Criticism /2 ed
      Film Theory and Criticism /3 ed
      Film and the Liberal Arts
      Awake in the Dark
      Against Interpretation

5592 Sontag, Susan.
"Theatre and Film" [NOTE: Also called "Film and Theatre."]
   IN: Styles of Radical Will
      Film Theory and Criticism /1 ed
      Film Theory and Criticism /2 ed
      Film Theory and Criticism /3 ed
      Film Theory and Criticism /4 ed
      Perspectives on the Study of Film
      Film And/As Literature

5593 Sontag, Susan.
"Against Interpretation."
   IN: Film And/As Literature
      Against Interpretation

5594 Sontag, Susan.
"Fascinating Fascism."
   IN: Women and the Cinema
      Movies and Methods: An Anthology

5595 Sontag, Susan.
"Jack Smith's *Flaming Creatures*."
   IN: The New American Cinema
      Against Interpretation

5596 Sorell, Victor A.
"Ethnomusicology, Folklore, and History in the Filmmaker's Art: *The Ballad of Gregorio Cortez*."
   IN: Chicano Cinema

5596a Sorkin, Adam J.
"*On the Waterfront*: 'Like It Ain't Part of America'."
   IN: Columbia Pictures

5597 Sorlin, Pierre.
"A Breath of Sea Air: Jacques Tati's *Les Vacances de M. Hulot*."
   IN: French Film: Texts and Contexts

5598 Sorlin, Pierre.
"Historical Films as Tools for Historians."
   IN: Image as Artifact

5599 Sorlin, Pierre.
"The Struggle for Control of French Minds, 1940-1944."
   IN: Film & Radio Propaganda ...

5600 Sotto, Agustin V.
"The Celluloid Route of 'Genghis Khan'."
   IN: Readings in Philippine Cinema

5601 Souday, Paul.
"On the Cinema."
   IN: French Film Theory and Criticism /v. 1

5602 Soupault, Philippe.
"Cinema U.S.A."

"Rage and Glory."
IN: The Shadow and Its Shadow

5603 **Soupault, Philippe.**
"Note 1 on the Cinema."
IN: French Film Theory and Criticism /v. 1

5604 **Soupault, Philippe.**
"*Jean de la Lune* or Cinema on the Wrong Track."
IN: French Film Theory and Criticism /v. 2

5605 **Southern, Terry.**
"The Screenwriter."
IN: Movie People

5606 *Sovetskii ekran*, **editorial.**
"The Rightist Danger in Cinema."
IN: The Film Factory

5607 **Sovkino Workers' Conference Resolution.**
"Sovkino's New Course (extract)."
IN: The Film Factory

5608 **Sovnarkom of the RSFSR.**
"Decree on the Establishment of Sovkino."
IN: The Film Factory

Sparrow, Felicity. SEE: Nicolson, Annabel; SEE: Rhodes, Lis.

5609 **Sparshott, F.E.**
"Basic Film Aesthetics."
IN: Film Theory and Criticism /1 ed
Film Theory and Criticism /2 ed
Film Theory and Criticism /3 ed

5610 **Spears, Jack.**
"The Civil War on the Screen."
"Nazimova." [RE: Alla Nazimova.]
"Edwin S. Porter: Motion Picture Pioneer."
"Louis Wolheim."
IN: The Civil War on the Screen ...

5611 **Spears, Jack.**
"The Movies of World War I."
"Max Linder, Comedy's Tragic Genius."
"Norma Talmadge."
"Comic Strips on the Screen."
"Mary Pickford's Directors."
"Colleen Moore."
"Chaplin's Collaborators."
"Baseball on the Screen."
"Marshall Neilan."
"The Doctor on the Screen."
"Robert Florey."
"The Indian on the Screen."
IN: Hollywood: The Golden Era

5612 **Spears, Ross.**
"Regional Filmmaking: The James Agee Film Project."
IN: The South and Film

Spector, Craig. SEE: Skipp, John.

5613 **Spehr, Paul C.**
"Filmmaking at the American Mutoscope and Biograph Company 1900-1906."

"Some Still Fragments of a Moving Past: Edison Films in the Library of Congress."
IN: Wonderful Inventions

5614 **Spehr, Paul C.**
"Pathé Frères."
IN: The First Tycoons

5615 **Spehr, Paul.**
"Before *The Birth of a Nation*: American Films, 1907-1914."
IN: The American Film Heritage

5616 **Spellerberg, James.**
"Technology and Ideology in the Cinema."
IN: Film Theory and Criticism /3 ed

Spence, Louise. SEE: Stam, Robert.

5617 **Spiegel, Alan.**
"The Cinematic Text: Rohmer's *The Marquise of O ...* from the Story by Heinrich von Kleist."
IN: Modern European Filmmakers ...

5618 **Spielberg, Steven.**
"Steven Spielberg." [Interview by Judith Crist.]
IN: Take 22

5619 **Spigel, Lynn.**
"From Domestic Space to Outer Space: The 1960s Fantastic Family Sit-Com."
IN: Close Encounters

5620 **Spigelgass, Leonard.**
"It's Not 'How' It Came To Be, But 'What' Came To Be—" [RE: an interview.]
IN: Blueprint on Babylon

5621 **Spoto, Donald M.**
"*Vertigo*: The Cure Is Worse Than the Dis-Ease."
IN: The Classic Cinema

5622 **Spottiswoode, Raymond.**
"Mainly Mechanical."
IN: Ideas on Film

5623 **Spring, D.W.**
"Soviet Newsreel and the Great Patriotic War."
IN: Propaganda, Politics and Film

Spring, Lori. SEE: Jacobowitz, Florence.

5624 **Springer, Claudia.**
"Comprehension and Crisis: Reporter Films and the Third World."
IN: Unspeakable Images

5625 **Spry, Robin.**
"*Action: The Quebec Crisis of 1970* [Interview with] Robin Spry."
IN: The Documentary Conscience

5626 **Sragow, Michael.**
"*All Night Long.*"
"*Blow Out.*"
"*Under Fire.*"
"*Southern Comfort.*"
"*Personal Best.*"

IN: Produced and Abandoned

Srebnick, Walter. SEE: Raubicheck, Walter.

5627 **Stabler, Bob.**
"Bob Stabler." [An interview.]
IN: Producers on Producing

5628 **Stacey, Jackie.**
"Desperately Seeking Difference."
IN: Issues in Feminist Film Criticism
The Female Gaze

5628a **Stacey, Jackie.**
"Feminine Fascinations: Forms of Identification in
Star-Audience Relations."
IN: Stardom

5629 **Stack, Dennis.**
"Reborn Midland Reflects Many-Splendored Past."
IN: The Movies: An American Idiom

5630 **Stack, Oswald.**
"Pier Paolo Pasolini."
IN: Cinema: A Critical Dictionary

5631 **Stack, Robert.**
"The Kiss Heard 'Round the World."
IN: Bedside Hollywood

5632 **Staehling, Richard.**
"From *Rock Around the Clock* to *The Trip*: The Truth
about Teen Movies."
IN: Kings of the Bs

5633 **Stahl, Jerry.**
"*Cafe Flesh*: Midnight Hit for a Pornographic Age."
IN: Omni's Screen Flights ...

5634 **Staiger, Janet.**
"Blueprints for Feature Films: Hollywood's Continuity
Scripts."
IN: The American Film Industry /rev ed

5635 **Staiger, Janet.**
"Combination and Litigation: Structures of U.S. Film
Distribution, 1896-1917."
IN: Early Cinema ...

5636 **Staiger, Janet.**
"Dividing Labor for Production Control: Thomas Ince
and the Rise of the Studio System."
IN: Cinema Examined
The American Movie Industry

5637 **Staiger, Janet.**
"Mass-Produced Photoplays: Economic and
Signifying Practices in the First Years of
Hollywood."
IN: Movies and Methods /v. 2
The Hollywood Film Industry

5638 **Staiger, Janet.**
"Reception Studies: The Death of the Reader."
IN: The Cinematic Text

5639 **Staiger, Janet.**
"The Hollywood Mode of Production to 1930."
"The Hollywood Mode of Production, 1930-60."

IN: The Classical Hollywood Cinema

5640 **Staiger, Janet.**
"This Moving Image I Have Before Me."
IN: Image as Artifact

5640a **Staiger, Janet.**
"Seeing Stars."
IN: Stardom

Staiger, Janet. SEE: Bordwell, David.

5641 **Stakhanov, Alexei.**
"My Suggestion to Soviet Cinema."
IN: The Film Factory

5642 **Stalin, Joseph.**
"Congratulations to Soviet Cinema on Its Fifteenth
Anniversary."
IN: The Film Factory

5643 **Stam, Robert.**
"Translinguistics and Semiotics."
"Language, Difference, and Power."
"Film, Literature, and the Carnivalesque."
"Of Cannibals and Carnivals."
"The Grotesque Body and Cinematic Eroticism."
"From Dialogism to *Zelig*."
IN: Subversive Pleasures

5643a **Stam, Robert, Robert Burgoyne and Sandy
Flitterman-Lewis.**
"Semiotics and the Philosophy of Language."
"The Founders of Semiotics."
"Russian Formalism."
"The Bakhtin School."
"Prague Structuralism."
"Jakobson's Communications Paradigm."
"The Advent of Structuralism."
"Post-Structuralism: The Critique of the Sign."
"The Cinematic Sign."
"Minimal Units and Their Cinematic Articulation."
"Cinema: *langue* or *langage*."
"The Grand Syntagmatique."
"The Eight Syntagmatic Types."
"Codes and Subcodes."
"Textual System."
"Textual Analysis."
"Filmic Punctuation."
"The Semiotics of Filmic Sound."
"Language in the Cinema."
"Beyond Saussure."
"The Semiotics of Narrative."
"Film as a Narrative Art: Formalist Approaches."
"Contemporary Models of Formal Structure."
"The Structuralist Analysis of Narrative."
"Plot Analysis: The Proppian Model."
"Semantic and Syntactic Approaches."
"The Problem of Point-of-View."
"Focalization and Filtration."
"Narration in Film."
"Types of Filmic Narrator."
"Character Narration."

"Gender in Voice-Over Narration."
"Unreliability."
"The Cinematic Narrator."
"Enunciation and Cinematic Narration."
"Cognitive Approaches to Narration."
"Recent Theories of the Cinematic Narrator."
"Tense."
"Psychoanalytic Theory."
"Psychoanalytic Film Theory."
"The Cinematic Apparatus."
"The Spectator."
"Enunciation."
"The Gaze."
"Feminist Film Theory."
"Cinematic Realism."
"Ideology and the Camera."
"The Classic Realist Text."
"Cinematic écriture."
"From 'Work' to 'Text'."
"The Contradictory Text."
"The Nature of Reflexivity."
"The Politics of Reflexivity."
"Intertextuality."
"Transtextuality."
"Discourse."
"Social Semiotics."
 IN: New Vocabularies in Film Semiotics

5644 **Stam, Robert.**
"Bakhtinian Translinguistics: A Postscriptum."
"Film and Language: From Metz to Bakhtin."
"Hitchcock and Buñuel: Desire and the Law."
 IN: The Cinematic Text

5645 **Stam, Robert.**
"Hitchcock and Buñuel: Authority, Desire, and the Absurd." [NOTE: This is a variation on the essay "Hitchcock and Buñuel: Desire and the Law."]
 IN: Hitchcock's Re-Released Films

5646 **Stam, Robert.**
"*Land in Anguish*."
"Formal Innovation and Radical Critique in *The Fall*."
"On the Margins: Brazilian Avant-Garde Cinema."
 IN: Brazilian Cinema

5647 **Stam, Robert.**
"*The Hour of the Furnaces* and the Two Avant-Gardes." [RE: Argentina.]
 IN: Reviewing Histories
  The Social Documentary ...

5648 **Stam, Robert.**
"Bakhtin, Polyphony, and Ethnic/Racial Representation."
 IN: Unspeakable Images

5649 **Stam, Robert.**
"Blacks in Brazilian Cinema."
 IN: Film and Politics in the Third World

5650 **Stam, Robert and Ismail Xavier.**
"Transformations of National Allegory: Brazilian Cinema from Dictatorship to Redemocratization."

 IN: Resisting Images

5651 **Stam, Robert and Louise Spence.**
"Colonialism, Racism, and Representation: An Introduction."
 IN: Movies and Methods /v. 2

5652 **Stam, Robert and Roberta Pearson.**
"Hitchcock's *Rear Window*: Reflexivity and the Critique of Voyeurism."
 IN: A Hitchcock Reader

Stam, Robert. SEE: Johnson, Randal.

5653 **Stamelman, Peter.**
"A Chat with Mel Blanc."
 IN: The American Animated Cartoon

5654 **Stanhope, Selwyn A.**
"Watching D.W. Griffith Shoot *The Birth of a Nation*."
 IN: Focus on The Birth of a Nation

5655 **Stanislavski, Constantin.**
"When Acting Is an Art."
 IN: Star Texts

5656 **Stanley, Kim.**
"Kim Stanley." [Interview by John Kobal.]
 IN: People Will Talk

5657 **Stanwyck, Barbara.**
"Barbara Stanwyck." [Interview by John Kobal.]
 IN: People Will Talk

Stapes, Terry. SEE: Cook, Pam.

5658 **Staples, Donald E.**
"The Auteur Theory Re-examined."
 IN: The Emergence of Film Art /1 ed
  The Emergence of Film Art /2 ed

5659 **Starr, Cecile.**
"Two Movie Books."
"Our Talking Pictures."
"Looking Forward."
"For Health and Happiness."
"Films with a Purpose."
"Kid Stuff."
"Films for Learning."
"Films, Films Everywhere."
 IN: Ideas on Film

5660 **Starr, Cecile.**
"Through the Psychiatric Looking Glass."
 IN: The Documentary Tradition /1 ed
  The Documentary Tradition /2 ed

5661 **Stead, Peter.**
"The People and the Pictures. The British Working Class and Film in the 1930s."
 IN: Propaganda, Politics and Film

5662 **Stead, Peter.**
"The People as Stars: Feature Films as National Expressions."
 IN: Britain and the Cinema ...

5663 **Steele, Robert.**
"Film and Aesthetics."
　IN: Sight, Sound, and Society
　　Crossroads to the Cinema

5664 **Steele, Robert.**
"The Good-Bad and Bad-Good in Movies: *Bonnie and Clyde* and *In Cold Blood*."
　IN: Focus on Bonnie and Clyde

5665 **Steene, Birgitta.**
"*The Seventh Seal*: An Existential Vision."
"*The Seventh Seal*: Film as Doomsday Metaphor."
"Words and Whisperings: An Interview with Ingmar Bergman."
　IN: Focus on The Seventh Seal

5666 **Steene, Birgitta.**
"Bergman's Portrait of Women: Sexism or Subjective Metaphor."
　IN: Sexual Stratagems

5667 **Steene, Birgitta.**
"Film as Theater: Geissendörfer's *The Wild Duck* from the Play by Henrik Ibsen."
　IN: Modern European Filmmakers ...

5668 **Stefano, Joseph.**
"Joseph Stefano." [Interview by Stanley Wiater.]
　IN: Dark Visions

5669 **Steiger, Rod.**
"The Actor."
　IN: Movie People

5670 **Stein, Elliot.**
"Buñuel's Golden Bowl." [RE: *Belle de Jour*.]
　IN: The World of Luis Buñuel
　　The Classic Cinema

5671 **Stein, Elliott.**
"Ernest Schoedsack and Merian Cooper."
"Frank Capra."
"Roland West."
"Tod Browning."
　IN: Cinema: A Critical Dictionary

Stein, Susan. SEE: Nicolson, Annabel.

5672 **Steinberg, David.**
"David Steinberg." [Interview by Charles Higham.]
　IN: Celebrity Circus

5673 **Steiner, Max.**
"Max Steiner: The Music Director."
　IN: The Real Tinsel

5674 **Steinmetz, Andres.**
"Educational Innovation and Evaluation."
　IN: Perspectives on the Study of Film

5675 **Stempel, Tom.**
"Mel Brooks."
"Philip Dunne."
　IN: Dictionary of Literary Biography /v. 26

5676 **Sten, Anna.**
"Anna Sten." [Interview by John Kobal.]
　IN: People Will Talk

5677 **Stephanick, Michael.**
"The Most Advanced Film Screened in Class This Year: A Catalogue of Effects."
　IN: Focus on Citizen Kane

5678 **Stephens, Lenora Clodfelter.**
"Black Women in Film."
　IN: The South and Film

5679 **Stephenson, Ralph.**
"Animation, Characteristics and Definition."
"Early Animation to the Twenties."
"Disney and His Contemporaries."
"Postwar America: UPA, Avery and Avant-Garde."
"Animation in Canada and Britain."
"French Animation from Cohl to Kamler."
"Polish Animation at Home and Abroad."
"Puppets and Cartoons in Czechoslovakia."
"Yugoslavia, The Rise and Shine of Zagreb."
"Humour and Artistry in Italy."
"Animation in the Balkans and Russia."
"Other Countries: Germany, Japan, Scandinavia."
"Present Trends, Abstract and Computer Animation."
　IN: The Animated Film

5680 **Stephenson, Ralph and Jean R. Debrix.**
"[From:] *The Cinema as Art*."
　IN: Film and Literature: Contrasts ...

5681 **Stephenson, William.**
"Fawn Bites Lion: Or, How MGM Tried to Film *The Yearling* in Florida."
　IN: The South and Film

5682 **Stern, Adele H.**
"Using Films in Teaching English Composition."
　IN: The Compleat Guide to Film Study

Stern, Dagmar. SEE: Gollub, Christian-Albrecht.

5683 **Stern, Lesley.**
"Independent Feminist Film-making in Australia."
　IN: An Australian Film Reader

5684 **Stern, Michael.**
"*Pylon* [novel by] William Faulkner. From the Folklore of Speed to *Danse Macabre*." [RE: *The Tarnished Angels*.]
　IN: The Modern American Novel ...

5685 **Stern, Michael.**
"Making Culture into Nature."
　IN: Alien Zone

5686 **Stern, Seymour.**
"D.W. Griffith's *Intolerance*."
　IN: The Essential Cinema /v. 1

5687 **Stern, Seymour.**
"Griffith: Pioneer of the Film Art."
　IN: Introduction to the Art of the Movies

5714 **Stoney, George.**
"All My Babies: research."
IN: Film: Book 1

5715 **Stoney, George.**
"*A Cry for Help*." [Interview by Alan Rosenthal.]
IN: The New Documentary in Action

5716 **Storaro, Vittorio.**
"Vittorio Storaro." [Interview by Dennis Schaefer and Larry Salvato.]
IN: Masters of Light

5717 **Storck, Henri.**
"Henri Storck." [Interview by G. Roy Levin.]
IN: Documentary Explorations

5718 **Stothart, Herbert.**
"Film Music."
IN: Behind the Screen

5719 **Stott, William.**
"Other People's Images: A Case History."
IN: Fair Use and Free Inquiry

5720 **Stout, Alan.**
"*The Back of Beyond*."
IN: An Australian Film Reader

Strand, Chick. SEE: Kinder, Marsha.

5721 **Strand, Paul.**
"*Les Maisons de la misère*."
IN: The Documentary Tradition /1 ed
The Documentary Tradition /2 ed

5722 **Strasberg, Lee.**
"A Dream of Passion: The Development of the Method."
IN: Star Texts

5723 **Stratton, David.**
"'I'd Rather Be Frivolous Than Boring': Tim Burstall."
"Lucky Man: Bruce Beresford."
"Mystery and Imagination: Peter Weir."
"Will the Real Filmmaker Please Stand Up?: Michael Thornhill."
"Gentle Craftsman: Ken Hannam."
"Actors' Director: Tom Jeffrey."
"In a Hostile World: Fred Schepisi."
"Chronicler of the Underdogs: Donald Crombie."
"Explorations of the Bizarre: Jim Sharman."
"Carlton Cinema: John Duigan."
"The Quiet Men: Tom Cowan, Esben Storm, Paul Cox."
"First from the Film School: Phil Noyce, Gill Armstrong."
IN: The Last New Wave

5724 **Straub, Jean-Marie.**
"Letter to the Export-Union."
"Bitburg: A Text."
"Fire: Alfred Edel."
IN: West German Filmmakers on Film

5725 **Straub, Jean-Marie and Danièle Huillet.**
"Direct Sound: An Interview."
IN: Film Sound
Film Theory and Criticism /4 ed

5726 **Straubhaar, Joseph Dean and Gayle King.**
"Effects of Television on Film in Argentina, Brazil, and Mexico."
IN: Current Research in Film /v. 3

5727 **Strauss, Theodore.**
"The Giant Shinnies Down the Beanstalk—Flaherty's *The Land*."
IN: The Documentary Tradition /1 ed
The Documentary Tradition /2 ed

5728 **Straw, Will.**
"The Myth of Total Cinema History."
IN: Explorations in Film Theory

5729 **Strawn, Linda May.**
"Samuel Z. Arkoff." [Interview.]
"Steve Broidy." [Interview.]
"William Castle." [Interview.]
IN: Kings of the Bs

5730 **Strebel, Elizabeth Grottle.**
"Imperialist Iconography of Anglo-Boer War Film Footage."
IN: Film Before Griffith

5731 **Strebel, Elizabeth Grottle.**
"Political Polarisation and French Cinema, 1934-39."
IN: Propaganda, Politics and Film

5732 **Strebel, Elizabeth Grottle.**
"Jean Renoir and the Popular Front."
IN: Feature Films as History

5733 **Strebel, Elizabeth.**
"Vichy Cinema and Propaganda."
IN: Film & Radio Propaganda ...

5734 **Street, Douglas.**
"*Pinocchio* [novel by] Carlo Collodi. *Pinocchio*—From Picaro to Pipsqueak."
IN: Children's Novels and the Movies

5735 **Strick, Philip.**
"*Cries and Whispers*."
IN: Sight and Sound

5736 **Strick, Philip.**
"Buster Keaton—The Great Stone Face."
"D.W. Griffith—Giving Birth."
IN: Movies of the Silent Years

5737 **Strick, Philip.**
"The Metropolis Wars: The City as Character in Science Fiction Films."
IN: Omni's Screen Flights ...

5738 **Strobel, Hans Rolf and Heinrich Tichawsky.**
"We Have Work to Do."
IN: West German Filmmakers on Film

5739 **Strock, Herbert L.**
"Herbert L. Strock." [An interview.]

IN: <u>Interviews with B ...</u>

Stroheim, Erich von. SEE: von Stroheim, Erich.

5740 **Struss, Karl.**
"Karl Struss." [Interviews by Charles Higham.]
IN: <u>Hollywood Cameramen</u>

5741 **Stuart, Andrea.**
"*The Color Purple*: In Defence [*sic*] of Happy Endings."
IN: <u>The Female Gaze</u>

5742 **Stuart, Fredric.**
"The Effects of Television on the Motion Picture Industry: 1948-1960."
IN: <u>The American Movie Industry</u>

5743 **Studlar, Gaylyn.**
"Masochism, Masquerade, and the Erotic Metamorphoses of Marlene Dietrich."
IN: <u>Fabrications</u>

5744 **Studlar, Gaylyn.**
"Masochism and the Perverse Pleasures of the Cinema."
IN: <u>Movies and Methods /v. 2</u>
<u>Film Theory and Criticism /4 ed</u>

5745 **Studlar, Gaylyn.**
"Midnight S/Excess: Cult Configurations of 'Femininity' and the Perverse."
IN: <u>The Cult Film Experience</u>

5746 **Studlar, Gaylyn and David Desser.**
"Never Having to Say You're Sorry: Rambo's Rewriting of the Vietnam War."
IN: <u>From Hanoi to Hollywood</u>

5747 **Stulberg, Gordon.**
"Film Company Management."
IN: <u>The Movie Business Book</u>

5748 **Stull, William.**
"The Primrose, Magenta and Blue Green Path of Color Movies." [RE: *Becky Sharp*.]
IN: <u>Celebrity Articles ...</u>

5749 **Sturges, John.**
"How the West Was Lost!"
IN: <u>Hollywood Directors 1941-1976</u>

5750 **Sturges, Preston.**
"Preston Sturges." [Interview by Andrew Sarris.]
IN: <u>Interviews with Film Directors</u>
<u>Hollywood Voices</u>

5751 **Subcommittee to Investigate Juvenile Delinquency, The.**
"[From:] Motion Pictures and Juvenile Delinquency."
"[From:] Television and Juvenile Delinquency."
IN: <u>Film and Society</u>

5752 **Suckow, Sherrie and Evan Kleiman.**
"[A History of Italian Cinema:] The 50's."
IN: <u>Italian Cinema</u>

5753 **Sufrin, Mark.**
"Filming Skid Row." [RE: *On the Bowery*.]

IN: <u>The Documentary Tradition /1 ed</u>
<u>The Documentary Tradition /2 ed</u>

5754 **Sugy, Catherine.**
"Black Men or Good Niggers?"
IN: <u>Film and the Liberal Arts</u>

5755 **Suid, Lawrence H.**
"Hollywood and the Military Image: An Overview."
"A Standard for the Future--*The Big Parade*; *What Price Glory?*; *Wings*."
"World War II: Fantasy--Creating an Image; Senate Investigations; *Air Force*; *Bataan*; *Sahara*."
"World War II: Reality--*Destination Tokyo*; *Thirty Seconds Over Tokyo*; *The Story of G.I. Joe*."
"World War II Refought--*Task Force*; *Battleground*; *Twelve O'Clock High*."
"The Image of the Marines and John Wayne--*Sands of Iwo Jima*; The John Wayne Image."
"A Different Image--The Korean Conflict; New Interpretations of World War II; *From Here to Eternity*; *The Caine Mutiny*."
"The Most Ambitious Undertaking--Re-Creating *The Longest Day*; Sylvester's Re-Evaluation of Military Assistance." [RE: Arthur Sylvester.]
"A Marriage Ends--A New Look at Cooperation; Antiwar Themes in Hollywood Films."
"The Military as Enemy--*Dr. Strangelove*; *Fail Safe*; *Seven Days in May*; *The Bedford Incident*; *The Americanization of Emily*."
"Wayne, Women, and Vietnam--Women's Roles; *The Green Berets*; Hawks and Doves."
"Film Biography as Reality--*Bridge at Remagen*; *Battle of the Bulge*; *Patton*: The Nineteen-Year Struggle; Delays and Disagreements; Developing the Character: Devil or Saint?; Production of *Patton*; Inteprepations."
"Illusion and Reality of War--*M*A*S*H*; *Catch-22*; *Tora! Tora! Tora!*; Renewed Controversy."
"Fiction and History in the 1970s--*The Last Detail*; *Cinderella Liberty*; World War II Nostalgia; *A Bridge Too Far*."
"Hollywood and Vietnam: A Beginning."
IN: <u>Guts & Glory</u>

5756 **Suid, Lawrence.**
"The Pentagon and Hollywood: *Dr. Strangelove or: How I Learned to Stop Worrying and Love the Bomb*."
IN: <u>American History/American Film</u>

5757 **Sukenick, Ronald.**
"Film Digression."
IN: <u>Writing in a Film Age</u>

5758 **Sukhdev, S.**
"S. Sukhdev." [Interview.]
IN: <u>Indian Cinema Superbazaar</u>

5759 **Surowiec, Catherine A.**
"Maurice Jaubert: Poet of Music."
IN: <u>Rediscovering French Film</u>

5760 **Survage, Léopold.**
"Colored Rhythm."
IN: <u>French Film Theory and Criticism /v. 1</u>

5761 **Sussex, Elizabeth.**
"Getting It Right."
IN: New Challenges for Documentary

5762 **Suter, Jacquelyn.**
"Feminine Discourse in *Christopher Strong*."
IN: Feminism and Film Theory

5763 **Sutherland, Allan T.**
"The Yorkshire Pioneers."
IN: Film Before Griffith

5764 **Sutherland, Donald.**
"Reflections of a Star."
IN: Anatomy of the Movies

5765 **Sutton, Martin.**
"Patterns of Meaning in the Musical."
IN: Genre: The Musical

5766 **Sutton, Martin.**
"Superego Confrontation on *Forbidden Planet*."
IN: Omni's Screen Flights ...

5767 **Sutton, Ronald E.**
"Film Study: The Seventies and Beyond."
IN: The Compleat Guide to Film Study

5768 **Suttor, Timothy L.**
"Ken Russell."
IN: Religion in Film

5769 **Swallow, Norman.**
"The Current Affairs Documentary."
IN: The Documentary Tradition /1 ed
The Documentary Tradition /2 ed

5770 **Swann, Paul.**
"Hollywood in Britain: The Postwar Embargo on Exporting Feature Films to Britain."
IN: Current Research in Film /v. 3

5771 **Swanson, Gloria.**
"*Sunset Boulevard*."
IN: Bedside Hollywood

5772 **Swanson, Gloria.**
"Gloria Swanson." [Interview by John Kobal.]
IN: People Will Talk

5773 **Sweeney, James Johnson.**
"Léger and Cinesthetic."
IN: Introduction to the Art of the Movies

Sweeney, Kevin W. SEE: Hemmeter, Thomas.

5774 **Sweet, Blanche.**
"Blanche Sweet: The Player."
IN: The Real Tinsel

5775 **Swerling, Jo.**
"*Lifeboat*, Script Excerpt."
IN: Propaganda on Film

5776 **Switzgable, Meg.**
"Meg Switzgable." [Interview by Lynn Fieldman Miller.]
IN: The Hand That Holds the Camera

5777 **Syberberg, Hans Jürgen.**
"We Live in a Dead Country."
"Mein Führer - Our Hitler. The Meaning of Small Words."
"The Abode of the Gods."
"Media Response to Fassbinder's *Berlin Alexanderplatz*."
IN: West German Filmmakers on Film

5778 **Sylbert, Anthea.**
"The Costume Designer."
IN: Filmmakers on Filmmaking /v. 1

5779 **Tadao Sato.**
"Change in the Image of Mother in Japanese Cinema."
"The Multilayered Nature of the Tradition of Acting in Japanese Cinema."
IN: Cinema and Cultural Identity

5780 **Tait, Archie.**
"Distributing the Product."
IN: British Cinema Now

5781 **Talbot, Daniel.**
"Historic Hearings--From TV to Screen." [RE: *Point of Order!*]
IN: The Documentary Tradition /1 ed
The Documentary Tradition /2 ed

Talbot, David. SEE: Zheutlin, Barbara.

5782 **Talbott, Gloria.**
"Gloria Talbott." [An interview.]
IN: Interviews with B ...

5783 **Tallents, Sir Stephen.**
"The Documentary Film."
IN: Nonfiction Film Theory and Criticism

5784 **Talmadge, Norma.**
"Close-Ups."
IN: The American Film Industry

5785 **Tambling, Jeremy.**
"Ideology in the Cinema; Rewriting *Carmen*."
"Film Aspiring to the Condition of Opera."
"The Work of Mechanical Reproduction in Opera."
"Musicals, Opera and Film."
"*Owen Wingrave* and Television Opera."
"Opera as 'Culinary Art': Bergman's *Magic Flute*."
"The Modernist and Minimalist Aesthetic: *Moses und Aron*."
"Losey's 'Fenomeni Morbosi': *Don Giovanni*."
"Between the Spectacle and the Specular: *La traviata*."
"The Fusion of Brecht and Wagner: Syberberg's *Parsifal*."
IN: Opera, Ideology and Film

5786 **Tandava, G.**
"The Documentary: Systematic Images."
IN: Indian Cinema Superbazaar

5787 **Tanner, Alain.**
"Irony is a double-edged weapon ..."
IN: The Cineaste Interviews

5788 Tanner, Louise.
"The Celluloid Safety Valve."
   IN: The Movies: An American Idiom

5789 Tapiovaara, Nyrki.
"Film in the Social Stuggle."
   IN: Cinema in Finland

5790 Taradash, Daniel.
"'I Don't Know, I've Never Read One Of His First
   Drafts'--" [RE: an interview.]
   IN: Blueprint on Babylon

5791 Taradash, Daniel.
"Daniel Taradash: Triumph and Chaos." [Interview by
   David Thomson.]
   IN: Backstory 2

Tarkington, Ralfe G. SEE: Matthews, Glenn E.

5792 Tarratt, Margaret.
"Monsters from the Id."
   IN: Film Genre
       Film Genre Reader

5793 Tassone, Aldo.
"From Romagna to Rome: The Voyage of a Visionary
   Chronicler (*Roma* and *Amarcord*)."
   IN: Federico Fellini

5794 Tatum, Stephen.
"The Classic Westerner: Gary Cooper."
   IN: Shooting Stars

5795 Tavel, Ronald.
"Shortcomings of the Sexual Metaphor in New York's
   Independent Films."
   IN: The New American Cinema

5796 Tavernier, Bertrand.
"Blending the personal with the political ..."
   IN: The Cineaste Interviews

5796a Tavernier-Courbin, Jacqueline.
"The Social Function of Humor in Charles Chaplin's
   Movies."
   IN: Charlie Chaplin

5797 Taylor, Al and Sue Roy (editors).
"Cecil Holland."
"Jack Pierce."
"Jack and Bob Dawn."
"The Baus." [RE: George, Gordon and Robert Bau.]
"Clay Campbell."
"Lee Greenway."
"William Tuttle."
"Emile LaVigne."
"Charles Schram."
"The Norins." [RE: Josef, Gustaf and John Norin.]
"Ben Nye, Sr."
"Howard Smit."
"Philip W.N. Leakey."
"Roy Ashton."
"Robert Schiffer."
"Stuart Freeborn."
"Dick Smith."
"Christopher Tucker."
"John Chambers."
"Fred Blau."
"Thomas Burman."
"Ken Chase."
"Stan Winston."
"Rick Baker."
"Morton K. Greenspoon."
   IN: Making a Monster

5798 Taylor, Anna-Marie.
"*Lucía*."
   IN: Sexual Stratagems

5799 Taylor, Bella.
"Martin Scorsese."
   IN: Close-Up: The Contemporary Director

5800 Taylor, Clyde.
"Africa."
   IN: World Cinema Since 1945

5801 Taylor, Clyde.
"Black Cinema in the Post-aesthetic Era."
   IN: Questions of Third Cinema

5802 Taylor, Clyde.
"Decolorizing the Image: New U.S. Black Cinema."
"Third World Cinema: One Struggle, Many Fronts."
   IN: Jump Cut

5803 Taylor, Clyde.
"The Colonialist Subtext in *Platoon*."
   IN: From Hanoi to Hollywood

5804 Taylor, Clyde.
"We Don't Need Another Hero: Anti-Theses on
   Aesthetics."
   IN: Critical Perspectives on Black ...

5805 Taylor, John Russell.
"F.W. Murnau--Master of Light."
"Gloria Swanson."
"Speechless Hitchcock."
"*Metropolis*."
   IN: Movies of the Silent Years

5806 Taylor, John Russell.
"Federico Fellini."
"Michelangelo Antonioni."
"Luis Buñuel."
"Robert Bresson."
"Ingmar Bergman."
"Alfred Hitchcock."
"The New Wave: François Truffaut, Jean-Luc Godard,
   Alain Resnais."
   IN: Cinema Eye, Cinema Ear

5807 Taylor, John Russell.
"Lindsay Anderson and Free Cinema."
"Anthony Asquith."
"Claude Autant-Lara."
"René Clair."
"Jean Cocteau."
"Federico Fellini."

"Robert Hamer and Ealing Comedy."
"Michael Powell."
"Satyajit Ray."
"Carol Reed and David Lean."
"Leni Riefenstahl."
"Robert Siodmak."
"James Whale."
"Robert Wise."
    IN: <u>Cinema: A Critical Dictionary</u>

5808 Taylor, John Russell.
"Claude Chabrol."
"Pier Paola Pasolini."
"Lindsay Anderson."
"Stanley Kubrick."
"Andy Warhol/Paul Morrissey."
"Satyajit Ray."
"Miklós Jancsó."
"Dušan Makavejev."
    IN: <u>Directors and Directions</u>

5809 Taylor, John Russell.
"Tell Me Lies."
    IN: <u>Focus on Orson Welles</u>

5810 Taylor, John Russell.
"Buñuel's Mexican Films."
"*I vitelloni* and *La strada*."
    IN: <u>Great Film Directors</u>

5811 Taylor, John Russell.
"Letter: Critical Attitudes."
    IN: <u>Sight and Sound</u>

5812 Taylor, John Russell.
"*The Seventh Seal*."
    IN: <u>Focus on The Seventh Seal</u>

5813 Taylor, John Russell and Arthur Jackson.
"What Is a Musical?"
    IN: <u>Crossroads to the Cinema</u>

5814 Taylor, Philip M.
"British Official Attitudes Towards Propaganda
    Abroad, 1918-39."
    IN: <u>Propaganda, Politics and Film</u>

5815 Taylor, Philip M.
"Propaganda in International Politics, 1919-1939."
    IN: <u>Film & Radio Propaganda ...</u>

5816 Taylor, Richard.
"*Hiroshima: A Document of the Atomic Bombing*."
    IN: <u>Nuclear War Films</u>

5817 Taylor, Richard.
"*Mother*."
"*October*."
"*Three Songs of Lenin*."
"*Alexander Nevsky*."
"*Triumph of the Will*."
"*The Wandering Jew*."
"*Uncle Kruger*."
"*Kolberg*."
    IN: <u>Film Propaganda</u>

5818 Taylor, Richard.
"Ideology as Mass Entertainment: Boris Shumyatsky
    and Soviet Cinema in the 1930s."
    IN: <u>Inside the Film Factory</u>

5819 Taylor, Richard.
"On the Red Front."
    IN: <u>Movies of the Silent Years</u>

5820 Taylor, Richard and Ian Christie.
"Entering the Film Factory."
    IN: <u>Inside the Film Factory</u>

Taylor, Richard. SEE: Shaheen, Jack G.

5821 Taylor, Robert.
"*The Last Hurrah* [novel by] Edwin O'Connor. John
    Ford's Boston."
    IN: <u>The Modern American Novel ...</u>

5822 Taylor, Samuel.
"A Talk by Samuel Taylor, Screenwriter of *Vertigo*."
    IN: <u>Hitchcock's Re-Released Films</u>

5823 Teas, Araminta.
"Hedda Hopper: *From Under My Hat*."
    IN: <u>Sight and Sound</u>

5824 Tebbel, John.
"U.S. Television Abroad: Big New Business."
    IN: <u>Film and Society</u>

Téchiné, André. SEE: Comolli, Jean-Louis.

Teddlie, Charles. SEE: Kindem, Gorham.

Tel Quel. SEE: Cahiers du Cinema.

5825 Telefilm International Magazine.
"[From:] An Exclusive Interview ... E. William Henry."
    IN: <u>Film and Society</u>

5826 Telotte, J.P.
"Beyond All Reason: The Nature of the Cult."
"*Casablanca* and the Larcenous Cult Film."
    IN: <u>The Cult Film Experience</u>

5827 Telotte, J.P.
"Faith and Idolatry in the Horror Film."
    IN: <u>Planks of Reason</u>

5828 Telotte, J.P.
"The Doubles of Fantasy and the Space of Desire."
    IN: <u>Alien Zone</u>

5829 Telotte, J.P.
"The Human Landscape of John Ford's South."
    IN: <u>The South and Film</u>

5830 Telotte, J.P.
"Through a Pumpkin's Eye: The Reflexive Nature of
    Horror."
    IN: <u>American Horrors</u>

5830a Telotte, J.P.
"*Film Noir* at Columbia: Fashion and Innovation."
    IN: <u>Columbia Pictures</u>

5831 **Teng Wenji.**
"Teng Wenji, Middle-Aged New Director." [Interview
by George S. Semsel.]
IN: Chinese Film

5832 **Tenney, Del.**
"Del Tenney." [An interview.]
IN: Interviews with B ...

5833 **Terayama, Shuji.**
"Shuji Terayama." [Interview by Joan Mellen.]
IN: Voices from the Japanese Cinema

5834 **Terry, Alice.**
"'If You Beat Me, I Wept': Alice Terry Reminisces
About Silent Films." [Interview by George C. Pratt.]
IN: Image on the Art ...

5835 **Teshigahara, Hiroshi.**
"Hiroshi Teshigahara." [Interview by Joan Mellen.]
IN: Voices from the Japanese Cinema

5836 **Tesson, Charles.**
"Gerardo de Leon, An Amazing Discovery."
"The Cult of the Image in Lino Brocka."
IN: Readings in Philippine Cinema

5837 **Testa, Bart.**
"*Un Certain Regard*: Characterization in the First
Years of the French New Wave."
IN: Making Visible the Invisible

5838 **Testa, Bart.**
"François Truffaut."
IN: Religion in Film

5839 **Testa, Bart.**
"Reflections on Makavejev: the Art Film and
Transgression."
IN: Before the Wall Came Down

5840 **Tevis, Charles V.**
"Censoring the Five-Cent Drama."
IN: The Movies in Our Midst

5840a **Tewkesbury, Joan.**
"Joan Tewkesbury." [Interview by Anthony Loeb.]
IN: Filmmakers in Conversation

5841 **Thalberg, Irving.**
"The Modern Photoplay."
IN: Film: Readings in the Mass Media
Introduction to the Photoplay
Film and Society

5842 **Thaxton, David.**
"*Mission to Moscow*."
IN: The American Film Heritage

5843 **Theisen, Earl.**
"The History of the Animated Cartoon."
"The History of Nitrocellulos as a Film Base."
IN: A Technological History ...

5844 **Thiher, Allen.**
"The Impressionist Avant-Garde."
"Surrealism's Enduring Bite: *Un Chien andalou*."

"The Surrealist Film: Man Ray and the Limits of
Metaphor."
"*Le Sang d'un Poéte*: Film as Orphism."
"From *Entr'acte* to *A Nous la Liberté*: René Clair and
the Order of Farce."
"Vigo's *Zéro de conduite*: Surrealism and the Myth of
Childhood."
"Jean Renoir and the Mimesis of History."
"Prévert and Carné's *Le Jour se lève*: Proletarian
Tragedy."
"Bresson's *Un condamné à mort*: The Semiotics of
Grace."
"The Existential Play in Truffaut's Early Films."
"*L'Année dernière à Marienbad*: The Narration of
Narration."
"Postmodern Dilemmas: Godard's *Alphaville* and
Deux ou trois choses que je sais d'elle."
"Afterword: Is Film a Language?"
IN: The Cinematic Muse

5845 **Thirard, P.-L.**
"Food for Thought." [RE: *Nazarin*.]
IN: The World of Luis Buñuel

5846 **Thomas, Bob.**
"Alfred Hitchcock."
"Assistant Director/Production Manager: Chico Day."
"From Assistant to Director: Wendell Franklin."
"Gordon Parks."
"Jack Lemmon."
IN: Directors in Action

Thomas, Dylan. SEE: Deren, Maya.

5847 **Thomas, Harry.**
"Harry Thomas." [An interview.]
IN: Interviews with B ...

5848 **Thomas, John.**
"Gobble, Gobble ... One of Us."
IN: Focus on The Horror Film

5849 **Thomas, Kevin.**
"*Cutter's Way*."
"*Night Moves*."
"*The Fury*."
IN: Produced and Abandoned

5850 **Thomas, Rosie.**
"India."
IN: World Cinema Since 1945

Thomas, Rosie. SEE: Gandhy, Behroze.

5851 **Thomas, Tony (editor).**
"Aaron Copland."
"Miklos Rozsa."
"David Raksin."
"Franz Waxman."
"Hugo Friedhofer."
"Max Steiner."
"Erich Wolfgang Korngold."
"Dimitri Tiomkin."
"Hans J. Salter."
"Bronislau Kaper."

"Alfred Newman."
"Bernard Herrmann."
"Elmer Bernstein."
"Henry Mancini."
"Fred Steiner."
"William Alwyn."
"John Addison."
"Jerry Fielding."
"Jerry Goldsmith."
"Leonard Rosenman."
    IN: Film Score

5852   **Thomas, Tony.**
"Sam Wood."
    IN: The Hollywood Professionals /v. 2

5853   **Thome, Rudolf.**
"That's Utopia: The Cinema of My Dreams."
"Thoughts about Filmmaking in the FRG."
    IN: West German Filmmakers on Film

5854   **Thompson, Frank.**
"Charles T. Barton."
    IN: Between Action and Cut

5855   **Thompson, Guadalupe Ochoa.**
"*Raíces de sangre*: Roots of Lineage, Sources of Life."
    IN: Chicano Cinema

5855a   **Thompson, John O.**
"Screen Acting and the Commutation Test."
    IN: Stardom

5856   **Thompson, Kristin.**
"Neoformalist Film Analysis: One Approach, Many
    Methods."
"'No, Lestrade, in This Case Nothing Was Left to
    Chance': Motivation and Delay in *Terror By Night*."
"Boredom on the Beach: Triviality and Humor in *Les
    Vacances de Monsieur Hulot*."
"Sawing Through the Bough: *Tout va bien* as a
    Brechtian Film."
"Duplicitous Narration and *Stage Fright*."
"Closure within a Dream? Point of View in *Laura*."
"Realism in the Cinema: *Bicycle Thieves*."
"An Aesthetic of Discrepancy: *The Rules of the
    Game*."
"*Play Time*: Comedy on the Edge of Percepton."
"Godard's Unknown Country: *Sauve qui peut (la vie)*."
"The Sheen of Armor, the Whinnies of Horses: Sparse
    Parametric Style in *Lancelot du Lac*."
"*Late Spring* and Ozu's Unreasonable Style."
    IN: Breaking the Glass Armor

5857   **Thompson, Kristin.**
"Non-Classical Spatial Structures in *Ivan the Terrible*:
    A Sample Analysis."
    IN: Explorations in National Cinemas

5858   **Thompson, Kristin.**
"The Concept of Cinematic Excess."
    IN: Narrative, Apparatus, Ideology

5859   **Thompson, Kristin.**
"Implications of the Cel Animation Technique."
    IN: The Cinematic Apparatus

5860   **Thompson, Kristin.**
"The Formulation of the Classical Style, 1909-28."
    IN: The Classical Hollywood Cinema

    Thompson, Kristin. SEE: Bordwell, David.

5861   **Thompson, Richard.**
"Sam Katzman: Jungle Sam, or, The Return of 'Poetic
    Justice, I'd Say'."
"*Thunder Road*: Maudit—'The Devil Got Him First'."
    IN: Kings of the Bs

5862   **Thompson, Richard.**
"Hawks at Seventy."
    IN: Focus on Howard Hawks

5863   **Thompson, Richard.**
"Meep-Meep!" [RE: Road Runner.] [NOTE: Also
    called "Meep Meep."]
    IN: The American Animated Cartoon
        Movies and Methods: An Anthology

5864   **Thompson, Richard.**
"Pronoun Trouble." [RE: Bugs Bunny and Daffy Duck.]
    IN: The American Animated Cartoon

5865   **Thompson, Richard and Tim Hunter.**
"Clint Eastwood."
    IN: American Directors /v. 2

5866   **Thoms, Albie.**
"Ken Hall."
"The Australian Avant-garde: 1972."
    IN: An Australian Film Reader

5867   **Thomson, David.**
"All Along the River." [RE: *Red River*.]
    IN: Sight and Sound

5868   **Thomson, David.**
"Directors and Directing."
"Screenwriters and Screenwriting."
    IN: Anatomy of the Movies

5869   **Thomson, David.**
"Godard."
"Hitchcock and Moralist Narrative."
"Renoir's Anecdotal Narrative."
    IN: Great Film Directors

5870   **Thomson, David.**
"In Pursuit of Reality."
"Lon Chaney—The Man of a Thousand Faces."
"Louise Brooks--A Lust for Life."
"They Had Faces Then."
    IN: Movies of the Silent Years

5871   **Thomson, David.**
"Narrative Viewpoint in *Vertigo*."
    IN: The Classic Cinema

5872   **Thomson, David.**
"Sex in Science Fiction Films: Romance or
    Engineering?"
"The Fear of Intelligence in Futuristic Films."
    IN: Omni's Screen Flights ...

5873 Thornhill, Michael.
"Strategies for an Industry—Government Intervention."
   IN: An Australian Film Reader

5874 Tian Zhuangzhuang.
"Tian Zhuangzhuang, Fifth Generation Director and Cinematographer." [Interview by George S. Semsel.]
   IN: Chinese Film

5875 Tibbetts, John C.
"Rowland Brown."
   IN: Between Action and Cut

Tichawsky, Heinrich. SEE: Strobel, Hans Rolf.

5876 Tiessen, Paul.
"Claude Jutra."
   IN: Religion in Film

5877 Tim, Tiny.
"Tiny Tim." [Interview by Charles Higham.]
   IN: Celebrity Circus

5878 Timberg, Bernard.
"New Forms of Media and the Challenge To Copyright Law."
   IN: Fair Use and Free Inquiry

Timberg, Bernard. SEE: Lawrence, John Shelton.

5879 Timberg, Sigmund.
"A Modernized Fair Use Code for Visual, Auditory, and Audiovisual Copyrights: Economic Context, Legal Issues, and the Laocöon Shortfall."
   IN: Fair Use and Free Inquiry

5880 *Time Magazine*.
"The People Own the Air."
   IN: Film and Society

5881 *Time Magazine*.
"The Shock of Freedom in Films."
"The Moonchild and the Fifth Beatle." [RE: Dustin Hoffman.]
   IN: The Movies: An American Idiom

5882 *Time Magazine*.
"An Angry Film—*Native Land*."
   IN: The Documentary Tradition /1 ed
       The Documentary Tradition /2 ed

5883 Tiomkin, Dmitri.
"Composing for Films."
   IN: Film and the Liberal Arts

5884 Tiongson, Nicanor G.
"From Stage to Screen: Philippine Dramatic Traditions and the Filipino Film."
   IN: Readings in Philippine Cinema

5885 Toback, James.
"James Toback." [Interview by John Andrew Gallagher.]
   IN: Film Directors on Directing

5886 Tobin, Genevieve.
"An Actress' Working Day."
   IN: Celebrity Articles ...

5887 Tobin, Yann.
"John M. Stahl."
"Mitchell Leisen."
   IN: American Directors /v. 1

5888 Todd, Janet M.
"*Dracula* [novel by] Bram Stoker; *Nosferatu the Vampyre* [film by] Werner Herzog. The Classic Vampire."
   IN: The English Novel and the Movies

5889 Toiviainen, Sakari.
"New Finnish Cinema."
"The Films of Risto Jarva."
   IN: Cinema in Finland

5890 Toiviainen, Sakari and Peter von Bagh.
"The Challenge of Nyrki Tapiovaara."
   IN: Cinema in Finland

5891 Toland, Greg.
"Composition of the Moving Image."
   IN: The Movies as Medium

5892 Toland, Greg.
"How I Broke the Rules in *Citizen Kane*."
   IN: Focus on Citizen Kane

5893 Tolstoy, Lev.
"It May Turn Out To Be a Powerful Thing."
   IN: Authors on Film

5894 Tomaselli, Keyan G. and Ruth Tomaselli.
"Before and After Television: The South African Cinema Audience."
   IN: Current Research in Film /v. 3

Tomaselli, Ruth. SEE: Tomaselli, Keyan G.

5895 Tomasulo, Frank P.
"The Politics of Ambivalence: *Apocalypse Now* as Prowar and Antiwar Film."
   IN: From Hanoi to Hollywood

5896 Tomlinson, Doug.
"'They Should Be Treated Like Cattle': Hitchcock and the Question of Performance."
   IN: Hitchcock's Re-Released Films

5897 Tomlinson, Doug.
"Performance in the Films of Robert Bresson: The Aesthetics of Denial."
   IN: Making Visible the Invisible

5898 Török, Jean Paul.
"'Look at the Sea': *Peeping Tom*."
   IN: Powell, Pressburger and Others

5899 Török, Jean-Paul.
"The Sensitive Spot." [RE: *Shoot the Piano Player*.]
   IN: Focus on Shoot the Piano Player

5900 Tosi, Mario.
"Mario Tosi." [Interview by Dennis Schaefer and Larry Salvato.]
   IN: Masters of Light

5901   Tourneur, Jacques.
        "Jacques Tourneur."
            IN: The Celluloid Muse

5902   Tourneur, Maurice.
        "Meeting the Public Demands."
            IN: Hollywood Directors 1914-1940

5903   Towne, Robert.
        "A Screenwriter on Screenwriting."
            IN: Anatomy of the Movies

5904   Towne, Robert.
        "Robert Towne." [Interviewed by John Brady.]
            IN: The Craft of the Screenwriter

5905   Towne, Robert.
        "The Screenwriter."
            IN: Filmmakers on Filmmaking /v. 2

5905a   Trachtenberg, Alan.
        "Photography/Cinematography."
            IN: Before Hollywood

5906   Trauberg, Leonid.
        "An Experiment Intelligible to the Millions."
        "The Red Clown to the Rescue!"
            IN: The Film Factory

        Trauberg, Leonid. SEE: Kozintsev, Grigori.

5907   Trauth, Denise M. and John L. Huffman.
        "Public Nuisance Laws: A New Mechanism for Film
            Censorship."
            IN: Current Research in Film /v. 1

5908   Travers, Peter.
        "*Henry: Portrait of a Serial Killer.*"
            IN: Produced and Abandoned

5909   Travolta, John.
        "John Travolta." [Interview by Rex Reed.]
            IN: Travolta to Keaton

5910   Treacher, Arthur.
        "How a Butler Would Raise Money for the Guild."
            IN: Celebrity Articles ...

5911   Tretyakov, S., V. Shklovsky, E. Shub, and O. Brik.
        "Symposium on Soviet Documentary."
            IN: The Documentary Tradition /1 ed
                The Documentary Tradition /2 ed

5912   Treviño, Jesus Salvador.
        "Form and Technique in Chicano Cinema."
            IN: Chicano Cinema

5913   Trimmer, Joseph F.
        "*The Virginian* [novel by] Owen Wister. Three Treks
            West." [RE: 1929 and 1946.]
            IN: The Classic American Novel ...

5914   Trimmer, Joseph F.
        "*The Virginian* [1929 and 1946]." [NOTE: Very nearly
            the same essay that appears in the previous entry.]
            IN: Western Movies

5915   Trotsky, Lev.
        "Vodka, the Church and the Cinema."
            IN: The Film Factory

        Trotti, Lemar. SEE: Clark, Walter Van Tilburg.

5916   Troy, William.
        "*M.*"
            IN: Awake in the Dark

5917   Troy, William.
        "Beauty and the Beast."
            IN: Focus on The Horror Film

5918   Truffaut, François.
        "Evolution of the New Wave [Truffaut in interview with
            Jean-Louis Comolli and Jean Narboni]."
            IN: Cahiers du Cinéma, 1960-1968

5919   Truffaut, François.
        "François Truffaut." [Interview by Andrew Sarris.]
            IN: Interviews with Film Directors

5920   Truffaut, François.
        "Aznavour Gives the Tone."
        "Adapting *Shoot the Piano Player.*"
        "Should Films Be Politically Committed?"
        "From an Interview."
            IN: Focus on Shoot the Piano Player

5921   Truffaut, François.
        "A Wonderful Certainty." [RE: *Johnny Guitar.*]
        "A Full View." [RE: CinemaScope.]
        "The Rogues are Weary [review of Jacques Becker's
            Touchez pas au grisbi]."
            IN: Cahiers du Cinéma, The 1950s

5922   Truffaut, François.
        "*Citizen Kane.*"
            IN: Focus on Citizen Kane

5923   Truffaut, François.
        "Interview."
        "Interview (second extract)."
            IN: The New Wave: Critical Landmarks

5924   Truffaut, François.
        "Loving Fritz Lang."
            IN: Great Film Directors

5925   Truffaut, François.
        "Chaplin and Bazin."
        "Charlie Chaplin Was a Man Just Like Any Other
            Man."
            IN: Essays on Chaplin

5926   Truffaut, François.
        "*Dr. Cyclops.*"
        "[From:] The *Journal of Fahrenheit 451.*"
            IN: Focus on The Science Fiction Film

5927   Truffaut, François.
        "François Truffaut." [Interview by Charles Higham.]
            IN: Celebrity Circus

5928   Truffaut, François.
        "A Certain Tendency of the French Cinema."

IN: <u>Movies and Methods: An Anthology</u>

5929 **Truffaut, François.**
"We Must Continue Making Progress."
IN: <u>Film: A Montage of Theories</u>

5930 **Truffaut, François.**
"François Truffaut." [Interview by Charles T. Samuels.]
IN: <u>Encountering Directors</u>

5931 **Truffaut, Francois.**
"Francois Truffaut." [Interview by John Andrew Gallagher.]
IN: <u>Film Directors on Directing</u>

Truffaut, François. SEE: Chabrol, Claude; SEE: Rohmer, Eric.

5932 **Trumbo, Dalton.**
"Carlton Moss: Our Cover Boy."
IN: <u>The Best of Rob Wagner's Script</u>

5933 **Trumbo, Dalton.**
"Everything In Life Is Comprised Of Religion--And Religion Is Nature--" [RE: an interview.]
IN: <u>Blueprint on Babylon</u>

5934 **Trumpener, Katie.**
"Fragments of the Mirror: Self-Reference, Mise-en-Abyme, *Vertigo*."
IN: <u>Hitchcock's Re-Released Films</u>

5935 **Tsiantis, Lee.**
"Samuel Fuller."
IN: <u>Dictionary of Literary Biography /v. 26</u>

5936 **Tsivian, Yuri.**
"Early Russian Cinema: Some Observations."
IN: <u>Inside the Film Factory</u>

5937 **Tsivian, Yuri.**
"Some Historical Footnotes to the Kuleshov Experiment."
IN: <u>Early Cinema ...</u>

5938 **Tuchman, Mitch.**
"'Independent' Producers, Independent Distributors."
IN: <u>Anatomy of the Movies</u>

5939 **Tucker, Jean E.**
"Voices from the Silents."
IN: <u>Wonderful Inventions</u>

5940 **Tucker, Judy.**
"The Continuity Person."
IN: <u>Crossroads to the Cinema</u>

5941 **Tudor, Andrew.**
"Eisenstein: Great Beginnings."
"The Problem of Context: John Grierson."
"Aesthetics of Realism: Bazin and Kracauer."
"Critical Method: Auteur and Genre."
IN: <u>Theories of Film</u>

5942 **Tudor, Andrew.**
"Genre."
IN: <u>Film Genre</u>
    <u>Film Genre Reader</u>

5943 **Tudor, Andrew.**
"Genre and Critical Methodology."
IN: <u>Movies and Methods: An Anthology</u>

5944 **Tudor, Andrew.**
"Grierson's Purposive Cinema."
"The Famous Case of German Expressionism."
"The Star/Audience Relationship."
IN: <u>Conflict and Control in the Cinema</u>

5945 **Tudor, Andrew.**
"On Alcohol and the Mystique of Media Effects."
IN: <u>Images of Alcoholism</u>

5946 **Tudor, Andrew.**
"The Aussie Picture Show."
IN: <u>An Australian Film Reader</u>

5947 **Tulloch, John.**
"Conventions of Dying: Structural Contrasts in Chekhov and Bergman."
"Mimetic Cinema: The Reflection of Horror."
"Cinema's Function: Grierson and the Documentary Idea."
"Cinema as a Social System: The Pattern of Hollywood."
"Cinema and Social Control: The John Wayne Syndrome."
"Films of Conflict: From Eisenstein to the Retro-Style Reaction."
"Cinema Auteurs: Western Structures."
"Mimesis or Marginality? Collective Belief & German Expressionism."
IN: <u>Conflict and Control in the Cinema</u>

5948 **Tulloch, John.**
"Raymond Longford's *The Sentimental Bloke*."
IN: <u>An Australian Film Reader</u>

5949 **Tully, Jim.**
"Mizner the Magnificent." [RE: Wilson Mizner.]
"Frank Capra."
IN: <u>The Best of Rob Wagner's Script</u>

5950 **Tung, Timothy.**
"The Work of Xie Jin: A Personal Letter to the Editor."
IN: <u>Film and Politics in the Third World</u>

Tuo, Li. SEE: Nuanxin, Zhang.

5951 **Turaj, Frank.**
"Poland: The Cinema of Moral Concern."
IN: <u>Post New Wave Cinema ...</u>

5952 **Turan, Kenneth.**
"*Chilly Scenes of Winter*."
"*The Stunt Man*."
IN: <u>Produced and Abandoned</u>

5953 **Turim, Maureen.**
"Poetic Realism as Psychoanalytical and Ideological Operation: Marcel Carné's *Le Jour se lève*."
IN: <u>French Film: Texts and Contexts</u>

5954 Turim, Maureen.
"Designing Women: The Emergence of the New
    Sweetheart Line."
IN: Fabrications

5955 Turim, Maureen.
"Gentlemen Consume Blondes."
IN: Movies and Methods /v. 2
    Issues in Feminist Film Criticism

5956 Turim, Maureen.
"Jean-Marie Straub and Danièle Huillet: Oblique
    Angles on Film as Ideological Intervention."
IN: New German Filmmakers

5957 Turim, Maureen.
"Textuality and Theatricality in Brecht and
    Straub/Huillet: *History Lessons*."
IN: German Film and Literature

5958 Turim, Maureen.
"The Place of Visual Illusions."
IN: The Cinematic Apparatus

5959 Turim, Maureen.
"The Retraction of State Funding of Film and Video
    Arts and Its Effects on Future Practice."
IN: Cinema Histories, Cinema Practices

5960 Turim, Maureen.
"*Main Street* [novel by] Sinclair Lewis. *I Married a
    Doctor*. Main Street Meets Hollywood."
IN: The Classic American Novel ...

Turim, Maureen. SEE: Mulvey, Laura.

5961 Turman, Lawrence.
"*The Marriage of a Young Stockbroker*."
IN: Directors in Action

5962 Turner, George E.
"*Creation*, the Lost Epic."
"*Frankenstein*, the Monster Classic."
"*The Monkey's Paw*—A Hollywood Jinx."
"*Flash Gordon*, An Interplanetary Gothic."
"*D.O.A.* [1950], a Walk-In Homicide."
"*Night of the Hunter*—Ritual Murder."
"A Single Length of *Rope*."
"Desert Madness of *The Lost Patrol* and *Bad Lands*."
"Kiss and Kill from *Out of the Past*."
"Man, *The Most Dangerous Game*."
"The Flight of *Wings*."
"Two Faces of *Dracula* [1931]."
"The Mighty Spectacle of *Gunga Din*."
"The Exquisite Evil of *Cat People* [1942]."
"The Mystique of *Laura*."
IN: The Cinema of Adventure, Romance & Terror

5963 Turner, George E.
"*The Hunchback of Notre Dame* [1923]."
IN: The Cinema of Adventure, Romance & Terror

5964 Turner, George E.
"The Evolution of Special Visual Effects."
IN: The ASC Treasury ...

Turner, George E. SEE: Price, Michael H.

5965 Turner, John W.
"*Little Big Man*."
IN: Western Movies

5966 Turner, John W.
"*Little Big Man*: The Novel and the Film." [NOTE: An
    abridged version of the essay in *Western Movies*.]
IN: The Pretend Indians

5967 Turner, Lana.
"A Stab of Relief."
IN: Bedside Hollywood

5968 Turney, Catherine.
"Catherine Turney." [Interview by Lee Server.]
IN: Screenwriter: Words Become Pictures

5969 Tuska, Jon.
"Critical Theories about Western Films."
"The Structure of the Western Film."
"John Ford."
"Howard Hawks."
"Henry Hathaway."
"Anthony Mann."
"Budd Boetticher."
"Sam Peckinpah."
"Jesse James."
"Billy the Kid."
"'Wild Bill' Hickok."
"Wyatt Earp."
"Heroes in Defeat."
"Legendary and Historical Reality."
"Women."
"Images of Indians."
IN: The American West in Film

5970 Tuska, Jon.
"In the Beginning: *The Great Train Robbery*."
"The Making of Broncho Billy: *Shootin' Mad*."
"The Western at Inceville: *The Invaders* and *On the
    Night Stage*."
"D.W. Griffith and the Western: *The Battle of
    Elderbush Gulch*."
"Colonel Selig Goes West: *The Spoilers* and *The
    Heart of Texas Ryan*."
"The Rise of Famous Players-Lasky: *The Squaw
    Man*."
"Universal in the Teens: *Straight Shooting* and *The
    Man with a Punch*."
"William S. Hart at Famous Players-Lasky: *Wagon
    Tracks* and *The Toll Gate*."
"The Western Epic Begins: *The Covered Wagon* and
    The Iron Horse."
"Universal in the Twenties: *The Border Sheriff* and
    The Flaming Frontier."
"The Fading of William S. Hart: *Tumbleweeds*."
"The Silent Zane Grey Westerns: *Wild Horse Mesa*
    and *The Vanishing American*."
"Indian Summer--The Saga of Fred Thomson:
    Thundering Hoofs."

"Fox Film Corporation in the Twenties: *The Gentle Cyclone* and *The Great K & A Train Robbery*."

"Tim McCoy at Metro-Goldwyn-Mayer: *Winners of the Wilderness*."

"Ken Maynard at First National: *The Red Raiders*."

"Universal In 1930: *Spurs*."

"The Western Serial in Transition--Part One: *The Indians Are Coming*."

"Classics of the Early Sound Era: *The Virginian* and *Law and Order*."

"Frontier Legends--Part One: *Billy the Kid* and *Pat Garrett and Billy the Kid*."

"The Western Serial in Transition--Part Two: *The Lightning Warrior*."

"Buck Jones at Columbia: *Men Without Law*."

"Tom Mix Rides Again: *Rider of Death Valley*."

"Tim McCoy at Columbia: *End of the Trail*."

"Hoot Gibson on Hard Times: *Cowboy Counsellor*."

"Ken Maynard at Universal: *The Strawberry Roan* and *Wheels of Destiny*."

"Buck Jones at Universal: *The Red Rider* and *The Ivory-Handled Guns*."

"The Autry Phenomenon—Part One: *In Old Santa Fe* and *Red River Valley*."

"The Coming of Cassidy: *Hop-a-long Cassidy* and *Hopalong Rides Again*."

"The Sound Zane Grey Westerns: *Man of the Forest* and *Heritage of the Desert*."

"The Three Mesquiteers: *Powdersmoke Range*, *The Bold Caballero* and *The Riders of the Whistling Skull*."

"The Golden Age of the Western Serial: *The Painted Stallion* and *Overland with Kit Carson*."

"George O'Brien in the Thirties: *Lawless Valley*."

"Cecil B. De Mille and Western Spectacle: *The Plainsman* and *Union Pacific*."

"Frontier Legends--Part Two: *Jesse James*, *The Return of Frank James*, *They Died with Their Boots On* and *Little Big Man*."

"The Duke with Spurs: *Stagecoach* and *The Dark Command*."

"Rebirth and Death: *Destry Rides Again* (1932) and *Destry Rides Again* (1939)."

"Charles Starrett at Columbia: *The Durango Kid*."

"'So Long, Rough Riders': *The Gunman from Bodie*."

"Universal in the Forties: *West of Carson City* and *Oklahoma Raiders*."

"The Revival of the Action Western: *The Cisco Kid in Old New Mexico*, *Wild Horse Mesa* and *Mojave Firebrand*."

"The King of the Cowboys: *Sunset in El Dorado* and *My Pal Trigger*."

"The Autry Phenomenon—Part Two: *The Cowboy and the Indians* and *Indian Territory*."

"Harry Sherman at United Artists: *American Empire* and *Buckskin Frontier*."

"Frontier Legends--Part Three: *My Darling Clementine*."

"David O. Selznick and the Western: *Duel in the Sun*."

"Howard Hawks: *Red River* and *Rio Bravo*."

"John Ford and the Indian Wars: *Fort Apache* and *She Wore a Yellow Ribbon*."

"New Directions at Columbia and Republic: *Coroner Creek* and *Hellfire*."

"The New Epics: *The Ox-Bow Incident*, *Shane* and *Wagon Master*."

"The Postwar Indians: *Broken Arrow* and *Run of the Arrow*."

"The Antisocial Western: *High Noon*, *Silver Lode* and *3:10 to Yuma*."

"John Wayne and the Indian: *Hondo* and *McLintock*."

"The Western Without Heroes: *Cat Ballou*, *Hang 'em High*, *Will Penny* and *Monte Walsh*."

"Sam Peckinpah and the Western with Only Villains: *Ride the High Country* and *The Wild Bunch*."

"The Duke Alone: *True Grit* and *The Cowboys*."

IN: <u>The Filming of the West</u>

5971   **Tuska, Jon.**
"*Trader Horn*: A Cinematograph."
"*Rain*: A Cinematograph."
"Visions of Armageddon: *War of the Worlds*."
"The American Western Cinema: 1903-Present."
"Yakima Canutt: A Career Study."
"Spencer Gordon Bennet: A Career Study."
"A Conversation with Dick Richards."
IN: <u>A Variable Harvest</u>

5972   **Tuska, Jon.**
"Alfred Hitchcock."
"Henry King."
"John Huston."
"Spencer Gordon Bennet."
IN: <u>Close-Up: The Hollywood Director</u>

5973   **Tuska, Jon.**
"Dick Richards."
"Roman Polanski."
"Sam Peckinpah."
IN: <u>Close-Up: The Contemporary Director</u>

5974   **Tuska, Jon.**
"H. Bruce Humberstone."
"Howard Hawks."
"Yakima Canutt."
IN: <u>Close Up: The Contract Director</u>

5975   **Tuska, Jon.**
"H. Bruce Humberstone."
"Henry King."
"Alfred Hitchcock."
"Howard Hawks."
"John Huston."
"Orson Welles."
"Roman Polanski."
"Sam Peckinpah."
IN: <u>Encounters with Filmmakers</u>

5976   **Tuska, Jon.**
"The American Western Cinema: 1903-Present."
IN: <u>Focus on The Western</u>

5977   **Tuttle, Frank.**
"Hollywood Bites Dog."
IN: <u>Hollywood Directors 1914-1940</u>

Twomey, Alfred E. SEE: McClure, Arthur.

5978 **Twomey, John.**
"From Eisenstein to Prime Time: the Film and Television Design Career of Nikolai Soloviov."
IN: Before the Wall Came Down

5979 **Tyler, Parker.**
"*Rashomon* as Modern Art."
IN: Renaissance of the Film
Focus on Rashomon

5980 **Tyler, Parker.**
"[From:] *Magic and Myth of the Movies*: Preface."
IN: Film Theory and Criticism /1 ed
Film Theory and Criticism /2 ed
Film Theory and Criticism /3 ed
Film Theory and Criticism /4 ed

5981 **Tyler, Parker.**
"A Preface to the Problems of the Experimental Film."
"For *Shadows*, Against *Pull My Daisy*."
"Orson Welles and the Big Experimental Film Cult."
IN: Film Culture Reader

5982 **Tyler, Parker.**
"Documentary Technique in Film Fiction."
"Leni Riefenstahl's *Olympia*."
IN: The Documentary Tradition /1 ed
The Documentary Tradition /2 ed

5983 **Tyler, Parker.**
"Hollywood's Surrealist Eye."
IN: Film: An Anthology

5984 **Tyler, Parker.**
"Is Film Criticism Only Propaganda?"
IN: The New American Cinema
Film: Readings in the Mass Media

5985 **Tyler, Parker.**
"Mirage of the Sunken Bathtub." [RE: John Ford.]
IN: Great Film Directors

5986 **Tyler, Parker.**
"Movies and the Human Image."
IN: Film: A Montage of Theories

5987 **Tyler, Parker.**
"The Film Sense and the Painting Sense."
IN: Film and the Liberal Arts

5988 **Tyler, Parker.**
"The Awful Fate of the Sex Goddess."
IN: Awake in the Dark

5989 **Tyler, Parker.**
"The Horse: Totem Animal of Male Power—An Essay in the Straight-Camp Style."
"Masterpieces by Antonioni and Bergman."
IN: Film Theory and Criticism /1 ed

5990 **Tyler, Parker.**
"The Daylight Dream."
IN: Crossroads to the Cinema

Tyler, Parker. SEE: Deren, Maya.

5991 **Tynan, Ken.**
"Toby Jug and Bottle." [RE: W.C. Fields.]
IN: Sight and Sound

5992 **Tyan [*sic*, Tynan], Kenneth.**
"Orson Welles."
IN: Focus on Orson Welles

5993 **Tynan, Kenneth.**
"Garbo."
IN: Film Theory and Criticism /1 ed
Film Theory and Criticism /2 ed
Film Theory and Criticism /3 ed

5994 **Tyndall, Andrew.**
"Cinema and the Superego."
IN: Cinema Histories, Cinema Practices

5995 **Tynjanov, Jurij.**
"On the Foundations of Cinema."
IN: Russian Formalist Film Theory

5996 **Tynyanov, Yuri.**
"On FEKS." [RE: Factory of the Eccentric Actor.]
IN: The Film Factory

5997 **Tynyanov, Yury.**
"The Fundamentals of Cinema."
IN: The Poetics of Cinema

5998 **Uher, Stefan.**
"Stefan Uher." [Interview by Antonín J. Liehm.]
IN: Closely Watched Films

5999 **Umland, Sam.**
"Sexual Freaks and Stereotypes in Recent Science Fiction and Fantasy Films: Loathing Begets Androgyny."
IN: Eros in the Mind's Eye

6000 **UNESCO/American Film Institute.**
"Africa: Ola Balogun."
"Belgium: Raymond Ravar."
"France: Gérard Lenne."
"India: Satish Bahadur."
"Japan: Naosuke Togawa."
"Mexico: Manuel González Casanova."
"Sweden: Bertil Lauritzen."
"Union of Soviet Socialist Republics: V. Zdan."
"United Kingdom: Keith Lucas."
"United States of America: George Stevens, Jr."
"Yugoslavia: Momcilo Ilic."
IN: The Education of the Film-maker

6001 **U.S. House of Representatives, Committee on Un-American Activities.**
"Hearings Regarding the Communist Infiltration of the Motion-Picture-Industry Activities in the United States."
"Hearings Regarding the Communist Infiltration of the Motion-Picture-Industry Activities in the United States (Second Week)."
"Communist Infiltration of Hollywood Motion-Picture."
IN: The Movies in Our Midst

6002 **U.S. Senate, Subcommittee of the Committee on Interstate Commerce.**
"Moving-Picture and Radio Propaganda."
IN: The Movies in Our Midst

6003 **United States Supreme Court.**
"Mutual Film Corp. v. Industrial Commission of Ohio."
"United States v. Paramount Pictures, Inc."
"Joseph Burstyn, Inc. v. Wilson, Commisioner of New York, et al."
IN: The Movies in Our Midst

Uram, Eugene M. SEE: Shaheen, Jack G.

6003a **Uricchio, William.**
"Television as History: Representations of German Television Broadcasting, 1935-1944."
IN: Framing the Past

6004 **Ursini, James.**
"Preston Sturges."
IN: Dictionary of Literary Biography /v. 26

6005 **Vaché, Jacques.**
"War Letter."
IN: The Shadow and Its Shadow

6006 **Vadim, Roger.**
"Roger Vadim." [Interview by Charles Higham.]
IN: Celebrity Circus

6007 **Vaines, Colin.**
"Film Music and Composers."
IN: Anatomy of the Movies

6008 **Valenti, Jack.**
"The Movie Rating System."
IN: The Movie Business Book

6008a **Valenti, Peter.**
"*The Treasure of the Sierra Madre*: Spiritual Quest and Studio Patriarchy."
IN: Image and Likeness

6009 **Valentin, Albert.**
"Introduction to Black and White Magic."
IN: The Shadow and Its Shadow

6010 **Valentino, Rudolph.**
"You're a Hell of a Sheik."
IN: Bedside Hollywood

6011 **Van Ackeren, Robert.**
"Relationships, Reality, and Realism."
"How a Film Classic Becomes a Video Clip."
IN: West German Filmmakers on Film

Van Bodegraven, Donna L. SEE: Martin, John.

Van Der Beek, Stan. SEE: VanDerBeek, Stan / Vanderbeek, Stan.

6012 **Van der Veer, Frank.**
"Matte Painting Technique."
IN: The ASC Treasury ...

6013 **Van Dongen, Helen.**
"Robert J. Flaherty: 1884-1951."
IN: Nonfiction Film Theory and Criticism

6014 **Van Dyke, W.S.**
"Rx for a Thin Man."
IN: Hollywood Directors 1914-1940

6015 **Van Dyke, Willard.**
"The Director on Location."
IN: Ideas on Film

6016 **Van Dyke, Willard.**
"The Interpretive Camera in Documentary Films."
IN: Nonfiction Film Theory and Criticism

6017 **Van Dyke, Willard.**
"Willard Van Dyke." [Interview by G. Roy Levin.]
IN: Documentary Explorations

6017a **Van Peebles, Melvin.**
"Melvin Van Peebles." [Interview by Anthony Loeb.]
IN: Filmmakers in Conversation

6018 **Van Wert, William.**
"Germaine Dulac: First Feminist Filmmaker."
IN: Women and the Cinema

6019 **Van Wert, William.**
"Last Words: Observations on a New Language."
IN: The Films of Werner Herzog

6020 **Vance, Mark.**
"*The Birth of a Nation*."
IN: Focus on The Birth of a Nation

6021 **Vanderbeek, Stan.**
"Compound Entendre."
IN: Film: A Montage of Theories

6022 **VanDerBeek, Stan.**
"Culture-Intercom."
IN: Sight, Sound, and Society

6023 **Vanderbeek, Stan.**
"Re: Vision."
IN: Perspectives on the Study of Film

6024 **VanDerBeek, Stan.**
"'Culture: Intercom' and Expanded Cinema."
IN: The New American Cinema

6025 **Vanderwood, Paul J.**
"An American Cold Warrior: *Viva Zapata!*"
IN: American History/American Film

6026 **Vane, Edwin T.**
"Edwin T. Vane." [An interview.]
IN: Producers on Producing

6027 **Varda, Agnes.**
"One Sings, the Other Doesn't."
IN: The Cineaste Interviews

6028 **Vardac, A. Nicholas.**
"Henry Irving."
"David Belasco."
"Steele MacKaye."
"George Méliès."
"D.W. Griffith."
"David Garrick."

IN: <u>Stage to Screen</u>

6029 Vardac, A. Nicholas.
"Realism and Romance: D.W. Griffith."
IN: <u>Focus on D.W. Griffith</u>
<u>Imitations of Life</u>

6030 Vardac, A. Nicholas.
"Griffith and *The Birth of a Nation*."
IN: <u>Focus on D.W. Griffith</u>

6031 Vargas, Alain.
"*Shoot the Piano Player*."
IN: <u>Focus on Shoot the Piano Player</u>

6032 *Variety*.
"The Littlest Rebel."
IN: <u>The Black Man on Film</u>

6033 Varney, Bill.
"Bill Varney [on Sound: Re-Recording]." [Interview by David Chell.]
IN: <u>Moviemakers at Work</u>

6034 Vartanian, Carolyn Reed.
"Women Next Door to War: *China Beach*."
IN: <u>Inventing Vietnam</u>

6035 Vas, Robert.
"*My Homeland* and *Nine Days in '26* [Interview with] Robert Vas."
IN: <u>The Documentary Conscience</u>

6036 Vas, Robert.
"*The Confrontation*."
IN: <u>Sight and Sound</u>

6037 Vas, Robert.
"Sorcerers or Apprentices: Some Aspects of the Propaganda Film."
IN: <u>Propaganda on Film</u>
<u>Sight, Sound, and Society</u>
<u>Crossroads to the Cinema</u>

6038 Vas, Robert.
"Arrival and Departure." [RE: *This Sporting Life*.]
IN: <u>Renaissance of the Film</u>

6039 Vasudev, Aruna.
"The Woman: Vamp or Victim?"
IN: <u>Indian Cinema Superbazaar</u>

6040 Vasudev, Aruna.
"The Woman: Myth and Reality in the Indian Cinema."
IN: <u>Cinema and Cultural Identity</u>

6041 Vasudev, Aruna and Philippe Lenglet.
"The Film Societies and the Film Press."
IN: <u>Indian Cinema Superbazaar</u>

6042 Vaughan, Dai.
"Let There be Lumière."
IN: <u>Early Cinema ...</u>

6043 Vaughan, Dai.
"Television Documentary Usage."
IN: <u>New Challenges for Documentary</u>

6044 Vaughn [*sic*, Vaughan], Dai.
"The Space between Shots."
IN: <u>Movies and Methods /v. 2</u>

6045 Vaughan, Dai.
"*The Man With the Movie Camera*."
IN: <u>The Documentary Tradition /1 ed</u>
<u>The Documentary Tradition /2 ed</u>

6046 Vaughn, Stephen.
"Financiers, Movie Producers, and the Church: Economic Origins of the Production Code."
IN: <u>Current Research in Film /v. 4</u>

6047 Vautier, René.
"The Word Brother and the Word Comrade."
IN: <u>Algerian Cinema</u>

6048 Vávra, Otakar.
"Otakar Vávra." [Interview by Antonín J. Liehm.]
IN: <u>Closely Watched Films</u>

6049 Vazquez, Emilio Rodriguez and Carlos Vicente Ibarra.
"Filmmaking in Nicaragua: From Insurrection to INCINE."
IN: <u>Cinema and Social Change ...</u>

6050 Velguth, Paul.
"Notes on the Musical Accompaniment to the Silent Films."
IN: <u>Art in Cinema</u>

6051 Venturini, Franco.
"Origins of Neo-Realism."
IN: <u>Springtime in Italy</u>

6052 Vernet, Marc.
"Blinking, Flickering, and Flashing of the Black-and-White Film."
IN: <u>Apparatus</u>

6053 Véronneau, Pierre.
"Children of Vertov in the Land of Brecht."
IN: <u>Show Us Life</u>

6054 Vertov, Dziga.
"WE: Variant of a Manifesto."
"The Fifth Issue of *Kinopravda*."
"Kinoks: A Revolution."
"On the Organization of a Film Experiment Station."
"Advertising Films."
"On the Significance of Newsreel."
"*Kinopravda* [1923]."
"On the Film Known as *Kinoglaz*."
"On the Significance of Nonacted Cinema."
"*Kinoglaz* (A Newsreel in Six Parts)."
"The Birth of Kino-Eye."
"On *Kinopravda*."
"Artistic Drama and Kino-Eye."
"The Essence of Kino-Eye."
"To the Kinoks of the South."
"*Kinopravda* and *Radiopravda*."
"The Same Thing from Different Angles."
"The Factory of Facts."

"Kino-Eye."
"On *The Eleventh Year*."
"*The Man with a Movie Camera*."
"From Kino-Eye to Radio-Eye."
"[From:] The History of the Kinoks."
"Letter from Berlin."
"Replies to Questions."
"Let's Discuss Ukrainfilm's First Sound Film:
    Symphony of the Donbas."
"First Steps."
"How We Made Our Film About Lenin."
"Without Words."
"I Wish to Share My Experience."
"*Three Songs of Lenin* and Kino-Eye."
"*Kinopravda* [1934]."
"My Latest Experiment."
"On the Organization of a Creative Laboratory."
"The Truth About the Heroic Struggle."
"In Defense of Newsreel."
"About Love for the Living Person."
"[From:] Notebooks, Diaries: 1924, 1926, 1927, 1931,
    1933, 1934 (On Mayakovsky; More on
    Mayakovsky; On My Illness), 1936 (*Lullaby*) 1937,
    1938, 1939, 1940, 1941, 1942, 1943, 1944, 1945,
    1953 (On Editing)."
"Draft of a Scenario Intended to Be Filmed During a
    Journey by the Agit-train, The Soviet Caucasus."
"The Adventures of Delegates en route to Moscow for
    a Congress of the Comintern."
"Outline for the Scenario of *The Eleventh Year*."
"*The Man with a Movie Camera* (A Visual Symphony)."
"Sound March (From *Symphony of the Donbas*)."
"*Symphony of the Donbas* (*Enthusiasm*)."
"*She* and *An Evening of Miniatures*."
"*A Young Woman Composer*."
"*A Day Throughout the World*."
"*The Girl at the Piano*."
"Letter from a Woman Tractor Driver."
"*To You, Front!*."
"A Minute of the World."
"Gallery of Film Portraits."
"*Little Anya*."
    IN: Kino-Eye

6055   **Vertov, Dziga.**
"Diary Entry."
"Fiction Film Drama and the Cine-Eye."
"More on Mayakovsky (extract)."
"My Illness."
"Speech to the First All-Union Conference on Sound
    Cinema."
"The *Cine-Pravda*."
"The Cine-Eyes. A Revolution."
"The *Cine-Pravda*: A Report to the Cine-Eyes."
"The Factory of Facts."
"The Radio-Eye's March."
"We. A Version of a Manifesto." [RE: Cine-Eye.]
"*Cine-Pravda* and *Radio-Pravda*."
"*The Eleventh Year*."
    IN: The Film Factory

6056   **Vertov, Dziga.**
"Film Directors: A Revolution."
"The Vertov Papers."
    IN: Apparatus

6057   **Vertov, Dziga.**
"Kino-Eye: The Embattled Documentarists."
    IN: Cinema in Revolution

6058   **Vertov, Dziga.**
"Selected Writings."
    IN: The Avant-Garde Film

6059   **Vertov, Dziga.**
"The Writings of Dziga Vertov."
    IN: Film Culture Reader

6060   **Vertov, Dziga.**
"'Kinoks-Revolution', Selections."
    IN: Film Makers on Film Making

6061   **Vestal, Stanley.**
"The Hollywooden Indian."
    IN: The Pretend Indians

Viany, Alex. SEE: de Andrade, Joaquim Pedro.

6062   **Vidor, King.**
"Bringing Pulham to the Screen." [RE: *H.M. Pulham,
    Esq.*]
    IN: Hollywood Directors 1941-1976

6063   **Vidor, King.**
"King Vidor."
    IN: The Celluloid Muse

6064   **Vidor, King.**
"King Vidor." [Interview by Richard Schickel.]
    IN: The Men Who Made the Movies

6065   **Vidor, King.**
"King Vidor." [Interview by Charles Higham.]
    IN: Celebrity Circus

6066   **Vidor, King.**
"Rubber Stamp Movies."
    IN: Hollywood Directors 1914-1940

6067   **Vieira, João Luiz.**
"From *High Noon* to *Jaws*: Carnival and Parody in
    Brazilian Cinema."
    IN: Brazilian Cinema

Vieira, João Luiz. SEE: Merena, Elizabeth.

6068   **Viera, John David.**
"Images as Property."
    IN: Image Ethics

6069   **Vieyra, Paulin Soumanou.**
"African Cinema: Solidarity and Difference."
    IN: Questions of Third Cinema

6070   **Vieyra, Paulin Soumanou.**
"Five Major Films by Sembene Ousmane."
    IN: Film and Politics in the Third World

6071   **Vigo, Jean.**
"Toward a Social Cinema."
IN: <u>French Film Theory and Criticism</u> /v. 2

6071a   **Vigouroux-Frey, Nicole.**
"Charlie Chaplin or the 'Vaudeville Dispossessed'."
IN: <u>Charlie Chaplin</u>

6072   **Villagra, Nelson.**
"The Actor at Home and in Exile." [RE: Chile.]
IN: <u>Cinema and Social Change ...</u>

6073   **Vincendeau, Ginette.**
"In the Name of the Father: Marcel Pagnol's 'trilogy'
Marius, Fanny, César."
"Therapeutic Realism: Maurice Pialat's *A nos amours.*"
IN: <u>French Film: Texts and Contexts</u>

6073a   **Vincent, William.**
"Rita Hayworth at Columbia: The Fabrication of a
Star."
IN: <u>Columbia Pictures</u>

6074   **Vinneuil, François.**
"Screen of the Week: *La Marseillaise.*"
"Screen of the Week: *Les Croix de bois.*"
"Screen of the Week: *La Rue sans nom.*"
"Screen of the Week: *La Kermesse héroïque.*"
"Screen of the Week: The Cinema Awards (1936)."
"Screen of the Week: *La Bête humaine.*"
"Screen of the Week: *La Règle du jeu.*"
IN: <u>French Film Theory and Criticism</u> /v. 2

6075   **Violante, Marcela Ferná.**
"Inside the Mexican Film Industry: A Woman's
Perspective."
IN: <u>Cinema and Social Change ...</u>

6076   **Violi, Patrizia.**
"Language and the Female Subject."
IN: <u>Off Screen</u>

6077   **Virilio, Paul.**
"Cataract Surgery: Cinema in the Year 2000."
IN: <u>Alien Zone</u>

6078   **Visconti, Luchino.**
"Anthropomorphic Cinema."
IN: <u>Springtime in Italy</u>

    Visconti, Luchino. SEE: Germi, Pietro.

6079   **Vitone, Phil.**
"Notes on Communication and Representation in the
Development of Educational Television."
IN: <u>Explorations in Film Theory</u>

6080   **Vittorini, Elio.**
"Politics and Culture: A Letter to Togliatti."
IN: <u>Springtime in Italy</u>

6081   **Viviani, Christian.**
"Who Is Without Sin: The Maternal Melodrama in
American Film, 1930-1939."
IN: <u>Imitations of Life</u>
     <u>Home Is Where the Heart Is</u>

6082   **Vizzard, Jack.**
"See No Evil."
IN: <u>The Movies in Our Midst</u>

6083   **Vlácil, František.**
"František Vlácil." [Interview by Antonín J. Liehm.]
IN: <u>Closely Watched Films</u>

6084   **Vlasopolos, Anca.**
"The 'Woman's Film' Genre and Our Modern
Transmutation: *Kramer vs. Kramer.*"
IN: <u>Women and Film</u>

6085   **Vogel, Amos.**
"On Miklos Jancso."
IN: <u>The Image Maker</u>

6086   **Vogel, Amos.**
"On Seeing a Mirage."
IN: <u>The Films of Werner Herzog</u>

6087   **Vogel, Amos.**
"The Film Society."
IN: <u>Ideas on Film</u>

6088   **Vogel, Amos.**
"Thirteen Confusions."
IN: <u>The New American Cinema</u>

6089   **Voight, Jon.**
"Jon Voight." [Interview by Rex Reed.]
IN: <u>Travolta to Keaton</u>

6090   **Volkman, Toby Alice.**
"Out of South Africa: *The Gods Must Be Crazy.*"
IN: <u>Image Ethics</u>

    von Bagh, Peter. SEE: Toiviainen, Sakari.

6091   **Von Brandenstein, Patrizia.**
"Patrizia Von Brandenstein [on Production Design]."
[Interview by David Chell.]
IN: <u>Moviemakers at Work</u>

6092   **Von Gunden, Kenneth.**
"*Beauty and the Beast*: The Classic Fairy Tale."
"*Conan the Barbarian*: Sword and Sorcery."
"*The Dark Crystal*: Other Worlds, Other Times."
"*Dragonslayer*: Mythic Beasts/Genrebuster."
"*The 5,000 Fingers of Dr. T*: A Child's Fantasy."
"*It's a Wonderful Life*: The Guardian Angel."
"*Jason and the Argonauts*: Ancient Mythology."
"*King Kong* [1933]: The Giant Monster."
"*Lost Horizon*: The Hidden Paradise."
"*Popeye*: The Comic Strip Hero."
"*Superman*: The Super Hero."
"*Thief of Bagdad* [1940]: Arabian Nights."
"*Time Bandits*: Child as Hero."
"*Topper*: The Ghost Story."
"*The Wizard of Oz*: The Fabulous Journey."
IN: <u>Flights of Fancy</u>

6093   **von Harbou, Thea.**
"[From:] *The Woman in the Moon.*"
IN: <u>Focus on The Science Fiction Film</u>

6094   **von Praunheim, Rosa.**
"Gay Film Culture."
"Erika from Würzburg: A Portrait of the Actress
    Magdalena Montezuma."
"With Fond Greetings to Champagne-Schroeter."
"From Beast to Beast."
    IN: West German Filmmakers on Film

6095   **von Sternberg, Josef.**
"More Light."
    IN: Hollywood Directors 1941-1976

6096   **von Sternberg, Josef.**
"Josef von Sternberg." [Interview by Andrew Sarris.]
    IN: Interviews with Film Directors

6097   **von Sternberg, Josef.**
"The von Sternberg Principle."
    IN: Sternberg

6098   **von Sternberg, Josef.**
"Acting in Film and Theatre."
    IN: Film Makers on Film Making
        Focus on Film and Theatre

6099   **von Sternberg, Joseph [*sic*, Josef].**
"Film as a Visual Art."
    IN: Film and the Liberal Arts

6100   **von Stroheim, Erich.**
"*The Merry Widow*."
    IN: Film Culture Reader

6101   **von Stroheim, Erich.**
"Erich von Stroheim." [Interview by Andrew Sarris.]
    IN: Interviews with Film Directors

6102   **von Stroheim, Erich.**
"The Seamy Side of Directing."
    IN: Hollywood Directors 1914-1940
        The First Film Makers

6103   **von Stroheim, Erich.**
"Introducing 'The Merry Widow'."
    IN: Film Makers on Film Making

6104   **von Stroheim, Erich.**
"Tribute to the Master."
    IN: Focus on D.W. Griffith

6105   **von Trotta, Margarethe.**
"Female Film Aesthetics."
"Working with Jutta Lampe."
    IN: West German Filmmakers on Film

6106   **von Zharen, W.M.**
"*Kidnapped* [novel by] Robert Louis Stevenson.
    Kidnapped—Improved Hodgepodge?"
    IN: Children's Novels and the Movies

6107   **Vonalt, Larry.**
"Looking Both Ways in *Casablanca*."
    IN: The Cult Film Experience

6108   **Vorkapich, Slavko.**
"Cinematics: Some Principles Underlying Effective
    Cinematography."
    IN: Hollywood Directors 1914-1940

6109   **Vorkapich, Slavko.**
"Toward True Cinema."
    IN: Perspectives on the Study of Film
        Introduction to the Art of the Movies
        Film: A Montage of Theories

6110   **Voznesensky, Alexel.**
"Open Letter to Nemirovich-Danchenko and
    Stanislavsky."
    IN: The Film Factory

6111   **Vronskaya, Jeanne.**
"The VGIK."
"Andrei Tarkovsky."
"Andron Mikhalkov-Konchalovsky."
"Tarkovsky's *Andrei Rublev*."
"Mikhalkov-Konchalovsky's *Asya's Happiness*."
"Elem Klimov's Bitter Satires."
"Larissa Shepitko."
"Alexei Saltykov."
"Mikhail Bogin."
"Pavel Lubimov."
"Alexander Mitta."
"Vladimir Fetin."
"Gleb Panfilov."
"Vassili Shukshin."
    IN: Young Soviet Film Makers

6112   **Vuillermoz, Emile.**
"Before the Screen."
"Before the Screen: *Les Frères corses*."
"Before the Screen: Hermes and Silence." [RE: reply
    to L'Herbier, "Hermes and Silence."]
"Before the Screen: *La Dixième Symphonie*."
"Before the Screen: Aesthetic."
"Abel Gance and *Napoléon*."
"*La Roue*."
"*Napoléon*."
    IN: French Film Theory and Criticism /v. 1

6113   **Vuillermoz, Emile.**
"A Case of Conscience."
    IN: French Film Theory and Criticism /v. 2

6114   **Wagenknecht, Edward.**
"Mary Pickford."
"Lillian Gish."
"Clarine Seymour."
"Geraldine Farrar."
"May McAvoy."
"The Duncan Sisters."
"Clara Bow."
"Charles Chaplin."
    IN: Stars of the Silents

6115   **Wagenknecht, Edward.**
"Came the Dawn."
    IN: The Movies in Our Midst

6116   **Wagenknecht, Edward.**
"*A Poor Little Rich Girl*."
    IN: The Rivals of D.W. Griffith

6117 Wagner, Geoffrey.
"The Problem of Popularity."
"*Citizen Kane.*"
"The Trials of Technique."
"*Les Liaisons Dangereuses* [1959]."
"The Reproduction of Reality."
"*Greed.*"
"*The Blue Angel.*"
"Psychology of Cinema."
"*The House of Usher.*"
"The Norms of Narration."
"*Face to Face.*"
"Three Modes of Adaptation (A:) Transposition."
"*Wuthering Heights.*"
"*Jane Eyre.*"
"*Madame Bovary.*"
"*Lord Jim.*"
"*Hunger.*"
"*Last Year at Marienbad.*"
"*1984.*"
"Three Modes of Adaptation (B:) Commentary."
"*The Heiress.*"
"*Catch-22.*"
"*A Clockwork Orange.*"
"*The Stranger* [1967]."
"Three Modes of Adaptation (C): Analogy."
"*Candide.*"
"*The Trial.*"
"*Cabaret.*"
"*Death in Venice.*"
"*Contempt.*"
     IN: The Novel and the Cinema

6118 Wagner, Natalie and R.J.
"Natalie & R.J. Wagner."
     IN: Travolta to Keaton

6119 Wagner, Rob.
"Will Rogers."
"Will Rogers—Fool."
     IN: The Best of Rob Wagner's Script

6120 Wagner, Robert W.
"Film, Reality, and Religion."
     IN: Celluloid and Symbol

6121 Wagner, Robert.
"Robert Wagner." [Interview by Charles Higham.]
     IN: Celebrity Circus

6122 Wajda, Andrzej.
"Between the permissible and the impermissible ..."
     IN: The Cineaste Interviews

6123 Wajda, Andrzej.
"Destroying the Commonplace."
     IN: Film Makers on Film Making

6124 Wajda, Andrzej.
"The Artist's Responsibility."
     IN: Politics, Art and Commitment ...

6125 Wald, Malvin.
"Carl Foreman."

     IN: Dictionary of Literary Biography /v. 26

6126 Wald, Malvin.
"James Poe."
     IN: Dictionary of Literary Biography /v. 44

6127 Waldman, Diane.
"The Justice Department Versus the National Film
     Board of Canada: An Update and Analysis."
     IN: Current Research in Film /v. 4

6128 Waldman, Diane.
"The Politics of Positive Images ... There's More to a
     Positive Image Than Meets the Eye." [NOTE: Also
     called "There's More to a Positive Image Than
     Meets the Eye."]
     IN: Jump Cut
         Issues in Feminist Film Criticism

Waldman, Diane. SEE: Walker, Janet.

6129 Walker, Alexander.
"Marlene Dietrich: At Heart a Gentlemen."
     IN: Women and the Cinema

6130 Walker, Janet.
"Couching Resistance: Women, Film, and Postwar
     Psychoanalytic Psychiatry."
     IN: Psychoanalysis and Cinema

6131 Walker, Janet.
"Hollywood, Freud and the Representation of Women:
     Regulation and Contradiction, 1945-early 60s."
     IN: Home Is Where the Heart Is

6132 Walker, Janet and Diane Waldman.
"John Huston's *Freud* and Textual Repression: A
     Psychoanalytic Feminist Reading."
     IN: Close Viewings

6133 Walker, John.
"Winners and Losers (Michael Winner at Home)."
"Decline and Fall (The End of the National Film
     Finance Corporation)."
"Monopoly Money (Thorn-EMI and Rank)."
"The Sinking of Lord Grade (Lew Grade's ITC)."
"Carry on Hammering (Hammer Horrors and 'Carry
     On' Films)."
"The Old Guard ... (Anderson, Schlesinger, Reisz,
     Richardson, Hitchcock, Neame, titillations and TV
     spin-offs)."
"... And the New (Loach, [Barney] Platts-Mills,
     Brownlow, [David] Hemmings, [Andrew] Sinclair,
     [Peter] Medak, [Chris] Petit, Losey, [Mike] Hodges,
     Frears, Yates, Attenborough, [Bill] Forsyth)."
"Fools and Visions (Monty Python, Alan Parker,
     Ridley Scott, John Boorman)."
"Rogue Talents (Nicholas Roeg and Ken Russell)."
"Twinkle, Twinkle British Stars (James Fox, Michael
     Caine, Robert Stephens, Glenda Jackson, United
     British Artists)."
"Building Jerusalem (David Puttnam and Goldcrest)."
"Enter the Amateurs (HandMade Films, Virgin Vision)."
"Producing the Goods (Don Boyd, Michael Relph,
     Lewis Gilbert, Skreba)."

"Through a Screen Darkly (Channel Four, independent cinemas, video and the new technology)."
IN: The Once and Future Film

6134 **Walker, Michael.**
"Jerzy Skolimowski."
IN: Second Wave

Walker, Michael. SEE: Cameron, Ian.

6135 **Walker, Roy.**
"In Fair Verona." [RE: *Romeo and Juliet*, 1954.]
IN: Focus on Shakespearean Films

6136 **Wall, Eileen.**
"How to See a Film."
IN: The Compleat Guide to Film Study

6137 **Wall, James M.**
"Biblical Spectaculars and Secular Man."
IN: Celluloid and Symbol
      Crossroads to the Cinema

6138 **Wall, James M.**
"François Truffaut."
IN: Three European Directors

6138a **Wall, James M.**
"*2001: A Space Odyssey* and the Search for a Center."
IN: Image and Likeness

Wallace, Earl. SEE: Kelley, William.

6139 **Wallace, Irving.**
"Outline of Eccentricity."
IN: The Best of Rob Wagner's Script

6140 **Wallace, Peggy A.**
"The Most Important Factor Was the 'Spirit': Leni Riefenstahl During the Filming of *The Blue Light*."
IN: Image on the Art ...

6141 **Wallace, Stephen.**
"Film Australia: Isolated and Middle Class."
IN: An Australian Film Reader

Wallach, Eli. SEE: Jackson, Anne.

6142 **Waller, Gregory A.**
"*Dracula: The Vampire Play* (1927), *Dracula* (1931), and *Dracula* (1927)."
"*Horror of Dracula*, Hammer's Dracula Films, *El Conde Dracula*."
"*Dracula* (1973) and *Count Dracula* (1977)."
"*Nosferatu, A Symphony of Horror* [1922] and *Nosferatu the Vampyre* [1979]."
IN: The Living and the Undead

6143 **Waller, Gregory A.**
"Rambo: Getting to Win This Time."
IN: From Hanoi to Hollywood

6144 **Waller, Gregory A.**
"Made-for-Television Horror Films."
IN: American Horrors

6145 **Waller, Gregory A.**
"Mickey, Walt, and Film Criticism from *Steamboat Willie* to *Bambi*."
IN: The American Animated Cartoon

6146 **Waller, Gregory A.**
"Midnight Movies, 1980-1985: A Market Study."
IN: The Cult Film Experience

6147 **Waller, Gregory.**
"Film and Theater."
IN: Film and the Arts in Symbiosis

6148 **Walling, William.**
"*All the King's Men* [novel by] Robert Penn Warren. In Which Humpty Dumpty Becomes King."
IN: The Modern American Novel ...

6149 **Walling, William.**
"*Chinatown*."
IN: Film in Society

6150 **Wallis, Hal.**
"The Studio Executive."
IN: Filmmakers on Filmmaking /v. 1

6151 **Wallis, Victor and John D. Barlow.**
"Democracy as Participation: *The Battle of Chile*."
IN: Show Us Life

6152 **Walsh, Andrea S.**
"Ma Joad: A Depression Ideal for Wartime Women." [RE: *The Grapes of Wrath*.]
"*Mrs. Miniver*. Coming of Age in Wartime."
"*Watch on the Rhine*: A Not So 'Tender Comrade'."
"*Since You Went Away*: An American Mrs. Miniver."
"From Traditional Mother to Independent Daughter: *A Tree Grows in Brooklyn*, *I Remember Mama*, *Little Women*."
"Going It Alone / Variations on a Maternal Theme: *Now, Voyager*--From Matrophobia to Self-Sacrificing Maternality."
"Unrequited Mother Love: *To Each His Own*."
"Dark Mirror: *Mildred Pierce*—Obsessional Mother-Evil Daughter."
"Career Heroines in 1940s Women's Films: *His Girl Friday*, *Woman of the Year*, *Adam's Rib*, *Lady in the Dark*."
"*His Girl Friday* to *Adam's Rib*: The Evolution of the Career Woman Comedy and Its Appeal for Female Audiences."
"*Lady in the Dark*: The Underside of the Dream of Female Success."
"In Suspicion and Distrust: The Women's Movie Encounters the *Film Noir*."
"A Diffuse Distrust: *Possessed*."
"Suspicion Confirmed: *Suspicion*, *Gaslight*, *Sleep My Love*."
"Suspicion Explored and Denied: *A Letter to Three Wives*."
"The Power and Potential of Undercurrent."
IN: Women's Film and Female Experience

6153 **Walsh, Martin.**
"The Complex Seer: Brecht and the Film."

"The Political Joke in *Happiness*."
"Political Formations in the Cinema of Jean-Marie Straub."
"*History Lesson*: Brecht and Straub/Huillet."
"*Introduction to Arnold Schoenberg's 'Accompaniment for a Cinematographic Scene'*."
"*Moses and Aaron*: Straub and Huillet's Schoenberg."
"Losey, Brecht and *Galileo*."
"Godard and Me: Jean-Pierre Gorin Talks."
"Draft Outline: The Brechtian Aspect of Radical Cinema."
    IN: <u>The Brechtian Aspect of Radical Cinema</u>

6154 Walsh, Raoul.
"Raoul Walsh." [Interview by Charles Higham.]
    IN: <u>Celebrity Circus</u>

6155 Walz, Eugene P.
"Creating a Film Studies Program at the University of Manitoba."
    IN: <u>Film Study in the Undergraduate Curriculum</u>

6156 Wanamaker, Marc.
"Hollywood Dawn."
"Thomas H. Ince—Father of the Western."
    IN: <u>Movies of the Silent Years</u>

6157 Wander, Brandon.
"Black Dreams: The Fantasy and Ritual of Black Films."
    IN: <u>Conflict and Control in the Cinema</u>

6158 Wanger, Walter.
"Walter Wanger: The Executive."
    IN: <u>The Real Tinsel</u>

Ward, Elizabeth. SEE: Silver, Alain.

6159 Warhol, Andy.
"Andy Warhol." [Interview by Joseph Gelmis.]
    IN: <u>The Film Director as Superstar</u>

6160 Warner, Harry M.
"Future Developments." [RE: sound.]
    IN: <u>The Movies in Our Midst</u>
        <u>The Story of the Films</u>

6161 Warner, Virginia.
"*The Negro Soldier*—A Challenge to Hollywood."
    IN: <u>The Documentary Tradition /1 ed</u>
        <u>The Documentary Tradition /2 ed</u>

6162 Warren, Jerry.
"Associated Distributors Productions, Inc."
    IN: <u>The New Poverty Row</u>

6163 Warren, Jerry.
"Jerry Warren." [An interview.]
    IN: <u>Interviews with B ...</u>

6164 Warshow, Paul.
"*They Shoot Horses, Don't They?* [novel by] Horace McCoy. The Unreal McCoy."
    IN: <u>The Modern American Novel ...</u>

6165 Warshow, Robert.
"The Anatomy of Falsehood." [RE: *Best Years of Our Lives*.]
"The Movie Camera and the American." [RE: *Death of a Salesman*.]
"A Feeling of Sad Dignity." [RE: Charles Chaplin.]
"The Flight from Europe."
"*Paisan*."
    IN: <u>The Immediate Experience</u>

6166 Warshow, Robert.
"Preface to *The Immediate Experience*."
    IN: <u>Awake in the Dark</u>
        <u>The Immediate Experience</u>

6167 Warshow, Robert.
"Movie Chronicle: The Westerner." [NOTE: Also called "The Westerner."]
    IN: <u>Film Theory and Criticism /1 ed</u>
        <u>Film Theory and Criticism /2 ed</u>
        <u>Film Theory and Criticism /3 ed</u>
        <u>Film Theory and Criticism /4 ed</u>
        <u>The American West on Film</u>
        <u>Focus on The Western</u>
        <u>Awake in the Dark</u>
        <u>Film: An Anthology</u>
        <u>The Immediate Experience</u>

6168 Warshow, Robert.
"The Gangster as Tragic Hero."
    IN: <u>Film and the Liberal Arts</u>
        <u>A Casebook on Film</u>
        <u>The Immediate Experience</u>

6169 Warshow, Robert.
"Re-Viewing the Russian Movies."
"Father and Son--and the FBI." [RE: *My Son John*.]
    IN: <u>Propaganda on Film</u>
        <u>The Immediate Experience</u>

6170 Warshow, Robert.
"*Monsieur Verdoux*."
    IN: <u>Great Film Directors</u>
        <u>The Immediate Experience</u>

6171 Warshow, Robert.
"*Day of Wrath*: The Enclosed Image."
    IN: <u>Film Theory and Criticism /1 ed</u>
        <u>Great Film Directors</u>
        <u>The Immediate Experience</u>

6172 Wasko, Janet.
"Early Ties Between the Film Industry and Banking."
"A New Era in Film Financing (1919-1926)."
"Case Study: D.W. Griffith."
"The Introduction of Sound and Financial Control (1927-1939)."
"Case Study: American Telephone & Telegraph Company."
"Case Study: Fox Film and Theater Corporations."
"Case Study: Radio-Keith-Orpheum Corporation."
"The Transitional Period and the Growth of Independent Production (1940-1960)."
"Case Study: The Bank of America."

"The Film Industry and Commercial Banks in the 1970s."
"Case Study: Walt Disney Productions."
"Case Study: MCA Inc./Universal Pictures."
"Case Study: Metro-Goldwyn-Mayer, Inc."
"Case Study: Twentieth Century-Fox Film Corporation."
"Case Study: Warner Communications Inc."
"Case Study: United Artists Corporation (Transamerica Corporation)."
"Case Study: Paramount Pictures (Gulf & Western Industries, Inc.)."
"Case Study: Columbia Pictures Industries, Inc."
"Case Study: Hollywood Banks in the 1970s."
   IN: Movies and Money

6173 **Wasko, Janet.**
"D.W. Griffith and the Banks: A Case Study in Film Financing."
   IN: The Hollywood Film Industry

6174 **Wasko, Janet.**
"Film Financing and Banking."
   IN: Film/Culture: Explorations ...

6175 **Wasko, Janet.**
"Hollywood, New Technologies and International Banking: A Formula for Financial Success."
   IN: Current Research in Film /v. 1

6176 **Wasserman, Albert.**
"*Sixty Minutes* [Interview with] Albert Wasserman."
   IN: The Documentary Conscience

6177 **Wasson, Richard.**
"*The Time Machine* [novel by] H.G. Wells; *The Time Machine* [film by] George Pal. Myths of The Future."
   IN: The English Novel and the Movies

6178 **Waterbury, Ruth.**
"Don't Go to Hollywood."
   IN: The Movies in Our Midst

6179 **Waters, John.**
"John Waters." [Interview by Scott MacDonald.]
   IN: A Critical Cinema

6180 **Watkins, Peter.**
"*The War Game*." [Interview by Alan Rosenthal.]
   IN: The New Documentary in Action

6180a **Watkins, Peter.**
"Peter Watkins." [Interview by Scott MacDonald.]
   IN: A Critical Cinema 2

6181 **Watkins, Peter.**
"Media Repression: A Personal Statement."
   IN: Explorations in Film Theory

6182 **Watt, Donald.**
"History on the Public Screen I."
   IN: The Historian and Film
      New Challenges for Documentary

6183 **Watt, Harry.**
"Interview [with] Harry Watt." [Interview by Eva Orbanz and Helmut Wietz.]
   IN: Journey To a Legend and Back

6184 **Watt, Harry.**
"You Start from Scratch in Australia."
   IN: An Australian Film Reader

6185 **Watts, Richard, Jr.**
"A Dying Art Offers a Masterpiece." [RE: *Passion of Joan of Arc*.]
   IN: Introduction to the Art of the Movies

6186 **Watts, Richard, Jr.**
"Films of a Moonstruck World." [RE: *A Midsummer Night's Dream*, 1935.]
   IN: Focus on Shakespearean Films

6187 **Watts, Richard, Jr.**
"D.W. Griffith: Social Crusader."
   IN: The Emergence of Film Art /1 ed
      The Emergence of Film Art /2 ed

6188 **Waugh, Dr. Karl T.**
"The Social Utility of the Photoplay."
   IN: Introduction to the Photoplay

6189 **Waugh, Thomas.**
"'Acting to Play Oneself': Notes on Performance in Documentary."
   IN: Making Visible the Invisible

6190 **Waugh, Thomas.**
"Beyond *Vérité*: Emile de Antonio and the New Documentary."
   IN: Movies and Methods /v. 2

6191 **Waugh, Thomas.**
"Filming the Cultural Revolution." [RE: China.]
   IN: New Challenges for Documentary

6192 **Waugh, Thomas.**
"Joris Ivens' *The Spanish Earth*: Committed Documentary and the Popular Front."
   IN: Show Us Life

6193 **Waugh, Thomas.**
"Lesbian and Gay Documentary: Minority Self-Imaging, Oppositional Film Practice, and the Question of Image Ethics.
   IN: Image Ethics

6194 **Waugh, Tom.**
"In Solidarity: Joris Ivens and the Birth of Cuban Cinema."
   IN: Jump Cut

6195 **Waugh, Tom and Chuck Kleinhans.**
"Gays, Straights, Film and the Left: A Discussion."
   IN: Jump Cut

6196 **Wayne, Jane Ellen.**
"John Barrymore."
"Fatty Arbuckle."
"Errol Flynn."
"Rudolph Valentino."

"Aly Kahn."
"Spencer Tracy."
"Clark Gable."
"John Garfield."
"John Gilbert."
IN: Kings of Tragedy

6197 **Wead, George.**
"*McTeague* [novel by] Frank Norris. Frank Norris: His Share of *Greed*."
IN: The Classic American Novel ...

6198 **Weales, Gerald.**
"*City Lights*."
"*She Done Him Wrong*."
"*Duck Soup*."
"*It's a Gift*."
"*Steamboat Round the Bend*."
"*Ruggles of Red Gap*."
"*Mr. Deeds Goes to Town*."
"*My Man Godfrey*."
"*Libeled Lady*."
"*Nothing Sacred*."
"*Bringing Up Baby*."
"*Destry Rides Again*."
IN: Canned Goods as Caviar

6199 **Weaver, Pat.**
"Pat Weaver." [An interview.]
IN: Producers on Producing

6200 **Webb, James R.**
"I Put A Sign On My Door; 'Scripts While You Wait'--" [RE: an interview.]
IN: Blueprint on Babylon

6201 **Webb, Michael (editor).**
"Spellbound in Darkness."
"Sending a Message."
"Production."
"Screenwriting."
"Directing the Picture."
"Production Design."
"Costume Design."
"Cinematography."
"Editing."
"Scoring."
"Special Effects."
"Star Power."
IN: Hollywood: Legend and Reality

6202 **Weber, Lois.**
"A Dream in Realization—An Interview."
IN: Hollywood Directors 1914-1940

6203 **Wedderburn, Alexander J.**
"Another Armat Intermittent Movement."
IN: A Technological History ...

6203a **Wees, William C.**
"The Camera-Eye: Dialectics of a Metaphor."
"The Cinematic Image as a Visualization of Sight."
"'The Untutored Eye'."
"'Giving Sight to the Medium': Stan Brakhage."

"'Working in Light': Kenneth Anger."
"Making Films for the Inner Eye: Jordan Belson, James Whitney, Paul Sharits."
"Balancing Eye and Mind: Michael Snow."
IN: Light Moving in Time

6204 **Wegner, Hart.**
"A Chronicle of Soil, Seasons and Weather: Jean Renoir's *The Southerner*."
IN: The South and Film

6205 **Wegner, Hart.**
"Film Studies at the University of Nevada, Las Vegas."
IN: Film Study in the Undergraduate Curriculum

6206 **Wegner, Hart.**
"Frederic Remington and John Ford: Dynamic and Static Composition Elements of *Fort Apache*."
IN: Explorations in National Cinemas

6207 **Weill, Kurt.**
"Music in the Movies."
IN: The Movies as Medium

6208 **Weinberg, Herman G.**
"Marco Polo, Modern Style." [RE: *La Croisière jaune*.]
IN: The Documentary Tradition /1 ed
The Documentary Tradition /2 ed

6209 **Weinberg, Herman G.**
"Coffee, Brandy, & Cigars X X X."
"A Footnote to *Foolish Wives*."
IN: Film Culture Reader

6210 **Weinberg, Herman G.**
"Erich von Stroheim."
IN: Introduction to the Art of the Movies

6211 **Weinberg, Herman G.**
"Stroheim's Pictorial Art."
IN: The First Film Makers

6212 **Weinberg, Herman G.**
"*The Great Dictator*."
IN: Focus on Chaplin

6213 **Weiner, Debra.**
"Interview with Ida Lupino."
IN: Women and the Cinema

6214 **Weinstein, Donald.**
"Flowers and Flight (Markopoulos's *Swain*)."
IN: The Essential Cinema /v. 1

6215 **Weir, Tom.**
"No Daydreams of Our Own: The Film as National Self-Expression."
IN: An Australian Film Reader

6216 **Weis, Elisabeth.**
"Consolidation of a Classical Style: *The Man Who Knew Too Much* [1934]."
IN: A Hitchcock Reader

6217 **Weis, Elisabeth.**
"Family Portraits."
IN: Sexual Stratagems

IN: The English Novel and the Movies

6244 **Welsch, Janice R.**
"The Film Program at Western Illinois University."
IN: Film Study in the Undergraduate Curriculum

6245 **Welsch, Janice.**
"Actress Archetypes in the 1950s: Doris Day, Marilyn Monroe, Elizabeth Taylor, Audrey Hepburn."
IN: Women and the Cinema

6246 **Welsch, Janice R. and Syndy M. Conger.**
"The Comic and the Grotesque in James Whale's Frankenstein Films."
IN: Planks of Reason

6247 **Welsh, James Michael.**
"The Film Program at Salisbury State College."
IN: Film Study in the Undergraduate Curriculum

6248 **Welsh, James Michael.**
"The Cinema of Intimacy: Peter Watkins's Portrait of the Artist as a Young Munch." [RE: *Edvard Munch.*]
IN: Explorations in National Cinemas

6248a **Welsh, Jim.**
"*A Soldier's Story*: A Paradigm for Justice."
IN: Columbia Pictures

6249 **Welsh, Michael E.**
"Western Film, Ronald Reagan, and the Western Metaphor."
IN: Shooting Stars

6250 **Welsh, Michael.**
"Origins of Western Film Companies, 1887-1920."
IN: Western Films: A Brief History

6251 **Wenden, D.J.**
"*Battleship Potemkin*: Film and Reality."
IN: Feature Films as History

6252 **Wenders, Wim.**
"Why Do You Make Films?"
"Time Sequences, Continuity of Movement: *Summer in the City* and *The Goalkeeper's Fear of the Penalty*."
"*The Scarlet Letter*."
"The heroes are the others: *False Movement*."
"*Kings of the Road*."
"*The American Friend*."
"Reverse Angle: New York City, March 1982."
"*Chambre 666*."
"*Film Thieves*."
"Goodbye to the booming voice of the old cinema: *The State of Things*."
"Impossible Stories."
"*Tokyo-Ga*."
"Like Flying Blind without Instruments: *Paris, Texas*."
"The growth of a small dependency."
"An attempted description of an indescribable film: *Wings of Desire*."
"For (not about) Ingmar Bergman."
"A history of imaginary films."
"*Le Souffle de l'Ange*."
IN: The Logic of Images

6253 **Wenders, Wim.**
"*Kelek*."
"*Red Sun*: Baby, You Can Drive My Car, and Maybe I'll Love You."
"Death Is No Solution: The German Film Director Fritz Lang."
"Emotion Pictures (Slowly Rockin' On)."
"Learning to Hear and See."
"That's Entertainment: Hitler."
"The *Filmverlag* against the Authors."
IN: West German Filmmakers on Film

6254 **Wenders, Wim.**
"Wim Wenders. [Interview by John Andrew Gallagher.]
IN: Film Directors on Directing

Wengraf, Susan. SEE: Artel, Linda.

Wensley, Chris. SEE: Giddings, Robert.

6255 **Werner, Gösta.**
"Frame by Frame: Scandinavian Film Reconstruction."
IN: Wonderful Inventions

6256 **Wertmuller, Lina.**
"You cannot make the revolution on film ..."
IN: The Cineaste Interviews

6257 **West, Ann.**
"The Concept of the Fantastic in *Vertigo*."
IN: Hitchcock's Re-Released Films

6258 **West, Dennis.**
"Cuba."
IN: World Cinema Since 1945

6259 **West, Jessamyn.**
"Example."
"Through a Glass Darkly."
IN: The Best of Rob Wagner's Script

6260 **West, Mae.**
"*My Little Chickadee*."
IN: Bedside Hollywood

6261 **West, Mae.**
"Mae West." [Interview by John Kobal.]
IN: People Will Talk

6262 **West, Mae.**
"Mae West." [Interview by Charles Higham.]
IN: Celebrity Circus

6263 **West, Mark.**
"*Chitty Chitty Bang Bang* [novel by] Ian Fleming. Fleming's Flying Flivver Flops on Film."
IN: Children's Novels and the Movies

6264 **Westerbeck, Colin L.**
"Stars vs. Actors: The Importance of Being Oscar."
IN: The Movie Star: The National ...

6265 **Westerbeck, Colin L., Jr.**
"*The Heartbreak Kid*."
"*Nashville*."
"*Day for Night*."
"*Young Frankenstein*."

IN: Movie Comedy

6266 Westerbeck, Colin L., Jr.
"The Dark Night of the Soul of Robert Bresson."
IN: The Emergence of Film Art /2 ed

6267 Westheimer, Joseph.
"Optical Effects."
IN: The ASC Treasury ...

6268 Westin, Alan F.
"The *Miracle* Case: The Supreme Court and the Movies."
IN: The Movies in Our Midst

6269 Westmore, Michael.
"Michael Westmore [on Makeup]." [Interview by David Chell.]
IN: Moviemakers at Work

6270 Westmore, Perc.
"Makeup."
IN: Hollywood Speaks!

6271 Wexler, Haskell.
"Haskell Wexler." [Interview by Dennis Schaefer and Larry Salvato.]
IN: Masters of Light

6272 Wexler, Haskell.
"Haskell Wexler." [Interview by Kris Malkiewicz.]
IN: Film Lighting

6273 Wexman, Virginia Wright.
"The Trauma of Infancy in Roman Polanski's *Rosemary's Baby*."
IN: American Horrors

6274 Wexman, Virginia Wright.
"Kinesics and Film Acting: Humphrey Bogart in *The Maltese Falcon* and *The Big Sleep*."
IN: Star Texts

Weyergans, François. SEE: Comolli, Jean-Louis.

6275 Whitaker, Claire.
"Hollywood Transformed: Interviews with Lesbian Viewers."
IN: Jump Cut

6276 Whitaker, Sheila.
"Declarations of Independence."
IN: British Cinema Now

6277 Whitaker, Sheila.
"Feminism and Exhibition."
IN: Films for Women

6278 White, Armond.
"*Distant Voices, Still Lives*."
IN: Produced and Abandoned

6279 White, Dennis L.
"The Poetics of Horror: More than Meets the Eye."
IN: Cinema Examined
     Film Genre

6280 White, G. Edward.
"Roosevelt, Remington, Wister: Consensus and the West."
IN: The American West on Film

6281 White, Kenneth.
"Animated Cartoons [1931]."
"F.W. Murnau."
"Garbo and Dietrich."
"Movie Chronicle [1930]."
"The Style of Ernst Lubitsch."
IN: Hound & Horn

6282 White, Raymond E.
"Ken Maynard: Daredevil on Horseback."
IN: Shooting Stars

6283 White, Susan.
"Male Bonding, Hollywood Orientalism, and the Repression of the Feminine in Kubrick's *Full Metal Jacket*."
IN: Inventing Vietnam

6284 White, Timothy R.
"Hollywood's Attempt at Appropriating Television: The Case of Paramount Pictures."
IN: Hollywood in the Age of Television

6285 Whitebait, William.
"Rouquier's *Farrebique*."
IN: The Documentary Tradition /1 ed
     The Documentary Tradition /2 ed

6286 Whitlock, Albert.
"Special Photographic Techniques for *Earthquake*."
IN: The ASC Treasury ...

6287 Whitney, Helen.
"*Youth Terror*: The View from Behind the Gun [Interview with] Helen Whitney."
IN: The Documentary Conscience

6288 Whitney, John and James.
"Audio-Visual Music."
IN: Art in Cinema
     The Avant-Garde Film

Whitney, James. SEE: Whitney, John.

6289 Whitney, Simon N.
"Antitrust Policies and the Motion Picture Industry."
IN: The American Movie Industry

6290 Whittemore, Don and Philip Alan Ceccettini.
"Pioneers of the Cinema: Charles Chaplin, Erich von Stroheim."
"In Search of Commercial Success, Hollywood Hires Its Competition: Ernst Lubitsch, Michael Curtiz, Victor Seastrom, James Whale, Alfred Hitchcock."
"In Pursuit of Art and Culture, Hollywood Goes Highbrow: F.W. Murnau, Paul Fejos and Slavko Vorkapich."
"Europe in Disorder, Emigration in the 1930s: Fritz Lang, Otto Preminger."
"The New Hollywood: Milos Forman."
IN: Passport to Hollywood

6291 **Wiater, Stanley.**
"Disturbo 13: The Most Disturbing Horror Films Ever Made."
IN: Cut!: Horror Writers ...

6292 **Wicking, Christopher.**
"Thrillers."
IN: Anatomy of the Movies

6293 **Wicks, Ulrich.**
"Borges, Bertolucci, and Metafiction."
IN: Narrative Strategies

6294 **Widen, Gregory.**
"Gregory Widen." [Interview by William Froug.]
IN: The New Screenwriter Looks ...

6295 **Wiegand, Wilfried.**
"The Doll in the Doll: Observations on Fassbinder's Films."
"Interview with Rainer Werner Fassbinder."
IN: Fassbinder

6296 **Wiegman, Robyn.**
"Black Bodies/American Commodities: Gender, Race, and the Bourgeois Ideal in Contemporary Film."
IN: Unspeakable Images

6297 **Wiener, Tom.**
"Robert Rossen."
IN: Dictionary of Literary Biography /v. 26

6298 **Wiese, Michael.**
"Michael Wiese." [An interview.]
IN: Producers on Producing

6299 **Wigal, Donald.**
"Film Today and Tomorrow."
"Suggested Film Program Groupings."
IN: Screen Experience

6300 **Wilbur, Crane.**
"*I Was a Communist for the FBI*, Scene from Final Shooting Script."
IN: Propaganda on Film

6301 **Wilbur, Richard.**
"A Poet and the Movies."
IN: Film and the Liberal Arts
Man and the Movies
Film And/As Literature

6302 **Wilde, Cornel.**
"*No Blade of Grass*: A Warning for Our Time."
IN: Omni's Screen Flights ...

6303 **Wildenhahn, Klaus.**
"The Method of Direct Observation: Two Examples."
IN: West German Filmmakers on Film

6304 **Wildenhahn, Klaus.**
"Approaches to the Legend." [RE: Free Cinema Movement.]
IN: Journey To a Legend and Back

6305 **Wilder, Billy.**
"Billy Wilder."
IN: The Celluloid Muse

6306 **Wilder, Billy.**
"One Head Is Better Than Two."
IN: Hollywood Directors 1941-1976

6307 **Wilder, Billy and I.A.L. Diamond.**
"The Screenwriter."
IN: Filmmakers on Filmmaking /v. 1

6307a **Wilder, Gene.**
"Gene Wilder, actor-director-screenwriter." [Interview by Constance Nash and Virginia Oakey.]
IN: The Screenwriter's Handbook

6308 **Wilke, Jane.**
"Clark Gable."
"Bette Davis."
"Rock Hudson."
"Elizabeth Taylor."
"John Wayne."
"Barbara Stanwyck."
"Tony Curtis."
"June Allyson."
IN: Confessions of an Ex-Fan Magazine Writer

6309 **Wilkerson, William R.**
"The International Film."
IN: Film and Society

6310 **Willemen, Paul.**
"Cinematic Discourse: The Problem of Inner Speech."
IN: Cinema and Language

6311 **Willemen, Paul.**
"On Realism in the Cinema."
IN: Screen Reader 1

6312 **Willemen, Paul.**
"The Third Cinema Question: Notes and Reflections."
IN: Questions of Third Cinema

6313 **Willemen, Paul.**
"Voyeurism, The Look, and Dwoskin."
IN: Narrative, Apparatus, Ideology

Willemen, Paul. SEE: Johnston, Claire.

6314 **Willett, Ralph.**
"The Nation in Crisis: Hollywood's Response to the 1940s."
IN: Cinema, Politics and Society in America

6315 **Williams, Alan.**
"The Lumière Organization and 'Documentary Realism'."
IN: Film Before Griffith

6316 **Williams, Alan.**
"Godard's Use of Sound."
IN: Film Sound

6317 **Williams, Alan.**
"Keeping the Circle Turning: Ophuls's *La Ronde* from the Play by Arthur Schnitzler."
IN: Modern European Filmmakers ...

6318 **Williams, Alan.**
"Reading Ophüls Reading Schnitzler: *Liebelei*."

IN: German Film and Literature

6319 Williams, Alan.
"The Musical Film and Recorded Popular Music."
  IN: Genre: The Musical

6320 Williams, Billy.
"Billy Williams." [Interview by Dennis Schaefer and Larry Salvato.]
  IN: Masters of Light

6321 Williams, Christopher.
"Politics and Production."
"The Deep Focus Question: Some Comments on Patrick Ogle's Article."
  IN: Screen Reader 1

6322 Williams, Linda.
"The Image." [RE: Jean Goudal; Antonin Artaud; Robert Denos; Sigmund Freud; Jacques Lacan.]
"*Un Chien andalou*." [RE: metaphor; metonymy; figures (of speech); Roman Jakobson.]
"*L'Age d'or*." [RE: myth; interdiction and transgression; diegesis.]
"Contemporary Surrealism: Buñuel's *Phantom of Liberty* and *That Obscure Object of Desire*."
"Conclusion: The Figures of Desire."
  IN: Figures of Desire

6323 Williams, Linda.
"'Something Else Beside a Mother': *Stella Dallas* and the Maternal Melodrama." [NOTE: Also called "'Something Else Beside a Mother': *Stella Dallas*."]
  IN: Issues in Feminist Film Criticism
      Imitations of Life
      Home Is Where the Heart Is

6324 Williams, Linda.
"*Personal Best*: Women in Love."
  IN: Films for Women

6325 Williams, Linda.
"*What You Take for Granted*."
  IN: New Challenges for Documentary

6326 Williams, Linda.
"Feminist Film Theory: *Mildred Pierce* and the Second World War."
  IN: Female Spectators

6327 Williams, Linda.
"Film Body: An Implantation of Perversions."
  IN: Explorations in Film Theory
      Narrative, Apparatus, Ideology

6328 Williams, Linda.
"The Critical Grasp: Buñuelian Cinema and Its Critics."
  IN: Dada and Surrealist Film

6329 Williams, Linda.
"Three Figures of Desire."
  IN: Cinema and Language

6330 Williams, Linda.
"Type and Stereotype: Chicano Images in Film."
  IN: Chicano Cinema

6331 Williams, Linda.
"When the Woman Looks."
  IN: Re-vision
      Film Theory and Criticism /4 ed

6332 Williams, Linda and B. Ruby Rich.
"The Right of Re-Vision: Michelle Citron's *Daughter Rite*."
  IN: Movies and Methods /v. 2

Williams, Linda. SEE: Doane, Mary Ann.

6333 Williams, Paul.
"*Out of it*."
  IN: Directors in Action

6334 Williams, Raymond.
"Realism, Naturalism, and Their Alternatives."
  IN: Explorations in Film Theory

6335 Williams, Raymond.
"British Film History: New Perspectives."
  IN: British Cinema History

6336 Williams, Tony.
"Missing in Action--The Vietnam Construction of the Movie Star."
  IN: From Hanoi to Hollywood

6337 Williams, Tony.
"Narrative Patterns and Mythic Trajectories in Mid-1980s Vietnam Movies."
  IN: Inventing Vietnam

6338 Williams, Tony.
"*Assault on Precinct 13*: The Mechanics of Repression."
  IN: American Nightmare

6339 Williams, Wenmouth, Jr., and Mitchell E. Shapiro.
"A Study of the Effects In-Home Entertainment Alternatives Have on Film Attendance."
  IN: Current Research in Film /v. 1

6340 Williamson, Bruce.
"*The Last American Hero*."
"*The Offence*."
"*F/X*."
"*Hair*."
  IN: Produced and Abandoned

6341 Williamson, Bruce.
"*The Loves of a Blonde*."
"The Late Chaplin."
  IN: Movie Comedy

6342 Williamson, Bruce.
"Brigitte Bardot."
"Al Pacino."
  IN: The Movie Star: The National ...

6343 Willinger, Laszlo.
"Laszlo Willinger." [Interview by John Kobal.]
  IN: People Will Talk

6344 Willis, Ellen.
"Is Lina Wertmuller Just One of the Boys?"

IN: <u>Women and the Cinema</u>

6345 Willis, Ellen.
"*Deep Throat*: Hard to Swallow."
IN: <u>Sexuality in the Movies</u>

6346 Willis, Gordon.
"Gordon Willis." [Interview by Dennis Schaefer and
Larry Salvato.]
IN: <u>Masters of Light</u>

6347 Willis, Jack.
"*Hard Times in the Country*." [Interview by Alan
Rosenthal.]
IN: <u>The New Documentary in Action</u>

6348 Wills, David.
"Slit Screen."
IN: <u>Dada and Surrealist Film</u>

6349 Wilmington, Michael.
"Andrei Tarkovsky: Russia's Science Fiction Poet."
IN: <u>Omni's Screen Flights ...</u>

6350 Wilmington, Michael.
"*Salvador*."
"*Danny Boy*."
"*The Best of Times*."
IN: <u>Produced and Abandoned</u>

6351 Wilmington, Michael.
"*Dumbo*."
IN: <u>The American Animated Cartoon</u>

Wilmington, Michael. SEE: McBride, Joseph.

6352 Wilson, David.
"Peter Bogdanovich."
"Robert Altman."
"Sam Fuller."
IN: <u>Close-Up: The Contemporary Director</u>

6353 Wilson, David.
"William Wellman."
IN: <u>Close-Up: The Hollywood Director</u>

6354 Wilson, David.
"A Television Election?"
IN: <u>Sight and Sound</u>

6355 Wilson, David.
"Alberto Cavalcanti."
"British Documentary Movement."
"James Ivory."
"Karel Reisz."
"Marcel Ophuls."
"Maurice Pialat."
"Mikhail Romm."
"Rainer Werner Fassbinder."
IN: <u>Cinema: A Critical Dictionary</u>

6356 Wilson, Edmund.
"The New Chaplin Comedy."
IN: <u>Great Film Directors</u>

6357 Wilson, Elizabeth.
"All the Rage."

IN: <u>Fabrications</u>

6358 Wilson, George M.
"Film, Perception, and Point of View."
"Fritz Lang's *You Only Live Once*."
"Coherence and Transparency in Classical Narrative
Film."
"Alfred Hitchcock's *North by Northwest*."
"Some Modes of Nonomniscience."
"Max Ophuls' *Letter from an Unknown Woman*."
"On Narrators and Narration in Film."
"Josef von Sternberg's *The Devil Is a Woman*."
"Nicholas Ray's *Rebel without a Cause*."
"Morals for Method." [RE: Colin MacCabe, "The
Classic Realist Text."]
IN: <u>Narration in Light</u>

6359 Wilson, Patricia.
"The Founding of the Northeast Film Studio,
1946-1949."
IN: <u>Chinese Film</u>

6360 Wilson, Robert A.
"The Horror Film as American Folk Art."
IN: <u>Conflict and Control in the Cinema</u>

6361 Winer, Robert.
"Witnessing and Bearing Witness: The Ontogeny of
Encounter in the Films of Peter Weir."
IN: <u>Images in Our Souls</u>

6362 Winetrobe, Maury.
"Maury Winetrobe." [Interview by Vincent LoBrutto.]
IN: <u>Selected Takes</u>

6363 Winetrout, Kenneth.
"The New Age of the Visible: A Call To Study."
IN: <u>Sight, Sound, and Society</u>

6364 Wing, W.E.
"Tom Ince of Inceville."
IN: <u>The First Film Makers</u>

6365 Winge, John H.
"Some New American Documentaries—In Defense of
Liberty."
IN: <u>The Documentary Tradition /1 ed</u>
<u>The Documentary Tradition /2 ed</u>

6366 Winner, Michael.
"Michael Winner." [Interview by Rex Reed.]
IN: <u>Travolta to Keaton</u>

6367 Winnington, Richard.
"*Bicycle Thieves*."
IN: <u>Sight and Sound</u>

6368 Winogura, Dale.
"Abby Mann."
"Niven Busch."
IN: <u>Dictionary of Literary Biography /v. 44</u>

6369 Winogura, Dale.
"Arthur Laurents."
IN: <u>Dictionary of Literary Biography /v. 26</u>

"*Sweet Sweetback's Baadasssss Song*: The Black Experience."
"*Deep Throat*: Pornography at Large."
"*Heavy Traffic*: The New Animation."
"*Sleeper*: Comedy for the Future."
"*Nashville*: New Forms."
"*Seven Beauties*: A Leading Woman Director."
IN: Landmark Films

6389 **Wolf, William.**
"Wasn't That Just Lovely, the Way His Head Exploded?" [RE: *The Wild Bunch*.]
IN: The American West on Film

6390 **Wolfe, Charles.**
"Busby Berkeley."
"Cecil B. De Mille."
"Mervyn LeRoy."
IN: American Directors /v. 1

6391 **Wolfe, Charles.**
"*Mr. Smith Goes to Washington*: Democratic Forums and Representational Forms."
IN: Close Viewings

6391a **Wolfe, Charles.**
"The Return of Jimmy Stewart: The Publicity Photograph as Text."
IN: Stardom

6392 **Wolfe, Judy.**
"The Filmmaker and Human Rights: Some Reflections."
IN: Forbidden Films

6393 **Wolfe, Ralph Haven.**
"Robert E. Sherwood."
IN: Dictionary of Literary Biography /v. 26

6394 **Wolfe, Tom.**
"Loverboy of the Bourgeoisie." [RE: Cary Grant.]
IN: Film: Readings in the Mass Media

6395 **Wolfenstein, Martha and Nathan Leites.**
"Movies: A Psychological Study."
IN: Film: An Anthology

6396 **Wolff, Perry.**
"Perry Wolff." [An interview.]
IN: Producers on Producing

Wolfson, Kim. SEE: Norden, Martin F.

6397 **Wolitzer, Meg.**
"*Shadow of a Doubt*."
IN: The Movie That Changed My Life

6398 **Woll, Allen L.**
"Bandits and Lovers: Hispanic Images in American Film."
IN: The Kaleidoscopic Lens

6399 **Woll, Allen L.**
"Ramon Novarro and the Myth of the Latin Lover."
"Douglas Fairbanks as *The Americano*."
"Dolores Del Rio."
"Wallace Beery in *Viva Villa!*."

"RKO's *Hi Gaucho*."
"Carmen Miranda and *The Gang's All Here*."
"Lupe Velez as *Mexican Spitfire*."
"Elia Kazan's *Viva Zapata!*."
"Herbert Biberman's *Salt of the Earth*."
"*Che!*."
"*Bananas*."
IN: The Latin Image in American Film

6400 **Wollen, Peter.**
"Cinema and Semiology."
"*North by Northwest*: a Morphological Analysis."
"Hybrid Plots in *Psycho*."
"The Hermeneutic Code."
"*Citizen Kane*."
"Art in Revolution." [RE: Bolshevism.]
"The Two Avant-Gardes."
"'Ontology' and 'Materialism' in Film." [RE: Andre Bazin.]
"Semiotic Counter-Strategies: Retrospect 1982."
IN: Readings and Writings

6401 **Wollen, Peter.**
"[From:] *Signs and Meaning in the Cinema*: The Auteur Theory."
IN: Film Theory and Criticism /1 ed
Film Theory and Criticism /2 ed
Film Theory and Criticism /3 ed
Film Theory and Criticism /4 ed

6402 **Wollen, Peter.**
"Eisenstein's Aesthetics."
"The Semiology of the Cinema."
IN: Signs and Meaning in the Cinema

6403 **Wollen, Peter.**
"John Ford."
"The Auteur Theory [extract]."
IN: Theories of Authorship

6404 **Wollen, Peter.**
"The Auteur Theory: John Ford."
IN: Conflict and Control in the Cinema

6405 **Wollen, Peter.**
"The *Auteur* Theory."
IN: Movies and Methods: An Anthology
Signs and Meaning in the Cinema

6406 **Wollen, Peter.**
"*Friendship's Death* (complete script)."
IN: Close Encounters

6407 **Wollen, Peter.**
"Afterward [to the *Cahier* articles on *Young Mr. Lincoln*]."
IN: Screen Reader 1

6408 **Wollen, Peter.**
"Cinema and Technology: A Historical Overview."
[NOTE: Also called "Cinema and Technology."]
[SEE: Christian Metz, "Discussion".]
IN: The Cinematic Apparatus
Readings and Writings

6409 Wollen, Peter.
"Cinema and Semiology: Some Points of Contact."
IN: <u>Movies and Methods: An Anthology</u>

6410 Wollen, Peter.
"Godard and Counter Cinema: *Vent d'Est*."
IN: <u>Movies and Methods /v. 2</u>
<u>Narrative, Apparatus, Ideology</u>
<u>Readings and Writings</u>

6411 Wollen, Peter.
"Some Thoughts Arising from Stanley Mitchell's
Article [on Marinetti and Mayakovsky]."
IN: <u>Screen Reader 1</u>

**Wollen, Peter. SEE: Comolli, Jean-Louis; SEE:
Metz, Christian.**

6412 Wollscheidt, Michael G.
"*Fail Safe*."
IN: <u>Nuclear War Films</u>

6413 Wolper, David.
"David Wolper." [An interview.]
IN: <u>Producers on Producing</u>

6414 Omitted

6415 Wood, Charles W.
"With the Bunk Left Out." [RE: *A Woman of Paris*.]
IN: <u>Focus on Chaplin</u>

6416 Wood, Gerald C.
"Horror Film."
IN: <u>Handbook of American Film Genres</u>

6417 Wood, Jerry.
"Film Study in the Small Liberal Arts College:
Carson-Newman College."
IN: <u>Film Study in the Undergraduate Curriculum</u>

6418 Wood, Michael.
"Dietrich: Empress of Signs."
IN: <u>Women and Film</u>

6419 Wood, Michael.
"The Corruption of Accidents: Buñuel's *That Obscure
Object of Desire* from the Novel *The Woman and
the Puppet* by Pierre Louys*."
IN: <u>Modern European Filmmakers ...</u>

6420 Wood, Michael.
"The Fierce Imagination of Luis Buñuel."
IN: <u>Great Film Directors</u>

6421 Wood, Natalie.
"Natalie Wood." [Interview by Rex Reed.]
IN: <u>Travolta to Keaton</u>

6422 Wood, Richard (editor).
The Documents:
"Depicting the Military Image on the Screen,
1913-1916."
"Mexico, 1914-1916."
"Preparedness, 1915-1917."
"American Entry into War, 1917."
"Wilson, *Pershing's Crusaders*, and *Hearts of the
World*."

"The Committee on Public Information and Film
Policy."
"The CPI at Home and Abroad."
"The Aftermath of War."
IN: <u>Film and Propaganda in America /v. 1</u>

6423 Wood, Robert E.
"Don't Dream It: Performance and *The Rocky Horror
Picture Show*."
IN: <u>The Cult Film Experience</u>

6424 Wood, Robin.
"Big Game: Confessions of an Unreconstructed
Humanist."
"In Defence of Art: On Current Tendencies in Film
Criticism."
"Levin and the Jam: Realism and Ideology."
"The Play of Light and Shade: *The Scarlet Empress*."
"Ewig hin der Liebe Glück ... *Letter from an Unknown
Woman*."
"Welles, Shakespeare and Webster: *Touch of Evil*."
"Images of Childhood."
"Reflections on the Auteur Theory."
"Hawks De-Wollenized."
"The Shadow Worlds of Jacques Tourneur: *Cat
People* and *I Walked with a Zombie*."
"The Ghost Princess and the Seaweed Gatherer:
Ugetsu Monogatari and *Sansho Dayu*."
IN: <u>Personal Views</u>

6425 Wood, Robin.
"Alan J. Pakula and Robert Mulligan."
"Anthony Mann."
"Arthur Penn."
"Bernardo Bertolucci."
"Budd Boetticher."
"Charles Laughton."
"Don Siegel."
"Dušan Makavejev."
"Fritz Lang: 1936-60."
"Jacques Tourneur."
"John Ford."
"John Huston."
"Ken Russell."
"Leo McCarey."
"Roberto Rossellini."
"Robert Altman."
"Sam Peckinpah."
"Stanley Kubrick."
IN: <u>Cinema: A Critical Dictionary</u>

6426 Wood, Robin.
"Apocalypse Now: Notes on the Living Dead." [RE:
Night of the Living Dead; *Dawn of the Dead*.]
"Introduction [to the Horror Film]."
"The Dark Mirror: Murnau's *Nosferatu*."
"World of Gods & Monsters: The Films of Larry
Cohen."
"*Der Erlkönig*: The Ambiguities of Horror."
"*Sisters*."
IN: <u>American Nightmare</u>

6427 **Wood, Robin.**
"Attitudes in *Advise and Consent*."
"*Exodus*."
"*La Baie des Anges*."
"*Tokyo Story*."
    IN: <u>Movie Reader</u>

6428 **Wood, Robin.**
"Ideology, Genre, Auteur."
    IN: <u>Film Theory and Criticism /4 ed</u>
        <u>Film Genre Reader</u>

6429 **Wood, Robin.**
"*Night of the Hunter* [novel by] Davis Grubb. Charles Laughton on Grubb Street."
    IN: <u>The Modern American Novel ...</u>

6430 **Wood, Robin.**
"*Rio Bravo*."
    IN: <u>Focus on Howard Hawks</u>
        <u>Western Movies</u>

6431 **Wood, Robin.**
"An Introduction to the American Horror Film."
    IN: <u>Planks of Reason</u>
        <u>Movies and Methods /v. 2</u>

6432 **Wood, Robin.**
"Art and Ideology: Notes on *Silk Stockings*."
    IN: <u>Genre: The Musical</u>

6433 **Wood, Robin.**
"Dusan Makavejev."
    IN: <u>Second Wave</u>

6434 **Wood, Robin.**
"Images and Women."
    IN: <u>Issues in Feminist Film Criticism</u>

6435 **Wood, Robin.**
"Quo Vadis Bruce Beresford?"
    IN: <u>An Australian Film Reader</u>

6436 **Wood, Robin.**
"Responsibilities of a Gay Film Critic."
    IN: <u>Movies and Methods /v. 2</u>

6437 **Wood, Robin.**
"Retrospective."
"Male Desire, Male Anxiety: The Essential Hitchcock."
"*Strangers on a Train*."
    IN: <u>A Hitchcock Reader</u>

6438 **Wood, Robin.**
"Returning the Look: *Eyes of a Stranger*."
    IN: <u>American Horrors</u>

6439 **Wood, Robin.**
"Shall We Gather at the River? The Late Films of John Ford."
    IN: <u>Theories of Authorship</u>

6440 **Wood, Robin.**
"Sternberg's *Empress*: The Play of Light and Shade."
"The Lure of Irresponsibility: *Scarface* and *Bringing Up Baby*."
    IN: <u>Great Film Directors</u>

6441 **Wood, Robin.**
"The Men Who Knew Too Much (and the women who knew much better)."
    IN: <u>Hitchcock's Re-Released Films</u>

6442 **Wood, Robin.**
"Thematic Structure in *Vertigo*."
    IN: <u>The Classic Cinema</u>

6443 **Wood, Robin.**
"Why We Should Take Hitchcock Seriously."
    IN: <u>Focus on Hitchcock</u>

6444 **Wood, Robin.**
"*Psycho*."
    IN: <u>Crossroads to the Cinema</u>

6445 **Wood, Robin.**
"*To Have* (written) *and Have Not* (directed)."
    IN: <u>Movies and Methods: An Anthology</u>

Wood, Robin. SEE: Cameron, Ian.

6446 **Woods, Frank.**
"Deliberation and Repose." [RE: D.W. Griffith.]
    IN: <u>The First Film Makers</u>

6447 **Woods, Frank.**
"Growth and Development." [RE: the photoplay.]
    IN: <u>Introduction to the Photoplay</u>

6448 **Woods, Gregory.**
"A Work Journal of the Straub/Huillet Film, *Moses and Aaron*."
    IN: <u>Apparatus</u>

Woodward, Joanne. SEE: Newman, Paul.

6449 **Woodward, Katherine S.**
"European Anti-Melodrama: Godard, Truffaut, and Fassbinder."
    IN: <u>Imitations of Life</u>

6450 **Woolf, Virginia.**
"The Movies and Reality."
    IN: <u>Authors on Film</u>
        <u>Film And/As Literature</u>

6451 **Woollacott, Janet.**
"The James Bond Films: Conditions of Production."
    IN: <u>British Cinema History</u>

6452 **Woolner, Lawrence H.**
"Dimension Pictures."
    IN: <u>The New Poverty Row</u>

6453 **Woolsey, Ralph.**
"Ralph Woolsey." [Interview by Kris Malkiewicz.]
    IN: <u>Film Lighting</u>

6454 **Worrell, Denise.**
"Madonna Is Her Given Name."
"The Eternal Childhood of Steven Spielberg."
"Steve Martin in Color."
"Plain-Wrap Superstar Paul Newman."
"Nastassia Kinski: Wild Child."
"David Lean on the Far Horizon."

"Bob Dylan Down Executioner's Row."
"The Dark Side of George Lucas."
"Very Very Bette Midler."
"Oliver Stone Goes to War."
"Michael Jackson in Never-Never Land."
    IN: Icons: Intimate Portraits

6455 Worth, Sol.
"Film as a Non-Art: An Approach to the Study of Film."
    IN: Perspectives on the Study of Film

6456 Worth, Sol.
"Pictures Can't Say Ain't."
    IN: Film/Culture: Explorations ...

6457 Wright, Basil.
"*Land Without Bread* and *Spanish Earth*."
    IN: The Documentary Tradition /1 ed
        The Documentary Tradition /2 ed

6458 Wright, Basil.
"Basil Wright." [Interview by G. Roy Levin.]
    IN: Documentary Explorations

6459 Wright, Basil.
"Handling the Camera."
    IN: A Casebook on Film
        Footnotes to the Film

6460 Wright, Basil.
"Interview [with] Basil Wright." [Interview by Eva Orbanz and Helmut Wietz.]
    IN: Journey To a Legend and Back

6461 Wright, Basil and B. Vivian Braun.
"Manifesto: Dialogue on Sound."
    IN: Film Sound

6462 Wright, Elsa Gress.
"*Gertrude*."
    IN: Renaissance of the Film

6463 Wright, Judith Hess.
"Genre Film and the Status Quo."
    IN: Film Genre Reader

6464 Wright, Will.
"Individuals and Values: The Structure of the Classical Western."
    IN: Conflict and Control in the Cinema

6465 Wu Yigong.
"To Be a Loyal Artist to the People."
    IN: Chinese Film Theory

6466 Wu Yigong.
"We Must Become Film Artists Who Deeply Love the People."
    IN: Perspectives on Chinese Cinema

6467 Wyatt, Robert O. and David P. Badger.
"What Newspaper Film Critics Value in Film and Film Criticism: A National Survey."
    IN: Current Research in Film /v. 4

6468 Wyborny, Klaus.
"Unordered Notes on Conventional Narrative Film."
    IN: West German Filmmakers on Film

6469 Wyler, William.
"No Magic Wand."
    IN: Hollywood Directors 1941-1976

6470 Wyler, William.
"William Wyler." [Interview by Charles Higham.]
    IN: Celebrity Circus

6471 "X".
"Hollywood Meets Frankenstein." [RE: HUAC.]
    IN: The Movies in Our Midst

6472 Xavier, Ismail.
"*Black God, White Devil*: The Representation of History."
    IN: Brazilian Cinema

6473 Xavier, Ismail.
"*Iracema*: Transcending Cinema Verité."
    IN: The Social Documentary ...

Xavier, Ismail. SEE: Stam, Robert.

6474 Xia Hong.
"Film Theory in the People's Republic of China: The New Era."
    IN: Chinese Film

6475 Xie Fei.
"My View of the Concept of Film."
    IN: Chinese Film Theory

6476 Xie Fengsong.
"Xie Fengsong, Scriptwriter." [Interview by George S. Semsel.]
    IN: Chinese Film

6477 Xie Jin.
"Xie Jin, Director of the Third Generation." [Interview by George S. Semsel.]
    IN: Chinese Film

6478 Yacowar, Maurice.
"*The Glass Menagerie*."
"*A Streetcar Named Desire*."
"*The Rose Tattoo*."
"*Baby Doll*."
"*Cat on a Hot Tin Roof*."
"*Suddenly Last Summer*."
"*The Fugitive Kind*."
"*Summer and Smoke*."
"*The Roman Spring of Mrs. Stone*."
"*Sweet Bird of Youth*."
"*Period of Adjustment*."
"*The Night of the Iguana*."
"*This Property Is Condemned*."
"*BOOM*."
"*Last of the Mobile Hot-shots*."
    IN: Tennessee Williams and Film

6479 Yacowar, Maurice.
"Hitchcock's Imagery and Art."
    IN: A Hitchcock Reader

6480 **Yacowar, Maurice.**
"Private and Public Visions: *Zabriskie Point* and *Billy Jack*."
IN: <u>Movies as Artifacts</u>

6481 **Yacowar, Maurice.**
"The Bug in the Rug: Notes on the Disaster Genre."
IN: <u>Film Genre</u>
<u>Film Genre Reader</u>

6482 **Yagher, Kevin.**
"Kevin Yagher." [Interview by Stanley Wiater.]
IN: <u>Dark Visions</u>

6483 **Yakovlev, Nikolai.**
"The Nihilists from ARK." [RE: Association of Revolutionary Cinematography.]
IN: <u>The Film Factory</u>

6484 **Yampolsky, Mikhail.**
"Kuleshov's Experiments and the New Anthropology of the Actor."
IN: <u>Inside the Film Factory</u>

6485 **Yang Ni.**
"Film Is Film: A Response to Tan Peisheng."
IN: <u>Chinese Film Theory</u>

6486 **Yang Ping.**
"A Director Who is Trying to Change the Audience: A Chat with Young Director Tian Zhuangzhuang."
IN: <u>Perspectives on Chinese Cinema</u>

6487 **Yarbro, Chelsea Quinn.**
"On *Freaks*."
IN: <u>Cut!: Horror Writers ...</u>

6488 **Yates, John.**
"Godfather Saga: The Death of the Family."
IN: <u>Movies as Artifacts</u>

6489 **Yau, C.M. Esther.**
"*Yellow Earth*: Western Analysis and a Non-Western Text."
IN: <u>Perspectives on Chinese Cinema</u>

6490 **Yau, Esther.**
"China."
IN: <u>World Cinema Since 1945</u>

6491 **Yeck, Joanne.**
"Anita Loos."
"Sidney Howard."
IN: <u>Dictionary of Literary Biography /v. 26</u>

6492 **Yellen, Linda.**
"Linda Yellen." [Interview by Lynn Fieldman Miller.]
IN: <u>The Hand That Holds the Camera</u>

6493 **Yellin, David G.**
"*Countdown to Zero*."
IN: <u>Nuclear War Films</u>

6494 **Yglesias, J.**
"*Intruder in the Dust* Another Evasive Film on the Negro."
IN: <u>The Black Man on Film</u>

6495 **Yhcam.**
"Cinematography."
IN: <u>French Film Theory and Criticism /v. 1</u>

6496 **Yi-Yu Cho Woo, Catherine.**
"The Chinese Montage: From Poetry and Painting to the Silver Screen."
IN: <u>Perspectives on Chinese Cinema</u>

6497 **Yin Tingru.**
"Yin Tingru, Actress." [Interview by George S. Semsel.]
IN: <u>Chinese Film</u>

6498 **Yoggy, Gary A.**
"When Television Wore Six-Guns: Cowboy Heroes on TV."
IN: <u>Shooting Stars</u>

6499 **Yordan, Philip.**
"Philip Yordan: The Chameleon." [Interview by Patrick McGilligan.]
IN: <u>Backstory 2</u>

6500 **Youdelman, Jeffrey.**
"Narration, Invention, and History."
IN: <u>New Challenges for Documentary</u>

6501 **Young, Andrew.**
"Family Pictures."
IN: <u>From Limelight to Satellite</u>

6502 **Young, Colin.**
"*The Seventh Seal*."
IN: <u>Focus on The Seventh Seal</u>

6503 **Young, Colin.**
"A Critique and Some Comments on Creating an American Film Institute."
IN: <u>Film Study in Higher Education</u>

6504 **Young, Colin.**
"Cinema of Common Sense: A View of Cinéma Vérité."
IN: <u>The Emergence of Film Art /1 ed</u>
<u>The Emergence of Film Art /2 ed</u>

6505 **Young, Colin.**
"Nobody Dies / Patriotism in Hollywood."
IN: <u>Film: Book 2</u>

6506 **Young, Loretta.**
"Loretta Young." [Interview by John Kobal.]
IN: <u>People Will Talk</u>

6507 **Young, Robert.**
"Robert Young." [Interview by Charles Higham.]
IN: <u>Celebrity Circus</u>

6508 **Young, Stark.**
"What Maisie Knows: Mae West."
IN: <u>Women and the Cinema</u>

6509 **Young, Vernon.**
"The Witness Point: Definitions of Film Art."
IN: <u>The Art of Cinema</u>

"The Whole World Is Watching (Mark Rosenberg; 'Katherine' [*sic*, Katharine]: The Making of an Exception; Mike Gray; Bruce Green; Jesus Salvador Trevino; Lynn Phillips)."
IN: Creative Differences

6538 **Zheutlin, Barbara.**
"The Politics of Documentary: A Symposium."
IN: New Challenges for Documentary

6539 *Zhizn iskusstva*, **editorial.**
"*October*–The Results of the Discussion."
"Theatre or Cinema?"
IN: The Film Factory

6540 **Zhong Dianfei.**
"Film Form and Film's National Form."
IN: Chinese Film Theory

6541 **Zhu Dake.**
"The Drawback of Xie Jin's Model."
IN: Chinese Film Theory

6542 **Zierold, Norman J.**
"The Trials of Jackie Coogan."
"Baby Leroy."
"What Was Shirley Temple Really Like?"
"Jane Withers: Dixie's Dainty Dewdrop."
"The True Judy." [RE: Judy Garland.]
"Little Lord Bartholomew."
"Edna Mae Durbin, alias Deanna."
"The Mick." [RE: Mickey Rooney]
"Jackie Cooper."
IN: The Child Stars

6543 **Zierold, Norman.**
"The Selznick Saga."
"'Uncle Carl' Laemmle."
"'Samuel Goldwyn Presents'."
"The Gentlemen from Paramount." [RE: B.P. Schulberg; Jesse Lasky; Cecil B. DeMille; Adolph Zukor.]
"'White Fang'." [RE: Harry Cohn.]
"The Brothers Warner."
"The 'Goy' Studio: Twentieth Century-Fox."
"Mayer's-*Ganz-Mispochen*."
IN: The Moguls

6544 **Zierold, Norman.**
"Theda Bara: The Wickedest Woman in the World."
"Barbara LaMarr: The Too-Beautiful Girl."
"Pola Negri: The Wildcat."
"Mae Murray: The Girl with the Bee-Stung Lips."
"Clara Bow: The 'It' Girl."
IN: Sex Goddesses of the Silent Screen

6545 **Zierold, Norman.**
"The Films' Forgotten Man: William Fox."
IN: The First Tycoons
The Moguls

6546 **Ziesmer, Jerry.**
"Travails of a Trainee." [RE: assistant director.]
IN: Directors in Action

6547 **Ziewer, Christian.**
"The Aesthetics of the 'Worker Film'."
"Last Words for Wolfgang Staudte."
IN: West German Filmmakers on Film

6548 **Zimbert, Richard.**
"Business Affairs and the Production/Financing/Distributing Agreement."
IN: The Movie Business Book

6549 **Zimmerman, Bonnie.**
"Daughters of Darkness: The Lesbian Vampire on Film."
IN: Planks of Reason

6550 **Zimmerman, Patricia R.**
"Entrepreneurs, Engineers, and Hobbyists: The Formation of a Definition of Amateur Film, 1897-1923."
IN: Current Research in Film /v. 3

6550a **Zimring, Michael.**
"Michael Zimring, literary agent." [Interview by Constance Nash and Virginia Oakey.]
IN: The Screenwriter's Handbook

6551 **Zinnemann, Fred.**
"Different Perspective."
IN: Hollywood Directors 1941-1976

6552 **Zinnemann, Fred.**
"Fred Zinnemann." [Interview by Rex Reed.]
IN: Travolta to Keaton

6553 **Zito, Stephen F.**
"The Black Film Experience."
IN: The American Film Heritage

6554 **Ziv, Frederic W.**
"Frederic W. Ziv." [An interview.]
IN: Producers on Producing

6555 **Zolotow, Maurice.**
"Billy Wilder."
IN: Close-Up: The Hollywood Director

6556 **Zsigmond, Vilmos.**
"Vilmos Zsigmond." [Interview by Dennis Schaefer and Larry Salvato.]
IN: Masters of Light

6557 **Zsigmond, Vilmos.**
"Vilmos Zsigmond." [Interview by Kris Malkiewicz.]
IN: Film Lighting

6558 **Zucker, Carole.**
"'I Am Dietrich and Dietrich Is Me': An Investigation of Performance Style in *Morocco* and *Shanghai Express*."
IN: Making Visible the Invisible

6559 **Zukor, Adolph.**
"Adolph Zukor: The Executive."
IN: The Real Tinsel

6560 **Zukor, Adolph.**
"I Felt the Freedom in the Air."
"Nobody Would Make Big Pictures."

"Operating in a Turmoil."
IN: <u>The First Tycoons</u>

6561 **Zukor, Adolph.**
"Origin and Growth of the Movies."
IN: <u>The Movies in Our Midst</u>
<u>The Story of the Films</u>

6562 **Zunser, Jesse.**
"*Rashomon.*"
IN: <u>Focus on Rashomon</u>

6563 **Zwerin, Charlotte.**
"*Salesman.*" [Interview by Alan Rosenthal.]
IN: <u>The New Documentary in Action</u>

-A-

A BOUT DE SOUFFLE (see: BREATHLESS)

A NOS AMOURS (Maurice Pialat, France, 1983) **6073**

A NOUS LA LIBERTE (Rene Clair, France, 1931) **2556, 5844**

A PROPOS DE NICE (Jean Vigo, France, 1930) **3190**

AAKALER SANDHANEY [In Search of Famine] (Mrinal Sen, India [Bengali], 1980) **1412**

AAKROSH [Cry of the Wounded] (Govind Nihalani, India [Hindi], 1980) **1412**

AB Svenska Biografteatern **2134**

abandoned, seduced and **1988**

Abbott and Costello **3848, 3850**

ABBOTT AND COSTELLO MEET FRANKENSTEIN (Charles Barton, U.S., 1948) **2546**

Abbott, Bud (SEE: Abbott and Costello)

ABC [American Broadcasting Company] **419**

abjection, an imaginary **1330**

abode of the gods **5777**

abreaction, cinematic **3673**

absence, femininity as **1590**

absence, structures of **2333**

abstract film **3518, 3578**

abstraction **1404, 1506**

absurd, cinema of the **2244**

absurd, growing up **2847**

absurd, the **5645**

absurd, theater of the **4323**

absurdist as box-office draw **2640**

absurdities **912**

academic subject, film as **5318**

Academy, the [Academy of Motion Picture Arts and Sciences] **3524**

access and consent **2708**

accessibility **79**

accidents, corruption of **6419**

accounting, creative **3693**

ACCUSED, THE (Jonathan Kaplan, U.S., 1988) **3833**

ACE IN THE HOLE [The Big Carnival] (Billy Wilder, U.S., 1951) **2546, 5082**

achievement, fantasies of **4064**

Achternbusch, Herbert **4883**

acinema **3770**

acoustic landscape, the visual and **1984**

acoustic world **349**

acquisitions executive **804**

ACROSS THE BRIDGE (Ken Annakin, G.B., 1957) **4642**

ACROSS THE PACIFIC (John Huston, U.S., 1942) **2546, 2556**

act, picture and **4226**

act, the **1806**

acted image, the **4359**

acting (SEE ALSO: actor; player) **207, 748, 761, 819, 1610, 1859, 2472, 2764, 3345, 3822, 3894, 4375, 4762, 4763, 5655, 6054, 6098, 6273**

acting, screen **5855a**

acting, a semiotic approach to **4563**

acting, Soviet school of **5417**

acting and behaving **3345**

acting as action, film **1015**

acting in Japanese cinema **5779**

acting in the seventies **4792**

acting to play oneself **6189**

Action (journal) **36**

action **951, 1536, 1894**

action, analogy of **1948**

action, film acting as **1015**

action, theatrical **3430**

action film, the continuous **3638**

ACTION: THE QUEBEC CRISIS OF 1970 (Robin Spry, Canada, 1970) **5625**

action-adventure (SEE ALSO: adventure) **951, 1635, 1976, 3514**

actor /-s (SEE ALSO: acting; player) **392, 971, 1179a, 1898, 2745, 2747, 2868, 3209, 3434, 3693, 4503, 4685, 4757, 4977, 5198, 5447, 5669, 6072**

actor, anthropology of the **6484**

actor, film **4333a**

actor, the eccentric **2230**

actor and text **2219**

actor from the acting **3209**

actor politicians of South India **2512**

actors, character **963**

actors, stars vs. **6264**

actor's art, the **4350**

actor's director **5723**

actors vs. directors **5198**

actress /-es **358, 1445, 5886**

actress, Shakespeare

actress archetypes **6245**

actress as signifier, the **1982, 1990**

actuality, history and **3283**

actuality, illusion of **4746**

actuelle, l' **5321**

adagio dancer **4543**

Adams, Nick **305**

Adams, Richard **3065**

ADAM'S RIB (George Cukor, U.S., 1949) **1046, 4842, 6152**

AGEE: A FILM (Ross Spears, U.S., 1980) **3840**

Agee Film Project **5612**

Agel, Henri **174**

agency, literary **6224**

agent **804, 4105, 6223**

agent, literary **5051**

aggression **4371**

aggression, love of **2013**

agit-train **6054**

agitator, cine- **2741**

agitprop, artisanship and **2564**

agreement, distributing **6548**

agreement, production (SEE: production agreement)

agreement, production/financing/distributing **6548**

AGUIRRE, THE WRATH OF GOD (Werner Herzog, Germany, 1972) **3569**

AIGLE A DEUX TETES, L' (Jean Cocteau, France, 1947) **1179a**

ain't, pictures can't say **6456**

air, people own the **5880**

AIR FORCE (Howard Hawks, U.S., 1943) **5755**

AIRPLANE! (Jim Abrahams, David Zucker & Jerry Zucker, U.S., 1980) **2213**

AJANTRIK [The Mechanical Man] (Ritwik Ghatak, India [Bengali], 1958) **1412**

Ajax **5009**

Akerman, Chantal **3918, 4503, 5049**

Akomfrah, John **2147**

ALAMBRISTA! (Robert M. Young, U.S [Chicano], 1976) **385**

Alamo, murder at the **4305**

Alassane, Moustapha **4636**

ALBERT PINTO KO GUSSA KYON AATA HAI [What Makes Alberto Pinto Angry] (Saeed Mirza, India [Hindi], 1980) **1412**

Albert, Edward **4855**

alchemy, biological **953**

alcohol (and media effects) **5945**

alcohol and the movies **3644**

alcoholic as hero, the **2423**

alcoholism **910, 4954**

Alcott, Louisa May **1801, 2199**

Aldrich, Robert **1304, 5200, 5402**

Alea, Tomas Gutierrez **1633**

alegoria, alegria **3033**

ALEXANDER NEVSKY (Sergei Eisenstein, USSR, 1938) **1759, 5817**

Alexander the Great **1758**

Alexandrov, Grigori **1758**

"Alfalfa" (SEE: Switzer, Carl)

ALFIE (Lewis Gilbert, G.B., 1966) **5249**

Algeria **121, 487, 4213, 5151**

Ali, Muhammad **1722**

ALI: FEAR EATS THE SOUL [Fear Eats the Soul] (Rainer Werner Fassbinder, Germany, 1974) **3980, 5125**

ALIBI (Roland West, U.S., 1929) **1471**

Alice Adams (book by Booth Tarkington) **5308**

ALICE ADAMS (George Stevens, U.S., 1935) **3233, 5308**

ALICE DOESN'T LIVE HERE ANYMORE (Martin Scorsese, U.S., 1975) **1538**

ALICE IN THE CITIES (Wim Wenders, Germany, 1974) **2849**

ALICE IN WONDERLAND (Norman Z. McLeod, U.S., 1933) **4044**

Alice's Adventures in Wonderland (book by Lewis Carroll) **4044**

ALICE'S ADVENTURES IN WONDERLAND (William Sterling, G.B., 1972) **4044**

ALICE'S RESTAURANT (Arthur Penn, U.S., 1969) **2243, 2277**

ALIEN (Ridley Scott, U.S., 1979) **147, 1329, 2149, 2433, 3192, 4370, 4399, 4565**

alien/father, child/ **5569**

alien Messiah, the **5124**

alienated generation **4644**

alienated vision, the **3421**

alienation **584, 2346, 2910**

alienation, structures of **3555**

alienation effect **761**

ALIMONY LOVERS (Harold Perkins, U.S., 1969) **1471**

ALL ABOUT EVE (Joseph L. Mankiewicz, U.S., 1950) **472, 2546, 3088**

all ears **5371**

All My Babies **5714**

ALL NIGHT LONG (Jean-Claude Tramont, U.S., 1981) **5626**

ALL QUIET ON THE WESTERN FRONT (Lewis Milestone, U.S., 1930) **821, 1116, 3406, 3569, 4205**

ALL THAT HEAVEN ALLOWS (Douglas Sirk, U.S., 1955) **585, 2097, 2579, 3570**

ALL THAT JAZZ (Bob Fosse, U.S., 1979) **553a**

ALL THAT MONEY CAN BUY [The Devil and Daniel Webster] (William Dieterle, U.S, 1941) **2546**

All the King's Men (book by Robert Penn Warren) **1450, 6148**

ALL THE KING'S MEN (Robert Rossen, U.S., 1949) **1116, 1450, 6148**

all the president's men **2329**

ALL THE PRESIDENT'S MEN (Alan J. Pakula, U.S., 1976) **1116, 4060, 4842**

all the rage **6357**

ALL-ROUND REDUCED PERSONALITY. See: REDUPERS

All-Union State Cinema Institute. SEE: VGIK

alla [*sic*] **5692**

animals, cruelty to **229**

animals in motion **4335**

ANIMATED ART OF THE BROTHERS QUAY, THE (Stephen & Timothy Quay, U.S.-G.B., 1978-87) **4788**

animated cartoon, music and the **3054, 4398**

animated film in China **4783**

animation (SEE ALSO: cartoons) **41, 888, 1185, 1380, 2404, 3165, 3384, 3822, 4654, 5543, 5679, 5843, 6281**

animation, avant-garde **5503**

animation, Balkan **5679**

animation, British **891, 5679**

animation, Canadian **5679**

animation, cel **5859**

animation, computer **5679**

animation, Czech **5679**

animation, French **5679**

animation, German **5679**

animation, Italian **5679**

animation, Japanese **5679**

animation, Polish **5679**

animation, puppet **5679**

animation, Russian **5679**

animation, Scandinavian **5679**

animation, suspended **42**

animation, women and cartoon **3927**

animation, Yugoslavian **5679**

animation effects (SEE ALSO: special effects; visual effects) **4550**

animator, voice **612**

Ann-Margaret **4855**

ANNA (Jurek Bogajewicz & Agnieszka Holland, Poland, 1987) **1689**

ANNA CHRISTIE (Clarence Brown, U.S., 1930) **2556**

annals of anality **4556**

ANNE OF THE INDIES (Jacques Tourneur, U.S., 1951) **3043**

ANNEE DERNIERE A MARIENBAD, L' (See: LAST YEAR AT MARIENBAD)

ANNIE GET YOUR GUN (George Sidney, U.S., 1950) **2045**

ANNIE HALL (Woody Allen, U.S., 1977) **553a, 2213, 2276, 3569**

another fine mess **5492**

ANOTHER WOMAN (Woody Allen, U.S., 1988) **3833**

Ansah, Kwaw **4636**

Ansikte, Ingmars **1006**

antecedents **4778**

anthropologist's eye **1818**

anthropology of the actor **6484**

anthropomorphic cinema **6078**

anti-cartoon **2465**

Anti-Communism **1116**

anti-hero **4644**

anti-illusionism **1811**

anti-information film, the **3228**

anti-melodrama, European **6449**

anti-myth **844**

anti-narrative of violence **830**

anti-porn **4906**

anti-semitism **5423, 5424**

anti-teater **3169**

anti-theses on aesthetics **5804**

anti-visual **1658**

anti-war themes (in Hollywood films) **5755, 5895**

ANTICIPATION [episode: Le Plus Vieux Metier du Monde] (Jean-Luc Godard, France, 1967) **1217**

ANTICIPATIONS OF THE NIGHT (Stan Brakhage, U.S., 1958) **3228, 3661**

antidotes, cinematic **4793**

antihero, comic **2206**

antisocial Western, the **5970**

antitrust legislation **5311**

antitrust policies **6289**

antitrust suit **697**

Antoine Doinel cycle, the **4226**

Antoine, Andre **1509**

ANTONIA (Jill Godmilow & Judy Collins, U.S., 1974) **2319**

antoniennui, no (SEE ALSO: Antonioni, Michelangelo) **5193**

Antonio, Emile de (SEE: de Antonio, Emile)

ANTONIO DAS MORTES (Glauber Rocha, Brazil, 1969) **997**

Antonioni, Michelangelo (SEE ALSO: antoniennui, no) **234, 1165, 1309, 1404, 1538, 1950, 2181, 2276, 2317, 2510, 2860, 2968, 3268, 4853, 5066, 5406a, 5806, 5989, 6383**

anxiety **4399**

anxiety, male **6437**

ANY NUMBER CAN PLAY (Mervyn LeRoy, U.S., 1949) **2045**

anything can happen **3211**

APACHE (Robert Aldrich, U.S., 1954) **585**

APARAJITO [The Unvanquished] (Satyajit Ray, India, 1956) (SEE ALSO: Apu Trilogy, The) **4902**

apes and essences **4204**

apocalypse **5383, 6426**

apocalypse and resurrection **3033**

APOCALYPSE NOW (Francis Ford Coppola, U.S., 1979) **553a, 720, 1116, 2213, 2529, 2689, 2965, 3570, 4508, 4515, 5895**

apocalyptic cinema **3963**

Apostles, the twelve **1759**

apotheosis **2145**

Baldwin, Stanley **4807**

Balkan animation **5679**

BALL OF FIRE (Howard Hawks, U.S., 1941) **488**

Ball, Lucille **4099, 4251, 4853**

Ball, Suzan **1353**

ballad, the **4572**

BALLAD OF AN UNSUNG HERO (Isaac Artenstein, U.S. [Chicano], n.d.) **3218**

BALLAD OF CABLE HOGUE, THE (Sam Peckinpah, U.S., 1970) **5250**

BALLAD OF GREGORIO CORTEZ, THE (Robert Young, U.S., 1982) **5038, 5596**

ballads, bullets or **5115**

Ballantine's scotch **3936**

ballerina, the new **1488**

ballet **3346**

BALLET MECANIQUE, LE (Fernand Leger, France, 1924) **2093, 3271, 3518**

balloons (for silent film titles) **1551**

Balogun, Ola **4636, 6000**

BALTHAZAR (See: AU HASARD BALTHAZAR)

BAMBI (Walt Disney, U.S., 1942) **366, 987, 1897, 2404, 6145**

banality, the cult of **2414**

BANANAS (Woody Allen, U.S., 1971) **553a, 2442, 6399**

BAND WAGON, THE (Vincente Minnelli, U.S., 1953) **2045, 2546, 5585**

BANDE A PART (Jean-Luc Godard, France, 1964) **1198**

BANDERA, LA (Julien Duvivier, France, 1935) **3567**

bandits and lovers **6398**

BANDITS OF ORGOSOLO, THE (Vittorio De Seta, Italy, 1961) **1972**

bandwagon, boys on the **4645**

Bangladesh **3610**

BANK DICK, THE (Eddie Cline, U.S., 1940) **2177**

Bank of America, The **6172**

bank, the **2208**

bankers **1228**

banking **6172, 6174**

banking, international **6175**

bankruptcy of cinema as art **5688**

banks, commercial **6172**

banks, (D.W.) Griffith and the **6173**

BAPTISM OF FIRE (see: FEUERTAUFE)

Bara, Theda **4251, 4725, 6544**

BARBAROSA (Fred Schepisi, U.S., 1982) **4788**

BARBED WIRE (Rowland V. Lee, U.S., 1927) **821**

Barbera, Joseph (SEE: Hanna and Barbera)

Bardem, Juan Antonio **2759, 5309**

Bardot, Brigitte **462, 1179a, 6342**

BARGAIN, THE (Reginald Barker, U.S., 1914) **4292**

Barker, Clive **280**

BARKLEYS OF BROADWAY, THE (Charles Walters, U.S., 1949) **2045**

Barn Burning (story by William Faulkner) **4639**

Barnet, Boris **1754, 2273**

baroque, the American **5191**

Baroque translation **3068**

BARREN LIVES (see: VIDAS SECAS)

Barrett, Rona **2592**

Barrow, Clyde (SEE ALSO: Bonnie and Clyde; BONNIE AND CLYDE) **1**

Barry Lyndon (book by W.M. Thackeray) **3305, 5492**

BARRY LYNDON (Stanley Kubrick, G.B., 1975) **3305, 3645, 3749, 5492**

BARRY McKENZIE [The Adventures of Barry McKenzie] (Bruce Beresford, Australia, 1972) **2777**

BARRY McKENZIE HOLDS HIS OWN (Bruce Beresford, Australia, 1974) **2777**

Barry, Iris **4026, 5692**

Barrymore, John **5251, 6196**

Barrymores, the **3258**

barter, erotic **1598**

Barthes, Roland **1253, 2856**

Bartholomew, Freddy **6542**

Barton, Charles T. **5854**

BAS-FONDS, LES [The Lower Depths] (Jean Renoir, France, 1936) **2277, 2281, 2556, 3490, 5142**

baseball (on the screen) **5611**

basic concepts **3387**

basic film aesthetics **5609**

basics, back to **1013**

Bass, Saul **2248**

Bassori, Timite **4636**

BAT, THE (Roland West, U.S., 1926) **3818**

BAT WHISPERS, THE (Roland West, U.S., 1930) **3818**

BATAAN (Tay Garnett, U.S., 1943) **1379, 5755**

BATAILLE DU RAIL, LA (Rene Clement, France, 1946) **433**

Bates, Barbara **1353**

Bates, Norman (character) **1678**

Bathily, Moussa **4636**

bathtub, sunken **5985**

BATMAN (Tim Burton, U.S., 1989) **2213**

Battcock, Gregory **4336**

battle, into **5082**

BATTLE BEYOND THE STARS (Jimmy T. Murakami, U.S., 1980) **5228**

BATTLE CRY OF PEACE, THE (J. Stuart Blackton, U.S., 1915) **821**

BELLS OF ATLANTIS (Ian Hugo, U.S., 1952) **3661**

Belmondo, Jean-Paul **4853, 5198**

Belson, Jordan **6203a, 6515**

Belushi, John **1722, 2982**

Bemberg, Maria Luisa **4778**

BEN-HUR (Fred Niblo, U.S., 1925) **819, 1179a, 1376, 1978**

BEN-HUR (William Wyler, U.S., 1959) **212a**

BEN-HUR [chariot race, 1959 version] **3929**

Benchley, Robert **3849**

Benedek, Laslo **1304, 5402**

Benegal, Shyam **1412**

benevolence, divine **3510a**

Bengal filmmaker **379**

Benjamin, Walter **1924**

Bennent, David **5273**

Bennett Sisters, the **3258**

Bennett, Charles **3799**

Bennett, Spencer Gordon **5971, 5972**

Benning, James **5049**

Bentley, Irene **1742**

Benton, Robert **39, 1168**

Beresford, Bruce **5723, 6435**

Bereyso, Patti **6537**

Bergman, Ingmar **130, 135, 234, 521, 1006, 1049, 1309, 1312, 1454, 1538, 1655, 1722, 2277, 2449, 2509, 2555, 2595, 2801, 2828, 2862, 2968, 3270, 3287, 3533, 3725, 4622, 4850, 5245, 5264, 5319, 5472, 5665, 5806, 5947, 5989, 6252, 6528**

Bergman, Ingrid **1003, 1425, 1722, 2627, 4251**

Bergman's non-verbal sequences [re: Ingmar] **3834**

Bergman's portrait of women [re: Ingmar] **5666**

Berkeley, Busby **323, 1505, 2273, 4327, 5368, 6390**

BERKELEY REBELS, THE (Arthur Barron, CBS Reports, 1965) **386**

Berlanga, Luis Garcia **2759, 5309**

Berlin, finding a home in **3407**

Berlin, Irving **2694**

Berlin, letter from **6054**

BERLIN, SYMPHONY OF A CITY (Walter Ruttmann, Germany, 1927) **1086, 1089**

BERLIN ALEXANDERPLATZ (Rainer Werner Fassbinder, Germany, 1980) **4884, 5306, 5777**

Berman, Pandro S. **5402**

Bern, Paul **1003**

Bernal, Ishmael **2728**

Bernanos, Georges **179**

Bernstein, Elmer **4511, 5851**

Bertolucci, Bernardo **962, 1165, 1309, 2509, 3272, 3318, 4150, 4503, 5402, 6293, 6383, 6425**

Bertolucci, Giuseppe **6383**

Berton, Pierre **2806**

Bess (character) **3974**

Bessie, Alvah **1561, 4174**

BEST BOY (Ira Wohl, U.S., 1979) **5260**

BEST FOOT FORWARD (Edward Buzzell, U.S., 1943) **2045**

best friend **4816**

BEST MAN, THE (Franklin Schaffner, U.S., 1964) **1116**

BEST OF TIMES, THE (Roger Spottiswoode, U.S., 1986) **6350**

BEST YEARS OF OUR LIVES, THE (William Wyler, U.S., 1946) **2177, 2960, 6165**

BETE HUMAINE, LA (Jean Renoir, France, 1938) **1234, 2556, 3468, 5142, 6074**

BETRAYED (Costa-Gavras, U.S., 1988) **2449**

BETSY'S WEDDING (Alan Alda, U.S., 1990) **3833**

Betty Boop (character) **2404**

Beverly Hills **2846**

BEVERLY HILLS COP (Martin Brest, U.S., 1984) **2213**

BEYOND A REASONABLE DOUBT (Fritz Lang, U.S., 1956) **4957**

BEZHIN MEADOW (Sergei Eisenstein; unproduced) **5428**

BHAVNI BHAVAI [A Folk Tale] (Ketan Mehta, India [Gujarati], 1980) **1412**

BHUMIKA [The Role] (Shyam Benegal, India [Hindi], 1977) **1412**

BHUVAN SHOME (Mrinal Sen, India [Hindi], 1969) **1412**

bias **459**

Biberman, Herbert **1561**

biblical spectaculars **6137**

bibliographical essay, a **1867**

bibliography, the first **5531**

bibliography (of the musical film) **1959**

BICYCLE THIEVES, THE [The Bicycle Thief] (Vittorio De Sica, Italy, 1948) **447, 1179a, 1435, 1497, 2177, 2556, 3161, 3569, 3573, 3898, 4324, 5082, 5583, 5856, 6367**

BIDONE, IL [The Swindlers] (Federico Fellini, Italy, 1955) **70, 5082**

Bierbichler, Annamirl **34**

big brother's backyard **3280**

big caper film, the **3118**

BIG CARNIVAL, THE (see: ACE IN THE HOLE)

BIG CHILL, THE (Lawrence Kasdan, U.S., 1983) **1116**

BIG COUNTRY, A (Australia, 1980) **1456**

BIG EASY, THE (Jim McBride, U.S., 1987) **3832**

big game **6424**

BIG HEAT, THE (Fritz Lang, U.S., 1953) **585**

BIG PARADE, THE (King Vidor, U.S., 1925) **309, 821, 1116, 2946, 5755**

BIG SKY, THE (Howard Hawks, U.S., 1952) **5008**

Big Sleep, The (book by Raymond Chandler) **4585, 5385**

BREAKING POINT, THE (Michael Curtiz, U.S., 1950) **4641**

breaking toys **2152**

breakthroughs **4833**

breath of sea air, a **5597**

BREATHLESS [A Bout de souffle] (Jean-Luc Godard, France, 1959) **422, 2312, 2556, 3271, 3569, 3901, 6388**

Brecht, Bertolt / Brechtian **399, 775, 1621, 1811, 1859, 2127, 2449, 3048, 3513, 3590, 3779, 4223, 4323, 4687, 4688, 5785, 5856, 6053, 6153, 6225**

Brechtian criticism **1621**

Breen, Joe **3573**

Breer, Robert **5049**

Brenon, Herbert **2273**

Bresson, Robert **234, 236, 431, 1179a, 1309, 2509, 4899, 5097, 5102, 5163, 5292, 5501, 5505, 5588, 5806, 5897, 6266**

Breton, Andre **2404**

BRIDE COMES TO YELLOW SKY, THE (script by James Agee) **61**

BRIDE OF FRANKENSTEIN, THE (James Whale, U.S., 1935) **2177, 2546, 2911, 4429, 5585**

BRIDE WORE BLACK, THE (Francois Truffaut, France, 1967) **2556**

brides of Christ **2097**

BRIDGE AT REMAGEN, THE (John Guillermin, U.S., 1969) **5755**

BRIDGE ON THE RIVER KWAI, THE (David Lean, G.B., 1957) **5115**

BRIDGE TOO FAR, A (Richard Attenborough, G.B., 1977) **5755**

Bridges, James **5402**

Bridges, Jeff **4854**

BRIDGES-GO-ROUND (Shirley Clarke, U.S., 1958) **3661**

BRIEF ENCOUNTER (David Lean, G.B., 1945) **2213**

BRIGADOON (Vincente Minnelli, U.S., 1954) **2045**

BRIGHT LEAF (Michael Curtiz, U.S., 1950) **4427**

BRIGHT LIGHTS (Busby Berkeley, U.S., 1935)

BRIGHT LIGHTS, BIG CITY (James Bridges, U.S., 1988) **3832**

BRIGHTON ROCK (James Boulting, G.B., 1947) **4642**

brilliance, artificial **3942**

bringing it all back home **5568**

BRINGING UP BABY (Howard Hawks, U.S., 1938) **1046, 2546, 2556, 6198, 6440**

BRINNER EN ELD, DET [A Fire is Burning] (Gustaf Molander, Sweden, 1943) **2145**

Britain (SEE ALSO: British cinema/film; Great Britain; England) **1809, 2145, 4725, 4808**

Britain, Black independent film in **4109**

Britain, embargo on exporting feature films to **5770**

Britain, Hollywood and **3139**

Britain, Hollywood in **5770**

Britain, the 'other cinema' in **2629**

BRITAIN PREPARED (Wellington House, U.S., 1915) **821**

British animation **891, 5679**

British case, the **5082**

British cine-feminists **3148**

British cinema and the underworld **4319**

British cinema and war **1300, 4916**

British cinema, black **4667**

British cinema/film (SEE ALSO: England) **86, 87, 198, 1300, 3361, 3738, 4038, 4067, 4320, 4600, 5082**

British Colonial Africa **5557**

British documentaries in the war **2587**

British documentary movement **2765, 2970, 3734, 6355**

BRITISH EMPIRE, THE (Tom Haydon, et al., G.B. [BBC-TV], series in 1970s) **2659**

British Empire and monarchy **4918**

British feature films, women in **2594**

British film and British theatre **809**

British film history **6335**

British film techniques **198**

British films, women, realism and reality in **274**

British Free Cinema (SEE: Free Cinema; Direct Cinema; cinema verite)

British historical epics **3800**

British Imperial cinema **4917**

British 'New Wave' **2768**

British novels **4038**

British official attitudes **5814**

BRITISH SOUNDS (see: SEE YOU AT MAO)

British stars **6133**

British television **3284**

British wartime films **4916**

British working-class, the **5661**

broadcasting **96, 3290**

broadcasting and cinema **383, 1039**

broadcasting, Japanese overseas **5138**

BROADWAY (Paul Fejos, U.S., 1929) **5368**

Broadway, comedies from **2177**

Broadway, dramas from **2177**

Broadway, first night on **4802**

BROADWAY MELODY, THE (Harry Beaumont, U.S., 1929) **3406**

Broca, Philippe de **2277**

Brock University **2420**

Brocka, Lino **2502, 5836**

Broidy, Steve **5729**

BROKEN ARROW (Delmer Daves, U.S., 1950) **585, 4142, 5970**

BROKEN BLOSSOMS (D.W. Griffith, U.S., 1919) **52, 176, 3487, 3570, 3602, 3604, 3617, 4288, 4725**

broken cudgels **2345**

BROKEN JUG, THE (Gustav Ucicky, Germany, 1937) **5442**

brokers, the new power **3693**

Broncho Billy [G. W.] Anderson **821, 4726, 5970**

Bronson, Betty **4251**

Bronson, Charles **1722**

Bronson, Dan **804**

Bronzino, Il **2404**

BROOD, THE (David Cronenberg, Canada, 1979) **5260**

Brook, Peter **1442, 4856**

Brooks, David **1746**

Brooks, Louise **5870**

Brooks, Mel **1722, 2687, 4575, 5192, 5545, 5675**

Brooks, Richard **853, 1309, 2004**

Brossette, Stanley **804**

brothel **5276**

brother, can you spare a dime? **4258**

brother, the word **6047**

brothers killing brothers **2301**

BROTHERS RICO, THE (Phil Karlson, U.S., 1957) **5362**

Broughton, James **734**

Brown, Clarence **819, 1863, 2269, 3373**

Brown, Harry **1973, 4185**

Brown, Joe E. **3848**

Brown, Rowland **3373, 5875**

Brown and Carney **3850**

Brown is not Greene **4642**

Browning, Tod **801, 2509, 5056, 5671**

Brownlow, Kevin **6133**

Bruce, Lenny **2982**

Bruckman, Clyde **44**

BRUDER (Werner Hochbaum, Germany, 1929) **8**

Brusati, Franco **6383**

Brustellin, Alf **4023**

brutalists, movie **3101**

Bryher [pseudonym: Winifred Ellerman] **4026**

Bs, beyond the **4172**

Buchman, Sidney **718, 1168**

BUCK ROGERS (Ford Beebe & Saul A. Goodkind, U.S., 1939; serial) **4565**

Buckner, Robert **1649**

BUCKSKIN FRONTIER (Lesley Selander, U.S., 1943) **5970**

budget, over- **5119**

BUFFALO BILL AND THE INDIANS, OR SITTING BULL'S HISTORY LESSON (Robert Altman, U.S., 1976) **1347, 4195**

bug in the rug **6481**

bugle call **5414**

Bugs Bunny (character) **1424, 5864**

Bujold, Genevieve **4854**

Bulgaria **2819**

BULLDOG DRUMMOND (F. Richard Jones, U.S., 1929) **4737**

bullets **3077**

bullets or ballads **5115**

BULLITT (Peter Yates, U.S., 1968) **5585**

bunk left out, the **6415**

bunny, Otto's lost **5406a**

BUNNY LAKE IS MISSING (Otto Preminger, U.S., 1965) **1471**

Bunuel, Luis **234, 435, 962, 1165, 1238, 1239, 1309, 1511, 1743, 1948, 1971, 2128, 2276, 2333, 2404, 2509, 2582, 2759, 2968, 3377, 3379, 4091, 4194, 4574, 4843, 4927, 4934, 4973, 5265, 5644, 5645, 5806, 5810, 6328, 6420**

Burch, Noel **1724**

bureaucratization **4842**

Burgin, Victor **4299**

BURGLAR, THE (Valery Ogorodnikov, U.S.S.R., 1987) **2449**

Burkina Faso **4636**

Burma **3610**

Burman, Thomas **5797**

BURMESE HARP, THE (see: HARP OF BURMA, THE)

BURN! (Gillo Pontecorvo, France-Italy, 1969) **5111**

Burnett, Frances Hodgson **596, 6387**

Burnett, W.R. **885**

BURNING AN ILLUSION (Menelik Shabazz, G.B., 1981) **5225**

burning, keep the campfires **998**

BURNING, THE (Tom Maylam, U.S., 1981) **1576**

Burns, George **1722, 4854**

Burstall, Tim **5723**

Burstyn, Ellen **4854**

Burstyn, Joseph **6003**

BUS STOP (Joshua Logan, U.S., 1956) **4814**

"Bus Stop" pileup **2896**

Busch, Niven **6368**

Buscombe, Ed **1204**

business **361, 2353, 2479, 3463, 4503, 6548**

business, international **2496**

business affairs executive **804**

business and love **4427**

bust, boom and **4661**

BUTCH CASSIDY AND THE SUNDANCE KID (George Roy Hill, U.S., 1969) **2213, 4142, 5585**

butler, a **5910**

Butler, David **5220**

butterflies, vampires and **5371**

BWANA DEVIL (Arch Oboler, U.S., 1952) **4390**

Bwana Metro **4390**

BY DESIGN (Claude Jutra, Canada, 1981) **5260**

by guess and by God **5082**

-C-

CAA (SEE: Creative Artists Agency)

CABARET (Bob Fosse, U.S., 1972) **3569, 5585, 6117**

CABIN IN THE SKY (Vincente Minnelli, U.S., 1943) **2045**

"cabin" picture **3649**

CABINET OF DR. CALIGARI, THE (Robert Weine, U.S., 1919) (SEE ALSO: Caligari; Caligarism) **735, 856, 985, 1064, 1788, 1971, 3271, 3390, 3391, 3399, 3569, 3602, 3602, 3603, 3608, 4700, 4731, 4914, 5171**

CABIRIA (see: NIGHTS OF CABIRIA)

CACIQUE BANDEIRA [Boss Bandeira] (Hector Olivera, Argentina-Spain, 1975) **1317**

cadence **1509**

Cadillacs **4061**

cadres, cinema **4537**

caduceus, the **4889**

CAFE FLESH (Rinse Dream, U.S., 1982) **5633**

CAGE, THE (Sidney Peterson & Hy Hirsh, U.S., 1947) **4617**

Cagney, James **657, 1943, 3294, 3410, 4358, 4575**

Cahiers du Cinema (journal) **2312, 2772, 3590, 4500**

Cahn, Edward L. **1303**

CAIN AND MABEL (Lloyd Bacon, U.S., 1936) **4069**

CAINE MUTINY, THE (Edward Dmytryk, U.S., 1954) **5755**

Caine, Michael **1722, 4855, 6133**

Calcutta, Renoir in **4828**

Caldwell, Zoe **4850**

Calhoun, Lynda **6537**

California **4805**

Caligari, Dr. (character) **735, 3390, 3399**

Caligarism **3480**

CALIGULA (Tinto Brass, U.S., 1980) **1471**

Callahan, Inspector (Harry) (SEE: Inspector Callahan)

calumny, race **4, 1345**

Camelot **1857**

camera **1213, 1214, 1534, 4867**

camera, 8mm **3627**

camera, aesthetics of the mobile **2243**

camera, handling the **6459**

camera, ideology and the **5643a**

camera, in the face of the **5091**

camera, interpretive **6016**

camera, Japanese **4931**

camera, mobile **2243**

camera, moving **5587**

camera, presence of the **5090**

camera, subjective **3668**

camera and style **4933**

camera and the American, the movie **6165**

camera approach, a **2952**

camera as a god, the **703**

camera eye, the **739, 3500, 5492**

camera movement **683, 684**

camera on the move **4220**

camera operator **804**

camera reconnoiters, the **476**

camera style, non-bourgeois **2699, 2705**

camera viewpoint **4650**

camera writes, the **4226**

camera-eye, the **4323, 6203a**

camera-stylo **278**

camera, what is a **745**

cameraman (SEE ALSO: cinematographer) **24, 819, 820, 3370, 4163, 4221**

cameras, the men with the movie **3370**

Cameroon **4636**

CAMILLE (George Cukor, U.S., 1936) **52, 2556, 3143**

Camino, Jaime **5309**

camp **324**

camp fires burning **998**

campaign cynicism **5439**

Campbell, Clay **5797**

CAN'T STOP THE MUSIC (Nancy Walker, U.S., 1980) **4069**

Canada **2566, 3566, 4263**

Canada, National Film Board of (SEE: National Film Board of Canada)

Canadian animation **5679**

Canadian cinema **3551**

Canadian Feature Film Conundrum **4182**

Canadian feature films **4583**

Canadian Film Board Unit B **3055**

Canadian film industry **4581, 4582**

Canavi, Liliana **5703**

Canby, Vincent **602**

CANDIDATE, THE (Michael Ritchie, U.S., 1972) **1116, 5439**

CANDIDE (Jean Pierre Cassel, France, 1960) **6117**

CANDY (Christian Marquand, U.S., 1968) **1471**

Cannery Row (book by John Steinbeck) **4184**

CANNERY ROW (David S. Ward, U.S., 1982) **4184**

Cannes Film Festival **1179a, 2861**

CAT PEOPLE (Jacques Tourneur, U.S., 1942) **2192, 3673, 5962, 6424**

catalogue of effects **5677**

cataract surgery **6077**

Catch-22 (book by Joseph Heller) **2688, 3897, 6117**

CATCH-22 (Mike Nichols, U.S., 1970) **2688, 3897, 5755, 6117**

caterer **804**

Catholic, the **1142**

Catholicism **2266**

CATHY COME HOME (Jeremy Sandford [writer], G.B., 1966) **5176, 5177**

CATTLE ANNIE AND LITTLE BRITCHES (Lamont Johnson, U.S., 1980) **4791**

cattle, they should be treated like **5896**

CAUGHT (Max Ophuls, U.S., 1949) **1590**

cautionary fables **4351**

Cavalcanti, Alberto **4230, 6355**

Cavani, Liliana **6383**

Cavell, Stanley **2405**

CBS [Columbia Broadcasting System] **651, 2449**

CBS-Vanderbilt litigation **3260**

CEDDO (Ousmane Sembene, Senegal, 1976) **4294**

cel animation **5859**

celebrities, stars vs. **5251**

Celluloid Brassiere, The (book by Tennessee Williams) **4323**

celluloid German, the **3548**

celluloid mujeres **4247**

celluloid palimpsests **2118**

celluloid route **5600**

celluloid safety valve **5788**

celluloid sculptor **5371**

cellulose nitrate **1931a**

cellulos, nitro- **5843**

Cendrars, Blaise **3518**

censorship **4, 34, 160, 375, 590, 820, 1199, 1366, 1367, 1471, 2338, 2588, 2967, 3426, 3514, 3571, 3606, 3609, 4011, 4368, 4389, 4629, 4811, 5023, 5132, 5519, 5907**

censorship (in Britain) **4745, 4747, 4748**

censorship (in Spain) **2759**

censorship, self- **317**

censorship, state **5132**

censorship and the American occupation (of Japan) **2782**

censorship in France **141**

Center for Media Study **5380**

center, the search for a **6138a**

Central America **3280**

centralisation **4161**

century, the unpopular **2277**

certain regard, un **5837**

certain tendency, a **5928**

certainty, a wonderful **5921**

certainty, the uncertainty of **4252a**

CESAR (Marcel Pagnol, France, 1936) **6073**

Ceylon **3006**

Chabrol, Claude **233, 488, 945, 1309, 2509, 4169, 4226, 4503, 5808**

chain, links in a **4681**

chain, theater **1690**

chain-store strategy **2357**

Chaka, Carol **6537**

CHAKRA [The Vicious Circle] (Rabindra Dharmaraj, Hindi, 1980) **1412**

chamber cinema **3430**

CHAMBER MYSTERY, THE (Abraham S. Schomer, U.S., 1920) **1551**

Chamberlain, Richard **4855**

chambermaids, the two **4193**

Chambers, John **5797**

CHAMBRE 666: CANNES, MAY 1982 (Wim Wenders, U.S.-France, 1983) **6252**

chameleon, the **6499**

champagne-Schroeter **6094**

Champion, Gower **4853**

CHANCE MEETING (See: BLIND DATE)

CHANCE OF A LIFETIME, THE (Bernard Miles & Alan Osbiston, G.B., 1950) **5082**

CHANCES ARE (Emile Ardolino, U.S., 1989) **3833**

Chandragupta, Bansi **1412**

Chaneys, the (Lon and Lon, Jr.) **801, 5870**

CHANG (Merian C. Cooper & Ernest B. Schodsack, U.S., 1927) **821, 2476**

change, continuity and **596**

change, social **317, 5023, 5449**

change and decay **4639**

change of emphasis **5115**

changes **4299**

changes, slow **6537**

Channel Four (British television) **2396, 6133**

Channing, Carol **4854**

CHANT D'AMOUR, UN (Jean Genet, France, 1950) **1471**

CHANT OF JIMMIE BLACKSMITH, THE (Fred Schepisi, Australia, 1978) **4037, 5260**

chaos of cool **2277**

CHAPAYEV (Georgi and Sergei Vasiliev, U.S.S.R., 1934) **1953, 4730**

Chaplin, Charles (SEE ALSO: Tramp, the) **431, 434, 488, 707a, 735, 819, 821, 1003, 1178, 1179a, 1303, 1330a, 1720, 1722, 1912, 1999a, 2000, 2065, 2124a, 2177,**

grip; location manager; production designer;production manager; property master; set designer; sound editor; sound recordist; unit publicist)

Crichton, Michael **4565**

cricket **3162**

CRIES AND WHISPERS (Ingmar Bergman, Sweden, 1972) **4588, 5165, 5515, 5527, 5735**

crime **2177, 4431, 4682, 4842**

CRIME AND PUNISHMENT (Josef von Sternberg, U.S., 1935) **694**

Crime Does Not Pay **3849**

crime film (SEE ALSO: gangster film) **1253, 5585**

Crime Movies (book by Carlos Clarens) **747**

CRIME OF M. LANGE, THE [Le Crime de Monsieur Lange] (Jean Renoir, France, 1935) **699, 2278, 2445, 2556, 3569**

CRIME WITHOUT PASSION (Ben Hecht & Charles MacArthur, U.S., 1934) **4737**

CRIMES OF THE HEART (Bruce Beresford, U.S., 1986) **3832**

CRIMINAL LIFE OF ARCHIBALDO DE LA CRUZ, THE (Luis Bunuel, Mexico, 1955) **5008**

CRISIS (Richard Brooks, U.S., 1950) **2045**

crisis, comprehension and **5624**

crisis, film **5082**

crisis, patriarchal **5569**

crisis structure **3856**

CRISS CROSS (Robert Siodmak, U.S., 1949) **2014**

Crist, Judith **602, 4026**

critic /-s (SEE ALSO: reviewers) **945, 947, 1195, 1256, 3461, 3527, 4060, 5201, 5211, 5335, 5528**

critic, death of a **4408**

critic, gay film **6436**

critic, letter to a **5008**

critic, middle class film **5201**

critic, the feminist **3985**

critic, the proprioceptive **5406a**

critic to film-maker, from **2314**

critical attitudes **5811**

critical credo **5469**

critical dystopia **4586**

critical grasp **6328**

critical impasse, a **3014**

critical methodology **5941, 5943**

critical question, the **2857**

critical subjectivity **2220**

critical theory **2154**

criticism (SEE ALSO: reviews) **433, 925, 966, 1216, 1217, 1981, 2312, 2486, 2452, 2582, 2642, 2771, 2772, 3320, 3527, 4060, 4493, 4514, 4681, 5202, 5231, 5298, 5528, 5984, 6145, 6424, 6467**

criticism, adaptation as **5492**

criticism, archetypal **2856**

criticism, Brechtian **1621**

criticism, feminist film (SEE: feminist film criticism)

criticism, gay film **4068**

criticism, genre **1253**

criticism, ideological **2643, 4402**

criticism, literary **1974**

criticism, Marxist **4402**

criticism, phenomenological **2856**

criticism, post-Bazin **3773**

criticism, self- **2865**

criticism, social **1192**

criticism, structuralist **1724**

criticism and scholarship **1337**

criticism and self-criticism **1461**

criticism and/as history **4681**

criticism as creation **2081**

critics, my **5175**

critics, newspaper film **6467**

critics, the culture **4026**

critique, radical **5646**

critique plus auto-critique **3773**

CROCODILE DUNDEE (Peter Faiman, Australia, 1986) **2213**

CROISIERE JAUNE, LA [The Yellow Cruise], LA (Leon Poirier & Andre Sauvage, France, 1934) **6208**

CROIX DE BOIS, LES (Raymond Bernard, France, 1932) **4844, 6074**

Crombie, Donald **5723**

Cromwell, John **970, 4074**

Cronenberg, David **953**

cronyism **1391**

Crosby, Bing **4433**

cross, sign of the **6220**

cross-cultural analysis **3150**

cross-cutting **2195**

cross-section films **3396**

CROSSFIRE (Edward Dmytryk, U.S,. 1947) **3570**

CROSSROADS (Jack Conway, U.S., 1942) **842**

Crossroads [British television series] **3284**

Crosswaite, David **2250**

CROWD, THE (King Vidor, U.S., 1928) **1310, 1509, 1551, 3487**

crowd splendor, the picture of **3678**

Crowley, Mart **4850**

Crown Film Unit **1422**

CRUCIFIED LOVERS, THE (Kenji Mizoguchi, Japan, 1954) **488**

cruel cinema **4597**

cruelty, the self-critical cinema of **3773**

Czechoslovakia **1429, 2277, 2551, 3665, 4382, 5518**

-D-

dada **1812, 3379**

daffodils **4461**

Daffy Duck (character) **1423, 5864**

Dahl, Roald **5332**

DAISY KENYON (Otto Preminger, U.S., 1947) **2556**

Daisy Miller (book by Henry James) **4316**

DAISY MILLER (Peter Bogdanovich, U.S., 1974) **720, 1455, 4316**

Dale, Charlie (SEE: Smith and Dale)

Dali, Salvador **1975, 2404, 3379**

Dallas [television program] **190**

Dalton, Emmett **821**

DAM BUSTERS, THE (Michael Anderson, G.B., 1955) **2213**

DAMES (Ray Enright, U.S., 1934) **1982, 1991**

DAMNED, THE (Luchino Visconti, Italy, 1969) **3271, 3974**

dance **1179a, 1354, 1505, 4722, 4842**

dance, cine **4617**

DANCE, GIRL, DANCE (Dorothy Arzner, U.S., 1940) **1982, 3203**

dance, respond **738**

dance, the violent **5565**

dance film, three kinds of **5560**

dance musical **1505**

dance of danger **3272**

dancer, adagio **4543**

dancer from the dance **3549**

dancers, some notes for young **3223**

DANCING MOTHERS (Herbert Brenon, U.S., 1926) **3602**

Dandridge, Dorothy **2982**

dandy, the **3866**

dandyism **3173**

danger, dance of **3272**

danger, poetry and **1579**

Dangerfield, Rodney **1722**

DANIEL (Sidney Lumet, U.S., 1983) **1116**

Daniels, Bebe **5530**

Daniels, Bree (character) **2255**

Danish film (SEE ALSO: Denmark) **983**

Danning, Sybil **1722**

D'Annunzio **204**

DANNY BOY (Neil Jordan, Ireland-G.B., 1982) **6350**

DANTON (Andrzej Wajda, France-Poland, 1982) **1165**

Darcus, Jack **2806**

daredevil on horseback **6282**

DARK COMMAND (Raoul Walsh, U.S., 1940) **5970**

DARK CRYSTAL (Jim Henson & Frank Oz, G.B., 1983) **6092**

DARK MIRROR (Robert Siodmak, U.S., 1946) **1982**

DARK PASSAGE (Delmer Daves, U.S., 1947) **3958**

DARK STAR (John Carpenter, U.S., 1975) **4453**

darkness, an unshielding **2707**

darkness, daughters of **6549**

darkness, freedom before **5115**

darkness, those who walk in **4175**

darkness and the shadow **4836**

DARLING LILI (Blake Edwards, U.S., 1970) **4069**

Darth Vader (character) **1804**

Darwinism **4648**

dash, cutting a **4914**

Dassin, Jules **1304, 3990**

daughter, evil **6152**

daughter, independent **6152**

DAUGHTER RITE (Michelle Citron, U.S., 1978) **1957, 3143, 6332**

daughters, mothers and **3143**

daughters of darkness **6549**

Daughters of Vienna (book by Josef von Sternberg) **1616**

Daves, Delmer **718, 1168, 1303, 1973**

DAVID AND LISA (Frank Perry, U.S., 1963) **2910**

David Copperfield (book by Charles Dickens) **3750**

DAVID COPPERFIELD (George Cukor, U.S., 1935) **3750**

Davies, Carmel **804**

Davies, Freeman **804**

Davies, Marion **3258, 4251**

Davis, Bette **52, 3300, 4251, 4850, 4854, 6308**

Davis, Peter **2493**

Dawn, Bob **5797**

dawn, called the **4983**

dawn, came the **6115**

Dawn, Jack **5797**

Dawn, Norman O. **1968**

DAWN OF THE DEAD (George Romero, U.S., 1979) **6426**

Dawson, Jan **4026**

DAY AT THE RACES, A (Sam Wood, U.S., 1937) **2177**

DAY FOR NIGHT (Francois Truffaut, France, 1973) **2556, 6265**

DAY IN THE COUNTRY, A (Jean Renoir, France, 1936) **2556**

Day of the Locust (book by Nathanael West) **2400**

DAY OF THE LOCUST (John Schlesinger, U.S., 1975) **720, 2400**

DAY OF WRATH (Carl Dreyer, Denmark, 1943) **985, 2556, 3609, 6171**

DAY THE EARTH CAUGHT FIRE, THE (Val Guest, U.S., 1962) **2539**

Del Monte, Peter **6383**

Del Rio, Dolores **6399**

Del Ruth, Roy **5220**

deliberation and response **6446**

delinquency, script of **2268**

DELINQUENTS, THE (Robert Altman, U.S., 1957) **4005**

Deliverance (book by James Dickey) **458**

DELIVERANCE (John Boorman, U.S., 1972) **458, 5163**

Delluc, Prix Louis **313, 1310, 1971**

Delvaux, Paul **2404**

demi-docs **4684**

democracy, dictatorship to **2759**

democracy, searchlight on **2464**

democracy as participation **6151**

democratic forums **6391**

democratic society, a **1394**

democratizing documentary **898, 899**

demolishing comedy **2277**

demonic, descent into the **2189a**

demonic in American cinema, the **3962**

DEMONS DE L'AUBE, LES (Yves Allegret, France, 1946) **433**

Demy, Jacques **233, 990, 1309, 4503, 5402**

demythologized world (Fellini's) **1622**

Deneuve, Catherine **963, 2679**

denial, the aesthetics of **5897**

denial of difference **2111**

Dennis, Sandy **4853**

Denny, Reginald **819**

Denos, Robert **6322**

denotation, problems of **4129**

Denti, Jorge **2148**

denunciation **6383**

departure, arrival and **6038**

dependency, a small **6252**

dependency, cultural **4582**

Depression, the **754, 4557, 6152**

depth of field (SEE ALSO: deep focus) **1213, 1214**

Derek, Bo **4251**

Deren, Maya **251, 734, 1283, 2509, 2678, 4026, 4785**

derring-do **4737**

De's case **2301**

desert, warriors of the **5284**

DESERT BLOOM (Eugene Corr, U.S., 1985) **3832**

DESERT HEARTS (Donna Deitch, U.S., 1985) **3832**

DESERT VICTORY (Col. David Macdonald, U.S., 1943) **83, 1896**

DESERTER (V.I. Pudovkin, U.S.S.R., 1933) **5082**

design, creature **804**

designer, costume (SEE: costume designer)

designer, makeup (SEE: makeup artist)

designer, production (SEE: art director; set designer; production designer)

designer, set (SEE: art director; production designer; set designer)

designer, sound (SEE: sound designer; sound designing)

designing women **5954**

desire **1476, 2016, 5644, 5645**

DESIRE (Vojtech Jansny, Czechoslovakia, 1958) **2550**

desire, disembodied **3520**

desire, figures of **6322, 6329**

desire, male **6437**

desire, the space of **5828**

desire, time and **4218**

desire to desire, the **1992**

DESIRE UNDER THE ELMS (Delbert Mann, U.S., 1958) **1471**

Desnos, Robert **3379**

DESPAIR (Rainer Werner Fassbinder, Germany, 1978) **1538**

desperate art, the **3100**

DESPERATE CHARACTERS (Frank Gilroy, U.S., 1971) **2277**

DESPERATELY SEEKING SUSAN (Susan Seidelman, U.S., 1985) **1992, 3832**

desperation and meditation **179**

DESTINATION MOON (Irving Pichel, U.S., 1950) **2382, 2684**

DESTINATION TOKYO (Delmer Daves, U.S., 1943) **5755**

destiny, politics against **5008**

destruction of 'theatre' **3965**

destructive element **2990**

DESTRY RIDES AGAIN (George Marshall, U.S., 1939) **2546, 5970, 6198**

details, motifs and the director's commentaries **3161**

detective, bungling **2277**

detective film, hardboiled **5235**

DETECTIVE STORY (William Wyler, U.S., 1951) **3573**

detective's long goodbye **1165**

detente, Anglo-American **5425**

Deutschland, USA **3546**

DEUX OU TROIS CHOSES QUE JE SAIS D'ELLE (see: TWO OR THREE THINGS I KNOW ABOUT HER)

development **3990, 4714, 6447**

deviant, the **4512**

Devil, the **785, 5206, 5306**

DEVIL HORSE, THE (Fred Jackman, U.S., 1926) **821**

DEVIL IN MISS JONES, THE (Gerard Damiano, U.S., 1972) **1471, 1845**

-E-

eye-minded, engaging the **3329**

EYES OF A STRANGER (Ken Wiederhorn, U.S., 1981) **6438**

EYES OF LAURA MARS (Irvin Kershner, U.S., 1978) **1993**

-F-

fable and phenomena **6383**

fables, cautionary **4351**

fabricating the female body **2159**

fabrication of a star **6073a**

FACE IN THE CROWD, A (Elia Kazan, U.S., 1957) **3205**

face of man **344**

FACE OF WAR, THE (Tore Sjoberg, Sweden, 1964) **5268**

FACE TO FACE (John Braham, U.S, 1953) **6117**

FACES (John Cassavetes, U.S., 1968) **3271, 4660**

faces, they had **5870**

faces of men **343**

fact of fiction **5268**

factory of facts **6054, 6055**

Factory of the Eccentric Actor (SEE: FEKS)

facts, factory of **6054, 6055**

facts, manufacture of **5427**

facts and fiction **5082**

fade-out **2290**

fades, her image **4903**

Fadika, Kramo-Lancine **4636**

FAHRENHEIT 451 (Francois Truffaut, U.S., 1966) (SEE ALSO: Journal of Fahrenheit 451) **2556, 4570**

FAIL SAFE (Sidney Lumet, U.S., 1964) **5755, 6412**

failure, lesson of a **5008**

failures (movie) **4045**

fair dealing **3254**

fair play **1587**

fair use **96, 3220, 3524, 4474, 5879**

fair use code **5879**

Fairbanks, the **3258**

Fairbanks, Douglas **2273, 3602, 3963, 4914, 5082, 5248, 5251, 6399**

fairy tale **2277, 6092**

"fait divers" **1953**

faith and idolatry **5827**

faith and mountains **5008**

FALL, THE (Rui Guerra & Nelson Xavier, Brazil, 1978) **5646**

fall, decline and **6133**

FALL OF A NATION, THE (Thomas Dixon, U.S., 1916) **5414**

fallacy, the Hawksian **553a**

fallacy, the Hitchcockian **553a**

fallacy, the literary **553a**

fallacy, the television **553a**

FALLEN IDOL, THE (Carol Reed, G.B., 1948) **4034, 4642**

fallen woman, the **2755**

fallen women cycle **2967**

falling sickness **1972**

FALSE MOVEMENT (see: WRONG MOVEMENT)

falsehood, anatomy of a **6165**

Falstaff (character) **1075**

FALSTAFF (see: CHIMES AT MIDNIGHT)

FAME (Alan Parker, U.S., 1980) **4064**

FAME IS THE SPUR (John & Roy Boulting, G.B., 1946) **4921**

famiglia, la **2326**

family, death of a **3962a**

family, rescuing the **3963**

family, the **2013, 3145**

family, the absent **2630**

family, the exploding **4449**

family discourse **818**

family economy **5568**

family in Italy, the **2298**

family melodrama (SEE ALSO: domestic melodrama; melodrama) **1814, 3314, 3481, 5240, 5330**

family pictures **6501**

family plot **1018**

FAMILY PLOT (Alfred Hitchcock, U.S., 1976) **5377**

FAMILY PORTRAIT SITTINGS (Alfred Guzzetti, Italy, 1976) **5087**

family portraits **6217**

family sit-com, fantastic **5619**

Famous Players-Lasky **5970**

Famous Studios, Paramount/ **3851**

fan magazines (SEE: film magazines)

fan writing **3012**

FANNY (Marcel Pagnol, France, 1932) **6073**

FANNY (Joshua Logan, U.S., 1961) **3706**

fans, horror **801**

fans in early television **3877**

FANTASIA (Ben Sharpsteen [for Disney], U.S., 1940) **2213, 2404, 2546, 6388**

fantasies **425, 4299**

fantasies, Indian **4722**

fantasies, transcendent **593**

fantasies of achievement **4064**

fantasm **2018**

fantastic, the **888, 1608, 1815, 3451, 6257**

fantastic and magical worlds **548**

fantastic realism **2865**

fantasy **1677, 3016, 3916, 4488, 4586, 5075, 5539, 5999**

fantasy, a child's **6092**

female audience /-s **3985, 6152**

female authorship **3983**

female body, fabricating the **2159**

female body, filming the **1590**

female body, uncovering the **3986a**

female colossus, the **412**

female discourse **3143**

female film aesthetics **6105**

female friendship **1982**

female identity **2481, 4088**

female narration **3981**

female politics **3143**

female representation **109**

female resistence **3143**

female sexuality **3143, 3321**

female spectator **1591, 4629**

female spectatorship **2575**

female spy, the **3496**

female subject, the **6076**

female voice, the **5460**

feminine, repression of the **6283**

feminine, the monstrous **1329, 1330**

feminine discourse **5762**

feminine disruption **4714**

feminine fascinations **5628a**

femininity **2018, 4215, 5745**

femininity and the masquerade **3043**

femininity as absence **1590**

feminism **109, 412, 1730, 1802, 2016, 2159, 2642, 2643, 2736, 2856, 3145, 3149, 3192, 3918, 3925, 4064, 4099, 4154, 4216, 4299, 4399, 4414, 4630, 5172, 5300, 5327, 5743, 5954, 6357**

feminism, uncanny **4098**

feminism and exhibitionism **6277**

feminist **2018, 2221**

feminist, R-rated **4564**

feminist aesthetic **1849**

feminist critic, the **3985**

feminist criticism (SEE: feminist film criticism)

feminist discourse **841**

feminist documentary **3152, 3618**

feminist film **2220, 3143**

feminist film, psychoanalysis for **914**

feminist film, the independent **3143**

feminist film criticism **1600, 1724, 2306, 2307, 2308, 3146, 3986, 4908**

feminist film practice, towards a **3045**

feminist film teaching **1134**

feminist film theory **914, 1483, 2161, 3766, 5643a, 6326**

feminist filmmaker **6018**

feminist filmmaking (Australian) **5683**

feminist filmmaking, independent **5683**

feminist futures **1323**

feminist parable **5329**

feminist poetics **1477**

feminist reading, a psychoanalytic **6132**

feminist spectators **1807**

feminist theatre, American **3512**

feminists, the **4026**

feminists, British cine- **3148**

FEMME DOUCE, UNE (Robert Bresson, France, 1969) **985, 2556, 2573, 2856**

FEMME EST UNE FEMME, UNE [A Woman Is a Woman] (Jean-Luc Godard, France, 1964) **3865**

femme-filmecriture **2663**

fenonmeni morbosi **5785**

FERGHANA CANAL (Sergei Eisenstein; unproduced) **1757**

Ferguson, Graeme **2806**

Ferreri, Marco **1318, 6383**

Ferry, Emily **804**

festival /-s, film (SEE ALSO: Cannes Film Festival) **3, 826, 1179a, 2449, 3435, 3994, 4060, 4219, 4337, 5082**

Fetin, Vladimir **6111**

fetishism **3143**

FEUERTAUFE [Baptism of Fire] (newsreel, Germany, 1940) **6226**

Feuillade, Louis **3703, 5097, 5100**

Feuillade, the avenging spirit of **3703**

Feydeau, Jacques **2277**

Feyder, Jacques **5097, 5144**

Fibber McGee and Molly **3850**

fiction **3109, 3450**

fiction, cinematic structure in **4323**

fiction, fact of **5268**

fiction, facts and **5082**

fiction, the future of a **696a**

fiction film **4136**

fiction film and historical analysis, the **1954**

fiction film drama **6055**

fiction friction **3793**

fiction of fact **5268**

fidelity, film **3897**

field, discursive **27**

Field, Sally **963**

FIELD OF DREAMS (Phil Alden Robinson, U.S., 1989) **2767**

field of the author, absent **4500**

Fielding, Jerry **5851**

Fields, Gracie **4434, 4915**

Hollywood, Europeans in **1574**

Hollywood, fig leaves in **109**

Hollywood, first years of **5637**

Hollywood, investigation of **1391**

Hollywood, murder in **4305**

Hollywood, passage to **3975**

Hollywood, pre- **4122a**

Hollywood, sins of **14, 1636**

Hollywood, the decline of **3528**

Hollywood, the new **844, 5479, 6290**

Hollywood, the pattern of **5947**

Hollywood and Britain **3139**

Hollywood and Hibernia **1146**

Hollywood and sex **4431**

Hollywood banks (1970s) **6172**

Hollywood conversations **4869**

Hollywood cop **4860**

Hollywood dawn **6156**

Hollywood goes highbrow **6290**

Hollywood goes to war **4431**

Hollywood heroines **3938**

Hollywood hires its competition **6290**

Hollywood in Britain **5770**

Hollywood in the television age **2341**

Hollywood Indian, the **6061**

Hollywood journalism **3693**

Hollywood meets Frankenstein **6471**

Hollywood mode of production **5639**

Hollywood narrative, classic **2356, 6358**

Hollywood on trial **3110**

HOLLYWOOD SHUFFLE (Robert Townsend, U.S., 1987) **5038**

Hollywood style, classical **683, 690**

Hollywood Ten, the **5248**

Hollywood transformed **6275**

Hollywood-scandal **820**

Hollywood's holy war **4484**

Hollywood's response to the 1940s **6314**

Hollywood's surrealist eye **5983**

Hollywood's unconscious **3581**

Holmes, Burton **821**

Holmes, Sherlock **4819**

Holocaust, Fascism and the **2209a**

Holocaust, post- **5183**

Holy Grail, the milk separator and the **1760**

HOMBRE DE LA ESQUINA ROSADA [Man on the Pink Corner] (Rene Mugica, Argentina, 1962) **1317**

HOME FROM THE HILL (Vincente Minnelli, U.S., 1960) **1468, 3487**

home front, the (British) **2607**

home movies **1071**

home video **299**

HOMECOMING (see: HEIMKEHR)

homesteader **1611**

homily, tragedy and **985**

homoerotic imaginary **4110**

homogenization, product **4647**

homosexuality (SEE ALSO: gay ...) **4645**

HONDO (John Farrow, U.S., 1953) **5970**

Hondo, Med **4636**

honesty, creative **1759**

honesty or hokum **670**

Hong Kong cinema **1100, 3448, 3610, 4834**

hoodlums **5496**

Hooeyland **4323**

Hooper, Tobe **2287a**

HOPALONG CASSIDY (Howard Bretherton, U.S., 1935) **5970**

HOPALONG RIDES AGAIN (Lesley Selander, U.S., 1937) **5970**

hope **4343**

Hope, Bob **3848, 5251**

hope; comic rhythm, and ambiguity **1241a**

hopi, maternal **2069**

Hopkins, Bo **2841**

Hopkins, Miriam **1742**

Hopper, Hedda **5823**

HORA DE LOS HORNOS, LA (see: HOUR OF THE FURNACES, THE)

hormones **4343**

Hornaday, Jeffrey **804**

Hornbeck, William **819**

horrific **6243**

horror (SEE ALSO: monster movies) **122, 147, 1253, 1469, 1522, 1537, 1579, 2117, 2176, 2262, 2432, 2685, 2757, 2807, 3124, 3285, 3601, 3609, 3684, 4033, 4039, 4190, 4687, 4848, 4904, 5539, 5585, 5827, 5830, 6142, 6291, 6360, 6416, 6426, 6431**

horror, ambiguities of **6426**

horror, hard-on for **3495**

horror, poetics of **6279**

horror, reflexive nature of **5830**

horror, the reflections of **5947**

horror, the ultimate **4809**

horror and magic **3285**

horror and morality **3285**

horror fans **801**

HURDES, LAS [Land Without Bread] (Luis Bunuel, Spain, 1932) **1025, 1235, 3228, 3271, 6457**

HURRY TOMORROW (Richard Cohen & Kevin Rafferty, U.S., 1975) **1189**

Hurt, William **1722**

Hussey, Olivia **4850**

HUSTLE (Robert Aldrich, U.S., 1975) **1538**

hustling **2244**

Huston, John **64, 1303, 2244, 2381, 2510, 2968, 3646, 3990, 5402, 5544, 5972, 5975, 6425**

Huxley, Aldous **1432, 2982, 5409**

Hyams, Peter **5402**

hyper-realism **1811**

hyperdirect **5008**

hypertextual transformation **3716**

hyphens of the self **5163**

hypothesis **544**

HYPOTHESIS OF THE STOLEN PAINTING (Raoul Ruiz, France, 1978) **4579**

hysteria, male **4215**

-I-

I, A WOMAN (Mac Ahlberg, Sweden, 1965) **1471**

"I", private **3824**

I ACCUSE (see: ICH KLAGE AN)

I AM A JERUSALEMITE (Yehoram Gaon, Israel, 1971) **2962**

I AM CURIOUS YELLOW (Vilgot Sjoman, Sweden, 1967) **1471, 3597**

I AM JOAQUIN (Luis Valdez, U.S. [Chicano], n.d.) **2780**

I AM SANDRA (Gary Graver, U.S., 1970) **1471**

I CLOWNS (see: FELLINI'S CLOWNS)

I CONFESS (Alfred Hitchcock, U.S., 1953) **781**

I don't give a damn **3217**

I felt freedom in the air **6560**

I LOVE YOU, ROSA (Moshe Mizrahi, Israel, 1971-72) **2962**

I MARRIED A DOCTOR (Archie Mayo, U.S., 1936) **5960**

I MARRIED A WITCH (Rene Clair, U.S., 1941) **2546**

I NEVER SANG FOR MY FATHER (Gilbert Cates, U.S., 1970) **1038**

I REMEMBER MAMA (George Stevens, U.S., 1948) **6152**

I SEE A DARK STRANGER [The Adventuress] (Frank Launder & Sidney Gilliat, G.B. 1946) **3496**

I WALKED WITH A ZOMBIE (Jacques Tourneur, U.S., 1943) **6424**

I WANT TO LIVE! (Robert Wise, U.S., 1958) **2601**

I WAS A COMMUNIST FOR THE FBI (Gordon Douglas, U.S., 1951) **1379, 6300**

I WAS A MALE WAR BRIDE (Howard Hawks, U.S., 1949) **488, 2556**

I WAS A SPY (Victor Saville, G.B., 1933) **5082**

I WAS A TEENAGE WEREWOLF (Gene Fowler, U.S., 1957) **585**

I WAS BORN, BUT ... (Yasujiro Ozu, Japan, 1932) **4992**

I wish to share **6054**

Ibsen, Henrik **5667**

ICE (Robert Kramer, U.S., 1969) **3773**

ice, the mysteries of walking in **2835**

ICH KLAGE AN [I Accuse] (Wolfgang Liebeneiner, Germany, 1941) **6226**

Ichikawa, Kon **646, 1309, 2273, 2510**

ICI ET AILLEURS (Jean-Luc Godard & Anne-Marie Mieville, France, 1977) **4372**

icon /-s **1234, 1540, 3017**

icon, star as cult **3017**

iconography **123, 334, 2817, 4731**

iconography, imperialist **5730**

id, the **5792**

I'd rather be frivolous **5723**

idea /-s **3030, 5079, 5494**

idea, the visual **1658**

ideal, the Bourgeois **6296**

ideals, affects and **3487**

ideals, reaffirmation of American **4455**

ideas, cinema of **2452, 2456**

ideas, collision of **1779**

ideas, progression of **4869**

ideas, recent **5126**

ideas, some **6526**

ideas of origin **1048**

ideas on the cinema, some **6526**

"idee" **2018**

identification /-s **55, 175, 176, 2575, 4128**

identification, cinematic **2111**

identification, forms of **5628a**

identification, primary **1817**

identity **2346, 5272**

identity, cultural **1584**

identity, female **2481, 4088**

identity, national **5219a**

identity, sexuality and **3262**

ideogram **1765**

ideological class struggle **937**

ideological consensus **87**

ideological content **1758**

ideological criticism **2643, 4402**

ideological effects of cinematographic apparatus **417**

ideological form **553**

ideological foundations **409**

Jenkins, Jane **804**

Jennings, Al **821**

Jennings, Humphrey **162, 165, 2774, 4444, 4899**

JENSEITS DER STRASSE [Harbor Drift][Beyond the Street] (Leo Mittler, Germany, 1929) **8**

JERICHO (Henri Calef, France, 1946) **433**

Jersey, William C., Jr. **2950**

Jerusalem **6133**

Jerusalem, building **6133**

JESSE JAMES (Henry King, U.S., 1939) **4142, 5970**

Jesus (SEE: Christ)

Jeune Cinema Allemand (SEE: German Cinema, New)

Jew /-s (SEE ALSO: Jewish ...) **1548, 2150, 4175, 4606, 5169**

JEW SUSS (see: JUD SUSS)

Jew, evolutionary image of the **5169**

Jew, the Little **3115a**

JEWEL OF THE NILE (Lewis Teague, U.S., 1975) **3832**

Jewish cowboy **1054**

Jewish horror film **2117**

Jewish images **1847, 2119**

Jewish parody, American **4607**

Jewish world, the **4449a**

JEZEBEL (William Wyler, U.S., 1938) **3024**

Jires, Jaromil **2550, 3664**

Joad, Ma (SEE: Ma Joad)

JOAN OF ARC (Victor Fleming, U.S., 1948) **558**

JOE (John G. Avildson, U.S., 1970) **1804**

John Ford's Boston **5821**

John Wayne syndrome, the **5947**

JOHNNY CASH (Arthur Barron, U.S., 1969) **2645**

JOHNNY GUITAR (Nicholas Ray, U.S., 1954) **4142, 5585, 5921**

Johnson, Avril **2147**

Johnson, Chic (SEE: Olsen and Johnson)

Johnson, Junior **3315**

Johnson, Mr. and Mrs. Martin **821**

Johnson, Nunnally **669, 1268**

Johnston, Claire **544**

JOKE, THE (Jaromil Jires, Czechoslovakia, 1969) **2277**

jokes **4097**

jokes, penis-size **3581**

JOLI MAI, LE (Chris Marker, France, 1962) **3445**

JOLSON I and II (THE JOLSON STORY [see next entry] and JOLSON SINGS AGAIN [Henry Levin, U.S., 1949]) **323**

JOLSON STORY, THE (Alfred E. Green, U.S., 1946) **2546**

Jones, Buck **5970**

Jones, Chuck **41, 657, 3596**

Jones, James Earl **4850**

Jones, L.Q. **2841**

Jons **1613**

Joplin, Janice **2982**

Jordan, Jim (SEE: Fibber McGee and Molly)

Joseph Andrews (book by Henry Fielding) **3459**

JOSEPH ANDREWS (Tony Richardson, G.B., 1977) **3459**

Jost, Jon **5049**

JOUR DE FETE (Jacques Tati, France, 1949) **5082**

JOUR SE LEVE, LE (Marcel Carne, France, 1939) **141, 5844, 5953**

JOURNAL D'UN CURE DE CAMPAGNE, LE [Diary of a Country Priest] (Robert Bresson, France, 1951) **176, 3713, 4840**

JOURNAL D'UN FEMME DE CHAMBRE, LE [Journal of a Chamber Maid] (Jean Renoir, France, 1946) **4193**

JOURNAL D'UN FEMME DE CHAMBRE, LE (Luis Bunuel, France, 1964) **4193**

journal for 1991 **679a**

Journal of Fahrenheit 451, The (book by Francois Truffaut) **5926**

journal, movie **4081**

journalism, Hollywood **3693**

journalistic approach, the **921**

journey, the fabulous **6092**

JOURNEY INTO AUTUMN (see: DREAMS)

JOURNEY INTO FEAR (Norman Foster, U.S., 1942) **2546**

journey to the self **4809**

Joyce, James **3308, 4323**

JOYLESS STREET, THE (G.W. Pabst, Germany, 1925) **4629**

JUAREZ (William Dieterle, U.S., 1939) **1116**

JUD SUSS [Jew Suss] (Veit Harlan, Germany, 1940) **1953, 5082, 6226**

JUDEX (Louis Feuillade, France, 1916) **945, 4971**

JUDGE PRIEST (John Ford, U.S., 1934) **2556**

judgement **4373**

JUDGMENT AT NUREMBERG (Stanley Kramer, U.S., 1961) **2601, 4842**

JUDITH OF BETHULIA (D.W. Griffith, U.S., 1914) **5087**

Judy, the true **6542**

Jug, Toby **5992**

JUGEMENT DERNIER, LE (Rene Chanas, France, 1945) **433**

jukebox, national **5516**

JUKTI TAKKO AR GAPPO (Ritwik Ghatak, India, 1974) **3159**

JULES ET JIM [Jules and Jim] (Francois Truffaut, France, 1961) **1179a, 1920, 1889, 2443, 2556, 3107, 3271, 3569, 4034, 4035**

JULIA (Fred Zinnemann, U.S., 1977) **1116**

Julien, Isaac **2147**

JULIET OF THE SPIRITS (Federico Fellini, Italy, 1965) **1804, 2201, 5148**

-L-

LE JOURNAL D'UN CURE DE CAMPAGNE (see: JOURNAL D'UN CURE DE CAMPAGNE, LE)

LE JOURNAL D'UN FEMME DE CHAMBRE (see: JOURNAL D'UN FEMME DE CHAMBRE, LE)

LE JUGEMENT DERNIER (see: JUGEMENT DERNIER, LE)

LE MEPRIS (see: CONTEMPT)

LE MILLION (see: MILLION, LE)

LE MYSTERE PICASSO (see: MYSTERE PICASSO, LE)

LE PETIT SOLDAT (see: PETIT SOLDAT, LE)

LE PETIT THEATRE DE JEAN RENOIR (see: PETIT THEATRE DE JEAN RENOIR, LE)

LE SANG D'UN POETE (see: SANG D'UN POETE, LE)

LE SANG DES BETES (see: SANG DES BETES, LE)

LE TESTAMENT D'ORPHEE (see: TESTAMENT D'ORPHEE, LE)

Leacock, Richard **621, 2950, 3856, 3893, 5402**

lead man **804**

LEAD SHOES, THE (Sidney Peterson, U.S., 1949) **3661**

leadership **6226**

leading man, the **2029**

Leakey, Philip W.N. **5797**

Lean, David **4638, 4640, 5807, 6454**

learning, films for **5659**

learning not to be bitter **3865**

learning resources **2731**

learning to hear and see **6253**

LEAVE HER TO HEAVEN (John Stahl, U.S., 1945) **4880**

leaves of grass **2244**

L'ECLISSE (see: ECLISSE, L')

Lederer, Charles **1168, 3636**

Lee, Bruce **1003, 4305**

Lee, Christopher **801, 2807**

Leenhardt, Roger **232**

Lef (journal) (SEE: Novy Lef)

Lefebvre, Jean-Pierre **1066**

Left, the **2449, 6195**

left, loony **2449**

Left cinema **5578**

"left" front (of art) **4678**

Left Front, the **2168**

left literature, Argentine **4767**

left of the screen **4443**

left political filmmaking **854**

LEFT-HANDED WOMAN, THE (Peter Handke, Germany, 1977) **1288**

leftist film activity **4609**

legend, approaches to the (SEE: Free Cinema)

legend, the Southern **4119**

legendary (reality) **5969**

legends, frontier **5970**

Leger, Fernand **3518, 5773**

Leggett, Mike **2558**

Legion of Decency **3923**

legislation, antitrust **5311**

legitimacy, mistaken **1468**

LeGrice, Malcolm **2252**

Lehman, Ernest **1268, 1973, 4993**

Leisen, Mitchell **2273, 5887**

leisure **515, 3963**

Lejeune, C.A. **4026**

Lelouch, Claude **233, 1212**

Lemke, Karl **3878**

Lemmon, Jack **1349, 3822, 4855, 5846**

Leni, Paul **1144**

Lenin **3757, 6054**

Leninist Proportion **1929**

Lennart, Isobel **5526**

Lenne, Gerard **6000**

lens /-es **1485, 3810**

lens darkly, through a **3963**

Lenya, Lotte **4853**

Lenz (novel by Peter Schneider) **4020**

Leon, Gerardo de **2501, 5836**

Leonardo **2404, 3810**

Leone, Sergio **1270, 3129**

leopards and history **4014**

LePrince, L.A.A. **5316**

LeRoy, Mervyn **970, 3788, 4834, 6390**

LES ANGES DU PECHE (see: ANGES DU PECHE, LES)

LES AUTRES (see: AUTRES, LES)

LES BAS-FONDS (see: BAS-FONDS, LES)

LES BONNES FEMMES (see: BONNES FEMMES, LES)

LES CARABINIERS (see: CARABINIERS, LES)

LES CROIX DE BOIS (see: CROIX DE BOIS, LES)

LES DEMONS DE L'AUBE (see: DEMONS DE L'AUBE, LES)

LES ENFANTS DU PARADIS (see: ENFANTS DU PARADIS, LES)

LES ETOILE DE MIDI (see: ETOILE DE MIDI, LES)

LES FRERES CORSES (see: FRERES CORSES, LES)

LES GIRLS (see: GIRLS, LES)

LES LIAISONS DANGEREUSES 1960 (see: LIAISONS DANGEREUSES 1960, LES)

LES MAISONS DE LA MISERE (see: MAISONS DE LA MISERE, LES)

LES NOCES DE SABLE (see: NOCES DE SABLE, LES)

LES NUITS DE LA PLEINE LUNE (see: NUITS DE LA PLEINE LUNE, LES)

-M-

MEPHISTO (Istvan Szabo, Hungary, 1981) **3899**

MEPRIS, LE (see: CONTEMPT)

Mercer, Mabel **4854**

merchandising **636**

MERCHANT OF FOUR SEASONS, THE (Rainer Werner Fassbinder, Germany, 1972) **3555**

Mercouri, Melina **4853, 4854**

merging and symbiosis **2910**

MERMAIDS (Richard Benjamin, U.S., 1990) **3833**

merriment, macabre **1361**

MERRY WIDOW, THE (Erich von Stroheim, U.S., 1925) **323, 6100, 6103**

MERRY-GO-ROUND (Erich von Stroheim, U.S., 1923) **3602**

MESHES OF THE AFTERNOON (Maya Deren & Alexander Hammid, U.S., 1943) **1987**

mesquiteers, three **5970**

message, the **3708**

message, sending a **6201**

Messiah, the alien **5124**

Messina, Philip **4503**

Messter, Oskar **4352**

Meszaros, Marta **2220, 4778**

metacinema, radical **3857**

metafiction **6293**

metahermeneutics **4402**

metahistory **2069**

metamorphoses, erotic **5743**

metamorphosis **2685**

metaphor **4714, 5844, 6322**

metaphor, dialectics of a **6203a**

metaphor, doomsday **5665**

metaphor, sexual **5795**

metaphor, subjective **5666**

metaphor, the Western **6249**

metaphors, cinematic **2243**

metaphors, monster **4110a**

Metaphors on Vision (book by Stan Brakhage) **736**

metaphysics **1404, 1642**

metapsychological approaches **416**

metapsychological study, a **4136**

meter man, the **1816**

method, critical **5941**

method, the (acting) **5722**

method, the working **1510**

method performance **3501**

methodological propositions **4133**

methodology **2384**

methodology, critical **5941, 5943**

methos **4514**

metonymy **6322**

metrical film, theory of **3413**

Metro-Goldwyn-Mayer (SEE: MGM)

METROPOLIS (Fritz Lang, Germany, 1926) **8, 614, 867, 2556, 3398, 3569, 4545, 4735, 5805**

metropolis wars **5737**

metteur(s) en scene (SEE ALSO: mise-en-scene) **455, 4957**

Metz, Christian **174, 1253, 1724, 2519, 2591, 2699, 2856, 3773, 5644**

MEXICAN SPITFIRE (Leslie Goodwins, U.S., 1939) **6399**

Mexico **3280, 3589, 3808, 5726, 6000, 6075, 6422**

Mexico, citizen of **1511**

Meyer, Andy **3906**

Meyer, Russ **1719**

Meyerberg, Paul **804**

MGM **52, 2058, 2361, 2888, 3849, 3851, 4252, 5274, 6172**

MGM meets the atomic bomb **4861**

MGM screenplays **4639**

Michaelson, Steve **804**

Micheaux, Oscar **1556**

Michelangelo, animation's **967**

Michelson, Annette **4026**

Mick, the **6542**

MICKEY ONE (Arthur Penn, U.S., 1965) **1804, 5498**

Mickey Mouse (character) **1492, 2055, 6145**

microphone **3529**

Middle Ages **887**

middle American sky, the **4776**

middle class film critic **5201**

middle class security **8**

middle-aged new directors (Chinese) **6531, 6535**

midland, reborn **5629**

Midler, Bette **4855, 6454**

midnight, after **3196**

MIDNIGHT COWBOY (John Schlesinger, U.S., 1969) **580, 2784, 3110, 4714**

midnight movies **6146**

midnight s/excess **5745**

MIDSUMMER NIGHT'S DREAM, A (Max Reinhardt & William Dieterle, U.S., 1935) **2438, 3067, 3882, 6186**

MIDSUMMER NIGHT'S DREAM, A (Peter Hall, U.S., 1969) **3067, 3882, 3883**

midwest **2441**

Midwest Films **5455**

Mieze **5306**

Mighty Mouse (character) **3304**

MIGHTY QUINN, THE (Carl Schenkel, U.S., 1989) **1721**

Mikado, The (comic opera by Gilbert & Sullivan) **3701**

MY DARLING CLEMENTINE (John Ford, U.S., 1946) **585, 2556, 3570, 5970**

MY DINNER WITH ANDRE (Louis Malle, U.S., 1981) **5038**

MY FAVORITE WIFE (Garson Kanin, U.S., 1940) **2556**

MY FOUR YEARS IN GERMANY (William Nigh, U.S., 1918) **821**

MY HOMELAND (Robert Vas, G.B., 1976) **6035**

my illness **6055**

MY LITTLE CHICKADEE (Edward Cline, U.S., 1940) **3088, 6260**

MY MAN GODFREY (Gregory La Cava, U.S., 1936) **3233, 6198**

my mind's eye **5492**

MY NIGHT AT MAUD'S (see: MA NUIT CHEZ MAUD)

MY PAL TRIGGER (Frank McDonald, U.S., 1946) **5970**

MY SON JOHN (Leo McCarey, U.S., 1952) **1116, 6169**

MY UNCLE (see: MON ONCLE)

MY WAY HOME (Bill Douglas, G.B., 1978) **4420**

MYSTERE PICASSO, LE (Henri-Georges Clouzot, France, 1956) **1179a**

MYSTERES DE NEW YORK (compilation of Pearl White serials, France, 1915-16) **1543**

MYSTERIOUS MR. MOTO (Norman Foster, U.S., 1938) **2546**

MYSTERIOUS X, THE (Benjamin Christensen, Denmark, 1914) **4279**

mystery **5539**

mystery, no **4727**

mystery and imagination **5723**

MYSTERY OF KASPAR HAUSER, THE [Every Man for Himself and God Against All] (Werner Herzog, Germany, 1974) **1287**

MYSTERY OF PICASSO, THE (Henri-Georges Clouzot, France, 1956) **5008**

MYSTERY OF THE LEAPING FISH (w/ Douglas Fairbanks, U.S., 1916) **3602**

MYSTERY OF THE WAX MUSEUM (Michael Curtiz, U.S., 1933) **2546, 5368**

MYSTIC PIZZA (Donald Petrie, U.S., 1988) **3833**

Mystifying Movies (book by Noel Carroll) **1010**

mystique, the individualist **2244**

myth **4299, 4726, 5570, 6322**

myth, American **1058**

myth, anti- **844**

myth, embodiment of a **1761**

myth, ghetto **3131**

myth, socialist realist **3502**

myth, structural study of **3631**

myth, the deceptive **4909**

myth, the Oedipus **4299**

myth, the will to **2836a**

myth & murder **2104a**

myth maker **1977**

myth of entertainment **1960**

myth of informed consent **155**

myth of the Latin lover **6399**

myth of the savage **3066**

myth of total cinema **436**

myth of total cinema history, the **5728**

myth of woman, the **1179a**

mythic beasts **6092**

mythic discourse **1982**

mythic rites of passage **1171a**

mythic trajectories **6337**

mythical patterns **3920**

mythological, the **1555**

mythology, ancient **6092**

mythology, Fellini's **3274**

mythology, inversions of American **2689**

mythology, Moroccan society as **5541**

mythology, movie **5234**

mythology, the new **5068**

myths, cultural **5514**

myths, political **3777**

myths of women **3044**

-N-

NAACP (National Association for the Advancement of Colored People) **1345**

Nabokov, Vladimir **2276**

Nadia (SEE: "Fearless" Nadia)

naive cinema **5104**

NAKED AMAZON (Zygmunt Sulistrowski, Brazil, 1957) **1471**

Naked and the Dead, The (book by Norman Mailer) **3829**

NAKED AND THE DEAD, THE (Raoul Walsh, U.S., 1958) **3829**

NAKED CAME THE STRANGER (Henry Paris [pseudonym: Radley Metzger], U.S., 1975) **1471**

NAKED CITY, THE (Jules Dassin, U.S., 1948) **2546**

naked eye, invisible to the **1355**

naked girls **5278**

NAKED KISS, THE (Samuel Fuller, U.S., 1965) **2404**

NAKED TRUTH, THE [T. N. T.] (George Walters, U.S., 1924) **1471**

NANA, MOM AND ME (Amalie R. Rothschild, U.S., 1974) **5094**

Nanook (character) **2008**

NANOOK OF THE NORTH (Robert Flaherty, U.S., 1922) **974, 2006, 2556, 3271, 3603, 5410, 6388**

Napoleon **2169**

nations, the **1565**

Native Americans (SEE: Indians)

NATIVE LAND (Leo Hurwitz and Paul Strand, U.S., 1942) **98, 5018, 5882**

Native Son (book by Richard Wright) **832**

NATIVE SON (Pierre Chenal, U.S., 1951) **832, 1471**

NATIVE SON (Jerrold Freedman, U.S., 1986) **832**

native, return of the **6512**

natural noises **2097**

naturalism **747, 2140, 3228, 6334**

naturalism, super- **6511**

nature, making culture into **5685**

nature, modesty of **4563**

nature, multilayered **5779**

nature, toward re:programming **3281**

nature, religion is **5933**

nature and censorship **34**

nature and function **5507**

nature of cinema **3207, 3637**

NAVIGATOR, THE (Donald Crisp & Buster Keaton, U.S., 1924) **2556**

NAZARIN (Luis Bunuel, Mexico, 1958) **3449, 3922, 5325, 5845**

Nazi, film director as **2449**

Nazi cinema **6226, 6385**

Nazi war film **3397**

Nazi wartime newsreel propaganda **6227**

Nazimova, Alla **4251, 5610**

NBC (National Broadcasting Company) **3241**

Neal, Patricia **4850**

Neame, Ronald **5402, 6133**

NEAR DARK (Kathryn Bigelow, U.S., 1987) **5395**

NEAR THE BIG CHAKRA (Anne Severson, U.S., 1971) **5360a**

necessity and invention **3840a**

negative cutter **804**

negotiations, pleasurable **2304**

Negri, Pola **6544**

Negro cowboys **1688**

Negro, documentary film and the **5537**

Negro intellectual, the **1382**

Negro sings a song, when a **4328**

NEGRO SOLDIER, THE (Stuart Heisler, U.S., 1943) **1335, 1337, 1344, 6161**

Negroes (SEE ALSO: Afro-Americans; Black Americans) **1306, 1332, 1333, 1342, 2658, 6494**

neighbors **855**

NEIGHBOURS (Norman McLaren, Canada, 1952) **4052**

Neilan, Marshall **5611**

Nelson, Ralph **5221, 5402**

Nemech, Jan **1309, 2550**

Nemirovich-Danchenko, Vladimir **6110**

neo-neo-realism **1972**

neo-realism (SEE ALSO: Italian Neo-realism) **223, 318, 439, 447, 634, 1101, 1744, 1952, 2878, 2950, 3898, 4257, 5072, 5082, 6051, 6525**

neoformalism (SEE ALSO: formalism) **5856**

neoformalism, beyond **1936**

neorealist movement in England **1044**

Nesbitt's Passing Parade, John **3849**

NET Journal **363**

nether villainy **2277**

NETWORK (Sidney Lumet, U.S., 1976) **1116**

network oligopoly power **3688**

network style **5320**

networks, the **1640**

neurosis **482**

NEVER CRY WOLF (Carroll Ballard, U.S., 1983) **196**

NEVER GIVE A SUCKER AN EVEN BREAK (Edward Cline & Ralph Ceder, U.S., 1941) **2177, 2546**

never having to say you're sorry **5746**

NEVER ON SUNDAY (Jules Dassin, Greece, 1960) **1471**

New American cinema **3648b**

NEW BABYLON, THE [Novyi Vavilon] (Grigori Kozintsev & Leonid Trauberg, U.S.S.R., 1929) **297, 2145**

new boy **5055**

new Chinese cinema **4833**

new cinema **2863, 3231, 4323, 4964**

New Deal **5018, 5080**

New Deal Era, documentaries of the **5018**

new dog **5131**

new frontier, the **3963**

New Frontier, Kennedy's **2689**

New German Cinema **1287, 1823a, 2085, 2725, 5175**

New Latin American cinema **899, 3714, 3716**

New Orleans **5304**

New Russian Cinema **1758**

New Wave (SEE: French New Wave)

NEW WIZARD OF OZ, THE (see: HIS MAJESTY, THE SCARECROW OF OZ)

New World Pictures **398, 719**

New York **23, 2277, 2452, 2730, 6252**

New York, motion picture exhibition in **118**

New York avant-garde **4785**

New York Globe **2467**

New York Newsreel **747**

New York Times **964**

New Yorker (magazine) **4026**

Noel, Craig **3822**

noise **1245, 2969**

noises, natural **2097**

nomadic aesthetics **2155**

nonacted cinema **6054**

nonfiction film **393, 394**

nonfiction television **4456**

nonnarrative cinema **959**

nonomniscience, modes of **6358**

nonsense, another kind of **3160**

nonverbal level **2922**

non-art, film as a **6455**

non-book **4060**

non-bourgeois camera style **2699, 2705**

non-classical spatial structures **5857**

non-continuity **2507**

non-horror film, horrors of **5508**

non-market factors **2499**

non-played film, the **5417**

non-realist film, realist and **1165**

non-theatrical distribution **2051**

non-verbal sequences, Bergman's **3834**

non-Western text, a **6489**

Noonan and Mitchell **3850**

Norin, Gustaf **5797**

Norin, John **5797**

Norin, Josef **5797**

NORMA RAE (Martin Ritt, U.S., 1979) **1116**

Norman Bates (character) **1678**

Normand, Mabel **3848**

norms of narration **6117**

NORTE, EL (see: EL NORTE)

NORTH BY NORTHWEST (Alfred Hitchcock, U.S., 1959) **781, 1051, 2404, 2546, 2556, 2618, 3569, 4358, 5087, 5585, 6358, 6400**

NORTH OF 36 (Irvin Willat, U.S., 1924) **821**

North, Alex **4511**

Northeast Film Studio (China) **6359**

Norton, Rosanna **804**

Norwich Women's Film Weekend **4123**

NOSFERATU: A SYMPHONY OF HORROR (F.W. Murnau, Germany, 1922) **985, 2256, 3161, 3247, 3570, 3979, 3982, 5079, 6142, 6426**

NOSFERATU THE VAMPYRE (Werner Herzog, Germany, 1979) **3982, 5888, 6142**

nostalgia **887, 5019**

NOSTALGIA (Hollis Frampton, U.S., 1973) **1925**

NOSTALGIA (Andrei Tarkovsky, Italy, 1983) **3836**

not-for-profit media institutions, film and **2430**

note on the film, a **3489**

NOTEBOOK (Marie Menken, U.S., 1963) **266**

notebooks (of Dziga Vertov) **6054**

notes, two **4617**

notes on films **5559**

notes on some new movies **4080**

NOTES ON THE CIRCUS (Jonas Mekas, U.S., 1966) **958**

NOTHING BUT A MAN (Michael Roemer, U.S., 1964) **1337**

nothing but flames **3773**

NOTHING BUT THE BEST (Clive Donner, G.B., 1964) **1348**

NOTHING SACRED (William Wellman, U.S., 1937) **6198**

nothing, saying **5501**

nothingness over a mustache **434**

NOTORIOUS (Alfred Hitchcock, U.S., 1946) **29, 60, 2177, 2556, 2646a, 3161, 3520, 3570, 4215, 5377**

NOTTE, LA (Michelangelo Antonioni, Italy, 1961) **3180, 4439, 4446**

nouvelle vague (SEE ALSO: French New Wave) **501, 2449, 2950**

Novak, Kim **4251**

Novarro, Ramon **2982, 4305, 6399**

NOVECENTO (see: 1900)

novel /-s and film /-s (SEE ALSO: film and fiction) **624, 1093, 2138, 5588**

novel, cinematic **4323**

novel, how not to film a **5163**

novel, limits of the **624**

novel, the **4767**

novel, the classic **2254**

novel, the dime **5549**

novel, the new **4323**

novel, the picaresque **4843**

novel isn't a movie **796**

novelist /-s **4060, 4367**

novelist versus screenwriter **4643**

novelistic, the **3984**

novelistic film **5163**

novels, British **4038**

novels, filming **630**

NOVIJ VAVILON (see: NEW BABYLON, THE)

Novo, Cinema (SEE: Cinema Novo)

Novy Lef (journal) **773, 780, 5407**

NOW, VOYAGER (Irving Rapper, U.S., 1942) **694, 2013, 2177, 3454, 6152**

NOW ABOUT THESE WOMEN (Ingmar Bergman, Sweden, 1964) **945**

Noyce, Phil **5723**

Nuanxin, Zhang **4778**

nuclear power **1116**

OLD ENOUGH (Marisa Silver, U.S., 1984) **5038**

OLD GRINGO (Carlos Fuentes, U.S., 1989) **2449**

old guard, the **6133**

Old Man and the Sea, The (book by Ernest Hemingway) **4346**

OLD MAN AND THE SEA, THE (John Sturges, U.S., 1958) **1585, 3514, 4346, 4641**

old school ties **4921**

Olea, Pedro **5309**

oligopoly power, network **3688**

Olivas, Sal **804**

OLIVER TWIST (David Lean, G.B., 1948) **2546**

Olivier, Laurence **1442, 1609, 1638, 2510, 4855**

Olivier and the filming of Shakespeare **3882**

Olmi, Ermanno **3648a, 4169, 4503, 6383**

Olsen, Ole (SEE: Olsen and Johnson)

Olsen and Johnson **3850**

Olson's genealogy **5501**

OLYMPIADE [Olympia] (Leni Reifenstahl, Germany, 1938) **4944, 5982**

Olympian, the transient **4459**

Olympics in Rome, the **5008**

omniscience (SEE: nonomniscience)

ON A CLEAR DAY YOU CAN SEE FOREVER (Vincente Minnelli, U.S., 1970) **323**

on location **4855**

ON THE BEACH (Stanley Kramer, U.S., 1959) **3253, 3401**

ON THE BOWERY (Lionel Rogosin, U.S., 1957) **5082, 5753**

ON THE NIGHT STAGE (Thomas H. Ince, U.S., 1915) **5970**

ON THE TOWN (Gene Kelly & Stanley Donen, U.S., 1949) **2045, 2046**

ON THE WATERFRONT (Elia Kazan, U.S., 1954) **585, 1116, 2749, 2905a, 3569, 4324, 4358, 4384, 4842, 5596a**

ONCE UPON A TIME IN AMERICA (Sergio Leone, U.S., 1984) **3119**

ONDANONDU KALADALLI [Once Upon a Time] (Girish Karnad, India [Kannada], 1978) **1412**

One Flew Over the Cuckoo's Nest (book by Ken Kesey) **2637, 5524**

ONE FLEW OVER THE CUCKOO'S NEST (Milos Forman, U.S., 1975) **961, 2013, 2213, 2637, 3252a, 3569, 5524**

one head is better **6306**

ONE MORE RIVER (Beryl Fox & Douglas Leiterman, U.S., 1964) **3587**

one night stands **2470**

one plus one **812**

ONE PLUS ONE [Sympathy for the Devil] (Jean-Luc Godard, France, 1970) **2444, 3773**

ONE SINGS, THE OTHER DOESN'T (Agnes Varda, France, 1976) **6027**

one track mind **5324**

ONE WAY OR ANOTHER (Sara Gomez, Cuba, 1974) **1331, 3143**

O'Neal, Tatum **2640**

O'Neill, Eugene **4323**

ONLY ANGELS HAVE WINGS (Howard Hawks, U.S., 1939) **2556, 5368**

ONLY GAME IN TOWN, THE (George Stevens, U.S., 1970) **4069**

only seven years **6535**

ONLY THE STRONG (Institute for American Strategy, U.S., 1972) **5364**

ONLY TWO CAN PLAY (Sidney Gilliat, G.B., 1962) **2277**

Ontario Theatres Branch **880**

ontogeny **6361**

ontology **454, 4017, 6400**

OPEN CITY (see: ROME: OPEN CITY)

open road **2849**

opening **3161**

opera **5785**

opera singers **4529**

operatics of history **2439**

operator, early motion picture **1623**

operetta **323**

Ophuls, Max **232, 1953, 2277, 2544, 3353, 4899, 5152, 6318, 6355**

opposition **4947**

oppositional film **2629, 6193**

oppression **1915**

optical effects (SEE ALSO: special effects; visual effects) **6267**

optical effects coordinator, titles and **804**

optical printer **1664**

optical printing **1664**

ORAINGOZ IZEN GABE/TODAVIA SIN NOMBRE [Still Nameless] (Jose J. Bakedano, Spain, 1986) **1317**

oral literature **1560**

oral tradition **4946**

ORDEAL, THE (Life Photo Film Corp., U.S., 1914) **1471**

order, narrative **5126**

order, new terms for **5320**

order, the breakdown of **4924**

order and coherence in poetry **4923**

order and the space for spectacle **56**

ORDET (Carl Dreyer, Denmark, 1955) **1642, 4077**

ordinary, plight of the **2405**

ORDINARY FASCISM (Mikhail Romm, U.S.S.R., 1965) **2145**

Orestes **1509**

orgasmic woman, the **2449**

ORIENT EXPRESS (Paul Martin, U.S., 1933) **4642**

PAINTED STALLION, THE (Alan James, U.S., 1937) **5970**

PAINTED VEIL, THE (Richard Boleslawsky, U.S., 1934) **2556**

painter, matte (SEE: matte painter)

painter looks at films **5082**

painters, modern **3518**

painters, theater by **2215**

painter's ideas **2488**

painting **176, 5082**

painting, matte (SEE: matte painting)

painting and cinema **431, 3575, 4424**

painting sense **5987**

paintings, classical **212a**

PAISAN (Roberto Rossellini, Italy, 1946) **1234, 2556, 6165**

Pakistan **3610**

Pakula, Alan J. **6425**

Pal, George **614, 5402**

PAL JOEY (George Sidney, U.S., 1957) **2177**

palace, the theater **3963**

palaces, picture **1545, 2362, 2364**

Palcy, Euzhan **4778**

palimpsest **2532a**

palimpsests, celluloid **2118**

PALM BEACH (Albie Thoms, Australia, 1979) **2805**

PALM BEACH STORY, THE (Preston Sturges, U.S., 1942) **2546, 3233**

palm trees **4983**

Panama, Norman **3436**

PANAMA HATTIE (Norman Z. McLeod, U.S., 1942) **2045**

pancake, once a **814**

PANDORA AND THE FLYING DUTCHMAN (Albert Lewin, U.S., 1951) **3958**

PANDORA'S BOX (G.W. Pabst, Germany, 1929) **1310, 1598, 1816, 3570**

Panfilov, Gleb **6111**

PANIC IN THE STREETS (Elia Kazan, U.S., 1950) **585**

PANIC IN YEAR ZERO (Ray Milland, U.S., 1962) **5364**

Pantagruel **1758**

pantomime **1463**

Papas, Irene **4850**

paper prints **4416**

paper to film (SEE ALSO: film and fiction/literature) **4417**

paperbacks, films and **3976**

paperwork **776**

Papousek, Jaroslav **2550**

parable, feminist **5329**

PARACELSUS (G.W. Pabst, Germany, 1943) **2120**

paradigm /-s **1016, 5511**

paradigm for justice **6203a**

paradigm of redemption **2646a**

paradigmatic axes, syntagmatic and **1711**

paradigmatic structure **143**

PARADINE CASE, THE (Alfred Hitchcock, U.S., 1948) **3570**

paradise **4264**

paradise, the hidden **6092**

paradise lost **2244**

Paradjanov, Sergei **1540**

paradox **4264, 4401**

paradox, embodiment of **2124a**

paradoxes of realism **4269**

Paraguay **3280**

paralysis in motion **857**

parametric style **5856**

Paramount, gentlemen from **6543**

Paramount Case **1230**

Paramount Decrees **1229, 1231**

Paramount Pictures **2361, 3586, 3849, 4252, 4803, 5274, 6172**

Paramount Pictures (and television) **6284**

Paramount Pictures, United States v. **6003**

Paramount/Famous Studios **3851**

paranoia **1116, 2013, 5036**

paranoids have enemies, even **2432**

parenthesis **1910**

PARENTS (Bob Balaban, U.S., 1989) **5048**

PARENTS TERRIBLES, LES [The Storm Within] (Jean Cocteau, France, 1948) **1179a**

Paris **2040, 2260, 4506**

Paris, cinematurgy of **4506**

PARIS, TEXAS (Wim Wenders, Germany, 1984) **6252**

PARIS DOES STRANGE THINGS (Jean Renoir, France, 1956) **5008**

PARIS NOUS APPARTIENT [Paris Belongs to Us] (Jacques Rivette, France, 1960) **3974**

Parker, Alan **2523, 6133**

Parker, Bonnie (SEE ALSO: Bonnie and Clyde) **1**

Parks, Gordon **2509, 5846**

Parlata Plays, Inc. (Parlata Company) **5531**

parody **2207, 4814**

parody, American Jewish **4607**

parody, carnival and **6067**

parodying genre **2904**

Parrish, Robert **1304**

PARSIFAL (Hans Jurgen Syberberg, Germany, 1982) **5785**

Parsons, Louella **6229**

PART-TIME WORK OF A DOMESTIC SLAVE (Alexander Kluge, Germany, 1974) **3200**

participatory cinema **4798**

Peebles, Melvin Van (SEE: Van Peebles, Melvin)

PEEPING TOM (Michael Powell, G.B., 1960) **1118, 5898**

PEEPING TOMS (Uri Zohar, Israel, 1972-73) **2962**

PEGGY SUE GOT MARRIED (Francis Coppola, U.S., 1986) **3832**

Peisheng, Tan **6485**

pen, shooting with a **5707**

pen, the hired **4060**

penance as a paradigm of redemption **2646a**

penis **2143**

penis-size jokes **3581**

Penn, Arthur **1221, 1304, 1309, 2244, 2773, 3356, 3698, 5402, 6425**

Pennebaker, D.A. **3856**

PENNIES FROM HEAVEN (Herbert Ross, U.S., 1981) **3091**

Pennsylvania **4389**

PENNY SERENADE (George Stevens, U.S., 1941) **2556, 3233**

Pentagon, the **5756**

pentagram **2069, 2070, 4848**

people, a sad-looking people **4626**

people, drama of the **4388**

people, real **2007**

people, the **5661**

people, the lighter **4975**

people as stars, the **5662**

people own the air **5880**

people to people **5082**

People's Republic of China (SEE: China)

Peppard, George **4853**

perceiving, the passion for **4128**

perception **158, 175, 6358**

perception, edge of **5856**

perception of ethics **3175**

perceptual process, art and the **4401**

Perelman, S.J. **45**

PERFORMANCE (Nicolas Roeg & Donald Cammell, G.B., 1970) **2100**

performance **4401, 5897**

performance, genre and **1467**

performance, method **3501**

performance, question of **5896**

performance and genre **1467**

performance frame, the **4361**

performance in documentary **6189**

performance style **6558**

performers **963, 1982**

peril, the movies in **5340**

PERIOD OF ADJUSTMENT (George Roy Hill, U.S., 1962) **6478**

period-style **5321**

periodical reviews **2796**

Perkins, Gil **4599**

permissible (and impermissible) **6122**

Perrault, Charles **325**

Perret, Leonce **873**

Perrine, Valerie **4854**

Perry, Eleanor **3733, 5526**

PERSHING'S CRUSADERS (Committee on Public Information, U.S., 1918) **6422**

PERSONA (Ingmar Bergman, Sweden, 1967) **716, 747, 879, 1982, 2856, 3188, 3569, 4714, 5501, 5589, 5590**

personal, the **5796**

personal, political is **5331**

PERSONAL BEST (Robert Towne, U.S., 1982) **1807, 5626, 6324**

personal experience, the **3853**

personal film, the **5498**

personal vision, the **5057**

personality **31**

personality, glut of the **3761a**

personality, property and the **3034**

personality, the cult of **2244**

personality, the new **3963**

personality-in-process **2220**

perspective /-s **1213, 1214, 1758, 1761**

perspective, different **6551**

perspective, the distancing **4504**

perspective reperceived **3228**

Peru **3280**

perverse **5745**

perverse pleasures **5744**

perversion **29, 482**

perversions, implantation of **6327**

pessimistic, political and **2752**

Pete Smith Specialties, The **3849**

PETER IBBETSON (Henry Hathaway, U.S., 1935) **3958**

Peters, Bernadette **4251**

Peters, Susan **1353**

Peterson, Sidney **734**

PETIT SOLDAT, LE (Jean-Luc Godard, France, 1963) **3865**

PETIT THEATRE DE JEAN RENOIR, LE [The Little Theater of Jean Renoir] (Jean Renoir, France, 1971) **2278, 5008**

Petit, Chris **6133**

Petri, Elio **4150, 4503**

PETRIFIED FOREST, THE (Archie May, U.S., 1936) **694**

Petronius **1562, 4249**

Petrov-Bytov's platform **4669**

Petrova, Olga **5530**

Pett, John **3418**

PETULIA (Richard Lester, U.S., 1968) **2277**

PHAEDRA (Jules Dassin, Greece, 1962) **4031**

phallic domination **3143**

phantasmagorical world **4029**

Phantom (of the Opera) **2311**

phantom, shining **1965**

PHANTOM CHARIOT, THE (Victor Seastrom, Sweden, 1921) **3602, 3603**

PHANTOM INDIA (Louis Malle, France-India, 1967-68) **2296**

PHANTOM LADY (Robert Siodmak, U.S., 1944) **2014**

PHANTOM OF LIBERTE, THE (Luis Bunuel, France, 1974) **721, 4091, 6322**

PHANTOM OF THE PARADISE, THE (Brian De Palma, U.S., 1974) **4910**

PHENIX CITY STORY, THE (Phil Karlson, U.S., 1955) **542, 5362**

phenomena, fable and **6383**

phenomena, psychopathic **4622**

phenomenological criticism **2856**

phenomenology **174, 185, 318, 1165**

phenomenon, cinematic **1797, 1798**

PHILADELPHIA STORY, THE (George Cukor, U.S., 1940) **1046, 2280, 2428, 2546**

Philippe, Gerard **1179a**

Philippine film history **3753**

Philippine movies **786, 1024, 1434, 1459, 2073, 2175, 3461, 3610, 3924, 5884**

Philistine **1142**

Phillips, Lynn **6537**

Philoctetes **4848**

Philosophical Problems of Classical Film Theory (book by Noel Carroll) **1009**

philosophy, literature and **1856**

philosophy, practical **48**

phobia, success **2432**

Photo League, the Workers Film and **98**

photogenic golden calf **4877**

photogenics, matters of **126a**

photogenics of sports, the **5008**

photogenie **25, 1837, 1841**

photograph and screen **1047**

photographer, still **804**

photographers, five **4299**

photographic agony, the **2069**

photographic effect **1739**

photographic image, ambiguity of the **2336**

photographic image, ontology of the **454**

photographic techniques, special **24, 6286**

photography ... (SEE ALSO: cinematography ...)

photography (still) **4159, 5905a**

photography, director of (SEE ALSO: cinematographer; cameraman) **804, 2871, 5371**

photography, film and **524**

photography, influence of **3730**

photography, public **2708**

photography, stills as **1553**

photoplay, the **1490, 3585, 3630, 4108, 4308, 6447**

photoplay, the intimate **3677**

photoplay, the modern **5841**

photoplays, mass-produced **5637**

photoplays and the stage **3679**

Phutane, Ramdas **1412**

physical existence **3386**

Pialat, Maurice **6355**

Picabia, Francis **3379**

picaresque novel **4843**

picaro to pipsqueak, from **5734**

Picasso, Pablo **2452, 3518**

Picazo, Miguel **5309**

Pick, Lupu **1971**

Pickford, Mary **819, 983, 1408, 2273, 2592, 2755, 3703, 3963, 4251, 4725, 5611, 6114**

Pickford's directors, Mary **5611**

PICKPOCKET (Robert Bresson, France, 1958) **1179a, 3228**

PICKUP ON SOUTH STREET (Samuel Fuller, U.S., 1953) **5362**

PICNIC (Joshua Logan, U.S., 1956) **2097**

PICNIC AT HANGING ROCK (Peter Weir, Australia, 1975) **2901, 3535, 4037**

pictorial beauty **4108**

pictorial eye, the **4323**

picture, the big **2297**

picture and act **4226**

PICTURE OF DORIAN GRAY, THE (Albert Lewin, U.S., 1945) **2546**

picture palaces **1545, 2362, 2364**

picture plays **2821**

picture show, the last **4060**

picture shows, the first **2821**

pictures, educational **3849**

pictures, nobody would make big **6560**

pictures, the whole equation of **5236**

pictures can't say ain't **6456**

pictures in small country **3700**

pie, how to throw a **5354**

ROME: OPEN CITY [Open City] (Roberto Rossellini, Italy, 1945) **753, 2556, 3271, 3898, 6388**

Romeo and Juliet (play by William Shakespeare) **1129**

ROMEO AND JULIET (George Cukor, U.S., 1936) **2438, 3882**

ROMEO AND JULIET (Renato Castellani, G.B., 1954) **3069, 3472, 3882, 6135**

ROMEO AND JULIET (Franco Zeffirelli, Italy, 1968) **1129, 1609, 3067, 3882**

Romero, George **4503**

Romm, Mikhail **6355**

RONDE, LA (Max Ophuls, France, 1959) **1471, 1520, 2442, 5082, 6317**

ROOM AT THE TOP (Jack Clayton, G.B., 1959) **985, 6388**

Room, Abram **5097**

Rooney, Mickey **6542**

Roosevelt, Theodore **6280**

ROPE (Alfred Hitchcock, U.S., 1948) **423, 2409, 2692, 4600, 5962**

Rose, Reginald **3142**

ROSE, THE (Mark Rydell, U.S., 1979) **2013**

ROSE TATTOO, THE (Daniel Mann, U.S., 1955) **6478**

ROSEMARY'S BABY (Roman Polanski, U.S., 1968) **727, 1804, 3271, 5585, 6273**

Rosen, Marjorie **1724, 4026**

Rosenberg, Mark **6537**

Rosenman, Leonard **4511, 5851**

Roshal, Grigori **3502**

Rosher, Charles **819**

Rosi, Francesco **1165, 1309, 4150, 4610**

Ross, Katherine **4854**

Rossall, Kerry **804**

Rossellini, Roberto **753, 2276, 3773, 4957, 5014, 5402, 6425**

Rossen, Robert **705, 1318**

Rota, Nino **2383**

Rothman, Stephanie **4564**

ROTHSCHILDS AKTIEN VON WATERLOO [The Rothschilds' Shares in Waterloo] (Erich Waschneck, Germany, 1940) **6226**

Rouch, Jean **233, 1971, 2950, 4503**

ROUE, LA (Abel Gance, France, 1922) **1136, 3518, 3575, 3602, 6112**

rough beasts slouching **4018**

rough riders, so long **5970**

roughing it **2244**

Rouquier, Georges **232**

route, celluloid **5600**

Rowan and Martin **3850**

Rowe, Clint **804**

ROYAL FAMILY (Richard Cawston, G.B., 1968) **1059, 3005**

ROYAL WEDDING (Stanley Donen, U.S., 1951) **2045**

Rozier, Jacques **2950**

Rozsa, Miklos **4511, 5851**

RSFSD [Russian Soviet Federated Socialist Republic] **3757**

RUBY GENTRY (King Vidor, U.S., 1952) **3487**

RUE SANS NOM, LA (Pierre Chenal, France, 1934) **6074**

rugged era, a **5542**

RUGGLES OF RED GAP (Leo McCarey, U.S., 1935) **6198**

Ruiz, Raul **1746, 4579, 4813**

rule and its exception, the **4869**

RULER, THE (see: HERRSCHER, DER)

RULES OF THE GAME, THE [La Regle du Jeu] (Jean Renoir, France, 1939) **1520, 2183, 2282, 2556, 3052, 3271, 3569, 3609, 3612, 3623, 3686, 5087, 5142, 5856, 6075**

RUMBLE FISH (Francis Ford Coppola, U.S., 1978) **2767**

RUMOURS OF WAR (Peter Jones, G.B., 1972; BBC-TV) **5711**

RUMPLESTILTSKIN (Raymond B. West, U.S., 1914) **3371**

RUN OF THE ARROW (Samuel Fuller, U.S., 1957) **5970**

RUNAWAY (Standish D. Lawder, U.S., 1969) **266**

runner, distance **6239**

Ruspoli, Marlo **2950**

Russell, Gail **1353**

Russell, Ken **2509, 4638, 4640, 4855, 5768, 6133, 6425**

Russell, Rosalind **4251**

Russfilm **6**

Russia (SEE ALSO: Soviet ...) **4725**

Russia, a salute to **1086**

Russia after the Revolution **2145**

Russia House (book by John Le Carre) **2449**

Russia in the 20s **936**

Russian adaptations (of Shakespeare) **3882**

Russian animation **5679**

Russian Association of Proletarian Writers (SEE: RAPP)

Russian avant-garde **2449**

Russian cinema/movies (SEE ALSO: Soviet cinema) **2452, 5936, 6169**

Russian classic, a new **2276**

Russian example, the **2451**

Russian Formalism **5643a**

Russian formalist film theory **1710, 2234**

Russian Soviet Federated Socialist Republic (SEE: RSFSD)

Russia's science fiction poet **6349**

Ruth, Roy Del (SEE: Del Ruth, Roy)

Ruttenberg, Joseph **1505**

Ruttmann, Walter **3518**

RUY BLAS (Pierre Billon, France, 1944) **1179a**

Rx **6014**

silents, voices from the **5939**

SILK STOCKINGS (Rouben Mamoulian, U.S., 1957) **2045, 6432**

SILKWOOD (Mike Nichols, U.S., 1983) **1116**

silliest film **6242**

Silliphant, Stirling **1151**

Silver, Joan Micklin **2510, 4503, 4778**

Silver, Raphael D. **4503**

SILVER LODE (Allan Dwan, U.S., 1954) **5970**

Simenon, Georges **3824**

Simon, John **602**

SIMON OF THE DESERT (Luis Bunuel, Spain, 1965) **3103**

simplicity of true greatness, the **4458**

simplification **2571**

simultaneity and stillness **985**

sin, the wages of **4175**

sin, who is without **6081**

Sinai **3871**

SINCE YOU WENT AWAY (John Cromwell, U.S., 1944) **6152**

SINCERELY YOURS (Gordon Douglas, U.S., 1955) **4069**

Sinclair, Andrew **6133**

SINDERELLA (David Hamilton Grant & Ron Inkpen [creators], G.B., 1972) **1471**

SING AS WE GO (Basil Dean, G.B., 1934) **2546**

sing it one more time, let's **3901**

Singapore **3610**

singer, the saloon **5230**

SINGIN' IN THE RAIN (Stanley Donen & Gene Kelly, U.S., 1952) **472, 2045, 2213, 2546, 3569, 5585, 6388**

singing and dancing (SEE: musicals)

SINGING FOOL, THE (Lloyd Bacon, U.S., 1928) **2368**

sinification **1149**

Sinkel, Bernhard **4023**

sins of Hollywood **14, 1636**

Sintzenich, Arthur H.C. "Hal" **379**

Siodmak, Curt **3799**

Siodmak, Robert **1303, 3990, 5807**

Sioux, a man named **1979**

Sirk, Douglas **488, 1303, 2544, 4299, 4302, 4531, 5402**

sister, modern **5230**

Sister Carrie (book by Theodore Dreiser) **2202**

SISTER CARRIE (see: CARRIE)

sisters **1982**

SISTERS (Brian De Palma, U.S., 1973) **6426**

SISTERS, OR THE BALANCE OF HAPPINESS (Margarethe von Trotta, Germany, 1979) **1982**

sisters of the night **3201**

sit-com, fantastic family **5619**

situation comedy (SEE: comedy, situation)

six authors in pursuit of **4442**

six guns, when television wore **6498**

Six Guns and Society (book by Will Wright) **747**

SIXTEEN IN WEBSTER GROVES (Arthur Barron, U.S., 1967) **386**

16mm, in praise of **1179a**

sixth art **973, 2169**

sixth sense **4612**

sixties, the **428, 1116**

sixties, superstar of the **787**

sixties political documentary **4881**

Sixty Minutes (television program) **6176**

69 (Robert Breer, U.S., 1968) **266**

sixty years of cinema **5082**

Sjeberg, Alf **1318**

Sjoman, Vilgot **5402**

Sjostrom, Victor (SEE Seastrom, Victor)

skeleton **727**

Skelton, Red **3848**

skid row **5753**

SKIN DEEP (Blake Edwards, U.S., 1989) **3833**

skin flick **1091, 1998**

skin head **4110**

Skinner, B.F. **2856**

Skolimowski, Jerzy **1165, 1309, 2277, 2510, 3666, 6134**

Skreba (production company) **6133**

sky, fragments of **1837**

Skywalker, Luke (character) **1804**

slasher film **1162**

Slaughterhouse-Five (book by Kurt Vonnegut) **1581**

SLAUGHTERHOUSE-FIVE (George Roy Hill, U.S., 1972) **720, 1581**

SLAVE OF LOVE, A (Nikita Milhalkov, U.S.S.R., 1976) **2276**

Slavic stereotype **2322**

SLEEP (Andy Warhol, U.S., 1963) **2214**

sleep, psychology of **2801**

SLEEP MY LOVE (Douglas Sirk, U.S., 1948) **6152**

sleep of reason, the **2432**

SLEEPER (Woody Allen, U.S., 1973) **255, 2638, 6388**

SLEEPING BEAUTY (Clyde Geronimi [for Disney], U.S., 1959) **2404**

sleight of hand, no **4727**

slit screen **6348**

Sloman, Edward **819**

slow up **5387**

slow-motion sound **1839**

SMALL BACK ROOM, THE (Michael Powell & Emeric Pressburger, G.B., 1949) **1681**

temporal multiplicity **852**

temporality **2196**

10 (Blake Edwards, U.S., 1979) **1538**

ten commandments (of the cowboy) **307**

TEN COMMANDMENTS, THE (Cecil B. DeMille, U.S., 1956) **2177, 2404**

TEN DAYS THAT SHOOK THE WORLD (see: OCTOBER)

tenacity **3429**

tendencies, current **6424**

tendencies, new **200**

tendency, a certain **5928**

tendentious **2221**

tender comrade **6152**

TENDER IS THE NIGHT (Henry King, U.S., 1962) **1588**

TENDER TRAP, THE (Charles Walters, U.S., 1955) **2097**

TENNESSEE JOHNSON (William Dieterle, U.S., 1942) **1335**

tennis **4576**

tense **5643a**

tense, the question of the present **1415**

tension, tempo and **1533**

TENT OF MIRACLES (Nelson Pereira dos Santos, Brazil, 1977) **3266**

10TH VICTIM, THE (Elio Petri, Italy, 1965) **5393**

TEOREMA (Pier Paolo Pasolini, Italy, 1968) **3898**

TEQUILA SUNRISE (Robert Towne, U.S., 1988) **2449**

TERMINAL ISLAND (Stephanie Rothman, U.S., 1973) **5086**

terminus and tantrum **6383**

terms, film **6530**

terms, stipulation of **2069**

terms for order, new **5320**

terms of dismemberment **4884**

TERRA TREMA, LA (Luchino Visconti, Italy, 1948) **2556, 3271**

terror **954, 1165**

terror, titans of **3609**

TERROR BY NIGHT (Roy William Neill, U.S., 1946) **5856**

terror of daylight **3132**

TERROR TRAIN (Roger Spottiswoode, U.S., 1980) **1576**

terror trends, trans-Atlantic **4786a**

terror-film **4731**

terrorism **3145, 4702**

terrorism, political **4702**

Terry, Alice **5530**

Terry, Paul **3851**

Terrytoons **3851**

TESS (Roman Polanski, G.B.-France, 1979) **720**

tesseract **2069**

test, screen **3505**

test, the commutation **5855a**

test case **5082**

TESTAMENT D'ORPHEE, LE (Jean Cocteau, France, 1959) **1179a**

testimony **1391**

Tex Arcana **5243**

Texas **1206, 3582**

Texas (Austin) **2821**

TEXAS CHAINSAW MASSACRE, THE (Tobe Hooper, U.S., 1974) **5383**

text (SEE ALSO: intertextuality; transtextuality) **5643a**

text, a **5724**

text, a collective **929**

text, a non-Western **6489**

text, actor and **2219**

text, film **3426**

text, heterogeneous **3674**

text, larding the **1585**

text, master **1725**

text, paternity and **1609**

text, pre-text and **218**

text, progressive **1308**

text, spectator-in-the- **817**

text, the accessiblity of the **79**

text, the cinematic **5617**

text, the classic realist **5643a**

text, the contradictory **5643a**

text, the dialogic **1982**

text, the publicity photograph as **6391a**

text, the vulnerable **176**

text and subject **5041**

text and subtext **3285**

text and the film **2780**

texts, early **2312**

textual analysis **5643a**

textual mechanism **1202**

textual poaching **3012**

textual politics **3424**

textual repression **6132**

textual system **5643a**

textuality **5041, 5957**

texture, milieu and **1313**

texture, open **5498**

Thalberg, Irving **819**

thanatos **2836a**

Thanhouser Company **5531**

thank heaven for little girls **4547**

Tykociner, Joseph T. **76, 4027**

Tyler, Parker **2404**

type /-s **1048, 6330**

types, character **4029**

typewriter, the polychrome **1890**

Tyson, Jim **804**

Tytla, Vlad **967**

-U-

UFA (studio) **3887**

UGETSU MONOGARTARI (Kenji Mizoguchi, Japan, 1953) **3569, 4029, 4902, 6424**

Uggams, Leslie **4853**

Ugland, Rudy **804**

Uher, Stefan **2550**

U.K. (SEE ALSO: Britain; England; Great Britain) **6000**

Ukrainfilm **6054**

Ullmann, Linn **1722**

Ullmann, Liv **2639, 4855**

Ulm Institute **3323**

Ulmer, Edgar G. **488, 659, 4076**

ultrarealism **1967**

Ulysses (book by James Joyce) **396**

ULYSSES (Joseph Strick, U.S., 1967) **396, 6388**

ULZANA'S RAID (Robert Aldrich, U.S., 1972) **1208, 4341**

UMBERTO D (Vittorio De Sica, Italy, 1952) **443, 2556, 3898, 5082, 6511**

un certain regard **5837**

UN CHANT D'AMOUR (see: CHANT D'AMOUR, UN)

UN CHIEN ANDALOU (see: CHIEN ANDALOU, UN)

UN CONDAMNE A MORT S'EST ECHAPPE (see: CONDEMNED MAN ESCAPES, A)

UN SEUL AMOUR (see: SEUL AMOUR, UN)

Un Tal Lucas (SEE: Tal Lucas, Un)

uncanny feminism **4098**

uncertainty, images of **2582**

uncertainty of certainty, the **4252a**

UNCLE KRUGER (see: OHM KRUGER)

uncoded images **3674**

unconforming, the **3318**

unconformist, the **3319**

unconscious, Hollywood's **3581**

unconscious, poetry of the **2019**

unconscious, the male **4299**

unconscious, the patriarchal **4216**

uncontrolled cinema, for an **3553**

unconventional masterpiece, an **3604**

UNCOUNTED ENEMY: A VIETNAM DECEPTION (CBS television, 1982) **459**

undead, the assorted **2545**

undefeated, the **4641**

UNDER CAPRICORN (Alfred Hitchcock, G.B., 1949) **488, 781**

UNDER FIRE (Roger Spottiswoode, U.S., 1983) **1116, 5626**

UNDER MY SKIN (Jean Negulesco, U.S., 1950) **4641**

under skin **2277**

UNDER THE CHERRY MOON (Prince, U.S., 1986) **2799**

UNDER THE ROOFS OF PARIS (see: SOUS LES TOITS DE PARIS)

UNDER THE VOLCANO (John Huston, U.S., 1984) **720**

undercurrent **6152**

underdevelopment, a trajectory within **2369**

underdogs **5723**

UNDERGROUND (Emile de Antonio, Mary Lampson & Haskell Wexler, U.S., 1978) **1462**

underground and in exile **4552**

underground film /-s (SEE ALSO: avant-garde ...) **1899, 4085, 4551, 5213**

underwater filmmaking **2010**

UNDERWATER! (John Sturges, U.S., 1955) **4069**

UNDERWORLD U.S.A. (Samuel Fuller, U.S., 1960) **585, 2404**

underworld, British cinema and the **4319**

undocumented workers **3808**

UNE FEMME DOUCE (see: FEMME DOUCE, UNE)

UNE FEMME EST UNE FEMME (see: FEMME EST UNE FEMME, UNE)

UNE SI JOLIE PETITE PLAGE (see: SI JOLIE PETITE PLAGE, UNE)

UNE VIE (see: VIE, UNE)

unfaithfulness, the virtues of **3458**

unfinished business **6537**

unheimlich maneuver, an **2112**

UNION MAIDS (Julia Reichert & James Klein, U.S., 1976) **2389, 4857**

Union of Soviet Film Workers **3429**

Union of Soviet Socialist Republics (SEE: Russia ...; U.S.S.R. ...)

UNION PACIFIC (Cecil B. DeMille, U.S., 1939) **5970**

unique and extraordinary **2584**

unit publicist **804**

United Artists **352, 353, 3968, 6172**

United British Artists **6133**

United States, view from the **5582**

United States spoke Spanish, if the **4991**

United States v. Paramount Pictures **6003**

units, minimal **5643a**

voice, cultural **5224**

voice, goodbye to the booming **6252**

voice, narrative **1828**

voice, the female **5460**

voice, women and the authorial **3520**

voice animator **612**

voice of silence, the **5114**

voice of the other **553**

voice-over **1165**

voice-over narration **5643a**

voices from the silents **5939**

Voight, Jon **4850**

VOIX HUMAINE, LA (Jean Cocteau & Roberto Rossellini, Italy, 1948) **1179a**

von Kleist, Heinrich **5617**

VON RYAN'S EXPRESS (Mark Robson, U.S., 1965) **1804**

von Sternberg, Josef **250, 427, 758, 819, 1094, 1303, 1404, 1683, 2510, 2968, 3788, 4480, 4482, 5158, 5402, 5550**

von Sternberg principle, the **6097**

von Stroheim, Erich **435, 820, 821, 1977, 3474, 3602, 3603, 3788, 4596, 4725, 5046, 5047, 5402, 6210, 6211, 6290**

von Trotta, Margarethe **2343, 4778**

Vorkapich, Slavko **6290**

vote, explanation of a **5008**

voyage of a visionary chronicler **5793**

VOYAGE TO ITALY [Viaggio in Italia] (Roberto Rossellini, Italy, 1953) **835, 2556, 5009**

VOYAGE TO THE BOTTOM OF THE SEA (Irwin Allen, U.S, 1961) **511**

voyeurism **5652, 6313**

voyeurisms, two **4132, 4135**

-W-

wages of sin, the **4175**

Wagner, Richard **5785**

WAGON MASTER (John Ford, U.S., 1950) **5970**

WAGON TRACKS (Lambert Hillyer, U.S., 1919) **5970**

WAITING FOR FIDEL (Michael Ruddo, Canada, 1974) **5109**

Wajda, Andrzej **1165, 1309, 2509, 2968, 4152, 4382, 4899**

WAKE IN FRIGHT [Outback] (Ted Kotcheff, Australia, 1971) **4037**

WAKE ISLAND (John Farrow, U.S., 1942) **1379**

Walas, Chris **804**

WALK IN THE SUN (Lewis Milestone, U.S., 1945) **5082, 5115**

walk up! **559**

WALKABOUT (Nicolas Roeg, Australia, 1971) **2856**

Walker, Robert **2982**

walking stick, the **572**

Wallin, Dan **804**

Walsh, Raoul **968, 1252, 1303, 1318, 5402**

Walt Disney Productions (SEE: Disney, Productions; Disney, Walt)

Walters, Charles **3941**

Walthall, Henry B. **5530**

Wan brothers, the **4783**

wanderer, enchanted **1281**

WANDERING JEW, THE (Fritz Hippler, Germany, 1940) **5817**

war (SEE ALSO: antiwar) **849, 1424, 2177, 2463, 2529, 3496, 3648a, 4143, 4389, 4431, 4498, 4745, 5577, 5585, 5895**

war, aftermath of **6422**

war, America's lost **711**

war, American entry into **6422**

war, British cinema and **1300**

war, British documentaries in the **2587**

war, comics and the **972**

war, films on **5577**

war, fragments of **3658**

war, Hollywood goes to **4431**

war, how TV covers **4180**

war, illusion and reality of **5755**

war, lion returns to **5115**

war, men at **4641**

war, peace and **224**

war, women next door to **6034**

war among the lion tamers **2888**

war and madness **2013**

war and the military image **6226**

war film, Nazi **3397**

war films, Australian **4515**

WAR GAME, THE (Peter Watkins, G.B., 1967) **5055, 5364, 6180**

WAR GAMES (John Badham, U.S., 1983) **332**

war letter **6005**

WAR LORD, THE (Franklin Schaffner, U.S., 1965) **1804**

WAR OF THE WORLDS (Byron Haskin, U.S., 1953) **5971**

war themes, anti- **5755, 5895**

WAR WAGON, THE (Burt Kennedy, U.S., 1967) **3102**

war woman, the post- **4880**

wardrobe **2775**

Warhol, Andy **414, 2404, 2510, 3354, 5402, 5808**

Warner, Harry **5542**

Warner Bros. (studio) **52, 561, 1423, 2151, 2358, 2361, 2367, 2427, 2515, 3258, 3849, 3851, 4252, 4391, 5080, 5274, 5368, 6543**

Warner Communications Inc. **2515, 6172**

word brother **6047**

WORD IS OUT (Arthur Bressan, Jr., U.S., 1977) **285**

word play **4501**

words **5665**

words, fighting **2984**

words, filming **833**

words, without **6054**

words and images **3520**

words and movies **3415**

WORDS AND MUSIC (Norman Taurog, U.S., 1948) **2045**

words per page **5379**

work **1428, 4333**

work, my **5023**

worker film **104, 1758, 1761, 6547**

workers, undocumented **3808**

Workers Film and Photo League **98**

Workers' Film Movement, the **2809**

working class, the **8, 3773, 4780**

WORKING CLASS GOES DIRECTLY TO HEAVEN, THE (Elio Petri, Italy, 1972) **3773**

working conditions, dependent **2210**

WORKING GIRL (Mike Nichols, U.S., 1988) **3833**

working girl, the **2755**

WORKING GIRLS (Lizzy Borden, U.S., 1986) **3832**

working in film, status of **4296**

working method, the **1510**

working with a friend **3465**

working woman, the **4842**

working-class, the British **5661**

working-class film heros **3315**

working-class films **5695**

working-class heroines **2389**

working-class history **2547**

world, the **5082**

world, a moonstruck **6186**

world, demythologized (Fellini's) **1622**

world, in a hostile **5723**

world, reel **4055**

world, self and **3586**

world, shaking the **3627**

WORLD, THE FLESH, AND THE DEVIL, THE (Ranald MacDougall, U.S., 1959) **4467**

world, the Jewish **4449a**

world, the mad sad **4739**

world, way of the **2244**

WORLD APART, A (Chris Menges, U.S., 1988) **3833**

WORLD AT WAR (John Pett, G.B., 1974-75; Thames Television) **3418**

world beyond **4194**

World in a Frame, The (book by Leo Braudy) **748, 749**

WORLD OF APU, THE (Satyajit Ray, India, 1959) (SEE ALSO: Apu Trilogy, The) **4902**

World Viewed, The (book by Stanley Cavell) **1047, 1048**

World War I **820, 2145, 2946, 2976, 2979, 5255, 5611**

World War II **98, 1116, 1335, 1471, 1810, 2013, 2976, 3133, 3782, 3800, 4431, 4498, 4748, 4785, 4808, 5110, 5755, 6326**

World War II, Soviet style **5110**

worlds, between two **3351**

worlds, magical **548**

worlds, other **6092**

Woronov, Mary **2287a**

Worth, Nicholas **2287a**

WOZZECK (Georg Klaren, Germany, 1947) **2833**

WR: THE MYSTERIES OF THE ORGANISM (Dusan Makavejev, Yugoslavia, 1971) **467, 3773**

wrangler **804**

Wray, Fay **147**

Wright, Prescott **1185**

Wright, Teresa **488**

write for movies **4060**

write stuff that's serious, you **4966**

writer /-s (SEE ALSO: screenplay; screenwriting; screenwriter; script) **975, 1917, 1965, 3693, 4409, 4506, 5186, 5371**

writer, the 'Eastern' **5299**

writer in film, the **4020**

writer-director, the **5454**

writerly film, reading the **3823**

writer's view, the **4026**

writing (SEE ALSO: screenplay; screenwriter; screenwriting; script) **1211, 1276, 2038, 2126, 2679, 3960, 4503**

writing, literature and **4634**

writing, narrative **1856**

writing, the sacrament of **4840**

writing, twisted **2692**

writing of history, the **742, 1953**

writing on the wall **5082**

WRITTEN ON THE WIND (Douglas Sirk, U.S., 1956) **1468, 3569, 4491**

WRONG MAN, THE (Alfred Hitchcock, U.S., 1956) **781, 1552, 2556, 5013**

WRONG MOVE (see: WRONG MOVEMENT)

WRONG MOVEMENT [Wrong Move][False Movement] (Wim Wenders, Germany, 1975) **2581, 4020, 6252**

wrong side, the **2493**

wrong side of the tracks, the **3487**

wrong track **5604**

ABOUT THE AUTHOR

STEPHEN E. BOWLES earned his Ph.D. in film from Northwestern University. Since the early 1970s, he has been teaching film and literature on the university level. For the past twenty years, Dr. Bowles has taught film history, theory and screenwriting in the Motion Pictures Program at the University of Miami where he has served as director and originator of the graduate program. He has published six books including *Sidney Lumet* (Boston: G. K. Hall & Co., 1979), a critical biography of the director, and the three-volume set *Index to Critical Film Reviews* (New York: Burt Franklin & Co., 1974-75). In addition to his teaching and publishing, Dr. Bowles is co-founder and assistant director of the prestigious international Miami Film Festival. Dr. Bowles is also an award-winning screenwriter whose next book will be a text on the screenwriting process.